The Illustrated Encyclopedia of JAZZ

a Salamander book

Published by

H·A·R·M·O·N·Y B·O·O·K·S
NEW YORK

A Salamander Book

First published 1978 in the United States by
Harmony Books, a division of Crown Publishers, Inc.
All rights reserved under the International Copyright
Union by Harmony Books. No part of this book may be
utilized or reproduced in any form or by any means,
electronic or mechanical, including photocopying,
recording, or by any information storage and retrieval
system, without permission in writing from the Publisher.

Harmony Books
A division of Crown Publishers, Inc.
One Park Avenue, New York, New York 10016
Published in Canada by General Publishing
Company, Limited

First published in the United Kingdom in 1978 by
Salamander Books Limited

© Salamander Books Ltd 1978
27 Old Gloucester Street, London WC1, United Kingdom

Second impression 1979

Case, Brian
The Illustrated Encyclopedia of Jazz
Includes discographies
1. Jazz music – bio-bibliography. 2. Jazz music –
discography. I. Britt, Stan, joint author. II. Title.
ML102.J3C34   785.4 2 0922 (B)   77-27647
ISBN 0-517-53343-X

Printed and bound by Henri Proost, Turnhout, Belgium

All correspondence concerning the content of this
volume should be addressed to Salamander Books
Limited

Credits

Authors:	Brian Case and Stan Britt
Consultant:	Joseph Abend
Photographs:	Val Wilmer
Editor:	Trisha Palmer
Design:	Roger Hyde and Barry Savage
Filmset by:	SX Composing, England
Color reproduction by:	Metric Reproductions Ltd, England
	Paramount Litho Ltd, England

Acknowledgements

The Publishers wish to express their sincere thanks to
Val Wilmer, who took the photographs used in this book.
Val Wilmer is a British journalist and photographer who
has worked extensively in the music field; her pictures
have appeared in publications throughout the world,
notably in her own books, *Jazz People*, *The Face of Black
Music* and *As Serious As Your Life*. Her work has also been
seen in her own and group exhibitions and in two films.
As a journalist, Val Wilmer has been associated with the
British publication *Melody Maker* since the mid-1960s;
she was also the London correspondent for the American
publications *Down Beat* and *Hit Parader* for several
years, and is now UK correspondent for *Jazz Magazine*
(Paris) and *Swing Journal* (Tokyo).

Publisher's Note

Each entry in this book has a selective
discography, giving the record title
followed by the US and UK labels in
brackets; if the second label is
European rather than English, this is
stated. If a record has a different
title in America and the UK, the US
title and label are followed by the UK
title and label.

The Authors acknowledge the debt they owe to such publications as Leonard Feather's *New Edition: The Encyclopedia of Jazz*, John Chilton's *Who's Who of Jazz* Jorgen Grunnet Jepsen's *Jazz Records A-Z*, Mike Ledbitter and Neil Slaven's *Blues Records 1943-1966*, and *Jazz On Record (A Critical Guide to the First Fifty Years)* by Albert McCarthy, Alun Morgan, Paul Oliver and Max Harrison.

We would also like to thank the following record companies who supplied record sleeves for use in the book: Ace of Hearts, America, Atlantic, Black Lion, Blue Note, Bluesway, Candid, Capitol, CBS, Classic Jazz, Collector's Classics, Contemporary, Delmark, DJM, Dooto, ECM, EMI, Epic, Epitaph, Esoteric, ESP, Family, Fontana, Fountain, Herwin, HMV, Impulse, Island, Japo, Jazz Archive, Jazz Kings, Jazz Panorama, Jazz Society, JCOA, Virgin, London, MCA, MGM, Milestone, Mode, Ogun, Old Masters, Oldie Blues, Pablo, Parlophone, Polydor, Prestige, Pye, Queen-Disc, RCA, Riverside, Savoy, 77 Records, Shoestring, Solid State, Sonet, Spotlite, Survival, Tax, Telefunken, Transatlantic, Vanguard, Vocalion, Vogue, Wave, Wing, World Record Club, Xtra.

Special thanks is given to the following for their valuable help: Hugh Attwooll, Peter Barnett, Roy Carter, Sue Baker, Chris Ellis, Wally Leaf, Andrew Carnegie, Howard Harding, Pat Stead, Fred Dellar, Simon Frodsham, Lindsay Edwards, Allan Garrick, Nick Highton, Ron Steggles, David Hughes, Colin Smith, George Hulme, Dave Machray, Buzz Carter, Charlie McCutcheon, Carol Stein, Harry Pleasants, Ray Purslow, Don Stone, Franco Chen, John Roberts.

Authors

The entries in this book represent the highly individual styles of two internationally respected music journalists, both of whom have been jazz enthusiasts for many years. Brian Case has written on Modern Jazz and Stan Britt on Mainstream/Traditional jazz, we would like to thank them both for their extensive research and help.

BRIAN CASE, for whom jazz has been a consuming interest for the past 27 years, has been a writer on the subject since the early '70s. He has interviewed over 150 musicians, most of whom appear in this book, and his articles have appeared in the British publications *Let It Rock, Black Music, Time Out, Inside London, Into Jazz, New Musical Express, Jazz Journal* and *The Observer.* He has contributed a chapter to the book *Jazz Now,* and has also written sleeve notes for albums by James Moody, Eric Dolphy and Harry Edison. Prior to his jazz-writing days he wrote a play, *Our Kid,* for British radio, and a novel *The Users* was published in 1968 by Peter Davies in the UK and Citadel/Simon and Schuster in the USA.

STAN BRITT, born in Beckenham, Kent, has been a freelance writer and occasional broadcaster for the past ten years and more, commenting almost exclusively on the music scene in general and jazz and blues in particular. Before that, he spent 15 years in various editorial capacities with two leading Fleet Street newspapers and has also served periods within the press offices of a couple of leading UK record companies. A regular contributor to diverse music publications such as *Billboard, Music Week, Melody Maker, Home Organist & Leisure Time* and *Album Tracking,* and the perpetrator of scores of sleeve notes for jazz and other music albums, he lives in South London surrounded by a huge collection of records, reference books and memorabilia, all pertaining to a subject which, one way or another, consumes most of his time: music.

Introduction

Of necessity, events happen alphabetically in this encyclopedia. Styles, schools, descendants, march in an orderly fashion from A to Z and from crude origins to contemporary sophistication. Improvised music doesn't happen that way. The genealogical tree of jazz is more like a monkey puzzle, with clear and direct descendants as rare as navels in Eden, so that labels can never be more than a convenient shorthand. The jazz lineage, a less tidy affair than the Christian marriage, is constantly subject to re-alignment.

A label that reads 'New Thing' or 'New Wave' or 'Modernist' is clearly bound for imminent redundancy. Records, too, put an unreal focus onto one area of a musician's working life: improvisers have good nights and nightmares. The economics of the jazz world—nightclubs, the road, poverty, the fads and pressures of record companies—taxes creativity, making a miracle of the artistic survival of even the most average performer.

Few artists are even in output. Some hit their peak in a brief outburst, and then level out. Others tire of the diet of integrity and crusts, and contract into the security of formula music. Sometimes—as in the '40s and '60s—a musical revolution in methods will overtake a player and shunt his work up the siding of public indifference. Like any healthy organism, jazz is not concerned exclusively with the latest and greatest: it is about the continuation of traditions. To talk about the vacuum left by the death of a Charlie Parker or a John Coltrane is to miss the point. Great innovators spring out of the rich soil of yesterday's traditions which were the day before's revolutions.

Jazz fans love to squabble: Trad fans versus Modernists, Acoustic versus Electric, Chords versus Free. The writers have made strenuous efforts to expunge personal bias and bigotry, but no doubt some of the entries—and absences—will provoke controversy. The Blues gets short shrift for reasons of space; it deserves a volume to itself. Jazz-Rock, a development away from the mainstream, gains inclusion as the most likely point of entry for the prospective jazz fan of today, rather than for its musical content. Recent developments in European improvised music—or indeed in Japan, for jazz is now an international phenomenon—cannot be adequately dealt with in a guide which covers over half a century of recorded music.

Albums have been included that are no longer available. Commerce has little conscience in the area of heritage, and the dedicated jazz collector can usually be found haunting the second-hand record bins. Where possible, the readily available has been preferred over the obscure, but in the mercurial world of record repackaging flux is the only constant.

Jazz is a live music. Any local musician dug over a year in your neighborhood club or pub will give you a truer picture of jazz than a one-off glimpse of an American giant.

Left: the late altoman Julian Cannonball Adderley with brother Nat. His band struck it rich in early '60s Soul boom.

Muhal Richard Abrams

After several years of playing Hard Bop with the Modern Jazz Two + 3, Chicago pianist Muhal Richard Abrams founded the Experimental Band to widen the scope of jazz. This led to his establishment of the Association for the Advancement of Creative Musicians (AACM) in 1965, which attracted many of Chicago's finest young players, Roscoe Mitchell, Joseph Jarman, Lester Bowie, Malachi Favors, Charles Clark, Steve McCall, Henry Threadgill, Bill Brimfield, Fred Anderson, Kalaparusha Maurice McIntyre, Lester Lashley, Leo Smith, Anthony Braxton, Leroy Jenkins, Jack de Johnette. Muhal's first album **Levels & Degrees Of Light,** though marred by indistinct recording, gives a fair idea of his exploratory scores. Moods fluctuate between eeriness – **Levels & Degrees,** which features the straight, wordless soprano voice and violent outbursts of unison chaos. **The Bird Song** pitches a read poem against a texture of shrill, sweet instruments such as bird whistles. His next album **Young At Heart, Wise In Time** has plenty of his piano which had evolved by now into a complex mixture of Bop, stride, and avant-garde tone clusters and dissonances.

Muhal's influence upon Chicago's jazzmen has been immense. The Art Ensemble and Anthony Braxton owe much to him and to the free, experimental atmosphere which he established. He can be heard playing piano with the Art Ensemble (**Fanfare For The Warriors**) and piano and oboe on an early album of Joseph Jarman's (**As If It Were The Seasons**) as well as piano, cello and alto clarinet on Braxton's debut album, **Three Compositions of New Jazz.**

Recordings:
Muhal Richard Abrams, Levels & Degrees Of Light (Delmark/Delmark)
Muhal Richard Abrams, Young At Heart, Wise In Time (Delmark/Delmark)
Art Ensemble Of Chicago, Fanfare For The Warriors (Atlantic/Atlantic)
Joseph Jarman, As If It Were The Seasons (Delmark/Delmark)
Anthony Braxton, Three Compositions Of New Jazz (Delmark/Delmark)
Duet (Arista/Arista)

Cannonball Adderley

Julian 'Cannonball' Adderley was born in 1928 in Florida, moving to New York and emphatically into the big league in 1955. Basically a Charlie Parker disciple, the altoist had plenty of bite and a rhythmic directness that became more pronounced in his later work. The meeting with Miles Davis – **Somethin' Else** – proved something of a comeuppance, for the trumpeter was playing with such concision that Cannonball sounded positively garrulous. His work in the Miles Davis group from 1957 – **Milestones, Kind Of Blue** – was interesting for the strides he made, learning how to use space, understatement and substitute chords. Chords and modes were very much a preoccupation in that band, with Miles and Coltrane both stretching to escape conventional harmony. Cannonball's association with arranger Gil Evans resulted in a masterly album, **Pacific Standard Time,** which deployed the altoist's legato style in orchestrations which reinterpreted jazz classics – **Manteca, Round Midnight, King Porter Stomp.**

Somethin' Else (Blue Note): it's Miles ahead on this session.

Adderley's contract with Riverside paired him with guitarist Wes Montgomery, pianist Bill Evans and a host of other musicians, but the big breakthrough came with his formation of a quintet. The first album, **Them Dirty Blues,** in which he shared the front-line with his trumpeter brother, Nat, sold more than the rest of his output combined. Bobby Timmons' soul hit number **This Here** may have had a lot to do with this success, and the unit increasingly featured these bluesy backbeat numbers – **Work Song (The Japanese Concerts)** and **Mercy, Mercy, Mercy (Mercy, Mercy, Mercy).** With Timmons at the piano, lured away from Art Blakey's Messengers, and the strong rhythm team of Sam Jones on bass and Louis Hayes on drums, the quintet became the spearhead of the commercially successful soul wave. Joe Zawinul joined the band, replacing Timmons, and wrote **Mercy,** and multi-instrumentalist Yusef Lateef was added.

While neither of the Adderley brothers was particularly original, their music, by its heavy emphasis on the roots, helped to popularize jazz at a time when radical upheavals – atonality, polyrhythmic complexity, tonal expressionism – was clearing the halls. Happy music, and none the worse for that. Cannonball's death (of a stroke, on August 8, 1975) hit jazz hard, for he was a kindly man, always ready to promote young talent – for example, Wes Montgomery.

Recordings:
Somethin' Else (Blue Note/Blue Note)
Miles Davis, Milestones (CBS/CBS)
Miles Davis, Kind Of Blue (CBS/CBS)
Gil Evans, Pacific Standard Time (Blue Note/Blue Note)
Them Dirty Blues, Now Cannonball & Eight Giants (Milestone/Milestone)
The Japanese Concerts (Milestone/Milestone)
Mercy, Mercy, Mercy (Capitol/Capitol)
Phenix (Fantasy/—)
Coast To Coast (Milestone/Milestone)

Bernard Addison

Although not a fashionable name amongst jazz guitarists these days, Bernard S. Addison (born Annapolis, Maryland, 1905) was one of the very best players to emerge from the 1920s. Basically a rhythm-section guitarist, using chord style, Addison's consistent playing added considerable impetus and drive both to the numerous bands with which he was associated, as well as to a vast number of recording sessions in which he participated. He played mandolin at early age. At first, he worked with several little-known bands, including Sonny Thompson's (with which he came to New York). Between 1925–1929 he was employed mostly at Small's, playing guitar and banjo, later as bandleader. He used guitar only from 1928. He also played with Claude Hopkins, a former schoolfriend (jointly, they led another band in the early 1920s). He was a member of the big band (♦) accompanying Louis Armstrong (♦) at New York's Cocoanut Grove – **V.S.O.P. (Very Special Old Phonography), 1928-1930, Vols 5 & 6** – in 1930; the same year Addison recorded with

Bubber Miley's (♦) Mileage Makers – **Bubber Miley & His Friends: 1929-1931.** He added much zest to the rhythm section of the Fletcher Henderson (♦) Orchestra (1933–1934) **(Fletcher Henderson Story** and **Fletcher Henderson Story, Vol 4, Complete Fletcher Henderson/Fletcher Henderson Story, Vol 2** and **The Big Bands/Ridin' In Rhythm).**

Before Henderson, he had appeared with Art Tatum (♦). During the Henderson period he recorded with fellow sidemen, including Coleman Hawkins (♦) and Henry 'Red' Allen (♦) **(Recordings Made Between 1930 and 1941)** – and with Horace Henderson (♦) **(The Big Bands/Ridin' In Rhythm),** both in 1933. After Fletcher Henderson, Addison became accompanist to Adelaide Hall (the pair had worked together previously, with Tatum); then the guitarist brought his own band into New York clubs Famous Door and Adrian's Tap Room for seasons (1935). He recorded again with Allen and Horace Henderson in '35 **(Henry Allen & His Orchestra 1934-1935)** and, in celebration of his band's engagement at Adrian Rollini's (♦) 48th Street club, recorded the band (with multi-instrumentalist Rollini present) for Victor.

These recordings (the same band, under Freddie Jenkins' name, cut other sides at the date) probably demonstrate best of all the rhythmic thrust Addison invariably imparted to this and other musical outfits with which he was associated. He worked as sole accompanist to vocal group the Mills Brothers (1936–1938), travelling with them to Europe ('36), during which time he recorded with Benny Carter (♦) who was then resident in the UK **(Swingin' At Maida Vale).** Around this time he worked also in a two-guitar band, with Teddy Bunn (♦); with Mezz Mezzrow **(The Big Apple),** then with violinist Stuff Smith (♦) (1938–1939). He led his own groups, worked with Sidney Bechet (♦) **(Sidney Bechet, Vol 2),** Coleman Hawkins **(The Big Sounds Of Coleman Hawkins & Chu Berry)** and Red Allen **(Harlem On Saturday Night)** – all 1940, before conscription into the US Army. He led his own Services unit, after which he joined Snub Mosley's band, then worked for several years in Canada, and was a member of the all-star Fletcher Henderson Reunion Band **(The Big Reunion)** in 1957.

During the latter half of 1950s he toured with the Ink Spots, then accompanied Juanita Hall (1960) and the same year appeared at the Newport Jazz Festival with Eubie Blake (♦). He also recorded with the pianist-composer on **Wizard Of The Ragtime Piano.** He continued working as a single act throughout the 1960s, and recorded in New York, together with trumpeter Johnny Letman and altoist Pete Brown (♦) **(Pete's Last Date).** But by this time Bernard Addison had become a student of classical guitar, then a guitar tutor.

Recordings:
Louis Armstrong, V.S.O.P. (Very Special Old Phonography), 1928-1930, Vols 5 & 6 (CBS – France)
Bubber Miley & His Friends 1929-1931 (RCA Victor – France)

The Fletcher Henderson Story (Columbia)/
The Fletcher Henderson Story, Vol 4 (CBS)
Coleman Hawkins, Recordings Made Between 1930 & 1941 (CBS – France)
Jelly Roll Morton, Vols 1, 7 (RCA Victor – France)
Various, The Big Bands (Prestige)/
Ridin' In Rhythm (World Records)
Henry Allen & His Orchestra 1934-1935 (Collector's Classics)
Various, Adrian Rollini & His Friends, Vol 1: 'Tap Room Special' (RCA Victor – France)
The Complete Fletcher Henderson (RCA Victor)/
Fletcher Henderson, Vol 2 (RCA Victor – France)
Benny Carter, Swingin' At Maida Vale (—/Ace of Clubs)
Milton 'Mezz' Mezzrow (Frankie Newton), The Big Apple (RCA Victor – France)
The Big Sounds Of Coleman Hawkins & Chu Berry (—/London)
Various, Harlem On Saturday Night (—/Ace of Clubs)
The Fletcher Henderson All Stars, The Big Reunion (Jazztone/—)
Pete Brown, Pete's Last Date (—/77)*
*Originally issued as **Bernard Addison, High In A Basement** (—/77)

Joe Albany

Born 1924, the legendary pianist has had to wait until the '70s to receive his critical due. One of the finest white Bebop pianists of the '40s – along with George Wallington, Al Haig and Dodo Marmarosa – Albany played with Charlie Parker, though recordings of their collaboration were not issued until 1976 **(Yardbird In Lotus Land).** For many years, his reputation was based on two records, **The Aladdin Sessions** and **The Right Combination,** separated by an eleven year gap. The former features the pianist on four tracks with Lester Young, and the later date, now deleted, was

Proto-Bopper (Spotlite): Joe Albany in pensive mood.

an informal session recorded in engineer Ralph Garretson's living room, and catches the vastly talented Albany with that other great recluse, tenorist Warne Marsh. Fourteen years elapsed before he surfaced on record again, this time unaccompanied and as good as ever **(Joe Albany At Home).** Since then, there has been a steady flow of albums, and

it looks as if his career has finally settled.

Technically, Joe Albany has everything: touch, timing and a limitless fund of devices to express the range of his imagination. There is a lyrical intensity about his best work that recalls the flights of Parker, his last influence.

Recordings:
Lester Young, The Aladdin Sessions (Blue Note/Blue Note)
Charlie Parker, Yardbird In Lotus Land (—/Spotlite)
The Right Combination (—/Riverside)
Joe Albany At Home (—/Spotlite)
Proto-Bopper (—/Spotlite)
Birdtown Birds (—/Steeplechase)
Joe Albany & Niels Pedersen (—/Steeplechase)

Henry 'Red' Allen

Henry James 'Red' Allen (born New Orleans, Louisiana, 1908; died New York City, 1967) was, together with Louis Armstrong (♦) and Roy Eldridge (♦), the outstanding trumpet stylist of the 1930s. Son of a New Orleans brass-band leader, Henry Allen (1877–1952), Red Allen started on violin and alto-horn, before switching to trumpet. After local work with leading New Orleans musicians like George Lewis (♦) and John Handy (♦), as well as with Sidney Desvignes aboard the SS *Island Queen,* Allen became a member of the King Oliver (♦) Jazz Band, 1927. Record debut – with Clarence Williams (♦) same year. Then returned to New Orleans, to work with Walter Pichon and on riverboats with Fate Marable (1928–29). Back in New York (1929), Allen recorded under his own name for first time **(Henry Red Allen & His New York Orchestra, Vols 1, 2: 1929)** in company with blues singer Victoria Spivey, and instrumentalists Albert Nicholas (♦), J. C. Higginbotham (♦), Charlie Holmes and Luis Russell (♦), all colleagues in band led by Russell, and of which Allen became a prominent member same year. Music produced at these sessions was of uniformly high standard, with Allen's trumpet playing the individual highlight. Already, as these

Above: 'Red' Allen – one of the advance guard of players to emerge from the late 1920s, early 1930s.

records show, Allen's basic style had been formed; a style which, although obviously influenced by Armstrong, had its own individualism. His playing was distinguished by positive allegiance to the beat, but with rhythmic flexibility few other trumpeters of the period possessed, and an overtly emotional projection; technically, few faults. And Allen's idiosyncratic tonal effects – glissandos, smears, achieved by adroit tonguing – made him, along with Armstrong, a member of the advance guard of the late-1920s/early-1930s. With Russell, recorded a series of extraordinary solos.

As with Oliver, already Allen was beginning to think in terms of other than two- and four-bar symmetry. His strong, brassy tone, his fierce attack, together with forward-looking harmonic conception, are demonstrated most handsomely in finest solos with Russell, including **Saratoga Shout, Doctor Blues, Jersey Lightning, Panama, Song Of The Swanee (The Luis Russell Story)** and **It Should Be You, Feeling Drowsy (Henry Red Allen, Vol 1).**

Allen left Russell (1932), worked with Charlie Johnson (1933), then joined Fletcher Henderson (♦), with whom he had worked, briefly, in '32. With Henderson, took several startlingly brilliant solos, on a variety of material, including **Wrappin' It Up, Rug Cutter's Swing (Henderson – 1934), 'Yeah Man!, Queer Notions, King Porter Stomp (The Fletcher Henderson Story/The Fletcher Henderson Story, Vol 4),** and **Night Life, Nagasaki,** and a different version of **Queer Notions (Jazz Pioneers/Ridin' In Rhythm).**

With Coleman Hawkins (♦), a colleague of his with Henderson, Allen often produced his best work while, in turn, stimulating the tenorist (eg the two versions of **Queer Notions** cited above). From a Hawkins record date of 1933, Allen's trumpet burned incandescently, on **Jamaica Shout** and **Heartbreak Blues (Jazz Pioneers/Ridin' In Rhythm). Ride, Red, Ride, St Louis Wiggle, Harlem Heat,** and **Red Rhythm** are four other sides which find Allen's

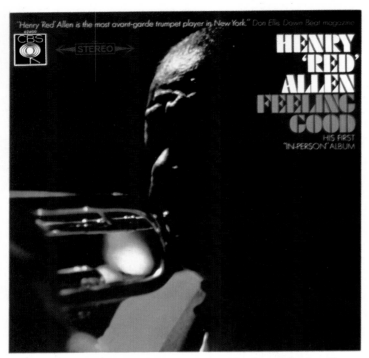

"Henry 'Red' Allen is the most avant-garde trumpet player in New York." Don Ellis Down Beat magazine

Feeling Good (CBS). Red Allen was called by Don Ellis: '... the most creative and avant-garde trumpet player in New York'.

playing at its most expressive – this time as a member of The Mills Blue Rhythm Band.

Also recorded with Billie Holiday (♦) (1937), **The Golden Years, Vol 2**, as well as with Sidney Bechet (♦) (1941), **Sleepy Time Down South** and James P. Johnson (♦), **Father Of The Stride Piano**. Allen recorded fine solos with King Oliver (**King Oliver, Vol 2: 1929-1930**), Jelly Roll Morton (**Jelly Roll Morton & His Red Hot Peppers (1927-1930), Vol 1**), and Lionel Hampton (♦) (**Lionel Hampton's Best Records, Vol 3: 1939-1940**). More of the Allen-Russell combination can be found within **Luis Russell & His Louisiana Swing Orchestra**.

Apart from his various recording activities of the 1930s-into-the-1940s, Allen's post-Henderson career encompassed a 25-month stint with the Mills Blue Rhythm Band, and a three-and-a-half-year spell with big band accompanying Louis Armstrong (**V.S.O.P. (Very Special Old Phonography, 1928-1930), Vols 5 & 6**).

Formed own sextet (end of 1940), of which long-time Allen associate, J. C. Higginbotham, was important member from beginning until 1947 (**The Very Great Henry Red Allen, Vol 1**). This series of Allen-led bands, with the leader's flaring trumpet and friendly vocals its focal points, lasted into the 1950s, having completed lengthy residencies in major clubs throughout US. Between 1954-65, Allen featured as regular attraction at the Metropole, New York.

First trip to Europe was with band of Kid Ory (♦) (1959), returning to Britain as solo act on several occasions during 1960s. Shortly after completing the last of these, in 1967, Allen died in New York of cancer.

One of Allen's finest record dates during latter part of his career took place in March, 1957, in the company of old friends like Hawkins, Higginbotham, Buster Bailey (♦), and Cozy Cole (♦). Session produced much superior jazz from all concerned, including

a series of magnificent trumpet solos on each of the ten recorded items, with those on **I Cover The Waterfront, Sweet Lorraine, 'S Wonderful** and a re-make of **Ride, Red, Ride** being especially praiseworthy (**The Very Great Henry Red Allen, Vol 2**). Allen's playing was, in fact, comparable to the best of his more youthful days; like that to be found on a famous session put together by Spike Hughes (**Spike Hughes & His All American Orchestra**).

During latter part of his career, Red Allen was guest in three important TV specials, *Chicago & All That Jazz, The Sound Of Jazz* and *Profile Of The Arts.* Allen's timeless playing, exemplified by two albums made at the tail-end of his career, **The Henry Allen Memorial Album/Mr Allen – Henry Red Allen** and **Feeling Good** was summed up by Don Ellis (♦), a trumpet player from a different era, in the following widely syndicated quote from 1965: 'Red Allen is the most creative and avant-garde trumpet player in New York'.

Recordings:
King Oliver, Vols 1, 2
(RCA Victor – France)
Henry 'Red' Allen, Vols 1-4
(RCA Victor – France)
Luis Russell & His Louisiana Swing Orchestra *(Columbia/—)*
The Luis Russell Story
(—/Parlophone)
The Fletcher Henderson Story
(Columbia)/
The Fletcher Henderson Story, Vol 4 *(CBS)*
The Complete Fletcher Henderson *(RCA Victor)/*
Fletcher Henderson, Vols 1-3
(RCA Victor – France)
Various, Jazz Pioneers
(Prestige)/
Ridin' In Rhythm
(World Records)
Fletcher Henderson, Henderson – 1934
(—/Ace of Hearts)
Coleman Hawkins, Recordings Made Between 1930 and 1941
(CBS – France)

Spike Hughes & His All American Orchestra
(London/Ace of Clubs)
The Mills Blue Rhythm Band
(Jazz Panorama – Sweden)
Jelly Roll Morton & His Red Hot Peppers (1927-1930), Vol 1
(RCA Victor – France)
Billie Holiday, The Golden Years, Vol 2 *(Columbia/CBS)*
Sidney Bechet, Vol 1: 'Sleepy Time Down South'
(RCA Victor – France)
James P. Johnson, Father Of The Stride Piano *(Columbia/—)*
Henry Allen & His Orchestra Vols 1-4 *(Collector's Classics/—)*
The Very Great Henry Red Allen, Vols 1, 2 *(Rarities/—)*
Various, Harlem On Saturday Night *(—/Ace of Hearts)*
Lionel Hampton's Best Records, Vol 3 (1939-1940)
(RCA Victor – France)
Louis Armstrong, V.S.O.P. (Very Special Old Phonography), 1928-1930, Vols 5 & 6 *(CBS – France)*
Louis Armstrong, Swing That Music *(MCA/Coral)*
The Henry Allen Memorial Album *(Prestige)/*
Mr. Allen – Henry Red Allen *(Xtra)*
Henry Allen, Feeling Good *(Columbia/CBS)*

Mose Allison

The pianist composer was born in Tippo, Mississippi, in 1927, and early blues influences such as Tampa Red, Memphis Slim and Sonny Boy Williamson permeate his work, despite later Bebop overlays. His first composition, a series of impressionistic vignettes, **The Back Country Suite (Mose Allison)** remains his best work, and makes a lighter, less self-conscious use of the roots than was usually the case in the late '50s. His singing on numbers like **Blues** or **One Room Country Shack** has an odd appeal, and influenced Georgie Fame. His occasional trumpet playing on later albums is shaky. Allison is an excellent sideman, with Al Cohn, for example, but the charm of his early suites was never recaptured.

Recordings:
Mose Allison *(Prestige/Prestige)*

Albert Ammons

Albert C. Ammons (born Chicago, Illinois, 1907) was perhaps the best-known and foremost exponent of boogie-woogie piano, a style of playing easily recognized by the repetitive ostinato figure played by the left hand, eight beats to the bar, complemented by powerful rhythmic right-hand work.

Ammons, father of the late tenor-saxophonist Eugene 'Gene' Ammons (♦), came to the fore during 1920s as pianist who appeared at numerous clubs in his native city. First began playing piano at ten, and was featured with Francois Moseley's Louisiana Stompers in 1929; then, as second pianist with William Barbee & His Headquarters (1930–31). By 1934 Ammons had put together own small combo, Chicago-based,

which lasted until 1938. 1936: recording debut with band that also included trumpeter Guy Kelly, bassist Israel Crosby (♦), and drummer Jimmy Hoskins; **Boogie Woogie Stomp**.

Left Chicago in '38 in company with fellow pianist Meade Lux Lewis (♦), at behest of John Hammond. In New York, the pair teamed up with another piano player, Pete Johnson (♦), all three working together, or solo, often with blues shouter Joe Turner (♦). The coming together of the three coincided with sudden craze for eight-to-a-bar music. Trio played at one of Hammond's Spirituals To Swing concerts (December '38) (**John Hammond's Spirituals To Swing**) with Ammons taking part in three-piano showcase (**Cavalcade Of Boogie**) as well as accompanying country-blues singer-guitarist Big Bill Broonzy (♦). Ammons also recorded in 1938 for Library of Congress (**The Complete Library Of Congress Boogie Woogie Recordings**), and the Ammons-Lewis-Johnson triumvirate cut a torrid two-part **Boogie Woogie Prayer (Cafe Society Swing & The Boogie Woogie)** in December, a perfect definition of superior boogie-woogie playing. **Cafe Society Rag**, from same session, and with a Turner vocal, identified an important New York venue for the boogie trio. February, '39: Ammons and Johnson (apart) recorded two boogie woogie pieces each with trumpeter Harry James (♦), (**Cafe Society Swing & The Boogie Woogie**), an unlikely combination which worked well for all three.

In 1939, too, Ammons recorded several times for Blue Note (**Blue Note's Three Decades Of Jazz – 1939 to 1949 – Vol 1**), as soloist (**Boogie Woogie Stomp**), and as member of Frankie Newton's Port of Harlem Jazzmen (**Port Of Harlem Blues**). More Ammons solo discs came same year for another famous jazz label, Riverside (**Giants Of Boogie Woogie**). At end of 1939, Ammons guested, again, at a further Spirituals to Swing concert (**John Hammond's Spirituals To Swing**), contributing two solid choruses to jam-session work-out on **Lady Be Good**, in company with Basie (♦) Orchestra and the Goodman (♦) Sextet. Ammons-Johnson duo (with rather unnecessary addition of Jimmy Hoskins' drums) laid down some fine boogie sounds for Victor in May, 1941 (**29 Boogie Woogie Originaux**), but it was to be Ammons' last recordings until 1944, due to a musicians' union ban on recordings and to an unfortunate accident which resulted in the pianist cutting off the tip of one finger in attempting to slice a sandwich. He was back in action, for in-person performances, not long after the incident. At this time, Ammons and Johnson worked regularly together, appearing in major US cities – they were great favorites amongst the Hollywood fraternity – but by 1944, Ammons was in recording studios again, this time for Commodore, alone, and in company with his Rhythm Kings (**Commodore Jazz, Vol 1**), who included Hot Lips Page (♦), Don Byas (♦), Big Sid Catlett (♦), Vic Dickenson, and his old Chicago associate, Israel Crosby. As well as the other's playing on this date, Ammons' powerful keyboard work, especially on **Bottom**

Blues, invariably takes solo honors, inspired no doubt by Catlett's catalytic drumming.

Between 1946 and 1949 Ammons recorded for Mercury.

Typical of the music Ammons produced for Mercury is that to be found on **Boogie Woogie Piano Stylings** and **'Jug' Sessions**, the former marred only by some ordinary or indifferent material, the latter featuring on tracks like **St Louis Blues**, Ammons' son, Gene. 1946: Joe Turner and Ammons re-united for National recording date **(Joe Turner Sings The Blues, Vol 2)**, with both big men sounding as electrifying as before. There was, however, a mid-1940s interruption to Ammons' career, due to temporary paralysis of both hands.

He returned to Chicago for the last ten years of his life, where he lived and continued to work. The only deviation from this was in 1949 when he joined Lionel Hampton (♦), recording as well as touring with the vibesman's band. But Albert Ammons, whose Jimmy Yancey (♦) influenced playing had given much pleasure to so many over the years died in December 1949.

Recordings:
Albert Ammons, Boogie Woogie Stomp
(Swaggie–Australia)
Various, John Hammond's Spirituals To Swing
(Vanguard/Vanguard)
Various, The Complete Library Of Congress Boogie Woogie Recordings *(Jazz Piano/—)*
Various, Cafe Society Swing & The Boogie Woogie
(Swingfan – Germany)
Various, Blue Note's Three Decades Of Jazz – 1939 to 1949 – Vol 1 *(Blue Note/—)*
Various, Kings Of Boogie Woogie *(Blue Note/—)*
Various, Giants Of Boogie Woogie *(Riverside/—)*
Various, 29 Boogie Woogie Originaux
(RCA Victor – France)
Various, Commodore Jazz, Vol 1
(—/London)
Various, Boogie Woogie Man
(RCA Victor – France)
Gene Ammons, 'Jug' Sessions
(EmArcy/—)
Various, Boogie Woogie Trio
(—/Storyville)
Albert Ammons, Boogie Woogie Piano Stylings
(Mercury – Holland)

Gene Ammons

Born 1925, the son of boogie-woogie pianist Albert Ammons, tenor man Gene 'Jug' Ammons was one of Chicago's favorite sons. At the age of 18, he was playing with the King Kolax band, then in the sax section of Billy Eckstine's band. In 1949, he succeeded Stan Getz in the Woody Herman Herd. Starting under the influence of Lester Young, Ammons is best known for the complete antithesis of that style. Big-toned, forthright, often closer to R&B, Ammons projects a party spirit on most occasions. In 1950, he formed an ideal two-tenor combo with Sonny Stitt – simple, functional heads, driving solos, blistering chase choruses. There is little to choose between their albums, **Soul Summit, Blues**

Up & Down or **You Talk That Talk**, for the spirit of rugged spontaneity surges through every number. Their final album together, made shortly before Ammons' death in 1974 **(Together Again For The Last Time)**, displays a shrinking of technique, some sloppy note production, but a compensating excitement. His opening solo on **Saxification** says it all – the overwhelming attack, big, blunt, honking, macho sound, the ends of his notes abrupt as a punch in the mouth. Ballads usually ended up as blues, **The More I**

Together Again For The Last Time (Prestige): great tenor team.

See You and **I'll Close My Eyes** feature reiterated phrases and grandstanding finales. Soul sax players like King Curtis owe a great deal to Jug.

Recordings:
Gene Ammons & Dodo Marmarosa, Jug & Dodo
(Prestige/Prestige)
Ammons & Stitt, Soul Summit
(Prestige/—)
Blues Up & Down *(Prestige/—)*
You Talk That Talk *(Prestige/—)*
Together For The Last Time
(Prestige/—)
Red Top *(Savoy/Savoy)*

Ivie Anderson

Duke Ellington's (♦) choice of vocalists to work with his various orchestras was too often singularly lacking in the kind of perception which enabled him to select instrumentalists whose talents were absolutely appropriate for his needs. But if Ellington employed but one really great vocalist, then that vocalist has to be Ivie Anderson (born Gilroy, California, 1904). Ivie, a sensitive, musicianly, always tuneful singer, worked with Ellington from February 1931 to August 1942. Even when faced with such daunting material as **Oh, Babe!, Maybe Someday** or **Five O'Clock Whistle (The Duke 1940)**, she succeeded, most times, in producing an eminently satisfactory performance.

Ivie Anderson, who died in Los Angeles in 1949, made very few recordings under her own name. But a January 1946 date **(Ivie Anderson & Her All Stars)**, in company with first-class musicians like Charlie Mingus (♦), Lucky Thompson (♦), and Willie Smith (♦), and with band arranged/conducted by Phil Moore, produced some generally first-class singing, best of all on **Empty Bed Blues** and a reprise of **I Got It Bad**, the latter one of her most celebrated

feature items with Ellington, viz **The Works Of Duke Ellington, Vol 16** and **In A Mellotone**.

Other Anderson-associated items from the Ellington songbook include **It Don't Mean A Thing (The Complete Duke, Vol 3: 1930-1932), Rocks In My Bed (In A Mellotone), I'm Checking Out Goodbye (The Ellington Era, Vol 2)** and **I Don't Mind (The Works Of Duke Ellington, Vol 18)**. As well as her many in-person appearances and recordings with the Duke Ellington Orchestra, Ivie Anderson also participated in the Marx Brothers' 1937 movie *A Day At The Races*.

The singer received vocal training initially between 9–13 at a convent, then studied for two years in Washington, DC. Her first professional engagement was in Los Angeles. She toured as dancer-singer; worked with several bands as singer only, including Paul Howard's and Anson Weeks' between 1925–30, and made Australian tour with Sonny Clay. Before joining Ellington she worked with Earl Hines (♦) in *Grand Terrace Revue* (1930). Opened her own restaurant in Los Angeles after leaving Ellington (1942), still singing regularly on West Coast. An asthmatic complaint restricted her appearances thereafter.

Perhaps the finest collection of Ivie Anderson recordings yet released is **Ivie Anderson**, which encapsulates some memorable vocalizing with Ellington. Included are such choice examples of the lady's art as **It Don't Mean A Thing, Happy As The Day Is Long, Shoe Shine Boy, Truckin', Get Yourself A New Dream** and **There's A Lull In My Life**.

Recordings:
Ivie Anderson *(Columbia/—)*
Ivie Anderson & Her All Stars
(Tops/Gala)
The Works Of Duke Ellington, Vols 10, 16, 17, 18
(RCA Victor – France)
The Complete Duke Ellington, Vols 3 (1930-1932), Vol 5 (1932-1933), Vol 6 (1933-1936), Vol 7 (1936-1937) *(CBS – France)*
Duke Ellington, The Ellington Era, Vol 2 *(Columbia/CBS)*
Duke Ellington, In A Mellotone
(RCA Victor/RCA Victor)
Duke Ellington, Vintage Duke
(Trip)
Duke Ellington *(Trip)/*
All That Jazz: Duke Ellington
(DJM)
Duke Ellington, The Duke 1940
(Jazz Society/—)

Arkestra
♦ *Sun Ra*

Louis Armstrong

Louis Armstrong (born New Orleans, 1900), formerly of the Crescent City's Coloured Waifs Home and the best-known jazz musician of his or any other generation, has few rivals for the title of the greatest of all instrumental soloists. And apart from Billie Holiday (♦) (one of the innumerable artists deeply influenced by Armstrong), he remains the greatest jazz vocalist of all time.

Armstrong's development, from an apparently hesitant cornettist (practically untutored) to a position of positive omnipotence, was astonishing. After various mundane non-musical jobs, the young Armstrong formed a band (together with drummer, Joe Lindsey); then, at 18, joined Kid Ory (♦). Worked with Fate Marable, both on Mississippi riverboats and in more conventional settings, between 1918–21. In the latter year, returned to city of his birth, played in marching bands as well as with jazz bands of Zutty Singleton (♦), Papa Celestin, and others. Most significant job yet was to follow: in 1922 Louis Armstrong joined Creole Jazz Band of King Oliver (♦), like Armstrong a trumpeter of immense importance and ability. Between 1922 and 1924 the two-part team of Armstrong and his mentor was to produce some of the most remarkable music in jazz history.

Cornettists, with Armstrong ostensibly operating as second string to Oliver, are at their most sublime on **Mabel's Dream** (both takes), **Canal Street Blues, Riverside Blues, Snake Rag (Louis Armstrong/King Oliver)** and **Tears, Buddy's Habit** and **Chattanooga Stomp (West End Blues). Tears** was important for the burgeoning talent; not only did he co-compose the piece with Lillian Hardin (the band's pianist and soon to become his second wife), but Louis' nine breaks, each executed impeccably and with rare feeling, point to the kind of virtuoso solo performances he was to produce with frightening regularity in the very near future **(Chimes Blues (Louis Armstrong/King Oliver)**, Armstrong's first solo on records, is less than average). **Weather Bird**

Louis Armstrong & Kid Oliver (Milestone) – 'remarkable'.

Adam And Eve Had The Blues (CBS). 'Twenties classics.

Rag (Louis Armstrong/King Oliver) is a glorious example of both Armstrong and Oliver operating in a non-solo capacity but providing superlative breaks in tandem.

When, in June 1924, Armstrong left an already fading Oliver, he had, even at this stage, left an indelible mark on jazz. With his induction into the Fletcher Henderson (♦) Orchestra as featured trumpet soloist, in September, '24, Armstrong's career took another major step forward. With Henderson, the virtuoso trumpet player really came into focus. His solos on Henderson recordings like **How Come You Do Me Like You Do?, Everybody Loves My Baby, Shanghai Shuffle, Alabamy Bound** and **Copenhagen (Louis Armstrong With Fletcher Henderson, 1924-1925)** are extraordinary in showing off Armstrong's unsurpassed tone, his inexhaustible stamina and fierce attack. His rhythmic powers too are remarkable, with Armstrong breaking up time in a way that made him stand out, with ease, amongst an already star-studded Henderson band (eg Hawkins, Buster Bailey, Redman, Joe Smith, et al). Next landmark came to pass with the advent of his Hot Five and Hot Seven recordings which have long since passed into the realms of jazz immortality. Chronologically, the Hot Five was first, with Armstrong leading the brothers Johnny Dodds (♦) and Warren 'Baby' Dodds (♦), Kid Ory, Lillian Hardin Armstrong (they were married by this time) and Johnny St Cyr through a series of classic performances. The Hot Five was an ideal setting for Armstrong's dexterity, yet only Johnny Dodds could compete with his all-round brilliance, if not technically, then in terms of pure jazz and emotional depth. A few odd failures or disappointments for Armstrong (eg, **King Of The Zulus**), but generally he sustained incredible heights through the Hot Five recordings (made between 1925–1927). **Cornet Chop Suey (The Louis Armstrong Legend)** is probably Armstrong's first real *tour de force*, but his playing on such as **Heebie Jeebies, Jazz Lips, Skid-Da-De-Dat** and **Gut Bucket Blues (The Louis Armstrong Legend)** are not far behind. The Hot Seven (1927) produced even more Armstrong fireworks: **Twelfth Street Rag, Melancholy Blues, Wild Man Blues,** and the electrifying **Potato Head Blues (The Louis Armstrong Legend)** set new standards of jazz performance and solo virtuosity. So too did Armstrong's playing on other items: **Gully Low Blues, S.O.L. Blues, Struttin' With Some Barbecue, Once In A While, Savoy Blues** – last three titles reverting to Hot Five format, with blues guitarist Lonnie Johnson (♦) added to **Barbecue** and **Savoy Blues (The Louis Armstrong Legend)**. By mid-1928, Armstrong had produced still further gems, this time with his Savoy Ballroom Five: **Fireworks, Skip The Gutter** and the magisterial **West End Blues**, with its awesome opening cadenza and final chorus that reaches the ultimate in building to a technical-emotional climax (all **The Louis Armstrong Legend)**.

In July 1928, Armstrong recorded with big band accompaniment, this one Carroll Dickerson's **(The Louis Armstrong Legend)**. It was a context in which the Armstrong horn was to be heard, regularly, during most of the next decade. Before finally embarking on this format full-time, there were more Savoy Ballroom Five recordings (seven, actually, with Don Redman (♦) added), including beautifully structured solos on **Basin Street Blues** (over dismal vocal-cum-instrumental background) **(The Louis Armstrong Legend)**. And there were inspired duets between Armstrong and an Armstrong-influenced pianist named Earl Hines (♦). At this time, Hines probably was the only instrumentalist in jazz who could offer real challenge to Louis Armstrong, in terms of all-round musical excellence and dazzling solo work. Both men struck sparks off each other – demonstrably so on **Savoyager's Stomp, Muggles,** and the mind-boggling **Weather Bird. Weather Bird**, like **West End Blues**,

Above: Louis Armstrong. With Ellington, the most celebrated jazz figure – equalled only by the immortal Charlie Parker.

another composition by Armstrong's old boss King Oliver, remains forever one of the all-time great jazz duets (all **The Louis Armstrong Legend)**. Armstrong knocked off yet further opulent trumpet solos on **I Can't Give You Anything But Love** and **Mahogany Hall Stomp (V.S.O.P. (Very Special Old Phonography), Vols 5 & 6)** with an all-star aggregation, including Jack Teagarden (♦), Joe Sullivan (♦), Lonnie Johnson and Luis Russell (♦), the last-named pianist-leader at the disc date. Russell's star-studded orchestra, along with other big bands (Les Hite, Zilner Randolph, etc) provided backdrop to Armstrong's trumpet for several years. Although these bands produced accompaniments that never remotely approached Armstrong's genius, the succession of one majestic solo after another continued unabated: **When You're Smiling, I'm A Ding Dong Daddy, Confessin' (V.S.O.P., Vols 5 & 6), Body and Soul, Sweethearts On Parade, Shine, Star Dust, Wrap Your Troubles In Dreams (V.S.O.P., Vols 7 & 8)** and **I Gotta Right To Sing The Blues, Dusky Stevedore (Louis Armstrong: July 4, 1900/July 6, 1971)**. By the time the last two items were recorded (1933), the accompanying orchestras were, in every way, nothing more than a cushion to accentuate the bravura work of the Armstrong horn and its owner's equally inimitable gravel voice. At this point, it is important to lay stress on the fact that, aside of his cornet/trumpet playing, Armstrong's *vocal* contributions to jazz had been considerable, even thus far.

From basic scat of **Heebie Jeebies, Gully Low Blues** and the like, to the more 'conventional' jazz singing of **I Can't Give You Anything But Love, I Ain't Got Nobody** and **I'm A Ding Dong Daddy**, Armstrong had become one of the great jazz vocalists. His voice had warmth, exuded personality, was rhythmically exciting; all in all, a perfect adjunct to the trumpet playing. Whilst on singing, it is also worth noting that Armstrong took part in an impressive number of recordings during 1920s, as accompanist to numerous blues (or blues-influenced) singers. Most notable of these involved Bessie Smith (♦) and Ma Rainey (♦). The Rainey tracks, **See See Rider Blues, Jelly Bean Blues** and **Countin' The Blues (Ma Rainey),** date from 1924, and demonstrate not only that Armstrong had a natural feel for the genre, but also that, at 24 years old, his blues-playing was astonishingly mature. With Smith, the following year, this side of his art had improved more than marginally. **St Louis Blues (The Empress)**, probably is the optimum Armstrong-Smith recording, the former's muted horn sounding at times like a logical extension of Bessie's magnificent vocalism. **Cold In Hand Blues, Reckless Blues, Sobbin' Hearted Blues (The Empress), I Ain't Gonna Play No Second Fiddle** and **Careless Love (Nobody's Blues But Mine)** are yet more supreme examples of one more magical combination. During the 1920s, the Armstrong trumpet was heard with singers as diverse as Virginia Liston, Margaret Johnson, Sippie Wallace, Eva Taylor (wife of Clarence Williams (♦)), Hociel Thomas, Clarence Todd (all **Adam & Eve Had The Blues)**; Bertha 'Chippie' Hill, Butterbeans and Susie, Cleo Gibson, Sara Martin, Victoria Spivey, Mamie Smith (all **Jazz Sounds Of The Twenties, Vol 4)** and Maggie Jones, Nolan Welsh, Clara Smith **(Rare Recordings Of The Twenties, Vol 1)**. Overall, the standard of the Armstrong contributions to these and other recordings is astonishingly high. Later in his career, he was to combine his vocal-instrumental talents with other more pop-orientated singers, the most successful collaboration being between Ella Fitzgerald (♦) and Louis Armstrong. This team worked together on record (and in person) on many occasions, nowhere better than during **Porgy & Bess** and **Ella & Louis, Vols 1 & 2/The Special Magic Of Ella & Louis, Vols 1 & 2)**. Louis Armstrong, the Virtuoso, tended to diminish during the latter

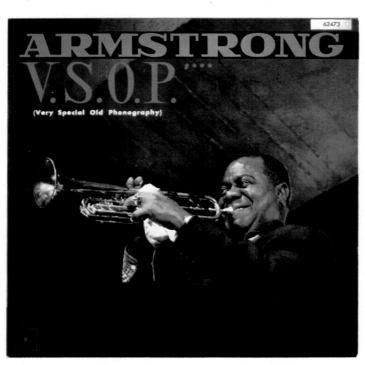

V.S.O.P. (Very Special Old Phonography), Vol 4 (CBS, France). Louis, in some Very Special Performances . . .

portion of the 1930s (and thereafter), but there remained occasions when his trumpet could soar to incomparable heights. Three such performances are: **Struttin With Some Barbecue** (a remake, and one of the few that can be said to be superior to the original), **Jubilee** and **Swing That Music (Complete Recorded Works 1935-1945)**, the latter title containing four trumpet choruses astonishing even by Louis' own incredible standards, with a stretched-out high-note climax that is unmatched. Armstrong-with-big-band-backing concept continued into the 1940s, but the decade started promisingly with a stimulating record date that reunited Louis with Sidney Bechet **(Complete Recorded Works 1935-1945)**, with both men trying to outplay the other throughout four titles, best of which is **Coal Cart Blues**. Armstrong had worked alongside Bechet during 1929, with Clarence Williams' Blue Five **(Adam & Eve Had The Blues)** and **Louis Armstrong/Sidney Bechet With The Clarence Williams Blue Five,** and with Josephine Beatty/Red Onion Jazz Babies **(Louis Armstrong In New York, 1924-1926).**

1947: first edition of Louis Armstrong & His All Stars, with cornet of Bobby Hackett (♦) a welcome additional voice, playing some delightful obbligato to Louis' vocals which, since the 1930s, had tended to be more and more a regular feature of recordings, concerts, etc. Also most welcome, the voice and trombone of Jack Teagarden, and the controlled explosiveness of Sidney Catlett's drumming. There are fine studio recordings by this band **(Louis Armstrong: July 4, 1900/July 6, 1971)**, and it was indeed fortuitous that one of its first concerts, at Town Hall in May '47, was recorded for posterity **(Satchmo's Greatest Hits, Vols 4, 5 & 6)**. There were many moments of magic thereafter, including generally top-class albums like **Louis Armstrong Joue W. C. Handy/ Ambassador Satch/Satch Plays Fats,** but often the all-star set-up failed to inspire its leader into producing, during the 1950s/1960s, playing which compared with his innovatory days of the 1920s/1930s. Significant or otherwise, it was during this latter part of his career – following wholly successful international tours which took him to far-off places like Africa, Australia, Europe, the Far East and behind a portion of the Iron Curtain – that Louis Armstrong became an even bigger international music celebrity, his ever-growing number of fans coming more from a strictly non-jazz audience – the people, in fact, who enjoyed his totally charismatic personality and warmth as much as his more specific contributions to jazz – probably more so. The kind who enjoyed his big box office movies like *Hello Dolly!, High Society, A Man Called Adam* or *Where The Boys Meet The Girls.* Or the audience which made his recordings like **Hello Dolly** and **What A Wonderful World** into enormous international successes **(World** went to No. 1 on the US Hit Parade in 1967).

It must be said, though, that by this time the Armstrong All Stars concept (often called a musical circus) had become far removed from that of 20 years before. And as the latter years were to prove, even someone as indomitable as Louis Armstrong could be stricken with poor health, to the extent that, during the final period of his life there was very little of the glorious trumpet playing of the past; indeed, the accent was mostly on focusing attention to his singing, something that even time and illness could not dim. Concerts, club appearances, records, TV, movies, documentaries – during his most distinguished career Louis Armstrong conquered them all. He, more than any other jazzman, must have brought the music (of which he was Ambassador No. 1) into areas where jazz was anathema. His larger-than-life personality and immense warmth endeared him to millions. It is true that his most important contributions to jazz (as well as to music of this century) were made, for the most part, prior to 1940. Yet right up to the last appearances, even during the final inconsistent records, there was always something magical about seeing and/or hearing Louis Armstrong playing trumpet and singing, regardless of context or situation. Aside from the above facts, Armstrong appeared in over 35 motion pictures or film shorts; he was the subject of at least one definitive TV special (CBS, 1956 – *Satchmo The Great)*; was the recipient of innumerable trophies and honours (musical and otherwise), was the winner of countless popularity and critics' polls, and was a long-standing advertisement for Swiss Kriss laxatives which he consumed in large, regular supplies. He played Bottom, onstage, in a 1939 musical production of the Shakespeare travesty, *Swingin' The Dream,* and starred in film specials in Germany and Denmark.

Books by or about the man include: *Satchmo, My Life In New Orleans,* Louis Armstrong; *Swing That Music,* Louis Armstrong; *Louis Armstrong,* Albert McCarthy; *Louis Armstrong,* Hughes Panassie; *Horn Of Plenty,* Robert Goffin; *Trumpeter's Tale – The Story Of Young Louis Armstrong,* Jeanette Eaton; *Louis Armstrong: A Self-Portrait/The Interview,* Richard Merryman; *From Satchmo To Miles,* Leonard Feather; *Celebrating The Duke, And Louis, Bessie, Billie, Bird, Carmen, Miles, Dizzy And Other Heroes,* Ralph J. Gleason; *Louis: The Louis Armstrong Story 1900-1971,* Max Jones, John Chilton; *Jazz Masters Of The 20's.* Richard Hadlock.

In 1956, Armstrong, assisted by as many relevant musicians as could be assembled at that time, helped put together **Satchmo: A Musical Autobiography,** a four-LP set retracing his career in jazz thus far, with the principal participant adding his own narrative. He died on July 6, 1971.

Recordings:
Louis Armstrong & King Oliver (Milestone)
King Oliver's Jazz Band, 1925 (Smithsonian Collection/—)
King Oliver's Jazz Band (—/Parlophone)
Ma Rainey (Milestone)
Bessie Smith, The Empress (Columbia/CBS)
Bessie Smith, Nobody's Blues But Mine (Columbia/CBS)
Various, Adam & Eve Had The Blues (CBS/France)
Various, Jazz Sounds Of The Twenties, Vol 4 (Columbia – Italy)
Various, Rare Recordings Of The Twenties, Vol 1 (CBS – France)
Louis Armstrong In New York, 1924-1926 (Riverside/Riverside)
Young Louis Armstrong, 1932-1933 (Bluebird/—)
Louis Armstrong: July 4, 1900/July 6, 1971 (RCA Victor/RCA Victor)

Complete Recorded Works 1935-1945 (MCA – France)
Various, Tootin' Through The Roof (Onyx/Polydor)
Louis Armstrong, Vols 1-3 (—/Saga)
The First Esquire Concert, Vols 1, 2 (—/Saga)
The Second Esquire Concert, Vols 1, 2 (—/Saga)
The Metronome All Stars/The Esquire All Stars (RCA Victor – France)
Louis Armstrong, Louis At The Movies (Privateer)
Satchmo's Greatest, Vols 1-5 (RCA Victor – France)
Satchmo At Symphony Hall, Vols 1, 2 (Decca/Coral)
Louis Armstrong, Swing That Music (Coral)
Louis Armstrong Joue W. C. Handy/Ambassador Satch/ Satch Plays Fats (CBS – France)
Louis Armstrong With Fletcher Henderson 1924-1925 (—/VJM)
Louis Armstrong/Ella Fitzgerald, 'Porgy & Bess' (Verve/Verve)
Louis Armstrong/Ella Fitzgerald, Ella & Louis (Verve)/ **The Special Magic Of Ella & Louis, Vols 1, 2** (Verve)
Louis Armstrong, 'Satchmo The Great' (Columbia Special Products/—)
Louis Armstrong/Duke Ellington, The Beautiful Americans (Roulette)
Louis Armstrong, Vols 1, 2 (Trip)/ **All That Jazz: Louis Armstrong** (DJM)

Art Ensemble of Chicago

In 1965, pianist Muhal Richard Abrams established the Association for the Advancement of Creative Musicians (AACM) out of a sense of dissatisfaction with the constraints of group music. In this workshop atmosphere, the third wave of the avant-garde was born, in many ways the most extreme development to date. The first releases on Delmark **(Abrams: Levels & Degrees Of Light, Joseph Jarman: Song For** and **Roscoe Mitchell: Sound)** showed a very high level of musicianship by hitherto unknowns, and many of the devices later to become the hallmark of AACM music. **The Little Suite (Sound)** pointed the way ahead, and it still is a shocker. Firstly, the players' originality is collective. In the course of this performance they handle upwards of twenty instruments, playing off textures against each other with great humor and surreal sense of theatre. The history of the music

Fanfare For The Warriors (Atlantic): Chicago's finest.

becomes a ragbag of quotes and references within the fabric of a piece – fragments from tent shows, field hollers, bugle calls, blues harmonica, Bebop and New Wave. From all this activity, the definitive group emerged: Roscoe Mitchell, Joseph Jarman, playing between them almost the entire saxophone family, flutes, clarinets, drums, sirens, whistles, gongs, bells, vibes etc; Lester Bowie on trumpet, flugelhorn, drums, steer horn etc; Malachi Favors on bass etc. The first album from what was to become the Art Ensemble of Chicago, was on the obscure Nessa

label **(Numbers 1 & 2)**, although variants of the group **(Congliptious** and **Old Quartet)** follow the same policy. There's a sense of games being played in extremis about much of this music; melody, harmony and rhythm being subjected to the same discontinuity as the plot in the modern novel. Indeterminacy rules, and much of the skill rests upon the reactions of the musicians towards each other, their reflexes. Lester Bowie is probably the key personality, with a solo style, **Jazz Death? (Congliptious)**, that most closely corresponds to the kaleidoscopic methods of the group. Mitchell and Jarman follow broadly the Dolphy-Coltrane trajectory on any one saxophone, but chop about so rapidly that this orthodoxy is obscured.

In 1969 the Art Ensemble embarked for France, establishing a greater reputation there than they had in America. An incredible spate of recording followed, all of it excellent. Arguably the best works are the longest, **Reese And The Smooth Ones,** and the slowly rising dynamic level of **People In Sorrow;** but amazing passages abound throughout their albums. The moving instrumental lament that follows the recitation of the poem **Ericka (A Jackson In Your House),** or the accurate Bebop of **Dexterity (Message To Our Folks),** shows that they can operate more conventionally.

Joined by drummer Don Moye, their first regular drummer since Philip Wilson left, they cut an album with Bowie's wife, the singer Fontella Bass **(Les Stances A Sophie).** Over a Motown beat, she renders the erotic words of **Theme De Yoyo,** while the tumbling, free-form saxes, gourds and gym whistles heckle and strafe.

Returning to the United States, the Art Ensemble made their first festival appearance at the Ann Arbor Blues & Jazz Festival in 1972, which was recorded for Atlantic **(Bap-tizum).** At last, American audiences proved receptive, though the Atlantic contract produced only one further album **(Fanfare For The Warriors)** on which they were rejoined by Muhal Richard Abrams, before being discontinued.

In many ways their music resembles that of Charles Ives, but with the speedo haywire. A little tune will peep out, tiptoe through the funhouse flak, gather confidence as the musicians soar into unanimity, falter into a broken puppet Petrushka waltz-time, and abruptly flop! Some indwelling suspicion of conventional beauty causes them to pull the rug out from under the listener's expectations, open trap doors. Their impatient, scratchy kind of energy ensures that the Art Ensemble will never settle for formula, and, more radically, that their music will have more to do with process rather than product.

Recordings:
Roscoe Mitchell, Sound (Delmark/Delmark)
Roscoe Mitchell, Congliptious (Nessa/Nessa)
Roscoe Mitchell, Old Quartet (Nessa/Nessa)
Roscoe Mitchell, Solo Saxophone Concerts (Sackville/Sackville)
Joseph Jarman, Song For (Delmark/Delmark)
Joseph Jarman, As If It Were The Seasons (Delmark/Delmark)
Lester Bowie Numbers 1 & 2 (Nessa/Nessa)
Lester Bowie, Gittin' To Know You All (/MPS – Germany)
Lester Bowie, Fast Last! (Muse/—)
Art Ensemble Of Chicago, Reese And The Smooth Ones (—/BYG – France)
Art Ensemble Of Chicago, Message To Our Folks (—/BYG – France)
Art Ensemble Of Chicago, A Jackson In Your House (—/BYG – France)
Art Ensemble Of Chicago, People In Sorrow (Nessa/Nessa)
Art Ensemble Of Chicago, Les Stances A Sophie (Nessa/Nessa)
Art Ensemble Of Chicago, Tutankhamun (Arista Freedom/Arista Freedom)
Art Ensemble Of Chicago, Chi Congo (Paula/Decca)
Art Ensemble Of Chicago, Phase One (Prestige/America)
Art Ensemble Of Chicago, Bap-tizum (Atlantic/Atlantic)
Art Ensemble Of Chicago, Fanfare For The Warriors (Atlantic/Atlantic)
Old/Quartet (Nessa/Nessa)

George Auld

Born Toronto, Canada, 1919, George Auld (real name: John Altwerger) established a reputation during the middle-to-late 1930s/early-1940s as an all-round accomplished musician and a tenor-saxophone soloist of some distinction. Also plays alto- and soprano-sax and clarinet with much efficiency, though not often in a solo capacity. Moved from Toronto to Brooklyn aged ten, won the Rudy Wiedoft scholarship two years later (playing alto). After hearing Coleman Hawkins (♦), switched to tenor in 1936.

First major engagement with own band, at Nick's, New York, after which joined big band of Bunny Berigan (♦), as featured tenor soloist (1937–8). His Hawkins-inspired solos with Berigan second only to leader's trumpet contributions in value. Many recordings with Berigan, including solid, jumping solos on items such as **Mahogany Hall Stomp, Can't Help Lovin' Dat Man** and **Prisoner's Song (Bunny Berigan & His Orchestra)**. Also featured on numerous broadcast dates with

Berigan on **Bunny Berigan - Leader & Sideman** and **Down By The Old Mill Stream**. Heard live, Auld's playing is even more assured and rewarding.

Moved on to Artie Shaw (♦) for stay of approximately one year (1938–9), until Shaw disbanded ('39), again as premier saxophone soloist. With Shaw, featured prominently on **Jungle Drums, Serenade To A Savage, I Didn't Know What Time It Was (Artie Shaw & His Orchestra, Vol 2)** and **My Heart Stood Still, Carioca, One Night Stand (Concerto For Clarinet)**. When Shaw reformed, in 1941, Auld again occupied first tenor solo chair. Featured in numbers like **Solid Sam (Concerto For Clarinet)** and **St James' Infirmary (Artie Shaw & His Orchestra, Vol 2)**.

In between, Auld had starred with Benny Goodman (♦) Orchestra **(All-Time Greatest Hits** and **Solid Gold Instrumental Hits)**, during which period the influence of Lester Young (♦) was apparent in his work, although Hawkins' style was still predominant.

Finest recordings during 1940, with Goodman Septet, including **Gilly, Waiting For Benny, A Smo-o-o-oth One (Charlie Christian With BG Sextet & Orchestra)** and **Benny's Bugle, On The Alamo, As Long As I Live (Solo Flight)**. Also in 1940, recorded with Billie Holiday (♦), playing tenor on two tracks, alto on four **(God Bless The Child)**.

After Shaw disbanded for second time (beginning of '42), Auld gigged with his own band on regular basis, until a brief period of service in US Army (1943). Then more small-group work followed, in fall of '43, by first own big band. Dizzy Gillespie (♦) recorded with band in 1945 **(Dizzy's Delight: The Big Bands)**. Around this time, Auld encountered bop but Lester Young influence became stronger. Illness during 1946 meant disbandment of big band, followed by exit from New York. Returned to work in 1947 and worked, briefly, with Billy Eckstine (♦) Orchestra (1948). Put together a particularly fine ten-piece mainstream-modern band in 1949, then spent just under a year as actor in Broadway play The Rat Race. Short stay with Count Basie (♦) Octet (1950) **(Count Basie, Vol 3)**; then fronted superior quintet, including Tiny Kahn, Lou Levy and Frank Rosolino. After further illness, moved to West Coast, this time to Las Vegas. Led variety of bands through the 1960s, made tour of Japan (1964) and was re-united with Goodman (1966).

During past 15–20 years has made many album dates, some falling into semi-jazz mood music category. From time to time, however, could still produce satisfying tenor playing in a definite jazz bag, as on dates with Buddy De Franco (♦) **(. . . Plays Benny Goodman)**, Barney Kessel (♦) **(To Swing Or Not To Swing)**, Maynard Ferguson (♦) **(Stratospheric)**, and Dinah Washington (♦) **(The Original Soul Sister)**. And his playing on own sessions, like **Georgie Auld Plays The Winners** and **Georgie Auld In The Land Of Hi-Fi** has been of a uniformly high standard. In 1977 took supporting role in film **New York, New York**, proving himself a thoroughly competent actor as well as ghosting for tenor-playing Robert De Niro.

Recordings:
Bunny Berigan & His Orchestra (RCA Victor/RCA Victor)
Bunny Berigan, Down By The Old Mill Stream (Jazz Archives/—)
Bunny Berigan - Leader & Sideman (Jazz Archives/—)
Artie Shaw, Concerto For Clarinet (RCA Victor/RCA Victor)
Artie Shaw & His Orchestra, Vol 2 (RCA Victor/RCA Victor)
Charlie Christian/Benny Goodman, Solo Flight (Columbia/CBS – Realm)
Charlie Christian With The Benny Goodman Sextet & Orchestra (Columbia/CBS – Realm)
Charlie Christian/Lester Young, Together 1940 (Jazz Archives/—)
Benny Goodman, All-Time Greatest Hits (Columbia/CBS)
Dizzy Gillespie, Dizzy's Delight (The Big Bands) (Phoenix/—)
Benny Goodman, Solid Gold Instrumental Hits (Columbia/CBS)
Billie Holiday, God Bless The Child (Columbia/CBS)
Count Basie, Vol 3 (RCA Victor – France)
Georgie Auld In The Land Of Hi-Fi (EmArcy/EmArcy)
Barney Kessel, To Swing Or Not To Swing (Contemporary/Contemporary)
Maynard Ferguson, Stratospheric (EmArcy/—)
Dinah Washington, The Original Soul Sister (EmArcy/Fontana)
Georgie Auld Plays The Winners (Philips/—)

Albert Ayler

Born 1936, died 1970, the great tenorman's brief career provoked fanatical reactions from both ends of the spectrum. Following the innovations of Ornette Coleman and Cecil Taylor, the second wave of New Thing players – Ayler,

Bells (ESP): the notorious one-sided album, Ayler and artwork.

Shepp, Pharoah Sanders – showed a ferocity in their playing that has never been equalled. The emotional ante had risen in assertion of the black identity, in rejection of European standards of taste and acceptability, and the rise parallels Afro-American political developments in the mid-60s.

Ayler's apprenticeship lay in R&B bands, where the tenor is used at the extremes of its register, and this characterizes all of his later work. His two earliest recordings, now difficult to obtain, sound more shocking than they were because of the orthodox Hard Bop context of his Scandinavian sidemen. The first album in compatible surroundings **(Spiritual Unity)**, featured the tenorist with bassist Gary Peacock and the drummer Sunny Murray, whose dramatic, almost frightening crescendos and silences add greatly to the atmosphere of Gothic intensity. **Ghosts, Second Variation** is a musical exorcism of overwhelming force, and Ayler never bettered this performance. The same trio feature on the posthumously released live session **Prophesy** and the mood is again Cormanesque. The same year, 1964, saw three more sessions with larger groups, each including Murray. Ayler recorded soundtrack music for an underground film (New York Eye & Ear Control)

Above: late tenorman Albert Ayler with his brother, trumpeter Don. Revolutionary or traditionalist?

New Grass (Impulse): Albert's rock 'n' roll album, other side up.

in company with Ornette Coleman's trumpeter, Don Cherry, altoman John Tchicai and trombonist Roswell Rudd, and the results are chaotic. Ayler's move into collective improvisation made more sense when he re-activated the readymade tradition of New Orleans and this was foreshadowed **(Spirits)** in the funeral procession atmosphere of **Witches And Devils** with trumpeter Norman Howard. The collaboration with Don Cherry reaches its peak on **Vibrations** and brings into focus the tenor player's outlandish romanticism on **Mothers.**

The search for ethnic roots showed Ayler's groups back with New Orleans ensemble playing throughout 1965, with spectacular high register work in his solos, **Spirits Rejoice** and **Bells.**

Ayler's contract with Impulse led to a broadening of his range, and a consequent dilution of content in the cause of communication. Thus, the debut album **In Greenwich Village** has a skirling Balkan flavour and the joys **(Truth Is Marching In)** and sorrows **(For John Coltrane)** move the listener in a direct and simple way. **Love Cry** saw a pretty re-working of his standard themes, **Ghosts** and **Bells** played fairly straight by Ayler and his brother, trumpeter Don, the horns augmented by the harpsichord of Call Cobbs. The complexity on this album comes from the amazingly fleet drumming of Milford Graves, who embroiders beneath the simple statements. Ayler's rock 'n' roll album **New Grass** upset his followers no end. The meeting between Ayler's avant garde tenor and the tight beat of Pretty Purdie with yeah-yeah lyrics, broke down the categories in some ways, but demonstrated too, that Free players needed more rhythmic space.

A concert performance, **Nuits De La Fondation Maeght,** showed a return to form, but Ayler's development was cut short by his death in the Hudson River in mysterious circumstances.

Albert Ayler's overwhelming impact tends to conceal the fact that he was something of a throwback, a pre-Bebop player with declared roots in Lester Young and Sidney Bechet, and a sound that goes all the way back to the field holler and the brass band. Belches, shrieks, wide register leaps, a vibrato as broad as a busker's and as sentimental as a locket, plus an agility in moving his line in and out of focus, all served to confuse the issue. He had an amazing sense of form and a unique imagination. His themes and his group concept all point to a search for some ethnic root that

springs straight from raw emotion. His critics mistook his work, seeing a gross, bumpkin naivety, and missing the communicative power and freshness.

Recordings:
Spiritual Unity *(ESP/ESP)*
Prophesy *(ESP/ESP)*
New York Eye & Ear Control *(ESP/ESP)*
Vibrations *(Arista Freedom/—)*
Spirits Rejoice *(ESP/ESP)*
Bells *(ESP/ESP)*
Albert Ayler In Greenwich) Village *(Impulse/Impulse)*
Love Cry *(Impulse/Impulse)*
New Grass *(Impulse/Impulse)*
Nuits De La Fondation Maeght *(Shandar – France)*

Derek Bailey

Guitarist Derek Bailey is a leading figure in the European free music scene, pioneering an investigation of sound and texture through electronic variation. Associated with John Stevens' Spontaneous Music Ensemble in the '60s **(So What Do You Think?)** and the London Jazz Composers Orchestra, Bailey formed a trio with trombonist Paul Rutherford and bassist Barry Guy **(Iskra 1903).** His work in the duo and solo situation is unfailingly inventive and cliche-free, his tonal manipulations always at the service of the music. A stimulating concert with multi-instrumentalist Anthony Braxton in 1974, was recorded **(Duo)** and finds both musicians exploring tonal areas and producing startlingly original music through creative friction rather than solo and support. The same general comment applies to the great guitarist's work with saxophonist Evan Parker dating back to an album from 1970 **(The Topography Of The Lungs)** which also includes the Dutch drummer, Han Bennink, and continuing through to a magnificently spiky concert performance in 1975 **(The London Concert).**

Currently, Bailey's fascination with totally free improvisation has led to the establishment of Company, an international pool of free musicians, Parker, Steve Beresford, Braxton, Steve Lacy, Rutherford, and Lol Coxhill, who play together without forming a permanent group, and the first album **(Company 1)** using Bailey, Parker, cellist Tristan Honsinger and bassist Maarten van Regteren Altena, thoroughly justifies the experiment. From 1971 the guitarist has also been giving solo recitals, and albums like **Derek Bailey Solo** and **Lot 74 – Solo Improvisations** confirm his reputation as the most original guitarist on the scene.

Recordings:
SME, So What Do You Think? *(—/Tangent)*
Iskra 1903 *(—/Incus)*
Duo *(Emanem/Emanem)*
The Topography Of The Lungs *(—/Incus)*
The London Concert *(—/Incus)*
Company 1 *(—/Incus)*
Derek Bailey Solo *(—/Incus)*
Lot 74 – Solo Improvisations *(—/Incus)*
Derek Bailey & Tristan Honsinger *(—/Incus)*
Music Improvisation Company *(—/Incus)*

Mildred Bailey

Mildred Bailey was, like Ethel Waters (♦) before her, and Dinah Washington (♦) after, one of those jazz singers who, not content with excelling in one musical genre, had sufficient talent to conquer others. In Mildred Bailey's case she could sing an eloquent blues, had the kind of vocal delivery that appealed to those uninterested in either blues or jazz, and could even make a fair stab at gospel singing. Born Mildred Rinker (in Tekoa, Washington, 1907), sister of Al Rinker (of Rhythm Boys – Bing Crosby–Paul Whiteman fame), was schooled in Spokane, began in music as a song demonstrator, then worked in a West Coast revue.

Her initial reputation was achieved through regular work on radio station KMTR as well as at other venues in California. Paul Whiteman (♦) signed her to sing with his large orchestra. Worked with Whiteman between 1929–33 (Whiteman probably was first bandleader to feature a solo girl vocalist) during which time she recorded such superb sides as **Stop The Sun Stop The Moon** and **Rockin' Chair (Paul Whiteman & His Orchestra);** the last-named as closely associated with the name Mildred Bailey as it was to become in later years with vocal-instrumental duo of Louis Armstrong (♦) and Jack Teagarden (♦).

During last year with Whiteman she married the bandleader's ex-xylophone player Red Norvo (♦). They were divorced in 1945. Norvo was to work with her regularly, from 1935 until the end of the 1930s. Her first record had orchestra conducted by Eddie Lang (♦) (1929): Hoagy Carmichael's **What Kind O' Man Is You (Her Greatest Performances 1929-1946, Vol 1).** As with her Whiteman recordings, Mildred Bailey's debut disc spotlighted her impeccable timing, her undoubted jazz phrasing, and the quiet depth she imparted to

Mildred Bailey, Her Greatest Performances 1929-1946 (CBS).

all kinds of lyrics. Little doubt, she was to become one of the top female jazz singers. Interesting too that while she was deeply influenced by black singers and musicians, her singing, on material such as Alberta Hunter's **Downhearted Blues (Her Greatest Performances, Vol 2), St Louis Blues (Vol 3)** and **Me & The Blues (Vol 3),** never was self-consciously aimed at singing 'black'.

Her curious (yet never unpleasant) high-register voice was rarely, if ever, off-pitch or off-key. Hers was a truly effortless kind of

singing, the type which enabled her to encompass a wide variety of material (eg **Old Folks, Peace, Brother!, Gulf Coast Blues** and **There'll Be Some Changes Made** (all **Vol 3**)). Her sense of humor was subtly projected on apposite material, like **Arthur Murray Taught Me Dancing In A Hurry** (**Vol 3**) and **Week End Of A Private Secretary (Vol 2),** recorded in 1942 and 1938 respectively. And on recordings like **'Tain't What You Do** and **St Louis Blues (Vol 2)** she worked with the John Kirby (♦) Orchestra (augmented by the presence of Red Norvo).

Her finest accompaniments of the period came from her then husband's band, and studio outfits assembled by arranger-composer Eddie Sauter (♦), with outstanding charts written by Sauter for both. She worked also with Benny Goodman (♦) (**Vol 1** and **Recordings Made Between 1930 & 1941),** her singing of Frank Loesser's **Junk Man** on the latter disc achieving some minor recognition, saleswise; she recorded too with Alec Wilder's classically-orientated octet (**Vol 3**) and numerous others with Norvo and studio bands under her own name (viz Mildred Bailey & Her Oxford Greys). Broadcast with Benny Goodman in 1939 (**Benny Goodman, His Stars & His Guests)** but next year worked strictly as a solo act.

Although beset by recurring illnesses during the 1940s, caused as much as anything by constant problems of overweight, she was given her own radio series via the CBS network *(The Mildred Bailey Radio Show – 1944-45).* Bailey's consistency of performance on these shows made her a firm favourite, with fans as well as with musicians. Her love for jazz ensured that invariably musicians of the calibre of Norvo, Teddy Wilson (♦) and Charlie Shavers (♦) were also on hand. 1940s recordings show little or no diminution of her powers (**All Of Me** and **First Esquire Jazz Concert, Vol 1),** but by 1949 her health had deteriorated alarmingly; during that year she was treated for heart and diabetes complaints. Sang again in 1950-1, but was forced thereafter to spend what remained of her life in a New York hospital where she died in December, '51. Mildred Bailey's singing was to deeply influence many other vocalists, including Ella Fitzgerald (♦), Peggy Lee (♦), Lee Wiley (♦), Mabel Mercer and Maxine Sullivan (♦).

Recordings:
Paul Whiteman & His Orchestra *(RCA Victor/RCA Victor)*
Mildred Bailey, Her Greatest Performances 1929-1946 *(Columbia)/*
Her Greatest Performances 1929-1946, Vols 1-3 *(CBS)*
Mildred Bailey, All Of Me *(Monmouth – Evergreen/Ember)*
The Mildred Bailey Radio Show 1944-1945 *(Sunbeam)*
Mildred Bailey, Me & The Blues *(Regal)/*
Rockin' Chair Lady *(CBS – Realm)*
Various, Recordings Made Between 1930 & 1941 *(CBS – France)*
Tommy Dorsey/Jimmy Dorsey/ Eddie Lang, Tommy, Jimmy & Eddie, 1928-29 *(—/Parlophone)*

Buster Bailey

William C. 'Buster' Bailey (born Memphis, Tennessee, 1902) ranks as one of the most accomplished clarinettists to appear thus far on the jazz scene. He was also a fine saxophonist. His soprano-sax accompaniment to blues singer Alberta Hunter on a 1924 recording of **Everybody Loves My Baby (Louis Armstrong In New York, 1924-1925)** is excellent; and his playing of the same instrument as a sideman for Clarence Williams (♦) **(Louis Armstrong/Sidney Bechet With The Clarence Williams Blue Five)** offers further evidence of his abilities in this direction. Also played alto-sax with modest solo success, eg on a 1935 recording by singer Putney Dandridge's Orchestra **(The Boss Of The Bass)**.

But it is as clarinettist that Bailey is primarily remembered. Bailey, who received a thorough musical education before embarking on a career as a professional musician, toured with orchestra of legendary W. C. Handy (♦) (1917–19); later an important sideman in the bands of Erskine Tate (1919–23), King Oliver (♦) (1923–4), Fletcher Henderson (♦) (1924–7, 1927–8, 1934, 1935–7). Started with clarinet at 13, studying under Franz Schoeppe (Chicago Symphony Orchestra). Bailey's impeccable playing was a major asset to the innumerable musical outfits with which he played.

In addition to the above, other bands with which he was associated in the early part of his career included Noble Sissle (with whom he toured Europe in '29, subsequently playing again with the same band 1931–3); Edgar Hayes (1929), Dave Nelson (1930), Mills Blue Rhythm Band (1934–5), Stuff Smith (♦) (1937).

Although it can be said that Bailey's academic tone and general approach lacked the warmth and vibrancy of contemporaries like Bechet (♦), Bigard (♦), Noone (♦), et al, his playing lacked absolutely nothing in terms of flexibility and all-round technical skills. It was these gifts, and an enviable ability to adapt to practically any musical surroundings, which made him constantly in demand throughout a lengthy career. For example, although never a major instrumentalist in the genre, Bailey was a sufficiently gifted blues player to be called upon to accompany singers of the calibre of Ma Rainey (♦) **(Ma Rainey)**, Bessie Smith **(The Empress** and **Nobody's Blues But Mine)**, Alberta Hunter and Trixie Smith (both **Louis Armstrong In New York, 1924-1925)**.

Bailey's clarinet also featured on recordings by other more jazz-orientated vocal performers: Billie Holiday (♦) **(The Lester Young Story, Vol 1)**, Mildred Bailey (♦) **(Her Greatest Performances 1929-1946)** and Midge Williams and Maxine Sullivan (♦) (both **Boss Of The Bass)**.

From a purely instrumental standpoint, Bailey's immaculate playing made him an obvious choice as clarinettist with the John Kirby (♦) Sextet **(Boss Of The Bass, John Kirby & His Orchestra 1941-1942** and **The Biggest Little Band In The Land)**, for whom he was a constituent member for seven years (1937–44), and again, for

much shorter spells, in 1945 and 1946. Successfully recorded with all kinds of bands. Apart from those noted above, he also recorded with Lil Armstrong **(Harlem On Saturday Night)**, Teddy Wilson (♦) **(Teddy Wilson & His All-Stars** and **The Teddy Wilson)**, Henry 'Red' Allen (♦) **(Henry 'Red' Allen All Stars, Vol 4** and **Henry Allen & His Orchestra 1934-1935)**, Bubber Miley **(Bubber Miley & His Friends)** and Wingy Manone (♦) and Chu Berry (♦) **(Chew, Choo, Chu & Co.)**. Under his own leadership, though, Bailey fared less successfully. An admirable showcase for his talents **(All About Memphis)** took place in 1958. In a quartet setting, Bailey's reworkings of **Beale Street Blues** and **Memphis Blues** are as good examples of his abilities as a clarinet player as anything he recorded elsewhere in his lifetime. His playing on three septet tracks is as good if not better than that of colleagues Vic Dickenson (♦), Herman Autrey (♦) and Hilton Jefferson (♦).

During the last 20 years of his life, spent mostly in New York, he worked with Eddie Condon (♦), Red Allen, Wilbur De Paris (♦) and Wild Bill Davison (♦). Also played in pit band of New York production of *Porgy and Bess*, worked with symphony orchestras and in TV studios, and appeared in film *Splendor In The Grass*. After working with Saints & Sinners band, joined the Louis Armstrong (♦) All Stars. Died in his sleep, at his home in Brooklyn, in 1967.

Recordings:
Various, Louis Armstrong In New York, 1924-1925
(Riverside/Riverside)
Louis Armstrong/Sidney Bechet With The Clarence Williams Blue Five
(CBS – France)
Fletcher Henderson, The Henderson Pathes (1923-1925)
(—/Fountain)
The Fletcher Henderson Story
(Columbia)
The Fletcher Henderson Story
(CBS)
Ma Rainey *(Milestone/—)*
Bessie Smith, The Empress
(Columbia/CBS)
Bessie Smith, Nobody's Blues But Mine *(Columbia/CBS)*
Bubber Miley & His Friends (1929-1931)
(RCA Victor – France)
Henry Allen & His Orchestra (1934-1935)
(Collector's Classics/—)
Henry 'Red' Allen All Stars, Vol 4 *(RCA Victor – France)*
King Oliver/Dave Nelson, Vol 3 (1929-1931)
(RCA Victor – France)
The Teddy Wilson
(CBS/Sony – Japan)
Teddy Wilson & His All Stars
(Columbia/CBS)
Wingy Manone/Chu Berry, Chew, Choo, Chu & Co.
(RCA Victor – France)
Various, Harlem On Saturday Night *(—/Ace of Hearts)*
Billie Holiday/Lester Young, The Lester Young Story, Vol 1
(Columbia/CBS)
John Kirby, Boss Of The Bass
(Columbia/—)
Mildred Bailey, Her Greatest Performances, 1929-1946
(Columbia/CBS)
John Kirby & His Orchestra 1941-1942
(RCA Victor – Germany)

John Kirby, The Biggest Little Band In The Land
(Trip/DJM)
The Complete Lionel Hampton
(Bluebird/—)
Lionel Hampton's Best Records, Vol 1 (1937-1938)
(RCA Victor – France)
Various, Frankie Newton At The Onyx Club *(Tax – Sweden)*
Buster Bailey, All About Memphis *(Felsted/Felsted)*

Chet Baker

Born 1929, the trumpeter's early career was attended with phenomenal luck, which turned spectacularly sour. 1952 saw him working with Charlie Parker on the West Coast **(Bird On The Coast)** and in the same year joining baritone saxist Gerry Mulligan's famous pianoless quartet. Still very much an apprentice, Baker's work with the group is distinguished less by technique than by his tone, which has an unforgettable plaintive quality, **My Funny Valentine** for example **(Gerry Mulligan Quartet)**. Numbers like **Walkin' Shoes, Bernie's Tune,** show the bright, skating lines of the trumpet as an excellent foil to the burly baritone. But Baker's cool approach sounds diffuse against the ascetic logic of altoist Lee Konitz, who joined the Quartet for recording sessions in 1953 **(Revelation)**. Also in that year, Baker topped Metronome's trumpet poll, and established his own quartet with pianist Russ Freeman. His work became more outgoing and assured, but none of the recordings remains in the catalogue **(Jazz At Ann Arbor), (Chet Baker – Russ Freeman Quartet)**.

Association with composers like Freeman, Twardzik and Zieff seemed to develop his limited range, and the group that he bought to Europe in 1955 **(Chet Baker In Paris)** represents the high water mark of promise. Unfortunately, pianist Dick Twardzik died of an overdose at the age of 24, leaving behind a handful of tantalizing examples of his originality, eg **The Girl From Greenland**. Baker's own career began to suffer from narcotics, arrests, headlines, and a critical backlash against his playing that had been so over-praised at the outset. In fact, many of his subsequent albums are excellent – **Playboys, Chet Baker & Crew, Chet In New York** – all unfortunately difficult to obtain. In recent years, he has made a comeback **(Baby Breeze)** and his courage and determination shine through his playing.

It is difficult to separate the music from the myth. Chet Baker's good looks, youth and fragile, introverted tone attracted a cult following in the '50s, which his subsequent and tragic track record did nothing to dispel. A likeness to James Dean and a sound reminiscent of Bix Beiderbecke gave a generation of jazz fans their 'Doomed Youth'. Miles Davis was his main inspiration, but there is a sincerity and emotional honesty about his playing that is very moving.

Recordings:
Bird On The Coast
(Jazz Showcase/—)

Playboys (Vogue): rare collectors' item, period cover.

Gerry Mulligan Quartet
(Prestige/Prestige)
Gerry Mulligan – Lee Konitz, Revelation
(Blue Note/Blue Note)
Chet Baker In Paris
(—/Blue Star, Barclay – France)
Chet Baker, Baby Breeze
(Limelight/Mercury)

Shorty Baker

Harold 'Shorty' Baker was the kind of first-rate trumpeter to call upon for practically any kind of work, but especially in a big-band context where his versatility and flexibility enabled him to take any one of the trumpet chairs with ease. He was the ideal section leader and an admirable, elegant soloist, which is why Duke Ellington (♦) tended to make good use of his not inconsiderable services at various times between 1938–62. The longest single period which Baker (born St Louis, Mo, 1914) spent as a member of the Ellington trumpet section was seven years (1946–52), but he was a constant asset, however lengthy (or otherwise) the time he spent in Ducal surroundings. Baker's superior tone, superb control and gorgeously melodic phrasing were all amply in evidence when Ellington allocated him solo space on choice material such as **Mood Indigo** and **Willow, Weep For Me (Ellington Indigos)**. And he could rise to the challenge of participating in the premier performance of an important Ellington work like **Black, Brown & Beige (Black, Brown & Beige)** in typically professional style.

Saxophonist Johnny Hodges (♦) also valued the services of Shorty Baker, using him on several record dates. It was Hodges who was a colleague of Baker's at a Billy Strayhorn (♦) record date in 1959, during which the trumpeter's warm, mellifluous playing was a stand-out part of the generally superior proceedings, nowhere better illustrated than during his solo on **You Brought A New Kind Of Love To Me**. A later session, co-featuring the trumpets of Baker and Doc Cheatham (♦), produced further elegantly swinging music **(Shorty & Doc)** without resulting in anything particularly significant or important. Aside from his work with Ellington, Baker worked with other noted bandleaders such as Fate Marable, Erskine Tate, Don Redman (♦) (1936–8), Teddy Wilson (♦), Andy Kirk (1940–2), Ben Webster (♦), Hodges (1954), Claude Hopkins (♦), and Bud Freeman (♦), as well as periodically leading his own small groups. Baker, who started his musical life as a drummer, was forced to retire from playing about 1964-5. After an operation in '65 he died from throat cancer in a New York Hospital in 1966.

Recordings:
Duke Ellington, Masterpieces By Ellington
(Columbia/CBS – Holland)
Duke Ellington, Solitude
(Columbia/Philips)
Ella Fitzgerald Sings The Duke Ellington Songbook, Vol 2
(Verve/Verve)
Duke Ellington, Ellington Indigos *(Columbia/—)*
Duke Ellington, Ellington Jazz Party *(Columbia/CBS – France)*
The World Of Duke Ellington
(Columbia)/
The Duke: Edward Kennedy Ellington (1899-1974) *(CBS)*
Duke Ellington, Ellington In Concert, Vol 2
(—/World Record Club)
Billy Strayhorn, Cue For Saxophone
(Master Jazz Recordings/ Vocalion)
Johnny Hodges, The Jeep Is Jumpin' *(Verve)*
Johnny Hodges, Mellow Tone
(—/Vogue)
Johnny Hodges, Used To Be Duke *(Verve/Verve)*
Various, Great Ellingtonians Play A Tribute To Duke Ellington *(—/Double-Up)*
Shorty Baker/Doc Cheatham, Shorty & Doc
(Prestige-Swingville/—)

Paul Barbarin

Born New Orleans, 1901, Barbarin, together with Zutty Singleton (♦) and Baby Dodds (♦), was most gifted drummer to emerge from Crescent City. Came from a very musical family – father brass player; three brothers (best known: Louis Barbarin) also musicians; Paul Barbarin was uncle to guitarist/banjoist Danny Barker (♦). Worked with legendary New Orleans jazz figures, like Buddie Petit, Freddie Keppard (♦), Jimmie Noone (♦) and King Oliver (♦) **(King Oliver's Dixie Syncopators: 1926-1928** and **King Oliver, Vols 1, 3).** But it was as drummer with Luis Russell (♦) **(Luis Russell & His Louisiana Swing Orchestra** and **The Luis Russell Story)** that Barbarin's fine musicianship and unswerving beat was heard to best advantage. Sounded impressive too when Russell band was used as virtual backdrop for artistry of Louis Armstrong (♦) **(Complete Recorded Works 1935-1945).** On record, Barbarin was also heard at his best in company with one-time Russell colleague, Henry Allen (♦) **(Henry 'Red' Allen, Vols 1-3** and **Henry Allen & His Orchestra 1934-1935).** His death, in 1969, happened during a New Orleans marching parade in which Barbarin was an active participant.

Recordings:
King Oliver's Dixie Syncopators (1926-1928)
(MCA – Germany)
King Oliver & His Orchestra, Vols 1, 3 *(RCA Victor – France)*
Luis Russell & His Louisiana Swing Orchestra *(Columbia/—)*

Paul Barbarin & His New Orleans Band (Vogue).

The Luis Russell Story
(—/Parlophone)
Louis Armstrong, V.S.O.P. **(Very Special Old Phonography), Vols 5 & 6** *(CBS – France)*
Henry 'Red' Allen, Vols 1-3 *(RCA Victor – France)*
Henry Allen & His Orchestra 1934-1935 *(Collector's Classics)*
Paul Barbarin/Sharkey Bonano, New Orleans Contrasts *(Riverside/—)*

Leandro 'Gato' Barbieri

Born in Argentina, the tenorman worked with bandleader Lalo Schifrin before moving to Italy in search of a jazz environment. Quite a few American New Wave players fetched up in Rome in the mid-'60s, and Barbieri was fortunate in joining up with Ornette Coleman's trumpeter, Don Cherry. The two albums that Blue Note recorded are classics of free group improvisation **(Complete Communion** and **Symphony For Improvisers)** and show Cherry's brilliant use of the young sideman. A player of enormous power and force, Barbieri tends to operate a very short trajectory, screaming up into the extreme

upper register within a few bars, and then back to ground level before starting again. Cherry, deploying tempo changes, demanding interaction, prevents those rhetorical spirals and leads his lowering hurricane in a quadrille. Barbieri also recorded with expatriates like Steve Lacy **(Nuovi Sentimenti)** and South African pianist Dollar Brand **(Confluence)**, a duo album of stark drama which unites the florid gestures of the tenor with the mission hall blues of the piano.

Barbieri's re-discovery of his Latin American roots led to a series of albums for Impulse which introduced a wider audience to his work, but seems to have led artistically to predictability. There have been several attempts to merge the two cultures – Gillespie and the Cuban drummer Chano Pozo in the '40s, altoman Bud Shank and Brazilian guitarist Laurindo Almeida, Stan Getz and Gilberto, Jobim and Bonfa in the '50s. Barbieri's hybrid centres on the tango, but in spite of the dense rhythmic activity – congas, shakers and rattlers – there is a static feel to the music. The best albums from this period remain the first **(The Third World)**, which has the advantage of major contributions by Charlie Haden and Roswell Rudd, and the second **(Fenix)**, which has a tenor solo of great balance, as well as the customary vehemence, in **Carnavalito**.

A vast battery of ethnic instruments surround the tenorist on an attractive album recorded in Buenos Aires **(Chapter One)**. Most of his later work hinges upon lush and beefy romanticism, with high-register kamikaze missions, over latin rhythms **(El Pampero** and **Live In New York)**. His appearance on composer Carla Bley's **Tropic Appetites** and the sound track for *Last Tango in Paris* rather confirms that his best work results from collaboration.

His style owes a good deal to Rollins and Coltrane, though the manner is more florid and melodramatic. His initial impact on the listener is overwhelming – the

spine-chilling screams, the huge drive – but, like Pharoah Sanders, his undoubted power tends to be dissipated through lack of structure.

Recordings:
Don Cherry, Complete Communion
(Blue Note/Blue Note)
Don Cherry, Symphony For Improvisers
(Blue Note/Blue Note)
Giorgio Gaslini, Nuovi Sentimenti *(—/HMV – Italy)*
Gato Barbieri – Dollar Brand, Confluence
(Arista Freedom/Arista Freedom)
The Third World
(Flying Dutchman/—)
Fenix *(Flying Dutchman)*
El Pampero
(Flying Dutchman/RCA Victor)
Chapter One *(Impulse/Impulse)*
Live In New York
(Impulse/Impulse)
Carla Bley, Tropic Appetites
(Watt/Watt)

Danny Barker

Daniel 'Danny' Barker (born New Orleans, 1909) has had a remarkably diverse career as both guitarist and banjoist (and sometimes singer), since, as a youth, first receiving musical tuition from Barney Bigard (♦) on clarinet and uncle Paul Barbarin (♦) on drums, respectively. Switched to banjo, guitar, studying briefly with Bernard Addison (♦). Barker, whose father was Onward Brass Band member, played first regular job with trumpeter Willie Pajeaud, but began really to establish name with Lee Collins (♦) (late-1920s), touring with the trumpeter's band. To New York, 1930. Gigged with numerous outfits, including Dave Nelson **(King Oliver/Dave Nelson, Vol 3: 1929/1931)**; Albert Nicholas (♦) 1935 **(Adrian Rollini & His Friends, Vol 1: 'Tap Room Special')**; James P. Johnson (♦), Lucky Millinder (♦), 1937-8, Benny Carter (♦), 1938-9. Then, for seven years, became guitarist for Cab Calloway (♦), whose band he joined in 1939. With Calloway, toured and recorded extensively **(Chu, 16 Cab Calloway Classics** and **Penguin Swing)**.

During 1930s, was regularly called upon by other top musicians for all kinds of record dates. These included Lionel Hampton (♦) **(The Complete Lionel Hampton: 1937-1941/Lionel Hampton's Best Records, Vols 2, 3, 5)**, Henry Allen (♦) **(Henry Allen & His Orchestra 1933-1934)**, Billy Kyle (♦) **(Swing Street, Vol 1)** and Chu Berry **The Big Sounds Of Coleman Hawkins & Chu Berry)**. Others with whom he worked during this period: Teddy Wilson (♦), Buster Bailey (♦), Adrian Rollini (♦), Wingy Manone, Ethel Waters (♦). Recorded in company with Charlie Parker (♦), Dizzy Gillespie (♦), under leadership of Sir Charles Thompson in 1945 **(The Fabulous Apollo Sessions)** and with Sidney Bechet (♦), Mezz Mezzrow same year, at one of their important King dates **(The Prodigious Bechet-Mezzrow Quintet & Septet)**.

Left Calloway in '46, to lead own combo, accompanying blues singer Blue Lu Barker (his wife). Performed similar function, 1949.

Above: 'Gato' Barbieri, Argentinian tenorman who found fame with a heady mixture of Free and Latin.

Rest of '40s spent with Millinder, again, Bunk Johnson (♦), Albert Nicholas, and on numerous occasions – concerts, radio, records – with Bechet (**Sidney Bechet & Friends, This Is Jazz, Vols 1, 2** and **This Is Jazz**). Worked often with Conrad Janis during 1950s, and as freelance during this and following decades (including stint on banjo with Paul Barbarin, 1954–55). Supported Eubie Blake (♦) at 1960 Newport Jazz Festival, took part in important TV special, *World of Jazz*, featuring Billie Holiday (♦) (**Billie Holiday, Vol 1**), and important record dates, like that featuring Pee Wee Russell (♦) (**Jam Session At Swingville**). Fronted own all-banjo band at 1964 New York World Fair. Appointed assistant to curator of New Orleans Jazz Museum after returning to live in the city, where he still can be heard playing his banjo and guitar.

Recordings:
Adrian Rollini & His Friends, Vol 1: 'Tap Room Special' *(RCA Victor – France)*
King Oliver/Dave Nelson, Vol 3: 1929/1931 *(RCA Victor – France)*
16 Cab Calloway Classics *(CBS – France)*
Chu Berry, Penguin Swing *(Jazz Archives)*
Chu Berry, Chu *(Epic/Epic – France)*
Various, Swing Street, Vol 1 *(Tax – Sweden)*
The Complete Lionel Hampton *(Bluebird)/*
Lionel Hampton's Best Records, Vols 2, 3, 5 *(RCA Victor – France)*
Henry Allen & His Orchestra 1933-1934 *(Collector's Classics)*
Louis Armstrong, Louis With Guest Stars *(—/MCA – Germany)*
Chu Berry, The Big Sounds Of Coleman Hawkins & Chu Berry *(—/London)*
Sidney Bechet, The Prodigious Bechet-Mezzrow Quintet & Septet *(—/Festival – France)*
The Genius Of Sidney Bechet *(Jazzology/—)*
This Is Jazz *(Jazzology/—)*
This Is Jazz, Vols 1, 2 *(Rarities)*
Various (Including Pee Wee Russell), Jam Session At Swingville *(Prestige/Prestige)*
Billie Holiday, Vol 1 *(Columbia/CBS)*
LaVern Baker Sings Bessie Smith *(Atlantic/Atlantic)*

George Barnes

George Barnes (born Chicago Heights, Illinois, 1921) became acquainted with guitar from very early age. Father, music teacher, gave lessons. Had his own band – four-piece – during middle-to-late-1930s with which he toured Middle West region of the US. Joined NBC as staffman, 1939. On request, joined band which Bud Freeman (♦) put together for Chicago residency (1942). After which he served in US Army (1942–6). Back in civilian life, Barnes worked regularly on radio (ABC) in Chicago. Left Chicago for New York City ('51) to work inside TV, radio and recording studios. During 1950s/1960s, played variety of jazz gigs but was involved more in studio pop-type work. Recorded

with Lawson-Haggart Band and with Ernie Royal Sextet. A capable rhythm guitarist, and a pleasing, unflashy soloist deriving basically from George Van Epps-Carl Kress-Dick McDonough school of guitar playing, his work often tends to lack real excitement and drive. Found fresh (and wider) popularity through his sympathetic playing opposite Ruby Braff (♦) within context of short-lived (1973–5) Ruby Braff-George Barnes Quartet. Content to leave lion's share of solo work to superior solo abilities of Braff, Barnes nevertheless was perfect foil to his partner. Demonstrated most effectively on record, **To Fred Astaire, With Love,** and, best of all, on **The Ruby Braff-George Barnes Quartet/The Best I've Heard,** part of which is recorded live, and **Salutes Rodgers & Hart.** Indeed, Barnes' involvement with jazz, particularly on record, has been more pronounced in recent times, including a brace of albums cut with Joe Venuti (♦) (**Gems** and **Joe Venuti & George Barnes - Live At The Concord Summer Festival**) both containing examples of his work that are as good as anything from previous years, in some cases superior in terms of all-round excellence. Similarly, his own **Swing Guitars** has many moments of delightful, filigree guitar picking of much subtlety and finesse. Barnes died of a heart attack in Concord, California, in September 1977.

Recordings:
The Ruby Braff-George Barnes

Quartet/The Best I've Heard *(Vogue)*
Ruby Braff/George Barnes, Braff/Barnes Quartet Salutes Rodgers & Hart *(Concord/—)*
George Barnes, Swing Guitars *(Famous Door/—)*
George Barnes/Joe Venuti, Gems *(Concord/—)*
Joe Venuti & George Barnes - Live At The Concord Summer Festival *(Concord/—)*
Blues Going Up *(Concord Jazz/—)*

Charlie Barnet

Charles Daly Barnet (born New York City, 1913) was born to wealthy parents, and raised by mother and a grandfather, who both wanted for the youngster to become corporation lawyer. Barnet, Jr, opted to become full-time jazz musician. Piano lessons at very early age, then on to saxophone at 12. Led first band four years later (aboard steamship); later, played for numerous ship's bands – for Cunard, Red Star, Panama-Pacific, making trips to Europe, South and Central America. By the time Barnet left Rumsey Academy and put together first (land-based) big band (1933) was already playing alto-, tenor- and soprano-saxophones and clarinet. First recorded examples of his sax playing, with Red Norvo (♦) 1934, give fair indication that

basically 'jump' style was already more or less formulated (**Swing Street, Vol 3**). Influences also apparent: admiration for Coleman Hawkins (♦) reflected on tenor; for Johnny Hodges (♦) on soprano and some alto; strong elements of Pete Brown (♦), especially from rhythmic standpoint, apparent on all three instruments. Never an extra-ordinarily gifted improviser, Barnet always was one of jazz's hardest-driving players. Band-leading/playing career interrupted in 1935 when he disbanded, temporarily moving to Hollywood to become film actor (with parts in two 1936 movies).

Final breakthrough, as bandleader, in 1939, aided by new RCA-Bluebird contract. (Barnet had recorded for label couple of years before (**The Complete Charlie Barnet, Vol 1**) without commercial success). Subsequent discs on Bluebird became major sellers. These included **Cherokee, Pompton Turnpike, Charleston Alley** and **Redskin Rhumba** (**Charlie Barnet, Vol 1**). Barnet, keen Ellington (♦) lover who had played chimes on latter's Victor recording of **Ring Dem Bells** in 1930, made sure own band was Ellington-influenced. Often featured Ducal material, such as **Gal From Joe's, Echoes Of Harlem, Harlem Speaks** and **Lament For Lost Love** (**Charlie Barnet, Vol 2**). Employed first-class arrangers, principally Horace Henderson (♦), Skip Martin, and, most notably, the

Below: Silver Star Swing Series Present Charlie Barnet & His Orchestra (MCA Coral, Germany).

18

Charlie Barnet, Vol 1 (RCA Victor) – top class big band.

gifted Billy May, whose work often has exhibited genuine humor. Barnet himself also contributed scores. Records apart, other major breakthrough came with band's residence at Famous Door, 52nd Street.

From 1939 until early-1950s, Barnet continued to lead succession of excellent big bands, boasting variety of impressive soloists. Very anti-racial, as shown by choice of sidemen through the years, Barnet at various times employed series of top-class black musicians, including: Roy Eldridge (♦), Peanuts Holland, Howard McGhee (♦), Clark Terry (♦), Charlie Shavers (♦), Dizzy Gillespie (♦) and Oscar Pettiford.

Although 1939-43 bands failed to attain the immense popularity of some other basically white 'swing bands' (ie mostly jazz-influenced dance bands), undoubtedly Barnet's were amongst the most jazz-conscious and hardest-swinging. Mid-1940s Barnet bands followed suit, including amongst personnel listings such names as Buddy De Franco (♦), Dodo Marmarosa (♦), Al Killian (♦), Eddie Safranski, Lawrence Brown (♦), Barney Kessel (♦). Switched record labels, from Victor to Decca, and the recording of **Skyliner (Silver Star Swing Series Presents)** became one of the band's biggest hits. In 1949, formed a fine bebop-based outfit, with arrangers Walter

'Gil' Fuller and Manny Albam, and instrumentalists such as Rolf Ericsson, Claude Williamson, Maynard Ferguson (♦), Tiny Kahn, Dick Hafer **(Bebop Spoken Here).** Sounded much more 'authentic' than, say, Goodman band of the period, though Barnet himself made no stylistic changes to his own playing. Disbanded October, 1949.

During following two decades led jazz units, both large and small, at intermittent periods, including record dates. Very little connection with Bebop (or post-bop) about these activities. Best of the latterday recordings was **Big Band 1967** which recaptured the essence of peak days.

During his career Charlie Barnet (he also married 11 times) was a poll-winning instrumentalist **(Benny Carter 1945 + The Metronome All-Stars).** During its halcyon days the Charlie Barnet Orchestra appeared in several films, or film shorts **(Film Tracks Of Charlie Barnet).**

Recordings:
Various, Swing Street, Vol. 3 *(Epic/Columbia)*
The Complete Charlie Barnet, Vol 1: 1935-1937 *(Bluebird/—)*
Charlie Barnet, Vols 1, 2 *(RCA Victor/RCA Victor)*
Charlie Barnet, King Of The Saxophone *(Trip)/* **Charlie Barnet & His Orchestra** *(DJM)*
Charlie Barnet, Rhapsody In Barnet *(Swing Era)*
Charlie Barnet & His Orchestra, Vol 1 *(Sounds of Swing)*
Film Tracks Of Charlie Barnet *(Joyce)*
Charlie Barnet & His Orchestra 1944-1949 *(Golden Era)*
Benny Carter 1945 + The Metronome All-Stars *(Queen Disc – Italy)*
Charlie Barnet, Some Like It Hot *(Swing Era)*
The Big Band Sound Of Charlie Barnet *(—/Verve)*
Charlie Barnet/Benny Goodman *(Capitol/One-Up)*
Charlie Barnet, Big Band 1967 *(—/Vocalion)*

Count Basie

William 'Count' Basie (born Red Bank, New Jersey, 1904) remains one of the supreme jazz catalysts after more than 50 years as a practising professional musician and a more or less uninterrupted period of 45 years as bandleader. In the latter role, the name 'Basie' connotes all that is best in big-band jazz. At least since 1935, when Basie took over remnants of Bennie Moten (♦) Kansas City Orchestra which, in turn, metamorphosed into Count Basie Orchestra. Basie, leading outfit called Barons of Rhythm, including Buster Smith, alto-sax, was discovered by impresario John Hammond, broadcasting from Reno Club, KC. Hammond helped put together first Basie big band, playing major role in getting its first national tour. Bill Basie was dubbed 'The Count' before leaving Kansas City. Following 'out of town' appearances, first important New York gig was residency at Roseland Ballroom.

First recordings, 1937 **(The Best Of Basie),** showed a dynamic outfit, with major soloists in Lester Young (♦), Herschel Evans (♦), Buck Clayton (♦), and Basie himself. Ensemble-wise, a certain raggedness, soon to be obviated with suitable replacements. Band evinced genuine shouting excitement, and underpinning everything was extraordinary rhythm section, comprising, Basie apart, drummer Jo Jones, bassist Walter Page, and guitarist Claude Williams (soon to be replaced by the far superior Freddie Green, still with Basie today, and since his inception a most vital cog in the wheel of all subsequent Basie-led aggregations). Vocals handled by Jimmy Rushing (♦), at first alone, then assisted by Helen Humes and, on occasion, by sax-section leader Earle Warren.
Roseland Shuffle (The Best Of Basie (1937-38)), as well as documenting the band's New York opening, remains archetypal example of this embryonic stage: introduced by Basie's piano and rhythm section, solos supported by constant riffing by various sections of band in what has long since become known as Kansas City style. (For chronology's

sake, small contingent from main band, including Young, had already made first recordings, with a quartet of sides recorded in Chicago, 1936 under pickup title of Smith-Jones, Inc.) As exciting as the band sounded on record, in live performance it was even more uplifting. Airshot performances from 1937 **(The Count At The Chatterbox, Count Basie & His Orchestra/William & The Famous Door** and **Basie Live!/Count Basie Live),** although often short on hi-fi, give more than adequate representation of just how and why it soon became respected as one of top three big bands. Basie composition called **One O'Clock Jump,** soon to become forever thereafter its theme, also recorded in '37. With Green replacing Williams and Warren taking over from Caughey Roberts on alto-sax and clarinet, band received further boost when Billie Holiday (♦) joined in same year. However, she was to stay for less than one year during which time she was unable to record with Basie, being personally contracted to another label. Despite initial breakthrough, top commercial success still eluded Basie band. This came only after month-long residency at Savoy Ballroom (January, '38), followed by six-month stint at Famous Door (engineered by agent Willard Alexander), with SRO audiences nightly at latter. This tremendous success was built through early-1940s, even though major blows, like death of Herschel Evans (1939), and drafting of key figures (Buck Clayton, Jones, Jack Washington), did not help; nor did the exiting of cornerstone sidemen like Young, Page, Benny Morton, or Don Byas. But from late-1930s through the next decade, the records continued to flow unabated; **Super Chief, Blues By Basie, Basie's Back In Town, One O'Clock Jump** and **Basie's Best.** And when sizzling big-band jazz for American Servicemen (by way of V-Discs) was called for, Count Basie Orchestra catered splendidly **(Count Basie: V-Discs, 1944-45** and **Count Basie: The V-Discs, Vol 2).**

Final years of World War II had seen appearance into band's ranks of new faces such as Joe Newman, Emmett Berry (♦), Al Killian, Eugene 'Snooky' Young, J. J. Johnson (♦), Eli Robinson, Illinois Jacquet (♦), Rudy Rutherford, Rodney Richardson and Shadow Wilson. (Buddy Rich (♦) sometimes acted as explosive deputy to Wilson.) By mid-1940s, even seemingly indestructible Basie band was feeling big-band draught. By 1947, even with continued support from Rushing, long-serving Harry Edison, and despite return of Page and Jones and replacement of Jacquet by Paul Gonsalves (♦), both band and repertoire had become stylised. Material-wise, the band was at lowest ebb. Ironically, Basie (surely not everyone's idea of a pop-style hitmaker) notched up what must be his only Hit Parade smash hit during this period. With Edison's wretched vocal, and very little of what could be called pure Basie, band's

Below: William 'Count' Basie – the Kid from Red Bank, New Jersey. Legendary leader of all-time legendary big band.

19

Above: Count Basie, after 50 years as a pro, still the supreme catalyst. And a bandleader in every way.

William & The Famous Door (DJM). First legendary band of the one-and-only Count Basie – 'live' on 52nd Street!

recording of novelty, **Open The Door, Richard!**, topped the US Charts at beginning of '47. By 1950, Basie had been forced to cut down to eight pieces, the first and only time since mid-1930s he had been without a big band under his leadership. First line-up had Basie leading Edison, Dickie Wells, Georgie Auld (♦), Gene Ammons (♦), Al McKibbon, Gus Johnson, and omnipresent Green; finally, octet comprising Charlie Rouse (♦) (replaced by Wardell Gray (♦)), Serge Chaloff (♦), Clark Terry (♦), Buddy De Franco (♦) (replaced by Marshall Royal), Jimmy Lewis, Johnson (or Buddy Rich). The latter octet(s) played music often influenced by contemporary jazz sounds. One version of octet appeared on its own and in support of Billie Holiday, in a splendid film short made in 1950.

Basie reverted to big-band formula in 1951, initially for recording purposes **(One O'Clock Jump)**, with a superior array of soloists; Gray, Lucky Thompson, Paul Quinichette, Eddie 'Lockjaw' Davis (♦), Newman, Charlie Shavers (♦), Terry, plus Lewis-Green-Johnson-Basie rhythm section. Of these, Johnson, Green, Newman and especially Davis, were to play important roles in Basie big-band renascence. Apart from customary superb solos, Gray's feature **Little Pony** attained something of 'in' reputation with fellow musicians and discerning fans; solo, notated and with words fitted to notes, phrases, etc, by Jon Hendricks, it was later reactivated in an extraordinary fashion by remarkable Lambert, Hendricks and Ross vocal group (with Annie Ross (♦) singing Gray's solo). Arrangers-composers Buster Harding **(Bleep Bop Blues, Nails, Howzit)**, Neal Hefti **(Fancy Meeting You, Little Pony)**, and Ernie Wilkins **(Bread, Bootsie, Hob Nail Boogie)** provided just the right of explosive material, blues-based with accent firmly on swing.

Wilkins, Hefti, Johnny Mandel and saxist-flautist Frank Wess were to exert considerable influence on direction with 'new' (1952) Basie band, first efforts of which were superbly encapsulated on two very successful Norman Granz-supervised LPS **(Count Basie Dance Sessions, Nos 1 &2/Sixteen Men Swinging)**, with Wilkins present also as member of sax section. Johnson, Green, Newman, Wilkins, together with Frank Foster, Eddie Jones and Charlie Fowlkes were each to make substantial contributions in rejuvenated band of this period, and thereafter. Even more than in earlier years, this 'new' Basie unit offered a togetherness that was almost hypnotic, with a delicious and unparalleled penchant for ultimate in relaxed rhythmic performance, and a unique sense of dynamic range – from a blistering scream to a muted whisper – which immediately elevated it to the big-band pantheon. Its pinnacle was reached in 1959 with the album which on its original release was entitled **The Atomic Mr Basie (The Atomic Mr Basie, Chairman Of The Board/The Atomic Mr Chairman)**. Solo-wise, the disc presents probably the finest collection of individual statements by Basieites since the war-time period, with especially rewarding contributions from Eddie Davis **(Whirly Bird**, and others), Frank Wess **(Splanky)**, Joe Newman, Thad Jones (♦), and William Basie **(The Kid From Red Bank)**.

But it is the sheer powerhouse dynamism of the band as a collective unit which must take pride of place (alongside Neal Hefti's finest-ever writing for Basie's, or for that matter any other band with whom he has been associated). Prior to **The Atomic Mr Basie**, this powerhouse aggregation had made a succession of top-notch LPs, including **The Band Of Distinction, Li'l Ol' Groovemaker, Basie At Newport, Easin' It** and **Kansas City Suite**. Last-named comprised a series of typically fine arrangements-compositions from Benny Carter (♦) which suited the band to perfection. A single popular recording of the 1950s/1960s (and indeed thereafter) was organist Wild Bill Davis' arrangement of **April In Paris (April In Paris)** with its one-more-thrice endings.

Although the Count Basie Orchestra of post-1952 did produce talented soloists like Newman, Thad Jones, Frank Foster, Frank Wess, Benny Powell and Eddie Davis, it is true that, in comparison with the pre-war/war-time bands it came off second-best. But, then, for this post-war outfit, its basic strength lay in that unflagging ensemble togetherness. One important figure appeared during the 1950s; his name – Joe Williams. A singer whose basically superior voice allowed him to encompass urban blues, R&B and standard pop (including ballads), with utmost

efficiency – if no more. Onstage, Williams' charismatic personality and big handsome voice helped immensely in the Basie 'comeback'; certainly, it is true to say also that behind Williams the band tended often to swing more potently than without his presence. Williams, who sang with Basie between 1955–8, first recorded with the band in 1955, at what, in the event, turned out to be by far the finest collaboration, on record, by the pair **(Count Basie Swings, Joe Williams Sings)**, including musically exciting versions of **Please Send Me Someone To Love, Roll 'Em, Pete, Alright, Okay, You Win** and **Every Day I Have The Blues**, latter a Memphis Slim (♦) tune that became Williams' first hit.

Frankly, following the opulence and electricity of **The Atomic Mr Basie**, the Count Basie Orchestra rarely has produced work of comparable stature. Of course, sometimes repertoire has been less than adequate (viz James Bond movie themes, Beatles tunes and excerpts from *Mary Poppins*). But many times since then band itself has seemed to be going through the motions, often playing over-familiar material in lackluster, even boring fashion. Ironically, its popularity has tended to soar during latterday period, thus its appeal today stretches well outside any thinly-disguised jazz boundaries. Nowadays, it is not at all uncommon for Count Basie Orchestra to play regular lucrative engagements at nightspots in Las Vegas. It has appeared on the bill of Royal Variety Show, in London, before Queen Elizabeth II. It has also recorded (as well as appeared in concert) with more pop-based vocal artists such as Billy Eckstine (♦), Tony Bennett, Mills Bros, Sammy Davis Jr, Kay Starr, Bing Crosby (♦), and Frank Sinatra (who has worked extensively with Basie & Co, on record and in person, including joint appearance at 1965 Newport Jazz Festival). In more definite jazz vein, Ella Fitzgerald (♦) has performed extremely capably in company with the Basie Orchestra **(On The Sunny Side Of The Street** and **Ella & Basie).** Perhaps best of all vocalist-band collaborations (of those who have not worked regularly with Basie) is to be found on **No Count Sarah** which produced vocal-instrumental fireworks from Sarah Vaughan (♦) and the band seldom heard, before or since. Whilst the reputation of the band itself might have lessened during past 10–15 years, the reputation and ability of its leader have remained undiminished. For example, during past five years Basie has been recorded outside as well as inside big-band format, which has meant constant re-evaluation of his pre-eminence as a piano player of first order. Right from earliest days, Basie has been a very

Basie Big Band (Pablo) – The Count and his men, 1975.

The Best Of Count Basie, Vol 2 (MCA Coral, Germany).

Super Chief (CBS). Justly celebrated soloists like Lester Young and Buck Clayton feature on this Basie classic.

good pianist. His early days with Bennie Moten (♦) **(Moten's Blues)**, indicate a useful performer whose antecedents come from Harlem-stride school, exemplified by Willie 'The Lion' Smith (♦), James P. Johnson (♦) and Fats Waller (♦).(Indeed, it was Waller, his initial inspiration, who had given fledgling Basie some basic tuition.) Later, outside own big band, Basie's superbly economic piano style (he developed an individual approach which was, in fact, an abbreviated version of Waller-type stride, using time and space to devastating effect) was heard most helpfully as part of Benny Goodman (♦) Sextet **(Solo Flight** and **Charlie Christian - Lester Young Together 1940)** or with the Metronome All Stars **(Benny Carter 1945 + The Metronome All Stars)**.

Basie also gave life to a star-studded Goodman jam session of '38 **(Famous Carnegie Hall Concert)**, as well as to important recording sessions by Lester Young **(Lester Young Leaps Again!** and **Pres/The Complete Savoy Recordings)** and Jo Jones **(The Jo Jones Special)**.

In more recent times, record producer Norman Granz has placed Basie's timeless keyboard artistry within an intriguing variety of small-group jazz company, ranging from basic piano-trio setting, with Ray Brown (♦) and Louis Bellson (♦) **(For The First Time)**, to situations involving more varied instrumentation. In such circumstances **(Basie & Zoot, Basie Jam, Nos 1 & 2** and **Count Basie Jam Session At The Montreux Jazz Festival 1975)** the Kid From Red Bank has acted as catalyst supreme, eliciting from the likes of Roy Eldridge (♦), Lockjaw Davis, Joe Pass (♦), Johnny Griffin (♦), Harry Edison, Clark Terry, Benny Carter and J. J. Johnson (♦), superior solo performances. Nothing new for Basie and Granz – Basie had done the same thing for the producer in early-1950s when Basie's piano (and organ too) had paced a line-up that included Stan Getz (♦), Carter, Buddy Rich, and ex-Basieites Edison, Wardell Gray and DeFranco, through some fine musical moments at a fine studio jam session **(Jam Sessions, Nos 2 & 3)**.

Basie's occasional outings at the organ have demonstrated a pleasing transference of piano technique to the electrical instrument, preferable at up-tempo. Especially memorable here is Basie's organ work with Illinois Jacquet **(Illinois Jacquet & His Orchestra)** as well as with Oscar Peterson (♦) **(Satch & Josh)** and own small-band recordings **(Count Basie Sextet, For The First Time, Basie Jam**, etc.), and on rarer occasions on big-band albums **(Dance Session No 1)**. In late-1976 Basie was hospitalized with a heart attack. But by early next year was back on the road again, in time for yet another European tour; at 74, as indomitable as ever. How much longer his band can continue to turn out same kind of music and still retain its popularity is anybody's guess. Certainly, change of musical direction (and policy?) is overdue, although it is doubtful, at this late stage of the game, whether any such changes will take place. Though a strictly one-off affair, the band's 1970 LP **Afrique,** arranged and conducted by Oliver Nelson (♦), and with music by Nelson, Gabor Szabo, Albert Ayler (♦), and Pharoah Sanders (♦), demonstrated that change, and dramatic change at that, was indeed possible. Whatever happens, it is true that the Basie band, like the leader himself, remains an implacable, immovable force that can still, when the adrenalin is flowing, rise to the heights like no other outfit, anywhere. There is much about the early Basie in *Jazz Style In Kansas City & The Southwest* by Ross Russell. Also of interest is *Count Basie & His Orchestra* by Ray Horricks.

Recordings:
Count Basie, Good Morning Blues *(MCA/—)*
The Count Swings Out (1937-38) *(—/MCA – Germany)*
Count Basie, The Best Of Basie (1937-38) *(—/MCA – Germany)*
Count Basie, The Blues I Like To Hear (1938-39) *(—/MCA – Germany)*

Count Basie, Super Chief *(Columbia/CBS)*
Lester Young With The Count Basie Orchestra *(Epic/Epic – France)*
Lester Young, The Lester Young Story, Vol 3/Enter The Count *(Columbia/CBS)*
The Count At The Chatterbox 1937 *(Jazz Archives/—)*
Count Basie & His Orchestra *(Trip)*/William & The Famous Door *(DJM)*
Blues By Basie *(Columbia/Philips)*
Basie's Back In Town *(Epic/Philips)*
One O'Clock Jump *(Columbia/Fontana)*
Various, John Hammond's Spirituals To Swing *(Vanguard/Vanguard)*
Various, Famous Carnegie Hall Concert *(Columbia/CBS)*
Count Basie, Basie's Best *(Columbia/CBS)*
Count Basie: The V-Discs – 1944-45 *(Jazz Society/—)*
Count Basie: The V-Discs, Vol 2 *(Jazz Society/—)*
Count Basie *(RCA Victor – France)*
Basie Live! *(Trip)*/Count Basie Live *(DJM)*
Blues By Basie *(Tax – Sweden)*
Count Basie, April In Paris *(Clef/Columbia-Clef)*
Count Basie Dance Sessions, Nos 1 & 2 *(Clef)*/
Sixteen Men Swinging *(Verve)*
Count Basie, The Band Of Distinction *(Verve/HMV)*
The Atomic Mr Basie *(Roulette)*, Chairman Of The Board *(Roulette)*/
The Atomic Mr Chairman *(Vogue)*
Count Basie: The Soloist 1941/1959 *(Jazz Anthology/—)*
Count Basie *(—/Vogue)*
Count Basie, Kansas City Suite *(Roulette/Columbia)*
Count Basie, The Newport Years, Vol VI *(Verve)*/The Live Big Band Sound Of Count Basie *(Verve)*
Count Basie, Afrique *(Flying Dutchman/Philips)*
Various, Jazz At The Santa Monica *(Pablo/Pablo)*
Charlie Christian/Lester Young, Together 1940 *(Jazz Archives/—)*
Lester Young Leaps Again! *(EmArcy/Fontana)*
Lester Young, Pres/The Complete Savoy Recordings *(Savoy/Savoy)*
Benny Carter 1945 + The Metronome All-Stars *(Queen Disc – Italy)*
Various, Jam Sessions Nos 2 & 3 *(Verve/Columbia – Clef)*
Illinois Jacquet & His Orchestra *(Verve/Columbia – Clef (EP))*
Count Basie, For The First Time *(Pablo/Pablo)*
Count Basie/Joe Turner, The Bosses *(Pablo/Pablo)*
Count Basie Jam Session At The Montreux Jazz Festival 1975 *(Pablo/Pablo)*
Count Basie, Basie Jam No 2 *(Pablo/Pablo)*
Count Basie/Zoot Sims, Basie & Zoot *(Pablo/Pablo)*
Count Basie Swings, Joe Williams Sings *(Verve)*/
Swingin' With The Count *(Verve)*
Joe Williams – Count Basie *(Vogue/Vogue)*
Count Basie/Sarah Vaughan, No Count Sarah *(Mercury)*/
Sassy *(Fontana)*
Lambert, Hendricks & Ross, Sing Along With Basie *(Roulette/Columbia)*
Count Basie/Ella Fitzgerald, On The Sunny Side Of The Street *(Verve/Verve)*
Montreux '77: Count Basie Big Band *(Pablo Live/Pablo Live)*
Montreux '77: Count Basie Jam *(Pablo Live/Pablo Live)*
Count Basie, The Atomic Period *(Rarities/—)*

Sidney Bechet

Sidney Bechet (born New Orleans, 1897) was amongst the first truly masterful jazz soloists, youngest of seven children in a musical family. First instrument was clarinet; as a child, he sat in with legendary Freddie Keppard, and marched with another New Orleans trumpeter Manuel Perez, and throughout his career remained one of finest of all clarinettists. Even though, eventually, clarinet took second place to soprano-sax, the latter instrument which Bechet, single-handed, turned into powerful form of expression within jazz vernacular. Other early jazz figures with whom Bechet was associated: Lorenzo Tio (a tutor for Bechet), Buddie Petit, John Robichaux, Bunk Johnson (♦); Bechet even played cornet during New Orleans street parades. Left Crescent City for good in 1917 (had worked for first time with King Oliver (♦) the year before), moving on to Chicago, then New York. Became a member of Southern Syncopated Orchestra led by Will Marion Cook, 1919 (second time) and went to Europe. Left Cook in London, by which time he added soprano to his clarinet, playing regularly in the British capital (and Paris), before deportation to the US ('21).

Same year recorded for first time. Briefly with Duke Ellington (♦) and James P. Johnson (♦), and in same year (1925) toured with *Revue Negre*, as a member of Claude Hopkins (♦) Orchestra which accompanied Josephine Baker.

1926: toured Russia, visited Berlin, organized band for another *Revue Negre*, re-visiting Europe following year. With Noble Sissle for season in Paris (1928), subsequently serving jail sentence in French capital for involvement in shooting incident. Returned to US, rejoining Sissle, toured with Ellington (1932), then organized the first of his celebrated New Orleans Feetwarmers (with cornettist Tommy Ladnier (♦)). Retired from music, becoming proprietor, with Ladnier, of a New York tailoring establishment. But by 1934 had rejoined Sissle, a situation which remained unchanged until 1938. Worked with own and other bands at Nick's, New York jazz club (1938), followed by a lengthy season at Momart Astoria with Willie 'The Lion' Smith (♦), with whom he had worked previously. Regular and much-respected figure on New York jazz scene from then until 1951 with many appearances at the famous Eddie Condon (♦) wartime Town Hall concerts, as well as innumerable concert and club dates in the Big Apple, and cities

Jazz Classics, Vol 1 (Blue Note) - gems by Bechet.

like Boston and Chicago. Appeared at Nice Jazz Festival (1949), where he jammed with Charlie Parker (♦) and others. Returned the following year.

From 1951 until his death (in 1959), Paris was to become more or less permanent home for Bechet although he made infrequent trips back to the States for special guest appearances, recordings, etc. Visited Britain (1956), South America (1957). In Paris, though, Bechet became something of an institution, a particular favourite amongst Left Bank fraternity. Took part in 1955 movie *Blues*.

Until John Coltrane (♦) made it his secondary instrument, Sidney Bechet's position as jazz's premier exponent of soprano-saxophone was unchallenged. Using combination of impassioned emotionalism (heightened by use of heavy and wide vibrato) and an unremitting attack, Bechet's fierce playing of the instrument was powerful enough to combat the challenge of all others, including trumpets, in any ensemble. Only Louis Armstrong (♦) **(Louis With Guest Stars)** seemed able to resist Bechet, whose approach to ensemble playing was that invariably taken by the trumpet. In his earlier days, often in Armstrong's company, Bechet provided stimulating accompaniments and solos to a variety of blues

singers, including Bessie Smith (♦), Mamie Smith, and Margaret Johnson. And with Clarence Williams (♦) (Bechet's first recordings of note were with Williams' Blue Five in 1923) he further enhanced vocal records of the 1920s by such as Virginia Liston, Sippie Wallace, Eva Taylor **(Adam & Eve Had The Blues).** With Williams, Bechet first locked horns with Armstrong **(Louis Armstrong/Sidney Bechet With The Clarence Williams Blue Five),** the pair sounding beautifully expressive on **Texas Moaner Blues, Papa De Dad', Just Wait Till You See** and the first get-together on **Coal Cart Blues.**

Bechet added his soaring sound to Jelly Roll Morton's (♦) New Orleans Jazzmen recording date of 1939, a few months after his own matchless recording of **Summertime (Jazz Classics, Vol 1)** for Blue Note; probably first-ever success on record for jazz ballad performance. Following year, in company with Muggsy Spanier (♦), he committed to record a series of superbly structured solos (in the context, and for Bechet, his flowing solos were admirably restrained) which rank with his finest work elsewhere **(Ragtime Jazz/ Tribute To Bechet).**

For Blue Note, Bechet recorded some of his most memorable solos **(Jazz Classics, Vols 1, 2)** including poignant clarinet duets with Albert Nicholas (♦) in 1946; a splendid Bechet Blue Note Quartet date with Teddy Bunn (♦) from 1940; the Bechet Blue Note Jazzmen sides (with Sidney DeParis (♦), Vic Dickenson (♦), et al) from 1944; more fine jazz in company of Max Kaminsky (♦), Art Hodes (♦) and the like, from '45; and some joyful, freewheeling music (with Wild Bill Davison (♦), and Hodes, again) from 1949.

Then, of course, there were the marvellously integrated, beautifully felt performances by the Feetwarmers **(Sidney Bechet, Vols 1-3).** And the equally famous recordings which juxtaposed Bechet's ecstatic soprano and clarinet opposite the simple, but heartfelt clarinet of Mezz Mezzrow, made in 1945 for the King Jazz label – (Mezzrow-Bechet Quintet) – to be repeated (although not as closely argued as '45) two years later **(The Prodigious Bechet-Mezzrow Quintet & Septet).** Even though a more gifted front-line partner (eg Armstrong) might have resulted in music of even greater significance, the Bechet-Mezzrow sessions find the New Orleans man achieving moments of total inspiration, rare even in the most exalted jazz circles. During his latter period as one of France's adopted sons, Bechet continued to work extensively, both in live performance as well as on record, using mostly local musicians, although readily taking opportunity to assert his undiminished authority in the company of visiting US jazzmen, as with **Refreshing Tracks, Vol 1.** And his rare trips back home often produced satisfying results **(Sidney Bechet At Storyville).** Fronted all-star band of Americans at Brussels International Fair (1958). Autobiography, *Treat It Gentle*, published in 1960.

Of all the non-trumpet front-line instrumentalists, Sidney Bechet was, without doubt, the most powerful voice. A virtuoso performer, and a complete individualist, Bechet remains one of jazz's most important soloists.

Recordings:
Louis Armstrong/Sidney Bechet, With The Clarence Williams Blue Five *(CBS – France)*
Clarence Williams, Adam & Eve Had The Blues *(CBS – France)*
Sidney Bechet, The Rarest ... Vol 1 *(After Hours)*
Sidney Bechet, Blackstick (1931-1938) *(MCA-Coral – Germany)*
Various, John Hammond's Spirituals To Swing *(Vanguard)/* **The Legendary John Hammond's Carnegie Hall Concerts 1938/39 From Spirituals To Swing** *(Vogue)*
Sidney Bechet, Unique Sidney *(CBS – France)*
Various, The Panassie Sessions *(RCA Victor/RCA Victor – France)*
Jelly Roll Morton & His Red Hot Peppers/New Orleans Jazzmen, Vol 2 (1926-1939) *(RCA Victor – France)*
Sidney Bechet, Vols 1-3 *(RCA Victor – France)*
Louis Armstrong, Louis With Guest Stars *(MCA Coral – Germany)*
Sidney Bechet, Jazz Classics, Vols 1, 2 *(Blue Note)*
Sidney Bechet/Muggsy Spanier, Ragtime Jazz (Olympic)/ Tribute To Bechet *(Ember)*
Sidney Bechet 1949 *(Barclay)*
Bechet/Mezzrow Quintet *(Concert Hall)*
The Prodigious Bechet/ Mezzrow Quintet & Septet *(Festival – France)*
Eddie Condon, The Eddie Condon Concerts, Vol 2 *(Chiaroscuro/—)*
Various, 'This Is Jazz', Vols 1, 2 *(Rarities)*

Sidney Bechet Album *(—/Saga)*
The Genius Of Sidney Bechet *(Jazzology/—)*
Sidney Bechet & Friends *(For Discriminating Collectors)*
Sidney Bechet At Storyville *(Storyville/Vogue)*
Sidney Bechet, Refreshing Tracks Vols 1 & 2 *(—/Vogue)*
Sidney Bechet, His Way *(Pumpkin/—)*
Sidney Bechet *(Musidisc – France)*

Bix Beiderbecke

More has been written over the years since his death about Leon Bix Beiderbecke (born Davenport, Iowa, 1903) than about the remarkable music he produced during a tragically short career. Indeed, it was not until 1974, with the publication of *Bix: Man & Legend*, written by Richard M. Sudhalter and Philip R. Evans, with William Dean-Myatt, that a totally comprehensive, scholarly and apparently near-flawless account of the life and music of Beiderbecke, complete with discography, made available a more or less satisfactory (and satisfying) account of the man's *music*, as well as his private life. Beiderbecke, who started at piano aged three, moved to cornet at 14, and graduated, musically, through school and local children's band, first evinced a genuine interest in becoming full-time jazzman during his high school period (1919-21).

In 1921 Beiderbecke played on riverboats, enrolled at Lake Forest Military Academy, near Chicago (he was expelled a year later) before taking jobs with several Chicago-based bands. Also in '21 sat in with Elmer Schoebel band. Joined the Wolverines (1923), making record debut with latter in 1924. Those early recordings **(Bix Beiderbecke & The Chicago**

Bix Beiderbecke & The Chicago Cornets (Milestone).

Cornets) show a rather tentative young musician, but thereafter he was to produce a series of recorded performances, on B-flat cornet, that were not only masterfully lyrical and supremely logical in development but also totally unlike anything produced at that time, either by the great black trumpet players or their white counterparts. Further Wolverines recordings demonstrate a growth in stature and confidence, and the formation of a style that was an intriguing counterpoint to those already in use – as personified in

Below: Sidney Bechet, Jazz Immortal. Magisterial and influential soloist (both on soprano-sax and clarinet).

the work of say, King Oliver (♦), Louis Armstrong (♦), Tommy Ladnier (♦) and Freddie Keppard.

Beiderbecke's was a style which was to exercise its own influence, swiftly and lastingly. Amongst those to be deeply influenced by Beiderbecke were Red Nichols (♦), Jimmy McPartland, Bobby Hackett (♦) and Rex Stewart (♦), who showed his admiration for Beiderbecke by producing a solo of Bixian style during a recording by the Fletcher Henderson Orchestra of Beiderbecke's own classic showcase, Singin' The Blues.

Beiderbecke left the Wolverines in November, '24, to join the orchestra of Charlie Straight, but more important was his association during 1925–6 with the band led by saxist Frankie Trumbauer (♦), a name soon to be closely associated with Beiderbecke's. Then both became members of Jean Goldkette Orchestra until temporary disbandment in autumn of 1927. By which time, Beiderbecke had recorded with, amongst other units, the Sioux City Six and his own Rhythm Jugglers (Bix Beiderbecke & The Chicago Cornets), Trumbauer (The Golden Days Of Jazz: Bix Beiderbecke) and the Goldkette band (The Bix Beiderbecke Legend).

With Trumbauer, Beiderbecke recorded two remarkable trio sides (also featuring guitarist Eddie Lang (♦)) Wringin' & Twistin' and For No Reason At All In C, not to mention the previously noted Singing The Blues, the latter containing probably the single most brilliant solo Beiderbecke produced on record, and certainly one of the most influential, much-copied and widely-discussed solos in jazz history. Of less import, but even more intriguing perhaps was an unaccompanied piano solo recorded same year, In A Mist. Both composition (it was written by Beiderbecke) and performance are cast in a distinctly Debussy-like mold. I'm Coming Virginia (also with Trumbauer) is another significant track that dates from 1927: beautifully sculpted, effortlessly delivered (The Golden Days Of Jazz: Bix Beiderbecke). Other important recordings during that year, made under the banner of Bix Beiderbecke & His Gang, included such influential sides as Jazz Me Blues and Since My Best Gal Turned Me Down (Bix Beiderbecke & His Gang).

Of equal importance was the occasion when Beiderbecke, together with Trumbauer, became a member of the Paul Whiteman (♦) Orchestra, the most popular and successful musical aggregation on the US music scene. With Whiteman, Beiderbecke was to receive the kind of international exposure he could not have accomplished alone. Conversely, jazz content of Whiteman's band was given decided boost with Beiderbecke's induction into its ranks (The Bix Beiderbecke Legend), especially on individual numbers like You Took Advantage Of Me, Changes, There Ain't No Sweet Man Worth The Salt Of My Tears, Love Nest and Dardanella. Often he was given a mere eight bars. But the eloquence of his playing, even when featured briefly, was in stark contrast to the often ponderous and heavy-handed swing of the huge orchestra.

During this period as principal jazz soloist with Whiteman, Beider-

becke began to lose his growing battle with alcoholism. Absent from the band on several occasions (once, when Whiteman was in Hollywood to make the famous early talkie, The King Of Jazz) Beiderbecke's health deteriorated so alarmingly that, after leaving for second time, in 1929, he never worked with Whiteman again.

Apart from freelance recordings, a rather pathetic final record date of his own, and some erratic live engagements, it was the end of the Bix Beiderbecke Story. He died in his Queen's, New York, apartment, August 6, 1931 – aged 28 – from lobar pneumonia with oedema of the brain. His body was taken to his native Davenport, where he was buried five days later. The Beiderbecke legend was given fictional renaissance many years after his death by Dorothy Baker's best-selling novel Young Man With A Horn, whose principal character obviously was based on the hard-drinking Bix Beiderbecke. Of other, non-fiction and, of course, more important publications about Beiderbecke, the following deserve individual recommendation: Bugles For Beiderbecke, by Charles H. Wareing & George Garlick, the best, next to the Sudhalter-Evans-Dean-Myatt tome; Richard Hadlock's chapter on Beiderbecke in his Jazz of the Twenties; Gunther Schuller's treatise on Bix in Early Jazz; and Burnett James' Bix Beiderbecke.

With his records being issued and re-issued at impressively regular intervals, the Legend of Bix Beiderbecke, the musical legend, retains its popularity and importance almost 50 years after his death.

Recordings:
Bix Beiderbecke & The Chicago Cornets (Milestone)
Bix Beiderbecke Story, Vols 1-3 (Columbia/CBS – France)
Bix Beiderbecke Legend (RCA Victor – France)
Bix Beiderbecke, Bix & His Gang (—/Parlophone)
Jack Teagarden Classics (Family – Italy)

Louis Bellson

Louis Bellson (born Louis Balassoni, in Rock Falls, Ill, 1924) has worked in all manner of jazz contexts since very youthful age. Respected big-band percussionist, has worked with Duke Ellington (♦), Harry James (♦), Tommy Dorsey (♦) and Count Basie (♦), spending more than one period during his career with each, and Ted Fio Rito, as well as leading a succession of healthy-sounding big bands of his own.

A formidable technician, but one who uses his considerable skills constructively and with infinite taste, Bellson is also equally at home within the framework of small-combo jazz. He has worked with countless small bands over many years, including better-known outfits such as the Benny Goodman Quintet and the more disparate Jazz at the Philharmonic all-stars.

Bellson, who during the mid-1940s innovated concept of twin bass drums as part of the drummer's basic kit, brought a completely new and fresh approach to

Louis Bellson At The Thunderbird (Impulse).

the Ellington orchestra during his two-year spell. From all-round standpoint, must be considered the most accomplished drummer employed, for any length of time, by Ellington. During this period (1950–2), Bellson's reputation was further enhanced, this time as composer and arranger. Amongst his written contributions for Ellington, the best-known include The Hawk Talks (affectionate dedication to Harry James), Ting-a-Ling and Skin Deep. Bellson's immaculate drumming featured extensively during latter, released originally as two-part single recording which achieved pop-type sales when released (1953).

Apart from work with big bands and small combos, Bellson often has accompanied top-line singers (viz Tony Bennett, Louis Armstrong (♦), Ella Fitzgerald (♦) and Pearl Bailey). In fact, Bellson married singer-comedienne-actress Pearl Bailey in 1953. In small-group setting, Bellson has proved demonstrably tasteful, always attentive accompanist, especially when accompanying pianists of the calibre of Count Basie (Basie Jam and For The First Time), Art Tatum (♦) (Tatum Group Masterpieces), Oscar Peterson (♦) (with Basie) (Satch & Josh) and Duke Ellington (Duke's Big Four).

Under his own name, Bellson has recorded many albums, none of which has proved to be of inestimable importance, but each containing much good music and all-round superior musicianship. Amongst the best of these have been several in-person recordings, including Louis Bellson At The Flamingo, Big Band At The Summit and Louis Bellson's Septet Recorded Live At The 1976 Concord Jazz Festival. Similarly, Bellson can be heard at his best during a live recording with Count Basie, Basie In Sweden.

As a person, Bellson is universally recognized as an endearing, genuinely modest jazz man. Thankfully, too, his modesty reaches into his musical make-up. Even when leading his own bands Bellson rarely hogs the solo limelight (unlike the vast majority of drummers). Possibly his lengthiest solo on record is to be found during yet another live performance, this time as a member of the Jazz at the Philharmonic troupe (The Exciting Battle/JATP Stockholm '55). But that is the exception, rather than the rule. Almost invariably, where he permits himself solo space at any length he prefers to integrate his drumnastics intelligently, within basic ensemble framework, as he does with great success during a recording of his own London Suite (Louie In London).

The former boy-wonder drummer, whose teens were spent winning all kinds of drumming contests, remains one of the handful of real virtuoso performers; constantly in demand, readily and easily adaptable, and a thorough profession to his proverbial finger-tips.

Recordings:
The World Of Duke Ellington, Vol 2 (Columbia)/
The World Of Duke Ellington, Vol 1 (CBS)
The World Of Duke Ellington, Vol 3 (Columbia)
The World Of Duke Ellington, Vol 2 (CBS)
Duke Ellington, A Tone Parallel To Harlem (CBS – France)
Duke Ellington Concert At Carnegie Hall (Trip/DJM)
Duke Ellington & The Ellingtonians (—/Vogue – France)
Duke Ellington, Duke's Big 4 (Pablo/Pablo)
Art Tatum, The Tatum Group Masterpieces (Pablo/Pablo)
Count Basie, Basie Jam (Pablo/Pablo)
Count Basie, Basie Jam No 2 (Pablo/Pablo)
Count Basie, For The First Time (Pablo/Pablo)
Count Basie Jam Session At The Montreux Jazz Festival 1975 (Pablo/Pablo)
Count Basie, Basie In Sweden (Roulette/Columbia)
Duke Ellington, Ellington Uptown (Columbia/CBS – France)
Various, The Exciting Battle/ J.A.T.P. Stockholm '55 (Pablo/Pablo)
Various, The Gillespie Jam Sessions (Norgran/Verve)
Various, Jazz Giants (Verve/Columbia – Clef)
Ella Fitzgerald/Louis Armstrong, The Special Magic Of Ella & Louis, Vol 2 (—/Verve)
Various (Including Louis Bellson), Kings Of Swing, Vol 2 (—/Verve)
Louis Bellson/(Mills Blue Rhythm Band), Big Bands! (Onyx/Polydor)
Louis Bellson, At The Flamingo (Verve/Columbia)
Louie In London (—/Pye)
The Louis Bellson Explosion (Pablo/Pablo)
At The Thunderbird (Impulse/—)
Big Band At The Summit (Roulette/Columbia)
Louis Bellson's Septet Recorded Live At The Concord Jazz Festival (Concord Jazz/—)
Louis Bellson, Prime Time (Concord Jazz/—)

George Benson

Guitarist George Benson's early contribution to jazz gets overlooked in the light of his current commercial success in the Easy Listening field. Born in Pittsburgh, Benson started out as a singer, and learned guitar changes with organist Jack McDuff, a partnership that produced his best work (George Benson & Jack McDuff). A contract with Creed Taylor's CTI label saw Benson in a formula setting of highly arranged funk (Body Talk, White Rabbit and Good King Bad) – all big-selling albums. A change to Warner Brothers put him in the millionaire bracket with a re-make of guitarist Gabor Szabo's hit **Breezin'**.

Recordings:
George Benson & Jack McDuff (*Prestige/Prestige*)
Body Talk (*CTI/CTI*)
White Rabbit (*CTI/CTI*)
Good King Bad (*CTI/CTI*)
Breezin' (*Warner/Warner*)
In Flight (*Warner/Warner*)

Bunny Berigan

Roland Bernard 'Bunny' Berigan (born Fox Lake, Hilbert, Calumet, Wisconsin, 1907) has the dubious distinction of figuring prominently amongst the all-time list of notable jazzmen who died at tragically early ages. Was less than 30 when he died in 1933 (in New York, from a combination of pneumonia and haemorrhage, accentuated by alcoholism). Berigan's death was a real tragedy insofar as his was a talent of comprehensive proportions. A first-class technician, Berigan's playing was noted for its fire and sheer emotionalism. Berigan exhibited a fierce attack, yet never was less than lyrical. His work in the lower register of his instrument was especially memorable, far superior to most other jazz trumpet players.

Came from a musical family, first learning violin before turning to trumpet. At 13 was playing in a local band. Played regularly for University of Wisconsin dance units, even though he was not a student, and likewise as teenager sat in with New Orleans Rhythm Kings. After working with several Wisconsin bands, made first trip to New York in 1928. Finally, moved from home to New York to join danceband of Hal Kemp (1930). Toured Europe with Kemp during major portion of that year. Returning to New York, freelanced, then became member of Fred Rich's outfit. 1931: Berigan's horn added to Dorsey Bros Orchestra that took part in Broadway show *Everybody Welcome*; the same year he completed summer season with Smith Ballew. During early-1930s, also became prolific session man (radio, recordings).

Major break-through came when signed by Paul Whiteman (♦) (1932–3), after which played, briefly, with Abe Lyman before becoming regular staffman with CBS. Between 1932 and 1935, when he joined Benny Goodman (♦), recorded prolifically, with the likes of the Boswell Sisters, Dorsey Bros Orchestra, Mound City Blue Blowers (**The Great Soloists: Bunny Berigan 1932-1937**), Adrian Rollini (♦) (**Adrian Rollini & His Orchestra 1933-34**).

His reputation as constantly rewarding trumpet soloist, influenced jointly by power and fire of Armstrong (♦) and Oliver (♦) and the lyricism of Beiderbecke (♦), was matched by the respect he earned from a personal standpoint. Whilst Berigan's reputation soared with Goodman, truth to say, the latter's band benefited most from the flaring trumpet solos its latest star acquisition produced. Both on record (**Benny Goodman, Vols 5, 7**) and in person (**A Jam Session With Benny Goodman 1935-37** and **Benny Goodman & His Orchestra Featuring Bunny Berigan**) Beri-

gan vied with Goodman's clarinet for top solo honors, and often won. During his stay with Goodman, Berigan's solos on **King Porter Stomp, Sometimes I'm Happy, Blue Skies** and others, overnight became individual statements of near-classic proportions. More studio work (CBS, ARC) followed departure from Goodman, then brief associations with Red McKenzie, Red Norvo (♦) and Ray Noble, plus recording date with Billie Holiday (♦) (**The Billie Holiday Story, Vol 1**) and others, under his own name (**The Great Soloists: Bunny Berigan 1932-1937**). At one of latter Berigan first recorded **I Can't Get Started (Take It Bunny!)** a song that was to play a significant part in his musical life after he re-recorded it with his own orchestra in 1937. Other important record dates included two in December, 1935, made specifically for UK market, during which Berigan inspired musicians like Bud Freeman (♦), Cliff Jackson, Cozy Cole (♦) and Jess Stacy (♦) to produce of their best (**Swing Classics 1935/Jazz In The Thirties**).

After participating in recordings with Tommy Dorsey (♦), which produced more Berigan excellence on, for example, **Song Of India, Melody In F, Marie** and **Liebestraum (Tommy Dorsey & His Orchestra)** Bunny Berigan, with Dorsey's blessing, put together his own big band (1937).

During the following years (1937–40) Berigan's alcoholism worsened, and although he delivered numerous glorious performances, there were times when his playing was erratic, even downright poor. Noted musicians who worked with Berigan's post-1937 big band included drummers Davey Tough (♦), Buddy Rich (♦) and George Wettling (♦); tenorist George Auld (♦); trombonists Sonny Lee and Ray Conniff; pianists Joe Bushkin and Joe Lippman (the latter also arranged for the band); and saxists-clarinettists Gus Bivona, Mike Doty and Joe Dixon.

Whilst it never achieved any extraordinary musical heights, Bunny Berigan's Orchestra often was better than some other of the many white big bands spawned by the 'Swing Era'. Hardly surprising, but Berigan's trumpet was focal point, and as its records testify (**Bunny Berigan & His Orchestra**) there were few occasions when he did not execute solos of superlative standards. His statements, for example, on **Can't Help Lovin' Dat Man, Prisoner's Song, Jelly Roll Blues, Mahogany Hall Stomp** (interesting comparison to Armstrong's immortal version) and, above all, **I Can't Get Started With You,** indeed rank with the great trumpet solos of the decade. **I Can't Get Started,** with warm, friendly vocal contribution from Berigan to add to his definitive trumpet statement, has long since assumed legendary proportions amongst jazz buffs. And this was the nearest he came to producing a hit record. Certainly, the Berigan orchestra managed to acquire for itself an ample share of radio broadcasts, and numerous superior examples of its worth have been made available over the years, including '**Down By The Old Mill Stream**' - Bunny In The '30s, **Bunny Berigan - Leader & Sideman, Shanghai Shuffle** and **Bunny Berigan, Vols**

Bunny Berigan, Vol 2 (Shoestring) – 'on the air'.

1, 2. Unfortunately, Bunny Berigan was not the most disciplined of bandleaders and this, together with his drinking problem and a penchant towards over-generosity, resulted in the orchestra's eventual demise.

Faced with bankruptcy, Berigan rejoined Tommy Dorsey (one of his staunchest admirers, always) in March, '40. Dorsey made sure that his ailing friend received his share of solos, as on **Hallelujah (That Sentimental Gentleman)** from a June, 1940 broadcast. By August, though, Berigan was again leading his own (small) band, in New York. Then, he put together what was to be his last big band, toured (including Hollywood, where he recorded his contribution to soundtrack of *Syncopation*), but contracted pneumonia in April '42. Although discharged from hospital in May, and did in fact play a few club dates, he was admitted to New York Polyclinic Hospital end of same month, at which venue he passed away on June 2.

Together with Bix Beiderbecke (whose own tragically short life followed a similar pathway), Bunny Berigan was the greatest white trumpet player to be produced from the 1920s/1930s period – indeed, one of the greatest of all-time – and truly a giant performer on his chosen instrument.

Recordings:
Bunny Berigan, The Great Soloists: Bunny Berigan (1932-1937) (*Biograph*)
Benny Goodman & His Orchestra Featuring Bunny Berigan (*Golden Era*)
Benny Goodman, Vols 5, 7 (*RCA Victor – France*)
A Jam Session With Benny Goodman 1935-1937 (*Sunbeam*)
Billie Holiday, The Billie Holiday Story, Vol 1 (*Columbia/CBS*)
Adrian Rollini & His Orchestra 1933-1934 (*Sunbeam*)
Bunny Berigan, His Trumpet & Orchestra: Original 1937-1939 Recordings (*RCA Victor Vintage/—*)
Bunny Berigan, Take It Bunny! (*Epic/—*)
Various (Including Bunny Berigan), Swing Classics 1935 (*Prestige*)/
Jazz In The Thirties (*World Records*)
Bunny Berigan, 'Down By The Old Mill Stream' - Bunny In The '30s (*Jazz Archives*)
Bunny Berigan, Great Dance Bands Of The Thirties (*RCA Victor*)/
Bunny Berigan & His Orchestra (*RCA Victor*)

Bunny Berigan, Through The Years - Bunny Berigan - Leader & Sideman (*Jazz Archives*)
Bunny Berigan, Vols 1, 2 (*Shoestring*)
Bunny Berigan 1936 (*Coral – Germany*)
Tommy Dorsey & His Orchestra, Vols 1, 2 (*RCA Victor*)
The Metronome All Stars (Esquire All Stars) (*RCA Victor – France*)
Tommy Dorsey, That Sentimental Gentleman (*RCA Victor/—*)

Chu Berry

Leon 'Chu' Berry (born Wheeling, West Virginia, 1910) probably was, together with Ben Webster (♦) and Bud Freeman (♦), third most important tenor-saxophonist during the period from mid-1930s until his premature death in 1941 (behind Coleman Hawkins (♦) and Lester Young (♦)). Certainly, it was no minor tragedy when Berry died in October, '41, from severe head injuries, following a car crash.

Coming from a musical family, Berry played alto-sax at high school. During three years at college, played both alto- and tenor-saxes (he moved on to the bigger horn, permanently, after hearing Hawkins). After turning down the offer of a career as professional footballer, Berry decided on a career in music, starting with Sammy Stewart band (1929–30), followed by spells with Cecil Scott, Otto Hardwick, Kaiser Marshall, Walter Pichon, Earl Jackson and Benny Carter (♦), (1932, and again in 1933). Like Carter, Berry also worked with Charlie Johnson (1932–3); then with Teddy Hill (1933–5) and Fletcher Henderson (♦) (1935-7) (**The Fletcher Henderson Story/The Fletcher Henderson Story, Vol 4**) before joining Cab Calloway (♦) in '37.

With Calloway, Chu Berry recorded some of his finest solos (**16 Cab Calloway Classics**), individual classics such as **Ghost Of A Chance, Lonesome Nights, Take The 'A' Train** and his own **At The Clambake Carnival.** With Lionel Hampton (♦), too, Berry's rich-toned, rolling style (Hawkins-influenced, no doubt, with less staccato in delivery and less overtly rhapsodic on ballads) found a happy stomping ground (**The Complete Lionel Hampton/Lionel Hampton's Best Records, Vols 2, 3, 5**) nowhere better showcased than on **Sweethearts On Parade (Vol 2).** Whilst with Calloway, Berry participated in a marvellously rewarding record date, featuring Roy Eldridge (♦), Sidney Catlett (♦) and others, which resulted in magnificent playing by front-line pair of Berry and Eldridge on **Sittin' In, Stardust, Body & Soul** and **Forty Six West Fifty Two (The Big Sounds Of Coleman Hawkins & Chu Berry).** With Eldridge, Berry had previously recorded under Gene Krupa's (♦) leadership, in 1936, at another successful date in which both played a major role in proceedings, notably during **Swing Is Here (Benny Goodman, Vol 4: 1935-1939).** Berry always sounded comfortable too with Teddy Wilson (♦), and during the late-1930s, the

Chu (Epic, France). The quintessence of Chu Berry.

pianist used his tenor-sax to considerable advantage at several recording sessions **(Teddy Wilson & His All-Stars)** and **(The Teddy Wilson).**

Surprising, perhaps, but Berry also sounded inspired and at top of his game when he recorded (in '38) as a member of Wingy Manone's Orchestra **(Chew, Choo, Chu & Co.** and **Wingy Manone, Vol 1).**

Although it has been stated in some publications that Chu Berry joined Count Basie (♦) Orchestra, this is erroneous. He did not take the place of Herschel Evans (♦), but did, however, deputize for him at recording date that produced **Oh! Lady Be Good** and a Jimmy Rushing (♦) feature, **Evil Blues.**

Amongst other impressive examples of Berry's big-toned, totally swinging tenor-sax style are to be found several 1937 recordings made under his own name **(Chu Berry & His Stompy Stevedores)**, also during his Calloway period. Notable amongst these are **Limehouse Blues, Chuberry Jam, Too Marvelous For Words** and **Indiana** (all 'Chu'). His work with Spike Hughes **(Spike Hughes & His All American Orchestra)** from four years before the Stompy Stevedores dates, once again illustrates the magnitude of his loss at such a ridiculously youthful stage in his development, musically and personally.

Recordings:
Spike Hughes & His All American Orchestra
(London/Ace of Clubs)
Benny Goodman, Vol 4 (1935-1939)
(RCA Victor – France)
Chu Berry, 'Chu' *(Epic – France)*
Chu Berry, Penguin Swing: Chu Berry Featured With Cab Calloway
(Jazz Archives)
16 Cab Calloway Classics
(CBS – France)
Mildred Bailey, Her Greatest Performances, 1929-1946, Vols 1, 2 *(Columbia/CBS)*
The Fletcher Henderson Story *(Columbia)/*
The Fletcher Henderson Story, Vol 4 *(CBS)*
The Complete Lionel Hampton *(RCA Victor)/*
Lionel Hampton's Best Records, Vols 2, 3, 5
(RCA Victor – France)
The Chocolate Dandies
(—/Parlophone)
Benny Carter – 1933 *(Prestige)/*
Various (Including Benny Carter), Ridin' In Rhythm
(World Records)
Teddy Wilson & His All-Stars
(Columbia/CBS – Holland)

The Teddy Wilson
(CBS Sony – Japan)
Chu Berry, Chew, Choo, Chu & Co. *(RCA Victor – France)*
Wingy Manone, Vol 1
(RCA Victor)
The Big Sounds Of Coleman Hawkins & Chu Berry
(—/London)
Coleman Hawkins/Chu Berry, Immortal Swing Sessions
(Sonet/—)

Emmett Berry

Though Emmett Berry was born in Macon, Georgia (1916), he was brought up in Cleveland, Ohio. Played with local bands at first, then for a year with J. Frank Terry's Chicago Nightingales, leaving latter band in New York (1933). Freelanced in New York until joining Fletcher Henderson (♦) (1936–9) **(Fletcher Henderson Story/Fletcher Henderson Story, Vol 4)** producing series of warm, uncomplicated solos on individual recordings like **Chris & His Gang, Rhythm Of The Tambourine** and **Back In Your Own Backyard.**

Berry's was (and is) typically mainstream style; its root point being Louis Armstrong (♦), with other influences like Buck Clayton (♦), Harry Edison (♦) and Roy Eldridge (♦), sometimes discernible. Joined Horace Henderson (♦), when brother Fletcher disbanded in '39; then found employment with Earl Hines (♦), Teddy Wilson (♦). With Raymond Scott band at CBS, also appeared with Teddy Wilson (again), Don Redman (♦), Benny Carter (♦) and with one of the last editions of John Kirby Sextet (1944-5). In 1945, worked with 52nd Street-based band of Eddie Heywood (♦) (he had recorded with the pianist a couple of years before) **(Begin The Beguine).** Later in '45, switched to Count Basie (♦), staying until Basie disbanded in 1950 **(Sugar Hill Shuffle, Count Basie With Illinois Jacquet** and **Count Basie).** With Jimmy Rushing (♦) (1950), then full-time with orchestra of Johnny Hodges (♦) **(The Jeep Is Jumpin')** (1951–4). With Earl Hines (♦), then Cootie Williams (♦), touring Europe with Sammy Price's (♦) Bluesicians (1955-6). With Price, recorded some of his finest trumpet playing, especially so on **Swingin' The Berries** which was a notch or two above **Swingin' Paris Style.**

During 1950s/1960s, closely associated with 'mainstream' revival, working many times alongside Buck Clayton, most notably with studio recordings like **Songs For Swingers** and **One For Buck.** In person too, Berry has toured with Clayton on several occasions, including European trips in 1959 and 1961, the latter with addition of Jimmy Witherspoon (♦) **(Buck Clayton & Jimmy Witherspoon Live In Paris).** On West Coast early 1960s, New York mainly since then.

Continues to play consistently well in numerous (mostly small-group) settings, often in company of Buddy Tate (♦), with whom he had recorded some fiercely swinging tracks in Los Angeles, 1947 **(Jumpin' On The West Coast!).**

Recordings:
The Fletcher Henderson Story
(Columbia)/

The Fletcher Henderson Story, Vol 4 *(CBS)*
Count Basie/(Jimmy Witherspoon), Blue Moods In The Shade Of Kansas City
(RCA Victor – France)
Eddie Heywood, Begin The Beguine *(Mainstream/Fontana)*
Various (Including Illinois Jacquet), The Tenor Sax Album *(Savoy/Savoy)*
Don Byas, Savoy Jam Party
(Savoy)
Count Basie, Vols 1-3
(RCA Victor – France)
Teddy Wilson, B Flat Swing
(Jazz Archives)
Jimmy Rushing, Listen To The Blues *(Vanguard)/***The Essential Jimmy Rushing**
(Vogue)
The Jo Jones Special
*(Vanguard)/***The Essential Jo Jones** *(Vogue)*
Johnny Hodges, The Jeep Is Jumpin' *(—/Verve)*
Sammy Price, Swingin' Paris Style *(—/Vogue)*
Sammy Price, Swingin' The Berries *(—/Columbia)*
Buck Clayton, Songs For Swingers *(Columbia/Philips)*
Buck Clayton, One for Buck
(World Record Club)
Buck Clayton & Jimmy Witherspoon Live In Paris
(—/Vogue)
Count Basie, Sugar Hill Shuffle *(—/Windmill)*
Count Basie With Illinois Jacquet *(—/Saga)*
Buddy Tate, Jumpin' On The West Coast
(Black Lion/Black Lion)

Barney Bigard

Not only is Leon Albany 'Barney' Bigard one of the very finest of the many gifted clarinet players to come from New Orleans, he is also the single most important performer on his instrument to have worked with the Duke Ellington Orchestra. Bigard, born in 1906, joined Ellington at end of 1927, after gaining valuable experience with several noted bandleaders, both in New Orleans and Chicago, including Albert Nicholas (♦), Luis Russell (♦) and King Oliver (♦). Brother of drummer Alex Bigard, he also brought his tenor-sax into the Ellington fold, although this latter instrument afforded him comparatively little solo space of any consequence; his premier importance with the band was as clarinettist, another of a succession of star solo instrumentalists to be uniquely showcased. Within the framework of music composed and arranged by Ellington, the stature of players like Barney Bigard often was raised in a way that, in all probability, would not have occurred in situations elsewhere. Certainly, before or since his almost-15 years with Ellington, Bigard rarely has been heard to better advantage. Bigard, one of the few to use the Albert (as opposed to the more popular Boehm) system of clarinet playing, always was an original player, but his originality was never more apparent than during his Ellington tenure. Possessor of a beautifully evocative tone, especially in the chalumeau register, Bigard is a warm, fluent improviser who has never needed to show off his undoubted technical skills in any pyrotechnic fashion. Outside

Ellington, Bigard has proved his worth in a variety of bands, most memorably in 1929, as member of the Jelly Roll Morton (♦) Trio **(Jelly Roll Morton (1929), Vol 6)**, his graceful, yet deeply-felt playing on **Smilin' The Blues Away** being exquisite.

With Ellington, Bigard really came into his own. Ellington's tone poem for Bigard's clarinet was the 1936 **Clarinet Lament**; a masterpiece of orchestration which allows Bigard to give full rein to his expressive powers, elegant drive and impressive technique **(The Complete Duke Ellington, Vol 7)**. Another early Bigard-Ellington masterpiece is to be found in the 1940 **Across The Track Blues (The Works Of Duke Ellington, Vol 12)** which, even to a casual listener, is ample evidence of his mastery as a blues performer. That blues superiority has been apparent throughout Bigard's career, and was certainly present during Ellington's 1928 recording of **The Mooche (Duke Ellington In Harlem).** And a trio of different recordings of **Saturday Night Function** from the following year **(The Works Of Duke Ellington, Vol 2, The Complete Duke Ellington, Vol 2: 1928-1930** and **Rare Duke Ellington Masterpieces)** are further superb examples of his prowess as a bluesman.

On tenor-sax, he was an ordinary soloist, one of his best contributions to Ellington on this instrument remains that on **Hot Feet (The Works Of Duke Ellington, Vol 3).** He was a competent, never brilliant, tenorist with Ellington, Oliver and Russell (though he rarely played the instrument after leaving the former).

After leaving Ellington, in 1942, Bigard worked with own bands, with Freddie Slack (1942–3); undertook some studio work; became a member of Kid Ory's (♦) band (1946), then worked as a member of the Louis Armstrong (♦) All Stars (1947–52). Subsequently, rejoined All Stars for two periods – 1953–5, 1960–1. Even with a supreme catalyst like Louis Armstrong, Bigard rarely recaptured the brilliance he had demonstrated with Duke Ellington. There were times, however, when he did produce fluent playing which was more than reminiscent of the past and Ellington, including a handful of Armstrong recordings **(Satch Plays Fats** and **Louis Armstrong, Vol 3).** But even those recordings under his own name rarely showed him at anywhere near his best. Better were those with Shelly Manne **(Shelly Manne & Co.),** Art Hodes (♦) **(Bucket's Got A Hole In It),** Ben Webster (♦) and Benny Carter (♦) **(BBB & Co.).** Just how inconsistent – and disappointing – his post-Ellington playing could be, is demonstrated, amply, throughout a record date which juxtaposed the keyboard skills of Bigard's former boss with Armstrong and All Stars **(The Beautiful Americans).** Since the 1960s Bigard has accepted selective gigs, and even a short British tour in the early-1970s. Jimmy Hamilton (♦), his eventual replacement with Ellington, gave distinguished service during his lengthy period with latter's band. Somehow, though, he never, to everyone's total satisfaction, filled the void created by Barney Bigard's departure.

Recordings:
**The Complete Duke Ellington,
Vols 1-7** *(CBS – France)*
**The Works Of Duke Ellington,
Vols 1-18** *(RCA Victor – France)*
Duke Ellington In Harlem
(Jazz Panorama)
**Duke Ellington, At His Very
Best** *(RCA Victor/RCA Victor)*
Duke Ellington, In A Mellotone
(RCA Victor/RCA Victor)
**Rare Duke Ellington
Masterpieces** *(—/VJM)*
**Duke Ellington, Hot In Harlem
(1928-1929)**
(Decca/MCA – Germany)
**Duke Ellington, Rockin' In
Rhythm (1929-1931)**
(Decca/MCA – Germany)
Duke Ellington, The Duke 1940
(Jazz Society)
King Oliver's Dixie Syncopators
(—/MCA – Germany)
Jelly Roll Morton, Vol 6 (1929)
(RCA Victor – France)
**Luis Russell & His Louisiana
Swing Orchestra** *(Columbia/—)*
**Louis Armstrong, Satch Plays
Fats** *(Columbia/CBS – France)*
Louis Armstrong, Vol 3
(—/Saga)
**Various (Including Barney
Bigard), Ellington Sidemen**
(Columbia/Philips)
**Art Hodes, Bucket's Got A Hole
In It: Barney Bigard With
Art Hodes** *(Delmark)*
**Barney Bigard/Benny Carter/
Ben Webster, BBB & Co.**
(Prestige-Swingville/Xtra)
Shelly Manne & Co.
(Flying Dutchman/—)
**Louis Armstrong/Duke
Ellington, The Beautiful
Americans** *(Roulette)*

Black Artists Group

Originally based in St Louis, this
group of avant-garde musicians
seem to be working similar collective areas to Chicago's AACM.
There is the same concentration on
a wide variety of instruments to
provide an ever-changing texture
to the music. To date, BAG's leading lights appear to be Oliver
Lake, Charles 'Bobo' Shaw (an
interesting composer of Asian-
influenced works) and Lester
Bowie's brother, Joseph. The one
album under the collective name
(Black Artists Group In Paris)
is a sensitive and dynamically
controlled piece, with fine alto
and trombone contributions from
Lake and Bowie respectively.

Recordings:
Black Artists Group In Paris
(BAG/BAG)
Joseph Bowie - Oliver Lake
(Sackville/—)
**Wildflowers, The New York
Loft Sessions** *(Douglas/—)*
Charles Bobo Shaw, Junk Trap
(—/Black Saint)
**Human Arts Ensemble, Live In
Trio Performance**
(—/Circle Records)

Ed Blackwell

One of the great pioneers of free
drumming – in company with
Sonny Murray and Milford Graves
– Ed Blackwell's main body of
work remains within the group
context of Ornette Coleman's

*Above: Ed Blackwell and Charlie Haden, drum and bass
pioneers with Ornette Coleman's trailblazing Quartet.*

Quartet and Don Cherry's units.
Born in New Orleans, his drum
concept fitted perfectly the needs
of the new collective music –
indeed, traditional New Orleans
march rhythms combine with an
African and Afro-Cuban influence
in his work. A master craftsman,
his pre-occupation with shifting
metres and sonics made him the
ideal partner for Ornette, although
it was Blackwell's student, Billy
Higgins, who cut the first albums
with the alto player.
The nature of Ornette's music –
the rapid shifts of tempo, the mobile
textures, the rocking swing –
placed immense responsibilities
on the drummer. It was a highly
specialized function, and Blackwell, unlike Higgins – a looser,
less asymmetrical player – doesn't
seem to have worked much outside the free school. The leader's
wish that rhythm should flow as
naturally as patterns of breathing
set enormous problems for his
group, particularly on the level of
avoiding collision. Blackwell's
style is simpler, less cluttered than
most drummers'; a tight snare
sound dominates, propelling the
rolling tattoo figures and often
echoing the alto phrases. It is concentrated playing that deftly avoids
the equally innovative use of
rhythm by bassists like Charlie
Haden, Scott La Faro or Jimmy
Garrison.
Blackwell's solo feature on **T & T
(Ornette!)** shows the close links
between rhythm and melody in
the new music, as well as the drummer's African leanings. Comparisons between Blackwell and Higgins can be drawn from their
paired solos **(Free Jazz** and
Twins) with the former's heart of
darkness drum rolls followed by
Higgins' flaring cymbal work.
Again, the drummer's work with
Ornette's trumpeter, Don Cherry,
is pivotal. The music constantly
changes direction and requires a
rare blend of self-effacement and
initiative **(Complete Communion, Symphony For Improvisers** and **Where Is Brooklyn).**
Cherry's composition for a large
group **(Relativity Suite)** features
Blackwell on **March Of The Hob-
bits.** The interaction between
trumpeter and drummer is most

clearly shown on the two albums
made for the deleted French label,
BYG **(Mu, Parts One & Two)** a
duo that never sounds remotely
restricted in textural range.
Ill-health has dogged Blackwell's
career (in fact, he's on a kidney
machine three times a week) and
recent years have seen few
albums.

Recordings:
Ornette Coleman:
This Is Our Music
(Atlantic/Atlantic)
Ornette! *(Atlantic/Atlantic)*
Art Of The Improviser
(Atlantic/Atlantic)
Ornette On Tenor
(Atlantic/Atlantic)
Free Jazz *(Atlantic/Atlantic)*
Twins *(Atlantic/Atlantic)*
Science Fiction
(Columbia/Columbia)
Friends And Neighbours
(Flying Dutchman/—)
Don Cherry:
Complete Communion
(Blue Note/Blue Note)
Symphony For Improvisers
(Blue Note/Blue Note)
Where Is Brooklyn?
(Blue Note/Blue Note)
Relativity Suite *(JCOA/Virgin)*
Mu, Parts One & Two
(BYG – France)
Old & New Dreams
(—/Black Saint – Italy)

Eubie Blake

There is little doubt that of all
living jazzmen, James Hubert Blake
(born Baltimore, Maryland, 1883)
is one of the most remarkable.
Not only because, at 95, he must be
the oldest practising jazz musician,
but because he retains such remarkable facility as a pianist.
Extraordinary to realize that Blake
was playing ragtime piano when
that musical form was first in
vogue. Not at all surprising, his
playing today has raggy overtones
and indeed he still plays ragtime
tunes at concert performances.
Not a noted practitioner of stride
piano, nevertheless he can occasionally evoke, with his strong,
two-handed playing, that school

of jazz expression; likewise, basic
blues.
Today Eubie Blake sings in a
modest friendly manner, and his
prowess as raconteur has been
positively documented in various
record projects of more recent
times. Blake's parents, both former
slaves, offered musical encouragement to their son, who showed
early interest, playing organ from
six. Deeply influenced by the
playing of itinerant black pianist
Jesse Pickett (to whom he first
listened in late-1890s). Composed
first ragtime tune **(Charleston
Rag)** in 1899. First regular job in a
sporting house. Initial professional
stage appearance with a Dr
Frazier's Medicine Show, Fairfield, Pennsylvania (1901), playing
melodion and executing buck
dance on back of a truck.
Toured as buck dancer before
going to New York (1902), returning to Baltimore following year for
work as relief pianist in saloon bar
joint; later in 1903 worked at
another sporting house. Gigged
at various establishments, including Goldfield House where he
was resident for some time. Atlantic City was his next home and
workplace (between 1905–14).
During 1914 was heard by visiting
piano giant James P. Johnson (♦)
who called Blake 'one of the foremost pianists of all time'. Met lyricist Noble Sissle during spring of
1915. Pair decided to go into song-
writing partnership. First joint
composition **(It's All Your Fault)**
popularized by Sophie Tucker in
her show. (Blake's first copy-
righted/published tune: **Chevy
Chase,** 1914.)
Prompted by black orchestra
leader James Reese Europe, Blake
and Sissle teamed up with successful vaudeville team Flournoy
Miller-Aubrey Lyles to produce
Shuffle Along, as a genuine black
musical comedy show (legendary
cabaret artiste Josephine Baker a
member of chorus line; Florence
Mills one of the singers). Sissle-
Blake team contributed strongly
to **Elsie** (1923), and to revues by
Cochran and André Charlot. In
1930, in collaboration with Andy
Razaf, Blake composed **Memories
Of You** – probably his best-ever
pop tune. **I'm Just Wild About
Harry,** his other most familiar
composition (used as Harry
Truman's presidential campaign
song in '48 US election) originated
from score of **Shuffle Along;
Memories Of You** was written for
Blackbirds Of 1930. Although
Blake continued to write music
for shows, mostly with Sissle, much
of his output was not used. Blake-
Sissle partnership renewed during
World War II: together they toured
with their own USO show, Blake
playing piano and conducting
orchestra.
Blake enrolled at New York University after ceasefire, obtaining
degree in music with specific
reference to Schillinger system.
Inactive professionally for several
years, Blake's 'comeback' was
gradual, via concerts, club appearances, benefits, etc, often being
reunited with Sissle. That his piano-
playing powers remained undiminished was illustrated by release of
Wizard Of The Ragtime Piano
in 1959, with sparkling keyboard
contributions sympathetically accompanied by Bernard Addison
(♦), Milt Hinton (or George
Duvivier), and Panama Francis
(or Charlie Persip). Noble Sissle

Above: James Hubert 'Eubie' Blake, the Peter Pan of jazz and ragtime. At 95, seemingly indestructible as ever.

1917-1929, Vol 1 *(Biograph)*
Eubie Blake - Blues & Ragtime, Vol 2 *(Biograph)*
Eubie Blake, Wizard Of The Ragtime Piano *(20th Century Fox/—)*
Eubie Blake, The Marches I Played On The Old Ragtime Piano *(20th Century Fox/—)*
The Eighty-six Years Of Eubie Blake *(Columbia/CBS – Holland)*
Eubie Blake, From Rags To Classics *(Eubie Blake Music/London)*
Eubie Blake, At The Piano *(Eubie Blake Music/London)*
Eubie Blake/Joan Morris/ William Bolcomb, Wild About Eubie *(Columbia/—)*
Eubie Blake, 91 Years Young *(RCA Victor – France)*

vocalized on **I'm Just Wild About Harry.**

One other first-class album of the comeback period is **The Marches I Played On The Old Ragtime Piano,** but it was not until release, in 1973, of **The 86 Years Of Eubie Blake** that total proof of his undiminished talents was produced. Through four sides of a fascinating double-LP set, Blake musically and verbally highlighted important events during his career, at same time citing examples of significant musical influences. Throughout, Blake's strong, ragtime-into-stride playing is astonishingly well-preserved. Vocally, Blake is as charming as ever, with fellow veteran Sissle helping out on three numbers.

Since approximately 1969, when Eubie Blake captivated an enthusiastic audience at that year's Newport Jazz Festival, his career has been much less than static. He has recorded at fairly regular intervals, giving still further insights into his own music as well as that by other ragtime, blues, jazz and vaudeville/pop composers of a bygone age he remembers so well **(Eubie Blake At The Piano** and **From Rags To Classics)** and has continued to make a series of absorbing live appearances, including **91 Years Young,** recorded in concert at the 1974 Montreux Jazz Festival.

With the sudden rush of interest in ragtime during the early-1970s, it must have amused – and delighted – Eubie Blake to find that many of his earliest recordings **(Eubie Blake - Blues & Ragtime, Vols 1 & 2)** made perhaps unexpected appearances in modern record catalogues. If there is a true living legend of jazz, one whose career literally spans its history from beginning until the present, then it is most definitely James Hubert Blake . . .

Recordings:
Eubie Blake - Blues & Ragtime

Art Blakey

Born 1919, drummer Art Blakey remains one of the greatest players and combo leaders in the history of jazz. There is such a furious commitment about his playing that soloists are forced to exert themselves, and any notion of coasting goes by the board. Generations of young players have learned their craft in Blakey's groups, left to lead their own groups, leaving him to break in another batch. Along with drummer Max Roach, it was Blakey's contention that drums were frontline instruments. History has proved them right, but initially their dominant role and parallel interchanges with the horns led to critical accusations of obtrusiveness.

It was this conception of heightened rhythmic activity that led to the formation of The Jazz Messengers in 1954 by Blakey and pianist Horace Silver. Their first album – **Horace Silver & The Jazz Messengers** – has tremendous punch, both drummer and pianist working together to lift the horns, trumpeter Kenny Dorham and tenorist Hank Mobley, on an urgent tide of riffs and accents. A live set **(At The Cafe Bohemia)** has the magnificent **Soft Winds** solo by Dorham, but the general standard of playing is so high that it seems pointless to single out performances. The interaction between drums, piano and the horns is the very essence of Hard Bop.

With the departure of Silver, the main onus of stoking the boilers fell on Blakey, and subsequent albums with altoist Jackie McLean and trumpeter Bill Hardman show an increase in domination from the drums **(Night In Tunisia).** The meeting with Monk **(Art Blakey's Jazz Messengers With Thelonious Monk)** produced fine, considered music, and both albums featured the unsinkable tenor of Johnny Griffin. Large drum ensembles **(Orgy In Rhythm** and **The Drum Suite)** were a preoccupation of Blakey's in the mid-50s, and showed his links with the music of Africa, home of the drum.

The next Messengers line-up laid emphasis on funk. Pianist Bobby Timmons' tune **Moanin'** heralded a return to the gospel atmosphere of Silver's **The Preacher,** and was soon followed by **Dat Dere (The Big Beat).** Musical directorship passed from tenorman Benny Golson to trumpeter Lee Morgan, a player of great style and poise, as displayed on **It's Only A Paper Moon (The Big Beat)** and the front line, if that term has any meaning in Blakey's groups, was brought up to strength by tenorman Wayne Shorter. Shorter's writing soon came to dominate the band book, and a succession of excellent albums restored the ascendancy of the Messengers **(Freedom Rider** and **Night In Tunisia).** Trumpeter Freddie Hubbard took over from Morgan with no loss of striking power. There is very little to choose between **Buhaina's Delight, Mosaic** and **Free For All,** and the eventual break-up of this unit (Shorter moving to Miles Davis' Quintet) would have been as discouraging to anyone less resilient than Blakey. In fact, the 1968 re-

Above: Art Blakey, veteran drummer and leader of Jazz Messengers, surely Hard Bop's hardest-hitting combo.

cording at Slugs **(Art Blakey & The Jazz Messengers Live!)** shows the old powerhouse driving the horns, Bill Hardman again, trombonist Julian Priester and tenorman Billy Harper, with his unquenchable enthusiasm.

Art Blakey has recorded with a wide range of musicians outside his own group, bringing urgency and sensitivity to the rhythm sections. His contributions to the Thelonious Monk trios **(Thelonious Monk),** and early quintets **(Genius Of Modern Music),** show his compatibility with the percussive keyboard style.

His drum style is unmistakable, the chunk of the hi-hat squashing down in the silence before the

Free For All (Blue Note): one of the best from a great band.

figures start to roll across the skins like big wooden skittle alley balls, the abrupt pause, a flashing woodpecker rattle of sticks on snarerim before the final titanic swell. Blakey took the bop style from Kenny Clarke and reduced it to its irreduceable essentials. At the centre of his work is the drum roll, tiny tumblings which build to landslide proportions. Weak players tend to be overpowered by his backing, but as a make-orbreak academy, Blakey's groups are second to none.

Drum Suite (Columbia): Art Blakey's Jazz Messengers, the leader's titanic drumming plus four other drummers.

Recordings:

Horace Silver & The Jazz Messengers
(Blue Note/Blue Note)
The Jazz Messengers At The Cafe Bohemia
(Blue Note/Blue Note)
A Night In Tunisia
(Vik/RCA Victor)
Art Blakey's Jazz Messengers With Thelonious Monk
(Atlantic/Atlantic)
Orgy In Rhythm
(Blue Note/Blue Note)
The Drum Suite
(Columbia/CBS)
Moanin' (Blue Note/Blue Note)
The Big Beat
(Blue Note/Blue Note)
Freedom Rider
(Blue Note/Blue Note)
Night In Tunisia
(Blue Note/Blue Note)
Buhaina's Delight
(Blue Note/Blue Note)
Mosaic (Blue Note/Blue Note)
Free For All
(Blue Note/Blue Note)
Art Blakey & The Jazz Messengers Live! (—/DJM)
Thelonious Monk
(Prestige/Prestige)
Thelonious Monk, Genius Of Modern Music
(Blue Note/Blue Note)
Art Blakey & The Jazz Messengers, Gypsy Folk Tales (Roulette/Pye)

Jimmy Blanton

Jimmy Blanton's life and musical career were both cut drastically short due to his premature death through tuberculosis in 1942. He was 21 years old. Blanton's death was a particularly unfortunate occurrence, for within the space of two years he had achieved, virtually single-handed, a complete breakthrough in the concept of bass playing in jazz. Instead of merely providing only a rock-solid accompaniment to front-line soloists, Blanton conceived his role along the lines of a horn, utilizing harmonic, melodic and rhythmic ideas that hitherto were unknown to jazz bassists. In those two years, Blanton emancipated the role of the bass player in jazz, and pioneered most, if not all, the directions it was to take in subsequent years. To an already star-studded Duke Ellington (♦) Orchestra, with whom he spent these vital two years, he imparted a rhythmic subtlety that even that great organization had not possessed before Blanton's inception into the ranks of Ellingtonia in the fall of 1939.

Before Blanton probably the only bassman possessing anywhere near his sophistication and subtlety was John Kirby (♦). But with Blanton, the thoughts and ideas for a whole new generation of bass players were crystallized: his fleet-fingered plucking certainly did have profound effect upon the work of Oscar Pettiford, Charles Mingus (♦), and Ray Brown, to name the three finest post-Blanton bassists who would carry on his pioneering efforts a stage further. (When, over 30 years later, Norman Granz persuaded Ellington to re-record a selection of the extraordinary Ellington-Blanton bass duets, the choice of Brown as bassist was obvious and appropriate **(This One's For Blanton).)**

The original Ellington-Blanton duets **(The World Of Duke Ellington, Vols 11, 14, 15)** today retain their freshness and vitality, especially studio-made masterpieces like **Pitter Panther Patter** and **Mr J. B. Blues (Vol 11).** Of the many sides which Blanton recorded in his two years with the full Ellington orchestra, probably his most memorable individual performances were encapsulated during **Jack The Bear** and **Ko-Ko (The Works Of Duke Ellington, Vol 9)** wherein his superb articulation and beautifully resonant tone are amply displayed, and his unflagging drive lifts the band to further heights of inspiration and achievement. Similarly during **Bojangles, Conga Brava, Harlem Airshaft (Vol 10); John Hardy's Wife (Vol 14)** and **Take The 'A' Train** and **Jumpin' Punkins (Vol 15),** Blanton's inspired playing adds that vital extra, exciting dimension to already impressive performances.

During his all-too-short period with Ellington (Blanton left the band in late-1941, after being taken seriously ill, and died in a sanitarium near Los Angeles in July, '42) the bassist took part in numerous bands-within-the-band recording projects, under the leadership of Barney Bigard (♦), Johnny Hodges (♦), Rex Stewart (♦), and Cootie Williams (♦). Here, too, his unique gifts never failed to enhance the respective sessions.

Jimmy Blanton (born Chattanooga, Tennessee, 1921) started out as violinist, studying theory with an uncle. Turned his attention to bass whilst at college and played in college and local bands. Made riverboat trips with bands of Fate Marable during summer vacations, and after moving to St Louis, became member of Jeter-Pillars Orchestra (1937), continuing to work with Marable during summer. Ellington heard him play in St Louis, signed him, and for a while Blanton and Billy Taylor were both employed as bassists with Ellington band (Taylor left at beginning of 1940).

Like Charlie Christian (♦) and Lester Young (♦) in their own individual ways, Jimmy Blanton was an innovator of real importance, whose playing looked forward to the Bebop innovations which he never lived to hear or, sadly, be part of.

Recordings:
Duke Ellington, The Jimmy Blanton Years
(Queen Disc – Italy)
The Works Of Duke Ellington, Vols 9-17
(RCA Victor – France)
Duke Ellington, The Duke 1940
(Jazz Society)
Duke Ellington, At His Very Best
(RCA Victor/RCA Victor)
Duke Ellington, Braggin' In Brass 1936-1939 (Tax – Sweden)
Duke Ellington 1937-1939
(Tax – Sweden)
Duke Ellington, The Ellington Era, Vol 2 (Columbia/CBS)
Duke Ellington/Ray Brown, This One's For Blanton
(Pablo/Pablo)

Carla Bley

Pianist/composer Carla Bley's importance as a musician is difficult to separate from her importance as organizer of a musical environment for others. In 1964 she and her husband, composer Michael Mantler, established the Jazz Composers Orchestra Association from the remains of the Jazz Composers Guild, with the aim of setting up a pool of talent on a non-profit making co-operative basis, issuing its own albums and giving each member a chance to write for the orchestra. Thus, Carla Bley's piano playing has contributed to the success of works by Don Cherry **(Relativity Suite),** Clifford Thornton **(The Gardens Of Harlem),** Grachan Moncur III **(Echoes Of Prayers).** Her own work, a jazz opera of staggering dimensions **(Escalator Over The Hill)** with lyrics by poet Paul Haines, also makes use of the talents of Cherry, Barbieri, Rudd, Haden and singer-bass guitarist Jack Bruce. Her next work, again collaborating with Haines **(Tropic Appetites),** is conceived on a smaller scale and has sterling contributions by Barbieri and Howard Johnson. Mantler's composition based on Samuel Beckett **(No Answer),** has the liturgical voice of Jack Bruce, Don Cherry's trumpet and Carla Bley on piano, creating that sparse and terminal atmosphere.

Outside the JCOA, she has written a notable composition **(A Genuine Tong Funeral)** around a nucleus of the Gary Burton Quartet, with orchestral textures that tug against that polished unit. Bassist Charlie Haden's suite **(Liberation Music)** was mainly arranged by Carla Bley.

She plays most keyboards, piano, organ, synthesizer etc, with great sensitivity. Most recently, she worked with Jack Bruce's short-lived band, her first move towards rock.

Recordings:
Don Cherry, Relativity Suite
(JCOA/Virgin)
Clifford Thornton, The Gardens Of Harlem (JCOA/Virgin)
Grachan Moncur III, Echoes Of Prayers (JCOA/Virgin)
Escalator Over The Hill
(JCOA/Virgin)
Tropic Appetites (Watt/Watt)
Michael Mantler, No Answer
(Watt/Watt)
Carla Bley-Gary Burton, A Genuine Tong Funeral
(RCA/RCA)
Charlie Haden, Liberation Music (Impulse/Impulse)

Paul Bley

Born 1932 in Canada, pianist Paul Bley took over Oscar Peterson's bassist and drummer when the maestro moved to the United States in 1949. Despite popularity and success for the trio, Bley too upped stakes and went to New York's Juilliard to extend his studies. By 1954 he was playing at

Above: Carla Bley and Mike Mantler, proprietors of the Jazz Composers Orchestra Association and stations out.

top venues like Birdland, and the following year worked briefly with Chet Baker. Bley seems to be naturally of the avant-garde, restless, experimental – as he says, 'chord changes have never interfered with my own way of hearing melody'. Ornette Coleman and Don Cherry gravitated to the Bley group in Los Angeles in 1958, which gave a recorded preview **(The Fabulous Paul Bley Quintet)** of the musical revolution to come with Coleman's series of Atlantic albums. In 1960 Bley was working with another experimenter, George Russell **(Jazz In The Space Age)** playing duets with fellow pianist, Bill Evans, on **Chromatic Universe**. He next spent three years with Jimmy Giuffre, and on albums like **Fusion** and **Thesis** showed great empathy for Giuffre's terse austerity, fractured lines and unstated pulse. After a year with tenorman Sonny Rollins **(Sonny Meets Hawk)** Bley formed his own trio with Steve Swallow on bass and Barry Altschul on drums, and released a stream of impressive albums for ESP and ECM **(Closer, Ballads, Open, To Love, Paul Bley & Gary Peacock** and **Bley NHOP)**. Bley's favourite compositions, **Closer** and **Mr Joy**, figure time and again, each version a further disciplined

Paul Bley (Wing): the pianist way back when. Rare album.

advance on the heart of the matter. Most recently he has set up his own label, Improvising Artists, and released albums with clarinettist Giuffre **(Quiet Song)**, with tenorman John Gilmore **(Turning Point)** and solo **(Alone Again)**.

In a quiet way Paul Bley has collected quite a few firsts. His pioneering work on the West Coast with Coleman put him in advance of many of the New Wave players in New York. He was the first to perform publicly on the synthesizer in 1969 – and soon returned to the acoustic piano. Unlike most of the New Wave pianists, Bley's style is spare and subtle, introverted and extremely concentrated. His chords are complex and many-layered. Inner voicings are constantly shifting, altering the structure of his pieces. He makes intelligent and sensitive use of the strings inside the piano, plucking and taking up the chord on the keyboard. Radicalism doesn't have to shout, and Bley's originality repays careful listening.

Recordings:
The Fabulous Paul Bley Quintet (—/America – France)
George Russell, Jazz In The Space Age (Decca/—)
Jimmy Giuffre, Fusion (Verve/—)
Jimmy Giuffre, Thesis
(Verve/—)
Sonny Rollins, Sonny Meets Hawk (RCA/RCA – France)
Paul Bley, Closer (ESP/ESP)
Ballads (ECM/ECM)
Open, To Love (ECM/ECM)
Paul Bley & Gary Peacock (ECM/ECM)
Paul Bley, Niels Henning Orsted Pedersen (—/Steeplechase)
Alone Again (Improvising Artists/Improvising Artists)
Quiet Song (Improvising Artists/Improvising Artists)
Turning Point (Improvising Artists/Improvising Artists)

Earl Bostic

Earl Bostic's hairy tone and basic, hard-driving rhythmic style made him one of the first cross-over jazz artists – in Bostic's case, from jazz to R&B. Born in Tulsa, Oklahoma, 1913, Bostic started on altosax, clarinet, and after studying music at Xavier University, New Orleans, work followed with numerous outfits (including Charlie Creath-Fate Marable, Don Redman (♦) and Edgar Hayes).

In 1939, Bostic fronted own band in New York, sometimes playing also baritone-sax, trumpet, guitar. In 1941, worked in Harlem with Hot Lips Page (♦). 1943: joined Lionel Hampton (♦), he had previously played at one of the vibraharpist's legendary late-1930s all-star record dates **(The Complete Lionel Hampton/Lionel Hampton's Best Records, Vols 3, 5)**. Stayed with Hampton's wildly-swinging big band for about a year **(Steppin' Out: Lionel Hampton, Vol 1: 1942-1944)**. Subsequently, worked with small groups, mostly under own leadership.

During 1950s attained a pop-size reputation as best-selling record artist with R&B-styled hits of standards like **Temptation, Flamingo, Sleep, Cherokee, You Go To My Head** and **Moonglow**. Many of the innumerable LPs he made during last 15 years of his life (Bostic died of a second heart attack in 1965, he was stricken by an initial heart seizure in '56) are of interest more to R&B fans than jazz collectors. But they always swung, with Bostic's sandpaper-edged tone and wailing sax projecting its basic message to great effect. Bostic, who during his career penned arrangements for, among others, Paul Whiteman (♦), Artie Shaw (♦), Hot Lips Page and Louis Prima, was also a composer of some merit: **Let Me Off Uptown** (a hit for Gene Krupa (♦) and **The Major & The Minor** (recorded by Alvino Rey), are amongst his better-known tunes.

Recordings:
The Complete Lionel Hampton (RCA Victor)/
Lionel Hampton's Best Records, Vols 3, 5 (RCA Victor – France)
Steppin' Out: Lionel Hampton, Vol 1 (1942-1944) (MCA – Germany)
Various, Swing Classics, Vol 2 (1944/45) (—/Polydor)
Earl Bostic, Bostic Showcase Of Swinging Dance Hits (—/Parlophone) (EP)
Earl Bostic (King/—)
Various (Including Hot Lips Page), The Sax Scene

Above: trumpeter Bobby Bradford, a player of fine logic and precise articulation.

(—/London)
Various (Including Buck Ram, Hot Lips Page, The Changing Face Of Harlem, Vol 1 (Savoy/Savoy)

Lester Bowie
♦ *Art Ensemble of Chicago*

Bobby Bradford

Born 1934 in Mississippi, the trumpeter paid his dues with Leo Wright, Buster Smith, Wardell Gray, Eric Dolphy and Gerald Wilson. Most importantly, he began playing with revolutionary altoman Ornette Coleman, in the Los Angeles area from 1953. After four years in USAF bands, Bradford studied music at the University of Texas. Between 1961–3, he rejoined Ornette in New York, but unfortunately no records resulted. Back in Los Angeles, he formed the New Art Jazz Ensemble with multi-reed man, John Carter. In the '70s, Bradford made several trips to Europe, and recorded with the fine British drummer, John Stevens.

A more orthodox, brass-toned player than Ornette's habitual partner, Don Cherry, Bradford's presence on numbers like **Law Years** and **The Jungle Is A Skyscraper (Science Fiction)** brings a deliberate and considered quality to the music. Again, elegance and freedom combined in his own West Coast band with fellow Texan, John Carter, and several excellent musicianly albums followed. The first **(Seeking)** featured the compositions of Carter and covered a wide spectrum of moods in which interaction between the horns and the rhythm section – Tom Williamson, bass, Bruz Freeman, drums – was distinguished by thought and restraint. There is real blues feeling on numbers like **The Sunday Afternoon Jazz Blues Society (Self Determination Music)** which works better than the longer,

more rambling pieces. The group deserves to be better known: logic and excitement are infrequent stable-mates.

Bobby Bradford's writing is prominently featured on his album with John Stevens, Trevor Watts and Kent Carter **(Love's Dream)** and the overall feeling is very much in line with Ornette's quartets. Sitting in with Stevens' Spontaneous Music Ensemble **(Bobby Bradford, John Stevens & SME)** Bradford submerges his personality in the dense collective textures.

Recordings:
Ornette Coleman, Science Fiction (Columbia/CBS)
Seeking (Revelation/—)
Flight For Four (Flying Dutchman/—)
Self Determination Music (Flying Dutchman/—)
Love's Dream (Emanem/Emanem)
Bobby Bradford, John Stevens & SME (—/Freedom)

Tiny Bradshaw

Myron 'Tiny' Bradshaw (born Youngstown, Ohio, 1905) was a drummer-pianist-singer during his musical career, but is best remembered for leading a big band that swung the blues and played good, solid, blues-based jazz and R&B from 1934 – the year it made its New York debut – until early-1950s.

Prior to 1934 Bradshaw, who had majored in psychology at Wilberforce University, Ohio, had sung with Horace Henderson's (♦) Collegians, then with Marion Hardy's Alabamians, the Savoy Bearcats, Mills Blue Rhythm Band, and Luis Russell (♦). Like the bands of Lucky Millinder (♦) and Todd Rhodes, Bradshaw recorded for important R&B label, King (between 1949–58). With King, Bradshaw notched up several hit records, including **Big Town** (with vocal by noted R&B artist Roy Brown) and **Soft**.

During last 10–15 years of its life, Bradshaw orchestra tended to concentrate more on R&B, although its allegiance to jazz never was forgotten completely. Bradshaw himself, after years of extensive nationwide tours and recording, finally became domiciled in Chicago. But it was in Cincinnati, Ohio – in 1958 – that Tiny Bradshaw died. Prior to his death, he had suffered two strokes, the last of which had precipitated his enforced retirement from the music business. Amongst list of musicians who worked with Bradshaw, at one stage or another, can be counted the following: trumpeters Bill Hardman, Henry Glover; saxists Sonny Stitt, Red Prysock, George 'Big Nick' Nicholas, Charlie Fowlkes, Sil Austin; bassist Sam Jones; and singer Arthur Prysock. Blues guitarist-singer Lonnie Johnson (♦) recorded with the band in 1951.

Recordings:
Various (including Tiny Bradshaw), Kings Of Rhythm & Blues (Polydor)

Ruby Braff

A marvellously eloquent, always mellifluous player, Reuben 'Ruby' Braff (born Boston, Mass, 1927) is something of a throwback to jazz of pre-World War II except that where Braff is concerned his music sounds fresh and, despite strong influences (ie Armstrong (♦), Berigan (♦), Hackett (♦), James (♦)), he does not slavishly copy any of the

great trumpeters/cornettists of the past.

A self-taught musician, Braff has tended to concentrate almost exclusively on the warmer sound of the cornet (like, for example, Nat Adderley). His career has seen its share of ups and downs – the latter occurring because of a peculiar situation in the 1950s whereby an up-and-coming player like Braff was unable to find sufficient work because his style was considered out of date. Even in the 'down' days, however, Braff managed to attract the attention of record labels and producers; his not inconsiderable discography thus far gives ample evidence that Braff has been a model of consistency, in various, mostly 'mainstream', settings.

Braff first came to notice of record-buyers through an appearance as sideman on a 1953 Vic Dickenson (♦) record date (**Vic Dickenson Showcase / The Essential Vic Dickenson**). He tended to steal solo limelight from long-established veterans like Dickenson, Ed Hall (♦) and Sir Charles Thompson. His ballad-playing **I Cover The Waterfront** was exquisite, sensitive; his blowing on faster items (**Jeepers Creepers, Keepin' Out Of Mischief Now**) was rhythmically subtle, with Braff exhibiting commendable controlled power, even at moments of climax. Whatever the mood, his playing maintained an impressive sense of logicality and lyricism that showed his obvious debt to Hackett. Further exposure – and in many ways a deeper insight into Braff's technique and mode of self-expression – came the

Below: a thoughtful Ruby Braff 'takes five', after producing yet another superbly mellifluous cornet solo.

Two By Two (Fontana) – Ruby Braff, with Ellis Larkins, a cornet and piano duet.

following year when he appeared as one-third of Mel Powell Trio (**Thigamagig**), then, with a tribute to Billie Holiday (♦) (**Holiday In Braff**), followed by an absolutely delightful cornet-piano date with Ellis Larkins (**Two By Two**), and a reunion date with Dickenson, this time with Braff as leader (**The Ruby Braff Special**). In this kind of basically mainstream company, Braff usually is to be heard at his most relaxed, which probably explains why his participation in George Wein's touring Newport All Stars packages (**Tribute To Duke, The Newport All Stars** and **Midnight Concert In Paris**) has usually found him operating at or near to his very best. Much the same can be said with regard to his live appearance at the diner owned by Mr and Mrs Ralph Sutton (♦), with mine host helping out on piano (**Sunnie's Side Of The Street**).

More recently, Braff's unique brand of unruffled elegance has been gorgeously showcased in the chamber setting of the Ruby Braff–George Barnes Quartet – a combo which was fully operational between 1973–5. With Braff providing the basic spark for the group, ably assisted by guitarist Barnes, plus rhythm guitar and bass, the cornettist had ample opportunity to demonstrate, once again, his dexterity and, in particular, just how effective it can be in utilizing an essentially extrovert instrument sotto voce and still produce music that is of exceptional quality. Indeed, the only complaint one can offer against the quartet was that there were times when the presence of a drummer and/or another horn might have injected more fire into proceedings. Certainly, it is true to say that Ruby Braff operates at a more emotionally satisfying level in more buoyant surroundings. Rather like his 1967 recording date with Buddy Tate (♦), George Wein, et al (**Hear Me Talkin'!**) or, in more recent, post Braff-Barnes, times, in company with such as Jimmie Rowles, Bucky Pizzarelli and Vic Dickenson (**Them There Eyes**).

Recordings:
Vic Dickenson Showcase (Vanguard)/**The Essential Vic Dickenson** (Vogue)
Mel Powell, Thigamagig (Vanguard/Vanguard)
Ruby Braff, Holiday In Braff (Bethlehem/London)
Ruby Braff, Ruby Got Rhythm (—/Black Lion)
Ruby Braff/Ellis Larkins, Two By Two (Vanguard/Fontana)
Ruby Braff At Newport

(Verve/Columbia – Clef)
Various, The Newport All Stars (Black Lion/Black Lion)
The Newport All Stars, Tribute To Duke (MPS)
The Newport All Stars, Midnight Concert In Paris (—/Philips)
Ruby Braff/Ralph Sutton, On Sunnie's Side Of The Street (Blue Angel Jazz Club/—)
Ruby Braff & His Men (RCA Victor/—)
Ruby Braff, Hear Me Talkin'! (Black Lion)
The Ruby Braff–George Barnes Quartet (Chiaroscuro)/
The Best I've Heard . . . (Vogue)
Ruby Braff & His International Jazz Quartet Plus Three (Chiaroscuro)/
The Grand Reunion (Chiaroscuro)/
Bugle Call Rag (Vogue)
The Ruby Braff Special (Vanguard/Vanguard)
Ruby Braff, Them There Eyes (Sonet)

Dollar Brand

At a time when Afro-Americans were once more looking to Africa as their spiritual and cultural home, and the word 'Uhuru' began to appear on the album sleeves of post-'60s jazz, the genuine article erupted on to the music scene. Pianist Dollar Brand is a South African Moslem for whom the function of music is both a celebration and a prayer; it has not lost its social role in Africa as it has in the West. A melange of influences runs through his playing – Ellington and Monk mix with mission

Ancient Africa (Japo): hypnotic piano from Dollar Brand.

hall hymns and zikr, the repetition of the holy attributes of Allah. The first album (**Anatomy Of A South African Village**) covers a wider selection of material than is normally associated with him. Later releases (**African Piano, African Sketchbook** and **Ancient Africa**) convey the unique flavour of his playing in which originals like **Xaba** or **Bra Joe From Kilimanjaro** bed down into the mesmerizing fabric of his improvisation. His duo album with Argentinian tenorman, Leandro 'Gato' Barbieri (**Confluence**) has an overwhelming impact, a starkly religious atmosphere that is both measured and passionate.

A percussive, repetitive player, Brand uses rumbling left-hand figures and a lot of pedal to sustain the dense, droning climate. It is almost as if he beats upon the piano to release its inner voicings, proceeding at the tempo of a stately cortège. His flute playing, too, has a multi-vocal quality in which the piped notes mingle with the humming voice and the percussive poppings of his fingers on the holes.

Recordings:
Anatomy Of A South African Village (—/Fontana)
African Piano (Japo/Japo)
African Sketchbook (Enja/Enja)
Ancient Africa (Japo/Japo)
Confluence (Arista Freedom/ Arista Freedom)
The Journey (—/Chiaroscuro)
Good News From Africa (—/Enja)
Children Of Africa (—/Enja)

Anthony Braxton

The most gifted instrumentalist of Chicago's AACM, Anthony Braxton's debut album **(Three Compositions Of New Jazz)** showed not only the fast, confident alto player, but also a highly distinctive approach to group improvising. Braxton's compositions, usually named with formulae, are diagrams which allow great scope for interaction and improvisation, so his choice of partners is crucial. His music is well served here by trumpeter Leo Smith and violinist Leroy Jenkins, habitual cohorts. His next album, **For Alto**, offers four sides of unaccompanied saxophone, a daring and at that time unprecedented idea which succeeds through intelligent programming. **To Composer John Cage** is the most savagely violent

playing on record, whereas **Dedicated To Ann And Peter Allen** meanders gently and lyrically through passages of silence. Further developments in group music followed, including five versions of **Small Composition (This Time)** which effectively shows the process whereby Braxton erodes the melody in favour of textural variation.

The short-lived group, Circle **(Circle Paris - Concert)**, comprising Braxton, pianist Chick Corea, bassist Dave Holland and drummer Barry Altschul, is less angular than previous collaborations, pretty at times, and always empathetic. Duets between Braxton and Corea feature on **The Complete Braxton** as well as encounters with trumpeter Kenny Wheeler. Braxton has an affinity for the European Free Music scene, and has worked fruitfully with others besides Wheeler, notably with that pioneer of avant-garde guitar, Derek Bailey **(Duo)**. Neither player complements the other in the traditional sense, but their separate lines establish an amazing continuity of feeling.

Braxton's writing covers an enormously wide area of sound, re-interpreting traditions such as Bebop, **Donna Lee (Donna Lee)**, the Cool School, **You Go To My Head (Donna Lee)**, the chord-change ballad **You Stepped Out Of A Dream (Five Pieces '75)**, as well as near-straight music pieces like the **Side Two, Cut Two** unaccompanied four saxophone composition – **New York, Fall '74**.

Below: multi-instrumentalist Anthony Braxton playing chess. In lean times he has earned his living at the game.

3 Compositions Of New Jazz (Delmark): Braxton's debut.

Integrated with this activity is Braxton's increasing armory of instruments. His interest in extremes of register has led him to take up the sopranino, the lumbering contrabass clarinet on **Goodbye Porkpie Hat (In The Tradition)** and, most recently, the clarinet. Anthony Braxton is, in fact, a one-man jazz crusade.

Recordings:
Three Compositions Of New Jazz (Delmark/Delmark)
For Alto (Delmark/Delmark)
This Time (—/BYG – France)
Circle Paris - Concert (ECM/ECM)
The Complete Braxton (Arista/Arista)
Duo (Emanem/Emanem)
Donna Lee (—/America – France)
Five Pieces '75 (Arista/Arista)
New York, Fall '74 (Arista/Arista)
In The Tradition (—/Steeplechase)
Duets (Arista/Arista)
Concerts: Berlin – Montreux (Arista/Arista)
Creative Orchestra Music 1976 (Arista/—)

Bob Brookmeyer

Mainly known as a sideman with Stan Getz, Gerry Mulligan and Jimmy Giuffre, Kansas City born valve-trombonist Bob Brookmeyer is a musician of all-round gifts. His trombone playing avoids the rapid-fire evenness of the modern school in favour of a wider bag of effects. A broad, historically-ranging approach has produced several albums under his own name that are robust, witty and inventive **(Traditionalism Revisited** and **Blues Hot & Cool)**. His later work with trumpeter Clark Terry **(Terry-Brookmeyer Quintet)** was a meeting of temperamentally similar players and resulted in warm, optimistic music. Brookmeyer is also a competent pianist and much in demand as a composer and arranger.

Recordings:
Getz At The Shrine (Verve/—)
The Fabulous Gerry Mulligan Quartet (—/Vogue)
The Jimmy Giuffre Trio, Trav'lin' Light (Atlantic/—)
Traditionalism Revisited (Pacific Jazz/Vogue)
Blues Hot & Cool (Verve/—)
The Clark Terry-Bob Brookmeyer Quintet (Mainstream/—)

Big Bill Broonzy

Big Bill Broonzy's death (in Chicago in 1958) robbed the blues world of one of its finest practitioners: a highly-rhythmic, flexible guitarist, a singer of great expressivity, and a composer whose songs invariably were remarkably real to life. But Broonzy (born William Lee Conley Broonzy, in Scott, Mississippi, 1893) did not die poverty-stricken and unrecognized in his lifetime, as was the fate of so many country bluesmen, great or otherwise. Indeed, during the last ten years of his life, Broonzy's reputation was international, and in some parts of the world he had become something approaching a cult figure.

One of seven children, Broonzy's musical interests were encouraged by an uncle. Raised in Arkansas, where he worked as a sharecropper and part-time preacher (he also worked, at one stage, as a coal-miner). His mother, who remembered the days of slavery, died in 1957, aged 102.

Broonzy's first instrument was violin, which he played at country hops. In 1917 he enlisted in US Army. After two years was demobilized and made his home in Chicago, by which time he was developing into a first-class guitarist who mixed freely with other itinerant bluesmen, including Papa Charlie Jackson, who taught Broonzy how to play guitar.

Recording debut found him playing a country reel **(Blues Origin)**, but thereafter his became one of the most familiar names on blues recording dates – his own and innumerable others, featuring all

'Big Bill' Broonzy (Bluebird RCA, France) – blues, '34-'35.

kinds of musicians. Amongst the latter can be numbered Georgia Tom Dorsey **(Georgia Tom)**, Sonny Boy Williamson **(Blues Classics By Sonny Boy Williamson** and **Sonny Boy Williamson, Vol 1)**, and Broonzy's brother-in-law, Washboard Sam **(Feeling Lowdown)**. Amongst Broonzy's own earliest recordings **(The Young Big Bill Broonzy 1928-1935)** there are superior examples of his skills, such as **Mississippi River Blues** (1934), **Stove Pipe Stomp** (1932), **Long Tall Mama** (1932) and the bleak **Starvation Blues** (1928). Superb recordings by Broonzy from the years 1936–41 can be found within **Big Bill's Blues** including tremendously evocative performances of Broonzy numbers as vividly real as **Southern Flood Blues, When I Been Drinking, Just A Dream** (one of his finest of all blues compositions), **All By Myself** and **Big Bill Blues**.

Despite his prolificity as recording artist, Broonzy was employed often in a non-musical capacity; between 1930–50, for example, he owned a farm in Arkansas, and was working it when John Hammond brought him to New York to appear at his Spirituals to Swing concert **(John Hammond's Spirituals To Swing)** in 1938, and again the following year.

By late-1940s he was working as janitor at Iowa State College, but Broonzy continued to record and to make appearances in and around Chicago.

Visited Europe, 1951, 1953, where he attained enormous following. During second European tour Broonzy recorded contents of **Big Bill Broonzy: All Them Blues**. 1951: Broonzy recorded an even better collection of blues **(Big Bill Broonzy)** with several stand-out performances of fine blues like **Hollerin' & Cryin', Back Water Blues, Low Down Blues**, plus a fresh reworking of **Big Bill Blues**. By this time his repertoire had broadened in size and scope – he must have written, in all, over 300 songs during his career.

However, there were times when his performances, in concert and on record, tended towards the bland. In between the two visits to Europe mentioned above, he toured the continent also in 1952, in tandem with Mahalia Jackson. Alone, he was to return for further sell-out appearances in each year between 1955–7. During 1955 trip he recorded in London, Paris, Baarn and, extensively, in Copenhagen. He continued to be active inside recording studios during '56 and '57 – in '56 was taped in live performance, alone, and on a couple of items together with voice and banjo of Pete Seeger **(Pete Seeger & Big Bill Broonzy In Concert)** and the following year appeared on record with the duo of Brownie McGhee and Sonny Terry **(Blues With Big Bill Broonzy, Sonny Terry, Brownie McGhee)**, the album also containing an interview with Broonzy. He was to repeat the singing-playing-talking format during what turned out to be his final recording dates **(Last Session)** in July, '57. Broonzy's vibrant singing and guitar playing was silenced forever in 1958 when this influential folk-blues artist of exceptional talents died of cancer.

Recordings:
Big Bill Broonzy/Sonny Boy Williamson, Big Bill & Sonny Boy (—/RCA Victor)
Jazz Gillum, Vol 1 (—/RCA Victor – France)
Washboard Sam (Blues Classics/—)
Big Bill Broonzy (—/Vogue)
Trouble In Mind (Blues Classics/—)
Big Bill Broonzy (—/Vogue)
Pete Seeger & Big Bill Broonzy In Concert (Verve/Verve)
Blues With Big Bill Broonzy, Sonny Terry, Brownie McGhee (Folkways/—)
Big Bill Broonzy, Last Session (Verve/Verve)
Various, Country Blues Encores (Origin/—)
Georgia Tom Dorsey, Georgia Tom (Riverside)
Big Bill Broonzy, Big Bill's Blues (CBS-Realm)
The Young Big Bill Broonzy 1928-1935 (Yazoo)
Big Bill Broonzy Sings Country

Blues (—/Xtra)
Big Bill Broonzy: All Them Blues (DJM)
Washboard Sam, Feeling Lowdown (RCA Victor/RCA Victor)
Blues Classics By Sonny Boy Williamson (Blues Classics)
Various, John Hammond's Spirituals To Swing (Vanguard/Vanguard)
Sonny Boy Williamson, Vol 1 (RCA Victor – France)
Big Bill Broonzy (Vogue – France)

Clifford Brown

Trumpeter Clifford Brown's death in a car accident at the age of 26 robbed jazz of one of its finest talents. His recording career is spanned **(The Beginning And The End)** by his 1952 debut with an R&B unit, Chris Powell and The Blue Flames, and his final, informal jam session recorded in an instrument shop on the eve of his death in 1956. Listening to those last tracks – **Walkin', Donna Lee** and **Night In Tunisia** – it's easy to see why Brownie became a legend. His sound is unmistakable; bright, warm, bubbling with vivacity. There is a joy and a clarity about his work that posterity has proved irreplaceable, and the heritage of hot trumpet – Gillespie, Navarro, Brown – passed into the very different approach of Miles Davis.

Brownie's work for the Blue Note label featured the trumpeter as both leader and sideman, and this has led to a good deal of overlapping on the albums. **Get Happy** turns up on **The Eminent J. J. Johnson** and **Brownie Eyes**; six tracks from **Brownie Eyes** are duplicated on Clifford Brown's **Memorial Album**. Numbers like **Brownie Speaks** or **Cherokee** show off his lyricism at up-tempos, the multi-note, tripping attack

The Complete Paris Collection (Vogue): multiples of a genius.

riding the furious drumming of Philly Joe Jones and Art Blakey. He turns up on a Tadd Dameron session **(The Arrangers' Touch)** as part of a ninetet, and his muted trumpet is featured on **Theme Of No Repeat**. The same year, 1953, found Brownie in the Lionel Hampton Band that visited Europe. Despite the leader's ban on individual bandsmen recording, the trumpeter dodged the manager by hopping down the hotel fire escape and cutting an unofficial midnight recording session with trumpeter Art Farmer and the Swedish All-Stars. **Lover Come Back To Me** and **Stockholm Sweetnin'** are classic performances. Further tracks were made in Paris **(The Complete Paris Collection)** with

groups of various sizes and combinations of Hampton sidemen, American expatriates and French jazzmen from the 17-piece big band to the quartet. Pianist Henri Renaud plays on most of the tracks, and helped with the organization. There are several takes of numbers like **Brown Skins, Keepin' Up With Jonesy, Salute To The Bandbox** and **The Song Is You** – all featuring the astonishingly mature 22-year-old trumpeter. As the Hard Bop trumpeter, Clifford Brown fitted perfectly into the heated atmosphere of the Art Blakey-Horace Silver combo, later to become The Jazz Messengers. Blue Note recorded the band live **(A Night At Birdland)** and caught the driving excitement, the trumpeter's perfectly executed double-tempo runs and long, supple phrases. His gorgeous tone and melodic fertility made him an excellent foil for singers like Sarah Vaughan and Helen Merrill, and even kept him clear of schmaltz on an album with strings.

1954 saw Brownie accorded recognition in the Down Beat Critics' Poll, and – more significantly – the start of one of the great partnerships of jazz. Master drummer Max Roach, convinced of the economic viability of a Hard Bop unit on the West Coast, contacted the trumpeter to return with him to Los Angeles. Before the unit finally settled down with a permanent personnel, various pianists like Kenny Drew and Carl Perkins, saxophonists like Herb Geller and Walter Benton sat in. The definitive personnel comprised Roach and Brownie, either Sonny Rollins or Harold Land on tenor, Richie Powell on piano and George Morrow on bass. This unit was every bit as good as The Jazz Messengers, or Horace Silver's groups, and the output is uniformly excellent.

At Basin Street, Daahoud, Remember Clifford, Study In Brown and **Three Giants** display the great variety of moods and rhythms the group was capable of, from the unusual time-signatures of **Valse Hot** and **Love Is A Many Splendored Thing** to the trumpet-drums duets of **Mildama**. Most of the writing came from within the band, Brownie's **Sandu, Daahoud, Joy Spring**; Rollins' **Pent-Up House**; Land's **Lands End** and Powell's **Gertrude's Bounce**, many of which have passed into jazz standards.

Recordings:
Memorial Album (Blue Note/Blue Note)
Brownie Eyes (Blue Note/Blue Note)
The Beginning And The End (Columbia/CBS)
The Eminent Jay Jay Johnson (Blue Note/Blue Note)
Gil Evans-Tadd Dameron, The Arrangers' Touch (Prestige/Prestige)
The Complete Paris Collection (—/Vogue – Pye)
Art Blakey At Birdland (Blue Note/Blue Note)
Max Roach-Clifford Brown In Concert (GNP/—)
Clifford Brown All Stars (Mercury/—)
At Basin Street (Trip/Trip)
Daahoud (Mainstream/Mainstream)
Remember Clifford (Trip/Mercury)

Three Giants (Prestige/Prestige)
Study In Brown (Trip/Trip)
Raw Genius (—/Victor – Japan)

Lawrence Brown

Lawrence Brown (born Lawrence, Kansas, 1905) was raised in Pasadena, California, where he studied medicine at local Junior College. Son of professional pianist, he tried piano, violin, tuba before moving on, finally, to trombone. Worked with various bands (including those of Paul Howard and Les Hite) until joining Duke Ellington (1932). Very adaptable musician, he can play straight ballad performances, or switch to fiery, almost tailgate trombone, and, with varying degrees of success, even took over Joseph 'Tricky Sam' Nanton's (♦) plunger-mute role when latter died. Spent the years 1932–51 as one-third of uniquely contrasting trombone team – Nanton, with his 'jungle' plungering, Cuban Juan Tizol, with his straight, slightly exotic Latin-tinged valve-trombone, and Brown. Tizol and Nanton were to be Brown's regular colleagues for 12 years.

During first of two spells with Ellington, Brown's sometimes flamboyant, almost eccentric, trombone style was more or less formulated, although at no time with Ellington did his solo work surpass that of Nanton.

Included among his most notable achievements in a solo capacity are the following: **Ducky Wucky (The Complete Duke Ellington, Vol 4: 1932); Rose Of The Rio Grande, Prelude To A Kiss (Ellington Era, Vol 1); Little Posey (Ellington Era, Vol 2); (There Is No) Greater Love (The Complete Duke Ellington, Vol 7: 1936-1937); Transblucency (At His Very Best); Don't Get Around Much Anymore, Blue Cellophane (The Indispensable Duke Ellington)** and **Solitude, Cocktails For Two, Blue Goose, Across The Track Blues, Flamingo, John Hardy's Wife** and **After All** (all **The Works Of Duke Ellington, Vols 8-10, 12, 14, 15)**. One of Ellington's finest showcases for the Brown trombone was **Golden Cross (The Golden Duke)**, recorded in 1947.

Brown was also on hand to help out with recording activities of the various Ellington small combos, adding his own distinctive voice to the respective ensemble voicings and his own brand of solo trombone where necessary **(The Works Of Duke Ellington, Vols 13, 16, 17** and **Hodge Podge)**.

Lawrence Brown joined newly-formed Johnny Hodges (♦) band when both gave notice to Ellington in 1951. Stayed with Hodges until 1955, recording regularly with the altoist **(The Jeep Is Jumpin')**. He was to record with Hodges at frequent intervals up until latter's death in 1970. Prior to rejoining Ellington in 1960, Brown's services were used extensively for studio work. Left Ellington, finally, in 1970.

Not a particularly impressive blues player, Brown's contributions to an important Joe Turner (♦) recording date in the 1950s **(Boss Of The Blues)** surely must have

Above: veteran trombonist Lawrence Brown, an Ellingtonian of some distinction, and a sideman for 30 years.

Above: altoman Marion Brown with trumpeter Leo Smith. Both men have extended the frontiers of modern music.

surprised even his most fervent admirers. His recordings with other leading musicians did, however, vary in terms of outright success and importance. There are good, solid, if rarely exceptional Lawrence Brown solos to be found on record dates by the likes of Lionel Hampton (♦) **(The Complete Lionel Hampton/ Lionel Hampton's Best Records, Vols 1, 2, 5)** and Earl Hines (♦) **(Once Upon A Time).**

A first-rate section leader, Brown's solo contributions to the Ellington band might seem much less than those by other instrumentalists. But his all-round competence and reliability never was in doubt.

Recordings:
Duke Ellington, The Ellington Era, Vols 1, 2 *(Columbia/CBS)*
The Complete Duke Ellington, Vols 4, 7 *(CBS – France)*
The Works Of Duke Ellington, Vols 8-17 *(RCA Victor – France)*
The Indispensable Duke Ellington, Vols 1, 2 *(RCA Victor/RCA Victor)*
Duke Ellington, At His Very Best *(RCA Victor/RCA Victor)*
Duke Ellington, The Golden Duke *(Prestige/Prestige)*
Johnny Hodges, Hodge Podge *(Epic/CBS – Realm)*
Rex Stewart Memorial *(CBS – Realm)*
Duke Ellington, Liberian Suite/ (A Tone Parallel To Harlem) *(CBS – France)*
The Second Big Band Sound Of Duke Ellington & His Orchestra *(Verve/Verve)*
Duke Ellington, The Great Paris Concert *(Atlantic/Atlantic)*
Duke Ellington, The Duke 1940 *(Jazz Society)*
Duke Ellington, Souvenirs *(Reprise)*
Johnny Hodges, The Jeep Is Jumpin' *(—/Verve)*
Joe Turner, Boss Of The Blues *(Atlantic/Atlantic)*
Earl Hines, Once Upon A Time *(Impulse/Impulse)*
The Complete Lionel Hampton
(RCA Victor)/
Lionel Hampton's Best Records, Vols 1, 2, 5 *(RCA Victor – France)*
Duke Ellington/Johnny Hodges, Blues Summit *(Verve)/* **Side By Side - (Back To Back)** *(Verve)*

Marion Brown

Born in Georgia, 1935, altoist Marion Brown is part of the second generation of New Thing players, though stylistically more traditional than most. His debut album for ESP **(Marion Brown)** showed a careful player of melodic gifts, not given to the tonal distortions and extremes of the period, and capable of developing a musical argument. After a stint with Sun Ra, and encouragement from Ornette Coleman and Archie Shepp, Brown began to arrive at an original voice. He takes interesting solos on albums by Shepp **(Fire Music)** and Coltrane **(Ascension),** though his most impassioned playing is to be found in the trio context **(Porto Novo)** with Dutch bassist Van Regteben Altena and the startingly original Han Bennink on drums. A larger group with Anthony Braxton, Bennie Maupin and Chick Corea **(Afternoon Of A Georgia Faun)** produced pastoral and pastel music of gentle charm, dappled with flutes and voices. **Djinji's Corner** operates on the principles of musical chairs. Brown's Impulse output has been varied, and variable **(Three For Shepp, Sweet Earth Flying** and **Geechee Recollections)** but there is always a clear line of development in his career.

Recordings:
Marion Brown Quartet *(ESP/ESP)*
Archie Shepp, Fire Music *(Impulse/Impulse)*
John Coltrane, Ascension *(Impulse/Impulse)*
Porto Novo

Porto Novo (Polydor): the soulful-looking altoist Marion Brown meets the Dutch powerhouse, Han Bennink, no quarter given.

(Arista-Freedom/Polydor)
Afternoon Of A Georgia Faun *(ECM/ECM)*
Three For Shepp *(Impulse/Impulse)*
Sweet Earth Flying *(Impulse/Impulse)*
Geechee Recollections *(Impulse/Impulse)*
Reeds 'n' Vibes *(Improvising Artists Inc/ —)*

Pete Brown

Only one thing prevented James Ostend 'Pete' Brown (born Baltimore, Maryland, 1906) from reaching the top as an alto-saxophonist; during his career there was always someone around who was that much more important, someone who was just that much better than him. In the 1930s, for instance, Brown was matched against ne plus ultra altoists like Benny Carter (♦) and Johnny Hodges (♦); in the 1940s, with the arrival of Bebop and ancillary jazz schools, he had to contend with Charlie Parker (♦), Sonny Stitt (♦) and Lee Konitz (♦). (Brown's flirtation with bebop can be described in one word: disastrous.) Brown was a superb individualist (if hardly an innovator or catalyst amongst altoists), the possessor of a hard, rather sour tone – the antithesis of anything remotely cloying or over-sentimental – with an obvious desire to swing prodigiously and often, and an ability to engender genuine excitement to any kind of musical environment he happened to be part of at any given time. Pete Brown also knew more than enough about the art of playing the blues. Unfortunately, his was a talent which fell below that of genius, or even near-genius. He did not demonstrate any new pathways down which other jazzmen might make further explorations: he did, however, influence other players during a colorful career, principally, Louis Jordan (♦), Bruce Turner (♦) and, most of all, Charlie Barnet (♦). The Brown approach to playing alto-sax, and the kind of bands he either led or was part of during the 1930s through the 1950s, both offer clear-cut definitions of such vague terminology as 'jump music' and 'jump band'; no-nonsense jazz that just swung (or jumped).

Geographically, Brown's reputation ultimately was established (and maintained) along New York's 52nd Street, during late-1930s/early-1940s. But his musical career per se commenced with violin, which he played at a Baltimore cinema, from the age of 12, and at high school concerts. Brown, who was also proficient on trumpet, switched to alto- and tenor-saxophones in 1924 playing first in theatres then with various bands. To New York in 1927: Brown began doubling on trumpet (temporarily) following year. Between 1930–7, he established an enviable reputation as a consistently hard-swinging altoist with a penchant for igniting jam session-type gatherings, or record dates. His worrying, driving alto was heard in a variety of small-band settings during this period, including those led by Willie 'The Lion' Smith (♦) (**The Swinging Cub Men**), Jimmie Noone (♦) (**Jimmie Noone: 1937-1941**) and, most frequently, Frankie Newton (♦) (**Frankie Newton At The Onyx Club**).

Together with Newton, Brown was featured at one of Hugues Panassie's special recording dates, in 1939 (**The Big Apple** and **The Panassie Sessions**). Newton and Brown co-led a fine and popular small combo that resided for a while at Kelly's Stables (1940). Both were featured in what was the embryo of the John Kirby (♦) Sextet (**Boss Of The Bass**).

During 1940s Brown continued to record at regular intervals (**Lowdown Blues** and **Saxophones**), but with the advent of Charlie Parker et ses confrères, his star waned, popularity-wise. Brown suffered more than most of his 1930s contemporaries. He was unable to come to terms with its phraseology etc, in the way which Coleman Hawkins (♦) or Benny Carter endeavored to understand its workings.

His playing on quasi-bop dates like **Greatest Of The Small Bands, Vol 2,** indicates his stylistic problems in trying to conform with new modes of expression. Brown was to remain indelibly a mid-period altoist, as his playing on early-1940s recordings such as **The Swinging Small Bands 2: 1940-1944** demonstrates, convincingly and happily. Occasional forays into beboppery (**Sir Charles Thompson**) were embarrassing, to say the least. But proof that he could still rise to the occasion – on his own clearly-defined terms – came at irregular

intervals during last years of his life.

His later recordings, like **The Newport Years,** tended mostly to be as inconsistent as his failing health, which meant his in-person appearances became much less frequent than in previous years. However, that he could still echo his finest work from better times is documented on a splendid Joe Turner (♦) record date (**Boss Of The Blues**) which contains at least one superlative example of his skills as a blue soloist, on **Morning Glories.** Both **Boss Of The Blues** and the self-explanatory **Pete's Last Date** find him in mutually profitable surroundings and consequently in irrepressible, splendid form. By 1963 Pete Brown had lost his battle with his health problems, and he died in New York the same year – still without just recognition for his not inconsiderable talents.

Recordings:
John Kirby, Boss Of The Bass (Columbia/—)
Willie 'The Lion' Smith, The Swinging Cub Men (—/Ace of Hearts)
Frankie Newton At The Onyx Club (Tax – Sweden)
Jimmie Noone 1937-1941 (Collector's Classics)
Various, Swingin' Clarinets (—/London)
Mezz Mezzrow/Frankie Newton, The Big Apple (RCA Victor – France)
Various (Including Pete Brown), The Swinging Small Bands 2 (1940-1944) (MCA – Germany)
Pete Brown/Jonah Jones, Lowdown Blues (Jazz Showcase)
Various, The Panassie Sessions (RCA Victor – France)
Various (Including Pete Brown), Saxophones (—/Mercury)
Various, Greatest Of The Small Bands, Vol 2 (RCA Victor – France)
Joe Turner, The Boss Of The Blues (Atlantic/Atlantic)
Various, The Newport Years (Verve/Columbia – Clef)
Pete Brown (Bethlehem/London)
Pete Brown, Pete's Last Date (77/77)

Sandy Brown

In truth, there have been few truly original jazz musicians originating from Great Britain. Without doubt, Alexander 'Sandy' Brown (born Izatnagar, India, 1929, but to all intents and purposes a red-blooded Scotsman) was one. A clarinettist who came to the forefront of British jazz during 1950s with an original approach to his instrument and an enviably broad-minded approach to jazz. Brown's basic technique was more than adequate, although hardly in the Goodman (♦)-De Franco (♦) class. But it was his very idiosyncratic phraseology, his hard-brush timbre and often hair-raising rhythmic involvement with his music that made him stand out, not only in British jazz circles, but universally. A most eminently satisfying blues player, he remains, even after his tragically premature death in March 1975, a memorable player and a lovable character. A mag-

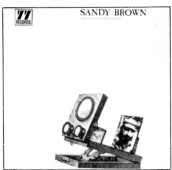

Sandy Brown With The Brian Lemon Trio (77 Records).

nificently earthy soloist, he could raise the level of an already admirable record session (**Doctor McJazz**) to unsuspected heights of passion and brilliance.

Brown, a self-taught musician, was a familiar figure on the British jazz scene in general and the London jazz scene in particular after leaving Scotland in 1946. Worked with such noted traditional figures as Humphrey Lyttelton (♦) and Chris Barber, frequently led own bands and appeared as guest soloist on countless other occasions.

But it was as co-leader of the Al Fairweather-Sandy Brown Jazz Band that Brown's individual reputation was really forged, at concert and club appearances as well as through the medium of several excellent mainstream-styled recordings, including **Doctor McJazz.** It was during this period (late-1950s/early-1960s) that Brown's clarinet playing mirrored his own widening interest in all kinds of jazz, gospel and even African music.

That Brown was labelled, erroneously, as a traditional clarinet player was something which, on rehearing his records, is obviously far from being the truth. Initially his premier influence was Johnny Dodds (♦), but other influences were added through the years; Ben Webster (♦), Charlie

Parker (♦), Louis Armstrong (♦), Duke Ellington (♦) and Charles Mingus (♦). A well-nigh perfect introduction of Sandy Brown's artistry is **McJazz Lives On!**, a superior compilation of some of his finest recordings. His pre-eminence as a bluesman can be judged from his impassioned, moving playing on **Careless Love** and, better still, on his own **Two Blue.** His admiration for gospel music manifests itself throughout **Oh Dong, Bang That Gong** (another Brown original) during which he thumps spiritedly through some primitive pianistics.

His clarinet is at its most melodic during a sensitively projected **Willow, Weep For Me.** And his wide tastes in jazz can be judged by the fact that other items to be found on this album include Benny Golson's **Blues March,** Mingus, and **Wednesday Night Prayer Meeting;** Nat Adderley's **Work Song;** and Teddy McRae's **Broadway,** plus several other Brown originals, each different in concept, mood and structure.

His talent as a composer of intriguing themes is a facet of Brown's talent which tends to be overlooked. A further string of Sandy Brown compositions is to be found within **Sandy Brown & The Brian Lemon Trio** including **Ebun, Legal Pete, Lucky Schiz & The Big Dealer,** and **Louis,** last-named a moving tribute to Louis Armstrong (♦).

Brown, a respected acoustical architect and, occasionally, a perceptive scribe on the subject of jazz, sometimes took the opportunity of essaying a friendly-sounding vocal chorus. As indeed he did in company with US blues pianist Sammy Price (♦) during recording of **Barrelhouse & Blues.** But here again, it is the rough eloquence and sheer driving force of his clarinet playing which remains longest in the memory. And even an acknowledged master of the idiom such as Price has to take second place to Brown's blues offering during a

supremely rewarding version of **In The Evening.**

Recordings:
Sandy Brown, McJazz
  (—/Nixa)
Sandy Brown/Al Fairweather, The Incredible McJazz
  (—/Columbia)
Sandy Brown, McJazz Lives On! (—/One-Up)
Sandy Brown With The Brian Lemon Trio (—/77)
Sammy Price, Barrelhouse & Blues (Black Lion)

Dave Brubeck

Immensely popular with the public and generally denigrated by the critics, pianist Dave Brubeck was the subject of heated arguments throughout the '50s. Classically-trained and influenced by modern composers like Darius Milhaud, Brubeck imported many classical devices into jazz, especially atonality, fugue and counterpoint. Bach, Beethoven and Chopin borrowings can be found throughout his work, and his touch is closer to the classical concert hall than the jazz club. Criticism centered on his lack of swing, pomposity of manner and the stultifying effect of his largely block-chorded solos. Most debates on the validity of Third Stream music – the merging of jazz and classical – have petered out during the less label-obsessed '60s and '70s, but the fact remains that Brubeck's work has lasted less well than Tristano's.

Starting with an Octet, Brubeck pared down to the famous Quartet, with altoist Paul Desmond. The early recordings remain the best, particularly those made during the quartet's tour of the college circuit. The Oberlin concert generates considerable emotion, possibly due to the freedom from inhibition (Brubeck and Desmond had quarrelled, the bassist given notice and the drummer had 'flu) and the music, particularly Desmond's solo on **The Way You Look To-night,** comes over with a rare virility. **Balcony Rock, Don't Worry 'Bout Me** and the Eastern flavoured **Le Souk** are again noteworthy for the melodic inventiveness of Desmond, whose tone has some of the purity and thin-spun sharpness of Konitz.

Brubeck's later experiments with unusual time signatures, **Blue Rondo A La Turk** in 9/8, and the internationally best-selling **Take Five** in 5/4 (**Time Out**) sound a little self-conscious against the pioneering work of Max Roach, and something of a set-piece in the context of the general freeing-up that was taking place around the late '50s. His extensive world tour in 1958 resulted in an album of pastiche based on ethnic music from Afghanistan, Turkey and Calcutta (**Dave Brubeck Quartet**).

Hard core jazz fans usually favour drummer Joe Morello, who joined the group in 1956, and bemoan the 19-year restriction on Desmond's talents. In fact, the altoist's work within the Quartet was as good as anything that he did outside **(The Paul Desmond Quartet Live)** and after recently rejoining for a

Left. pianist Dave Brubeck, '50s cult figure, often criticized for his classical approach and lack of swing.

Above: Newport 1958 (CBS). From the famous Festival, with Quartet members Paul Desmond, Joe Morello and Eugene Wright.

reunion tour Desmond died suddenly in 1977.

Recordings:
Time Out (Columbia/CBS)
Time Further Out
  (Columbia/CBS)
Dave Brubeck Quartet
  (Columbia/CBS)
Impressions Of Japan
  (Columbia/CBS)
Brubeck & Desmond, The Duets
  (A&M/A&M)
Paul Desmond Quartet Live
  (A&M/A&M)

Time Out (CBS): biggest hits.

Georg Brunis

Georg Brunis (born New Orleans, Louisiana, 1900) was one of the first white players really to latch on to the art of tailgate trombone playing, as epitomized by Kid Ory (♦). Originally known as George Clarence Brunies, he came from a musical family – brothers Albert 'Abbie' and Merritt (both trumpeters), Henry (trombone) and Richard, all played professionally, though none achieved the fame and reputation of Georg.

At the tender age of eight, Georg Brunis was playing peck horn with band of Papa Jack Laine. Later, played trombone with Alfred Laine (son of Jack Laine), then with Leon Rappolo (♦). 1919: switched from New Orleans to Chicago, to work with various local bands, leaving temporarily to work aboard a steam-boat. Two years later, joined Friars Society Orchestra which begat the New Orleans Rhythm Kings **(New Orleans Rhythm Kings).** Brunis' playing on recordings by NORK (1922–3) is a clear indication of how he, together with Miff Mole (♦), helped jazz trombone move away from almost obligatory reliance on tailgate playing. His rumbustious solos pointed the way to further developments, whilst his ensemble playing maintained a flexibility little known in jazz at the time, as exemplified by his work on **Tin Roof Blues (New Orleans Rhythm Kings).**

In 1924 – the year Brunis left NORK – he recorded with the Wolverines, alongside Bix Beiderbecke (♦) **(Bix Beiderbecke & The Chicago Cornets)** and his contributions to **Sensation** and **Lazy Daddy** totally confirm critic Max Harrison's sleeve-note assertion that Brunis was 'the ideal trombonist' for Beiderbecke. (Brunis' efforts on kazoo on **Lazy Daddy** are contrastingly forgettable.) Spent the period 1924–34 with band of clarinettist Ted Lewis – not the most pre-possessing occupation for a committed jazzman, although he did manage to include a trip to Europe as part of his stay. With Louis Prima in '34, and during 1934–5 recorded with another band calling itself the New Orleans Rhythm Kings **(Kings Of Jazz),** although Brunis was sole representative of the original outfit. His playing nevertheless, most notably on old NORK favourites such as **Tin Roof Blues** and **Sensation Rag,** demonstrated all the vigor and bite of the previous decade. Became house trombonist at Nick's, New York, favourite spot for Dixielanders, working with all leading figures from that genre. Added punch and experience to fine recordings for Commodore by Bobby Hackett (♦) **(Commo-**

dore, Vol 1) with whose band he had also worked previously, during 1937/8. Was seminal figure in success of Muggsy Spanier's (♦) Ragtimers in 1939 **(The Great 16)** and his joyously driving trombone rarely has been heard to better advantage; the interplay between Brunis and the leader's cornet also does much to ensure the undoubted success of the Ragtimers' Victor records.

When Spanier disbanded at end of '39, Brunis returned to Nick's before moving to Art Hodes' (♦) band (1940–1), then back to Nick's (1941–2). 1943–6: another lengthy spell with Ted Lewis. In '43, he recorded with his own Jazz Band and under leadership of Wild Bill Davison (♦) **(The Davison-Brunis Sessions, Vol 1),** both bands being identical in line-up. Music resulting from these dates remains, like the Spanier Ragtimers, archetypal white-Dixieland jazz at its finest; once again Brunis' contributions were admirable.

Format was repeated by Commodore in 1946, with only minimal changes in personnel of both bands **(The Davison-Brunis Sessions, Vol 3)** and the music was just as invigorating. Brunis worked regularly with the Eddie Condon band (1947–9), and for a while was a regular on the *This Is Jazz* radio series **(This Is Jazz: Muggsy Spanier** and **This Is Jazz: The Genius Of Sidney Bechet).**

Spent 1950s leading own bands, or with Hodes. Career during 1960s, although interrupted by serious illness towards end of decade, followed similar pattern. Was still fairly active, in his 70s, up until the time he died, in 1974.

Recordings:
Georg Brunis & His New Rhythm Kings (Jazzology/—)
New Orleans Rhythm Kings (Milestone)
Various, Bix Beiderbecke & The Chicago Cornets (Milestone)
Various, Kings Of Jazz (Swaggie – Australia)
Eddie Condon, Jam Sessions At Commodore (—/Ace of Hearts)
Muggsy Spanier, The Great 16 (RCA Victor/RCA Victor – France)
Eddie Condon, Commodore Condon Vol 1 (—/London)
The Davison-Brunis Sessions, Vols 1, 3 (—/London)
Various, That Toddlin' Town (—/Parlophone)
New Orleans Rhythm Kings, 1934-1935 (MCA – Germany)
Various, 'This Is Jazz', Vols 1, 2 (Rarities/—)
Various, 'This Is Jazz': Muggsy Spanier (Jazzology/—)
Various, 'This Is Jazz': The Genius Of Sidney Bechet (Jazzology/—)

Teddy Bunn

Although his has not been always a fashionable name amongst jazz guitarists, Theodore 'Teddy' Bunn (born Freeport, Long Island, 1909) has long since presented impressive credentials, of the kind which make him indisputably one of the giants on his chosen instrument.

Whether playing single-line solos, combining almost delicacy in approach with inner strength,

Above: Teddy Bunn, fine technician, notable blues player – one of the finest of all jazz guitar players.

or essaying chordal work, firmly strummed and with an enviable awareness of dynamics, Bunn has been one of the most consistently rewarding guitar players thus far to be produced by jazz.

Particularly sensitive in the blues idiom, Bunn, not surprisingly, has been featured often with both vocal and instrumental performers of a definite blues persuasion. Trixie Smith and Rosetta Crawford (**Out Came The Blues**) are just two blues singers with whom Bunn has recorded. He has also recorded with vaudeville-bluesmen Coot and Grant Wilson (**The Rarest Sidney Bechet, Vol 1**). And his guitar has been heard in company with clarinettist/soprano-saxist Sidney Bechet (♦), himself a comprehensively gifted blues player, on numerous occasions. Most notable Bechet-Bunn recordings include **The Complete Ladnier-Mezzrow-Bechet**, although, in truth, Bunn's solo opportunities here were few (he also sang on **If You See Me Comin'**, co-composed by Mezzrow, Bunn).

Took part in Bechet session ('39), from whence came celebrated version of **Summertime (Sidney Bechet Jazz Classics, Vol 1)**. At same date, with addition of Frankie Newton (♦) and J. C. Higginbotham (♦), Bechet-Bunn group cut two superb blues, **Pounding Heart Blues** and **Blues For Tommy Ladnier (Sidney Bechet Jazz Classics, Vol 2)** with guitarist contributing short but telling solo to

second title. 1940: Bunn once again inside recording studio with Bechet for further Blue Note date that produced, as part of quartet of fine tracks, a poised version of **Dear Old Southland (Sidney Bechet Jazz Classics, Vol 2)**. Later same year recorded with another noted blues instrumentalist, Oran 'Hot Lips' Page (♦), for Victor.

In quartet setting, Bunn produced series of solos which are as fine as anything he recorded elsewhere. Beautifully delineated statements on **Just Another Woman** and **Do It If You Wanna**, that are miniature masterpieces of blues-tinged jazz guitar. Bunn takes a couple of friendly vocals, but it is his guitar playing which, along with Page's own trumpet/vocal contributions, are focal points of session (**Feelin' High & Happy**).

Bunn's was very much a musical background; both parents and brother were all instrumentalists. First professional jazz experience in early-1920s; first recordings with Spencer Williams during same decade. Recorded with Duke Ellington (♦) Orchestra (1929) (**Hot In Harlem: 1928-1929** and **Cotton Club Days, Vol 1**), one of few non-Ellingtonians to do so. (In fact, Bunn did once work with Ellington, briefly, as deputy guitarist.)

In early-1930s name of Teddy Bunn became more widely known through his excellent playing with both Washboard Rhythm Kings and Washboard Serenaders

bands (**Washboard Rhythm Kings/Serenaders 1930-1933**). Reputation further enhanced as member of his next band, known first as Ben Bernie's Nephews, later changed to Spirits of Rhythm. Popularity of this band on 52nd Street, New York, considerable, especially during and because of important, lengthy stint at prominent jazz spots at that venue. Left group in 1937 to work for short period with John Kirby (♦). After leading own combos, rejoined Spirits of Rhythm, 1939. (Numerous references to band's activities in New York to be found in Arnold Shaw's *The Street That Never Slept*.) During '37, recorded with Jimmie Noone (♦) (**Jimmie Noone 1937-1941**) and, together with two other members of SOR, broadcast in support of Lionel Hampton (♦) (**Great Swing Jam Sessions, Vol 2**). 1938: in spite of the fact they had never previously met, musically or socially, Teddy Bunn and Johnny Dodds (♦) achieved considerable rapport at recording session that produced richly rewarding music, as illustrated by aural reference to tracks like **Wild Man Blues** and **Blues Galore (Harlem On Saturday Night)**. The Spirits of Rhythm moved to West Coast (1940); the same year he recorded with Lionel Hampton (**The Complete Lionel Hampton / Lionel Hampton's Best Records, Vol 4**) and under his own name, for Blue Note. The SOR disbanded and reformed on several occasions. Bunn settled in California, working with own bands (including his Waves of Rhythm), and others. Worked with Edgar Hayes on more than one occasion; likewise, Jack McVea. Brief spell with Louis Jordan (♦) (1959), toured with a rock show, but from 1960s was troubled with failing sight plus recurring illness, including heart attacks and strokes. He died in July 1978.

Recordings:
Washboard Kings/Washboard Serenaders 1930-1933
(RCA Victor – France)
Various, Swing Street, Vol 1
(Epic/Columbia)
Jimmie Noone, 1937-1941
(—/Collector's Classics)
Various (Including Johnny Dodds), Harlem On Saturday Night *(—/Ace of Hearts)*
The Rarest Sidney Bechet, Vol 1 *(—/After Hours)*
The Complete Ladnier-Mezzrow-Bechet
(RCA Victor – France)
Various, Blue Note's Three Decades Of Jazz (1939-1949), Vol 1 *(Blue Note/Blue Note)*
Sidney Bechet, Jazz Classics, Vols 1, 2 *(Blue Note/Blue Note)*
Various, Great Swing Jam Sessions, Vol 2 *(—/Saga)*
Hot Lips Page, Feelin' High & Happy *(RCA Victor/—)*
Duke Ellington, Hot In Harlem (1928-1929) *(MCA – Germany)*
Duke Ellington, Cotton Club Days, Vol 1 *(—/Ace of Hearts)*
The Complete Lionel Hampton *(Bluebird)/*
Lionel Hampton's Best Records, Vol 4
(RCA Victor – France)
Various (Including Rosetta Crawford, Trixie Smith), Out Came The Blues *(—/Coral)*
Various (Including Big Joe Turner), Roots Of Rock & Roll, Vol 2 *(Savoy/—)*

Kenny Burrell

Detroit guitarist Kenny Burrell is one of the most consistent players around. Veteran of countless Blue Note and Prestige sessions, he played with pretty well everybody in the post-Bop '50s from Coltrane to Jimmy Smith. Though usually associated with relaxed, after-hours blues, Burrell has fitted well into the more ambitious, arranged setting of the big band. With a star-studded studio band playing the arrangements of Gil Evans (**Guitar Forms**) Burrell really stretches out and shows the form that made him Duke Ellington's favorite guitarist. He repays the compliment in one of the few successful tributes to the maestro (**Ellington Is Forever**), which features his guitar and an amazing collection of sitters-in: Thad Jones, Snooky Young, Jon Faddis, Joe Henderson and Jimmy Smith.

Above: Kenny Burrell, master of after-hours ambience. Collaboration with Gil Evans produced a masterpiece.

Kenny Burrell seems to be one of the few gutsy ex-organ combo players not to decline into predictable blues licks or inflated soul productions. The catalogs list scores of available albums both as sideman and leader.

Recordings:
Jimmy Smith, Back At The Chicken Shack
(Blue Note/Blue Note)
Midnight Blue
(Blue Note/Blue Note)
All Day Long & All Night Long
(Prestige/Prestige)
Kenny Burrell & John Coltrane
(Prestige/Prestige)
Guitar Forms *(Verve/Verve)*
Ellington Is Forever
(—/Fantasy)

Gary Burton

Vibes player Gary Burton was born in 1943 in Indiana, and developed a phenomenal technique using three and four mallets at once. 1964-6 saw the virtuoso working with tenorman Stan Getz (**Getz Au Go Go** and **In Paris**) before launching out with his own group which included guitarist Larry Coryell. During the height of the psychedelic '60s, Burton appeared on the same bill as rock bands, playing that unlikely in-

Above: Gary Burton, wizard of multiple-mallet techniques on vibraphone. Improbable popularity in hippy '60s.

strument in beads and buckskins, and incorporating rock influences – particularly Coryell's feedback effects – as well as his own native hillbilly. The growth of non-jazz features shows in the comparison between two albums, **Duster** and **Lofty Fake Anagram**, and when the fashion bubble burst Burton's career found itself in the doldrums. A Montreux recording from 1971 (**Alone At Last**), which has a side of solo vibes, is accomplished but directionless. His best work results from challenging company, and Carla Bley's composition (**A Genuine Tong Funeral**) using the Gary Burton Quartet and JCOA musicians like Steve Lacy and Gato Barbieri, effectively harnesses his virtuosity.

As with pianists Keith Jarrett and Chick Corea, with both of whom he duetted (**Gary Burton With Keith Jarrett** and **Crystal Silence**), Burton's career benefited from collaboration with German record producer Manfred Eicher. In 1973 he made what was effectively a comeback album (**The New Quartet**), using unknown musicians; guitarist Michael Goodrick, bassist Abraham Laboriel and drummer Harry Blazer, and revealing splendid group interplay in a programme of Carla Bley, Jarrett, Corea and Mike Gibbs compositions. An album of mainly Mike Gibbs compositions, who also conducted **7 Songs For Quartet & Chamber Orchestra,** is clever, if frigid, Burton. A meeting with bassist Eberhard Weber (**Ring**) produced fine music from the jazz-rock feel of **Unfinished Sympathy** to Carla Bley's **Silent Spring.** Two duo albums featured Burton with bassist Steve Swallow (**Hotel Hello**), multi-tracked and many-layered interpretations of Swallow's complex themes, and Burton with guitarist Ralph Towner (**Matchbook**), a more overtly romantic session of great charm and empathy.

Recordings:
Stan Getz, Getz Au Go Go
  (Verve/Verve)
In Paris *(Verve/Verve)*
Duster *(RCA Victor/RCA Victor)*

Lofty Fake Anagram
  (RCA Victor/RCA Victor)
Alone At Last
  (Atlantic/Atlantic)
A Genuine Tong Funeral
  (RCA Victor/RCA Victor)
Gary Burton With Keith Jarrett
  (Atlantic/Atlantic)
Crystal Silence *(ECM/ECM)*
The New Quartet *(ECM/ECM)*
7 Songs For Quartet & Chamber Orchestra *(ECM/ECM)*
Ring *(ECM/ECM)*
Hotel Hello *(ECM/ECM)*
Matchbook *(ECM/ECM)*

Billy Butterfield

Technically skilled, warmly emotional, supremely melodic, and a gifted all-round player – that is as good a description as any of Charles William 'Billy' Butterfield (born Middleton, Ohio, 1917). With the added comment that he is as much at home playing in small or large jazz outfits as he is fitting into all kinds of musical contexts to be found inside TV, radio and recording studios as a coveted session player.

As a boy started on violin, bass and trombone before switching to trumpet (later adding flugelhorn) full-time. Studied medicine at Transylvania College, after graduation from high school. Played in college dance bands, then worked with little-known outfits before obtaining first really important professional job with Bob Crosby (♦), in 1937.

With Crosby, Butterfield became ideal foil to trumpet styles of Yank Lawson (♦) and Sterling Bose. Established an enviable reputation as solo player with solos like that on **I'm Free** (later known as **What's New?** and under latter banner achieving even greater popularity) (**South Rampart Street Parade**). With Bob Crosby's Bob Cats, Butterfield's solo talent likewise utilized to great advantage, most notably on **Mournin' Blues,** where the influence of Bix Beiderbecke (♦), via Bobby Hackett (♦), is clearly discernible (**Big Noise From Winnetka**). Butterfield stayed with Crosby until 1940, when he joined Bob Strong before accepting offer from Artie Shaw (♦), with whom he was to remain until 1941 (when Shaw disbanded).

During this time, Butterfield's mellifluous trumpet heard at its best on numerous Shavian items, including **Stardust, Concerto For Clarinet, Chantez Les Bas** and **Blues (Concerto For Clarinet).** As with Crosby, Butterfield played splendidly with Shaw's own small band (**Artie Shaw & His Gramercy Five**) and his driving muted solo did much to help **Summit Ridge Drive** become a million-selling disc several times over. Other Gramercy Five titles with excellent Butterfield contributions are **When The Quail Comes Back to San Quentin, My Blue Heaven** (particularly expressive plunger-mute solo) and **Keepin' Myself For You.**

Worked with Benny Goodman (♦) 1941–2 and featured eloquently with big band – **Something New (Benny Goodman Plays Solid Gold Instrumental Hits)** – is a fine example of his work with the clarinettist. In 1942, recorded with basically Goodman contingent for Commodore under leadership of Mel Powell (**Swingin' Clarinets**) contributing finely rounded, if brief, solos to session, especially appealing on **When Did You Leave Heaven?**

Left Goodman for Les Brown ('42), then became CBS staffman until entry into US Army (1945). Before service, Butterfield had taken part in a generally excellent record date (in 1944) at which his trumpet was matched opposite the laconic tenor-sax of Lester Young (♦) (**Pres/The Complete Savoy Recordings**). Also in '44, was featured at several of the legendary Eddie Condon (♦) Town Hall concerts, giving a fine account of himself during a fiercely swinging **Struttin' With Some Barbecue** at one such event (**Eddie Condon & His All Stars**). Same year, his trumpet and studio orchestra accompanied singer Margaret Whiting on a recording of **Moonlight In Vermont,** which became million-selling hit. After demobilization, put together own band which toured and recorded during 1946–7. Disbanded, played solo residency at Nick's, New York, before returning to studio work (also New York).

During late-1940s, into the 1950s, continued making records and in-person appearances with various leaders, including Condon (**We Called It Music, The Golden Days Of Jazz: Eddie Condon** and **Chicago & All That Jazz!**) as well as periodically fronting various own bands.

Produced some of his finest trumpet playing at all-star record date for Capitol in '56 (**Session At Riverside**). From time to time also worked again with Goodman, and taught trumpet. Then, in 1968, joined newly-formed World's Greatest Jazzband of Yank Lawson & Bob Haggart. In company with old friends and musically sympathetic players, Butterfield's playing took on new lease of life. Certainly, solos like **The Windmills Of Your Mind,** a duet with Lawson, **It Must Be Him (Extra!), This Is All I Ask (The WGJB Of Yank Lawson & Bob Haggart – Project 3/World Record Club)** and **What's New? (The WGJB Of Yank Lawson & Bob Haggart Live At The Roosevelt Grill)** must be ranked with his finest recorded solos taken from any time during his career. Since his first involvement with WGJB, Butterfield has made

equally praiseworthy guest appearances at various concerts given by the band, including **WGJB Of Yank Lawson & Bob Haggart In Concert, Vol 2, At Carnegie Hall** and has continued to tour successfully as a much-appreciated solo act.

Recordings:
Bob Crosby, South Rampart Street Parade *(—/MCA)*
Bob Crosby, Bob Crosby's Bob Cats 1938-1942
  (Swaggie – Australia)
Bob Crosby, Big Noise From Winnetka *(—/MCA)*
Artie Shaw, Concerto For Clarinet *(RCA Victor)*
Artie Shaw & His Gramercy Five *(—/RCA Victor)*
Benny Goodman Plays Solid Gold Instrumental Hits
  (Columbia/CBS)
Various, Swingin' Clarinets
  (—/London)
Lester Young, Pres/The Complete Savoy Recordings
  (Savoy/—)
Eddie Condon & His All Stars
  (Jazum/—)
Eddie Condon, We Called It Music *(—/Ace of Hearts)*
Eddie Condon, The Golden Days Of Jazz *(Columbia/CBS)*
Various, Chicago & All That Jazz! *(—/Verve)*
The World's Greatest Jazzband Of Yank Lawson & Bob Haggart Live At The Roosevelt Grill *(Atlantic)/*
Billy Butterfield, Watch What Happens *(—/77 Records)*
The WGJB Of Yank Lawson & Bob Haggart
  (Project 3/World Record Club)
Dick Wellstood/Billy Butterfield, Rapport *(—/77 Records)*
The WGJB Of Yank Lawson & Bob Haggart, In Concert/ At Carnegie Hall, Vol 2
  (World Jazz/—)
Jack Teagarden, Prince Of The Bone, Vol 2 (1928-1957)
  (RCA Victor – France)
Various, Session At Riverside
  (Capitol/Capitol – Holland)
The WGJB Of Yank Lawson & Bob Haggart Plays Duke Ellington *(World Jazz/—)*

Don Byas

Carlos Wesley 'Don' Byas (born Muskogee, Oklahoma, 1912) was a 'mid-period' tenor-saxophonist in the truest sense of that expression. He emerged during early-1930s, to be influenced primarily by Ben Webster (♦) and, particularly, Coleman Hawkins (♦). And Byas' peak years coincided with the advent of Bebop with which he associated himself with typical gusto and fervor. In the beginning, Byas had started his musical schooling on violin – his mother and father both played instruments – then transferred his allegiance to alto-saxophone. Before his 20th birthday, had gigged with bands like those of Bennie Moten (♦), Walter Page's Blue Devils, and during period at Langston College, Oklahoma, led own Don Byas Collegiate Ramblers. Switched to tenor-sax around this time (whilst with Bert Johnson's Sharps & Flats, 1933–5). Left latter band to settle in California, working with Lionel Hampton (♦), Eddie Barefield, Buck

Clayton (♦) (in 1937). With band accompanying Ethel Waters (♦) (1937–9), followed by short stays with Don Redman (♦), Lucky Millinder (♦), before joining Andy Kirk (♦) (1939–40). 1940: with Edgar Hayes, Benny Carter (♦). 1941: to Count Basie (♦), in place of exiting Lester Young (♦). Strongly featured during almost three-year stint with Basie band.

Solo highlights on record include **Sugar Blues** and **St Louis Blues (Superchief)**, both of which were, like **Bugle Blues** and **Royal Garden Blues (Blues By Basie)**, recorded by small contingent from full band; **Harvard Blues (Blues By Basie)** probably remains the best.

After leaving Basie, Byas made home in New York, quickly establishing himself as one of the most popular tenorists on 52nd Street. Worked alongside one of his idols, Coleman Hawkins (at Yacht Club), also with Dizzy Gillespie (♦) (at Onyx Club), in what must have been the first working Bebop band. Byas had recorded with Hawkins in 1944 (**Cattin'** and **Swing!**). During same year, took part (with Hawkins and Gillespie) in first known bop record date (**The Many Faces Of Jazz Vol 52: Coleman Hawkins**). Like Hawkins, Byas' speed of execution, harmonic awareness and alert mind enabled him to respond to the new music. But he never really became an out-and-out bebopper – tonally and rhythmically, his playing remained based in the music of a previous generation. Byas had recorded with Gillespie in Trummy Young's band in '44 (**Jazz 44**) and two years later was employed by the trumpeter as sideman for recording date which produced more clearly defined examples of bop (**Greatest Of The Small Bands, Vol 2**) soloing confidently on **52nd Street Theme**, **A Night In Tunisia** and **Ol' Man Rebop**.

Between 1944–6 Byas recorded numerous titles for Savoy, mostly at sessions under own name, and with sympathetic colleagues like Charlie Shavers (♦), Emmett Berry (♦), Clyde Hart and Max Roach (♦). Typical of the high standard of performances from the tenorist at these dates (**Savoy Jam Party**) are superior examples of his big-toned, rhapsodic ballad playing (**Candy** and **Sweet & Lovely**, both from 1944; **September In The Rain**, 1945; **They Say It's Wonderful** and **September Song**, 1946), plus a series of comprehensively swinging up-tempo gems like **Savoy Jam Party** and **Bass C-Jam** in '44; **How High The Moon** and **Cherokee** in '45; **St Louis Blues** and **I Found A New Baby** in '46. Two remarkable virtuoso-class performances (**Indiana** and **I Got Rhythm**) came from a New York Town Hall appearance in 1945 (**Town Hall Concert, Vol 3**). Same year 'The Don' led own bands at various jazz nightspots in the city, including Three Deuces. By September of 1946 Byas was in Europe, as principal soloist with Don Redman. After leaving Redman at tour's conclusion, decided to make his home in France. Later, moved to Amsterdam where, eventually, he settled for good, with Dutch wife

and family. 1950: featured with Duke Ellington (♦) Orchestra during its European tour that year; recorded with Ellington contingent (plus French pianist Raymond Fol), under Johnny Hodges' (♦) leadership (**Mellow Tone**).

Ten years later the emigré tenorist again toured Europe with fellow Americans, this time as member of Jazz At The Philharmonic troupe. During which his bristling, hard-hitting solos compared favorably with work of his colleagues: most interesting to hear Byas' thick tone, unflagging drive in company with two other tenor giants, Hawkins and Stan Getz (♦) (**JATP In Europe, Vol 1**) as well as part of a predominantly mainstream line-up (**JATP In Europe, Vol 3**).

In between, Byas had built up considerable reputation as solo act, visiting most European countries, including Britain, playing at festivals, concerts and in clubs. Twenty-four years after leaving

Anthropology (Black Lion) – tenorist Don Byas 'live' . . .

his home country, Byas returned principally for purpose of making Dutch documentary film about Don Byas. Appeared – to enthusiastic response – at 1970 Newport Jazz Festival and, briefly, elsewhere. 1971: toured Japan with Jazz Messengers of Art Blakey (♦), returning to Holland same year. During 1960s, Byas' playing underwent slight stylistic adjustments as he endeavored to incorporate (sometimes unsuccessfully) some of the devices of John Coltrane (♦) and Sonny Rollins (♦) (who both acknowledged Byas as personal influence). Basically, though, his bop-tinged mid-period style was maintained right up until the time of his death, from lung cancer, in 1972.

Typical of Byas' 1960s performances (and indeed of his playing up to his death) are those to be found on a two-tenor album from 1966 (**Ben Webster Meets Don Byas**). Better still, though, is **Anthropology** from three years before the Byas-Webster date, with Byas steaming through a typical live programme, including the title tune and **A Night In Tunisia** from his Gillespie-associated days, helped enormously by the efforts of the phenomenal Danish bassist Niels-Henning Ørsted-Pederson.

Recordings:
Count Basie, Blues By Basie
(Columbia/Philips)
Count Basie, Superchief
(Columbia/CBS)
Count Basie
(Queen Disc – Italy)
Count Basie, The V-Discs, Vol 2
(Jazz Society)

Coleman Hawkins, Cattin'
(—/Fontana)
Coleman Hawkins, Swing!
(—/Fontana)
Various, Jazz 44
(—/Black & Blue – France)
Coleman Hawkins, The Many Faces Of Jazz, Vol 52
(Mode – France)
The Greatest Of Dizzy Gillespie
(RCA Victor)/
Various, The Greatest Of The Small Bands, Vol 2
(RCA Victor – France)
Shelly Manne & Co.
(Flying Dutchman/—)
Various, Town Hall Concert, Vol 3 *(—/London)*
Don Byas, Savoy Jam Party
(Savoy)
Le Grand Don Byas
(Vogue – France)
Various, Mellow Tone *(Vogue)*
Don Byas, Live At The Montmartre *(Debut/Fontana)*
Don Byas Meets Ben Webster
(Prestige)/
Ben Webster Meets Don Byas
(BASF)
Don Byas, Ballads For Swingers
(—/Polydor)
Don Byas, Anthropology
(Black Lion/Black Lion)
Various, Jazz At The Philharmonic In Europe, Vols 1, 3 *(Verve/Verve)*

Charlie Byrd

Born 1925 in Virginia, guitarist Charlie Byrd achieved immense popularity on the bossa nova wave in the early '60s. Influenced by none of the usual guitar masters – Christian, Reinhardt – Byrd studied under classical master, Segovia, and much of his improvisation revolves around the classical flamenco. In fact, his status as a jazzman has often been questioned, though there are no doubts about his mastery of the instrument. A quiet, sensitive player, Byrd uses an acoustic classical guitar and concentrates on meandering melodies of great charm and limited drive. In 1959 he joined Woody Herman, and in 1961 took his trio on a State Department tour of Latin America. Collaborating with tenorman Stan Getz on one of the first bossa nova albums (**Jazz Samba**) Byrd began a long preoccupation with that form. The hit number **Desafinado** turns up on his Milestone double album **Latin Byrd** as well as versions of **One Note Samba** and other Jobim compositions. Most of his albums reveal a charming miniaturist, though the jazz content rather depends upon his colleagues.

Recordings:
Stan Getz, Jazz Samba
(Verve/Verve)
Latin Byrd *(Milestone/Milestone)*
Triste *(Improv/Improv)*

Donald Byrd

Donald Toussaint L'Ouverture Byrd was born in 1932 in Detroit, a city that had supplied many of the stalwarts of Bop and Hard Bop: Kenny Burrell, Pepper Adams, Sonny Stitt, Milt Jackson, Tommy Flanagan, Barry Harris and the three Jones boys, Thad, Elvin and Hank. After early experience as a

sideman with George Wallington, Art Blakey's Messengers and Max Roach, trumpeter Byrd found himself in the lucrative position of recording every day to keep up with the public appetite for long playing albums. Between 1955–8, he made sixty albums for Blue Note, Savoy and Prestige, sharing sessions with Monk, Coltrane, Rollins, Silver, Jackie McLean and Phil Woods. His playing at this time was immature, his tone thin, but – despite overexposure – his promise was clear. A good example **(House Of Byrd)** collates two mid-50s sessions, pairing with trumpeter Art Farmer, and sharing a quintet with altoist Phil Woods.

A period with altoist Gigi Gryce produced the Jazz Lab, in which the two music students could experiment with composition and harmony, and this bore fruit in Byrd's excellent Blue Note albums with baritone saxophonist, Pepper Adams. Two of these **(Royal Flush** and **The Cat Walk)** show that the trumpeter's writing on **Jorgie's, Shangri-La** and **The Cat Walk** avoided the clichés of the period

Royal Flush (Blue Note):
trumpet star before stardom.

and invented new routes to old destinations, while his playing gained in strength and lyricism.

A combination of factors led to Donald Byrd's subsequent disappearance from jazz circles in favor of fusion music. He attributes his change of direction to the ghetto riots, the influence of singer James Brown, both as a leader of his people and a musician, and the rise of Tamla Motown in his hometown. Byrd is a doctor of ethnomusicology, and believes that the black heritage is better represented today through Soul music, hence his Blue Note album, **Black Byrd,** that label's first million-seller, and a pretty diluted product in terms of jazz content. Byrd's protégé, Herbie Hancock, made a similar crossover. These days, the trumpeter plays with his own band, The Blackbyrds.

Recordings:
House Of Byrd
(Prestige/Prestige)
The Cat Walk
(Blue Note/Blue Note)
Royal Flush
(Blue Note/Blue Note)
Black Byrd
(Blue Note/Blue Note)

Cab Calloway

Cabell 'Cab' Calloway (born Rochester, New York, 1907) is remembered mostly as a jivey vocalist-cum-bandleader of the 1930s–'40s who found fame afresh

in another area of music – the stage musical – later in his career. Calloway, raised in Baltimore where he sometimes sang with local high-school group, studied at Chicago college when Calloway moved on from Baltimore to the Windy City in his teens. Appeared, together with sister Blanche, at Chicago's Loop Theatre; couple also appeared in a tabloid show. Cab Calloway worked as drummer and master of ceremonies around this time. With the Missourians in New York (1928), then back to Chicago to work with Alabamians (1929), combining job of MC with that of 'personality vocals'. Back again with Missourians then, after regularly undertaking bandleading chores, changed name of band to Cab Calloway & His Orchestra. 1931: commenced prestigious residency at New York's Cotton Club lasting, on and off, best part of a year. Already, Calloway – later to be dubbed His Highness of Hi-De-Ho – had established more of a reputation than band itself: recording, in 1931, of **Minnie The Moocher (The King Of Hi-Di-Ho)** tended to confirm this.

Unfortunately, most recordings tended to feature Calloway's averagely funny vocals – scarcely 'jazz singing' in any conceivable way – to the exclusion of all but a comparative handful of solos from his sidemen.

Cab Calloway & His Cotton Club Orchestra recorded some fairly good material for Victor 1933–4, including **Long About Midnight** and **Moonglow,** plus reprises from recent past of **Minnie The Moocher** and **Kickin' The Gong Around (Cab Calloway & His Orchestra 1933-1934).** Calloway and orchestra toured Europe (including Britain) in 1934. Calloway himself played alto-sax (apparently unconvincingly) on odd occasions during 1930s. Probably best jazz emanated from band of 1937–42 vintage. Principal soloist during most of this time was Chu Berry (♦), whose superior tenor-saxophone playing of **I Don't Stand A Ghost Of A Chance** (1940) became a popular recording and today is rightly looked upon as something of a classic **(Chu** and **16 Cab Calloway Classics).** At the time, Berry was most generously featured soloist with Calloway **(Penguin Swing)** but other notable instrumentalists (and their features) were: Hilton Jefferson (♦), **Willow, Weep For Me** (1940); Jonah Jones (♦), **Jonah Joins The Cab** (1941); Cozy Cole (♦), **Crescendo In Drums** and **Paradiddle** (both 1940); Milt Hinton, **Pluckin' The Bass** (1939); and a youthful trumpeter-arranger Dizzy Gillespie (♦), **Pickin' The Cabbage** and **Bye Bye Blues** (1940–1) (all **16 Cab Calloway Classics).**

Calloway band lasted until 1948 (when star sidemen mentioned had all long since departed). After break-up, Calloway toured with sextet, putting together big bands from time to time for rare engagements, including trips to Canada, South America. Calloway appeared as solo act in Britain (1948), head-lining London Palladium for season. Toured UK again, in similar fashion, in 1955.

For two years (1952–4 including London run), appeared as Sportin' Life in folk-opera *Porgy & Bess* (Original Broadway Cast LP: **Porgy**

& Bess). Was to repeat this role at various times during 1950s. Put together more big bands for seasons at various New York clubs, and elsewhere, during 1950s; midway through decade, undertook tour with Harlem Globetrotters. Was back, few years later, to more stage work, including leading role opposite Pearl Bailey in *Hello Dolly!* During a colorful lifetime in show business has appeared in numerous movies, including *The Big Broadcast of 1933, International House, The Singing Kid, Stormy Weather, Sensations of 1945* and *St Louis Blues.* Current venture in preparation – starring role in new black musical.

Recordings:
Chu Berry, Chu *(Epic)/*
Chu Berry & His Stompy Stevedores *(Epic – France)*
16 Cab Calloway Classics
(—/CBS – France)
Chu Berry, Penguin Swing: Chu Berry Featured With Cab Calloway *(Jazz Archives)*
Cab Calloway & His Orchestra 1933-1934
(RCA Victor – Germany)
Cab Calloway & His Cotton Club Orchestra
(—/RCA Victor – France)
The King Of Hi-De-Ho
(—/Ace of Hearts)

Harry Carney

There is very little argument to the categorical statement that, when

Above: Harry Carney – without a doubt, the most celebrated exponent of the baritone-sax in jazz history.

all is said and done, Harry Carney (born Boston, Massachusetts, 1910) was the greatest of all the baritone-saxophonists. Certainly, it could be said that Serge Chaloff (♦) was a more accomplished improviser and had more speed; and there have been times when Gerry Mulligan (♦) too has proved to be a more interesting soloist than Carney – especially at length. Having said that, Carney still was in a class of his own, omnipotent on an often cumbersome instrument for around 45 years, unchallenged in terms of sheer tonal quality, ability to swing (Carney was unbeatable in terms of rhythmic drive), and all-round competence.

He was the first to 'tame' the baritone, to make it sound something rather more than a kind of vaudeville throwback (Adrian Rollini (♦) undertook a similar mission in the late-1920s with the even more cumbersome bass-saxophone). Carney was also an accomplished soloist on alto-sax, clarinet and bass-clarinet. But it was the hugeness of his baritone-sax sound which became so integral a part of the overall sound of the textures and colours devised by Duke Ellington (♦) for his various orchestras. And it was to Ellington that Carney, like so many other Ducal soloists over the years, owed a priceless debt of gratitude for providing him with the kind of settings and situations which enabled his innate talent to blossom to the fullest. Carney remained a rock-like figure of absolute permanency within the Ellington fold, while others around him lasted a mere 15, 10, five or less years.

In all, Carney's residence with the Ellington band lasted from 1927 until his employer's death in 1974 – just six months before Carney himself passed away. Carney's death, like Ellington's, was something of a shock: both seemed blessed with an indomitable spirit, and seemingly unlimited reserves of physical, mental and spiritual stamina. And there was a special kind of relationship between Ellington and Carney that did not seem to exist between the bandleader and any of his other star pupils. For many years prior to Ellington's hospitalization, then subsequent death, Carney had not travelled on the Ellington band bus, being more gainfully employed by the leader to drive him from one gig to the next. As such, it is said he was one of the very few persons who can be said to have been something of a confidant of the Duke's. Later to become a prolific Poll-winner on baritone, Harry Howell Carney joined Ellington in 1927 (his first gig with the band was a one-nighter near the city of his birth) after having worked with local Boston bands, then leaving for New York together with friend altoist Charlie Holmes. His subsequent splendidly consistent work with Ellington and his ability to merge into practically any kind of jazz context found him regular work, when he could take time off from his intense involvement with the Ellington band, as a member of all kinds of musical outfits. Especially the kind of pick-up record-session bands put together by Teddy Wilson (♦) for singers of the calibre of Billie Holiday (♦) (**The Golden Years, Vol 2**) and to showcase the talents of the cream of available jazz instrumentalists (**Teddy Wilson & His All Stars**).

Carney's supremacy as baritone-saxist no doubt earned him a two-number spot on the star-studded bill of the legendary Goodman Carnegie Hall concert of January 1938 (**The 1938 Carnegie Hall Jazz Concert**) where his versatility made him an obvious choice for inclusion amongst the list of participants in the jam session on **Honeysuckle Rose**, and his matchless tone and magnificent control earned him an even more appropriate showcase, alongside the soprano-sax of Johnny Hodges (♦), during an unforgettable duet performance by both on the little-heard Ellington number **Blue Reverie**. Hodges, incidentally, clearly was the principal influence on Harry Carney's playing, and in the shaping of his style. Both his tonal superiority and his equally unsurpassed control owed much to Hodges' own masterful approach to his art; similarly, Carney's basically melodic, lyrical approach to improvisation was very much akin to Hodge's.

Always a major asset with whomever he appeared, Carney's cavernous baritone sound has been majestically and helpfully present throughout a string of first-rate record dates with Hodges as leader (**Ellingtonia '56, Johnny Hodges & The Ellington Men, Hodge Podge** and **Love In Swingtime 1938/9**). Carney performed a similar role in other all-star sessions, including those put together by Lionel Hampton (♦) (**The Complete Lionel Hampton/Lionel Hampton's Best Records, Vols 2, 5**). Likewise, with regard to 'official' all-star studio get-togethers like **The Metronome All Stars/The Esquire All Stars** and **Benny Carter 1945 + The Metronome All-Stars**) or organized live events cast in a similar vein (**Second Esquire Concert, Vol 2**) the latter as member of the Ellington Orchestra.

But it is as the anchor member of the most famous of all jazz aggregations that Carney's name is forever linked. And for anyone remotely interested in his work, it is Harry Carney's inimitable renderings of such as **Sophisticated Lady, Prelude To A Kiss** or **La Plus Belle Africaine** which more readily come to mind – the solos, and of course, that unique, all-encompassing sound which for 45 years gave the Ellington ensemble such body and strength.

Recordings:
The Works Of Duke Ellington, Vols 1-18
(RCA Victor – France)
The Complete Duke Ellington, Vols 1-7 *(CBS – France)*
Duke Ellington, Ellington In Concert, Vol 2
(—/World Record Club)
Duke Ellington, The Beginning (1926-1928) *(MCA – Germany)*
Duke Ellington, Hot In Harlem (1928-1929) *(MCA – Germany)*
Duke Ellington, Rockin' In Rhythm (1929-1931)
(MCA – Germany)
Duke Ellington, The Golden Duke *(Prestige/Prestige)*
Duke Ellington, Toodle-oo
(—/Vocalion)
Duke Ellington, Masterpieces By Ellington *(CBS – Holland)*
Duke Ellington, Such Sweet Thunder
(Columbia/CBS – Realm)
Duke Ellington, His Most Important Second War Concert
(—/Saga Pan)
Duke Ellington, Black, Brown & Beige *(Ariston – Italy)*
Duke Ellington, The Duke 1940
(Jazz Society)
Various (Including Duke Ellington), The Greatest Jazz Concert In The World
(Pablo/Pablo)
Duke Ellington, The Great Paris Concert *(Atlantic/—)*
Duke Ellington, The English Concert
(United Artists/United Artists)
Duke Ellington's 70th Birthday Concert
(Solid State/United Artists)
Duke Ellington, Latin American Suite *(Fantasy/—)*
Duke Ellington's Third Sacred Concert, The Majesty Of God, As Performed In Westminster Abbey
(RCA Victor/RCA Victor)
Various, Great Ellingtonians Play A Tribute To Duke Ellington *(—/Double-Up)*
Johnny Hodges, Hodge Podge
(Columbia/CBS – Realm)
Everybody Knows Johnny Hodges *(Impulse/Impulse)*
Johnny Hodges & The Ellington Men *(Verve)*
Duke Ellington Meets Coleman Hawkins *(Impulse/—)*
Billie Holiday, The Golden Years, Vol 2 *(Columbia/CBS)*
Various, The 1938 Carnegie Hall Jazz Concert *(Columbia/CBS)*
Various, The Second Esquire Concert, Vol 2 *(—/Saga)*
Benny Carter 1945 + The Metronome All-Stars
(Queen Disc – Italy)
The Metronome All Stars/ The Esquire All Stars
(RCA Victor – France)
The Complete Lionel Hampton
(RCA Victor)/
Lionel Hampton's Best Records, Vols 2, 5
(RCA Victor – France)
Teddy Wilson & His All Stars
(Columbia/CBS)
Rex Stewart Memorial
(—/CBS – Realm)
Johnny Hodges, Ellingtonia '56
(Verve/Columbia – Clef)
Johnny Hodges, Love In Swingtime 1938-39
(Tax – Sweden)
Duke Ellington, Souvenirs
(Reprise)

Blues Before Sunrise (Columbia). Leroy Carr, a blues legend as singer, pianist and especially as composer.

Leroy Carr

Pianist-singer-composer Leroy Carr (born Nashville, Tennessee, 1905) and guitarist Scrapper Blackwell comprised one of the great blues partnerships of all times. Carr's thoughtful blues piano and gentle, sensitive vocalism was given extra impetus through Blackwell's more astringent guitar work: deservedly, the duo became one of the best-loved in the history of vocal-instrumental blues. Carr's lyrics are amongst the most poetic and moving of all blues writers; blues like **Midnight Hour Blues, My Woman's Gone Wrong, Southbound Blues** and **Blues Before Sunrise** (all **Blues Before Sunrise**) and **How Long, How Long** (his most famous composition) are exquisite examples of folk-blues writing and thus have enriched the genre considerably.

After Carr's parents separated, when he was a child, he and his eldest sister were brought by their mother to Indianapolis. Leroy Carr taught himself to play piano at home (unbeknownst to his mother). Ran away to join circus, then enlisted in Army (having lied about his age). Married at 17, father of a daughter following year; became involved in bootlegging liquor, and eventually served term of imprisonment at State Farm. After taking job at meat-packing firm, Carr became full-time pianist-singer.

His name became widely known after teaming up with Blackwell. Pair became popular act, both in-person and on record. Rapport between them – with Blackwell adjusting his basically plangent style to accommodate the gentler approach, instrumentally and vocally, of his partner – was never less than effective. Sometimes it was extraordinary. (As indeed were the drinking habits of both.)

How Long, How Long (1928) was Carr's first recording (for Vocalion); it achieved almost overnight success. Session was produced by Blackwell at an Indianapolis radio station. Record has been reported as having sold over a million copies. Carr was to record the number several times, best of these later versions being **How Long, How Long Blues No 2 (Rural Blues)**.

Amongst an impressive list of other Carr-Blackwell collaborations are **Naptown Blues, Bread Baker, What More Can I Do?** and **How About Me? (Naptown Blues: 1929-1934)**; **My Woman's Gone Wrong, Midnight Hour Blues, Hustler's Blues, Corn Likker**

Blues Before Sunrise (CBS) – edition as released in UK.

Blues and **Hurry Down Sunrise (Blues Before Sunrise)**.

As moving as anything he recorded during his all-too-brief career are **Six Cold Feet In The Ground, Big Four Blues** and **Rocks In My Bed (Leroy Carr)** all from 1935. But just as exceptional (perhaps even more so) are **It's Too Short, Big Four Blues** and **Shining Pistol (Blues Before Sunrise)** with Carr's piano and voice and Blackwell's guitar augmented by additional presence of Josh White, on second guitar. Leroy Carr's premature death, in 1935, from nephritis accentuated by alcoholism, was a major tragedy for the world of blues.

Recordings:
Leroy Carr, Naptown Blues (1929-1934) *(Yazoo)*
Leroy Carr, Blues Before Sunrise *(Columbia/CBS)*
Leroy Carr, Rural Blues *(RBF/—)*
Leroy Carr, The Country Blues *(RBF/—)*
Leroy Carr *(—/RCA Victor) (EP)*

Benny Carter

Bennett Lester 'Benny' Carter (born New York City, 1907) assuredly is one of the most accomplished, multi-talented musicians to grace the jazz scene, in any era: an excellent trumpet player and clarinettist, proficient on tenor-sax, piano; a peerless alto-saxophonist; and a writer of immense imagination and all-round skills. Only as an occasional singer can any one aspect of his talents be said to be less than average. Carter's skills as arranger and composer place him high amongst the leaders of this field, his writing for the saxophone section being virtually in a class of its own. Exemplified magnificently on two LPs **(Further Definitions** and **Additions To Further Definitions)** from late-1960s. For anyone remotely interested in, or questing for knowledge about, the career of this remarkable musician, then attention must be focused primarily on his contributions to the evolution in jazz of alto-saxophone. For Carter usually is ranked (correctly) alongside Johnny Hodges (♦), Charlie Parker (♦) and Ornette Coleman (♦) in most, if not all, all-time listings of the top men on this particular instrument. The jazz-lovers' dream, a record date featuring three of the four, was realized in 1953 **(The Charlie Parker Sides/The Parker Jam Session)** when Carter, Hodges and Parker stood shoulder-to-shoulder inside a recording studio for the first, and only, occasion, along with several other jazz giants or near-giants. Carter's personal influence on the alto-sax during the 1930s was at least equal to that of Hodges, and he remains one of a handful of altoists who came to the forefront during that decade successfully to incorporate some of Parker's unique vocabulary into his own musical make-up, without losing his own identity.

Basically, Carter's approach to the alto involves an almost unsurpassed elegance of tone, a most definite sympathy to rhythm (achieved with what has long since been recognized as typical Carter subtlety), and a clean, uncluttered, flowing, essentially melodic mode of improvisation. Technically, his work on alto (as indeed with the several other instruments he has used during his lengthy career) is beyond reproach. Coming from a musical family – both Cuban Bennett (1902–1965), an accomplished trumpeter, and Darnell Howard (1895–1966), a noted clarinettist-violinist, were cousins – Benny Carter started on piano, adding, in turn, trumpet and C-melody sax. Vital change to alto-sax took place after first important engagement, with band of June Clark (1924). Same year, first worked with Earl Hines (♦) on baritone-sax, after which his musical experiences (and education) really began to pick up: Horace Henderson (♦), James P. Johnson (♦), Duke Ellington (♦), Fletcher Henderson (♦) **(The Fletcher Henderson Story/The Fletcher Henderson Story, Vols 2, 3)**, Charlie Johnson **(Charlie Johnson & His Orchestra 1927-1929)** and Chick Webb (♦). He worked with several of these bands on more than one occasion.

1931: appointed musical director of McKinney's Cotton Pickers **(McKinney's Cotton Pickers, Vols 2-5)**, a position he held for about a year. Carter also occupied a similar role with pseudonymous Chocolate Dandies band **(The Chocolate Dandies)** between 1930–3, during which time he also worked with Don Redman (♦), and he added trumpet as a regular 'double', still finding time to write scores for several bands for whom he had worked before joining Johnson and others with whom he did not work as an instrumentalist. Between 1932–4 became leader of own bands **(Benny Carter – 1933/Ridin' In Rhythm)** and in latter year also arranged for Benny Goodman (♦). Then came stints with Willie Bryant **(Willie Bryant/Jimmy Lunceford & Their Orchestras)** before Carter emigrated – temporarily – to Europe (1935).

In Paris, Carter's first job was with Willie Lewis Orchestra **(Willie Lewis Orchestra)**, but by 1936 he had crossed the English Channel to take up appointment as staff arranger for Henry Hall Orchestra (although he was not allowed to play). Permission was given for Carter to play on London record date featuring contingent from Hall band **(Swingin' At Maida Vale)**. Tour of Scandinavia (1936) then Holland, France (1937–8), documented in part with recordings made in Holland **(Benny Carter With The Ramblers & His Orchestra)**. In March, 1938, recorded in Paris with cosmopolitan band, including legendary Django Reinhardt (♦) **(Django & His American Friends, Vol 2)** and music which resulted from same was of consistently high quality; similarly pleasing results had been obtained from another Paris session involving Carter and Reinhardt a year before **(Django & His American Friends, Vol 1)**, this time with Coleman Hawkins (♦) helping Carter to act as catalyst.

After second Carter-Reinhardt date, returned to US. Between 1939–41, led own big band, at various times featuring noted instrumentalists such as Tyree Glenn (♦), Jonah Jones (♦), Jimmy Archey, Sidney De Paris (♦), Sonny White, Doc Cheatham (♦), Benny Morton (♦), Eddie Heywood (♦), Joe Thomas, J. C. Heard and Coleman Hawkins. Despite fine contribu-

Above: Benny Carter, multi-instrumentalist, composer, arranger, bandleader – truly a Jazz Giant in every sense.

tions from sidemen on recordings by these bands **(Melancholy Benny** and **Benny Carter & His Orchestra: 1940-1941)** it is the playing of its leader and his arrangements and compositions which linger longest in the memory. Indeed, his writing for the saxes on **All Of Me**, from 1940 **(Benny Carter & His Orchestra: 1940-41)** still sounds remarkable today. During 1940, Carter also recorded under Hawkins' leadership **(The Big Sounds Of Coleman Hawkins & Chu Berry)** and with Billie Holiday (♦) **(God Bless The Child)** contributing sensitive clarinet obbligato and solo to **St Louis Blues** at the singer's October 15 record date. In New York, Carter fronted sextet that included Dizzy Gillespie (♦) and Jimmy Hamilton (♦). (Carter had written superior arrangements for Cab Calloway (♦) Orchestra, of which Gillespie was then member, 1940.)

1943: moved to West Coast. In Hollywood, put together another big band which included some up-and-coming talent, like Max Roach (♦), Henry Coker, Al Grey, J. J. Johnson (♦), Joe Albany (♦), Porter Kilbert, Curley Russell. Once again, recordings **(Big Band Bounce** and **Live Sessions 1943/1945)** do reasonable justice to uniformly fine music produced by Carter and sidemen, further amplified by superior big-band music to be found within **Benny Carter 1945 + The Metronome All-Stars**. 1945: made permanent home in Hollywood. Throughout much of the late-1940s/early-1950s, live appearances drastically reduced. This was because he was to spend much time in Hollywood writing music for various films. Also appeared on screen, as himself, in several films, including *The Snows of Kilimanjaro, Stormy Weather, As Thousands Cheer* and *Clash By Night*. During 1950s, occasionally put together own bands, including big-band residency in Los Angeles in 1955; same year he assisted with musical score for *The Benny Goodman Story*. (Did likewise for *The Five Pennies*, as well as for highly-successful TV series *M-Squad*.)

Carter's interrupted recording career picked up somewhat when, in 1952, Norman Granz signed him to record series of albums for his Clef/Norgran labels **(The Formidable Benny Carter, New Jazz Sounds, etc)**. For Granz, he also participated in recordings with other top-name artists, including the Parker-Hodges-Carter-&-Co. session noted pre-

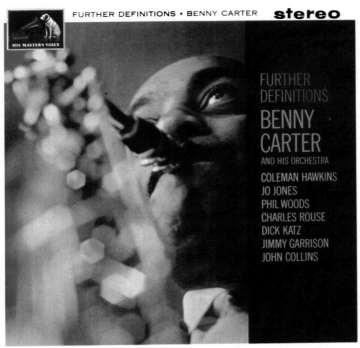

FURTHER
DEFINITIONS

BENNY
CARTER
AND HIS ORCHESTRA

COLEMAN HAWKINS
JO JONES
PHIL WOODS
CHARLES ROUSE
DICK KATZ
JIMMY GARRISON
JOHN COLLINS

Further Definitions (Impulse). Benny Carter's
compositions for saxes are as distinctive as
they are memorable.

viously, and a rewarding all-star date in 1953 which resulted in **Jam Session, Nos 2, 3.** Latter events were nothing new to Benny Carter. For instance, he had been meaningful contributor to three of Lionel Hampton's classic all-star dates of 1938–9 **(The Complete Lionel Hampton/Lionel Hampton's Best Records, Vols 2, 3, 5, 6)** and further proved his worth in this kind of organized jam session situation by taking solo honors during a similarly styled Capitol record date in 1955 **(Session At Midnight).** And that Carter's alto had lost none of its opulence or combative spirit during live performance was demonstrated most admirably when he toured for Granz with Jazz At The Philharmonic in 1953 **(JATP In Tokyo).** His **Flamingo** feature, in Ballad Medley portion of programme, was as graceful, elegant as ever; alongside his peers (eg Webster, Bill Harris, Eldridge, Willie Smith) his impassioned playing on the more rhythmic numbers lost nothing in comparison; and he proved during same tour probably best sax player to work with Gene Krupa (♦) Trio. Carter, at 47, reserved some of his greatest improvisations for another piano-sax-drums session (this one inside the studio) a year later. This time Carter was in company of drummer Louis Bellson (♦) and the jazz pianists' pianist, Art Tatum (♦). Never for one

moment overawed by the extravagancies of Tatum's keyboard style, Carter produced, even by his own high standards, astonishingly good solos throughout, especially on **Blues In B Flat, Undecided, Makin' Whoopee'** and his own **I'm Left With The Blues In My Heart.** That Carter could continue to co-exist in most kinds of jazz company was proved by a thoroughly enjoyable record date for Contemporary in late-1950s **(Benny Carter: Jazz Giant)** with Carter's undiminished artistry en rapport with sympathetic playing of Ben Webster, Barney Kessel (♦), Frank Rosolino, Jimmie Rowles (or André Previn), Leroy Vinnegar and Shelly Manne. Subsequent Contemporary session **(Swingin' The 20's)** with Vinnegar and Manne again present was not as successful because special guest Earl Hines (♦), whilst soloing admirably enough, seemed intent on going his own way elsewhere. Apart from his work on alto and trumpet, Carter also played piano on some tracks. Carter cut three LPs for United Artists between 1959–62, best of these being **The Benny Carter Jazz Calendar** with his deft, distinctive touch as writer being much in evidence. And as well as Carter and fellow saxists Hawkins, Charlie Rouse and Phil Woods (♦) playing, collectively and alone, it was Carter's inventive, fresh-sounding scores for **Further Definitions** that took pride of place at a '61 recording session, including a marvellous re-write for saxes of Hawkins' immortal **Body & Soul** solo from '39. Follow-up LP, **Additions To Further Definitions,** had two different saxes-with-rhythm line-ups, and although not as comprehensively successful as its successor, it did contain much Carter-inspired music-making, and more glorious writing for the reeds. Since early-1960s, Benny Carter has been, in turn, active and semi-active as a player. Has toured with JATP on several occasions **(Jazz At The Philharmonic In Europe, Vols 1, 3 (1960)** and **The Greatest Jazz Concert In The World (1967))** and more recently, **JATP At The Montreux Jazz Festival 1975.** Has also made numerous studio recordings with variety of musicians, but all of a similar free-swinging bent as of previous years. These have included musicians of the calibre of Barney Bigard (♦) and Ben Webster **(BBB & Co),** Milt Jackson and Joe Pass (♦) **(The King),** Dizzy Gillespie and Tommy Flanagan **(Carter, Gillespie, Inc)** and Count Basie, Eddie 'Lockjaw' Davis (♦) and Clark Terry (♦) **(Basie Jam No 2).** For a short period, in 1968, Carter lent his alto-sax sound to the Duke Ellington (♦) Orchestra. Seven years before he had performed a similar function with Count Basie, and in November, '60 had provided the Basie band with a collection of compositions/arrangements **(Kansas City Suite)** which ranked with anything it has been called upon to play during past 25 years. Carter's mid-1970s activities, rather than decreasing, appear to have expanded from previous decade. At turned 70, this incredibly well-preserved musician is as unquenchably prolific and musically outstanding as at any comparable period of a truly distinguished career.

Recordings:
Charlie Johnson-Lloyd Scott-Cecil Scott *(RCA Victor – France)*
McKinney's Cotton Pickers, Vols 2-5 (1928-1931)
(*RCA Victor – France*)
The Chocolate Dandies *(—/Parlophone)*
The Fletcher Henderson Story *(Columbia)/*
The Fletcher Henderson Story, Vols 2, 3 *(CBS)*
Benny Carter - 1933 *(Prestige)/*
Various, Ridin' In Rhythm *(World Records)*
Spike Hughes & His All-American Orchestra *(London/Ace of Clubs)*
Willie Bryant/(Jimmie Lunceford) & Their Orchestras *(Bluebird/—)*
Willie Lewis *(Pirate – Sweden)*
Benny Carter, Swingin' At Maida Vale *(—/Ace of Clubs)*
Benny Carter With The Ramblers & His Orchestra
(*—/Decca – France*)
Django Reinhardt & The American Jazz Giants *(Prestige)/*
Django & His American Friends, Vols 1, 2 *(HMV)*
The Complete Lionel Hampton *(Bluebird)/*
Lionel Hampton's Best Records, Vols 2, 3, 5, 6 *(RCA Victor – France)*
Coleman Hawkins/Roy Eldridge, Hawk & Roy *(Phoenix)*
Ethel Waters (1938-1941) *(RCA Victor – France)*
The Big Sounds Of Coleman Hawkins & (Chu Berry) *(—/London)*
Benny Carter, Melancholy Benny *(Tax – Sweden)*
Benny Carter, & His Orchestra: 1940-41 *(RCA Victor – France)*
Billie Holiday, God Bless The Child *(Columbia/CBS)*
Benny Carter, Big Band Bounce *(Capitol/Capitol – Holland)*
Benny Carter 1945 + The Metronome All-Stars *(Queen Disc – Italy)*
The Formidable Benny Carter *(Norgran/Columbia – Clef)*
Benny Carter, New Jazz Sounds *(Verve/Columbia – Clef)*
Various, The Charlie Parker Sides *(Verve/*
The Parker Jam Sessions *(Verve)*
Various, Jam Session, Nos 2, 3 *(Verve/Columbia – Clef)*
Various, J.A.T.P. In Tokyo *(Pablo/Pablo)*
Various, The Tatum Group Masterpieces *(Pablo/Pablo)*
Various, Session At Midnight *(Capitol/Capitol)*
Benny Carter: Jazz Giant *(Contemporary/Vogue – Contemporary)*
Benny Carter/Earl Hines, Swingin' The 20's
(*Contemporary/Vogue – Contemporary*)
The Benny Carter Jazz Calendar *(United Artists/United Artists)*
Count Basie, Kansas City Suite *(Roulette/Columbia)*
Benny Carter, Further Definitions *(Impulse/Impulse)*
Benny Carter, Additions To Further Definitions *(Impulse/HMV)*
Benny Carter/Barney Bigard/Ben Webster, BBB & Co.
(*Prestige – Swingville/Xtra*)
Various, The Greatest Jazz Concert In The World *(Pablo/Pablo)*
Benny Carter, The King *(Pablo/Pablo)*
Benny Carter/Dizzy Gillespie, Carter, Gillespie, Inc.
(*Pablo/Pablo*)
Montreux '77: Benny Carter 4 *(Pablo Live/Pablo Live)*
Count Basie, Basie Jam No. 2 *(Pablo/Pablo)*

BENNY CARTER AND HIS ORCHESTRA 1939/40
MELANCHOLY
BENNY

Melancholy Benny (Tax, Sweden). Between 1939 and 1940
(the date of these tracks), Benny Carter was leader of a fine
big band.

Wayman Carver

Wayman Alexander Carver (born Portsmouth, Virginia, 1905) will be remembered, if for no other reason than he was first musician to make extensive use of flute as solo instrument within the context of jazz, at time when its use, even as an addition to the usual big-band armoury of reeds, was uncommon.

Carver, an accomplished musician who also played saxophone and clarinet and was a noteworthy composer, left for New York at beginning of 1930s after leading own band and touring with J. Neal Montgomery's Collegiate Ramblers. Was reliable section man, an occasional soloist for, in sequence, Elmer Snowden (1931-2), Benny Carter (♦) (1933-4) and Chick Webb (♦) (1934-40). It was whilst with Webb that Carver established his reputation as jazz flute soloist.

His own favourite solo with Webb was Sweet Sue (Strictly Jive 1936-1938) and other fine examples of Carver's playing with same band are Down Home Rag (A Legend 1929-1936), I Got Rhythm and Hallelujah (both King Of The Savoy 1937-1939); former featuring Little Chicks, Webb's own band-within-the-band. Apart from recording with King Oliver (♦)/Dave Nelson band, in 1931 (King Oliver/Dave Nelson, Vol 3 (1929-1931) Carver's all-round abilities were recognized by Englishman Spike Hughes, who used his saxophone-flute playing for series of remarkable recordings made in '33, mostly as section man but also as flute soloist on How Come You Do Me Like You Do? and Sweet Sue, Just You (Spike Hughes & His All American Orchestra). Carver stayed with Webb when leader died and Ella Fitzgerald (♦) took over leadership. After leaving music business completely in 1940, returned following year to work with the singer. Ceased to be active full-time player for second – and final – time, becoming teacher, arranger. Was appointed Professor of Music at Clark College, Atlanta, Georgia. He died in 1967.

Recordings:
Chick Webb, A Legend (1929-1936) (MCA – Germany)
Chick Webb, King Of The Savoy (1937-1939) (MCA – Germany)
Chick Webb, Strictly Jive (1936-1938) (MCA – Germany)
Ella Fitzgerald/Chick Webb, Ella Swings The Band (1936-1939) (MCA – Germany)
Various (Including Chick Webb), Classics Of The Swing Years: The Treasury Of Golden Swing (—/Polydor)
King Oliver/Dave Nelson, Vol 3 (1929-1931) (RCA Victor – France)
Spike Hughes & His All American Orchestra (London/Ace of Clubs)

Big Sid Catlett

With Jo Jones (♦) and Davey Tough (♦), Sidney 'Big Sid' Catlett (born Evansville, Indiana, 1910)

was the finest drummer of the 1930s – and a frightening good drummer throughout the following decade.

An immensely powerful player with extraordinary flexibility – he could move from a thundering snare-drum press roll to a whispering side-drum comment in an instant – Catlett seemed at ease in all kinds of jazz company, big-band or small-group, ancient or modern. His career was as colorful as his life, his drumming being heard in the company of the best musicians available, including Louis Armstrong (♦), Charlie Parker (♦), Fletcher Henderson (♦), Benny Goodman (♦), Benny Carter (♦), Sidney Bechet (♦), Don Redman (♦) and, very briefly, Duke Ellington (♦) in 1945. As youngster, Catlett played piano, drums (taught the rudiments of drumming in Chicago, where his family had moved after he was born) and broke into music business with Darnell Howard (1928).

Amongst other leaders with whom he worked during early part of his career: Elmer Snowden, Benny Carter (Benny Carter - 1933/Ridin' In Rhythm), Rex Stewart, Spike Hughes (Spike Hughes & His All American Orchestra), Eddie Condon (♦) and Bud Freeman (♦) (Home Cooking). Recorded as member of the Chocolate Dandies (1933), under direction of Carter (The Chocolate Dandies) and worked also for Don Redman (Don Redman) the Dandies' previous musical director. Worked with other lesser-known bands, including several in Chicago, to which city he moved, again, in 1934. Joined Fletcher Henderson for period of just over six months (The Fletcher Henderson Story/The Fletcher Henderson Story, Vol 4) after which he became member of the Don Redman orchestra (1936-8).

Took part in famous Blues In C Sharp Minor recording session (1936) under leadership of Teddy Wilson (♦) (Teddy Wilson & His All Stars). Gave Louis Armstrong the kind of inspiring drumming he rarely received, before or afterwards, during his three main periods with various Armstrong bands: 1938-41, 1941-2 (Swing That Music and Complete Recorded Works 1935-1945) and 1947-9 (Satchmo's Greatest, Vols 4, 5, 6, Satchmo At Symphony Hall and Louis Armstrong, Vol 1). Louis Armstrong, Vol 3 covers the period 1939-49, in relation to concerts and broadcasts in which Catlett was an integral part of respective ensembles.

Catlett's relationship with Goodman has been reported as not being entirely amicable. During an on-off working relationship in '41, his drumming sparked band dynamically (Benny Goodman Plays Solid Gold Instrumental Hits). After approximately one-and-a-half years with Teddy Wilson (♦), became key figure in some of best jazz to be heard on 52nd Street. Jammed regularly with numerous other bands as well as leading own (including record dates). Participated in 1939 Blue Note session which produced Bechet's classic Summertime (Sidney Bechet Jazz Classics, Vol 1), also for same label in '39 recorded with Bechet, Frankie Newton (♦) (Sidney Bechet Jazz Classics, Vol 2). Same year, took

part in one of Lionel Hampton's (♦) celebrated jam-sessions (Henry 'Red' Allen All Stars, Vol 4: 1939-1957), his explosive accents and rock-steady beat inspiring Hampton, Red Allen (♦), Charlie Christian (♦), et al, to impressive heights of excitement and creation.

Involved in another splendid all-star gathering – concert at Metropolitan Opera House, NYC 1945, featuring musicians selected by board of experts of Esquire Magazine, published in its initial year book. Sound balance is not perfect, but it is instructive to hear Catlett catering for individual requirements of such as Armstrong, Hampton, Art Tatum (♦), Red Norvo (♦), and Billie Holiday (♦). Month later, performed like task in studio band fronted by Albert Ammons (♦) (Commodore Jazz, Vol 1) and including Don Byas (♦) and Vic Dickenson (♦). Ditto in respect of two productive dates under Coleman Hawkins' (♦) name (Swing! and Cattin'). From time to time, recorded with own bands.

In March 1944 led tightly-integrated quartet, featuring expressive tenor from Ben Webster (♦) (Sax Scene). The following January, with another top tenorman present, Illinois Jacquet (♦), recorded quartet of jumping tracks for Capitol (Swing Exercise). Nine months later, with Hawkins again principal soloist, led seven-piece unit through four Catlett originals, best of which is Before Long (52nd Street, Vol 1). Webster, in turn, used Catlett's incisive, sometimes tempestuous, drumming to good advantage in rewarding May 1946 session (The Big Three) with Catlett especially stimulating on Blues For Mr Brim and Dark Corners..

Catlett took part in two further important recording sessions, both co-featuring Sidney Bechet and Mezz Mezzrow (The Prodigious Sidney Bechet-Mezz Mezzrow Quintet & Septet). Here again, he fitted in with ease, contributing greatly to handsome drive imparted by rhythm section, and working well in tandem with George 'Pops' Foster's bass.

Although it could never be said that 'Big Sid' was a Bebop drummer per se, his sheer versatility allowed him to play alongside out-and-out Beboppers without sounding, like other drummers of his age, too clumsy and out-of-place. Though never consciously aping the Clarke (♦)-Roach (♦)-Blakey (♦)-Haynes (♦) school of drumming, and still retaining a basically Swing-period style, fitted easily into place when called upon to take part in a 1945 record date featuring Dizzy Gillespie (♦), Charlie Parker (♦) (Dizzy Gillespie: The Small Groups: 1945-1946).

Catlett, with his sharp, green-check suits, extrovert personality and gallery-fetching drumming, incorporated within his playing all the finest, most exciting elements of the finest of jazz percussion up until the arrival of so-called modern jazz. Even then, his influence on younger drummers continued to be felt; nowhere more obvious is that influence than in the playing of Philly Joe Jones, an acknowledged devotee of Catlett. Forced to quit touring because of illness (1949), became resident drummer at Chicago club, Jazz Ltd, but worked for

Eddie Condon (♦) in New York, and took part in ill-fated final concert by John Kirby (♦) band. Collapsed and died from heart attack, Chicago, 1951, following pneumonia at beginning of same year.

Recordings:
Benny Carter - 1933 (Prestige)/ Various, Ridin' In Rhythm (World Records)
Spike Hughes & His All American Orchestra (London/Ace of Clubs)
The Chocolate Dandies (—/Parlophone)
Bud Freeman, Home Cooking (Tax – Sweden)
Don Redman (CBS – Realm)
Teddy Wilson & His All Stars (Columbia/CBS)
The Fletcher Henderson Story (Columbia)
The Fletcher Henderson Story, Vol 4 (CBS)
Sidney Bechet Jazz Classics, Vol 1, 2 (Blue Note)
Henry 'Red' Allen, Vol 4 (1939-1957) (RCA Victor – France)
Various, Blue Note's Three Decades Of Jazz (1939-1949), Vol 1 (Blue Note)
Louis Armstrong, Swing That Music (Decca/Coral)
Benny Goodman Plays Solid Gold Instrumental Hits (Columbia/CBS)
Louis Armstrong, Satchmo's Greatest, Vols 4, 5, 6 (RCA Victor – France)
Various, The First Esquire Concert, Vol 1 (—/Saga)
Various, Commodore Jazz, Vol 1 (—/London)
Coleman Hawkins, Swing! (—/Fontana)
Coleman Hawkins, Cattin' (—/Fontana)
Various, Sax Scene (—/London)
Various, Swing Exercise (Capitol/Capitol – Holland)
The Prodigious Sidney Bechet - Mezz Mezzrow Quintet & Septet (Festival – France)
Dizzy Gillespie: The Small Groups (1945-1946) (Phoenix)
Various, 52nd Street, Vol 1 (Onyx/Polydor)
Various, The Big Three (Bob Thiele Music/RCA Victor)
Louis Armstrong, Vols 1, 3 (—/Saga)
Louis Armstrong, Satchmo At Symphony Hall (Decca/Coral)
Lester Young, Lester Leaps Again! (EmArcy/Fontana)

Serge Chaloff

Born 1923 in Boston, died 1957, baritone saxophonist Serge Chaloff's father and mother were both classical musicians. The best of the Bebop baritones, Chaloff worked with the bands of Georgie Auld and Jimmy Dorsey before joining Woody Herman in 1947. Chaloff is the second soloist on The Four Brothers (The Best Of Woody Herman) and featured on The Goof And I. Disgracefully, most of his best recordings have been deleted, but four tracks with alternate takes (Brothers & Other Mothers) give an idea of his agility on the big horn and his highly original turn of phrase.

Recordings:
The Best Of Woody Herman (—/CBS)
Brothers & Other Mothers

(Savoy/Savoy)
Blue Serge (Capitol/Capitol)

Ray Charles

The influence of Ray Charles on a broad spectrum of popular music during past 20-odd years has been almost immeasurable. Single-handed he was responsible (from middle-to-late-1950s period) in creating huge market for basically black soul music; his concerts, records attracted vast audiences – white and black – and did much in helping bring together various pop music forms.

Charles' own musical mixture comprises various elements of blues, R&B, gospel, jazz and pop. Gospel stems from his own religious (Baptist) upbringing and his participation in church music from very young age. As youngster, Charles also listened to jazz, blues, C&W and pop.

Amongst lengthy list of some who have helped shape his unique style can be numbered the following: Washboard Sam, Sonny Boy Williamson, Mahalia Jackson, Bud Powell (♦), Joe Turner (♦) (the singer), Muddy Waters (♦), Charles Brown, Hank Williams, Count Basie (♦), and Nat Cole (♦) (both as singer and pianist).

Ray Charles Robinson (born Albany, Georgia, 1932) became totally blind at six, yet taught himself to play piano, organ, alto-saxophone, clarinet, trumpet. Also learned to read and write music and make own arrangements (thanks to Braille) during his time at Florida school for deaf and blind. Left school to join danceband in mid-teens. Joined blues band of Lowell Fulsom (for a year), during which time he developed, vocally and pianistically. Played Apollo, alone, put together group to accompany singer Ruth Brown, then returned to Seattle where he had moved after leaving the dance-band. Put together another band for residency (it was sometimes known as Maxim Trio) and band achieved distinction of being first all-black unit to have sponsored TV show in Pacific Northwest.

Previously, in Seattle, Charles had formed a trio modelled closely on celebrated King Cole Trio, with leader's vocals often cast very much in Cole vein (in those days his style varied between Cole and Charles Brown), and between 1949–51 had recorded for Swing-time **(Ray Charles Blues)**. Recorded around 60 sides for the label, mostly unremarkable. With Swingtime's fortunes fading, Atlantic Records paid $2,500 for Charles' contract (1952).

Transformation from average-to-good R&B-based singer-pianist-composer was startling. By end of 1950s, Charles had notched up a string of huge-selling record hits, starting with **It Should've Been Me** (1953), and continuing with **I Got A Woman, Hallelujah, I Love Her So, A Fool For You, Drown In My Own Tears, Yes Indeed, Swanee River Rock, Night Time Is The Right Time, What'd I Say, Just For A Thrill** and **Don't Let The Sun Catch You Cryin'** (A 25th Anniversary In Show Business Salute To Ray Charles). Each number delivered with maximum of emotional impact, with Charles' impassioned singing sometimes ascending to falsetto

Above: 'The Genius' – that's the appellation long ago accorded Ray Charles, giant of blues, R&B and jazz . . .

range, and supported by own gospel-jazz piano and a rough, exciting big band riffing furiously behind him.

Whilst recordings demonstrated just how genuinely exciting Ray Charles could be, it was with his in-person appearances that conclusive judgments could be made. The combination of the Charles voice and piano, a basic-sounding rhythm section, hard-hitting band and, from 1957 onwards, a Gospel-based vocal group The Raelettes, tended to make his concerts seem reminiscent of a black church service, with Charles and vocal and band engaged in frantic call-and-response format, with totally involved audience adding its own presence in manner of gospel congregation.

During his stay with Atlantic Charles' jazz proclivities were given full reign in albums specifically designed to show off this side of his talents. Most notable of these are a brace of non-vocal albums **(Soul Brothers** and **Soul Meeting)**, both of which conjoin Charles' instrumental talents (as accomplished pianist, and average, Parker-influenced, weak-toned altoist) with the consummate vibraharp artistry of Milt Jackson. Also on Atlantic is **The Great Ray Charles**, another all-instrumental LP, with Charles' piano accompanied by six-piece band, arranged by Quincy Jones and Ernie Wilkins, apart from two fine trio tracks **(Black Coffee** and **Sweet Sixteen Bars)** which, perhaps more than most of his recordings, admirably define Charles' gospel-based, bop-tinged jazz piano style.

Moving to ABC Paramount (1959), Charles' very first single release (an updating of **Georgia On My Mind)** was a hit, the first of numerous others for the label **(25th Anniversary In Show Business Salute To Ray Charles)** to feature, along with more conventional jazz/

blues instrumentation, strings. Arranger for **Georgia** was Ralph Burns.

Over the years Charles has worked with numerous other top-rated jazz writers, including Marty Paich, Gerald Wilson, Gil Fuller, Quincy Jones and Ernie Wilkins. Paich supplied string scores for **Ray Charles & Betty Carter**, a superb, often moving collaboration between two artists both deserving to be called jazz singers, here framed in semi-jazz setting. The Charles-Carter idea was repeated three years after the first, and in many ways best, recording date ('61). After **Georgia** came more ABC hits: **Unchain My Heart, Hit The Road, Jack, One Mint Julep, I Can't Stop Loving You, You Are My Sunshine, Cryin' Time, Busted,** etc.

By this time he was featuring an ever-wider variety of material, including two award-winning albums in which he sang C&W songs **(Modern Sounds In Country & Western, Vols 1, 2** and **Together Again: Country & Western Meets Rhythm & Blues)** his own way. Better by far, though, were LPs like **Genius + Soul = Jazz** wherein Charles (on organ, and singing only on two tracks) is brought together with the Count Basie orchestra (circa 1960), minus its leader, with superior charts from Jones and Burns.

During latter part of 1960s, and through until the present, Charles has continued to tour with own big band and singers. Left ABC Paramount to start own label (Cross-over), which subsequently re-issued much of the Atlantic–ABC Paramount material.

Charles' health not at its best during end of last decade, helped not at all by addiction to heroin, a situation which led, at one period, to a jail sentence during which time he successfully took a cure. There is no doubt Ray Charles

remains a vital and compelling performer, a genuine talent of real importance and continuing influence. In truth, though, there have been many occasions during past decade when his music appears to have been stylized, and a series of inferior repetitions of the past. As a recording artist, for instance, he has been unable to recapture his almost magical appeal of the 1950s/1960s; and his concert appearances sometimes have given the impression of someone going through the motions, his heart not always completely into his music. There are occasions still when the real Ray Charles is revealed, once again, as the musically charismatic personality who can put other rivals

What'd I Say (Atlantic) – Ray Charles at his very best.

completely in the shade, seemingly without really trying.

Aural reference to Charles' live recordings **(Ray Charles Live - The Great Concerts, Ray Charles At Newport** and **Genius Live In Concert)** give more than adequate proof of his in-person greatness in the past. And just how much his very presence can add extra fuel to an already raging inferno can be judged from his impromptu appearance (he was already in the audience, before being called onstage) during a magnificent Aretha Franklin concert – **Live At Fillmore West.**

Recordings:
Ray Charles, Ray Charles Blues
(—/Ember)
The Best Of Ray Charles
(Atlantic/Atlantic)
The Genius Of Ray Charles
(Atlantic/Atlantic)
Ray Charles, What'd I Say
(Atlantic/Atlantic)
A 25th Anniversary Show Business Salute To Ray Charles (Atlantic/Atlantic)
Ray Charles At Newport
(Atlantic/Atlantic)
Ray Charles/Milt Jackson, Soul Brothers (Atlantic/Atlantic)
Ray Charles/Milt Jackson, Soul Meeting (Atlantic/Atlantic)
Ray Charles Live – The Great Concerts (Atlantic/—)
Ray Charles, Genius + Soul = Jazz (Impulse/HMV)
The Great Ray Charles
(Atlantic/London)
Ray Charles, The Genius After Hours (Atlantic/London)
Ray Charles, Modern Sounds In Country & Western, Vols 1, 2 (ABC-Paramount/HMV)
Ray Charles & Betty Carter
(ABC-Paramount/
Pathe Marconi – France)
Ray Charles, Genius Live In Concert
(ABC-Paramount/Blues Way)
Ray Charles Sings The Blues

(Atlantic)
Ray Charles, Sweet & Sour
(ABC-Paramount/—)
Ray Charles, The World Of Ray Charles, Vols 1, 2
(Crossover/London)
Focus On Ray Charles
(Crossover/London)
Ray Charles, Message To The People (Renaissance/Probe)

Doc Cheatham

For more than 50 years, Adolphus Anthony 'Doc' Cheatham (born Nashville, Tennessee, 1905) has been a trumpet player of the first order, an accomplished soloist as well as a top-class lead, without ever achieving the kind of recognition his talents most certainly deserve. To some extent, Cheatham has helped to foster the illusion that, as a soloist at least, his is a meager talent. And a succession of bandleaders often have tended to agree by utilizing his not inconsiderable services either as lead trumpeter only, or in another non-solo capacity within the brass section.

Cheatham, taught trumpet and music theory by Prof. N. C. Davis, in his home town, has been associated with mostly big bands. For example, amongst others, he worked in the 1920s with large-size outfits led by Marion Hardy (his first job as a professional),

Albert Wynn, Wilbur De Paris (♦) and Chick Webb (♦).

In following decade, Cheatham's trumpet was heard in such diverse outfits as McKinney's Cotton Pickers **(McKinney's Cotton Pickers, Vol 5: 1930-31)**, Cab Calloway (♦) **(Cab Calloway & His Orchestra 1933-1934** and **16 Cab Calloway Classics)** and Teddy Wilson (♦) **(Teddy Wilson & His Big Band 1939-1940).** Spent the years 1933–9 with Calloway, making his second trip to Europe with that band (in '34) – his first had taken place in 1929, as member of Sam Wooding Band.

First gig of 1940s was with Benny Carter (♦), with whom he recorded **My Favourite Blues (Benny Carter & His Orchestra: 1940-41),** one of his infrequent solos, but one which emphasizes his elegant, poised and warm style.

Worked on record, for Commodore, as part of band backing

Billie Holiday (♦) at famous 1944 date **(The 'Commodore' Days).** Leader at that session was Eddie Heywood (♦), for whom Cheatham was then playing trumpet **(Begin The Beguine).** (Prior to Heywood, Cheatham had worked with Fletcher Henderson (♦) and Teddy Hill.) Between 1952–5 worked with another fine small combo, led by Vic Dickenson (♦).

Cheatham's reputation was internationalized when he made two further overseas trips, this time as member of the Wilbur De Paris New Orleans Band; first, in 1957, to Africa then, in '60, to Europe. In between these tours, came another European jaunt (in 1958) with pianist Sammy Price (♦). Revisited African continent in 1960, touring with Herbie Mann's band. Member of the Benny Goodman (♦) Quintet/Sextet (1966–7). His trumpet regularly featured on showcase items like **When Sunny Gets Blue, I Can't Get Started** and **These Foolish Things.** Yet another trip to Europe – this time to Belgium – in August, '66, also with Goodman, to appear at Comblain-la-Tour Jazz Festival, live and on television. Same year was back in Europe with jazz package titled Top Brass, featuring several of the finest brassmen extant.

Below: Adolphus Anthony 'Doc' Cheatham, for over 50 years an accomplished (oft-neglected) horn player.

From early-1950s through 1960s, worked regularly in Afro-Cuban-styled bands, a genre in which he obviously feels at ease. The bands include: Marcelino Guerra, Perez Prado and Machito (various occasions, including Japanese tour in 1956).

During last decade, has continued to do most of the things he had performed so impeccably in the previous decades – recording (including jazz and session work), TV, in big band and small groups alike. A most dependable sideman, whose own individual talents have been showcased thoroughly on one occasion only – a two-LP collection **(Adolphus 'Doc' Cheatham)** – and in sympathetic quartet setting, he produces consistently fine playing throughout. Nothing startling or innovative: just honest-to-goodness professional trumpet work, showing his clarity of tone and superior con-

trol, not to mention a deceptively straightforward brand of swing. His superior ballad playing (eg **This Is All I Ask** and **That's All)** is complemented admirably by a selection of impressive up-tempo performances, all of which demonstrates that, as a soloist, Doc Cheatham has been lamentably and unforgivingly neglected during an otherwise wholly distinguished career. Perhaps the one other album which does full justice to his talents is **Shorty & Doc,** a delightfully unpretentious, easy-swinging set recorded in 1961, in company of another drastically underrated trumpet man, Harold 'Shorty' Baker (♦). During his career, Cheatham has been heard on record also with Ma Rainey (♦), Max Kaminsky(♦), Pee Wee Russell (♦), and Captain John Handy.

Recordings:
McKinney's Cotton Pickers, Vol 5 (1930-1931)
(RCA Victor – France)
Cab Calloway & His Orchestra 1933-1934
(RCA Victor – Germany)
Teddy Wilson & His Big Band 1939-40 (Tax – Sweden)
Eddie Heywood, Begin The Beguine (Mainstream/Fontana)
Wilbur DeParis, That's A Plenty (Atlantic/London)
Wilbur DeParis, The Wild Jazz Age (Atlantic/London)
Juanita Hall Sings The Blues
(Counterpoint/Society)
Shorty Baker/Doc Cheatham, Shorty & Doc
(Prestige – Swingville/—)
Billie Holiday, Vol 1
(—/SagaPan)
Adolphus 'Doc' Cheatham
(Jezebel/—)
Earl Hines, Swingin' Away
(—/Black Lion)
Doc & Sammy (Sackville/—)
Hey Doc!
(Black & Blue – France)
Buddy Tate, Jive At Five
(Mahogany/—)
Sammy Price Five
(Black & Blue – France)

Don Cherry

Born in Oklahoma City, 1936, the trumpeter played with orthodox groups before meeting Ornette Coleman in 1956, and falling completely under the influence of the altoist's revolutionary concepts. Cherry is present on all the classic Atlantics, the most compatible foil that the leader ever found. There are parallels for the sorcerer's apprentice role with the young Miles Davis in Charlie Parker's group; both trumpeters are tentative and at their best when restricting their ideas to ranges they can handle; both are most effective as an astringent contrast to their volcanic leaders. Cherry's sound on pocket trumpet is thin, his ideas fragmented and often inconclusive, and the impression is of a neurotic Boy Scout. Nevertheless, within the context of the music, his understanding of his leader's world is complete – contrapuntal numbers like **Mapa (Ornette On Tenor)** show his responsiveness. **Peace (Shape Of Jazz To Come)** displays his growing variety of method, and both **Face Of The Bass (Change Of The Century** and **WRU (Ornette!)** give him a chance to express himself before

the leader has mapped out the melodic possibilities. Expressive but rhythmically weak, Cherry's early work is overshadowed by both Ornette and his own subsequent development.

Cherry left the group and tried out the lessons he had learned with a variety of giants. Sessions with Coltrane **(The Avant-garde)** and Rollins **(Our Man In Jazz)** followed, both proving that Cherry's concept was both lighter and more radical. **Cherryco,** for example, finds Coltrane unable to utilize the theme without resort to the chord changes. The collaboration with tenorist Albert Ayler proved more suitable, although the dense collective **New York Eye And Ear Control** lacks the coherence of **Free Jazz.** The album that they made together in Copenhagen, 1964 **(Vibrations)** catches both players at their best.

Lessons in organizing the New York Contemporary Five, members including Archie Shepp and altoist John Tchicai, between 1963–4, stood Cherry in good stead when he assembled his own group. Now based in Europe, he chose the young Argentinian tenorist, Leandro 'Gato' Barbieri, Henry Grimes on bass and Ed Blackwell drums. The two albums for Blue

Above: Don Cherry, exponent of world music. After leaving Ornette, extensive travel altered his ambitions.

Note **(Complete Communion** and **Symphony For Improvisers)** are classics of the new music, rich in texture and melodic invention, offering a group empathy that holds the vast range of moods together. By now, Cherry possessed a formidable technique, and his lyrical gifts had been broadened by his travels and exposure to other ethnic musics. As a leader, shaping the direction of the group, his identity is as strongly imprinted as Ornette's was back in the old quartet days. His soloing over the massive Jazz Composers' Orchestra **(The Jazz Composers' Orchestra)** is spikily assured and attacking. However, increasingly there were signs that Cherry's fascination with other folk forms was leading him away from jazz; inevitable, perhaps, for non-harmonic new music has more in common with non-European idioms. The heavy emphasis on flutes and percussion make for an Eastern experience **(Eternal Rhythm)** and much of Cherry's subsequent work cannot be judged by Western 'Art Music' standards, for he seems to be aiming at a religious celebration. The duets with Ed Blackwell **(Mu, 1 & 2)** place him firmly within the jazz mainstream, and his trumpet playing here is angularly brilliant. A final composition **(Relativity Suite)** achieves a balance between his allegiances, from the Tibetan-sounding bells at the opening to the wild, jubilantly sung passage from Cherry.

In 1974, Don Cherry settled in Sweden, and although productive in the fields of schoolchildren's music and Eastern chant, it seemed unlikely that he would return to jazz. Always unpredictable, Cherry has recently re-surfaced with two excellent albums **Don Cherry** and **Old & New Dreams**.

Recordings:
Ornette Coleman's Atlantic Albums (Atlantic/Atlantic)
The Avant-garde (Atlantic/Atlantic)
Our Man In Jazz (RCA Victor/RCA Victor)
New York Eye And Ear Control (ESP/ESP)
Vibrations (Arista-Freedom/ Arista-Freedom)
New York Contemporary Five (Sonet/Sonet)
Complete Communion (Blue Note/Blue Note)
Symphony For Improvisers (Blue Note/Blue Note)
Jazz Composers' Orchestra (JCOA/JCOA Virgin)
Eternal Rhythm (BASF/BASF)
Mu, Parts 1 & 2 (—/BYG – France)
Relativity Suite (JCOA/JCOA Virgin)
Don Cherry (A&M/A&M)
Old & New Dreams (—/Black Saint – Italy)

Relativity Suite (JCOA Virgin): cover shot of a quilt made by Don Cherry's wife, Moki. Trumpet, voice, conch and suite by Don.

George Chisholm

George Chisholm (born Glasgow, Scotland, 1915) has been since the late-1930s probably the finest jazz trombonist produced in Britain. As early as 1936, Chisholm's worth as a technically assured, fiery player had been recognized by musicians outside the British Isles. It was in 1936 that Benny Carter (♦), at that time living and playing in Holland, invited him to participate in a recording session which took place in that country, in company with the Dutch band the Ramblers **(Benny Carter With The Ramblers & His Orchestra)**. Chisholm's perky trombone was second only to Carter's immaculate playing in terms of solo success on that date. Same year, he recorded in company of another famous US jazzman, the great saxophonist Coleman Hawkins (♦). And when Fats Waller (♦) visited London in 1939, during which time he undertook several recording engagements, George Chisholm's trombone was a welcome addition to the proceedings at one of these **(The Fats Waller Memorial Album)**.

Soloist and section man with bands of Teddy Joyce (1936), Ambrose (1938), BBC Showband (1952), Kenny Baker (on numerous occasions), Jack Parnell (1959), and a participant at special Hungarian relief fund London concert (1958, with Louis Armstrong (♦) headlining), Chisholm has attained a wide reputation during past 15 years as a very funny man (which he is). Unfortunately, his natural flair for comedy often has obscured the fact that he remains gifted trombonist who can deliver sensitive solos, in a 'serious' vein, with the best, as his playing on tracks like **Here's That Rainy Day, The Boy Next Door** and **Mood Indigo** (all **George Chisholm**) shows quite definitely.

Just how much he can add to the

excitement of a live performance – inspiring those around him to give of their very best – can be judged further by his expressive playing as guest at a concert by the Alex Welsh Band **(An Evening With Alex Welsh)**. And his ability to more than hold his own in distinguished company is manifestly displayed within the grooves of **Wild Bill Davison With The Freddy Randall Band**.

Recordings:
George Chisholm (—/Rediffusion)
Benny Carter With The Ramblers & His Orchestra (Decca – France)
The Fats Waller Memorial Album (—/Encore)
Various, British Jazz, Vols 1, 2 (—/BBC Records)
Various, Swingin' Britain – The Thirties (—/Decca)
George Chisholm, Jazz Today – Tribute To Benny Carter (—/Jazz Today)
An Evening With Alex Welsh (—/Black Lion)
Wild Bill Davison With Freddy Randall & His Band (—/Black Lion)

Charlie Christian

Guitarist Charlie Christian was, along with Thelonious Monk, Charlie Parker, Dizzy Gillespie and Kenny Clarke, one of the pioneers of Bebop. Some of the earliest Bop recordings from 1941 find Christian already into his mature style, single note runs and complex chord changes **(The Harlem Jazz Scene)**. Also present are Monk and Clarke and a Dizzy Gillespie still divided between his early influence, Roy Eldridge, and the new developments. **Swing To Bop** shows his intensely rhythmic use of riff, and throughout his blues feeling on the comparatively new instrument, the electric guitar, shows the influence of his Texas

After Hours (Esoteric): roots of the Bebop Revolution.

and Oklahoma upbringing. In 1939, he joined the Benny Goodman Sextet, and his profound influence on that unit, as well as future generations of guitarists, is shown on performances like **A Smo-o-o-oth One** and **Seven Come Eleven** where the pattern of riff, run and riff set the method of development. **Solo Flight** features the guitarist riding the Goodman Orchestra **(Charlie Christian With The Benny Goodman Sextet & Orchestra)**. Born in 1919, Christian died of tuberculosis in 1942.

Charlie Christian Live! (Jazz Archive): pioneering guitar.

Recordings:
Harlem Jazz Scene, 1941 (Esoteric/Society)
Charlie Christian With The Benny Goodman Sextet & Orchestra (Columbia/Realm)

Stanley Clarke

Bassist Stanley Clarke, like drummer Anthony Williams, was something of a teenage prodigy, playing with Horace Silver at 18. Born in Philadelphia in 1951, he began on violin and 'cello, later switching to acoustic and amplified bass. He made his reputation with pianist Chick Corea's jazz-rock outfit, Return To Forever, the unusual amount of elbow-room in the group's approach giving him plenty of solo space. Any of their albums **(Hymn To The 7th Galaxy, Light As A Feather, Where Have I Known You Before** and **No Mystery)** illustrate the subtle interaction between the musicians. Clarke's albums under his own name **(Stanley Clarke, Journey To Love** and **School Days)** commute between jazz and rock with astonishing passages of near-flamenco classical like **Spanish Phases For Strings & Bass (Stanley Clarke)** and multi-tracked vocal on **Just A Game (School Days)**. Superstar publicity has both inflated and detracted from his real status as a fine musician.

Recordings:
Return To Forever (ECM/ECM)
Hymn To The 7th Galaxy (Polydor/Polydor)
Light As A Feather (Polydor/Polydor)
Where Have I Known You Before (Polydor/Polydor)
No Mystery (Polydor/Polydor)
The Romantic Warrior (Columbia/CBS)
Stanley Clarke (Atlantic/Atlantic)
Journey To Love (Atlantic/Atlantic)
School Days (Atlantic/Atlantic)

Buck Clayton

Wilbur 'Buck' Clayton (born Parsons, Kansas, 1911) has had the kind of distinguished career that should be envy of most, if not all jazzmen. Started on piano, aged six, switched to trumpet at 16, taking lessons from father who played trumpet, tuba. Worked in several non-musical jobs on West Coast before returning to Kansas for completion of high school

Stanley Clarke

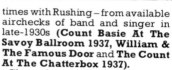

Stanley Clarke (Atlantic): prodigiously talented bass and bass-guitarist from Return To Forever, here calling the shots.

studies. Went back to Los Angeles to work with several local bands, before leading a 14-piece band, which later was heard by Teddy Weatherford who arranged for its residency in Shanghai. After which, Clayton led another big band in Los Angeles (1936), and his career really began to take shape when he joined Count Basie (♦) late '36. Since then has continued to demonstrate a consistency in performance that few other jazz trumpeters have matched.

Buck Clayton's first recordings, made in 1937, illustrate the kind of warm, delicate and relaxed swing that marks his playing at all times, as well as showcasing his basic all-round technique. A technique that is much influenced by Louis

One For Buck (World Record Club) . . . and one for his fans.

Armstrong (♦), coupled with much of the sensitivity, lyricism of Joe Smith. Those early recordings – as featured soloist with Basie, as well as soloist-accompanist on dates featuring Billie Holiday (♦) – also demonstrate that by this time Clayton's personal approach to trumpet was more or less formulated.

Over the years, with slight adjustments here and there, that style has remained virtually unchanged. His elegance of phrase and undeniable rhythmic powers added considerably to Basie-Holiday re-

cordings of '37 (and indeed, for both, thereafter). In addition, his astute use of various mutes, pleasingly evidenced on tracks like **Honeysuckle Rose** (briefly) and **Swinging At The Daisy Chain** further enhanced his growing reputation. Subsequent studio-made Basie-Clayton recordings **(The Best Of Count Basie, Jumpin' At The Woodside, You Can Depend On Basie, The Great Count Basie & His Orchestra, Super Chief, The Lester Young Story, Vol 3** and **Count Basie)** were to produce even more memorable Clayton trumpet work.

Of many consistently fine solos which Clayton delivered during his tenure with Basie, following must rank with best: **Smarty,**

Buck Clayton Jam Sessions (Vogue) – jazz at its best.

Swingin' The Blues, Jumpin' At The Woodside, Time Out, Topsy, Doggin' Around and **Fiesta In Blue**, plus two Basie sextet items, **Bugle Blues** and **Royal Garden Blues**. One should not forget Clayton's exquisite playing on tracks featuring blues singer Jimmy Rushing (♦) **(Blues I Love To Sing)** including **Good Morning Blues, Sent For You Yesterday & Here You Come Today, Blues In The Dark, Boo-Hoo** and **How Long Blues**. And there is potent evidence of Clayton's in-person abilities – with Basie, and some-

times with Rushing – from available airchecks of band and singer in late-1930s **(Count Basie At The Savoy Ballroom 1937, William & The Famous Door** and **The Count At The Chatterbox 1937).**

Clayton's sensitive contributions added an extra dimension to numerous Billie Holiday record dates, especially from this period. In 1937, for instance, made particularly significant contributions to such individual titles as **This Year's Kisses, Why Was I Born?, Mean To Me (The Lester Young Story, Vol 1** and **He's Funny That Way (The Lester Young Story, Vol 2).**

In '38, as member of a Lester Young (♦)-led pianoless Kansas City Six, Clayton produced some of his most expressive solo work **(Lester Young & The Kansas City Five** (sic)), nowhere better illustrated than on **Pagin' 'The Devil'** and **I Want A Little Girl.** Young-Clayton partnership also produced memorable results at subsequent reunions **(Spirituals To Swing** and, especially, **Lester Young Leaps Again!).**

Although hardly a typical Jazz At The Philharmonic representative, even in this pot-boiling atmosphere he never lost his poise and innate good taste **(Jazz At The Philharmonic 1946, Vol 2)** by which time Clayton not only had left Basie, but also had completed period of service in US Army. Since World War II he has toured with JATP (just under two years), appeared as featured soloist in all manner of pick-up groups, and has led succession of invariably top-class units, basically comprising mid-period jazzmen. In this latter respect, he has long since become the single most important individual with 'mainstream' jazz, a phrase coined many years ago by a leading critic to describe music that contains elements of both traditional and modern forms. Clayton too has been prime mover in organized jam sessions on record, made possible with advent of LP record. Majority of these, starting in 1953, were recorded for American Columbia label. Probably most celebrated is **Buck Clayton Jam Session**

Above: ex-Basie sideman Buck Clayton – his trumpet playing transcends stylistic categories, matures like the best wines.

comprising two extended tracks **(The Hucklebuck** and **Robbins Nest),** and included series of solos – some brilliant, some ordinary – from such as Urbie Green, Henderson Chambers, Joe Newman, Julian Dash, Sir Charles Thompson and, of course, Clayton himself. Jam sessions tended to vary in terms of artistic and creative success, depending upon chosen musicians; **The Golden Days Of Jazz: Swingin' Buck Clayton Jams Count Basie & Benny Goodman** exemplifies kind of magnificent-plus-mundane results which have emanated from similar Clayton-sponsored recorded jam sessions. One such recording that did produce mostly superior music was **Buck Clayton Band** which teamed Clayton with fellow trumpeter Ruby Braff (♦). Pair struck sparks off each other, inspiring rest of eight-piece band to give of individual and collective best. Clayton's own favorite jam session recording is **Songs For Swingers** dating from 1958, which also contains splendid tenor-saxophone playing by another Basie alumnus, Buddy Tate (♦). Earlier same year, Clayton contributed mightily to a Tate album date **Swinging Like . . . Tate!,** and earlier same month, shone brightly at two other mainstream dates, those fronted, respectively, by Coleman Hawkins (♦) **(The High & Mighty Hawk)** and Dicky Wells (♦) **(Trombone Four In Hand).**

In more recent times Buck Clayton was forced to give up playing trumpet completely, due to stomach, lip and hernia ailments. However, he has not ceased to be involved with jam session events. Indeed, he has produced several recordings in past few years, involving even wider range of musicians and styles. His enforced retirement from playing has, of necessity, thrown spotlight on to area of his talent that too often has gone unnoticed: composing, arranging. As member of Basie band, produced string of commendable charts (including **H&J**, **Down For Double**, **It's Sand, Man** and **Taps Miller**). Has also written for bands of Duke Ellington (♦) and Harry James (♦).

Since 1950s his uncomplicated compositions/arrangements have appeared at more regular intervals. After most recent efforts in this direction, including **Buck Clayton Jam Session, Vols 1, 2/ Buck Clayton Jam Session**, his writing (as well as his playing) has contributed handsomely to fine music found on more than one album by Humphrey Lyttelton (♦) band. Best of these probably is **Le Vrai Buck Clayton, Vol 2**. His talents as soloist, accompanist, composer, arranger and leader are encapsulated equally impressively throughout 1961 live double-LP collection reissued in its entirety during recent past **(Buck Clayton & Jimmy Witherspoon Live In Paris)**. In all these areas of music-making Buck Clayton has been, for around 45 years, a real credit to world of jazz – and unquestionably he remains one of its most professional as well as important contributors.

Recordings:
Count Basie, Swinging At The Daisy Chain (—/Coral)
Count Basie, Jumpin' At The Woodside (Brunswick/Coral)
Count Basie, You Can Depend On Basie (—/Coral)
The Best Of Count Basie (MCA Coral – Germany)
The Great Count Basie & His Orchestra (Joker – Italy)
Count Basie, Super Chief (Columbia/CBS)
Jimmy Rushing, Blues I Love To Sing (Brunswick/Ace of Hearts)
Count Basie At The Savoy Ballroom 1937 (Saga)
Count Basie & His Orchestra (Trip)/
William & The Famous Door (DJM)
Count Basie, The Count At The Chatterbox 1937 (Jazz Archives)
Lester Young & The Kansas City 5 (sic) (Mainstream/Stateside)
Various, John Hammond's Spirituals To Swing (Vanguard/Vanguard)
Lester Young, Lester Young Leaps Again! (EmArcy/Fontana)
Various, Jazz At The Philharmonic 1946, Vol 2 (Verve)
A Buck Clayton Jam Session (Columbia/CBS – Realm)
Swingin' Buck Clayton Jams Count Basie & Benny Goodman (CBS)
Buck Clayton Band (Vanguard/Vanguard)
Buck Clayton, Songs For Swingers (Columbia/Columbia)
Buddy Tate, Swinging Like . . . Tate! (Felsted/Felsted)
Coleman Hawkins, The High & Mighty Hawk (Felsted/Felsted)
Dicky Wells, Trombone Four In Hand (Felsted/Felsted)
Buck Clayton/Buddy Tate, Kansas City Nights (Prestige/—)
Various, Tootin' Through The Roof, Vol 2 (Onyx/Polydor)
Nat Pierce, Jam Session At The Savoy (RCA Victor – France)
Buck Clayton Jam Session, Vols 1, 2 (Chiaroscuro)/

Buck Clayton Jam Sessions (Vogue)
Jimmy Rushing, Who Was It Who Sang That Song (Master Jazz Recordings/—)
Buck Clayton & Jimmy Witherspoon Live In Paris (Vogue)
Buck Clayton, Jazz Party Time (Chiaroscuro)/**Jam Sessions, Vol 2** (Vogue)
One For Buck (World Record Club)
The Lester Young Story, Vols 1-3 (Columbia/CBS)
Buck Clayton/Roy Eldridge, Trumpet Summit (Pumpkin/—)

Rod Cless

George Roderick 'Rod' Cless (born Lennox, Iowa, 1907) was one of school of white jazzmen who emerged in middle- and late-1920s. A skilful clarinettist with liquid tone and light, attractive vibrato, playing was sometimes reminiscent of Frank Teschemacher (♦) (one of his premier influences) with whom he played in variety of bands in and around Chicago during latter half of 1920s. Cless – who also played alto-saxophone but rarely as soloist – worked with Jess Stacy (♦), Frank Snyder and Muggsy Spanier (♦). With latter, Cless recorded his finest solos **(The Great Sixteen)**, contributing greatly to undoubted success of legendary '39 Spanier's Ragtimers sessions.

Also recorded with Eddie Condon (♦), Max Kaminsky (♦) **(Dixieland Horn)**, Art Hodes (♦) **(The Funky Piano Of Art Hodes)** and Yank Lawson (♦). In person, worked with these and likes of Wild Bill Davison (♦), Marty Marsala, Georg Brunis (♦) and Bobby Hackett (♦). Cless died in 1944, in New York, of serious injuries sustained following heavy fall.

Recordings:
Muggsy Spanier, The Great Sixteen (RCA Victor/ RCA Victor – France)
The Funky Piano Of Art Hodes (Blue Note)
Max Kaminsky, Dixieland Horn (Commodore/Melodisc)

Arnett Cobb

Arnett Cleophus Cobb (born Houston, Texas, 1918) is one of long breed of Texan musicians whose hard-booting, highly-extrovert tenor-saxophone playing has for many years become integral part of jazz. Studied piano with grandmother as youngster, moved on to violin, trumpet, C-melody sax before turning, finally, to tenor-sax.
First professional work (aged 15) with band of drummer Frank Davis. Spent two years (1934–6) with another territorial band, that of Chester Boone. 1936: joined new outfit, put together by Milton Larkin (like Boone a trumpeter). Cobb stayed until 1942, when he moved on to Lionel Hampton (♦). With Hampton, Cobb's became familiar name, his exciting solos on feature items like **Flying Home No 2 (The Best Of Lionel Hampton)** and **Overtime (Steppin' Out: Lionel Hampton, Vol 2: 1942-**

The Fabulous Apollo Sessions – Arnett Cobb (Vogue).

1944) adding considerably to solo strength of band, and making Cobb more than adequate replacement for departed Illinois Jacquet (♦). 1947: left Hampton to put together own band.
Cobb's 1947 recordings with this six-piece band (for Apollo) **(The Fabulous Apollo Sessions)** demonstrate, most convincingly, that he was not just a wild, frenetic big-band blower, with little or nothing to say of any constructive consequence. At same time, excitement engendered by his playing on titles like **Go, Red, Go, Top Flight** and **Big League Blues**, proved he had lost none of his ability to produce genuinely exciting performances. Also, these tracks were to leave indelible mark on R&B music scene in general, then and later. 1948: Cobb forced to disband because of recurring back trouble, resulting in operation. Could not resume work until 1950 when he introduced new band. Again, though, career was interrupted by car crash (1956), resulting in serious injuries. Returned to Houston, to front another 16-piece band for residency at local club of which ultimately he became manager.
Emergence of soul jazz during late-1950s/early-1960s meant that, for a time, Cobb's masculine tenor sound was back in favour – certainly on record. For Prestige, for instance, he made a stack of always vitally swinging albums, with generally interesting selection of studio colleagues including Eddie 'Lockjaw' Davis (♦), Wild Bill Davison (♦) **(Blow, Arnett, Blow!)**, Coleman Hawkins (♦), Buddy Tate (♦) **(Very Saxy)**, Red Garland **(Sizzlin')** and Ray Bryant **(Party Time)**. And to show he could still handle ballads in prescribed fashion, he produced masterful readings of **Willow, Weep For Me, Blue & Sentimental** and **P.S. I Love You**, during admirable low-key date **(Ballads By Cobb)**.
Cobb's club work has continued since 1960s, although periods of ill-health have meant further interruptions to career. However, made first trip to Europe in 1973, as part of all-star package show. Following year, played Dunkirk Jazz Festival, returning in '75 with Milt Buckner's band, with whom he essayed a more formal European tour. These days, records by Arnett Cobb are conspicuous by their rarity. Certainly, though, there is much joyous, free-blowing music to be heard on **Jazz At Town Hall, Vol 1** with Cobb and Buckner being supported, with obvious enthusiasm, by drummer Panama Francis, and the man Cobb replaced with Lionel Hampton, 'way back in '42 – Illinois Jacquet.

Recordings:
The Best Of Lionel Hampton (—/MCA Coral – Germany)
Steppin' Out: Lionel Hampton, Vol 2 (1942-1944) (—/MCA – Germany)
Arnett Cobb, The Fabulous Apollo Sessions (Vogue – France)
Arnett Cobb, Blow, Arnett, Blow! (Prestige/—)
Arnett Cobb, Very Saxy (Prestige/Prestige)
Arnett Cobb, Sizzlin' (Prestige)
Arnett Cobb, Ballads By Cobb (Prestige – Moodsville)
Arnett Cobb/Illinois Jacquet, Jazz At Town Hall, Vol 1 (JRC/—)
Arnett Cobb & His Mob (Phoenix Jazz/—)

Al Cohn

Born 1925 in Brooklyn, tenorman Al Cohn, in company with Stan Getz, Allen Eager, Brew Moore and Zoot Sims, was initially influenced by Lester Young. Early performances in this idiom **(Brothers & Other Mothers)** featured Cohn with Getz and Sims, and in quartet performances with pianist George Wallington. A busy professional writer and arranger, Cohn's appearances on record have been infrequent, though his compositions – **The Goof And I**, for example, written for Serge Chaloff – often turn up in the jazz repertoire. Big band experience with Woody Herman, Buddy Rich and Artie Shaw gave him a robust, hard swinging sound, and in recent years a Rollins influence has flavored his style. Usually associated with tenorman Zoot Sims, much of his best work has been in that two-tenor relationship, both men plainly inspired by each other, both hewing to a swinging, melodic and infinitely cheerful approach **(Zootcase, Body & Soul** and **Motoring Along)**. They turn up together in a Miles Davis unit of 1953 **(Dig)**, playing Cohn originals like **Tasty Pudding**. A witty, reliable musician, Cohn's rare albums under his own name **(Play It Now)** are a guaranteed delight.

Recordings:
The Brothers & Other Mothers (Savoy/Savoy)
Zoot Sims, Zootcase (Prestige/Prestige)
Al Cohn - Zoot Sims, Body & Soul (Muse/—)
Motoring Along (Sonet/Sonet)
Al Cohn, Play It Now (Xanadu/—)
Miles Davis, Dig (Prestige/Prestige)

Motoring Along (Sonet): Al Cohn in familiar surroundings.

Nat King Cole

Nat King Cole, usually associated with the romantic vocal, was one of the finest jazz piano players of the '40s. Born in Alabama, 1919, he was initially influenced by Earl Hines, but soon developed his own distinctive style. An excellent compilation of his trios from 1944–9 illustrates the logic of his improvisational gifts **(Trio Days)**, while an album with trumpeter Charlie Shavers and tenorman Herbie Haymer from 1945, alternate takes and all, gives a wonderful sense of music in the making **(Anatomy Of A Jam Session)**. Classic trio performances by Lester Young, Cole and Buddy Rich originally billed the pianist as Aye Guy for contractual reasons **(The Genius Of Lester Young)**. His work in the turbulent JATP atmosphere accompanying tenormen Illinois Jacquet and Jack McVea can be found on a compilation of concerts **(Jazz At The Philharmonic 1944-6)**. At the start of the '50s, Cole's success as a singer drew him away from jazz; he died in 1965.

Recordings:
King Cole Trio, Trio Days
(Capitol/ —)
Anatomy Of A Jam Session
(Black Lion/Black Lion)
The Genius Of Lester Young
(Verve/Verve)
Jazz At The Philharmonic 1944-46 *(Verve/Verve)*

Anatomy Of A Jam Session (Black Lion): complete with chat.

Cozy Cole

William Randolph 'Cozy' Cole (born East Orange, New Jersey, 1909) took up drums and studied music at an early age (two brothers later became professional pianists) before Cole family moved to New York City. First drummed professionally, in late teens, with Wilbur Sweatman, then led own band.

Debut on records with Jelly Roll Morton (♦) **(Jelly Roll Morton & His Red Hot Peppers: 1927-1930, Vol 1)** in 1930. Worked with orchestra of Blanche Calloway (1931-2), then with string of first-rate bands – Benny Carter (♦), Willie Bryant **(Willie Bryant/ Jimmie Lunceford & Their Orchestras)**; Stuff Smith (♦) **(Stuff Smith & His Onyx Club Orchestra)** and Cab Calloway (♦).

With Smith, Cole produced some of his finest small-group drumming from this earlier period in his career; with Calloway, with whom he was mainstay of rhythm section

From The Very Beginning (MCA): a youthful-looking Nat King Cole from way back before his voice outsold his piano-playing.

between 1938–42, probably his best big-band playing **(Chu Berry Featured With Cab Calloway: 'Penguin Swing', 1937-1941** and **16 Cab Calloway Classics)**, latter containing no less than three excellent drum features for Cole: **Paradiddle, Ratamacue** and **Crescendo In Drums**; each satisfyingly integrated within framework of big-band arrangements.

Apart from brief spell with Raymond Scott ('42), Cole worked for year as CBS staffman, taking time off to lead own band on 52nd Street. Also featured in Broadway musicals *Carmen Jones* (1954) and *Seven Lively Arts* (1946).

Recorded series of fine sides in 1944, featuring Coleman Hawkins (♦) and Cole, with fine Earl Hines (♦) piano at one Hawkins-led session **(Swing!** and **Cattin')**. Further Cole-led sessions (with Hawkins, and others), late '44, resulted in equally fine music, with Cole's firm, yet never overpowering beat one of several plus factors **(Jazz 44)**. Early 1945: Cole took part in important embryonic bop record session, together with Charlie Parker (♦) and Dizzy Gillespie (♦) **(Dizzy Gillespie: The Small Groups: 1945-1946)** and even though his contributions therein only approximated the stylistic devices of that genre, it says much for his general adaptability that he fitted in with reasonable success and did not sound out of his depth. Briefly with Benny Goodman (♦) (1946), but mostly engaged in studio work between 1946-8. Fronted own combos, 1948-9, before joining Louis Armstrong (♦) All Stars (early '49) **(Louis Armstrong: July 4, 1900 - July 6, 1971** and **Louis Armstrong At The Pasadena)**. Appeared in film *Glenn Miller Story*, with Armstrong. Was regular at New York's Metropole during 1950s.

Started drum tuition school with close friend Gene Krupa (♦), and participated in splendid Henry 'Red' Allen (♦) record date ('57) **(Greatest Of The Small Bands, Vol 5)**. Achieved sudden, un-

expected commercial success when two-sided single disc, **Topsy**, an old Basie number, became million-selling hit (1958): **Topsy 1** ('A' side) reached US Top 30; then, **Topsy 2** ('B' side) went as high as third place in Charts.

Toured Europe with Jack Teagarden (♦) – Earl Hines All Stars (1957). After success with **Topsy** Cole toured with own band for a time; then, it was back to studio and club work. Toured Africa (1962–3) with own band. Since then has kept active in most areas of those spheres in which he has been a regular participant, including productive stint as member of quintet led by Jonah Jones (♦).

Apart from other film appearances, played on soundtrack of *The Strip*. Cozy Cole has been, for half a century now, one of the most all-round accomplished percussionists, universally recognized as tremendously versatile musician. True, there are times when his drumming has tended to become less than sparkling and stimulating – especially when compared to some of the efforts of those drummers who have emerged since early-1940s – but those occasions clearly have been outweighed by countless number of splendid performances he has given to all kinds of musicians, bands, record, concert and studio dates.

Apart from records already mentioned, there are comparatively few other recordings by Cozy Cole-led organizations which can be said to be totally memorable, or even important. Often these have tended to lack consistency, as with **Earl Hines – Cozy Cole**, or have promised much but, in the event, produced little of real substance.

Recordings:
Jelly Roll Morton & His Red Hot Peppers (1927-1930)
(RCA Victor – France)
Stuff Smith & His Onyx Club Orchestra *(Collector's)*
16 Cab Calloway Classics

(CBS – France)
Chu Berry Featured With Cab Calloway : 'Penguin Swing', 1937-1941 *(Jazz Archives)*
The Complete Lionel Hampton *(RCA Victor)/*
Lionel Hampton's Best Records, Vols 1, 2, 3, 5, 6 *(RCA Victor – France)*
Various, The Panassie Sessions 1938 *(RCA Victor – France)*
Willie Bryant/(Jimmie Lunceford) & Their Orchestras *(Bluebird/—)*
Chu Berry, Chew, Choo, Chu & Co. *(RCA Victor – France)*
Coleman Hawkins, Swing! *(Fontana)*
Coleman Hawkins, Cattin' *(Fontana)*
Various, The Greatest Of The Small Bands, Vol 5 *(RCA Victor – France)*
Dizzy Gillespie; The Small Groups (1945-1946) *(Phoenix)*
(Pete Johnson)/Cozy Cole, All Star Swing Groups *(Savoy/Savoy)*
Louis Armstrong: July 4, 1900 -July 6, 1971 *(RCA Victor/RCA Victor)*
Louis Armstrong At The Pasadena *(Decca/Coral)*
Jazz Giants: Cozy Cole/ Red Norvo *(Trip/—)*
Cozy Cole & His Orchestra *(Love/London)*
Earl Hines – Cozy Cole *(Felsted/Felsted)*

Bill Coleman

William Johnson 'Bill' Coleman is a sensitive, melodic trumpet player who seems to have spent more time (as an active professional musician anyway) in Paris, France, than in Paris, Kentucky (where he was born in 1904). A still greatly under-appreciated talent – especially in country of his birth – Coleman's mellow, probing, always swinging style was based firmly on much of the general Armstrong-influenced trumpet playing of the 1930s. It was his misfortune that during this decade there were, in addition to Armstrong, an exceptional number of important and gifted trumpeters (eg Allen (♦), Berigan (♦), Eldridge (♦), Clayton (♦) and Cootie Williams (♦), etc) whose efforts tended to obscure Coleman's own admirable work. Situation not helped greatly because this former Western Union messenger boy spent so much time away from the States.

After trying clarinet and C-melody sax, youthful Coleman decided on trumpet, making first-ever appearance with band led by J. C. Higginbotham (♦).

Professionally, career really started to gain momentum after coming

Bill Coleman A Paris, Volume 2 (1936-38) (Parlophone/EMI)

49

Above: trumpet veteran Bill Coleman – is he the most widely-traveled instrumentalist in jazz history?

to New York with band of Lloyd & Cecil Scott (1927). With Lloyd W. Scott before joining Luis Russell (♦) for first time, in 1929; stayed for longer spell between 1931–2 **(Luis Russell & His Louisiana Swing Orchestra** and **The Luis Russell Story).**

There were other bands between the two periods spent with Russell, and thereafter, but from a first-time standpoint, a five-month stay with Lucky Millinder was significant: with this band, made first of many trips to Europe (this one in '33). After leaving Millinder, with Benny Carter (♦), then joined Teddy Hill. By fall of 1935 had left for Europe, for second time (with Freddy Taylor). Instead of returning to US, worked in local Bombay band (1936–7). Worked with Willie Lewis Orchestra in Paris until end of 1938, then played residency in Egypt ('39), including appearance at wedding reception of Shah of Iran. Back to US to join Benny Carter (♦), Spring, 1940. Worked briefly with Fats Waller (♦) (Coleman previously had recorded with the pianist, in 1934) **(Fats Waller Memorial)** before becoming member of sextet led by another pianist, Teddy Wilson (♦), with whom he stayed for almost a year. With Andy Kirk (♦) (1941–2), then with Roger Kay, Noble Sissle, Ellis Larkins (1943). In between latter engagements, fronted own trio, on 52nd Street. Successively with Mary Lou Williams (♦), John Kirby (♦) and George Johnson (as co-leader), before USO tour with Herbie Cowens (Philippines, Japan). Then, from 1946, with Sy Oliver (♦) and Billy Kyle (♦), before

leaving, once again, for France, in 1948, where he decided to set up home.

Whilst in Europe has long since become firm favorite at jazz clubs and concerts and festivals. Has worked in Europe with touring Count Basie band (♦) (1961), been member of package shows as featured soloist. Has returned home on only few occasions. Despite his lengthy absences in all kinds of far-off countries and continents, Coleman's attractive sounding trumpet has been recorded at regular intervals during his career.

Not surprisingly, considering the amount of time he has spent in his adopted country, many of his best recordings have taken place in Paris (France). Apart from sessions in Paris with Willie Lewis Orchestra **(Bill Coleman A Paris, 1936-38, Vols 1, 2)**, has recorded numerous sides with local musicians, such as Stephane Grappelli (♦), Django Reinhardt (♦), and Alix Combelle, as well as resident or visiting Americans (viz Herman Chittison, Tommy Benford, Wilson Myers, Edgar 'Spider' Courance).

Amongst notable Coleman Paris-made recordings can be counted **Bill Street Blues, After You've Gone** and **Exactly Like You (Bill Coleman A Paris, 1936-38, Vol 2).** In France, also recorded with legendary Django Reinhardt **(Django Reinhardt & The American Jazz Giants/Django & His American Friends, Vol 2),** his dancing, elegant lines dovetailing effectively with guitarist's powerful rhythm and Romany tone.

Nearly 30 years later, trumpeter

was back in Europe, for annual Montreux Jazz Festival.

Together with French tenorist Guy Lafitte, Coleman produced warm, timeless blowing, some of which later found itself on record **(Mainstream At Montreux).** 1952: in company with Dicky Wells (♦), Zutty Singleton (♦) and Lafitte, was recorded during Paris concert, taking solo honours with ease – especially velvet-toned muted solo on **Solitude (Coleman Rarities).** Of US-made recordings, Coleman's work with tenor giants Coleman Hawkins (♦) and Lester Young (♦) rank with his finest achievements. Was present at a December, '43 Hawkins session which resulted in fine music-making from all present, including elegant trumpet on **Voodte** and **Stumpy.** Less than two weeks later, recorded with Young (with Dicky Wells again in attendance), contributing short precise contributions to **I'm Fer It Too** and **Hello Babe.** Opposite both tenormen, Coleman was, as usual, the perfect foil **(Classic Tenors),** perhaps a trifle overmodest in approach, but eminently respectful of the fact that Hawkins and Young respectively were the stars of both sessions.

Coleman and Young were matched together at further date, following year. Again, Coleman counterpointed some of Young's most glorious saxophone playing with the kind of felicitous trumpet work which Buck Clayton (♦) had contributed to Young dates in earlier times **(Lester Young & The Kansas City Five** (sic)**).** During one of his rare trips back home, Coleman's tasteful, graceful playing on a 1940 Joe Marsala (♦) date for Commodore **(Swingin' Clarinets)** was, like just about everything else he has accomplished during a fulfilling career, quietly superb, notably on **Three O'Clock Jump.** Of much more recent vintage, Bill Coleman's performances during 1967 London date **(Swingin' In London)** as front-line partner to Ben Webster (♦), proved he had lost little or nothing of his skills.

Recordings:
Charlie Johnson/Cecil Scott/ Lloyd Scott
(RCA Victor – France)
The Luis Russell Story
(—/Parlophone)
Luis Russell & His Louisiana Swing Orchestra
(Columbia/—)
Bill Coleman A Paris, 1936-38, Vol 1, 2 (—/Parlophone)
Fats Waller Memorial
(RCA Victor – France)
Django Reinhardt & The American Jazz Giants
(Prestige)/
Django & His American Friends, Vol 2 (HMV)
Various (Including Joe Marsala), Swingin' Clarinets
(—/London)
Lester Young/Coleman Hawkins, Classic Tenors
(Contact/Stateside)
Bill Coleman, Coleman Rarities
(Rarities/—)
Bill Coleman/Guy Lafitte, Mainstream At Montreux
(Black Lion/Black Lion)
Bill Coleman, Swingin' In London
(Black Lion/Black Lion)
Lester Young & The Kansas City Five (sic)
(Mainstream/Stateside)

Ornette Coleman

Born 1930 in Texas, Ornette Coleman was a largely self-taught musician, and by the age of 14 he was playing with carnival and R&B bands around the Fort Worth area. In the main, the jazz fraternity put him down as harmonically incompetent – not surprisingly, since he was groping towards the most radical innovation that jazz had yet experienced, a revolution that was to de-throne harmony. 'It was when I noticed that I was making mistakes that I realized that I was on the track of something.' By 1954 had most of his style together, and by 1956 a small group of musicians empathetic enough to provide the necessary context. Nevertheless, these were hungry years, with little chance of work, and by 1958 Ornette – in desperation – approached Contemporary records with a bunch of his compositions. Thanks to the openmindedness of producer Lester Koenig, he was invited to record them himself, plastic alto and all, and the two releases **Something Else** and **Tomorrow Is The Question,** though less than ideal in group terms (a piano was included on the debut album, and an orthodox if sympathetic rhythm section on the second) did publicly unveil the revolution.

Where musicians like Coltrane, Rollins, Mingus and Russell, sought to find a way out of the harmonic

Ornette (Atlantic): the one with Scott La Faro on bass.

maze of chord progressions, Ornette by-passed the problem. He based his improvisations on melodic and rhythmic planes, developing the solo along a freer-ranging logic than harmony had allowed. The music sounds like a non-European folk survival – direct and moving. Group interaction depended upon intuition to a greater degree than with more traditionally structured music, for there were no pre-set formulas to fall back upon. The demands have whittled the Coleman cohorts to a handful – trumpeter Don Cherry; bassists Charlie Haden, Scott La Faro, Jimmy Garrison and David Izenzon; drummers Ed Blackwell, Billy Higgins, Charles Moffett and Denardo Coleman; tenorman Dewey Redman.

The release of Ornette's albums on Atlantic is the fullest manifesto of the new music, and jazz was never the same again. Two armed camps developed out of the chord players and the free, though in fact the non-musician will find little difficulty in following Ornette's

Scott La Faro's bass **(Ornette!)** though staggeringly innovative, was too prone to ornamentation for the needs of the music, and lacked the selflessness and intuition of Haden's work. Ornette switched to tenor **(Ornette On Tenor)** because, controversially, 'the best statements Negroes have made, of what their soul is, have been on tenor saxophone'. The result was great music, with **Cross Breeding**, a solo of matchless symmetry and logic, contrasting with **Mapa**, which is contrapuntal throughout and group playing of the highest order.

The boldest experiment was yet to come with the double quartet album **(Free Jazz)** Ornette's regular quartet supplemented by Eric Dolphy, Freddie Hubbard, La Faro and both Higgins and Blackwell. Each man solos, backed by a free collective guided only by an open response to the stream of invention. It is themeless, unrehearsed, and kept from chaos mainly by the sheer aptness of the altoist's contributions. A classic album, influencing John Coltrane's 'Ascension' experiment, and giving rise to a flood of largely incoherent copyists.

In 1962, Ornette was recorded with his new trio, David Izenzon bass, Charles Moffett drums **(Town Hall)**; one example of an entirely new direction, a composition for string ensemble, **Dedication To Poets And Writers**, was included. The next two years were spent in semi-retirement at his New York studio, where he wrote and worked at two new instruments, the trumpet and the violin. Early in 1965 he returned to public performances with the trio, opening at the Village Vanguard, and then visiting Great Britain to play the legendary Fairfield Hall concert **(An Evening With Ornette Coleman)**.

Starting with a wind quintet composition, Ornette followed by unveiling his concept of trumpet and violin playing **(Falling Stars)** both used unconventionally and largely effective as tone colorings rather than precision instruments. His alto remained unchanged and unrivalled. Izenzon revealed himself as a master of arco bass playing and a considerable innovator, while Moffett – a Fort Worth friend of the leader's – proved himself to be the most conventionally swinging drummer that Ornette had used.

The same year saw the release of two Blue Note albums by the trio, caught live **(At The Golden Circle)** in Stockholm. The familiar medium-fast tempos of **Antiques, Dee Dee** and **Faces And Places** display the old rocking swing and fertile melodic imagination in full spate. A commission to compose a film score **(Chappaqua Suite)** led to a double album, but the music was judged to be too dominant for the screen images, and not used. The trio was expanded to include tenorist Pharoah Sanders and

Above: Ornette Coleman, the revolutionary altoist who changed the face of jazz improvisation. Much-lauded.

melodic line and logic, and might well wonder what all the fuss was about. Compositions like **Lonely Woman** or **Peace (The Shape Of Jazz To Come)** possess a beauty that would convert the most diehard listener, though the composer's tone might hoist a few eyebrows. Fiercely vocalized and shifting pitch to include squalling dissonances and searing cries, Ornette's alto alternates ambiguously between anguish and exaltation.

The Atlantic series from 1959–61 show the range of approaches possible within the new music. Performances like **Ramblin' (Change Of The Century)** have the feel of traditional Texas blues, rock as bucolically as a hoe-down. The leader's alto moves in short, jigging phrases, contrasting the attack with great attention to dynamics. The title track, like **Kaleidoscope (This Is Our Music)**, is fast and violent, the key centre discarded as the emotion demands. **Beauty Is A Rare Thing (This Is Our Music)** has a spaciousness about it, and a harrowing beauty that forms and disintegrates and reforms as the four players stretch out the motifs. The medium-fast tempo number, such as **C & D (Ornette!)**, **Congeniality (The Shape Of Jazz To Come)**, **Monk And The Nun (Twins)** and **The Fifth Of Beethoven (The Art Of the Improvisers)**, is the most typical.

Most of these albums comprise the quartet of Ornette, Don Cherry on pocket trumpet, Charlie Haden on bass and either Ed Blackwell or Billy Higgins on drums – a line-up that the leader has never bettered.

Chappaqua Suite (CBS): music for film 'Chappaqua', never used; the director felt its impact would unbalance the visuals.

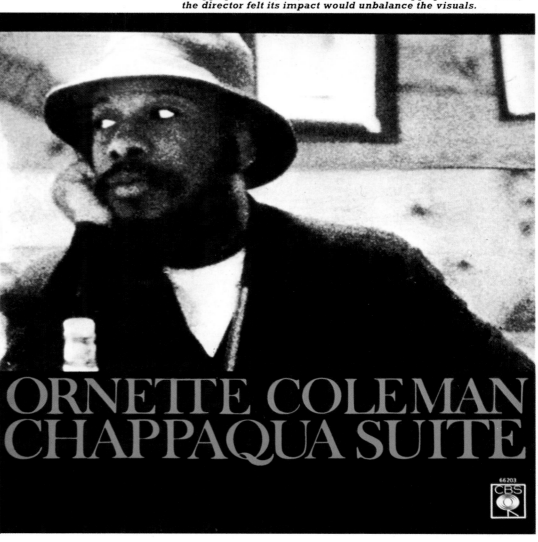

ORNETTE COLEMAN CHAPPAQUA SUITE

66.203

CBS

At The 'Golden Circle' Stockholm (Blue Note): classic session.

eleven woodwind, brass and strings players, and Ornette plays for most of the time over an economically written background.

Once again, controversy arose over the use of Ornette's ten-year-old son, Ornette Denardo, as the group's drummer **(The Empty Foxhole** and subsequently **Ornette At 12** and **Crisis).** Wayward, the youngster's playing certainly adds a random factor to the music. The leader's meeting with Coltrane's drummer, Elvin Jones **(New York Is Now** and **Love Call),** works well, but at the expense of Elvin's normal style; a meeting of giants, sympathetic but incompatible. By this time, Ornette had found another front line horn in tenorist Dewey Redman, another Fort Worth musician steeped in the blues tradition, and given to half-moaned, half-played tonal manipulations. An album from 1969 **(Crisis)** brings Don Cherry back into the group, and the high spot occurs with the hauntingly beautiful Charlie Haden composition, **Song For Che.**

Currently, Ornette Coleman seems to have retreated into retirement amid a flurry of rumours. His only recorded work in several years has been **O.C.** from an album of duets made by Charlie Haden **(Closeness)** which shows his genius unimpaired.

Ornette Coleman, like Cecil Taylor, pioneered free music. His influence is immeasurable. However, he remains one of the few improvisers imaginative enough to handle the rich pasturage of melodic freedom.

Recordings:
Something Else
 (Contemporary/Contemporary)
Tomorrow Is The Question
 (Contemporary/Contemporary)
The Shape Of Jazz To Come
 (Atlantic/Atlantic)
This Is Our Music
 (Atlantic/Atlantic)
Change Of The Century
 (Atlantic/Atlantic)
Ornette! *(Atlantic/Atlantic)*
Art Of The Improvisers
 (Atlantic/Atlantic)
Ornette On Tenor
 (Atlantic/Atlantic)
Free Jazz *(Atlantic/Atlantic)*
Twins *(Atlantic/Atlantic)*
Town Hall *(ESP/ESP)*
An Evening With Ornette
 Coleman/Ornette Coleman In
 Europe *(Polydor/—)*
At The Golden Circle
 (Blue Note/Blue Note)
Chappaqua Suite
 (Columbia/CBS)
The Empty Foxhole
 (Blue Note/Blue Note)
Ornette At 12 *(Impulse/Impulse)*
Crisis *(Impulse/Impulse)*

New York Is Now
 (Blue Note/Blue Note)
Love Call
 (Blue Note/Blue Note)
Charlie Haden, Closeness
 (A&M/A&M)
Dancing In Your Head
 (A&M/A&M)

Lee Collins

Lee Collins (born New Orleans, Louisiana, 1901) was archetypal New Orleans trumpeter: hot, with distinctive vibrato; good soloist and fine ensemble player. Influenced in turn by Bunk Johnson (♦) and Louis Armstrong (♦). Father also played trumpet and gave his son tuition. First professional job (at 15) in local New Orleans club. Put together band with bassist George 'Pops' Foster. Also played with Columbia Band, Young Tuxedo Orchestra, Papa Celestin, and others. Spent three years with drummer Zutty Singleton (♦) (1919–22). Toured with own band (1923). Joined King Oliver (♦) in Chicago (1924); in same year, appeared on record with Jelly Roll Morton (♦). As member of Morton's Kings of Jazz **(Jelly Roll Morton 1923/24)** Collins' overall contributions to titles like **Fish Tail Blues** and, most notably, **Weary Blues,** demonstrate awareness of Morton's personal approach to collective improvisation and overall ensemble rapport. Solo on **Weary Blues** has genuine poignancy.

Back to New Orleans, where he appeared with his own and other bands; toured with Prof Sherman Cook's Revue, and was co-leader (with tenorist David Jones) of Jones & Collins Astoria Eight, recorded by Victor in 1929 **(New Orleans, Vol 3).** The four titles recorded by this band have long since become recognized as classic examples of New Orleans jazz, using tight ensembles, and with front-line of Jones and Theodore Purnell, saxes, and Sidney Arodin, clarinet, receiving firm lead from Collins' trumpet. **Astoria Strut** and **Damp Weather** probably best examples on record of Hot Eight. Collins worked with Luis Russell (♦) in 1930 in New York; then, with Dave Peyton in Chicago (where he also worked with numerous other bands).

Formed own unit for touring, then undertook long residency in Calumet City. Returned once more to Chicago in '39, to work with own band and with others. Later, toured with Kid Ory (♦), worked with Art Hodes (♦) (1950–1). Invited by Mezz Mezzrow to join his band for 1951 European tour, but forced to return home because of illness. Recorded with Mezzrow in France **(Mezz Mezzrow & His Orchestra*** and **Mezz Mezzrow & His Orchestra*)** although neither disc shows Collins to any great advantage. 1953: with pianist Joe Sullivan (♦). 1954: toured with Mezzrow in fall, but once again struck down by illness which again compelled him to return home.

Suffered stroke, then chronic emphysema, both of which resulted in his being unable to play during final years of his life. Died Chicago 1960.

Recordings:
Various, New Orleans, Vol 3
 (RCA Victor – France)

Jelly Roll Morton 1923/24
 (Milestone)
*Mezz Mezzrow & His
 Orchestra *(Vogue – France)*
*Mezz Mezzrow & His
 Orchestra *(—/Vogue)*
*Different LP recordings

Alice Coltrane

Alice Coltrane, the great tenorman's second wife, replaced pianist McCoy Tyner in the John Coltrane group in January, 1966, and remained until Coltrane's death in 1967. Coltrane said of her that 'she continually senses the right colours, the right textures, of the sounds of the chords.' Her approach, like the new drummer, Rashied Ali's, was towards a looser, more diffuse design, and the change wrought by the newcomers can be heard on a version of **My Favourite Things (Coltrane Live At The Village Vanguard Again).** The release of some of her late husband's recordings found Alice dubbing Indian backgrounds **(Infinity)** and her own subsequent output has been characterized by a religious Eastern feel. Proficient on organ, harp and piano, Alice Coltrane's music concentrates on swirling, transcendental textures.

Recordings:
John Coltrane, Coltrane Live At
 The Village Vanguard Again
 (Impulse/Impulse)
John Coltrane, Concert In
 Japan *(Impulse/Impulse)*
McCoy Tyner, Extensions
 (Blue Note/Blue Note)
A Monastic Trio
 (Impulse/Impulse)
Journey In Satchidananda
 (Impulse/Impulse)
Lord Of Lords *(Impulse/Impulse)*
Ptah The El Daoud
 (Impulse/Impulse)
World Galaxy *(Impulse/Impulse)*

John Coltrane

Tenorman John Coltrane was born in North Carolina, 1926, and by his death in 1967, had become one of jazz's great touchstones of spiritual integrity, and a vital linking figure between the '50s and the New Thing. Beginning in R&B outfits, Coltrane joined Dizzy Gillespie in the early '50s, and the classic Miles Davis Quintet in 1955. With Miles, the tenorman showed a debt to Dexter Gordon, with passages of incoherence, and sudden landslides of considerable power and originality. **Round Midnight** gives an early hint of his emotional force **(Miles Davis, Tallest Trees).** Throughout the year and a half that he stayed with Miles, he worked on his style, trying, as he later told Wayne Shorter, to start in the middle of a sentence and move in both directions at once. In effect, the result was an outrush of arpeggios and semi-quavers spiralling up from the line. Chords obsessed him, and the move to Thelonious Monk's group in 1957 was the necessary next stage. Monk's harmonic sense was totally original, and Coltrane learned how to play buoyantly over the rhythmic staggers of **Monk's Mood** and the jolting, choppy tides of **Nutty (Thelonious Monk & John Coltrane).**

After the Bebop masters – Dizzy, Miles and Monk – he pushed out on his own. His best performances **Good Bait, Lush Life** and **Traneing In,** generated their own rhythmic impetus, the runs cascading into the famous 'sheets of sound', long, spearing legato notes arising from the complexity with chilling force **(More Lasting Than Bronze** and **John Coltrane).** A meeting with innovator Cecil Taylor **(Coltrane Time)** showed that although Coltrane was moving out of the strictures of Hard Bop, he was not

Left: John Coltrane, patron saint of contemporary tenor saxophonists. Also responsible for the soprano vogue.

by-passing the harmonic complex like Taylor or Ornette Coleman. Miles Davis, also casting about for a looser armature, came up with the modal timelessness of Indian music **(Kind Of Blue)** and Coltrane found the melodic freedom of that session highly relevant to his own search.

In 1959 he reached the first real plateau of maturity with two classic albums. His sound was uniformly strong over three octaves, and flexible enough to handle the delicacy of **Naima** or the headlong turbulence of **Mr P.C. (Giant Steps).** There was a new austerity and discipline in his playing, and the beginnings of a pre-occupation with split notes appeared on **Harmonique (Coltrane Jazz).** His soprano saxophone made its appearance on a number indelibly associated with him, the lyrically lovely **My Favorite Things,** and a great vogue for the instrument began. More important was the formation of the great quartet, McCoy Tyner piano, Jimmy Garrison bass, and Elvin Jones drums – a team chosen as a forcing house for his ceaseless explorations. Tyner's strength and dense chordal textures, his ability to sustain vamp figures which would check

COLTRANE

Coltrane (Impulse): a close-up of the most-imitated embouchure in post-Bop – and also, through dental decay, the most painful.

the leader's slide back into harmony: Garrison's stability and teamwork; Jones' multi-directional rhythms that surrounded Coltrane with choice. Between the 4/4 cymbal beat, the fierce counter-rhythms and the tenor's heavy, incantatory pulse, audiences had to find a new way to move to the music. Recording for Impulse, the quartet produced an unbroken series of exacting and exhilarating albums.

Many of the critics who had hailed **Giant Steps** gave an emphatic thumbs down to marathon performances like the seminal **Chasin' The Trane (Live At The**

Village Vanguard) but changed their minds with the four-part devotional work, **A Love Supreme,** which in turn became another breakoff point.

Between 1960–5, Coltrane had laid classic performances like **Blues Minor (Africa Brass), Transition (Transition)** and **Out Of This World (Coltrane),** the strong and tender reading of standard songs **(Ballads),** and had collaborated successfully with Eric Dolphy on tour and record. With Elvin Jones, he had pioneered a way of making the longer line breathe.

Next, Coltrane sought new stimulation in the young New Thing players. Fascinated by Ornette Coleman's **Free Jazz** experiment, he explored the possibilities of the free ensemble, augmenting the quartet with Archie Shepp, Pharoah Sanders, John Tchicai, Marion Brown, Freddie Hubbard, Dewey Johnson and Art Davis **(Ascension).** The dense, raging music cried out for a different rhythm, for a looser drummer than Elvin Jones. Coltrane took tenorman Pharoah Sanders into the group, stimulated by his writhing, high-energy playing, and added the mobile, flickering Rashied Ali on drums. The next phase has its riches and its confusions. Arguably, the finest album **(Meditations)** has the two tenormen plaiting, jostling, scouring

music to its emotional quick over the rhythmic groundswell without bogging down into chaos. A performance like **Naima (Live At The Village Vanguard Again)** with the leader's grandeur of expression sandwiching a convoluted solo from Sanders, has great symmetry. With the departure of Tyner and Jones, and their replacement by Alice Coltrane and Rashied Ali, Coltrane once again threw everything back into the melting pot, and this experimental phase was only terminated by his death. Group concept aside, late Coltrane is distinguished by the sheer majesty of his tone, particu-

Concert In Japan (Impulse): Coltrane and Pharoah, 1966.

larly evident on his duo album with Ali **(Interstellar Space)** and on **Offering** from his final album **Expression.** Like Sonny Rollins, his influence on jazz has been enormous and a flood of albums has been released posthumously. Quiet, introspective, humble, John Coltrane's life seems to have been almost totally dedicated to the musico-spiritual search.

Recordings:
Miles Davis, Tallest Trees
(Prestige/Prestige)
Thelonious Monk & John Coltrane (Milestone/Milestone)
More Lasting Than Bronze
(Prestige/Prestige)
John Coltrane (Prestige/Prestige)
Black Pearls (Prestige/Prestige)
Blue Train (Blue Note/Blue Note)
Paul Chambers & John Coltrane (Blue Note/Blue Note)
Coltrane Time
(United Artists)
Miles Davis, Kind Of Blue
(Columbia/CBS)
Giant Steps (Atlantic/Atlantic)
Coltrane Jazz
(Atlantic/Atlantic)
Don Cherry & John Coltrane, The Avant Garde
(Atlantic/Atlantic)
My Favorite Things
(Atlantic/Atlantic)
Live At The Village Vanguard
(Impulse/Impulse)
Live At Birdland
(Impulse/Impulse)
Crescent (Impulse/Impulse)
Coltrane (Impulse/Impulse)
Africa Brass (Impulse/Impulse)
Transition (Impulse/Impulse)
Sun Ship (Impulse/Impulse)
Ballads/The Gentle Side Of John Coltrane
(Impulse/Impulse)
A Love Supreme
(Impulse/Impulse)
Ascension (Impulse/Impulse)
Meditations (Impulse/Impulse)
Live In Seattle (Impulse/Impulse)
Concert In Japan
(Impulse/Impulse)
Live At The Village Vanguard Again (Impulse/Impulse)
Interstellar Space
(Impulse/Impulse)
Expression (Impulse/Impulse)
Om (Impulse/Impulse)
Kulu Se Mama (Impulse/Impulse)
Cosmic Music (Impulse/Impulse)

Eddie Condon

Albert Edwin Condon (born Goodland, 1905) was Hollywood publicity man's dream of archetypal jazzman: hard drinker, witty, something of a raconteur, characterful . . . in truth, Condon was all

Coltrane Live At The Village Vanguard Again! (Impulse).

these things and more. A living legend for most of his 69 years, whose influence, musically, was felt more than heard. A more than capable rhythm guitarist/banjoist, whose quietly propulsive strumming helped bolster up many a rhythm section. Never in any way a major soloist (nor even a player of minor significance, solo-wise) Condon's premier influence was as a kind of self-appointed entrepreneur, impresario, cheerleader, producer, as well as an indefatigable champion of what was (and is) basically a white-Dixieland jazz school.

A tough little man who taught himself to play, first ukelele, then banjo and guitar, Condon worked

Condon A La Carte (Ace of Hearts)

as semi-pro musician in his teens, and before he was 20 had played alongside an acknowledged giant like Bix Beiderbecke (◆). Condon associated himself with so-called Austin High School Gang (eg Krupa (◆), Freeman (◆), Teschemacher (◆), and it was with contingent of these and other Chicago-affiliated musicians that Condon (together with Red McKenzie, vocals, kazoo) produced first of McKenzie & Condon's Chicagoans recordings in December '27, **That Toddlin' Town - Chicago: 1926-28,** four titles which were to set both standard and style for future 'Chicago jazz'. Other examples of latter: recordings from following year involving Miff Mole (◆) & His Little Molers, Eddie Condon's Quartet and Condon's singularly titled Footwarmers **(That Toddlin' Town - Chicago: 1926-28).**

During next few years Condon was to record with impressive list of important jazzmen, including Jack Teagarden (◆) **(Jack Teagarden: Prince Of The Bone),** Louis Armstrong (◆) **(V.S.O.P.: Very Special Old Phonography, 1928-1930, Vols 5 & 6);** Red McKenzie's Mound City Blue Blowers **(Recordings Made Between 1930 & 1941).** Also participated, on

Eddie Condon's World of Jazz (CBS) - Condon and Friends . . .

banjo, in famous 1932 recording sessions under nominal leadership of meagerly-talented Billy Banks (**Billy Banks & His Rhythmmakers**) and it was with orchestra led by Condon that Bud Freeman was to record his most famous solo feature, **The Eel (Home Cooking)**.

Freeman and Condon were to remain close musical associates right up to latter's death. They worked together in clubs and at concerts on innumerable occasions through the years and recorded in each other's company prolifically, with either Condon playing on Freeman-led bands (**Chicagoans In New York**) or the tenorist guesting with Condon (**Chicago & All That Jazz**).

After serious stomach illness in 1936, Condon co-led, with clarinettist-saxist Joe Marsala (♦), fine little band. After working consistently in New York, especially at Dixieland emporium, Nick's, Condon worked with Bobby Hackett (♦) Bud Freeman's Summa Cum Laude Orchestra (**Chicago Styled**), then both Hackett and Marsala again. Then, in 1942, was responsible for putting together first-ever organized jam session before TV cameras. During this period the ever-gregarious Condon commenced own jam-session type series of concerts at New York's Town Hall, involving lengthy list of prominent jazzmen, most of whom had been Condon associates for several years.

Condon's Town Hall concerts (**The Eddie Condon Concerts Town Hall 1944-45: Featuring Pee Wee Russell** and **Eddie Condon Town Hall Concerts With Lee Wiley**) did much to help in revival of interest in more traditional jazz forms during 1940s, as well as providing much fine music. These also precipitated kind of studio jam-session recordings which Condon was to oversee in 1950s (**The Golden Days Of Jazz: Eddie Condon**) although there had been similar dates during late-1930s/early-1940s (**Jammin' At Condon's** and **The Roaring Twenties**), all of which permutated various line-ups of Condon favourites, with quality of music varying from the bland, even messy, to the bright, loosely disciplined and brilliant. Just how poor this kind of music can be is revealed all too illuminatingly on an ill-titled **Jazz As It Should Be Played**.

1945: opened own club, in Greenwich Village, which lasted 12 years. Club changed venue 13 years later. Condon's autobiography, *We Called It Music* (co-written with Thomas Sugrue) first published in 1948, year he started own jazz TV series.

Toured Britain in 1967 with own band; visited Japan, Australasia, '64. Underwent two major operations (1964, 1965); reduced own appearances at his club which closed doors in '67. But by 1970 was working in band co-led by Roy Eldridge (♦) and Kai Winding. Last recorded evidence of Condon probably dates from 1972 (**Jazz At The New School**) which demonstrated he was still carrying out the creed which he and others had long since laid down as the Dixielanders' textbook.

Full list of musicians who worked with Condon (who died in 1973) is comprehensive but would certainly include, apart from those already mentioned, Sidney Bechet (♦), Wild Bill Davison (♦), Cutty Cutshall, Lou McGarity, Bob Wilber (♦), Joe Bushkin, Gene Schroeder, Rex Stewart (♦), Vic Dickenson (♦), Edmond Hall (♦), Peanuts Hucko, George Wettling (♦), Billy Butterfield (♦), Jess Stacy (♦), Joe Sullivan (♦), Max Kaminsky (♦) and Brad Gowans.

Apart from the afore-mentioned autobiography, *Eddie Condon's Scrapbook of Jazz* (by Eddie Condon, with Hank O'Neal) is of absorbing interest to anyone remotely interested in the life and music of Eddie Condon and his numerous musical associates.

Recordings:
Various, That Toddlin' Town – Chicago (1926-1928)
(—/*Parlophone*)
Jack Teagarden, Vols 1, 2
(*RCA Victor – France*)
The Louis Armstrong Legend
(*World Records*)
Coleman Hawkins, Recordings Made Between 1930 & 1931
(*CBS – France*)
Billy Banks & His Rhythmmakers (—/*CBS – Realm*)
Bud Freeman, Home Cooking
(*Tax – Sweden*)
Bud Freeman, Chicago Styled
(*Swaggie – Australia*)
Various, Trombone Scene
(—/*London*)
Various, Great Swing Jam

Sessions, Vol 1 (—/*Saga*)
Various, Chicago Jazz
(*Decca/Coral*)
Eddie Condon, Condon A La Carte
(*Commodore/Ace of Hearts*)
Eddie Condon, Commodore Condon Vol 1 (—/*London*)
Bud Freeman, Chicagoans In New York (*Dawn Club/—*)
Various, The Davison-Brunis Sessions, Vols 1-3
(—/*London*)
The Eddie Condon Concerts, Town Hall 1944-45, Vols 1, 2
(*Chiaroscuro/—*)
Eddie Condon & His All Stars, Vols 1-18 (*Jazum/—*)
Jack Teagarden, Big T's Jazz
(—/*Ace of Hearts*)
Eddie Condon, We Called It Music (—/*Ace of Hearts*)
Eddie Condon, The Golden Days Of Jazz (*CBS/CBS*)
Various, Chicago & All That Jazz! (—/*Verve*)
Muggsy Spanier & His Ragtimers (—/*London*)
Eddie Condon's World Of Jazz
(*CBS – Holland*)

Chick Corea

Born in Boston, 1941, pianist Chick Corea's father was a jazz musician, and his earliest influences were Bud Powell and Horace Silver, while a classical training added the strands of Stravinsky, Ravel, Debussy and Bartok. Corea played with Blue Mitchell, Herbie Mann and Stan Getz (**Sweet Rain**), contributing the complex **Litha** and the lovely waltz **Windows** to the session, and eliciting some of Getz's best work by his sympathetic piano support. A period with Miles Davis during his transition to jazz-rock saw Corea sharing electric keyboard duties with Joe Zawinul (**In A Silent Way, Bitches Brew** and **Big Fun**); though an earlier album (**Filles de Kilimanjaro**) gives a clearer idea of his work.

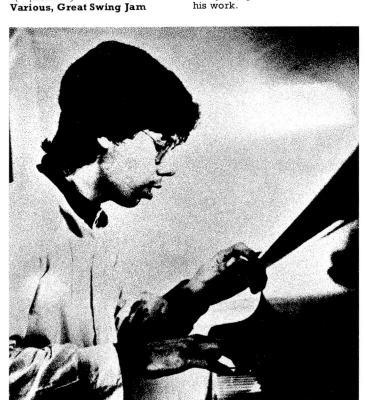

Typical of his playing in the late '60s – fierce, energetic – is an album with trumpeter Woody Shaw and saxophonist Joe Farrell (**Tones For Joan's Bones**) which is driven along on the surging drumming of Joe Chambers. His formation of Circle in 1970 with multi-instrumentalist Anthony Braxton, bassist Dave Holland and drummer Barry Altschul marked a change in direction. Free interplay is the keynote here, from the driving version of **Nefertiti** – a much wilder, looser performance than Miles' – to the dissonant piano in duet with Braxton's extremes of pitch on **Duet (Circle, Paris Concert).** The group broke up in 1971 when Corea left – 'I used to feel very limited and confined and I'd be into a compulsive experimentation on the bandstand' and recorded a pair of solo piano albums for ECM (**Piano Improvisations**). Fragile, introspective, the music draws extensively from classical, each piece meticulously constructed, from the Monk standard, **Trinkle Tinkle,** to the eight impressionistic vignettes of **Where Are You Now.**

The debut album by Corea's new group, **Return To Forever,** featured Joe Farrell, reeds; Stanley Clarke, bass; Airto Moreira, percussion; and Brazilian singer Flora Purim. With Corea on electric piano, and a return to the more overtly stated rhythm, the group played a chamber version of jazz-rock and were immensely successful. Subsequent albums (**Light As A Feather, Hymn The 7th Galaxy, No Mystery, Where Have I Known You Before** and **Romantic Warrior**) have seen personnel changes, with Corea and Clarke constant, and guitarist Al Di Meola replacing Farrell. Today, one of the crossover supergroups, Return To Forever is careful not to outstrip its following, and Corea in interview places a heavy premium on communication. A scientologist, he believes that his music has a mission, and himself draws inspiration from the scientologist poetry of Neville Potter (**Where Have I Known You Before**).

Recordings:
Stan Getz, Sweet Rain
(*Verve/Verve*)
Miles Davis:
   In A Silent Way
   (*Columbia/CBS*)
   Bitches Brew
   (*Columbia/CBS*)
   Big Fun (*Columbia/CBS*)
   Filles De Kilimanjaro
   (*Columbia/CBS*)
Tones For Joan's Bones
   (*Atlantic/Atlantic*)
Circling In
   (*Blue Note/Blue Note*)
Circle, Paris Concert
   (*ECM/ECM*)
Piano Improvisations, Vols 1 & 2 (*ECM/ECM*)
Return To Forever (*ECM/ECM*)
Light As A Feather
   (*Polydor/Polydor*)
Hymn The 7th Galaxy
   (*Polydor/Polydor*)
No Mystery
   (*Polydor/Polydor*)
Where Have I Known You Before (*Polydor/Polydor*)
Romantic Warrior
   (*Columbia/CBS*)

Left: pianist Chick Corea, whose career has moved from avant-garde to popular appeal. A devout Scientologist.

Curtis Counce

Bassist Curtis Counce was born in 1926 in Kansas City, and made his recording debut with Lester Young in 1946, followed by stints with Shorty Rogers and Stan Kenton. In 1956 he founded his quintet which lasted until the following year and represents his chief claim to fame. The Curtis Counce Group was arguably the most virile and consistently imaginative outfit on the West Coast in that period, and its four albums, **Landslide, Counceltation, Carl's Blues** and **Exploring The Future**, have not dated like much of that region's more self-consciously experimental music. Tenorman Harold Land, trumpeter Jack Sheldon, pianist Carl Perkins and drummer Frank Butler shared the writing dues with the leader, and between them created a personality that could compete with any combo on the more fashionable East Coast. Underrated at the time, especially Frank Butler whose technique was showcased on numbers like **A Fifth For Frank (Landslide)** and **The Butler Did It (Carl's Blues)**, the only member who continued to add to his reputation was Harold Land.

Recordings:
Landslide
(Contemporary/Contemporary)
Counceltation
(Contemporary/Contemporary)
Carl's Blues
(Contemporary/Contemporary)
Exploring The Future
(Dooto/—)

Ida Cox

Ida Cox (born Knoxville, Tennessee, 1889) was not only one of the most successful blues artists, she was one of the very best. As a child, sang in local African Methodist Choir. Ran away from home to work with F. S. Wolcott's Rabbit Foot Minstrels, making her first appearance at 14. Became solo performer, singing blues, as well as vaudeville and tent-show songs. First recording in June 1923 – even before Ma Rainey (♦).

Very first sides (for Paramount) were **Any Woman's Blues**, **'Bama Bound Blues** and **Lovin' Is The Thing I'm Wild About (Ida Cox, Vol 1)**. Accompanied only by piano of Lovie Austin, Cox demonstrated at this first session that hers indeed was a voice richly textured, beautifully expressive (especially on **Any Woman's Blues**), deeply immersed in blues idiom, and tinged by her vaudevillian experiences **(Lovin)**. Lovie Austin was to become important contributor in ensuring Cox's recordings were so uniformly superb, illustrative of blues singing at its best. **Bear-Mash Blues**, from a December '23 session **(Ida Cox, Vol 2)**, finds her singing with optimum feel, accompanied lovingly by pianist Jesse Crump. Crump, also organist, dancer and writer (he composed **Bear-Mash Blues** with Cox), became her husband in 1927. **Graveyard Dream Blues**, from Ida Cox's second record date **(Ida Cox, Vol 2)** must be considered, even by her consistently high standards, one of her very finest

Exploring The Future (Dooto): Curtis Counce taking that big step on behalf of the West Coast. Once rare, now re-issued.

offerings; a stark, electrifyingly real blues written by singer and projected in appropriately emphatic style. Lovie Austin apart, Jimmy O'Bryant, clarinet, and Tommy Ladnier, cornet, offer accompaniment which is, collectively and individually, beyond reproach. Austin (as leader of her Blues Serenaders, as well as capacity of solo pianist), together with Ladnier and O'Bryant, became basic ingredients of Ida Cox recordings, with minimal additional musicians used at different times. One important addition was Johnny Dodds (♦), who replaced O'Bryant at August '24 session **(Ida Cox, Vol 2)** that produced magnificent blues singing/playing to be found within **Wild Women Don't Have The Blues** and **Worried In**

Ida Cox, Volume 1 (Fountain) – 16 classic blues tracks.

Mind Blues. Dodds, although in more subordinate role than usual, still as omnipotent in this context as ever. Declamatory **Blues Ain't Nothin' Else But!**, with unknown accompaniment **(Ida Cox, Vol 2)** is another superlative example of Ida Cox's art.

In late-1920s, she formed own travelling show *Raisin' Cain* which continued through 1930s. After which she toured with Darktown Scandals troupe. Recorded at Carnegie Hall in 1939 **(John Hammond's Spirituals To Swing)** executing powerful **Four Day**

Creep, accompanied by Dicky Wells (♦), James P. Johnson (♦), Lester Young (♦), Buck Clayton (♦), et al. Same year, recorded with equally potent support from Hot Lips Page (♦), Lionel Hampton (♦), Ed Hall (♦), J. C. Higginbotham (♦) and others. **Hard Time Blues** is beautifully representative of overall quality of music resulting from session **(Hard Time Blues)**. Worked through 1950s regularly until career temporarily curtailed by stroke (1945). Retired to live in town of her birth.

Made comeback on record in 1961 when she proved she had retained some of her old potency. Stellar jazz line-up included Coleman Hawkins (♦), Roy Eldridge (♦), Jo Jones (♦) and Sammy Price (♦). This Riverside LP, **Blues For Rampart Street,** found her recapturing some of the charisma of past days, particularly on tracks like **Mama Goes Where Papa Goes, Hard Time Blues** and **Wild Women Don't Have The Blues**. Pitch and control often were uncertain throughout the two sessions but, at 72, power of her voice remarkably well preserved.

Recordings:
Ida Cox, Vols 1, 2
(—/Fountain)
King Oliver Plays The Blues
(Riverside/London)
Ida Cox, Blues Ain't Nothin' Else But *(Milestone/—)*
Ida Cox, Blues For Rampart Street *(Riverside/Riverside)*
Various, Ma Rainey & The Classic Blues Singers *(CBS)*
Various, John Hammond's Spirituals To Swing
(Vanguard/Vanguard)
Ida Cox, Hard Time Blues
(—/Fontana)

Jimmy Crawford

James Strickland 'Jimmy' Crawford (born Memphis, Tennessee, 1910) will always be associated primarily

with the Jimmie Lunceford (♦) Orchestra during its formative years and its peak period of artistic and commercial successes (1933–40). Crawford's driving drumming, whether in two- or four-beat style, was principal factor in band's superior rhythmic performances. Those who remember band during its halcyon years testify to the potency of its rhythm section, with Crawford as its key figure, with only Count Basie's (♦) rhythm team capable of out-swinging it. Crawford (whose first instrument was alto-horn) first met Lunceford as student at Manassas High School. Served in US Army (1943–5), playing with various Service outfits. Between 1945–9, mostly with Edmond Hall (♦), but also with Harry James (♦), briefly, in 1946, and Fletcher Henderson (♦) (1950). Has worked extensively in pit bands of Broadway shows (starting with *Pal Joey*) since early-1950s, and toured with Lena Horne show *Jamaica*. Outside of big-band work with Lunceford (any one available LP can be cited as excellent example of his abilities) a 1958 date with Buster Bailey (♦) **(All About Memphis)** ranks with his very best within small-combo context.

Recordings:
Jimmie Lunceford, Rhythm Is Our Business (1934-1935)
(MCA – Germany)
Jimmie Lunceford, Harlem Shout (1935-1938)
(MCA – Germany)
Jimmie Lunceford, For Dancers Only (1936-1937)
(MCA – Germany)
Jimmie Lunceford, Blues In The Night (1938-1942)
(MCA – Germany)
Jimmie Lunceford, Jimmie's Legacy (1934-1937)
(MCA – Germany)
Jimmie Lunceford, The Last Sparks (1941-1944)
(MCA – Germany)
Mills Blue Rhythm Band 1931/1934/Jimmie Lunceford & His Orchestra 1934
(RCA Victor – Germany)
Jimmie Lunceford, Lunceford Special
(Columbia/CBS – Realm)
Jimmie Lunceford, Takin' Off With Jimmie *(Tax – Sweden)*
Jimmie Lunceford, Memphis To Harlem (1930-1934)
(RCA Victor – France)
Don Redman & His All Stars
(Alamac)
Buster Bailey, All About Memphis *(Felsted/Felsted)*

Bing Crosby

Harry Lillis 'Bing' Crosby (born Tacoma, Washington, 1904) has been best known (and most widely respected) pop singer of past 50 years, with total record sales of almost unassailable proportions. Crosby, star of around 50 movies and Academy Award-winning actor, started his career in music business as solo singer who sometimes played drums. After experience in vaudeville, joined entourage of bandleader Paul Whiteman (♦), as solo vocalist and as member of vocal trio the Rhythm Boys, in 1927. During this time, Crosby's singing was much influenced by jazz – in fact, there is little doubt he could be classified

mono only

The Bing Crosby Story, Vol 1: The Early Jazz Years (1928-1932) (CBS). Bing, Duke, Dorseys, Whiteman et al.

as a jazz singer. With Whiteman, the jazz influence was especially strong on individual items like **Louisiana, From Monday On, You Took Advantage Of Me (The Bix Beiderbecke Legend); 'Tain't So, Honey, 'Taint So, After You've Gone (The Bing Crosby Story)**. Also recorded in company with numerous jazz musicians, from Bix Beiderbecke (♦), and Frankie Trumbauer (♦), Don Redman (♦), Dorsey Bros (♦) Orchestra and Duke Ellington (♦) (all **The Bing Crosby Story**).

With Ellington orchestra, he recorded a remarkably fine version of **St Louis Blues**. Other jazzmen with whom Crosby recorded include Lionel Hampton (♦), Woody Herman (♦), Jack Teagarden (♦), Joe Sullivan (♦), Count Basie (♦) (**Bing 'N' Basie**) and Louis Armstrong (♦). He worked many times with Armstrong over the years – on record, radio, television and films (**Louis Armstrong & Bing Crosby On Stage**). And although in later years Crosby's singing lost much of its initial basic jazz feel, still there were occasions when the jazz spark returned, as with his singing of **Now You Has Jazz**, during the 1956 film musical *High Society*, in company of Louis Armstrong and the Armstrong All Stars (**High Society, Original Film Soundtrack**).

When Crosby left Whiteman band he took with him Whiteman's guitarist Eddie Lang (♦). Lang, who can be heard on many Crosby recordings, worked as the singer's personal accompanist between 1930 and his death, two years later. On Lang's death, Crosby replaced him with another guitarist – Perry Botkin – simply because he sounded like and played in the style of Lang.

Crosby appeared at the London Palladium in 1976 and 1977; both seasons were extremely successful. Following the second season he went to Spain, primarily to rest. After completing a game of golf (a lifelong passion), he collapsed and died almost immediately from a heart attack, on October 14, 1977,

a month to the day after he had completed what was to be his final LP session in London. **Seasons**, while not especially indicative of Crosby's jazz abilities, contains some of the finest singing he had committed to record in a decade and a half. An appropriate way to close the book on an entertainer who had long since become one of the best-loved singers of the twentieth century.

Recordings:
The Bix Beiderbecke Legend *(RCA Victor – France)*
The Bing Crosby Story *(Columbia/CBS)*
Bing Crosby/Johnny Mercer, Mr Crosby & Mr Mercer *(—/MCA)*
Louis Armstrong & Bing Crosby On Stage *(—/Windmill)*
'High Society' (Original Film Soundtrack) *(Capitol/Capitol)*
Bing Crosby/Count Basie, Bing 'N' Basie *(Daybreak/Daybreak)*
The Early Jazz Years: 1928-1930 *(Columbia/CBS)*

Bob Crosby

George Robert 'Bob' Crosby (born Spokane, Washington, 1913) is one of a handful of successful bandleaders who did not play an instrument, could neither read nor write music, and was used only as an up-front personality to effect introductions, wave a casual baton (or arm), and generally look the part of (in his case) the handsome-and-well-groomed type – something which often seemed obligatory during Swing Era.

Crosby was set on career as lawyer after graduating from college. Instead, in 1932, became professional singer with orchestra of Anson Weeks. 1934: joined Dorsey Bros Orchestra. With Dorseys, Crosby's reputation as modest singer (certainly not in same class as his elder brother) began to grow amongst record collectors. His easy-going, if ultimately for-

gettable, vocals on tracks like **Basin Street Blues, Dinah, Lullaby Of Broadway, What A Difference A Day Made** and **It's Dark On Observatory Hill** (all **Bring Back The Good Times**) did help, however, to bring band to wider audience.

Took over group of musicians defecting from Ben Pollack (♦) Orchestra, including Gil Rodin, Eddie Miller (♦), Matty Matlock and Ray Bauduc. Thus, the Bob Crosby Orchestra was put together. Debut came early-1935, in New York. At first, it had like Pollack's band, strings, but this was passing phase, and Crosby Orchestra adopted policy of playing Dixieland favorites, augmenting these with new material in similar vein without strings. Soon it became No. 1 big-band specializing in orchestral Dixieland two-beat jazz. In early days, apart from names mentioned above, other notable sidemen appeared – sidemen whose presence would be vital to success of the Crosby outfit; Yank Lawson (♦) and Bob Haggart were two.

Other important musicians to give excellent service to the band: Irving Fazola (♦), Billy Butterfield (♦), Bob Zurke, Joe Sullivan (♦), Jess Stacy (♦), Muggsy Spanier (♦) and Eddie Miller (♦).

An important event in Bob Crosby Orchestra Story was advent of the Bob Cats, a fine band-from-within-the-band unit which produced the the best out-and-out jazz performances. Amongst host of well-remembered Bob Cats sides can be numbered **Who's Sorry Now?, Can't We Be Friends?, March Of The Bob Cats, Mournin' Blues, Jazz Me Blues** and **I Hear You Talking** (all **Bob Crosby's Bob Cats/Big Noise From Winnetka** and **Tin Roof Blues (The Bob Cats: Bob Crosby's Bob Cats 1938-42**). Especially popular pieces featured by the main orchestra included: **South Rampart Street Parade** (composed by Haggart, Bauduc), **I'm Prayin' Humble** (Haggart), **Honky Tonk Train Blues** (featuring Zurke), and **I'm Free** (later retitled **What's New?** after being given words by Johnny Burke) (all **Five Feet Of Swing/ South Rampart Street Parade**)...

From semi-novelty standpoint, success of **Big Noise From Winnetka (Bob Crosby's Bob Cats/ Big Noise From Winnetka)** featuring drummer Bauduc playing on strings of a whistling Haggart's bass, perhaps was the biggest surprise.

Although through the years Crosby was to lose key men – Kincaide, Lawson, Charlie Spivak, all at once; to Tommy Dorsey in '38; Butterfield, Fazola, in '40 – somehow adequate replacements (generally) were to be found. (In some cases, too, eg Lawson, departees were to return to the fold.) Eventually, by 1942, what had been basically the original Bob Crosby Orchestra fell apart, tenorist/clarinettist Miller taking a segment of the then current personnel to form own band.

Crosby, who had appeared in various films, alone and with band – *Let's Make Music, Sis Hopkins, Presenting Lily Mars* and *Holiday Inn* (soundtrack) – went solo to Hollywood. Appeared in further movies, including *As Thousands Cheer, Reveille With Beverly, See Here Private Hargrove*, etc. With US Marines (1944-5). Reformed new band on part-time

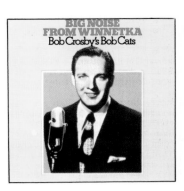

Big Noise From Winnetka (MCA) – made by the Bob Cats.

basis, for special engagements, but during late-1940s and 1950s, became better-known as TV, radio personality in solo capacity, often hosting own shows. Since 1960s, has been successful businessman outside music, although from time to time has assembled Crosby-type re-union bands, often containing well-known alumni, for special occasions not entirely divorced from nostalgia (Crosby toured Far East during latter portion of '64).

Recordings:
Bob Crosby, The Radio Years *(—/London)*
The Dorsey Bros., Bring Back The Good Times *(MCA – Germany)*
Bob Crosby & His Orchestra 1935-1956 *(Coral/Vogue – Coral)*
Bob Crosby, Five Feet Of Swing *(Decca)*
South Rampart Street Parade *(MCA)*
Bob Crosby's Bob Cats *(Decca)*
Big Noise From Winnetka *(MCA)*
The Bob Cats: Bob Crosby's Bob Cats 1938-42, Vol 2 *(Swaggie – Australia)*

Israel Crosby

The bassist (born Chicago, Illinois, 1919) firstly was a trumpet player, adding trombone, tuba. By 13, was playing regularly on all three instruments. At 15, became string bass player, working in Chicago with various leaders, including Albert Ammons (♦). Made debut on record with pianist Jess Stacy (♦), November 1935; three days later, recorded again with Stacy, this time as member of Gene Krupa's (♦) Chicagoans; one number, **Blues Of Israel**, dedicated to and featuring the talents of the young bass player (both sessions **Benny Goodman & The Giants Of Swing/Ridin' In Rhythm**). Worked with Fletcher Henderson (♦) (1936-8), Three Sharps & A Flat (1939), Horace Henderson (♦) (1940-1), Teddy Wilson (♦) (1941-3). 1944: started session work, an occupation which lasted on regular basis for several years. Worked with Ahmad Jamal Trio (1951-3), then again between 1957-62 (**But Not For Me/The Ahmad Jamal Trio At The Pershing**), as well as with Benny Goodman (1956-7), with whom he toured Asia. Finally, became member of George Shearing Quintet before dying of a blood clot, in his home town in 1962. Amongst other notable recording dates, Crosby's bass was powerfully present alongside Jimmie Noone (♦) **(Jimmie Noone 1937-41)** and during Teddy Wilson's celebrated **Blues In C Sharp Minor** session **(Teddy Wilson & His All Stars).**

Recordings:
Benny Goodman & The Giants Of Swing (Prestige)/
Various, Ridin' In Rhythm (World Records)
The Fletcher Henderson Story (Columbia)/
The Fletcher Henderson Story, Vol 4 (CBS)
Edmond Hall, Celestial Express (Blue Note)
Teddy Wilson & His All Stars (Columbia/CBS)
Jimmy Yancey, Lowdown Dirty Blues (Atlantic/Atlantic)
Jimmie Noone 1937-41 (Collector's Classics)
But Not For Me/The Ahmad Trio At The Pershing (Cadet/London)

Tadd Dameron

Born in Cleveland, 1917, died New York, 1965, pianist-arranger Tadley Dameron left a legacy of beauty. He arranged for Vido Musso and Harlan Leonard, making his debut as a pianist with Babs Gonzales' Three Bips & A Bop. He was adept at translating Bebop, essentially a combo music, to the needs of the big band, and **Good Bait** and **Our Delight,** written for Dizzy Gillespie's band **(In The Beginning)** and **Cool Breeze** written for Eckstine's, are

The Tadd Dameron Memorial Album (Prestige).

models of concision and lyricism **(Mr B. & The Band). If You Could See Me Now,** the first Bebop ballad, developed out of Gillespie's cadenza to **Groovin' High,** became a vehicle for both Eckstine and Sarah Vaughan. In 1949, he appeared as co-leader with Miles Davis at the Paris Jazz Festival.

Though modest about his piano playing, and usually restricting himself to accompanying, Dameron's talents went beyond 'arranger's' piano. Between 1947–9 he led his own group, which boasted such talents as trumpeter Fats Navarro, tenors Wardell Gray and Allen Eager, through his own compositions. **The Squirrel, Dameronia, Tadd Walk, Lady Bird, Jahbero, Symphonette** and **The Chase** have become jazz standards **(Prime Source),** and the combo was tighter than most Bebop units. Dameron led his band throughout a lengthy incumbency at the Royal Roost, and developed Navarro's talent to the full. He didn't find a comparable

Above: Tadd Dameron, sadly neglected in his lifetime, one of jazz's greatest composers for the combo.

player until trumpeter Clifford Brown in 1953 **(The Arranger's Touch)** and his muted solo on **Theme Of No Repeat** is a classic. Included on the same album is a later session which features **Fontainebleau,** a short composition in three movements of great textural beauty. A session with tenorman John Coltrane, though interesting, falls short of Dameron's high standards **(Mating Call)** though the deleted album **(The Magic Touch),** using a large ensemble, shows that his genius for voicings and the creation of inspiring springboards remained undimmed.

A great jazz composer, Dameron's work achieves the almost impossible in its balance between form and improvisation. As a judge of talent – Navarro, Eager, Brown, Sarah Vaughan – he ranks with Ellington and Miles Davis.

Recordings:
Dizzy Gillespie, In The Beginning (Prestige/Prestige)
Billy Eckstine, Mr B. & The Band (Savoy/Savoy)
Fats Navarro, Prime Source (Blue Note/Blue Note)
The Arranger's Touch (Prestige/Prestige)
Mating Call (Prestige/—)
Fats Navarro (Milestone/Milestone)
The Miles Davis-Tadd Dameron Quintet (Columbia/CBS)

Johnny Dankworth & Cleo Laine

Born 1927, John Dankworth, alto, soprano, clarinet, bandleader, composer, was one of the founder figures of British modern jazz. His influential Septet, 1950–3, put across the Bebop message **(A Lover & His Lass).** He has led a succession of big bands over the past two decades, taking the Newport Jazz Festival by storm in 1959.

Recruiting top British and American talent to perform his larger works, Dankworth has recorded several excellent concept albums **(What The Dickens, Zodiac Variations** and **Million Dollar Collection).** Often criticized for passionlessness and politeness, his music cannot be faulted on the technical level. A thorough professional, Dankworth has written movie scores and a classical piano concerto.

His wife, singer Cleo Laine, started with the Dankworth Septet in 1951, and their musical partnership has flourished ever since. An international star, she has sung everything from jazz to Schoenberg's Pierrot Lunaire. Most of her albums include jazz or jazz-influenced numbers, and her vocal range and flexibility are phenomenal.

Recordings:
A Lover & His Lass (—/Esquire)
What The Dickens (Fontana/Fontana)
Zodiac Variations (Fontana/Fontana)
Million Dollar Collection (Fontana/Fontana)
Cleo Laine Live At Carnegie Hall (RCA Victor/RCA Victor)
Born On A Friday (RCA Victor/RCA Victor)
I Am A Song (RCA Victor/RCA Victor)
Shakespeare & All That Jazz (Fontana/Fontana)
Best Friends (RCA Victor/RCA Victor)

Kenny Davern

From being a very competent, yet hardly inspired, clarinettist/saxophonist, John Kenneth 'Kenny' Davern (born Huntington, Long Island, New York, 1935) has developed over the years into an impressive musician whose all-round abilities these days are considerable. His collaboration with fellow saxist / clarinettist Bob

Wilber (♦), in the context of the estimable Soprano Summit has been of mutual benefit to both – not to mention jazz lovers. Certainly, Davern's has become increasingly an authoritative voice, whether on clarinet or sopranosax. Whether in the studio **(Soprano Summit** and **Chalumeau Blue)** or in live performance **(Soprano Summit In Concert)** there is little doubt that, like Wilber, in the past five years Davern has shown a musical development and maturity that is little short of astonishing. Other notable recorded evidence of this development, during the same period and before, can be judged from his work with Dick Wellstood (♦) **(Dick Wellstood & His Famous Orchestra Featuring Kenny Davern)** and with Wellstood, Eddie Condon (♦), Gene Krupa (♦) and Wild Bill Davison (♦) **(An Evening At The New School).** A long way perhaps from his earliest days in the music business, with such diverse leaders as Alfredito, Ralph Flanagan, Jack Teagarden (♦), all from early-1950s. Davern also led his own band, the Salty Dogs, in 1958.

Recordings:
Phil Napoleon & His Memphis Five (Capitol/EMI–Electrola – Germany)
Various, An Evening At The New School (Chiaroscuro/—)
Dick Wellstood & His Famous Orchestra Featuring Kenny Davern (Chiaroscuro/—)
Soprano Summit (World Jazz)
Soprano Summit In Concert (Concord Jazz/—)
Soprano Summit, Chalumeau Blue (Chiaroscuro/Pye)

Chalumeau Blue (Pye) – featuring Soprano Summit.

Eddie 'Lockjaw' Davis

Born in New York City, 1921, Eddie 'Lockjaw' Davis is largely self-taught. His early tenor influences, Coleman Hawkins, Ben Webster, Don Byas, formed his big-toned, aggressive style, but he has since developed into an immediately identifiable musician. His early experience with the big bands of Cootie Williams, Lucky Millinder, Andy Kirk and Louis Armstrong made him an ideal sideman for Count Basie, whom he joined in 1952. At a time when the Basie band needed an outsize personality in the ranks, Jaws fitted the bill, and the tracks on which he solos, **Flight Of The Foo Birds** and **After Supper (The Atomic Mr Basie),** leap with vigor and enthusiasm. His work with a studio big band **(Trane Whistle)** inspires

Straight Ahead (Pablo): Jaws doing what he does best.

Above: Eddie 'Lockjaw' Davis, whose honking tenor has saved many a session and revived the Basie band.

everybody and the three-trumpet chase on **Jaws,** followed by the man himself, is a knockout.

In 1955, Jaws teamed with Shirley Scott on organ for a series of straight-ahead bluesy albums **(The Cookbook)** which helped to establish the tenor and organ combo popularity during the late '50s. A number like **The Rev** shows what a master can do with a simple phrase, teasing, squeezing, delaying and hollering in that hoarse, staccato voice until it takes on the contours of emotional conviction. **Have Horn Will Blow** must be one of the hottest solos on record.

He found an ideal partner for a two-tenor band in Johnny Griffin **(The Toughest Tenors).** Sounding positively mainstream beside the mercurial, Bebop Griffin, Jaws' swaggering, melodramatic delivery gives these sessions the stature of a classic boxing bout. Excellent on numerous Norman Granz jam sessions, Lockjaw's feature album **(Straight Ahead)** with the Tommy Flanagan Trio shows all the 'towserish' tenacity that gave him his nickname, and also the Ben Websterish beefy, breathy tenderness on ballads like **I'll Never Be The Same.**

Recordings:
The Atomic Mr Basie
(Roulette/Vogue)
The Second Big Band Sound Of Count Basie (Verve/Verve)
Trane Whistle (Prestige/—)
The Cookbook
(Prestige/Prestige)
The Toughest Tenors
(Milestone/Milestone)
Straight Ahead (Pablo/Pablo)
Hey Lock! (Roulette/Pye)

Miles Davis

Trumpeter Miles Dewey Davis was born in Illinois in 1926, the family making a significant removal to East St Louis when Miles was two. His dentist father bought him a trumpet for his 13th birthday, and his teacher advised him to play without vibrato – 'you're gonna get old anyway and start shaking.' St Louis trumpeters had their own way of playing – sweet, smooth and spacious – quite unlike the pyrotechnic styles of Roy Eldridge and Dizzy Gillespie. Even this early in his career, it was sound that interested Miles.

In 1944, he got his first big break, playing in Billy Eckstine's orchestra which at that time included the cream of the young Bebop revolutionaries, Charlie Parker, Gillespie and Dexter Gordon. Lost in adulation, Miles enrolled at Juilliard School of Music in New York and spent most of his time tracking Parker through the nightspots. The inevitable happened, Bird encouraging the intimidated student to join him on the bandstand. As a foil to the tempestuous leader, Miles' trumpet was adequate, but his solo spots were marred by poor technique, a meager range and faulty intonation. What he did have was a unique emotional impact. He copied nobody, concentrated on the middle register where he was strongest, and worked tirelessly on the shape of his phrases. Most of Parker's Savoy and Dial output gives a good idea of Miles development in the middle '40s **(Bird - The Savoy Recordings** and **Charlie Parker On Dial).**

Leaving Bird in 1948, he studied with arranger Gil Evans, which led to the establishment of the vastly influential nine-piece band. The arrangements of Evans, Carisi and Gerry Mulligan blended the vitality of small combo Bebop with a greater range of sound texture and coloration. The band had a

Below: Miles Davis, still the most influential trumpeter; his groups have spawned innumerable imitations. Genius.

light sound and the instrumentation – apart from Miles' trumpet, Lee Konitz's alto and Mulligan's baritone – included a French horn and tuba. It was altogether too far-out for its time, and the band folded after two weeks, leaving recorded evidence **(Birth Of The Cool** and **Pre-Birth Of The Cool)** which set the pattern for jazz on the West Coast for the next decade.

The early '50s were tough on Miles. Bebop had outstripped its audience and the vogue was for singers. Nevertheless, two albums that the trumpeter cut for Blue Note in 1952-3-4 show an intense emotional involvement with his music. The spareness of his style was emerging as an original aesthetic rather than a cover up for limitations. Irrelevance is rigidly purged. Numbers like **The Leap** or **Take-Off** make use of pedal points, foreshadowing the later modal explorations of **Kind Of Blue.** Some critics contend that these albums are his best **(Miles Davis, 1 & 2).**

In 1954, Miles recorded **Blue 'n' Boogie** and **Walkin',** his way of proving that he could play as hot and funky as the old school, a rebuttal of veteran trumpeter Roy Eldridge's verdict 'it's mouse

music, man.' The same confident Miles cut the famous Christmas Eve session of that year with pianist Thelonious Monk and vibraphonist Milt Jackson **(Tallest Trees),** a session tense with quarrels between Miles and Monk. He speared out long legato notes across bar lines, biting them off abruptly in a style that showed trumpeters how to generate excitement without screaming. The lyrical placement and accenting of phrases made **Bags Groove** and **The Man I Love** into classics. In 1955, he found himself the hit of the Newport Jazz Festival: 'what's all the fuss? I always play like that.'

The quintet that set the pattern for most jazz combos in the '50s followed later in the year. Crucial to the blend of simplicity and multi-directional activity that has always characterized Miles' groups was the choice of drummer. Philly Joe Jones had the fire and inventiveness to lift the soloists, one of the great Hard Bop drummers, and bassist Paul Chambers played long, alert prowling lines. The anchorman was pianist Red Garland, tirelessly solid in his block chord approach. Sharing the front line on tenor was John Coltrane, later to be the greatest trailblazer of the '60s, but at this time still beset by problems. His sound was spinechilling, making

Kind Of Blue (CBS): the seminal modal experiment of Miles.

his entrances great dramatic events, and then following up with solos composed of fast, multi-note rows of chord changes. Coltrane and Miles were diametrically opposed in aims, the leader editing to the bone, and the contrast worked. Under Miles' direction, the band moved away from harmonic predictability, using fewer chord changes to give more prominence to melody. Any tracks show the unity and sheer streamlined superiority of this quintet (**Miles Davis** and **Workin' & Steamin'**).

With altoist Cannonball Adderley added, and pianist Bill Evans for Garland, Miles made one of the most influential albums of his career (**Kind Of Blue**) in which modes, rather than chords, are used as a basis for improvisation. The resultant music is beautiful, uncluttered and ageless. Miles' playing is epigrammatic, the purity of his tone singing.

Miles continued his collaboration with Gil Evans as featured soloist over a richly textured orchestra (**Sketches Of Spain, Porgy And Bess** and **Miles Ahead**), all of which sold well and helped to make his trumpet sound the most syndicated in jazz.

Having pioneered at least two new directions for jazz, and helped to promote the careers of future giants like Rollins, Coltrane, Philly Joe and Bill Evans, he decided to change direction again.

He signed up an unknown teenage drummer, Tony Williams, to provide a constantly challenging polyrhythmic surface, with Ron Carter on bass and Herbie Hancock on piano. The rhythm section was capable of playing in different times to each other, and the overall sound was lighter, lither and more sinuous than its predecessor. Following stints with those underrated tenormen, George Coleman (**My Funny Valentine** and **Four**), and Hank Mobley (**Friday & Saturday Nights – In Person**), Miles lured tenorman Wayne Shorter from Art Blakey's Jazz Messengers. Shorter was basically in the Coltrane bag, a hard, squalling, legato player, but with a jigging, snake-hipped attack that fitted Miles' new conception.

A series of fine albums followed (**ESP, Miles Smiles, Sorcerer, Nefertiti** and **Miles In The Sky**), of which **Miles Smiles** is the highpoint. As influential as the 1955 quintet, it brought the patterns of tension and release to big dipper proportions, avoided strong harmonic touchstones and made use of the rhythmic freedoms pioneered elsewhere. Miles was an outspoken critic of the New Wave – Ornette, Taylor, Dolphy, etc – and soon began looking elsewhere for his next development. The next album, **Filles De Kilimanjaro**, featured Hancock on electric piano and Carter on electric bass, with the flexible drumming of Williams stiffening up.

Miles' new conception was derived from West Coast acid rock, riff dominated with the trumpeter more economic than ever over a brocade of electric ripples. Using an enlarged personnel, Hancock, Chick Corea and Joe Zawinul on electric pianos, Dave Holland on bass, John McLaughlin on guitar, Shorter on soprano saxophone and Tony Williams on drums (all of whom went on to lead their own units), Miles cut what, from the

Above: Miles Davis' classic rhythm section – Jimmy Cobb (drums), Wynton Kelly (piano) and Paul Chambers (bass).

jazz fan's viewpoint, was to be his last album (**In A Silent Way**). Although labels are arbitrary, Miles Davis' subsequent output is of little interest to the jazz record collector.

Recordings:
Birth Of The Cool
  (Capitol/Capitol)
Pre-Birth Of The Cool
  (—/Durium Italian)
Miles Davis, Vols 1 & 2
  (Blue Note/Blue Note)
Walkin' *(Prestige/Prestige)*
Tallest Trees *(Prestige/Prestige)*
Miles Davis *(Prestige/Prestige)*
Workin' & Steamin'
  (Prestige/Prestige)
Milestones *(Columbia/CBS)*
Kind Of Blue *(Columbia/CBS)*
Sketches Of Spain
  (Columbia/CBS)
Porgy And Bess
  (Columbia/CBS)
Miles Ahead *(Columbia/CBS)*
My Funny Valentine
  (Columbia/CBS)
Four *(Columbia/CBS)*
Miles In Europe
  (Columbia/CBS)
Friday And Saturday Nights At The Blackhawk
  (Columbia/CBS)
ESP *(Columbia/CBS)*
Miles Smiles *(Columbia/CBS)*
Sorcerer *(Columbia/CBS)*

Nefertiti *(Columbia/CBS)*
Miles In The Sky
  (Columbia/CBS)
Filles De Kilimanjaro
  (Columbia/CBS)
Miles In Tokio
  (—/CBS Sony – Japan)
In A Silent Way
  (Columbia/CBS)
Water Babies *(Columbia/CBS)*
Miles Davis At Plugged Nickel, Chicago *(—/CBS Sony – Japan)*

Wild Bill Davison

William 'Wild Bill' Davison's birthplace was Defiance, Ohio (in 1906). It seems an appropriate name for a cornet player whose hard-hitting, passionate work has been an integral part of the white-Dixieland, Condon Gang-type jazz scene for around 45 years. Like his late friend and colleague of many years, Eddie Condon (♦), Davison seems to epitomize everyone's idea of the cynical, hard-drinking, hard-living jazzman whose formative years were spent learning his trade in the 1920s/1930s in Chicago, one of jazz' most important landmarks.

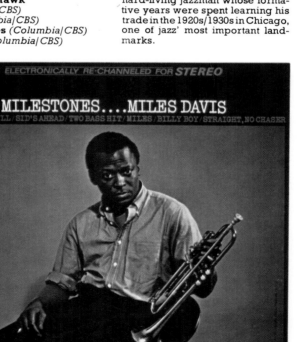

Milestones (Columbia): Miles Davis before the cross-over. Classic quintet plus 'Cannonball' Adderley. Shirt widely admired in 1958.

ESP (CBS): aptly-titled in view of the group interaction.

Davison's earliest playing was with local Ohio bands, before he left for the Windy City in 1927. 1931: put together own big band (which included, prior to his death, legendary clarinet player Frank Teschemacher (♦)), this outfit lasting approximately six months. After which Davison took his cornet to Milwaukee where he worked extensively between 1933–1, including leadership of several smaller groups. Took off again in 1941, this time for New York, where he had played previously, with Omer-Hicks Orchestra (1926), prior to leaving for Chicago. Led own popular band at Greenwich Village club, Nick's, in 1941, as well as working in Boston (1943). Worked in Katherine Dunham Revue ('43), and at Ryan's, New York, before being inducted into US Army (1943–5). With Art Hodes (♦), following demobilization, at Village Vanguard; fronted own outfit in St Louis, then became regular at Eddie Condon Club from 1945–57. Davison and his wife moved to Hollywood (1960), although he was never happy there. Toured with own band in 1962, then with Salt Lake City Six (1963). Took band into New York's Metropole following year. Since 1957, has been regular visitor to Europe where his hot-blooded cornet playing invariably receives warm reception.

On record, Davison's pull-no-punches solo work – basic in rhythmic concept, brassy in tonality – has been much documented on record. His recordings with Condon are admirably representative of his style (**The Golden Days Of Jazz: Eddie Condon** and **We Called It Music**), likewise his recorded work with Sidney Bechet (♦) (**Commodore Jazz, Vol 1**) and Eddie Edwards (**Eddie Edwards & His Original Dixieland Jazz Band**).

Just to show that he can be mellow, sensitive, even lyrical, his interpretations of standard ballads like **I Can't Get Started, Everything Happens To Me** and **You Took Advantage Of Me** (all **But Beautiful**) throw a different, and rarely heard, light on the work of a man who has carried on the traditions of the past with unremitting fervor and passion. (Before taking up trumpet, Davison played mandolin, banjo and guitar.)

Recordings:
Sidney Bechet Album *(—/Saga)*
The Davison-Brunis Sessions, Vols 1, 2 *(—/London)*
Tony Parenti - Ragtime
  (Riverside/London)
The Golden Days Of Jazz: Eddie Condon *(CBS – Holland)*

Various, Commodore Jazz,
Vol 1 (—/London)
Various, Trombone Scene
(—/London)
Wild Bill Davison & His
Jazzologists (Jazzology/—)
Wild Bill Davison, The Jazz
Giants (Sackville – Canada)
Eddie Condon, We Called It
Music (Ace of Hearts)
Wild Bill At The Bull Run
(Jazzology/—)
Various, Jazz At The New
School (Chiaroscuro/—)
Wild Bill Davison, Live At The
Rainbow Room
(Chiaroscuro/—)
Wild Bill Davison, But
Beautiful
(Storyville – Denmark)
Wild Bill Davison With Freddy
Randall & His Band
(Black Lion)

Blossom Dearie

The intriguingly named Miss
Dearie plays piano delicately, and
sings acrid and often witty songs
in a tiny voice. A perennially
popular nightclub entertainer.

Recordings:
My New Celebrity Is You
(Blossom Dearie/Blossom Dearie)

Buddy De Franco

Born Boniface Ferdinand Leonardo
De Franco in 1923, the clarinettist
who won the *Downbeat* Poll ten
years running is today largely a
forgotten man. De Franco was
the victim of fashion: the clarinet
supremacy of the Swing era had
faded, and Bebop found no place
for the instrument, thus De Franco's
virtuosity found little popular outlet. He turns up with the Metronome
All Stars of 1947 with Gillespie,
Bill Harris, Flip Phillips and Nat
King Cole on **Leap Here (All Star
Sessions)** and takes his orchestra
through the fiendishly complex
avant-garde George Russell composition, **A Bird In Igor's Yard
(Crosscurrents)**, also leading a
sextet with Jimmy Raney and
Max Roach on **Extrovert** and
Good For Nothing Joe. A meeting
with piano virtuoso Art Tatum
proved that De Franco was technically equipped to keep up with
that firework display, and he
plays brilliantly **(The Group
Masterpieces)**.

Art Tatum Group Masterpieces
(Pablo): De Franco also ran.

Recordings:
All Star Sessions (Capitol/—)
Crosscurrents (Capitol/Capitol)
**Art Tatum, The Group
Masterpieces** (Pablo/Pablo)
The Jazz Ambassadors, Vol 2
(Verve/Verve)
Borinquin (Sonet/Sonet)

Sidney De Paris

Sidney de Paris (born Crawfords-
ville, Indiana, 1905) never was a
virtuoso trumpet player like, for
example, Louis Armstrong (♦) or
Roy Eldridge (♦), but he was undoubtedly a gifted player – a
musician who made adroit use of
various mutes something of a
speciality – who tends still to be
overlooked when discussion on
top trumpeters is underway. But
de Paris, brother of trombonist-
bandleader Wilbur de Paris (1900–
73), proved his worth on countless
occasions, and in a variety of jazz
settings. True, his fierce growling
contributions to one of the legendary Panassie record dates, that of
November 21, 1938 **(The Complete Ladnier-Mezzrow-Bechet)**
were at variance with fellow trumpeter Tommy Ladnier (♦). But elsewhere he slotted easily into practically any given situation and
usually could be relied upon to
contribute handsomely.
Sidney de Paris' father was band-
master and music teacher. Played
first in local Washington, DC, band
(1924) before switching to New
York in '25. Worked in orchestra
of Charlie Johnson on two occasions (1926-7, 1928-30). With Johnson, de Paris first attracted attention as accomplished soloist: **Harlem Drag (Charlie Johnson -
Lloyd Scott - Cecil Scott)** was one
of his finest statements from this
early period. After Johnson, with
Benny Carter (♦), McKinney's Cotton Pickers, Vols 2, 3) soloing especially well with latter band on **Miss
Hannah (Vol 3)** in typical warm
fashion. Joined Don Redman (♦)

(1932–6), during which time recorded with the respected writer-
instrumentalist-bandleader, taking
fiery solos on such as **Nagasaki,
That Blue-Eyed Baby From
Memphis** and **That Dallas Man**,
and, best of all, a torrid plunger-
muted **Hot & Anxious** (all **Don
Redman**). Although he never
matched other man's irresistible
power and drive, de Paris was
ideal foil for Sidney Bechet (♦).
Following late-1930s work with
Mezz Mezzrow, Redman (again),
Zutty Singleton (♦), and employment with one of legendary Blackbirds revues (1938–9), de Paris
played with Bechet band of 1940.
On record, the Bechet–de Paris
pairing worked well. Though de
Paris' solos could not equal
Bechet's, he produced telling con-
tributions to **Wild Man Blues,
Nobody Knows The Way I Feel
Dis Mornin'** and **Old Man Blues**.
De Paris was to work again – on
record at least – with Bechet, on
more than one occasion in the
future. For instance, a productive
December 1944 session for Blue
Note **(Sidney Bechet Jazz Clas-
sics, Vols 1, 2)** contained ad-
mirable trumpet playing on **Jazz
Me Blues** and **Muskrat Ramble**.
De Paris also recorded for Blue
Note under own name (more pre-
cisely Sidney de Paris' Blue Note
Jazzmen and Sidney de Paris &
His Blue Note Stompers) **(de Paris
Dixie)** as well as with Edmond
Hall (♦) **(Original Blue Note Jazz,
Vol 1)**. During 1940–1, worked
with Benny Carter (♦) Orchestra,
also, briefly, with Charlie Barnet
(♦) big band. Recorded with Art
Hodes (♦), with whose band he
worked in 1942. Further big-band
work with Roy Eldridge (♦), following year, likewise with Claude
Hopkins (♦) (1946).
Not all Sidney de Paris' playing
during last decade of his life (he
died in 1967) was representative
of his best, but there are sufficient
examples of his pungent trumpet
(or flugelhorn) documented on
record which rekindle memories
of earlier times. Most of these

were recorded when he was
member of brother Wilbur's New
Orleans Jazz Band, and include
**Wilbur de Paris & His New
Orleans Jazz, The Wild Jazz
Age**, and, especially, **Callin' The
Blues** with Sidney de Paris' horn
spurring guest Jimmy Witherspoon (♦) into producing some
fine blues singing. (Sidney de
Paris had first worked with Wilbur
1927–8; brothers played together
again in early 1940s.)
From 1964 until his death, Sidney
de Paris worked more or less full-
time with brother's band (although
he did not visit Africa with that outfit in 1957), and with clarinettist
Omer Simeon (♦) provided the
individual musical highlights.

Recordings:
**Charlie Johnson (Lloyd Scott –
Cecil Scott)**
(RCA Victor – France)
**McKinney's Cotton Pickers
(1928-1929), Vols 2, 3**
(RCA Victor – France)
Don Redman (CBS – Realm)
**Various, The Complete
Ladnier-Mezzrow-Bechet**
(RCA Victor – France)
Sidney Bechet, Vol 2
(RCA Victor – France)
**Sidney Bechet Jazz Classics,
Vols 1, 2** (Blue Note)
**Jelly Roll Morton, Vol 2
(1926-1939)**
(RCA Victor – France)
Sidney de Paris, de Paris Dixie
(Blue Note)
**Wilbur de Paris & His New
Orleans Jazz**
(Atlantic/Atlantic)
**Wilbur de Paris, The Wild Jazz
Age** (Atlantic/Atlantic)
**Wilbur de Paris/Jimmy
Witherspoon**
(Atlantic/Atlantic)
**Various (Including Edmond
Hall), Original Blue Note Jazz,
Vol 1** (Blue Note)

Vic Dickenson

Victor 'Vic' Dickenson (born
Xenia, Ohio, 1906) is one of jazz'
most character-full instrumentalists, his droll, mocking trombone
often evoking all kinds of humorous moods; conversely, he can
project gentle sadness, or shouting
exuberance. His shaggy-dog tone
certainly helps in the projection
of his own delightfully eccentric
musical humor, assisted further
by an expert use of mutes (including his own 'spare' hand). There
have been times during a 50-years-
plus career when inspiration has
failed, and when he has tended to
fall back on over-used stock
phrases. But even in his late-
sixties and early-seventies, he has
still been able to call upon his
considerable varied resources
(and experience) to produce performances which continue to mark
him down as one of the most distinctive voices in jazz history.
His playing – open and muted – of
Constantly, a Dickenson original,
recorded during his early-1970s
tenure with the World's Greatest
Jazzband of Yank Lawson & Bob
Haggart **(World's Greatest Jazzband . . . Live At The Roosevelt
Grill)** proved he still was as gifted
as in previous years.
More recently – 1976 on both
occasions – his contributions to
record dates by Ruby Braff (♦)
(Them There Eyes) and another
with Dickenson himself as leader

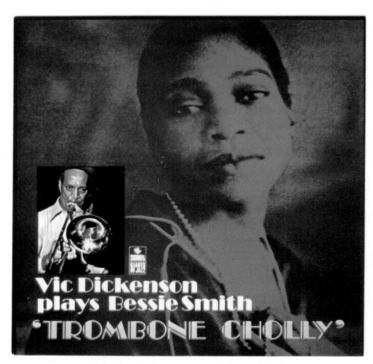

*Vic Dickenson Plays Bessie Smith 'Trombone Cholly' (Sonet).
Great jazz trombonist salutes great blues lady . . .*

(**Vic Dickenson Plays Bessie Smith: 'Trombone Cholly'**) found him in even better form. On latter album, the kind of basic sensitivity that does not always show in his work was realized, most eloquently, during a marvellously relaxed **Nobody Knows You When You're Down & Out.** After failing to come to grips with organ, an elder brother gave Vic Dickenson trombone. Played first tentative dates with this, before family moved *in toto* to Columbus, Ohio, where the young trombonist worked with more local outfits, before taking first professional job with Don Phillips, in Wisconsin.

For next five years, spent playing time in employment of numerous big bands, including those led by Speed Webb, Zack Whyte, Luis Russell (♦) (Dickenson made record debut, as singer, with latter, in '32) before moving to Kansas City. More playing experience with more bands, before first really significant engagement with Claude Hopkins (♦), with whom he was to spend almost four years.

Dickenson's growing reputation with Hopkins led to him joining Benny Carter (♦) Orchestra (1939), staying a year before replacing Benny Morton (♦) with Count Basie (♦). With Basie also for year, without much solo exposure; **Let Me See (Lester Young With The Count Basie Orchestra)** was his only real outing. No reflection on Dickenson's abilities, though, for Basie used few trombone soloists at the time.

After Basie, back with Carter, and more solo opportunities, including **My Favourite Blues** and **What A Diff'rence A Day Made** (both **Benny Carter & His Orchestra 1940-1941**). 1941: worked with Sidney Bechet (♦), both in clubs and on record (**Sidney Bechet, Vol 1**). Was to record again with Bechet on several occasions, first of these three years later, for Blue Note (**Sidney Bechet Jazz Classics, Vols 1, 2**) and also much later, in 1953 (**Sidney Bechet At Storyville, Vols 1, 2**) during one of Bechet's by then infrequent trips back to the US. Dickenson recorded for Blue Note in 1944, Bechet apart, in company with James P. Johnson (♦), Sidney de Paris (♦) (both **Blue Note's Three Decades Of Jazz - 1939 to 1949 - Vol 1**) and Art Hodes (♦) and Edmond Hall (♦) (both **Original Blue Note Jazz, Vol 1**). Durings 1940s, Dickenson's trombone heard with several fine small bands, including those of Frankie Newton (♦) (with whom he had recorded previously in accompaniment to Billie Holiday (♦)) (**The 'Commodore' Years**)), Eddie Heywood (♦) (**Begin The Beguine**) and Hot Lips Page (♦).

Apart from lengthy period of absence through ill-health, stayed with Heywood from 1943–6. Also played well on Lester Young's first record date after being discharged from Army (**The Aladdin Sessions**) and was even better at an Albert Ammons (♦) date for Commodore (**Commodore Jazz, Vol 1**).

During late-1940s, and 1950s, regularly led own bands, worked as solo act as well as for others (frequently in company of Bobby Hackett (♦)) during first half of 1950s. Pair often worked together too in more recent years, including 1968 record date (**This Is My Bag**), which showed Dickenson

Above: Vic Dickenson, important soloist on trombone and one of the most distinctive sounds on that instrument.

at both his best and his least inspiring. Experienced newly-found popularity in mid-1950s with revival of interest in 'mainstream' artists. Recordings for Vanguard, notably **Vic Dickenson Showcase**, received with much all-round acclaim, including **Jeepers Creepers**, with trombone solo which is encapsulation of quintessence of Vic Dickenson's greatness. Other excellent recordings of the period: Buck Clayton's (♦) (**Buckin' The Blues**) and Ruby Braff's (♦) (**Ruby Braff Special**) underlined fact that for too long he had been either underrated or taken for granted. Subsequent record sessions with Lester Young (**Prez & Teddy**) and Pee Wee Russell (♦) (**Jam Session At Swingville**) offered further conclusive proof.

Visited Europe for Cannes Jazz Festival (1958), returning again on several occasions, including tours with George Wein's All Stars (**Midnight Concert In Paris**) and as single performer. To Asia, Australia, with Eddie Condon (♦), in '64; with Wild Bill Davison (♦) (1961–2), co-led (with Red Richards) Saints & Sinners band for several years in same decade, and worked with Bobby Hackett band (1968–70) (**Bobby Hackett Live At The Roosevelt Grill**). Dickenson-Hackett partnership ended only

when trombonist accepted lucrative offer to join World's Greatest Jazz Band, touring and recording (**World's Greatest Jazz Band Of Yank Lawson & Bob Haggart Live At The Roosevelt Grill** and **Century Plaza**) for two to three years. Since then, has continued to work on freelance basis, often putting together fine little bands (**Vic Dickenson & His Quartet**) and continuing to be recorded fairly often by those who realize just how much color, humor and depth his trombone sound can add to a conventional jazz session, viz **Vic Dickenson.**

Recordings:
Benny Carter, Melancholy Benny (1939-1940)
(Tax – Sweden)
Benny Carter & His Orchestra (1940-1941)
(RCA Victor – France)
Sidney Bechet Jazz Classics, Vols 1, 2 *(Blue Note)*
Sidney Bechet, Vol 1
(RCA Victor – France)
Various (Including James P. Johnson/Sidney de Paris/ Sidney Bechet), Blue Note's Three Decades Of Jazz - 1939 to 1949 - Vol 1 *(Blue Note)*
Various, Jammin' At Sunset, Vol 1 *(Black Lion/Black Lion)*
Various (Including Albert

Ammons), Commodore Jazz, Vol 1 *(—/London)*
Lester Young, The Aladdin Sessions *(Blue Note)*
Sidney Bechet At Storyville, Vols 1, 2 *(Storyville/Vogue)*
Vic Dickenson Septet *(Vanguard/Vanguard)*
Ruby Braff Special *(Vanguard/Vanguard)*
Buck Clayton, Buckin' The Blues *(Vanguard/Vanguard)*
Various (Including Pee Wee Russell), Jam Session At Swingville *(Prestige/Prestige)*
Buddy Tate/Earle Warren, The Count's Men *(RCA Victor)*
Lester Young/Teddy Wilson, Prez & Teddy *(Verve)*
Vic Dickenson Showcase *(Vanguard)*/**The Essential Vic Dickenson** *(Vogue)*
Vic Dickenson *(RCA Victor/RCA Victor)*
Buck Clayton Jam Session Vols 1, 2 *(Chiaroscuro)*/ **Buck Clayton Jam Sessions** *(Vogue)*
Bobby Hackett Live At The Roosevelt Grill *(Chiaroscuro/—)*
Various, Midnight Concert In Paris *(—/Philips)*
Billie Holiday, The 'Commodore' Years *(—/Ace of Hearts)*
World's Greatest Jazzband Of Yank Lawson & Bob Haggart Live At The Roosevelt Grill *(Atlantic/Atlantic)*
Vic Dickenson Quartet *(Mahogany/—)*
Ruby Braff, Them There Eyes *(—/Sonet)*
Vic Dickenson Plays Bessie Smith/'Trombone Cholly' *(—/Sonet)*
Buddy Tate, Jive At Five *(Mahogany/—)*
Gentleman Of The Trombone *(Mahogany/—)*

Baby Dodds

Warren 'Baby' Dodds (born New Orleans, Louisiana, 1898; died Chicago, Illinois, 1959), together with Zutty Singleton (♦) and Paul Barbarin (♦), is representative of the very finest drumming to emerge from New Orleans during the early part of jazz history. At 14, worked in factory, but after drum tuition worked with Bunk Johnson (♦) in New Orleans parades. First important job with trumpeter Willie Hightower; then came prestigious gigs with Papa Celestin, Fate Marable (1918–23). Worked with King Oliver (♦) for a year (1922–3), joining brother Johnny Dodds (♦) who was already playing clarinet with the Creole Jazz Band. Dodds' famed press rolls, rock-steady beat, and an all-round flexibility which many contemporaries did not possess, earned him plaudits of big name leaders with whom he worked through the years. This meant he obtained regular work after leaving Oliver with Honore Dutrey, Freddie Keppard, Willie Hightower (again), Lil Armstrong, and Johnny Dodds (with whom he worked regularly at Kelly's Stables, 1927–9).

Dodds brothers played numerous varied engagements together in Chicago during 1930s, including regular appearances at the Three Deuces. Baby Dodds also helped brother run fleet of taxis during same decade. With Jimmie Noone (1940–1), Bunk Johnson (1945); at

47, drummer made first-ever trip to New York with trumpeter's band. With pianist Art Hodes (♦) for two years (1946–7), visited Europe with Mezz Mezzrow ('48) to appear at Nice Jazz Festival. Back in New York with Miff Mole (♦) (1948–9). Suffered stroke in spring of '49; a second in 1950. Was playing again in 1951, and in 1951–2 teamed up with trumpeter Natty Dominique (♦), with whom he had played in Johnny Dodds' Black Bottom Stompers and Washboard Band during late-1920s (**Clarinet King** and **The Complete Johnny Dodds**).

Taken ill in New York in '52, returned to Chicago for recuperation. Last major appearance in New York in 1952. Partially paralysed, Dodds nevertheless played from time to time until forced to retire completely in 1957.

Despite difficulties in recording drummers in pre-hi-fi days, Dodds' drumming skills were an integral part of other discs by King Oliver (**Louis Armstrong & King Oliver** and **West End Blues**), Louis Armstrong (**V.S.O.P. (Very Special Old Phonography), Vols 1 & 2, 3 & 4**), George Lewis (♦) (**George Lewis With Kid Shots**), Bunk Johnson (**Bunk Johnson's Band 1945**), Albert Nicholas (♦) (**Creole Reeds**), Sidney Bechet (♦) (**Sidney Bechet, Vols 2, 3** and **Jelly Roll Morton Vols 1, 2, 4**). But best examples of his talents are to be found on a trio of LPs (**Baby Dodds, Nos 1, 2, 3**) recorded in 1946, in which the younger Dodds gives a comprehensive and totally fascinating account of his approach to jazz drumming, verbally as well as percussionistically.

Recordings:
Louis Armstrong & King Oliver
(Milestone)
King Oliver, West End Blues
(CBS – France)
King Oliver's Jazz Band
(—/Parlophone)
Louis Armstrong, V.S.O.P. (Very Special Old Phonography), Vols 1 & 2, 3 & 4
(CBS – France)
Jelly Roll Morton, Vols 1, 2, 4
(RCA Victor – France)
George Lewis With Kid Shots
(American Music/—)
Bunk Johnson's Band 1945
(—/Storyville)
The Complete Johnny Dodds
(RCA Victor – France)
Sidney Bechet, Vols 2, 3
(RCA Victor – France)
Albert Nicholas, Creole Reeds
(Riverside/—)
Baby Dodds, Jazz A La Creole
(GHB)
Various, 'This Is Jazz', Vols 1, 2
(Rarities/—)
Johnny Dodds, Clarinet King
(—/Ace of Hearts)
Johnny Dodds, Weary Way Blues (Family – Italy)
Baby Dodds, 'Baby Dodds', Nos 1, 2, 3 (Disc/Melodisc)

Johnny Dodds

To most connoisseurs of early jazz Johnny Dodds (born New Orleans, Louisiana, 1892) was the greatest of all clarinet players. In many ways, Dodds – brother of drummer Warren 'Baby' Dodds (♦) and a clarinettist since 17 – *was* the greatest. He may have lacked the technical skills of Sidney Bechet (♦), Jimmie Noone (♦), or Barney

Weary Way Blues (Family, Italy) – Johnny Dodds 1927-29.

Bigard (♦), but he more than made up for any deficiencies with a warmth and passion which only Bechet surpassed.

Tutored by legendary New Orleansian Lorenzo Tio, worked with Kid Ory (♦), and marching bands (both in New Orleans); and on riverboats with Fate Marable; then back with Ory – all before 1920. In latter year, joined King Oliver (♦), working with trumpeter four years, in Chicago and California. Recorded first solos with Oliver, most eloquent of which are **Canal Street Blues** and **Mandy Lee Blues** (**Louis Armstrong & King Oliver**), demonstrating that his was a very basic jazz style; emotional, yet with a harsher (but not unmelodic) tone than, say, Noone. Dodds lacked nothing in ability as blues-player; his contributions to numerous recordings with singers like Ida Cox (♦) (**Ida Cox, Vol 2**) were demonstrably right in every way. With leader-pianist-composer Lovie Austin (**Lovie Austin & Her Blues Serenaders**) Dodds' abilities in blues genre very moving (eg **In The Alley Blues**). As member of Louis Armstrong's (♦) Hot Five/Seven combos, Dodds' playing reached new peaks. He was only member of either band to challenge Armstrong's omnipotence (if not his technical mastery) as soloist.

Recordings such as **Come Back Sweet Papa, Gut Bucket Blues, Willie The Weeper, Wild Man Blues, Melancholy Blues, Weary Blues (V.S.O.P. (Very Special Old Phonography), Vols 1 & 2)** and **Gully Low Blues, S.O.L. Blues (V.S.O.P., Vols 3 & 4)** benefit enormously from his presence as soloist and ensemble player. Equally superb recordings featuring Dodds' piping clarinet, assisted by Kid Ory (♦) and others from Hot Five (sans Armstrong), released under various titles: New Orleans Bootblacks and Wanderers (**Johnny Dodds & Kid Ory**) and Black Bottom Stompers (**Black Bottom Stompers, Vols 1, 2**). Yet further Dodds excellence to be found within **Weary Way Blues** and **Clarinet King**, latter containing exquisite clarinet, and with Armstrong comprehensively on form throughout.

Jelly Roll Morton (♦) made ample use of Dodds' expressive playing on records by his Red Hot Peppers and, even more impressively, in a trio setting, group completed by Morton and Baby Dodds (**Jelly Roll Morton, Vols 1, 2, 4**).

Dodds led own bands during 1930s. Made first (and only) trip to New York in 1938, to record with his Chicago Boys: long-time associate Lil Armstrong, Teddy Bunn

(♦); and Charlie Shavers and O'Neil Spencer from the John Kirby (♦) band. At 46, his powers seemed undiminished, as shown on five items, including further versions of **Wild Man Blues** and **Melancholy Blues (Harlem On Saturday Night)**. Less than three years later, Dodds had died after cerebral haemorrhage (he had moved back to Chicago in '38, suffering a heart attack there a year later).

Probably best all-round examples of Johnny Dodds' playing are to be found on **The Complete Johnny Dodds** with vibrant clarinet throughout sides by Morton (the Trio session), singer Sippie Wallace, Dixieland Jug Blowers, and Dodds' own orchestra, trio, and Washboard Band. Exceptional playing, even by Dodds' finest work elsewhere, particularly on items like **Blue Clarinet Stomp, Heah Me Talkin', Pencil Papa, Indigo Stomp, Mr Jelly Lord, Wolverine Blues** and **Carpet Alley Breakdown**. Apart from clarinet, Johnny Dodds also played alto-saxophone, although he was never in any way an outstanding soloist on this instrument.

Recordings:
King Oliver, West End Blues
(CBS – France)
Louis Armstrong & King Oliver
(Milestone)
Ida Cox, Vol 2 (Fountain)
Lovie Austin & Her Blues Serenaders (Fountain)
Johnny Dodds & Kid Ory
(Columbia)
Johnny Dodds, Black Bottom Stompers, Vols 1, 2
(Swaggie – Australia)
Jelly Roll Morton, Vols 1, 2, 4
(RCA Victor – France)
Louis Armstrong, V.S.O.P. (Very Special Old Phonography), Vols 1 & 2, 3 & 4
(CBS – France)
Johnny Dodds, Clarinet King
(Ace of Hearts)
Johnny Dodds, Weary Way Blues (Family – Italy)
The Complete Johnny Dodds
(RCA Victor – France)
Various, Harlem On Saturday Night (—/Ace of Hearts)

Eric Dolphy

Born 1928 in Los Angeles, the great multi-instrumentalist's earliest influence – in common with most of his generation – was Charlie Parker. Dolphy first came to prominence with the Chico Hamilton Quintet, playing with a passion that threatened to crack the effete confines of that unit. In 1960, he moved to New York to join Charlie Mingus, where his willingness to challenge conventions found a sympathetic environment. Before his death in 1964, Dolphy was in great demand, playing with Max Roach, George Russell, Ornette Coleman and – most notably – John Coltrane. He wrote the orchestrations for the **Africa Brass** album and joined the Coltrane group as a floating member, accompanying them on their tour of Europe – and staying on. From the career point of view, this was a bad move: the brilliant innovator and the pedestrian local talent. His death cut short his expansion from soloist into the fuller group conception of fellow pioneers like Coltrane and Coleman, and his final album, **Out To Lunch**, is a tragic reminder of his potential as a leader.

Dolphy was a transitional figure, neither doctrinaire New Thing, nor wholly content with the harmonic confines of Bebop. He seemed to hear differently, to hear high, so that his work on alto, **245 (Eric Dolphy), The Prophet (Five Spot)**, and **Love Me (Memorial)** takes on a shrill, keening quality. Extremes of vocalization mark his playing on both alto and bass clarinet, an instrument that he rescued from limbo and often used in duos with bass players. With Mingus, **What Love (Charlie Mingus Presents)** or Richard Davis, **Alone Together (Memorial)**, the dark sonorities are rich and ominous as a dungeon

Below: the late great Eric Dolphy, multi-instrumentalist supreme of the '60s. Alto, flute, bass-clarinet.

Out To Lunch (Blue Note): great cover, classic recording.

Eric Dolphy (Epitaph): half of a mammoth recording session.

door, whereas on **Music Matador (Memorial)** it snorts like a happy hippo. On both horns, the shape of his phrases is unpredictable, almost wayward, with abrupt, jagged lines flowering suddenly into decoration. His flute, by contrast, is all prettiness and delicacy, never more so than on **Gazzelloni (Out To Lunch)**.

Recordings:
Eric Dolphy (Prestige/Prestige)
Eric Dolphy At The Five Spot (Prestige/Prestige)
Charles Mingus Presents The Charles Mingus Quartet (CBS Barnaby/—)
Max Roach, Percussion Bitter Sweet (Impulse/Impulse)
George Russell, Outer Thoughts (Milestone/Milestone)
John Coltrane, Africa Brass (Impulse/Impulse)
Eric Dolphy Memorial (VeeJay/DJM)
Eric Dolphy, Out To Lunch (Blue Note/Blue Note)

Natty Dominique

Trumpeter Anatie 'Natty' Dominique (born New Orleans, 1896) was hardly a Louis Armstrong (♦) or King Oliver (♦). But he was a capable player, with warm tone, who did not try to attempt the kind of virtuosic feats his limited technique could not have coped with anyway. Dominique was most closely associated with Johnny Dodds (♦), with whom he worked from 1928 until his retirement from full-time employment in the music business in early-1940s. The Dodds–Dominique partnership was especially effective during a series of recordings, in 1928, by the former's Washboard Band, where Dominique graciously allows the clarinettist to dominate

proceedings, to advantage of both performance and listener **(The Complete Johnny Dodds)**.

Dominique's trumpet sounds particularly at ease in company of another clarinet player: Jimmie Noone (♦) **(Jimmie Noone 1937-1941)**. But he is no match for the litheness of a rhythmically more flexible Noone from a subsequent (1940) record date. He is better, though, at a 1926 session, accompanying blues vocalist Sippie Wallace **(Woman Of The Blues)** and likewise during **Baby** and **Oriental Man** (1927), and **Brown Bottom Bess** and **Lady Love** (1928) (all **Johnny Dodds & Kid Ory)**. Again, though, mixture of Dominique's martial-beat approach and an almost reluctant ensemble lead tends to lessen impact, and make his work appear forgettable. Dominique is fine in ensemble, but again non-assertive on Jelly Roll Morton's (♦) **Muddy Water Blues** and **Big Fat Ham (Jelly Roll Morton 1923/24)**, both dating from 1923. Here, his lack of positive lead lends an air of anonymity to his individual contributions on cornet. Probably finest playing on record dates back to 1927 when, once more in company of Johnny Dodds, Dominique recorded as member of pianist Jimmy Blythe's Owls. His playing here, whilst never likely to approach that of the classic New Orleans trumpeters, is in most ways admirable, not the least in its poignancy—not unlike Bunk Johnson (♦). As with other recordings, Dominique, opposite Dodds' more expressive and assured work, was a perfect foil.

Johnny Dodds, Clarinet King (—/Ace of Hearts)
Various (Including Sippie Wallace), Women Of The Blues (RCA Victor/RCA Victor)
Johnny Dodds & Kid Ory (Columbia)
The Complete Johnny Dodds (RCA Victor – France)
Johnny Dodds, Weary Way Blues (Family – Italy)
Jelly Roll Morton 1923/24 (Milestone)
Jimmie Noone 1937-1941 (Collector's Classics)

Kenny Dorham

Born 1924, McKinley Dorham served his apprenticeship during the hectic Bebop years, playing trumpet in the Dizzy Gillespie big band, and even acquitting himself honorably in chase choruses with the fabulous Fats Navarro **(Fats Navarro Memorial)**, an early influence. Dorham played with the Charlie Parker Quintet **(Historical Masterpieces)**, his tone already bitingly direct. In the mid-'50s, he was a founder member of The Jazz Messengers, the hard-hitting atmosphere and messianic drumming spurring the trumpeter to his best work, **Soft Winds (The Jazz Messengers At The Cafe Bohemia)**.

As the decade wore on, Dorham's Hard Bop style underwent moderate changes, he concentrated on his tone, burnishing it to a muscular lyricism on numbers like **Larue** and **My Old Flame (But Beautiful)**.

Before his death in 1972, he had formed a fruitful association with

Above: the late Kenny Dorham, unfairly overlooked Bebop giant of the trumpet. Diz, Fats and Miles got the plaudits.

the young tenorist, Joe Henderson, and their albums for Blue Note feature a wealth of original material utilizing modes and bossa nova rhythms. Kenny Dorham was unfortunate in his contemporaries, Gillespie and Navarro in the '40s, Miles Davis and Clifford Brown in the '50s. He was considerably more than merely reliable, and his work shows a steady and continuous development. A moving and melodic player, he could also drive like a row of sabres. If popularity polls ignored him, his fellow musicians did not, and he features on albums with Monk, Tadd Dameron, Rollins, Hank Mobley, Max Roach and – rather incongruously – with Cecil Taylor.

Recordings:
Fats Navarro Memorial (Savoy)
Charlie Parker, Historical Masterpieces (Archive of Folk & Jazz/MGM)
The Jazz Messengers At The Cafe Bohemia (Blue Note)
Kenny Dorham, But Beautiful (Milestone)
Kenny Dorham, Trompeta Toccata (Blue Note)
Kenny Dorham, Una Mas (Blue Note)
The Bopmasters (Impulse/—)

Jimmy Dorsey

James Dorsey (born Shenandoah, Philadelphia, 1904) was one of the most accomplished musicians produced by jazz of the Roaring Twenties. Dorsey, elder brother of Tommy Dorsey (♦), started on cornet, moved on to clarinet and alto-sax (occasionally baritone-sax too). Played cornet in band of Thomas F. Dorsey, his father, who taught him basic music knowledge. With brother Tommy, started both Dorsey's Novelty Six, then Dor-

seys' Wild Canaries; latter became one of first jazz outfits to broadcast.

After making recording debut with Billy Lustig's Scranton Sirens, joined California Ramblers (1924), then freelanced – on radio, records – with bands of Jean Goldkette, Henry Thies, Ray Miller, Vincent Lopez, Paul Whiteman (♦), Red Nichols (♦). By 1930, had joined Ted Lewis, with whom he toured Europe. Undertook more extensive studio-session work as well as helping Tommy Dorsey to run part-time Dorsey Bros bands which eventually (in 1934) became full-time Dorsey Bros Orchestra **(Dorsey Bros 1928, Dorsey Bros 1928-1929** and **Bring Back The Good Times)**. This 1934 band lasted for about a year before violent disagreement between the brothers led to younger Dorsey walking offstage during actual engagement – never to return in that band's lifetime.

Jimmy Dorsey continued to lead what was already a band of growing popularity. Gradually, Jimmy Dorsey Orchestra became leading participant in Swing Era, playing to enthusiastic ballroom audiences as well as producing hit records like **Amapola, Tangerine, My Prayer, Yours, Green Eyes, Besame Mucho** and **Star Eyes (The Great Jimmy Dorsey)**, each featuring vocal performances by Bob Eberly, Helen O'Connell and Kitty Kallen – alone or in pairs. Much of jazz content disappeared altogether, although on certain occasions **(Jimmy Dorsey & His Orchestra 1935-1942)** the commercial-pop aspects were (temporarily) forgotten and the band endeavored to swing with eloquent power, as with items such as **Stompin' At The Savoy, Major & Minor Stomp, Mutiny In The Brass Section** and **Waddlin' At The Waldorf**.

Despite demise of big-band era,

Dorsey continued to lead own orchestra until 1953 when he was finally reunited with Tommy as member of his brother's own orchestra. (Musically, pair had been reunited in 1947, when both appeared in semi-biographical movie, *The Fabulous Dorseys*).

On Tommy's death, in '56, Jimmy Dorsey assumed leadership of former's band, a position he held until following year when increasing ill-health forced him to retire. Same year, he died of cancer.

Jimmy Dorsey band took part in several World War II movies, including *The Fleet's In, 4 Jacks & A Jeep, That Girl From Paris* and *Shall We Dance?* As jazz instrumentalist, Dorsey's reputation probably is best remembered from earlier days, 'way back to the 1920s-through-the-1930s, when he worked with innumerable jazzmen, including Jack Teagarden (♦) (**J.T.** and **Jack Teagarden Classics**); Joe Venuti (♦), Eddie Lang (♦) and Adrian Rollini (♦) (**Benny Goodman & The Giants Of Swing/Jazz In The Thirties**); Miff Mole (♦) (**Miff Mole's Molers 1928-30**) and Red Nichols (♦) (**Red Nichols & His Five Pennies, 1926-1928**).

In the 1920s, his was the most important voice on alto-sax; on clarinet, too, his playing was always immaculate, although not quite as distinctive; on cornet (or trumpet), Dorsey could be a more-than-average 'hot' performer, as he proved in company with Venuti-Lang Blue Five (**Benny Goodman & The Giants Of Swing/Jazz In The Thirties**). On alto and clarinet, his always rhythmic playing was a decided asset, whether heard in context of Whiteman Orchestra (**The Bix Beiderbecke Legend**) or in proximity with such as Bix Beiderbecke (♦) and Frankie Trumbauer (♦) (**The Golden Days Of Jazz: Bix Beiderbecke**) or in all manner of bands with or without his brother (**Tommy, Jimmy & Eddie, 1928-29**). And even during the peak days of his orchestra, Jimmy Dorsey's jazz feel, coupled with his technical dexterity, could produce a supremely rewarding performance, as with his astonishingly good version of **I Got Rhythm**, as guest on one of Eddie Condon's (♦) legendary war-time concerts (**Eddie Condon & His All Stars, Vol 8**).

Recordings:
Tommy Dorsey/Jimmy Dorsey/ Eddie Lang, Tommy, Jimmy & Eddie 1928-29
(—/Parlophone)
The Bix Beiderbecke Legend
(RCA Victor – France)
The Charleston Chasers 1925-1928 (VJM)
Jack Teagarden Classics
(Family)
Jack Teagarden, 'J.T.'
(—/Ace of Hearts)
Various, Benny Goodman & The Giants Of Swing (Prestige)/ **Jazz In The Thirties**
(World Records)
Joe Venuti/Eddie Lang, The Sounds Of New York, Vol 2 (1927-1933)
(RCA Victor – France)
Miff Mole's Molers - 1927, With Sophie Tucker
(—/Parlophone)
Miff Mole's Molers 1928-30
(—/Parlophone)
Red Nichols & His Five Pennies, 1926-1928
(MCA Coral – Germany)

Dorsey Bros, 1928-1930
(The Old Masters/—)
Coleman Hawkins, Recordings Made Between 1930 & 1941
(CBS – France)
Dorsey Bros, Bring Back The Good Times
(MCA Coral – Germany)
Jimmy Dorsey & His Orchestra 1935-1942 (Swingfan – Germany)
The Great Jimmy Dorsey
(Ace of Hearts)

Tommy Dorsey

Tommy Dorsey (born Shenandoah, Pennsylvania, 1905), younger brother by one year of Jimmy Dorsey (♦), started his musical life as a trumpet player and trombonist but during the last 25 years of his life was renowned as leader of a jazz-influenced danceband who mostly featured himself as a trombone player with a gift for executing superbly controlled pianissimo ballad performances, each solo being a model – with or without mute – for any aspiring player on that instrument.

If either of the two Dorsey brothers could be said to have the shortest temper, then probably it was the younger; it was this red-blooded temperament which led to frequent clashes – even stand-up fights – not only with Jimmy Dorsey, but with a succession of sidemen he employed during his many years as bandleader.

Like Jimmy, Tommy Dorsey was taught to play trumpet by his musician-father. His trumpet play-

Tommy Dorsey, Vol 2 (RCA Victor). For years Tommy Dorsey fronted a successful jazz-based dance band.

ing in the early days was interesting insofar as, where most of his white contemporaries tended to follow the lyrical pathway of Bix Beiderbecke (♦), Dorsey's impassioned blowing obviously was primarily influenced by the 'hot' solos of the leading black hornmen. For example, his fierce solos on **It's Right Here For You** and **Tiger Rag**, both from a November 1928 recording date, likewise, **Daddy, Change Your Mind** and **You Can't Cheat A Cheater** from following April (all **Tommy, Jimmy & Eddie, 1928-29**) bear ample testimony to the emotional content in his trumpet work.

During 1927–8, worked as trombonist with the Paul Whiteman (♦) Orchestra. Perhaps his most famous solo feature with Whiteman was a first-class contribution to Don Redman's arrangement of **Whiteman Stomp (Paul Whiteman & His Orchestra)**. During the time when he was co-leading one of the early Dorsey Bros bands he recorded **I'm Getting Sentimental Over You**. By the time he had split with his brother and put together own band, Tommy Dorsey had re-recorded the tune (**Tommy Dorsey & His Orchestra**) and thereafter it was to become his very popular signature tune. From 1935, when he formed the Tommy Dorsey Orchestra – using remnants of Joe Haynes Orchestra – until his death in 1956, he was to prove one of the most popular as well as durable bandleaders.

The Tommy Dorsey Orchestra peaked between 1937–44, during which time top jazz sidemen like Bud Freeman (♦), Louis Bellson (♦), Gene Krupa (♦), Buddy Rich (♦), Charlie Shavers (♦), Max Kaminsky (♦), Bunny Berigan (♦), Buddy De Franco (♦), Joe Bushkin and Yank Lawson (♦) had passed through its ranks. Likewise, a host of superior pop singers, mostly on the first rungs of the ladder to success, notably Jack Leonard, Jo Stafford, Dick Haymes, Lucy Ann Polk and, most famous of all, Frank Sinatra.

Whilst arrangers Paul Weston and Axel Stordahl handled more commercial aspects of band's charts, Dorsey wisely utilized skills of such jazz-based writers as Dean Kincaide and Sy Oliver, in order to maintain the real spirit of jazz within the band, something all too often absent from many of Dorsey's big-band rivals of the Swing Era. The Clambake Seven – a small group taken from within the ranks of the orchestra – also helped to sustain the jazz interest (**Tommy Dorsey, The Clambake Seven**). Oliver was employed, not only as staff arranger, but on occasion as trumpeter and singer too. Dorsey himself featured less and less as a jazz soloist of any real importance, although there were times when the urge to become involved with undiluted jazz could not be resisted, for example as a sometime member of the Metronome All Stars (**Metronome All Stars/**

Esquire AllStars). Usually, though, Dorsey was content to produce one superb ballad performance after another (or supply ultra-smooth obbligato for his vocalists), as well as indulge in purely technical exercises like **Trombonology (Tommy Dorsey, Vol 2)**.

The Dorsey Orchestra featured in several films, including *Ship Ahoy!, Reveille With Beverly, Girl Crazy* and *A Song Is Born.*

Amongst its most popular discs can be numbered **After You've Gone, Lonesome Road** (two-part record arranged by Oliver) (both **Tommy Dorsey, Vol 2**) and **On The Sunny Side Of The Street, Marie** (featuring Berigan and with vocal by Leonard), **Hawaiian War Chant, Opus No. 1** and **Song Of India** (fine Berigan trumpet solo) (all **Tommy Dorsey & His Orchestra**). There were many others too, mostly featuring vocalists Sinatra, Stafford, the Pied Pipers, et al, but all basically conceived in a pop bag. For Tommy Dorsey, his involvement with jazz went back to his more youthful days, when he blew passionately – both on trombone and trumpet – in company of other eager, fresh-faced youngsters like Benny Goodman (♦) **(The Early B.G.)**, Joe Venuti (♦) and Eddie Lang (♦) **(The Golden Days Of Jazz/Stringing The Blues** and **The Sounds Of New York, Vol 2)**, Bix Beiderbecke (♦) **(The Bix Beiderbecke Legend)** and Adrian Rollini (♦) **(Jazz In The Thirties)**.

Recordings:
Tommy Dorsey/Jimmy Dorsey/ Eddie Lang, Tommy, Jimmy & Eddie - 1928-29
(—/Parlophone)
Tommy Dorsey & His Orchestra
(RCA Victor/RCA Victor)
Tommy Dorsey, Vol 2
(RCA Victor/RCA Victor)
The Best Of Tommy Dorsey, Vols 1-6 (RCA Victor – France)
Dorsey Bros, Bring Back The Good Times
(MCA Coral – Germany)
Dorsey Brothers 1928
(The Old Masters)
Dorsey Brothers 1928-1930
(The Old Masters)
The Chocolate Dandies
(—/Parlophone)
Benny Goodman, The Early B.G.
(Vocalion)
Joe Venuti/Eddie Lang, The Golden Days Of Jazz/Stringing The Blues (CBS – Holland)
Joe Venuti/Eddie Lang, The Sounds Of New York, Vol 2
(RCA Victor – France)
Bix Beiderbecke, The Bix Beiderbecke Legend
(RCA Victor – France)
Various (Including Adrian Rollini), Jazz In The Thirties
(World Records)
Various, Metronome All Stars/ Esquire All Stars
(RCA Victor – France)
Paul Whiteman & His Orchestra
(RCA Victor/RCA Victor)
Tommy Dorsey, The Clambake Seven (RCA Victor)

Hank Duncan

Henry 'Hank' Duncan (born Bowling Green, Kentucky, 1896; died Long Island, New York, 1968) was leader of his own bands as early in present century as 1918–19: first, in Louisville, then in Detroit. After which this Fats Waller

Above: Eddie Durham – trombonist, guitarist, writer. A talented, always reliable, man to have on your team.

(♦)-James P. Johnson (♦)-Luckey Roberts disciple moved to Buffalo and joined the Fess Williams band for five-year spell. 1931: worked for a while with King Oliver (♦), then with Sidney Bechet (♦) and Tommy Ladnier (♦), Charlie Turner's Arcadians (including stint as second pianist when Fats Waller toured with band). Duncan, who possessed huge hands, a helpful physical attribute for pianists of stride - cum - Harlem - rent - party proclivities, worked for many years as solo act in New York. 1939: became one-third of Zutty Singleton (♦) Trio.

During 1940s, worked with various name musicians, including Bechet and Mezz Mezzrow (Duncan had recorded as member of Bechet's New Orleans Feetwarmers **(Sidney Bechet, Vols 1, 2)** in 1932). Began lengthy housepianist tenure at New York's Nick's, in Greenwich Village (1947–63), interrupted only by one-and-a-half years (1955–56) together with Singleton and trumpeter Louis Metcalf, at Metropole.

After Nick's engagement finally concluded, Duncan did usual rounds of jazz clubs right up to his death. Never did get much opportunity to record alone, a 1944 date for Black & White appears to be only time he appeared on record under his own name. But apart from the Bechet sessions mentioned above, did appear on record in company with likes of Waller (1935) **(Fats Waller Mem-**

orial, Vol 1); Wild Bill Davison (♦) (1954) **(Wild Bill Davison & His Jazzologists)**; Tony Parenti (♦) (1955) **(Tony Parenti's All Stars)**; and ex-Waller reedman Gene Sedric's Honey Bears (1938).

Duncan was, without question, a fine 'strider' whose talents, in the end, never were fully realized – or sufficiently appreciated.

Recordings:
Sidney Bechet, Vols 1, 2
(RCA Victor – France)
Fats Waller Memorial, Vol 1
(RCA Victor – France)
Various (Including Gene Sedric), Swing Street, Vol 1
(Tax – Sweden)
Wild Bill Davison & His Jazzologists (Jazzology/—)
Tony Parenti's All Stars
(Jazztone/—)

Eddie Durham

Eddie Durham has spread his talents widely – as guitarist, trombonist, arranger, composer – in a most productive way. He never was the most remarkably gifted jazzman in any of these areas, but has always commanded respect of his fellow musicians for general reliability and an unfailing ability to produce the goods in a professional and expert manner. Comes from musical family – in fact, no less than six brothers have been

employed as musicians. Indeed, Durham's initial playing experience (as guitarist) was with so-called Durham Bros Orchestra.

After adding trombone, Durham (born St Marcos, Texas, 1906) worked with succession of Mid-Western bands during late-1920s, including Walter Page's Blue Devils. First major gig though, with Bennie Moten (♦) Orchestra (1929), with whom he stayed until 1933. Played trombone, guitar with Moten, began making reputation also as composer, arranger. Composed (or co-composed) variety of jump-style tunes, including **Every Day Blues (Bennie Moten's Kansas City Orchestra, Vol 3, 1929), You Made Me Happy, Oh! Eddie, Prof. Hot Stuff (... Vol 4, 1929-1930)** and **Lafayette (... Vol 5, 1929-1932)**. Took brief guitar solos on various numbers, best of which was probably **I Wanna Be Around My Baby All The Time (Vol 5, 1929-1932)**. Employed by Cab Calloway (♦), Andy Kirk (♦), before moving on to Willie Bryant, as staff arranger. Reputation further enhanced on joining Jimmie Lunceford (♦) where, again, his services as instrumentalist as well as writer became much in evidence. For Lunceford, arranged **Swingin' On C** (own composition), **Blues In The Groove, Wham (Re - Bop - Boom - Bam) (Takin' Off); Lunceford Special (Lunceford Special); Bird Of Paradise, Rhapsody Junior** (both with Eddie Wilcox) **(Rhythm Is Our Business)**; and **Pigeon Walk (For Dancers Only)**.

Solo-wise, chances were restricted with Lunceford, although his electric guitar playing (Durham was one of first jazzmen to use amplified instrument on regular basis at this time) on **He Ain't Got Rhythm (Jimmy's Legacy)**, makes it not at all difficult to understand why he was a major influence on Charlie Christian (♦). Left Lunceford for Count Basie (♦) (1937), as staff arranger and sideman. Continued to produce first-class compositions-arrangements, including **Topsy** (later to become a pop-size hit via a Cozy Cole (♦) disc), **Time Out** (with composer featured on guitar), **Out The Window (The Best Of Basie, 1937-1938)**.

With his services as writer becoming more and more in demand, left Basie mid-1938. For up-and-coming Glenn Miller Orchestra, wrote **Slip Horn Jive (Legendary Glenn Miller, Vol 2), Glen Island Special**, and arranged **Baby Me (Legendary Glenn Miller, Vol 3)**, whilst Miller made good use of **Wham (Re - Bop - Boom - Bam) (Legendary Glen Miller, Vol 4)**. Durham also provided Miller with fine chart for **I Want To Be Happy (Vol 4)**. Also wrote for bands of Artie Shaw (♦), Ina Ray Hutton, Jan Savitt.

Some more-than-reasonable mid-period jazz emanated from Durham-supervised record session of early-1940s **(The Swinging Small Bands 2, 1940-1944)** and he toured with all-girl band, International Sweethearts of Rhythm (1941–3), acting as musical director. Later, led his own all-female band. Continued to be active as writer, and sometimes instrumentalist, with various bands, singers through 1940s; during 1950s-1960s again busy, mostly in writing capacity – although did get to play with band calling itself Swingers, Inc.

Since late 1950s has also led own bands, mostly in and around New York. 1969: joined Buddy Tate (♦) band, playing trombone, guitar, and during early-1970s worked worked with Count's Men (unit led by former Basie colleague Earle Warren). Recorded in New York by British critic-author Albert McCarthy (**Eddie Durham**) in 1973, 1974, Durham had lost little of his instrumental-compositional talents. His guitar work – especially on his own **Blues For Mac** (an obvious dedication), and **Good Morning Blues** – is beyond reproach. Also in 1973, recorded with saxist-clarinettist Eddie Barefield (**Eddie Barefield**) with pleasing results. Amongst other Eddie Durham compositions, his most famous (more from a pop standpoint) must be **I Don't Want To Set The World On Fire.**

Recordings:
Bennie Moten's Kansas City Orchestra, Vols 3, 4, 5 (*RCA Victor – France*)
Jimmie Lunceford, Takin' Off (*Tax – Sweden*)
Jimmie Lunceford, Lunceford Special (*Columbia/CBS – Realm*)
Jimmie Lunceford, Rhythm Is Our Business (*MCA – Germany*)
Jimmie Lunceford, For Dancers Only (*MCA – Germany*)
Jimmie Lunceford, Jimmie's Legacy (*MCA – Germany*)
The Best Of Count Basie, 1937-1938 (*MCA – Germany*)
The Legendary Glenn Miller, Vols 2, 3, 4 (*RCA Victor/RCA Victor*)
Various (Including Eddie Durham), The Swinging Small Bands 2 (*MCA – Germany*)
Eddie Durham (*RCA Victor/RCA Victor*)
Eddie Barefield (*RCA Victor/RCA Victor*)

Allen Eager

Born 1927 in New York, tenorman Allen Eager is one of the enigmas of jazz. A concise, swinging player strongly based on the Lester Young style, Eager was one of the best tenors on 52nd Street in the '40s, but frequently left the scene for High Society, skiing, horse-riding and

car-racing, settling in Paris in the '50s. Some of his best blowing can be found on a Savoy compilation (**The Brothers & Other Mothers**) which features Lester's white disciples, Stan Getz, Al Cohn, Zoot Sims, Brew Moore and Serge Chaloff. His flowing drive on numbers like **Booby Hatch** is wildly exciting. Two years later, in 1948, he played in Tadd Dameron's sextets and septets, sharing the front line with players like Fats Navarro and Wardell Gray (**Prime Source** and **Good Bait**). Interesting to contrast his style with Gray's; both men are on the Lester-Bird axis, with Eager lighter, more floating in his attack, **Lady Bird** and **Jahbero.** In the early '50s, Eager played with Gerry Mulligan's large groups in company with Lee Konitz, Al Cohn and Zoot Sims, switching to alto for some tracks (**Revelation**). Nothing is available of his later work.

Recordings:
The Brothers & Other Mothers (*Savoy/Savoy*)
Fats Navarro, Prime Source (*Blue Note/Blue Note*)
Fats Navarro – Tadd Dameron, Good Bait (*Riverside/—*)
Gerry Mulligan – Lee Konitz, Revelation (*Blue Note/Blue Note*)

Billy Eckstine

Born 1914 in Pittsburg, singer Billy Eckstine became the first Afro-American pop idol. His rich, bass-baritone voice, perfect pitch and timing, gave him supremacy in the field of the romantic ballad, **I Apologize, Tenderly, Laura, No One But You (Greatest Hits).** In fact, Eckstine is a hipper musician than his pop following realize. From 1939–43, he was the vocalist with Earl Hines' band, forming his own big band 1944–7 which was years ahead of its time. Excited by the Bebop explosion, Eckstine recruited a band of young revolutionaries, including Charlie Parker, Dizzy Gillespie, Fats Navarro, Kenny Dorham, Miles Davis, Sonny

Stitt, John Jackson, Dexter Gordon, Wardell Gray, Gene Ammons, Leo Parker, Tommy Potter and Art Blakey. Arrangements by Dizzy Gillespie, Tadd Dameron, Budd Johnson and Jerry Valentine gave the band a distinctive, adventurous sound, and it was probably only the Eckstine vocals that gave it its commercial viability. Sarah Vaughan also sang with the band, showing an Eckstine influence in her wide vibrato. Proficient on trombone and trumpet, the leader took occasional solos, but gave generous space to Dexter Gordon, **Lonesome Lover Blues;** Gene Ammons, **Second Balcony Jump;** Wardell Gray, **Blues For Sale;** Fats Navarro, **Tell Me Pretty Baby.** Two albums catch the band at its peak (**Mr. B. & The Band** and **Together**), the latter album taken from radio broadcasts.

Eckstine has continued to record with jazz musicians from time to time, including the hilarious **I Left My Hat In Haiti** with Woody Herman, and **St. Louis Blues**, with the Metronome All-Stars, including Lester Young and Warne Marsh (**Greatest Hits**). With the sort of voice you could stand a spoon up in, the Eckstine baritone influenced many of the Bebop singers of the period.

Recordings:
Greatest Hits (*MGM/MGM*)
Mr. B. & The Band (*Savoy/Savoy*)
Together (*Spotlite/Spotlite*)

Harry Edison

Harry Edison (born Columbus, Ohio, 1915) remains, after 40 years, one of jazz's most gifted and distinctive trumpet players. His sweet-sour tone, deceptively casual approach to what is a straight kind of swing, and splendid all-round qualities have, since the mid-1930s, ensured that his services have been constantly in demand. For conventional jazz record sessions like **Jazz Giants '57/Jazz Giants, Jam Session, Nos 2, 3** and **Jammin' At Sunset,** or bread-and-butter studio sessions with jazz-influenced singers of the calibre of Ella Fitzgerald (♦) (**Sings The Cole Porter Song Book**) and Frank Sinatra (**Swing Easy/Songs For Young Lovers**), or for guest appearances at major international jazz festivals (**Newport In New York '72: The Jam Sessions, Vol 4** and **Jazz At The Santa Monica '72**). His own sound alone would make Edison's an individual voice, but his playing is even more easily identifiable when he uses a mute – result is a tight, choked sound, with tension created by resultant feeling of suppressed excitement that is not really suppressed at all.

After commencing on trumpet at 12, Edison's career in music began with work for local Ohio bands. Moved on to Alphonso Trent, then Jeter-Pillars, before gaining valuable, hard-blowing experience with R&B-inclined band of Lucky Millinder (♦), starting in February '37. Accepted invitation to replace Karl George in trumpet section of Count Basie (♦) Orchestra. Stayed with Basie until leader disbanded in February '50, during which time was employed continuously as a principal soloist. For Basie, Edison

produced string of memorable solos, including those on recordings like **Panassie Stomp, Jive At Five (You Can Depend On Basie); Shorty George, Texas Shuffle (Jumpin' At The Woodside); Every Tub, Bolero At The Savoy (Super Chief); Blow Top, Rock-A-Bye Basie, Louisiana, Moten Swing, Easy Does It (Lester Young With Count Basie & His Orchestra); Tuesday At Ten** (**Basie's Back In Town**); and **Taps Miller, The Killer** and **Avenue C** (**Basie's Best**). Also produced for Basie clutch of Kansas City-inspired compositions, including **H&J, Let Me See, Beaver Junction,** and the eminently durrable **Jive At Five.** After leaving Basie, worked with Jimmy Rushing (♦), Jazz At The Philharmonic (1950), then Buddy Rich (♦). Was employed by drummer for most of two-year period (1951–3). Rich has often used services of Edison – one of his favorite trumpet players – for live appearances and for record dates, in both small combo and big band contexts (**That's Rich** and **Buddy & Sweets**).

In 1953 undertook international tour as solo performer with revue of late Josephine Baker. Then moved to West Coast where he set up home, becoming regular studio musician, working often with top artists like Sinatra, Nat King Cole (♦), Nelson Riddle, etc. During period, recorded one of his finest albums, **Inventions/Sweet At The Haig,** live quartet date which showcased all his qualities in most admirable fashion. Around this time, however, Edison's work tended to fall short of greatness by penchant for overuse of musical clichés. From time to time, clichés have returned; mostly, though, he has continued to prove one of the most gifted practitioners of jazz trumpet-playing. Undismayed by advent (and eventual passing) of bop, Edison's fetching brand of mid-period jazz often has a quality of timelessness.

1958: moved back to New York, working mostly with own bands, personnel often including such as Ben Webster (♦), Jimmy Forrest (♦) and Joe Williams, the singer. With George Auld in '64, visited Europe with another JATP troupe same year. Continued to guest with top bands, like those of Rich, Louis Bellson (♦) (**Thunderbird**), and old boss, Basie; but by end of 1960s was working once again in California.

Apart from those mentioned above, has contributed handsomely to record dates involving Red Norvo (♦) (**Greatest Of The Small Bands, Vol 1**); Jimmy Witherspoon (♦) (**There's Good Rockin' Tonight**); Barney Kessel (♦) (**To Swing Or Not To Swing**); Lionel Hampton (♦) (**The Tatum Group Masterpieces**).

Own dates have been less frequent perhaps than one might have expected, but more often than not have resulted in music of highest quality, as with the admirable **Gee Baby, Ain't I Good To You/Blues For Basie** and **Walkin' With Sweets;** both LPs benefiting greatly by presence of Ben Webster. For Edison, a particularly rewarding date was that which placed his trumpet alongside giants like Duke Ellington (♦) and Johnny Hodges (♦). Even though there were occasions when the clichés were present, his contributions overall to the occasion

Below: Harry 'Sweets' Edison, perennial trumpet favorite of fellow trumpeters, Sinatra and jazz buffs alike.

(Blues Summit/Side By Side - Back To Back) seldom fell below a level of real inspiration. His work here is the epitome of utter relaxation.

In more recent times, has tended to come into spotlight again, following period of neglect. After early-1970s re-appearance with JATP **(Jazz At The Santa Monica '72)** Edison signed with Norman Granz' Pablo label. As a result, his playing, on records at least **(Oscar Peterson & Harry Edison, Basie Jam, The Trumpet Kings Meet Joe Turner, The Bosses** and, best of all thus far, **Edison's Lights)** give ample proof that, musically, he has taken on new lease of life. Apart from his many other achievements in an eminently satisfactory career, Edison's squeeze-note style was heard in Gjon Mili's film *Jammin' The Blues* **(Jammin' With Lester)** as front-line colleague to former Basie associates Lester Young (♦), Dicky Wells (♦), and Illinois Jacquet (♦).

Recordings:
Count Basie, You Can Depend On Basie (—/Coral)
Count Basie, Jumpin' At The Woodside (—/Coral)
Count Basie, Super Chief (Columbia/CBS)
Lester Young With Count Basie & His Orchestra (Epic – France)
Count Basie, Basie's Back In Town (Epic/Philips)
Count Basie, Basie's Best (CBS – Holland)
Harry Edison, Inventions (Pacific Jazz)/
Sweets At The Haig (Vogue)
Frank Sinatra, Swing Easy/ Songs For Young Lovers (Capitol/Capitol)
Ella Fitzgerald Sings The Cole Porter Song Book (Verve/Verve)
Various, Jammin' At Sunset (Black Lion/Black Lion)
Buddy Rich, That's Rich (—/Verve)
Buddy Rich, Buddy & Sweets (Verve/Verve)
Various, Jam Sessions, Nos 2, 3 (Verve/Columbia – Clef)
Barney Kessel, To Swing Or Not To Swing (Contemporary/ Vogue – Contemporary)
Various, Jazz Giants '57 (Verve)/ **Jazz Giants** (Columbia – Clef)
Harry Edison, Gee Baby, Ain't I Good To You (Verve)/ **Blues For Basie** (Verve)
Harry Edison, Walkin' With Sweets (Verve)
Jimmy Witherspoon, There's Good Rockin' Tonight (World Pacific/Fontana)
Art Tatum (Including Lionel Hampton), The Tatum Group Masterpieces (Pablo/Pablo)
Red Norvo, Greatest Of The Small Bands, Vol 1 (RCA Victor – France)
Duke Ellington/Johnny Hodges, Blues Summit (Verve)/ **Side By Side - Back To Back** (Verve)
Various, Jazz At The Santa Monica (Pablo/Pablo)
Various, Newport In New York '72: The Jam Sessions, Vol 4 (Atlantic/Atlantic)
The Trumpet Kings Meet Joe Turner (Pablo/Pablo)
Count Basie/Joe Turner, The Bosses (Pablo/Pablo)
Oscar Peterson & Harry Edison (Pablo/Pablo)
Count Basie, Basie Jam (Pablo/Pablo)

Harry Edison, Edison's Lights (Pablo/Pablo)
Various, Jammin' The Blues (Jazz Archives)
Louis Bellson, Thunderbird (Impulse/—)

Above: Roy Eldridge. In the history of jazz his contributions to trumpet have been of seminal importance.

Roy Eldridge

David Roy 'Little Jazz' Eldridge (born Pittsburgh, Pennsylvania, 1911) is one of the most important trumpet soloists in jazz history. A superb technician, and a player of extra-ordinary fire and emotional projection, Eldridge first played drums (at six), and received some tuition on trumpet from elder brother Joe Eldridge (1908–52), himself a first-class alto-saxophonist, violinist. After working with various little-known bands (including his own), first came into prominence with Horace Henderson's Dixie Stompers, then with Zach Whyte (both in '28), Speed Webb (1929–30), Cecil Scott, Elmer Snowden, Charlie Johnson, Teddy Hill, before co-leading (with brother Joe) local Pittsburgh outfit (1933). With McKinney's Cotton Pickers, then back with Teddy Hill, worked with another of his own bands, before, in 1935, became member of one of the principal jazz outfits of the period, that led by Fletcher Henderson (♦). Although Eldridge's trumpet was heard with Henderson for only a comparatively short period (1936-7), he carried on great tradition of superior trumpet soloists with band, producing red-hot solos on such as **Christopher Columbus, Stealin' Apples** and **Blue Lou** (all **The Fletcher Henderson Story/The Fletcher Henderson Story, Vol 4**). Around this time, was

catalyst supreme on some of the finest small-group recordings of 1930s: with Gene Krupa's (♦) Swing Band, in 1936 **(Benny Goodman, Vol 4: 1935-1939)**; with Teddy Wilson (♦) **(The Teddy Wilson** and **Teddy Wilson & His All Stars)**; as well as Wilson-led sessions involving singer Billie Holiday (♦) **(The Golden Years, Vols 1, 2** and **God Bless The Child)**. Eldridge was to work with Holiday in later years **(In Concert: Coleman Hawkins with Roy Eldridge & Billie Holiday** and **The Voice Of Jazz, Vol 7)**.

During 1937, brought exciting eight-piece band into Chicago's Three Deuces **(Roy Eldridge At The Three Deuces, Chicago - 1937)** which featured not only Joe Eldridge on alto, but some of his brother's most exceptional playing up to that time. Roy Eldridge was to become resident at Three Deuces between 1936–8, after which he toured States with same band. That same year left music business for a while to study radio-engineering. Comeback took place in November '38, at 52nd Street's Famous Door. Same month, recorded for Commodore, in company with tenorist Chu Berry (♦) **(The Big Sounds Of Coleman Hawkins & Chu Berry)**, and in January following year took one of his best-ever bands into Arcadia Ballroom, New York **(Arcadia Shuffle)** producing one dazzling, powerhouse solo after another.

His up-tempo statements, with double-time runs executed with facility hitherto unknown, obviously deeply influenced a young, up-coming Dizzy Gillespie (♦). Eldridge's ballad playing was warm and deeply-felt. And there was little doubt about his familiarity with and ability to 'feel' the blues.

Following prestigious residencies at the Apollo, Golden Gate Ballroom and Kelly's Stables (1939–40), he returned, in '41, to Chicago for further important season, this one at Capitol Lounge. Next, joined new Gene Krupa big band as featured soloist. With Krupa, established an even wider reputation, with key solo spots (as singer as well as trumpeter) on successful items like **Let Me Off Uptown, Little Jazz, Rockin' Chair** and **After You've Gone.**

After Krupa's band split in 1943, became, for a time, session player with Paul Baron Orchestra at CBS (1943–4), playing Mildred Bailey (♦) radio series. Toured with Artie Shaw (♦), again as featured soloist (1944–5) **(Artie Shaw Featuring Roy Eldridge, Artie Shaw & His Orchestra, Vol 2** and **Artie Shaw & His Gramercy Five)**. Eldridge, an always sensitive, sometimes explosive, character, had to undergo various Jim Crow experiences when touring with Shaw – despite conscious efforts by leader and his other sidemen to prevent such occurrences – which left a scar which lasts until today.

Returned to Krupa in 1949, after leading own bands, then toured Europe with Benny Goodman (♦) (1950). Signed with Norman Granz as solo recording artist and to tour with Granz' Jazz At The Philharmonic packages. In this latter environment, both best and worst of Eldridge could be found. The histrionic excesses of JATP sometimes, sadly, elicited from Eldridge tasteless squeals, shrill altissimo blowing that, however audience-rousing, failed to do his great

67

talent justice, in any way. However, there are times when his admittedly extrovert tendencies were channelled into something more memorable and lasting (**J.A.T.P. In Tokyo**).

Over the succeeding years, has continued to record with many of jazz's finest players, including Dizzy Gillespie (**Trumpet Kings** and **The Gillespie Jam Sessions**); Ben Webster (♦) (**Ben Webster & Associates / Ben Webster & Friends**); Stan Getz (♦) (**Nothing But The Blues**); Lester Young (♦) (**Prez & Teddy**); Buddy Tate (♦) (**Buddy Tate & His Buddies**); Gene Krupa and Buddy Rich (♦) (**Drum Battle**); Oscar Peterson (♦) (**Oscar Peterson & Roy Eldridge**); Peterson and Sonny Stitt (♦) (**Only The Blues/Sittin' In**); Bud Freeman (♦) (**Chicago**); and Johnny Hodges (♦) (**Blues A-Plenty**). Each of these albums contain much superb Eldridge, especially those with Getz, Peterson, Stitt, Webster and the two Gillespies.

One notable failure was on-record collaboration with Art Tatum (♦) (**The Tatum Group Masterpieces**) with Eldridge sounding not at all at ease, or anywhere near to his best. (There is rumour that Eldridge and Tatum recorded their contributions at different times, which might afford reasonable explanation for the meeting of two acknowledged giants not being a success.) During past 30 years there have been other, more successful, record sessions, including several which took place in Paris, under Eldridge's leadership, during 1950–1 (**Little Jazz Paris Session**) relating to his European trip with Benny Goodman. There were also excellent studio re-creations of Krupa's early days as bandleader in his own right (**The Big Band Sound Of Gene Krupa**) with Eldridge recalled to take his rightful place in premier trumpet soloist's chair. Amongst more recent recordings, there have been successful sessions with Joe Turner (♦) (**Nobody In Mind**) and Count Basie (♦) (**Count Basie Jam Session At The Montreux Jazz Festival 1975**).

Of records issued under his own name, best by far has been **The Nifty Cat** which combines all the virtues of his younger days with the maturity of the 60-year-old he was at time of recording. It is true to say, though, that Roy Eldridge has tended to show his age in recent years, a certain shrillness of tone, too wide vibrato and inability to hit notes with the power and accuracy of former times being obvious failings. But when he is 'on', Roy 'Little Jazz' Eldridge still retains most of those elements which long ago made him an acknowledged giant of jazz, as well as the vital link between those two other great trumpet stylists, Louis Armstrong (♦) and Dizzy Gillespie.

Recordings:
The Fletcher Henderson Story
(Columbia)/
The Fletcher Henderson Story, Vol 4 *(CBS)*
Benny Goodman, Vol 4 (1935-1939)
(RCA Victor – France)
The Teddy Wilson
(CBS/Sony – Japan)
Teddy Wilson & His All Stars
(Columbia/CBS)

Billie Holiday, The Golden Years, Vols 1, 2
(Columbia/CBS)
Billie Holiday, God Bless The Child *(Columbia/CBS)*
Billie Holiday, The Voice Of Jazz, Vol 7 *(Verve)*
Roy Eldridge At The Three Deuces, Chicago – 1937
(Jazz Archives)
The Big Sounds Of Coleman Hawkins & Chu Berry
(—/London)
Roy Eldridge, Arcadia Shuffle
(Jazz Archives)
Montreux '77: Roy Eldridge 4
(Pablo Live/Pablo Live)
Artie Shaw & His Orchestra, Vol 2 *(RCA Victor/RCA Victor)*
Artie Shaw & His Gramercy Five *(—/RCA Victor)*
Roy Eldridge, Little Jazz Paris Session *(—/Vogue)*
Coleman Hawkins, Swing!
(Fontana)
Roy Eldridge, Swing Along With Little Jazz
(MCA Coral – Germany)
Coleman Hawkins/Chu Berry, Immortal Swing Sessions
(—/Sonet)
Roy Eldridge/Tiny Grimes Never Too Old To Swing
(—/Sonet)
In Concert: Coleman Hawkins With Roy Eldridge & Billie Holiday *(Phoenix)*
Various, J.A.T.P. In Tokyo
(Pablo/Pablo)
Various, The Gillespie Jam Sessions *(Verve)*
Dizzy Gillespie/Roy Eldridge, Trumpet Kings *(Verve)*
Ben Webster & Associates
(Verve)/
Ben Webster & Friends
(Verve)
Herb Ellis/Stan Getz/Roy Eldridge, Nothing But The Blues *(Verve/Columbia – Clef)*
The Big Band Sound Of Gene Krupa *(Verve/Verve)*
Lester Young/Teddy Wilson, Prez & Teddy *(Verve)*
Buddy Tate & His Buddies
(Chiaroscuro/—)
Sonny Stitt/Roy Eldridge/Oscar Peterson, Only The Blues
(Verve)/
Sittin' In *(Verve)*
Bud Freeman, Chicago
(Black Lion/Black Lion)
Johnny Hodges, Blues A-Plenty
(Verve/HMV)
Art Tatum, The Tatum Group Masterpieces *(Pablo/Pablo)*
Joe Turner, Nobody In Mind
(Pablo/Pablo)
Count Basie, Montreux '77: Count Basie Jam
(Pablo Live/Pablo Live)
Oscar Peterson & Roy Eldridge
(Pablo/Pablo)
Various, Jazz At The Santa Monica '72 *(Pablo/Pablo)*
Roy Eldridge, The Nifty Cat
(Master Jazz Recordings/—)

The Eleventh House

An ex-sideman with vibraphonist Gary Burton, and flute player Herbie Mann, guitarist Larry Coryell crosses most musical divisions. His early career found him often closer to the string-bendings and feedback techniques of rock, for example, his solo feature on **Communications 9 (Jazz Composers Orchestra)**. Over the years, he has applied his technical brilliance to electric jazz-rock,

jazz, free music, acoustic classical guitar works and twelve-tone rows with equal facility. The guiding spirit behind The Eleventh House, which also features the bombastic drumming of Alphonse Mouzon, Coryell in this context often looks like a man in search of a direction. The music, falling within so many categories, the lovely, meditative acoustic guitar of **Eyes Of Love (Level One)**, a world away from the funk of **Kowloon Jag (Aspects)**. A meeting with fellow guitarist John McLaughlin (**Spaces**) resulted in some highly compatible improvisation, and Coryell's current move back into solo acoustic guitar (**The Lion & The Ram**) may well prove his most artistically satisfying decision.

Recordings:
At The Village Gate
(Vanguard/Vanguard)
Barefoot Boy
(Flying Dutchman/—)
Lady Coryell
(Vanguard/Vanguard)
Spaces *(Vanguard/Vanguard)*
Level One *(Arista/Arista)*
Aspects *(Arista/Arista)*
The Lion & The Ram
(Arista/Arista)

Duke Ellington

Because of the multiplicity and significance of his achievements within the field of music in general, and his unsurpassed contributions to jazz in particular, Edward Kennedy 'Duke' Ellington (born Washington, DC, 1899) remains one of the seminal figures of twentieth-century music. In total, the music produced by Ellington in over 55 years was colossal; and the overall standard of that prodigious output – written as well as played – is equal to any other comparable contributor to music of the past near-80 years. There is absolutely no comparison between Ellington's personal achievements and any other major musical innovator. For example, it is more than unlikely that at any time in the foreseeable future there will emerge another ultra-prolific composer and orchestrator who, during over a half-century of continuous writing, will also find time to lead, non-stop, a succession of orchestras or bands – undertaking regular recording dates and an exhausting year-by-year touring schedule, at home and abroad – play fine piano with those various aggregations, and act as official spokesman and master of ceremonies.

If the final story is ever told, it seems unlikely that a complete assessment of Ellington's output as writer can be made. Certainly, though, his compositions run into the thousands, extended works as well as shorter (usually 32-bar) 'tunes'. His capacity for work was almost inhuman, and Ellington's was a mind which continually explored the possibilities opened up by various outlets, other than those presented by his own orchestra. For example, Duke Ellington composed music for such stage shows as *Jump For Joy* and *My People*; he has written musical scores for movies like *Anatomy of a Murder* (**Anatomy Of A Murder**), *Assault On A Queen* and *Paris Blues*. During latter period of his career, Ellington was profoundly involved with a series of Sacred Concerts (he was a deeply religious man) for which, of course, he composed the music. (This latterday preoccupation was, for Ellington, his most important contribution to music of any kind. In truth, though, it might be said that in some ways – especially with regard to respective librettos – projects like **Concert Of Sacred Music, Second Sacred Concert**, and **Duke Ellington's Third Sacred Concert, The Majesty Of God**) were not as comprehensively successful as a majority of Ellington's other larger compositions.)

Blues Summit (Verve)– Duke Ellington & Johnny Hodges.

Duke Ellington At Carnegie Hall (Queen-Disc, Italy).

Ellington's involvement with extended works of secular nature resulted in music of extraordinary quality. First examples of Ellington extending his compositional genius beyond a basic 32-bar format came in 1931 with two-part **Creole Rhapsody (The Works Of Duke Ellington, Vol 6)** followed by the 1935 four-part **Reminiscin' In Tempo (The Ellington Era, 1927-1940, Vol 2** and **The Complete Duke Ellington, Vol 6: 1933-1936)**. Both allowed Ellington, master music painter, to fill his canvas with additional textures of color, contrast and excitement. Ellington's first composition in truly extended vein remains one of his most brilliantly evocative: **Black, Brown & Beige**. In many ways **Black, Brown & Beige** was an in-depth summation of Ellington's many achievements up to that time (1943). Because of a recording ban, only excerpts from the entire suite were committed to record (**The Works Of Duke, Vol 19**) although Ellington did record the piece in 1958, with gospel singer Mahalia Jackson reprising the moving **Come Sunday** vocal passage (**Black, Brown & Beige**). Best of all (and, of course, of historical signific-

Above: Edward Kennedy Ellington – 'The Duke'. Greatest contributor to the development of jazz, for all time.

Duke Ellington In Harlem (Jazz Panorama) – a youthful-looking Duke on a Swedish release.

ance) was complete **Black, Brown & Beige** as premiered at Carnegie Hall in January 1943 (**Duke Ellington: Black, Brown & Beige**). Other notable successes in an extended vein have been **Such Sweet Thunder, Liberian Suite/A Tone Parallel To Harlem: The Harlem Suite, A Drum Is A Woman, The Far East Suite, The Latin-American Suite, New World A-Coming: Harlem: The Golden Broom & The Green Apple, The Togo Brava Suite/The English Concert, Suite Thursday** (**Suite Thursday/Peer Gynt Suites Nos 1 & 2**) and **Deep South Suite** (last movement of which **Happy-Go-Lucky Local** is a magnificent 12-bar train blues). Superb as these and other extended works are, they are no better than the countless miniature masterpieces written by Ellington during his career. Many of these have not only become an integral part of jazz composing history, but are acknowledged as being meaningful contributions to standard library of popular song. Amongst most famous (and in many cases these rank with Ellington's finest) are following: **Sophisticated Lady, Do Nothing Till You Hear From Me** (originally known as **Concerto For Cootie** before lyric was written and its title changed), **I Got It Bad, I'm Beginning To See The Light, Solitude, Satin Doll, I Let A Song Go Out Of My Heart, Mood Indigo** (first recorded as **Dreamy Blues**), **In A Sentimental Mood, Drop Me Off At Harlem, Just Squeeze Me** and **Prelude To A Kiss** (probably his best-ever song).

Although his lyric-writing collaborators included John LaTouche, Johnny Mercer, Ted Koehler, Don George, Peggy Lee (♦), Johnny Burke and Mitchell Parish, often Ellington's songs were poorly served by inferior lyrics. An innovation by Ellington during 1920s was his use of a singer (Adelaide Hall) using her voice in a manner of a jazz instrumentalist. Adelaide Hall's wordless vocals on **Creole Love Call** and **Blues I Love To Sing (The Works Of Duke, Vol 1)** succeeded in a definite, if startling, fashion. Ellington was to use the human voice in similar manner more than once in future, including a stunning **Transblucency** from 1946 (**At His Very Best**), with Kat Davis as singer.

From an instrumental standpoint the list of masterpieces is, of course, even greater. For Ellington's genius extended to possessing an uncanny knack of selecting the kind of players whose wholly individual sounds and styles would suit his musical creations to perfection. Apart from their 'normal' use within a typical Ellington framework, several of his major soloists were accorded their own individual showcases, including Barney Bigard (♦), with **Clarinet Lament (The Complete Duke Ellington, Vol 7: 1936-1937)** and Cootie Williams (♦), with **Concerto For Cootie (The Works Of Duke, Vol 10)** and **Echoes Of Harlem (The Complete Duke Ellington, Vol 7: 1936-1937)**. As well as saluting his own musicians, Ellington also offered delicious tributes to other musical personalities, like jazz dancer Bill Robinson (**Bojangles**) and black comedian-vaudeville artist Bert Williams (**Portrait Of Bert Williams**) (both **The Works Of Duke, Vol 10**) and Willie 'The Lion' Smith (♦) (**Portrait Of The Lion (The Ellington Era, 1927-1940, Vol 1/The Ellington Era, 1927-1940, Vol 1 – Part 3)**).

Mostly, Ellington used material written by himself, or by his sidemen, including Mercer Ellington (♦), his son; Juan Tizol (**Caravan, Perdido, Bakiff, Conga Brava**, etc); Barney Bigard, and, most prominently, Billy Strayhorn (♦), his closest collaborator. But he was not averse to using compositions from other jazz writers or pop tunes. In latter category, not even Duke Ellington could make totally satisfying jazz out of score from *Mary Poppins* (**Souvenirs**), but was more successful with repertoire from two classical composers: Edvard Grieg (**Peer Gynt Suites Nos 1 & 2/Suite Thursday**) and Piotr Ilyich Tchaikovsky (**The Nutcracker Suite**). Like all great jazz organizations, Ellington orchestra was usually at its most exciting during live performance. Some other jazz big-bands

(viz Count Basie (♦), Jimmie Lunceford (♦), Chick Webb (♦)) are known to have out-swung it during the kind of cutting contests which once were possible in ballrooms and theatres. Certainly, though, recorded evidence has been made available over the years to prove that when the occasion was right, the band could drive, wail and stomp with the best. Such occasions are apparent during the following: **The Duke 1940, Ellington At Newport**, with its legendary 27 consecutive choruses by tenorist Paul Gonsalves (♦) during **Diminuendo & Crescendo In Blue; (The Great Paris Concert, The Greatest Jazz Concert In The World, The Togo Brava Suite/The English Concert** and **Duke Ellington's 70th Birthday Concert**). With such an embarrassment of riches throughout 50 years, it is no easy task to select a particular period that could be said to be representative of the absolute peak of Ellington's achievements. But the 1940–2 period found Duke Ellington scaling peaks of artistic invention that rarely have been approached, before or since. In many ways, the list of soloists at his disposal during this time could not be bettered, in terms of individual and collective brilliance: Williams, Rex Stewart (♦), Ray Nance (♦), Joseph 'Tricky Sam' Nanton (♦), Lawrence Brown (♦), Bigard, Ben Webster (♦), Harry Carney (♦), Johnny Hodges (♦), and the leader himself. The additional presence of bassist Jimmy Blanton (♦) until 1941 was another plus factor.

Between 1940 and 1942 Ellington wrote an astonishing number of classic

The Duke 1940 (Jazz Society). Unforgettable double LP.

Duke Ellington Meets Coleman Hawkins (Impulse).

masterpieces-in-miniature, including: **Ko-Ko, Jack The Bear (The Works Of Duke, Vol 9), Conga Brava, Concerto For Cootie, Cotton Tail, Don't Get Around Much Anymore, Bojangles, Portrait Of Bert Williams, Harlem Airshaft, Rumpus In Richmond (Vol 10), Sepia Panorama, In A Mellotone (Vol 11), Warm Valley, Across The Track Blues (Vol 12), Take The 'A' Train** (written by Strayhorn), **Blue Serge** (written by son Mercer) **(Vol 15), Chelsea Bridge** (also by Strayhorn), **C Jam Blues (Vol 17)**. Over the years, there were comparatively few 'outsiders' invited to participate in Ellingtonian activities (although drummers Elvin Jones (♦), Max Roach (♦) and trumpeters Dizzy Gillespie (♦) and Gerald Wilson deputized at various times).

Apart from previously mentioned Mahalia Jackson–Ellington session, visiting artists like Ella Fitzgerald (♦) (**. . . Sings The Duke Ellington Songbook, Vols 1, 2, Ella At Duke's Place** and **Ella & Duke At The Côte d'Azur**); Jimmy Rushing (♦) (**Jazz At The Plaza, Vol 2** and **Ellington Jazz Party**); Billie Holiday (♦) (**Jazz At The Plaza, Vol 2**); and Gillespie

MONO | AH 23   COTTON CLUB DAYS   DUKE ELLINGTON

COTTON CLUB DAYS

DUKE ELLINGTON

DUKE ELLINGTON AND HIS ORCHESTRA

Ace of Hearts

COTTON CLUB STOMP   BLACK AND TAN FANTASY
EAST ST. LOUIS TOODLE-OO   BIRMINGHAM BREAKDOWN
DOIN' THE VOOM VOOM   PADUCAH   WALL ST. WAIL
RENT PARTY BLUES   GOIN' NUTS   JOLLY WOG
HARLEM FLAT BLUES   HOME AGAIN BLUES

*Cotton Club Days (Ace of Hearts, Decca). Memories of
the early days of the inimitable Ellington orchestra.*

(Ellington Jazz Party), have all sat in, with generally worthwhile results.
A sit-in of a more unusual nature took place in 1961, when the full might of
both the Ellington and Basie bands met inside recording studio **(First
Time/Basie Meets Ellington)** in fierce and friendly musical combat. One aspect of Duke Ellington's lifetime in music which attracted less
attention than was merited (mostly due, like Count Basie, to a genuine
modest assessment of his own abilities in this direction) was his competence as a piano player. Ellington, apart from his talents as band pianist,
was a very good soloist – sometimes a superb one. His early recordings
show him to be an average-only solo player, **The Duke – 1926**, showing
traces of his prime influences, James P. Johnson (♦), Willie 'The Lion'
Smith (♦) and Luckey Roberts, but without their flair and drive. He was
no more than competent during the formative years of his orchestra
(Duke Ellington In Harlem, Duke Ellington, Vol 1, 1926-1928 and
Toodle-Oo) but by 1930s, even though he allowed himself little solo
space, there was a definite improvement. In 1941, recorded piano solos
(The Works Of Duke, Vol 15) which indicated he should feature himself
more at the keyboard with his band. Included was wistful, introspective
version of **Solitude,** about which there could be few complaints. The
impact of Jimmy Blanton was felt not only with the Ellington orchestra
during his brief tenure, but also on piano-playing of Ellington. The delightful duets pair recorded in 1940 **(The Works Of Duke, Vol 11)** demonstrate just how good a solo pianist (and accompanist) Ellington could be.
Six years later, Ellington and Billy Strayhorn recorded series of duets
with bassist Wendell Marshall **(The Golden Duke)** which, on the whole,
worked well; three years after which Ellington (in trio setting) produced
his finest playing yet **(Piano Reflections)** essaying a programme of
new as well as established material.

During 1960s and thereafter – mostly at prompting by others – Ellington
featured himself more at the piano. His work features throughout recordings such as **Solo** (an album which has remarkable, lengthy version of
Symphonie Pour Un Monde Meilleur and a typical medley of Ellington
tunes); **Duke Ellington - The Pianist** and **This One's For Blanton!** (a
tribute to Blanton, in company with bassist Ray Brown) and **Duke's Big 4.**
Perhaps finest examples of Ellington, solo pianist, emanate from a superb
studio date **Blues Summit/Back To Back & Side By Side** which featured
also talents of Harry Edison (♦) and Johnny Hodges (♦). Both latter musicians
played at their considerable best – but Ellington took solo honours with
ease. More fine Ellington piano highlighted recordings at which non-
Ellington instrumentalists like Max Roach (♦) and Charles Mingus (♦)
(Money Jungle), John Coltrane (♦) **(Duke Ellington Meets John
Coltrane)** and Coleman Hawkins (♦) **(Duke Ellington Meets Coleman
Hawkins)** were given joint top billing.

Biographically: Duke Ellington came from well-to-do Washington,
DC, family, and after winning poster-designing contest at high school
became proprietor (for a while) of own sign-writing business. First
played piano in public while at high school. After graduation, began to
play local gigs. First composition, **Soda Fountain Rag.** Concentrated
exclusively on music, playing piano with various bands, including Elmer
Snowden. Put together own Duke's Serenaders, then worked with Wilbur
Sweatman, in New York. 1924: took over leadership of Washingtonians
group, touring regularly, playing residencies (including lengthy stay
at Kentucky Club), before commencing important residency at Cotton
Club (1927–31), in Harlem, interrupted only by national tours and recording dates. Amongst the most important recordings to make an impact on the jazz world during this period were **East St Louis Toodle-oo**
(Ellington's first theme), **Black Beauty** and **Birmingham Breakdown**
(all **The Beginning: 1926-1928), The Mooche, Awful Sad** and **Jungle
Jamboree** (all **Hot In Harlem: 1928-1929); Mood Indigo, Rockin' In**

Rhythm and **Creole Rhapsody** (all **Rockin' In Rhythm: 1929-1931**).
Band also appeared in film *Check & Double Check* (1930), and made
its first trip to Europe (London, Paris) in 1939. Ellington wrote music for,
and his band participated in, revue *Jump For Joy*, which opened in Los
Angeles in 1941. First of legendary Carnegie Hall concerts took place in
1943 (featuring première of **Black, Brown & Beige)**, continuing annually,
up to and including 1950. In 1951, Ellington band combined with
Symphony of the Air for première of *Night Creature*, at same venue.
Ellington took trumpeter-violinist-singer Ray Nance and singer Kay
Davis on tour to UK (1948); full Ellington band (plus, of course, its leader)
returned ten years later and on numerous other occasions in subsequent
years. During 1960s, Ellington visited Far East, Middle East, India,
Australasia, etc, and constant schedule of touring – at home as well as
overseas – continued up until Ellington's death in May 1974. During his
career, Duke Ellington received innumerable honors and awards.
These included the President's Medal, the Springarn Medal, Presidential Medal of Freedom, 15 honorary degrees; was given Key to 18
cities (as far afield as Niigata, Japan, to Savannah, Georgia to Amsterdam,
Holland); and was presented before Her Majesty Queen Elizabeth II.
Ellington's long-awaited autobiography *Music Is My Mistress* was published in 1974. Other notable literary works on Duke Ellington include
following: *Duke – A Portrait of Duke Ellington* by Derek Jewell; *Duke
Ellington* by Barry Ulanov; *Duke Ellington: His Life & Music*, anthology,
edited by Pete Gammond; *Duke Ellington* by G. E. Lambert; *The World
of Duke Ellington* by Stanley Dance.

Of those musicians who contributed in making Ellingtonia such a terribly
important part of jazz history, following played, if not vital, important
roles in that story: Ivie Anderson (♦), Harold 'Shorty' Baker (♦), Louis
Bellson (♦), Barney Bigard (♦), Jimmy Blanton (♦), Lawrence Brown (♦),
Harry Carney (♦), Tyree Glenn (♦), Paul Gonsalves (♦), 'Sonny' Greer (♦),
'Toby' Hardwicke (♦), Johnny Hodges (♦), Quentin Jackson (♦), 'Bubber'
Miley (♦), Ray Nance (♦), 'Tricky Sam' Nanton (♦), Russell Procope (♦),
Al Sears (♦), Rex Stewart (♦), Billy Strayhorn (♦), Clark Terry (♦), Arthur
Whetsol (♦), 'Cootie' Williams (♦).

Recordings:
Duke Ellington, **The Duke – 1926** *(Riverside/London)*
Duke Ellington **In Harlem** *(Jazz Panorama – Sweden)*
Duke Ellington, **Vol 1 (1926-1929)** *(MCA Coral – Germany)*
Duke Ellington, **The Beginning (1926-1928)** *(Decca/MCA – Germany)*
Duke Ellington, **Hot In Harlem (1928-1929)** *(Decca/MCA – Germany)*
Duke Ellington, **Rockin' In Rhythm (1929-1931)**
  (Decca/MCA – Germany)
Duke Ellington, **Toodle-oo** *(—/Vocalion)*
Duke Ellington, **The Works Of Duke, Vols 1-18**
  (RCA Victor – France)
The Complete Duke Ellington, Vols 1-6 *(CBS – France)*
The Ellington Era, 1927-1940, Vols 1, 2 *(Columbia/CBS)*
Duke Ellington, **Braggin' In Brass 1936-1939** *(Tax – Sweden)*
Duke Ellington, **1937-1939** *(Tax – Sweden)*
Duke Ellington, **Masterpieces (1938-40)** *(RCA Victor – France)*
Duke Ellington, **Ellington Uptown** *(Columbia/Philips)*
Duke Ellington, **Masterpieces By Ellington**
  (Columbia/CBS – Holland)
Duke Ellington/Mahalia Jackson, **Black, Brown & Beige**
  (Columbia/CBS – Holland)
Duke Ellington: **Black, Brown & Beige** *(Ariston – Italy)*
Duke Ellington, **Liberian Suite/A Tone Parallel To Harlem**
  (Columbia/CBS – France)
Duke Ellington, **Peer Gynt Suites Nos 1 & 2/Suite Thursday**
  (Columbia/CBS)
Duke Ellington, **The Nutcracker Suite** *(Columbia/CBS)*
Duke Ellington, **A Drum Is A Woman** *(Columbia/Philips)*
Duke Ellington, **Such Sweet Thunder** *(Columbia/CBS – Realm)*
Duke Ellington, **New World A-Coming: Harlem: The Golden**
  Broom & The Green Apple *(Decca/—)*
Duke Ellington, **The Far East Suite** *(RCA Victor/RCA Victor)*
Duke Ellington, **The Latin-American Suite** *(Fantasy/—)*
Duke Ellington. **The Togo Brava Suite** *(United Artists)/*
  The English Concert *(Sunset)*
Duke Ellington, **Afro-Eurasian Eclipse** *(Fantasy/—)*
Duke Ellington, **Concert Of Sacred Music** *(RCA Victor/—)*
Duke Ellington, **Second Sacred Concert** *(Fantasy/—)*
Duke Ellington's **Third Sacred Concert, The Majesty of God, As**
  Performed In Westminster Abbey *(RCA Victor/RCA Victor)*
Duke Ellington, **The Duke 1940** *(Jazz Society/—)*
Duke Ellington, **Ellington At Newport** *(Columbia/CBS)*
Various (Including Duke Ellington), **The Greatest Jazz Concert In**
  The World *(Pablo/Pablo)*
Duke Ellington's **70th Birthday Concert** *(Solid State/United Artists)*
Ella Fitzgerald Sings The Duke Ellington Songbook, Vols 1, 2
  (Verve/Verve)
Ella Fitzgerald/Duke Ellington, **Ella At Duke's Place** *(Verve/Verve)*
Ella Fitzgerald/Duke Ellington, **Ella & Duke At The Côte d'Azur**
  (Verve/Verve)
Various (Including Ellington/Rushing/Gillespie/Holliday),
  Ellington Jazz Party *(Columbia/Philips)/*
Jazz At The Plaza, Vol 2 *(Columbia/CBS)*
Duke Ellington, **The Radio Transcriptions, Vols 1-5**
  (Hindsight/London)
Duke Ellington/Count Basie, **First Time** *(Columbia)/*
  Basie Meets Ellington *(Embassy)*
Duke Ellington, **Piano Reflections** *(Capitol/One-Up)*
Duke Ellington, **Solo** *(President – France)*
Duke Ellington – **The Pianist** *(Fantasy/—)*
Duke Ellington/Johnny Hodges, **Blues Summit** *(Verve)/*

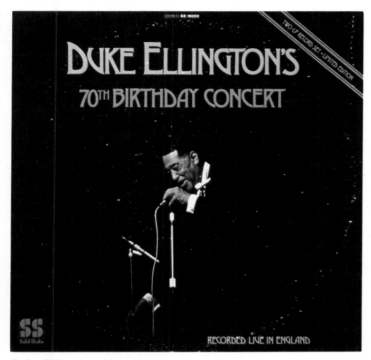

Duke Ellington's 70th Birthday Concert (Solid State).
The Ellington Band's own magnificent gift to its boss.

Back To Back & Side By Side (*Verve*)
Duke Ellington, Money Jungle (*United Artists/United Artists*)
Duke Ellington/Ray Brown, This One's For Blanton! (*Pablo/Pablo*)
Duke Ellington Meets John Coltrane *Impulse/Impulse*)
Duke Ellington Meets Coleman Hawkins (*Impulse/Impulse*)
Duke Ellington, The Great Paris Concert (*Atlantic/—*)
Duke Ellington . . . And His Mother Called Him Bill
   (*RCA Victor/RCA Victor*)
Duke Ellington, Souvenirs (*Reprise/Reprise*)
Duke Ellington, The Ellington Suites (*Pablo/Pablo*)

Mercer Ellington

To Mercer Kennedy Ellington (born Washington, DC, 1919) fell the utterly unenviable task of trying to achieve the almost impossible when, following the death of Duke Ellington (♦) in 1974, he agreed to become front man of his father's orchestra – the most celebrated and important jazz aggregation of all time. But in typically modest and unassuming fashion, Ellington, Jr, endeavored to pick up the pieces. A formidable task, especially with many of the most illustrious sidemen having died in recent past (viz Strayhorn (♦), Hodges (♦), Stewart (♦), Hardwicke (♦)) and with other major figures (Carney, 1974; Gonsalves, 1974; Nance, 1976, and Webster, 1974) soon to die. (Trumpeter Cootie Williams (♦), another seminal figure in Ellingtonia, was ill and hospitalized for a while; reedman Russell Procope (♦) was in semi-retirement; and neither Jimmy Hamilton (♦) nor Sam Woodyard, from previous line-ups, was available for touring). Still, Mercer Ellington – arranger, composer, trumpeter, and one-time tour manager for Duke Ellington band – was no newcomer to rigors of band-leading. As a youth had studied trumpet and alto-sax, subsequently enrolled as student at Columbia University, Juilliard, and New York University. Put together his very first band as long ago as 1939. (Dizzy Gillespie (♦), Clark Terry (♦), and Calvin Jackson were

amongst sidemen; Billy Strayhorn composed-arranged for the band prior to joining entourage of Ellington, Sr).

Following conscription into US Army, Mercer Ellington put together another big band, this one lasting until 1949 (singer Carmen McRae, then known as Carmen Clarke, worked with this outfit). 1950: Mercer played trumpet and E-flat horn with his father. Started own Mercer Records label (1950–2), leaving music altogether to work as salesman following its demise. Back again, as trumpeter and road manager for Cootie Williams' band (1954), then acted as general assistant to his father (1955–9), after which took up trumpet again – and bandleading.

Over the years, has written numerous durable jazz compositions, many of which have been featured by Duke Ellington Orchestra. Included are: **Things Ain't What They Used To Be** (also known as **Time's A-Wastin'**), **Piano Reflections (Greatest Jazz Concert In The World** and **The Works Of Duke, Vol 17); Moon Mist (His Most Important Second War Concert** and **Duke Ellington, Vol 2); Blue Serge (Duke Ellington, Vol 2, Duke Ellington, 1943-1946** and **In A Mellotone);** and **Jumpin' Punkins (The Works Of Duke, Vols 15, 17).**

Apart from sundry other contributions to the Duke Ellington repertoire, Mercer occasionally also helped his father on more ambitious scores, like **Latin American Suite.** His own album **Continuum** proved encouraging augury for future. Apart from own **Blue Serge,** this first Ellington album to be made after Duke Ellington's

passing included dedication to another Ellington alumnus, **Carney,** written by saxist Rick Henderson; plus a healthy selection of not over-familiar material by Duke or Strayhorn, including **Drop Me Off In Harlem, Rock Skippin' At The Blue Note, Ko-Ko, All Too Soon** and **Jump For Joy,** most of which had lain dormant for years.

It is, of course, impossible to forecast just how long Mercer Ellington can continue to carry the lifelong traditions of his illustrious father. It might well be he will achieve much, personally and artistically, if he concentrates more on his own writing – and that of others still living – using only those compositions of Duke Ellington that are of the unhackneyed, rarely heard, variety. Of recordings made by previous Mercer Ellington big bands, best are **Black & Tan Fantasy, Steppin' Into Swing Society** and **Colors In Rhythm.** Has also contributed to numerous record dates featuring alto-saxophone artistry of Johnny Hodges (♦), including exemplary **Bouquet Of Roses** and **Viscount,** for a 1950s recording date **(The Big Band Sound Of Johnny Hodges).**

Recordings:
Duke Ellington, Piano Reflections (*Capitol/One-Up*)
Duke Ellington, The Works Of Duke, Vols 14, 15, 17 (*RCA Victor – France*)
Duke Ellington, His Most Important Second War Concert (*—/Saga*)
Duke Ellington, Vol 2 (*—/Saga*)
Duke Ellington 1943-1946 (*Jazz Society*)
Various (Including Duke Ellington), The Greatest Jazz Concert In The World (*Pablo/Pablo*)
Duke Ellington, Latin American Suite (*Fantasy/—*)
Mercer Ellington, Steppin' Into Swing Society (*Coral/—*)
Mercer Ellington, Colors In Rhythm (*Coral/—*)
Mercer Ellington, Black & Tan Fantasy (*MCA/—*)
Mercer Ellington/Duke Ellington Orchestra, Continuum (*Fantasy/Fantasy*)
The Big Band Sound Of Johnny Hodges (*—/Verve*)

Don Ellis

Trumpeter Don Ellis was born in Los Angeles in 1934, and gained big band experience with Woody Herman, Claude Thornhill, Lionel Hampton and Charlie Barnet. He spent 1961–2 with the experimental units of George Russell **(Outer Thoughts),** cutting excellent solos on **Pan Daddy** and **The Stratus Seekers.** Much of Ellis' exploratory work was inspired by contemporary straight music rather than jazz, and performances like **Despair To Hope** sprang from John Cage's indeterminancy **(New Ideas).** Surprisingly, Ellis' 21-piece orchestra, using unusual meters, multividers and choirs, achieved great commercial success during the psychedelic '60s. In fact, the band had a walloping impact, never sounding in the least pretentious or Third Stream. The eeriness of **Milo's Theme** with its electronically-processed flutes is curiously plaintive, and the distant chorus and Indian dron-

ings of **Star Children** provides a highly original setting for Ellis' precise trumpet **(Shock Treat-Treatment).** An atmospheric live performance **(Don Ellis At Fillmore)** shows the leader's amazing instrumental control in the unaccompanied grotesqueries of **The Blues.** Hey Jude begins on trumpet, but so distorted by a ring modulator that it resembles Morton Subotnick's **The Wild Bull.** He has since turned to movie scores, including **The French Connection.**

Recordings:
George Russell, Outer Thoughts (*Milestone/Milestone*)
New Ideas (*Prestige/—*)
Electric Bath (*Columbia/CBS*)
Shock Treatment (*Columbia/CBS*)
Don Ellis At Fillmore (*Columbia/CBS*)

Booker Ervin

Born 1930 in Texas, Booker Telleferro Ervin was in the great tradition of big-toned Texas tenormen. During the '50s, he gigged around the South with R&B bands, moving

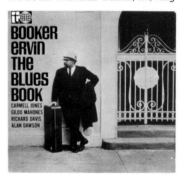

The Blues Book (Prestige):
one of Booker's great books.

to New York in 1958 where he joined Charlie Mingus' band. Between 1958–60, he was a featured soloist on numerous Mingus albums, most notably **Boogie Stop Shuffle (Mingus Ah-Um), Theme For Lester Young (Mingus, Mingus, Mingus, Mingus, Mingus), Lock 'Em Up (The Candid Recordings).** The raw, passionate strength of his playing fitted perfectly into the volcanic Mingus world, rhythmically forceful enough to ride the shifting ensemble textures.

A consistent player, the albums under his own name are uniformly excellent. The **Book** series for Prestige **(The Song Book, The Blues Book, The Space Book, The Freedom Book)** all feature him in compatible company, most often with pianist Jaki Byard, bassist Richard Davis and drummer Alan Dawson, and transcend the usual blowing session casualness. Ervin's unrelenting intensity is well to the fore on numbers like **Mojo (The Space Book)** and **One For Mort (The Blues Book),** while his majestic ballad technique is at its best on **There Is No Greater Love (The Space Book).** There is an hypnotic, incantatory strength about the tenorman's work, nowhere more evident than on **The Trance (The Trance)** which was recorded during his eighteen-month stay in Europe.

The posthumously released **Blues For You** from the 1965 Berlin Jazz Festival **(Lament For Booker)** runs for over 27 minutes and the tenor grips from start to finish.

Variously influenced by Dexter Gordon and John Coltrane, he shares that spearing legato cry. Harmonically adventurous, experimenting with modes, Booker Ervin's work was continually improving and his death in 1970 of a kidney disease cut short a career that was synonymous with integrity.

Recordings:
The Song Book
(Prestige/Prestige)
The Blues Book
(Prestige/Prestige)
The Space Book
(Prestige/Prestige)
The Freedom Book
(Prestige/Prestige)
The Trance (Prestige/Prestige)
Lament For Booker (—/Enja)

Bill Evans

Born in New Jersey, 1929, pianist Bill Evans has one of the most distinctive touches in jazz; four bars, and the identity is clear. He credits George Shearing for opening his ears to the beauties of tone, and Horace Silver and Bud Powell contributed to his formative period. After sessions as a sideman with George Russell and Charlie Mingus in the mid-50s, Evans joined Miles Davis on the classic **Kind Of Blue** album, contributing considerably more than backing. In fact, like Miles, the pianist was moving steadily towards greater concision, paring away excess to free melody and making use of modes to this end.

As a soloist, Bill Evans has tremendous, unshowy technique. Chords are meticulously dissected and rearranged, probed for inner resonances, the whole method used to lyrical ends. This introverted, romantic approach seemed to come out of left field in the violent, Hard Bop atmosphere of the late '50s, but in many respects Evans was in the forefront of developments. His work has influenced such pianists as Paul Bley (♦), Keith Jarrett (♦), Chick Corea (♦), Herbie Hancock (♦) and Joe Zawinul, themselves influential stylists in the late '60s and '70s. An Evans solo like **Peace Piece (Peace Piece & Other Pieces)** shows just how adventurous he was on this spontaneously evolving, harmonically free work.

He was one of the pioneers of free melodic interplay within the group, allowing the original members of his trio scope to create independent lines. The staggeringly original young bassist, Scott La Faro, roves parallel to the piano, building structures of his own, intersecting briefly with a walking line or synopsizing the piano's direction with an appropriate chord. The role of the drummer is less spectacular, but Paul Motian tracks the subtle rhythmic shifts and adds to the overall texture. This trio's debut album **(Spring Leaves)** shows a rare empathy on numbers like **Autumn Leaves** or **Blues In Green**, and also an attacking spirit not normally associated with Evans. A live session **(The Village Vanguard Sessions)** rises to the heights of simultane-

ous improvisation, a near-telepathic rapport between the three players that goes beyond the earlier album's achievement. **Solar** seems to move in several dimensions, while the reworking of **Milestones** sees Motian too working more loosely than usual in the foreground. **Jade Visions** explores similar emotional territory to **Peace Piece,** each note sustained like a glowing ember before being supplanted by the next. Possibly Evans' most popular composition, **Waltz For Debby,** receives a definitive treatment here, while versions of **Porgy** and **My Romance** are unexpectedly robust.

The tragic death of La Faro in a car accident in 1961 brought bassist Chuck Israels into the group, followed by Gary Peacock, the difficult role finally settling on the most sympathetic player of the lot, Eddie Gomez. Apart from Shelley Manne and Jack de

The Village Vanguard Sessions (Milestone): classic Evans.

Johnette, Evans has had difficulty in finding the perfect drummer. Various editions of the trio recorded Evans' familiar choice of standards, the range of mood comparatively narrow but the interpretation profound **(Trio '64, At Town Hall** and **The Tokyo Concert).** Bill Evans has also continued to record as a solo artist **(Alone** and **Conversations With Myself)** utilizing multi-tracking to excellent effect, so that the three pianos recede in dynamic perspective. A meeting with trumpeter Freddie Hubbard and guitarist Jim Hall **(Interplay)** resulted in some miraculous ensemble improvisation, though a festival meeting with the tigerish drummer, Tony Oxley, did not **(Live At The Festival).** Most recently he was recorded with the singer, Tony Bennett **(The Tony Bennett – Bill Evans Album)** which displays a shared love of the song form.

Recordings:
Peace Piece & Other Pieces
(Milestone/Milestone)
Spring Leaves
(Milestone/Milestone)
The Village Vanguard Sessions
(Milestone/Milestone)
Trio '64 (Verve/Verve)
At Town Hall (Verve/Verve)
The Tokyo Concert
(Fantasy/—)
Alone (Verve/Verve)
Conversations With Myself
(Verve/Verve)
Interplay (United Artists/—)
Live At The Festival
(Enja/Enja)
The Tony Bennett – Bill Evans Album (Fantasy/—)
Empathy (Verve/Verve)

Gil Evans

Born 1912, arranger Gil Evans is, along with Duke Ellington and Tadd Dameron, one of the greatest orchestrators in jazz. His deployment of instruments brings out the richness of tone in textures that almost activate the taste buds. Evans devises structures that are continually shifting and refining around the soloist, the writing never conflicting with that sense of spontaneity vital to jazz. Starting as an arranger with the Claude Thornhill orchestra in the early '40s, Evans' reputation grew beyond the dance band connection with his work for Miles Davis' 1949 nine-piece band. On **Boplicity** and **Moondreams (Birth Of The Cool)** Evans' characteristic blendings of French horn and tuba became widely influential. His first album with a unit of his own **(The Arranger's Touch)** has excellent playing from soprano saxophonist Steve Lacy on **Ella Speed** and **Just One Of Those Things,** and sumptuous use of French horn, muted trumpet and bassoon in the ensembles, while **Big Stuff** features lower register textures in a highly original arrangement.

The collaboration with Miles Davis was resumed in 1957, the soloist playing flugelhorn over Evans' voicings for a 19-piece orchestra **(Miles Ahead).** The album has ten pieces by different writers from Dave Brubeck to Johnny Carisi, and Davis' role is assimilated into the general orchestral fabric. The artistically successful partnership continued with two further albums; on **(Porgy & Bess),** the Gershwin score considerably altered on performances like **Summertime,** which is stately rather than crooning, and Davis riding the ensemble swells with great economy and his unique brand of choked melancholia. The final album **(Sketches Of Spain)** mixes flamenco patterns with jazz, and Davis' playing is often cast in a tragic mould. Throughout the series, Evans' writing is tailored to fit the trumpeter's musical temperament, the prevailing sadness of mood achieved through the quality of sound. Some critics have found Evans' work lacking in drive, swing, and the explosive power of impassioned playing – a shot-silk canvas. In fact, driving performances like Lacy's over a thrusting ensemble on **Straight No Chaser (Pacific Standard Time)** show that Evans' aesthetic is by no means effete. Budd Johnson's work on Don Redman's **Chant Of The Weed,** Jimmy Cleveland's trombone on **Ballad Of The Sad Young Men** and trumpeter Johnny Coles on Beiderbecke's **Davenport Blues** show no lack of virility. A programme of jazz classics featuring altoist Cannonball Adderley **(Pacific Standard Time)** includes **Lester Leaps In** and the brilliantly scored **Manteca,** with Adderley at his best on Monk's **Round Midnight** and Jelly Roll Morton's **King Porter Stomp.** Further albums followed on which the ensemble was showcased as much as the soloist, tonal combinations that seem to hover like painter Morris Louis' veils. The best of these **(Out Of The Cool, The Individualism Of Gil Evans** and **Gil Evans)** show a harmonic subtlety and originality of mind that

remains unsurpassed.

Recordings:
Miles Davis, Birth Of The Cool
(Capitol/Capitol)
Miles Davis, Miles Ahead
(Columbia/CBS)
Miles Davis, Porgy & Bess
(Columbia/CBS)
Miles Davis, Sketches Of Spain
(Columbia/CBS)
The Arranger's Touch
(Prestige/Prestige)
Pacific Standard Time
(Blue Note/Blue Note)
Out Of The Cool
(Impulse/Impulse)
The Individualism Of Gil Evans
(Verve/—)
Gil Evans (Ampex/—)

Herschel Evans

Herschel Evans (born Denton, Texas, 1909) came into prominence with the Count Basie (♦) Orchestra, which he joined in late-1936, staying until his premature death, through heart condition, in New York, 1939. He joined Basie as second tenor to Lester Young (♦) but it was soon obvious that Evans himself was exceptional. Not as intuitively gifted a soloist as Young, Evans was a powerfully rhythmic player, with his own variations on the more generally accepted (at that time) Coleman Hawkins (♦) approach to his instrument. His death was particularly tragic, because it seemed that he was yet to reach the peak of his powers.

Worked mostly with Texan bands from 1926–30. With Benny Moten (1933–5), Hot Lips Page (♦), Dave Peyton, the last-named in Los Angeles, where Evans decided to stay after leaving Peyton. Played with an early Lionel Hampton (♦) band based in California, before becoming member of Buck Clayton's (♦) band in *Brownskin Revue.* Both Clayton and Evans joined Basie at same time. Evans' tenor solos with Basie did not have the forward-looking, innovatory quality of Young's, but in their own way they compared favorably. Of the better examples of Evans in full flight, his contributions to **Doggin' Around** (an Evans contribution to Basie book), **John's Idea** and **Blue & Sentimental** stand out (all **Jumpin' At The Woodside**) being, simply, one of the great jazz tenor performances of all time. Other notable Evans solos with Basie: **Glory Of Love, Smarty, Georgianna** (all **The Count Swings Out 1937-1938)** and **Shout & Feel It, Every Tub** (both **Super Chief).**

Outside of Basie, Evans was an invaluable asset to any bandleader. Especially to the organizer of studio jam sessions like Lionel Hampton. Evans participated in one of Hampton's legendary all-star dates in July, '38, and his solos were full of his customary warmth and depth, particularly those on **Shoe Shiner's Drag (The Complete Lionel Hampton / Lionel Hampton's Best Records, Vol 2, 1938-1939)** and **Any Time At All (The Complete Lionel Hampton/ Lionel Hampton's Best Records, Vol 6, 1937-1941).**

In 1937, and again in 1938, Evans recorded in pick-up band under leadership of Harry James (♦) **(Harry James & His Orchestra,**

1936-1938) blowing fiercely on **One O'Clock Jump,** and rhapsodizing passionately on **Penthouse Serenade** and **I Can Dream, Can't I?** And he takes another beautifully constructed solo, in between vocal choruses, on Mildred Bailey's (♦) **Heaven Help This Heart Of Mine (Her Greatest Performances, Vol 2)** recorded in '37. With Basie, Evans sometimes took clarinet solos. However, his work on this instrument was hardly distinguished, nowhere as distinctive or moving as that of tenor rival Young. Evans solos on his 'doubling' instrument during band's recording of **Jumpin' At The Woodside (Jumpin' At The Woodside).** Tenor-sax was Herschel Evans' one-and-only instrument, and just how exciting he could sound, in live performance, can be judged from his individual statements on such items as **Oh, Lady Be Good** and **Swingin' At The Daisy Chain** from **The Count At The Chatterbox,** featuring the Basie band in full cry at Hotel William Penn, Pittsburgh, in 1937. Evans was an important influence on similar big-toned tenor players like Illinois Jacquet (♦), Buddy Tate (♦), Arnett Cobb (♦) and possibly Lucky Thompson.

Recordings:
Count Basie, Jumpin' At The Woodside (—/Coral)
Count Basie, The Count Swings Out (1937-1938) (MCA – Germany)
Count Basie, The Count At The Chatterbox (Jazz Archives/—)
Count Basie, Super Chief (Columbia/CBS)
The Complete Lionel Hampton (Bluebird)/
Lionel Hampton's Best Records, Vols 2, 6 (RCA Victor – France)
Harry James & His Orchestra 1936-1938 (The Old Masters/—)
Mildred Bailey, Her Greatest Performances (1929-1946) (Columbia/
Her Greatest Performances, Vol 2 (CBS)

Art Farmer

Trumpeter Art Farmer was born in Iowa, 1928, playing in the bands of Horace Henderson, Benny Carter and Lionel Hampton. In 1953 he went with Hamp's outfit to Europe and recorded several tracks with distinguished fellow bandsman, Clifford Brown, **Stockhold Sweetnin', Scuse These Blues, Falling In Love With Love** and **Lover Come Back To Me,** and the Swedish All Stars **(Clifford Brown Memorial).** The previous year, Farmer turned up on another historic session with tenorman Wardell Gray, playing his own **Farmer's Market (Central Avenue).** In fact, Farmer is an extremely adaptable musician, and has played with experimenters like George Russell as well as the Boppers.

A collection of his early work **(Farmer's Market)** finds him in a variety of groups including those of Sonny Rollins and Horace Silver. **Alone Together** is his best track, displaying a certain debt to the lean phrasing of Miles Davis, but technically superior. A session from 1955 is by the Art Farmer-Gigi Gryce Quintet, and in its meticulous charts shows an impatience

with the prevailing casual blowing sessions of Hard Bop. A later group, the Art Farmer-Benny Golson Jazztet **(Tonk)** and **(Farmer-Golson Jazztet)** proved an ideal setting for his lyrical gifts and considered approach.

Recordings:
Clifford Brown Memorial (Prestige/—)
Wardell Gray, Central Avenue (Prestige/Prestige)
Farmer's Market (Prestige/Prestige)
Tonk (Mercury/Mercury)
Farmer-Golson Jazztet (Cadet/—)
Portrait Of Art (Contemporary/—)
A Sleeping Bee (Sonet/Sonet)

Above: Art Farmer, co-leader with Benny Golson of the Jazztet, fine unit which gave McCoy Tyner his start.

Irving Fazola

Irving Henry Fazola's graceful phrasing and warm, liquid tone could only have come from New Orleans (where he was born in 1912). But Fazola, like fellow New Orleans clarinettist Edmond Hall (♦), skilfully adapted his basic style into one which fitted Swing Era of late-1930s, early-1940s, in admirable fashion. After starting on piano, Fazola switched to clarinet at 13. First professional engagement two years later, then regular gigs with such as Louis Prima, Sharkey Bonano, Armand Hug.
1935: worked in New Orleans with Ben Pollack (♦), then toured with same band. With bands of Gus Arnheim (1937), Glenn Miller (1937-8), and after rejoining Pollack, briefly, became member of Bob Crosby (♦) Orchestra/Bob Cats (1938). Was one of Crosby's star soloists. Fitted in beautifully with Dixie-swing concept of Crosby bands. Soloed eloquently,

and with feeling, as member of main orchestra on titles like **My Inspiration,** and witty interpretation of **Skaters' Waltz (South Rampart Street Parade)** and also with Bob Cats, on **Milk Cow Blues (Come On & Hear, Vol 2)** and **Spain, Hindustan, Mournin' Blues** and **Jazz Me Blues** (last-named, something of a classic Fazola statement) **(Big Noise From Winnetka).** After leaving Crosby in 1940, worked with Jimmy McPartland, in Chicago, before returning to New Orleans to join Tony Almerico Band (late '40).
1941: doubled on bassoon with innovative Claude Thornhill (♦) Orchestra, his Jimmie Noone (♦)-influenced clarinet sitting comfortably upon the fascinating background textures provided by Thornhill and fellow arranger Bill Borden **(Claude Thornhill At Glen Island Casino 1941** and **The Memorable Claude Thornhill).** Left to join Muggsy Spanier (♦) big band last day of 1941, remaining for approximately four months. During which time produced typically mellifluous contributions to Muggsy Spanier record date (January,'42) **(Muggsy Spanier)** with **Hesitating Blues** and **Can't We Be Friends?** being especially memorable.
Spent year with Teddy Powell Orchestra (1942-3) **(Teddy Powell & His Orchestra 1942-3)** then gigged with Georg Brunis (♦) in New York. With Horace Heidt Orchestra for one-and-a-half years, then, once again, back to New Orleans, where he led own band on radio (1943-7), also working clubs. During this period, renewed working acquaintance with Almerico and Louis Prima, also working with latter's brother, Leon (all between 1944-5). Worked regularly on local radio during much of 1948, and up until March 1949, when he died in his sleep, Irving Fazola continued to delight with his own brand of flowing, unhurried clarinet playing, as personified by results of his final recording

date in 1948 **(New Orleans Express).**

Recordings:
Bob Crosby, South Rampart Street Parade (MCA)
Bob Crosby, Come On & Hear, Vol 2 (—/Coral)
Bob Crosby, Big Noise From Winnetka (MCA)
The Memorable Claude Thornhill (Columbia/—)
Claude Thornhill At Glen Island Casino 1941 (Monmouth-Evergreen/—)
Muggsy Spanier (Decca/Ace of Hearts)
Teddy Powell & His Orchestra (1942-43) (First Time Records/—)
Harry James & His Orchestra, 1936-1938 (The Old Masters/—)
Various (Including Irving Fazola), New Orleans Express (EmArcy/EmArcy)

Maynard Ferguson

Born in Montreal, 1928, trumpeter Maynard Ferguson made his name with the Stan Kenton Orchestra, where his phenomenal upper register technique allowed him to scream an octave above the rest of the trumpet section **(Artistry In Jazz).** Shorty Rogers used him to good effect in his own driving band **(Blues Express)** and he also worked for the movie studios, notably on Cecil B. De Mille's *The Ten Commandments.* In 1956, he formed his own big band, using largely young unknowns who went on to establish a reputation – Slide Hampton, Don Ellis, Joe Farrell and Jaki Byard. The first and best album **(A Message From Newport)** has a colossal impact, largely due to the bite and precision of the brass. Subsequent Ferguson bands show a similar emphasis on hard swing, though his more recent work shows a disco orientation.

Recordings:
Stan Kenton, Artistry In Jazz (Capitol/—)
Shorty Rogers, Blues Express (RCA – France)
A Message From Newport (Roulette/—)
Alive & Well In London (Columbia(CBS)
Chameleon (Columbia/CBS)
Live At Jimmy's (Columbia/CBS)
Primal Scream (Columbia/CBS)

Ella Fitzgerald

Born 1918 in Virginia, singer Ella Fitzgerald got her first big break when she was spotted by altoist Benny Carter in the amateur hour at Harlem's Apollo. This led to bandleader Chick Webb taking her on as vocalist, and with her first smash hit, **A-Tisket A-Tasket,** her career was assured. She conducted Webb's orchestra after his death. In 1937, she won the Down Beat poll, and has gone on winning ever since. Over the years, her voice has matured from its first piping prettiness into a rich contralto. The old argument still continues over Ella's status as a jazz singer, and her lack of emotional depth. She does not move the listener like Billie Holiday, nor amaze with her imagination like Sarah

Vaughan, and her swoops through the scales are practised, glossy and often predictable. Nevertheless, her voice is an unrivalled instrument when handling the classier popular songs. Her signing to Norman Granz saw the release of a series of songbooks covering Jerome Kern & Johnny Mercer, Rodgers & Hart, Harold Arlen, Irving Berlin, Cole Porter and Duke Ellington, the latter – particularly with the small groups – being the most jazz-orientated. She is also a great favorite with Jazz at the Phil audiences, and her scat-singing on numbers like **Lady Be Good** or **How High The Moon** is by now obligatory. The recent re-emergence of Granz has produced a crop of fine Ella albums in the small group context (**Take Love Easy, Ella In London, Ella At Montreux** and **Ella & Oscar**).

Recordings:
Ella Fitzgerald & Louis Armstrong, Ella & Louis (Verve/Verve)
Ella Sings The Duke Ellington Songbook (Verve/Verve)
JATP In Tokyo (Verve/Verve)
Ella Fitzgerald & Joe Pass, Take Love Easy (Pablo/Pablo)
Ella In London (Pablo/Pablo)
Ella At Montreux (Pablo/Pablo)
Ella Fitzgerald & Oscar Peterson, Ella & Oscar (Pablo/Pablo)
These Are The Blues (Verve/Verve)

Bud Freeman

In April, 1977, Lawrence 'Bud' Freeman (born Chicago, Illinois, 1906) celebrated his 71st birthday by appearing at a London Soho restaurant. Freeman, who thrives on the fact that his dapper exterior and polite, articulate manner often leads to him being thought of as an Englishman, was in fine form during his birthday gig. From looks and bearing – and especially the vitality and crispness of his playing – it was little short of amazing to recall that Freeman had tried out his first saxophone – a C-melody sax to be precise – some 54 years previously (the switch to tenor followed two years later, in 1925).

Tonally, Freeman's work on tenor has been compared with that of Lester Young (♦); in actual fact, though the comparison is more or less correct, Freeman's tone has more of an edge than Young's; rhythmically, there are similarities with the earlier style of Coleman Hawkins (♦). Truer still is the fact that Bud Freeman always has been an individualist, instantly recognizable, and something of a style-setting innovator. Certainly, he remains the archetypal tenor player of so-called Chicago school, of which Freeman was one of the early protagonists. His playing is marked by a tenacious, joyful approach to the most basic of jazz tenets: swinging. Making excellent use of vibrato, he has a highly personal way of treating ballads – tender, yet without maudlin sentimentality – and his elliptical phrasing and almost deadpan tone are other aspects of his art which help make him the wholly distinctive player he is. Bud Freeman's musical training included some tuition from father of cornettist Jimmy McPartland. At beginning

of his career, was closely associated with Austin High School Gang, in Chicago; he and associates deeply affected by music of Louis Armstrong (♦), Jimmy Noone (♦), King Oliver (♦), Bix Beiderbecke (♦), the New Orleans Rhythm Kings, et al. Together with his Austin High colleagues, Freeman worked with a variety of bands between 1925-7, not always strictly jazz, mostly in Chicago.

1927: Freeman, Frank Teschemacher (♦) and McPartland recorded as members of (Red) McKenzie & (Eddie) Condon's Chicagoans. Results have long since passed into annals of recorded jazz as classic definitions of white 'Chicago' jazz (**That Toddlin' Town - Chicago: 1926-28**). Also in '27, Freeman joined orchestra of Ben Pollack (♦), with whom he was to remain for almost a year before joining a band aboard the *Ile de France*. Also worked for fortnight in Paris with drummer-friend Davey Tough (♦). Returning to US, Freeman joined Red Nichols (♦), before working with succession of jazz and dance bands, including Roger Wolfe Kahn, Zez Confrey (♦).

1935: with prestigious Ray Noble Orchestra, with Noble giving Freeman generous allocation of solo space (viz **Dinah (With All My Heart)** with tenorist producing bubbling, infectious solo). Spent two years (1936-8) as featured soloist with Tommy Dorsey (♦). Again, was given ample solo space, notably on such Dorsey items as **Smoke Gets In Your Eyes, Who?, Maple Leaf Rag, Marie (Tommy Dorsey & His Orchestra)** and **After You've Gone, That's A-Plenty, Blue Danube** and **Beale Street Blues (Tommy Dorsey, Vol II)**.

Joined Benny Goodman (♦), remaining for nine-month period in 1938.

1939: appointed nominal leader of Summa Cum Laude Orchestra (originally assembled for one-night gig by Eddie Condon previous year) whose members included, Condon and Freeman apart, Max Kaminsky (♦), Pee Wee Russell (♦) and Brad Gowans. Like those by McKenzie & Condon Chicagoans, recordings by the SCLO are coveted, rightly so, by aficionados of Chicago jazz.

Records testify handsomely (**Chicagoans In New York: Bud Freeman** and **Chicago Styled**) to freshness and spring-heeled vitality of band during its almost one-and-a-half-year lifetime. SCLO took part in short-lived revue *Swingin' That Dream*, also featuring Louis Armstrong and Benny Goodman Septet. Apart from comprehensive association with large-size bands during 1930s, Freeman worked with numerous small combos during decade, in person and on record.

Two important recording dates under Condon's leadership really established Bud Freeman as major soloist. Most significant for Freeman was feature item entitled **The Eel (Home Cooking)** which was recorded twice, at both sessions. In itself, **The Eel** encapsulates quintessence of Bud Freeman's approach to tenor-sax.

In 1938, demonstrated ability to more than hold his own even, in strongest company, eg Armstrong, Teagarden (♦), Waller (♦), laying down some of his most dynamic playing during broadcast date

Above: Tenorist Bud Freeman – 'always an individualist, instantly recognisable . . . a style-setting innovator . . .'

from New York (**All That Jazz: Louis Armstrong**). Freeman's long association with Condon continued productively into 1940s, with consistently high standard of overall performance both by various Condon-led bands in general and Freeman's tenor-sax in particular. Recording-wise, these collaborations ranged from a 1939 date which recaptured spirit if not essence of McKenzie & Condon Chicagoans (**Chicago Jazz**) through a trio of 1940 studio sessions, two in March (**Commodore Condon, Vol 1**) and one in July (under Freeman's name) (**Home Cooking**). In the mutually inspiring company of Condonites Russell, Hackett, Kaminsky, Teagarden, Mole (♦) and Tough, Freeman invariably gave of his very best during these occasions. When SCLO disbanded, toured with yet another big band – this one his own. Venture, however, lasted only few months before its leader joined combo of Joe Marsala (♦).

Following move back to city of his birth, plus another unsuccessful attempt at leading big band, Freeman served with US Army

(1943-5). Appointed leader of Service band at Ft George, Maryland; likewise for another band in Aleutian Islands. Out of uniform, was soon back on New York music scene, including regular work, once again, with Condon (1946-7). Early in '47, accepted offer to lead trio for hotel residence in Rio de Janeiro. Five years later, was to tour Chile, Peru. Some of Freeman's finest playing of 1950s captured on record during a 1954 Condon jam session in New York (**The Golden Days Of Jazz: Eddie Condon**). During this decade he studied with pianist-composer Lennie Tristano (♦), although he maintains this did nothing to change his musical thoughts or basic approach to jazz. Nor did it, for Freeman continued to sound as easily recognizable in 1950s as he had in company with rest of Louisiana Rhythm Kings in 1929 (**Jack Teagarden Classics**), or with Benny Goodman's Boys, also '29 (**The Early B.G.**), with Joe Venuti's Blue Six in '33 (**Benny Goodman & The Giants Of Swing/Jazz In The Thirties**), with Mezz Mezzrow's orchestra in '34 (**The Big Apple**) or leading his own Windy Five (including Bunny Berigan (♦)) (**Swing Classics - 1935/Jazz In The Thirties**).

On an all-star record date like

The Big Challenge it was intriguing to hear Freeman's tenor in tandem with Hawkins (**I'm Beginning To See The Light** and **Alphonse & Gaston**), as well as juxtaposed, one next to the other (**When Your Lover Has Gone**). Since 1950s, has continued to tour extensively, throughout the US and abroad. A regular visitor to the UK and Europe (including European trip in '67 as member of Jazz From A Swinging Era package), either as leader of own groups, or as solo act. Between 1969–70, was member of World's Greatest Jazzband, with which outfit he has toured and recorded on numerous occasions (**Live At The Roosevelt Grill, Extra!, The World's Greatest Jazzband Of Yank Lawson & Bob Haggart, The W.G.J.B. Of Yank Lawson & Bob Haggart** and **Century Plaza**). Has also appeared with saxist-clarinettist Bob Wilber (♦) (**Song Of The Tenor, The Music Of Hoagy Carmichael** and **The Compleat Bud Freeman**) to mutual advantage of both players. The musical compatibility of the duo is self-evident from overall contents of albums, just as it had been previously with Condon, Teschemacher, Tough and Ruby Braff (♦) (**Bud Freeman**).

Thus far, Bud Freeman has written two autobiographical books – *You Don't Look Like A Musician* and *If You Know Of A Better Life*.

Recordings:
**Various, That Toddlin' Town –
Chicago: 1926-28** (*Parlophone*)
**Benny Goodman, The Early
B.G.** (—/*Vocalion*)
**Various, Jack Teagarden
Classics** (*Family – Italy*)
Various, Swing Classics – 1935
(*Prestige*)/
Jazz In The Thirties
(*World Records*)
Bud Freeman, Home Cooking
Tax – Sweden)
**Bud Freeman, Chicagoans In
New York** (*Dawn Club*)
Bud Freeman, Chicago Styled
(*Swaggie – Australia*)
**Mezz Mezzrow/(Frankie
Newton), The Big Apple**
(*RCA Victor – France*)
Louis Armstrong (*Trip*)/
**All That Jazz: Louis
Armstrong** (*DJM*)
Benny Goodman, Vols 5, 7
(*RCA Victor – France*)
**Tommy Dorsey, Tommy
Dorsey & His Orchestra**
(*RCA Victor/RCA Victor*)
Tommy Dorsey, Vol II
(*RCA Victor/RCA Victor*)
**Various (Including Eddie
Condon), Chicago Jazz**
(—/*Coral*)
**Eddie Condon, Commodore
Condon, Vol 1** (—/*London*)
Lee Wiley, Sweet & Lowdown
(*Monmouth – Evergreen/*—)
**Various (Including Eddie
Condon/Bud Freeman), The
Commodore Years**
(*Atlantic/*—)
**Jack Teagarden, Vol 2:
'Prince Of The Bones'**
(*RCA Victor – France*)
**The Golden Days Of Jazz:
Eddie Condon** (*CBS – Holland*)
The Bud Freeman Trio
(—/*London*)
**Eddie Condon, Chicago & All
That Jazz!** (—/*Verve*)
Various, The Big Challenge
(*Jazztone/Concert Hall*)
The Compleat Bud Freeman
(*Monmouth – Evergreen/
Parlophone*)

*Home Cooking (Tax, Sweden) –
Bud Freeman at his best.*

**Bob Wilber/Maxine Sullivan,
The Music Of Hoagy
Carmichael**
(*Monmouth – Evergreen/
Parlophone*)
**The World's Greatest Jazzband
Of Yank Lawson & Bob
Haggart, Extra!**
(*Project 3/Parlophone*)
**The World's Greatest Jazzband
Of Yank Lawson & Bob
Haggart** (*Project 3/
World Record Club*)
**The World's Greatest Jazzband
Of Yank Lawson & Bob
Haggart – Live At The
Roosevelt Grill**
(*Atlantic/Atlantic*)
**The World's Greatest Jazzband
Of Yank Lawson & Bob
Haggart In Concert, Vol 2,
At Carnegie Hall**
(*World Jazz/*—)
**The World's Greatest Jazzband
of Yank Lawson & Bob
Haggart, Century Plaza**
(*World Pacific/*—)
Bud Freeman, The Joy Of Sax
(*Chiaroscuro/*—)
**Bud Freeman, Song Of The
Tenor** (*Philips*)

Slim Gaillard

The proto-typical '40s hipster, Gaillard sang, danced, played guitar and practically every other instrument, but is usually remembered for his jive talk. He had a string of hits, **Tutti Frutti, Flat Foot Floogie, Cement Mixer, A-Reet-a-Voutee**, some in partnership with bassist Slam Stewart. Charlie Parker and Dizzy Gillespie turned up on one of his novelty sessions, cutting four tracks including the splendid **Slim's Jam** (**Charlie Parker, Bird/The Savoy, Recordings**). A collection with Bam Brown, Harry The Hipster Gibson and Leo Watson, the most gymnastic of scat-singers, catches precisely the period flavor. **Avocado Seed Soup Symphony** is a surreal masterpiece (**Mc-Vouty**).

Recordings:
**Slim Gaillard & Bam Brown,
McVouty** (*Hep/Hep*)

Erroll Garner

Pianist Erroll Garner was one of jazz's great romantics. Basically a swing musician, his piano conception was firmly rooted in an orchestral style with a powerful, two-handed attack which built towards great crescendos. Rich chords and a percussive left hand that

*Concert By The Sea (CBS):
the late great Erroll Garner.*

drove with a tireless energy, warmth and humor and great melodic gifts made Garner a popular concert performer.

A session from 1947, Charlie Parker's first after his breakdown, found Garner coping well in an unsuitable setting, both men hitting the heights on **Cool Blues**, and accompanying singer Earl Coleman on **This Is Always**, which became a hit (**Charlie Parker On Dial, Vol 2**). Stunning Garner can be heard on **Blue Lou** from a Gene Norman concert with Wardell Gray (**Jazz Scene USA**), and a collection of excellent '40s performances by the diminutive titan in the more usual trio setting are on Savoy (**The Elf**).

A Columbia collection from the '50s gives a fine cross-section of his talent, from the lyrical **Am I Blue** and **Dreamy** – his own composition – to the charging **Avalon** (**Play It Again, Erroll!**). His most popular album (**Concert By The Sea**) has the performer pulling out all the stops, the long teasing introductions, the vast range of resource, the overwhelming attack. Playing mainly standards like **Autumn Leaves**, and **April In Paris**, Garner stamps his material with his own unique personality. A self-taught musician, Garner's inability to read music didn't prevent him from

writing some beautiful tunes, including **Misty**. Four compositions turn up on a late session from the '70s (**Magician**) which shows all the vitality of three decades ago, and the same determination to wring the listener's heartstrings.

Born in 1923, Garner died in 1977, leaving scores of albums behind on a multiplicity of labels.

Recordings:
**Charlie Parker On Dial,
Vol 2** (*Spotlite/Spotlite*)
Jazz Scene USA
(—/*Vogue – France*)
The Elf (*Savoy/Savoy*)
Play It Again, Erroll
(*Columbia/CBS*)
Concert By The Sea
(*Columbia/CBS*)
Magician (*London/Pye*)
The Greatest Garner
(*Atlantic/Atlantic*)

Stan Getz

Born 1927, Philadelphia, tenorman Stan Getz achieved fame early with his lyrical **Early Autumn** solo with Woody Herman's Second Herd, and as part of the **Four Brothers** saxophone feature (**Early Autumn**).

A Savoy collection from the late '40s assembles the white Lester Young disciples, Getz, Al Cohn, Serge Chaloff, Brew Moore and Allen Eager – **Lester's Gray Boys (Brothers & Other Mothers)**. More early Getz exemplifies the cool approach, subtle, unassertive playing that flows lyrically on ballads like **Indian Summer, Wrap Your Troubles In Dreams** and **Too Marvellous For Words** (**Stan Getz**).

Following a tour of Scandinavia which left scores of Getz imitators in its wake, the tenorman began to show more virility in his attack, and a live date from 1951 (**Getz At Storyville**) shows a rare blend of relaxation and drive. With model accompaniment, Al Haig on piano,

*West Coast Jazz (Columbia). Long-deleted Stan Getz
classic containing the 'Shine' solo. Cover art hip '50s.*

Above: Tenorman Stan Getz, enduring master of the ballad. Enjoyed commercial success with the bossa nova in the '60s.

Jimmy Raney, guitar, Tiny Khan, drums, Getz flows through up-tempo numbers like **Parker '51,** and **The Song Is You,** and endless melodic variations on **Thou Swell.** The '50s found him recording for Clef in a series of variable meetings with the giants. Most of these are deleted, but the session with Lionel Hampton produced the driving **Cherokee** and **Jumping At The Woodside,** and the more compatible date with West Coast musicians, trumpeter Conte Candoli and drummer Shelly Manne, found Getz in peak form, especially on the unaccompanied introduction to **Shine.** A session with Dizzy Gillespie, recently re-issued **(Diz & Getz)** shows the near-honking side of tenorman, subtlety thrown to the winds, as he responds to Gillespie's ebullience. In the mid-'50s, he formed a quintet with trombonist Bob Brookmeyer, but again none of their albums is currently available. An encounter with another trombonist, J. J. Johnson, at the Chicago Opera House, resulted in some of Getz's finest work, from the sinuous attack of **Crazy Rhythm** to the lyrical loveliness of **It Never Entered My Mind (Getz & J.J. 'Live').** A year later, Getz moved to Scandinavia, disenchanted with current jazz fashions, returning in 1961 and recording one of the few successful albums with strings **(Focus)** which owes much to the brilliant writing of Eddie Sauter.
Following in the footsteps of Gillespie and Bud Shank, Getz made a highly profitable fusion with Latin American music, cutting the first album of the bossa nova fad **(Jazz Samba)** which contained the hit **Desafinado.** He followed this up with two albums on which he collaborated with the Brazilians, Jobim and Bonfa **(Jazz Samba Encore** and **Getz-Gilberto),** the latter containing the Astrud Gilberto version of **Girl From Ipanema.**

By the mid-'60s, he was back in the straight-ahead groove again, leading a quartet of Gary Burton, vibes, Steve Swallow, bass and the great Roy Haynes, drums **(Getz Au Go-Go).** Though not attracted to the expressionism of the New Wave players, the tenorman did loosen up considerably under the influence of young sidemen, and albums like the two with pianist Chick Corea **(Captain Marvel** and **Sweet Rain)** show a greater degree of group interplay and shifting tempos than before.

Currently Stan Getz is one of the acknowledged masters of the tenor – not a radical innovator, but an artist who has always gone his own way, and concentrated on working out the details of his style. His tone is one of the loveliest in jazz, and can carry him through a fairly lush programme without losing the attention of the jazz fan **(The Special Magic Of Stan Getz & Burt Bacharach).**

Recordings:
Woody Herman, Early Autumn
 (Capitol/—)
Brothers & Other Mothers
 (Savoy/Savoy)
Stan Getz *(Prestige/Prestige)*
Getz At Storyville *(Roost/Sonet)*
Stan Getz - Dizzy Gillespie,
 Diz & Getz *(Verve/Verve)*
Getz & J.J. 'Live' *(Verve/Verve)*
Focus *(Verve/Verve)*

Jazz Samba *(Verve/Verve)*
Jazz Samba Encore
 (Verve/Verve)
Getz-Gilberto *(Verve/Verve)*
Getz Au Go-Go
 (Verve/Verve)
Captain Marvel
 (Verve/Verve)
Sweet Rain *(Verve/Verve)*
The Special Magic Of Stan
 Getz & Burt Bacharach
 (Verve/Verve)
The Peacocks *(Columbia/CBS)*

Terry Gibbs

Vibraphonist Terry Gibbs was born in New York, 1924. His style was based on Lionel Hampton's, and he first came to prominence with Woody Herman, 1948–9, moving on to the bands of Tommy Dorsey and Benny Goodman before branching out on his own. The best examples of his work in the catalog are the small group comprising Sam Jones, Louis Hayes and Kenny Burrell **(Take It From Me)** and the big band formed in 1959, including Conte Candoli, Frank Rosolino, Bill Perkins and Mel Lewis, a shouting, extrovert outfit **(The Big Band Sound Of Terry Gibbs).**

Recordings:
Take It From Me *(Impulse/—)*
The Big Band Sound Of Terry
 Gibbs *(Verve/Verve)*

Dizzy Gillespie

Born John Birks Gillespie in South Carolina, 1917, the trumpeter took over his idol, Roy Eldridge's chair in the Teddy Hill band, where his penchant for clowning and horse-play soon earned him his nickname (and gained him the sack from the Cab Calloway band). An early example of his playing can be found on **Kerouac** and **Stardust** from 1941 **(The Harlem Jazz Scene)** which contain both the Eldridge influence and some

of the harmonic ideas that led him into Bebop. A period as trumpeter and arranger with the revolutionary Billy Eckstine band of 1944 set the seal on his emergence as the leading trumpeter of the new music, and his small combo recordings between 1944–6 with young modernists like Milt Jackson and Al Haig – **52nd Street Theme, Night In Tunisia, Ol' Man Rebop, Anthropology (The Greatest Of Dizzy Gillespie)** or with tenormen Dexter Gordon or Sonny Stitt – **Blue 'n' Boogie, One Bass Hit, Oop Bop Sh'Bam, A Handful Of Gimme, That's Earl, Brother (In The Beginning)** are classics of the genre.

In 1945, collaboration with Bebop's greatest figure, Charlie Parker, produced the magnificent **Groovin' High, Dizzy Atmosphere, All The Things You Are, Salt Peanuts, Shaw 'Nuff, Lover Man** and **Hot House (In The Beginning)** while a vast and confusing tangle of recordings covers their work together in the studio, concert hall and broadcast **(Lullaby In Rhythm, The Definitive Charlie Parker, Vol 2, Bird & Diz, Diz 'n' Bird In Concert** and **The Quintet Of The Year),** all of it the finest music that modern jazz has to offer. Unlike Parker, however, Dizzy combined imaginative genius with a talent for public presentation and his beret, horn-rim glasses and goatee soon became the Bebop uniform.

In 1946 he organized a big band and worked with arrangers like Gil Fuller, Tadd Dameron, George Russell and John Lewis to transplant what was essentially a combo music into a wider format. The finest pieces, **Emanon, Things To Come** and **Our Delight (In The Beginning)** show the excitement and incredible technique of the band in playing the complex scores, while Dizzy's pioneering work with Latin American rhythms is illustrated by the blasting **Manteca** and **Cubano Be, Cubano Bop (The Greatest Of Dizzy Gillespie).** By late 1949 the crisis hit the

The Giant (America): Dizzy Gillespie's phenomenal cheek in action. Bent trumpet his standard instrument since 1954.

Above: Dizzy Gillespie, pioneer of Bebop, Afro-Cuban and the angled trumpet. Living history.

big band scene, and Dizzy was forced to pander to popular tastes with numbers like **You Stole My Wife You Horsethief (Strictly Bebop)** and in 1950 it was disbanded. A good deal of hilarious scat-singing accompanies some brilliant trumpet playing on numbers like **Swing Low, Sweet Cadillac** and **School Days** from a Salle Pleyel concert of 1953, while earlier combos, one including a young John Coltrane, showcase the leader's lyricism, drive and rhythmic assurance on **Tin Tin Deo** and **Birks Works; The Champ (Dee Gee Days)** was the biggest-selling Bebop number of the period.

A studio big band from 1954 showed that Dizzy could generate wild enthusiasm and excitement even in those frigid surroundings, and the arrangements by Buster Harding of numbers like **Hob Nail Special** or **Pile Driver** are eminently suitable **(The Big Band Sound Of Dizzy Gillespie)**. Other tracks on the album feature another studio band from 1955, and a regular big band which Dizzy assembled for a US State Department tour 1956–8. Numerous '50s jam sessions followed under the aegis of Norman Granz, including several with Dizzy's one-time mentor, Roy Eldridge **(Trumpet Kings** and **The Gillespie Jam Sessions)**, while an encounter with Stan Getz provokes the seamless tenorman to some of his wildest playing on record **(Diz And Getz)**. Using his regular quintet and familiar numbers, the trumpeter recorded wonderfully lyrical versions of **There Is No Greater Love** and **Moonglow (Have Trumpet, Will Excite)**.

The '60s saw no decline in powers though on some albums he seems less than fully committed, a charge that can hardly be levelled in the next decade. An album cut in Europe with the dynamic tenor-man Johnny Griffin **(The Giant)** has Dizzy playing throughout with daring and ferocity, lyrical on **Serenity**, incisive on **Stella By Starlight**. A new contract with

Granz's Pablo has produced a great renaissance, from the duet with Oscar Peterson **(Oscar Peterson & Dizzy Gillespie)**, the quartet with Joe Pass, Ray Brown and Mickey Roker **(Dizzy Gillespie's Big 4)** and the Montreux Festival recordings from 1975 **(Dizzy)**. A big band **(Dizzy Gillespie & Machito)** and a septet **(Bahiana)** continue Dizzy's fusion of jazz and Latin American music.

An undisputed trumpet master, Dizzy Gillespie's ability to swing at the softest volume, or to vary his attack from squeezed notes to high register screams remains unrivalled. His abilities as a conga drummer and singer are often overlooked amid his stage antics.

Recordings:
Charlie Christian, The Harlem Jazz Scene *(Esoteric/Saga)*
Charlie Parker, Lullaby In Rhythm *(Spotlite/Spotlite)*
The Definitive Charlie Parker, Vol 2 *(Verve/Metro)*
Bird & Diz *(—/Saga)*
Charlie Parker/Miles Davis/ Dizzy Gillespie *(Vogue/Vogue)*
The Quintet Of The Year *(Debut/Vogue)*
The Greatest Of Dizzy Gillespie *(RCA/RCA)*
In The Beginning *(Prestige/Prestige)*
Strictly Bebop *(Capitol/Capitol)*
Live At The Spotlite, '46 *(Hi-Fly/Hi-Fly)*
Trumpet Masters, Dizzy Gillespie *(GNP Crescendo/Vogue)*
Dee Gee Days *(Savoy/Savoy)*
The Big Band Sound Of Dizzy Gillespie *(Verve/Verve)*
Trumpet Kings *(Verve/Verve)*
The Gillespie Jam Sessions *(Verve/Verve)*
Stan Getz & Dizzy Gillespie *(Verve/Verve)*
Have Trumpet, Will Excite *(Verve/—)*
The Giant *(Prestige/America)*
Oscar Peterson & Dizzy Gillespie *(Pablo/Pablo)*
Dizzy Gillespie's Big 4 *(Pablo/Pablo)*

Dizzy *(Pablo/Pablo)*
Dizzy Gillespie & Machito *(Pablo/Pablo)*
Bahiana *(Pablo/Pablo)*
Dizzy's Party *(Pablo/Pablo)*
Diz & Getz *(Verve/Verve)*

Jimmy Giuffre

Multi-reed player Jimmy Giuffre's conception has developed further and foreshadowed more radical change over thirty years than most. Born in 1921, his best known early work was the composition **Four Brothers** for Woody Herman's 2nd Herd. A West Coast musician, Giuffre's output varied between the typical, chirpily swinging sessions with Shorty Rogers **(West Coast Jazz)** and the highly experimental **(Shelly Manne, The Three & The Two)** on which Giuffre, Rogers and Manne indulge in simultaneous improvising. Giuffre began to concentrate on the clarinet, restricting himself to the broody, breathy chalumeau register, and his writing grew spare and concerned with emotive sound qualities. A long-deleted album **(The Jimmy Giuffre Clarinet)** casts a reflective, pastoral mood, and shows his methodical advance into new territory. Two trio albums **(The Jimmy Giuffre Trio** and **Trav'lin' Light)** approach the often rustic themes with all the nimble footwork of maypole dancers, no individual predominating. Dispensing with the sounded beat and reviving a pre-harmonic melodic directness, Giuffre was ahead of Ornette Coleman, for example, by several years. His later trios with pianist Paul Bley and bassist Steve Swallow **(Free Fall, Fusion** and **Thesis)** brought this conception to its fullest ensemble realization. His most recent work, **Quiet Song**, confirms his status as one of

Below: Jimmy Giuffre (right) with swinging tenor-team Zoot Sims and Al Cohn. Cohn's heard this one before.

the few avant-garde clarinettists, and an artist of great originality.

Recordings:
Shorty Rogers, West Coast Jazz *(Atlantic/Atlantic)*
Shelly Manne, The Three & The Two *(Contemporary/—)*
The Jimmy Giuffre Clarinet *(Atlantic/—)*
The Jimmy Giuffre Trio *(Atlantic/—)*
Trav'lin' Light *(Atlantic/—)*
Free Fall *(Columbia/—)*
Fusion *(Verve/—)*
Thesis *(Verve/—)*
Paul Bley, Quiet Song *(Improvising Artists Inc/—)*
Mosquito Dance *(—/DJM)*

Tyree Glenn

Evans Tyree Glenn (born Corsicana, Texas, 1912; died 1974) amassed wealth of big-band experiences – Tommy Myles (1934–6); Charlie Echols (1936); Eddie Barefield (1936–7); Eddie Mallory (1937–9) (the band which accompanied singer Ethel Waters (♦)) **(Ethel Waters: 1938-1939)**; Benny Carter (♦) (1939); Cab Calloway (♦) (1939–46); Don Redman (♦) (with whom he came to Europe, in '46); and Duke Ellington (♦) (1947–51) before becoming a useful instrumentalist in a strictly small-combo context.

Glenn's premier instrument was trombone, but he also doubled (unusually for trombonist) on vibraphone. With Ellington, Glenn's trombone was used fairly extensively – especially during 1947. He could play warm open solos, as on **You Gotta Crawl Before You Walk, Boogie Bop Blues, Sultry Serenade, Three Cent Stomp,** or **How High The World Of Duke Ellington/The Duke: Edward Kennedy Ellington: 1899-1974)**, or effect a reasonable facsimile of the plunger-mute style as pioneered by his predecessor in Ellington band, Joseph 'Tricky Sam' Nanton (♦). **Hi 'Ya Sue**

(The World Of Duke Ellington, Vol 2/The World Of Duke Ellington) is an impressive example of his plunger technique. On vibes, was less featured with Ellington, **Dance No 2** from **Liberian Suite (Liberian Suite/Tone Parallel To Harlem)** and **Limehouse Blues (Ellington In Concert, Vol 1)** are two comparatively rare examples. With Calloway, his solos were more evenly divided.

From 1965-8, Glenn worked with Louis Armstrong (♦) All Stars, playing trombone, vibes and taking odd vocal (something he also accomplished with Calloway). Part-time actor in early-1950s, Glenn's feature item with Armstrong was his own **Tyree's Blues.** Best-known composition, though, is afore-mentioned **Sultry Serenade,** which, when retitled **How Could You Do A Thing Like That To Me?** and with lyric appended, received numerous recordings by top pop artists like Frank Sinatra.

Recordings:
Duke Ellington, Liberian Suite/ (A Tone Parallel To Harlem) *(CBS – France)*
The World Of Duke Ellington *(Columbia)/*
The Duke: Edward Kennedy Ellington (1899-1974) *(CBS)*
The World Of Duke Ellington, Vol 2 *(Columbia)/*
The World Of Duke Ellington *(CBS)*
Duke Ellington, Ellington In Concert, Vols 1, 2 *(—/World Record Club)*
16 Cab Calloway Classics *(CBS – France)*
'Penguin Swing': Chu Berry Featured With Cab Calloway & His Orchestra *(Jazz Archives/Jazz Archives)*
Melancholy Benny: Benny Carter & His Orchestra 1939/40 *(Tax – Sweden)*
Ethel Waters (1938-1939) *(RCA Victor – France)*
Don Redman & His All Stars *(Almac/—)*
Al Sears, The Greatest Of The Small Bands, Vol 5 *(RCA Victor – France)*
Various, Newport In New York '72: The Jam Session, Vol 3 *(Atlantic/Atlantic)*

Paul Gonsalves

During the 1950s, Paul Gonsalves (born Boston, Massachusetts, 1920) established himself as one of the leading tenor-saxophonists in jazz – a reputation he sustained, with consummate ease, up to the time of his death, in 1974. Gonsalves started out on guitar, an instrument he continued to play on odd occasions, especially in later years **(Great Ellingtonians Play A Tribute To Duke Ellington).** Was an average-to-good tenor player when he joined Duke Ellington (♦) in 1950. Previously, his playing experience had encompassed periods with Boston-based big band of Sabby Lewis (early-1940s), Count Basie (♦) (1946), and Dizzy Gillespie (♦) (1949-50). Apart from short spells away from the band for reasons of health or the occasion in '53 when he temporarily joined Tommy Dorsey (♦), Gonsalves was to remain with Ellington for the rest of his working life. Ellington generously featured

Above: Tenorist Paul Gonsalves: jazz immortality in 27 choruses, with Ellington, at Newport Jazz Festival, 1956.

Gonsalves in all kinds of settings – ballads, up-tempo swingers, blues. But it was a marathon, 27-chorus solo during band's electrifying appearance at 1956 Newport Jazz Festival that finally established tenorist's name as something of a household word (in the jazz world, anyway).

With benefit of hindsight, the extemporized solo **Ellington At Newport** tended to achieve a hallowed status from some quarters in excess of its true worth, but certainly Gonsalves' unflagging playing throughout **Diminuendo & Crescendo In Blue** generated a genuine and sustained excitement. However, Gonsalves' talent is best recalled as an Ellington soloist of real creativity, warmth and individuality on other items, such as **Solitude (Masterpieces By Ellington)** recorded in 1950, and probably his first major showcase with the band; **Happy Reunion (Ellington Presents)** from 1958; **Mount Harissa (The Far East Suite)** from '66; and **Circle Of Fourths (Such Sweet Thunder)** from '57. Overall, Gonsalves' recorded output with Ellington was excellent. Somehow, though, records he made under his own name rarely did his talents full justice. One of the best was a date featuring also Gonsalves' fellow Ellingtonian Ray Nance (♦) **(Just Sittin' & A-Rockin')** which contains quality tenor playing to grace any jazz situation. There are intriguing moments, too, during a London-recorded album **(Humming Bird)** with British trumpet player Kenny Wheeler vying for top solo honors.

With Johnny Hodges (♦), Gonsalves usually was to be found at his best: certainly his work throughout **Everybody Knows Johnny Hodges** is consistently rewarding. And in a Norman Granz-inspired all-star record date from '57, Gonsalves acquitted himself splendidly **(Sittin' In),** rubbing shoulders with such redoubtables as Coleman Hawkins (♦), Dizzy Gillespie (♦), Stan Getz (♦), and Wynton Kelly. His ballad feature for the date – a beautifully structured, breathy **Gone With The Wind** which shows his indebtedness to Ben Webster (♦) – is a perfect demonstration of his serpentine, sinewy brand of tenor-playing, with its highly individual harmonic approach. In its own unhistrionic way, a more appropriate encapsulation of the art of Paul Gonsalves than, say, 27 choruses of **Diminuendo & Crescendo In Blue.**

Recordings:
Duke Ellington, Ellington At Newport *(Columbia/CBS – France)*
The World Of Duke Ellington *(Columbia)/*
The Duke: Edward Kennedy Ellington (1899-1974) *(CBS)*
The World Of Duke Ellington, Vol 2 *(Columbia)/*
The World Of Duke Ellington *(CBS)*
Duke Ellington/Count Basie, Basie Meets Ellington *(Embassy)*
Duke Ellington & The Ellingtonians *(Vogue – France)*
Duke Ellington, The Cosmic Scene *(Columbia/Philips)*
Duke Ellington, Ellington Indigos *(Columbia)*
Duke Ellington, Ellington '55 *(Capitol)/*
Toast To The Duke *(World Record Club)*
Duke Ellington, Newport 1958 *(Columbia/Philips)*
Duke Ellington, Jazz At The Plaza *(Columbia/CBS)*
Duke Ellington's 70th Birthday Concert *(Solid State/United Artists)*
Duke Ellington, The Toga Brava Suite *(United Artists)/*
The English Concert *(United Artists)*
Duke Ellington, Soul Call *(Verve)/*
The Second Big Band Sound Of Duke Ellington *(Verve)*
Duke Ellington, Masterpieces By Ellington *(Columbia/CBS – Holland)*
Duke Ellington, Ellington Presents *(Bethlehem/Ember)*
Duke Ellington, The Far East Suite *(RCA Victor/RCA Victor)*
Duke Ellington, Such Sweet Thunder *(Columbia/CBS – Realm)*
Everybody Knows Johnny Hodges *(Impulse/Impulse)*
Various, The Greatest Jazz Concert In The World *(Pablo/Pablo)*
Various, Sittin' In *(Verve/Columbia – Clef)*
Paul Gonsalves/Ray Nance, Just Sittin' & A-Rockin' *(Black Lion/Black Lion)*
Paul Gonsalves, Humming Bird *(—/Deram)*
Paul Gonsalves, Boom-Jackie-Boom-Chick *(Vocalion)*
Paul Gonsalves, Tell It The Way It Is *(Impulse/HMV)*
Various, Great Ellingtonians Play A Tribute To Duke Ellington *(—/Double-Up)*
Count Basie *(RCA Victor – France)*
Paul Gonsalves & His All Stars *(Barclay/—)*

Benny Goodman

Benjamin David Goodman (born Chicago, Illinois, 1909) probably is the most technically accomplished clarinettist to make a living (primarily) from jazz. Goodman was 12 when he made first public appearance as player at a talent contest, imitating Ted Lewis; he is as much at home playing Clarinet Concertos of Mozart, Weber, et al, as he is playing music by Fletcher Henderson (♦), Eddie Sauter (♦), Mel Powell, or any one of the numerous standard pop composers. Indeed, since 1938, Goodman has worked, in person and on record, with leading personalities and aggregations from world of classical music. In 1940, for example, Goodman commissioned Bela Bartok to write **Contrasts,** which he recorded with violinist Joseph Szigeti. Aaron Copland's Clarinet Concerto and a similar piece by Paul Hindemith also have been written on commission from Benny Goodman. But, of course, it is as a jazz clarinet player, first and foremost, that Goodman inevitably will be remembered. Even as youngster, Goodman tended mostly to sound assured and comfortable, no doubt aware that his technical command was considerably better than his con-

The Early Benny Goodman (Vocalion, Decca). To some, the youthful B.G. produced jazz superior to his later work.

The Famous 1938 Carnegie Hall Jazz Concert (Columbia). Rightly acknowledged, one of the great live jazz records.

temporaries. There are those who feel that despite his increasing technical mastery during post-1930 period, Goodman's jazz playing during earliest part of career has rarely been surpassed. There is an element of truth in this, because there were times, after Goodman had ascended the mythical throne of the equally mythical King of Swing, when a comparative glibness tended to permeate his effortless improvizations. The passionate outpourings of his youth certainly had a more definite commitment, jazz-wise. Equally true, however, is the fact that the embryonic Goodman had not yet found his own voice, at that time sounding a sometimes strange amalgam of styles of influential clarinettists of 1920s – Frank Teschemacher (♦), Leon Rappolo, Jimmie Noone (♦) and, at times, even bizarre-sounding Ted Lewis. Still, recordings from Goodman's earlier period, with the Chicagoan leading his Benny Goodman's Boys, or playing role of sideman with Irving Mills & His Hotsy Totsy Gang, Red Nichols' (♦) Orchestra (all **The Early BG**) or Ben Pollack's Orchestra **(Ben Pollack & His Orchestra: 1933-1934)** show a genuine talent in the making. Probably most outstanding recordings of this time were those with Joe Venuti/Eddie Lang All Stars **(Nothing But Notes)**.

By early 1930s it was obvious too that, apart from his instrumental talents, Benny Goodman took to role of being leader with flair and relish. With assistance from John Hammond, Goodman fronted accompanying outfits on Billie Holiday's (♦) first recording dates, in 1933, 1935 **(The Golden Years, Vols 1, 2).** He was to play on numerous subsequent Holiday sessions **(The Lester Young Story, Vol 1, The Billie Holiday Story, Vol 1 and The Golden Years, Vols 1, 2)** producing immaculate clarinet performances which, admittedly, sometimes tended to sound a trifle reserved when measured against contributions by, say, Lester Young (♦), Buck Clayton (♦), Teddy Wilson (♦). (It was Hammond who had persuaded Goodman to join an all-star band, for one track only, on final recording date by Bessie Smith (♦), great blues artist, also in '33. He failed, however, to persuade Goodman to sign Holiday to sing with his band.) During early-1930s, as with previous decade, Goodman's appearances on record were many. Amongst those who benefited by his appearances were Red Nichols (with whom Goodman worked extensively between October 1929 – January 1930, and, on record at least, for a period thereafter) **(J.T.)**; Adrian Rollini (♦); Gene Krupa (♦) (both **Benny Goodman & The Giants Of Swing/Jazz In The Thirties).** Krupa was to become a seminal figure in meteoric rise to fame Goodman was to experience following ecstatic reaction to his music at dance date in August 1935, at Palomar Ballroom, LA, played by orchestra put together previous year. Palomar date, almost single-handed, signalled start of Swing Era. By end of 1930s, Goodman had indeed become 'King of Swing'. Krupa's drumming apart, notable sidemen whose instrumental talents, Goodman aside, helped contribute much to what became international success of clarinettist's bands – large and small – included trumpeters Bunny Berigan (♦), Ziggy Elman, and, especially, Harry James (♦), pianist Jess Stacy (♦), guitarist Charlie Christian (♦), and two important black musicians, Teddy Wilson (♦) and Lionel Hampton (♦), both of whom were prime movers in success of various Goodman small combos. But as far as the big band was concerned, most significant figure was Fletcher Henderson, himself an innovator of great importance in the field. Henderson, who from time to time played piano on Goodman small-group recordings, contributed impressive number of superb arrangements for Goodman – arrangements which already had been featured by Henderson-led big bands of previous years. Although by no stretch of the imagination could Goodman's solo strength be said to equal, let alone surpass, Henderson's, clarinettist's band performed these arrangements in a smoother, slicker, generally superior manner, technically speaking. Could be said Goodman band lacked the heart of Henderson's, and that in terms of

drive and depth it compared poorly with Henderson, Basie, Ellington, Lunceford, and most of the black big bands. Yet certainly it was not as emasculated as some have claimed, and there were times when it was lifted to exceptional heights, exemplified superbly throughout **(1938 Carnegie Hall Jazz Concert** and **The Big Band Sound Of Benny Goodman),** significantly, perhaps, both live recordings. Later, at beginning of 1940s, band achieved further splendor, thanks, in the main, to fresh-sounding arrangements–compositions by Eddie Sauter (♦), Mel Powell, Buster Harding and Jimmy Mundy **(Benny Goodman Plays Solid Gold Instrumental Hits).** With big-band era waning, Goodman flirted, half-heartedly, with bop; to most fans, flirtation was unsuccessful. But it was not for lack of trying; by such top instrumentalists/arrangers as tenorist Wardell Gray (♦), trumpeters Doug Mettome, Fats Navarro (♦) (present on one record date only), and arranger-composer Chico O'Farrill. Goodman himself made little or no effort to effect stylistic adjustments to accommodate bop phraseology in his own playing. Yet records from the period (1947–9) **(Bebop Spoken Here, Benny Goodman In Hollywood Featuring Wardell Gray** and **B.G.)** give lie to claims that the association was total failure – even though leader's heart remained, unshakeably, in pre-bop era. Since late-1940s, Goodman has continued to lead various groups – of all sizes – but in more recent times his activities as bandleader have been nothing like halcyon King-of-Swing days. Since first-time visit to London in 1949, has made numerous tours to many parts of the world, including successful visit to Russia (1962) (first US jazz outfit to be invited by Russians). Although achievements of various Goodman big bands have, over the years, produced much – musically, artistically, commercially – there is little doubt that most of the best jazz produced by Goodman-led groups has come from Trio (most famous, original, line-up: Teddy Wilson, Krupa, Goodman); Quartet (same as Trio, plus Hampton); plus variety of Quintets, Sextets, Septets, etc. (which have starred, most notably, George Auld (♦), Cootie Williams (♦), Count Basie (♦), Hampton, Johnny Guarnieri (♦), Christian, Gray, and Zoot Sims (♦). Christian, something of a Goodman protégé, came to fame with, and died whilst still officially a member of, the Goodman organization. It was he, more than anyone, who helped to make the small-combo sides of 1939–41 so memorable and of lasting value, both with his forward-looking guitar solos and his rhythmically infectious riff-type compositions. Certainly, Christian's very presence seemed to inspire Goodman into producing some of his finest playing at any time of what, when all is said and done, was an illustrious career **(The Genius Of Charlie Christian/Solo Flight, Charlie Christian With The Benny Goodman Sextet & Orchestra** and **Charlie Christian With Benny Goodman & The Sextet).**

A comprehensive bio-discography, B.G. – On the Record, researched, written by D. Russell O'Connor & Warren W. Hicks, first published in 1969. The Kingdom of Swing, co-written by Goodman and Irving Kolodin, first appeared 30 years before B.G. – On the Record. Goodman appeared in film A Song Is Born (1948), having acting as well as musical role. He and the orchestra featured in several movies, including Stage Door Canteen, Hollywood Hotel and The Big Broadcast of 1937. Many times a Poll-winner – as band-leader, clarinettist – also played soprano-, alto- and tenor-saxes on occasion; and during one eventful recording date in 1928, in addition to clarinet, he played baritone-sax **(Room 1411),** baritone and alto **(Blue),** and even cornet **(Jungle Blues),** (all **The Early B.G.).** But his doubling on instruments other than clarinet mostly took place during pre-1935 period. Did much to help break down racial barriers which existed in music business during 1930s, by hiring Hampton and Wilson on permanent basis, then Henderson and others. The Benny Goodman Story, a typical Hollywood interpretation of the life of a jazzman and with only barest biographical reference to his real life-story, completed and first shown in 1955.

Recordings:
Ben Pollack & His Orchestra: 1933-1934 (—/*VJM*)
Various (Including Benny Goodman), The Early B.G. (—/*Vocalion*)
Joe Venuti, Nothing But Notes (1931-1939) (*MCA – Coral – Germany*)
Benny Goodman, A Jazz Holiday (*MCA/—*)
Various, Benny Goodman & The Giants Of Swing (*Prestige*)/ **Jazz In The Thirties** (*World Records*)
Adrian Rollini & His Orchestra 1933-34 (*Sunbeam*)
Various (Including Benny Goodman), Recordings Made Between 1930 & 1941 (*CBS – France*)
A Jam Session With Benny Goodman 1935-37 (*Sunbeam*)
Benny Goodman & His Orchestra Featuring Bunny Berigan (*Golden Era*)
Benny Goodman, Vols 1-12 (*RCA Victor – France*)
The Complete Benny Goodman, Vols 1-3 (*RCA Victor/—*)
The Big Band Sound of Benny Goodman (—/*Verve*)
Benny Goodman Trio & Quartet Live 1937-38, Vols 1, 2 (*CBS – France*)
Benny Goodman, 1938 Carnegie Hall Jazz Concert (*Columbia/CBS*)
The Genius Of Charlie Christian (*Columbia*)/**Solo Flight** (*CBS*)
Charlie Christian With The Benny Goodman Sextet & Orchestra (*Columbia/CBS – Realm*)
Charlie Christian With Benny Goodman & The Sextet (*Jazz Archives*)
Benny Goodman, Plays Solid Gold Instrumental Hits (*Columbia/CBS*)
Various (Including Benny Goodman), Kings Of Swing (—/*Verve*)
Various (Including Benny Goodman), John Hammond's Spirituals To Swing (*Vanguard/Vogue*)
Benny Goodman In Hollywood Featuring Wardell Gray (*Swing Treasury*)
Benny Goodman, He's The King (*Donna Discs*)
Various, The Metronome All Stars/(Esquire All Stars) (*RCA Victor – France*)
Benny Goodman/(Charlie Barnet), Bebop Spoken Here (*Capitol/Capitol – Holland*)
Benny Goodman In Moscow, Vols 1, 2 (*RCA Victor/RCA Victor*)
Billie Holiday, The Golden Years, Vols 1, 2 (*Columbia/CBS*)
The Billie Holiday Story, Vol 1 (*Columbia/CBS*)
The Lester Young Story, Vol 1 (*Columbia/CBS*)
Benny Goodman, All-Time Greatest Hits (*Columbia/CBS*)

Dexter Gordon

Born Los Angeles, 1923, the son of a doctor, Dexter Gordon became *the* Bebop tenorman. Dexter served his apprenticeship in the big bands, blowing two-tenor chase choruses with Illinois Jacquet in Lionel Hampton's band from 1940-3. His style was a combination of the laid-back Lester Young and the huge tone of Coleman Hawkins, adapted to the more complex harmonic world of Charlie Parker. After Hamp, he spent a year home playing the clubs. Los Angeles around the mid-'40s was a jumping town, and Bird's visit set the seal on emergent Bebop. Central Avenue was the West Coast's 52nd Street.

Dexter joined Louis Armstrong's band for several months and then the more suitable environment of Billy Eckstine's band, which included Dizzy Gillespie, Sonny Stitt, Gene Ammons, Leo Parker and John Jackson, with Fats Navarro taking Dizzy's chair. Two-tenor chases were again a big feature with Dexter and Ammons cutting and carving at each other over Art Blakey's relentless drumming. With most of the musicians under 25, the band played with wild enthusiasm, preaching the message of Bebop. Dexter left in 1945 after 18 months and went to New York where he became a favorite along the 52nd Street clubs. He recorded **Blue 'n' Boogie** with Dizzy Gillespie (**In The Beginning**) and, with his own groups, including baritonist Leo

Doin' Allright (Blue Note): the tenor giant's resurgence.

Parker, Bud Powell or Tadd Dameron on piano and driving drummers like Blakey or Max Roach, cut a set of high-spirited tracks like **Dexter's Minor Mad, Blow Mr Dexter** and **Dexter Rides Again (Long Tall Dexter, The Savoy Sessions).**

Back in Los Angeles, Dexter teamed with tenorman Wardell Gray for a series of exhilarating chases like **The Chase** and **The Steeplechase (The Chase); Rocks 'n' Shoals (Jazz Concert-West Coast)** and, with tenorman Teddy Edwards, for **The Duel (The Foremost!).** A later re-union with Gray **(Move)** is included on the Prestige memorial album to Gray **(Central Avenue).**

Following Miles Davis' pace-setting **Birth Of The Cool** album, the West Coast jazz scene underwent a sea-change, and Dexter Gordon's robust, hard-driving style fell from grace. After a spell in Chino prison for narcotics, the tenorman made few recordings in the '50s, though his playing on a session with pianist Carl Perkins **(Dexter Blows Hot And Cool)** showed that he had lost none of his vigor. Strangely enough, it was acting that boosted his comeback. In 1960, he acted in and performed, and wrote music for Jack Gelber's play *The Connection.* The following year, he signed to Blue Note for a series of classic albums **(Doin' Allright, Dexter Calling, Go, A Swingin' Affair, Our Man In Paris** and **One Flight Up).** All the old virtues of drive, tone and imagination are here in abundance, the sardonic, guffawing quotes, the massive, loping swing. By this time, Hard Bop was in the ascendant and Dexter was back in fashion – in fact, the most influential tenorman, John Coltrane, had borrowed Dexter's legato, spearing cry. There is an incantatory power about Dexter's playing which makes the simplest, repeated phrases sound less predictable than inevitable. His double-tempo flights shed not an ounce of weight. His beefy treatment of ballads can be overwhelmingly moving; **Guess I'll Hang My Tears Out To Dry (Go)** and **You've Changed (Doin' Allright),** and his lasting affiliation to Bebop is displayed on **Scrapple From The Apple** and **A Night In Tunisia (Our Man In Paris)** where he shares the honors with other 52nd Street veterans like pianist Bud Powell and drummer Kenny Clarke. At 6 foot 5, Dexter Gordon seems to straddle sessions like an enforcer – always reliable, sometimes great.

In his time, he has influenced tenormen Gene Ammons, Allen Eager, Stan Getz, John Coltrane and Sonny Rollins. In 1962, he emigrated to Europe and now lives in Copenhagen. One of the most well-loved performers in jazz.

Recordings:
The Foremost! (*Onyx/Polydor*)
The Chase (—/*Spotlite*)
Dizzy Gillespie, In The Beginning (*Prestige/Prestige*)
Billy Eckstine, Together (—/*Spotlite*)
Long Tall Dexter, The Savoy Sessions (*Savoy/Savoy*)
The Hunt (*Savoy/Savoy*)
Dexter Blows Hot And Cool (*Dooto/—*)
Wardell Gray, Central Avenue (*Prestige/Prestige*)
Doin' Allright (*Blue Note/Blue Note*)
Dexter Calling (*Blue Note/Blue Note*)
Go (*Blue Note/Blue Note*)
A Swingin' Affair (*Blue Note/Blue Note*)
Our Man In Paris (*Blue Note/Blue Note*)
One Flight Up (*Blue Note/Blue Note*)
Montmartre Collection (*Black Lion/Black Lion*)
Blues Walk (*Black Lion/Black Lion*)
Homecoming (*Columbia/CBS*)
Sophisticated Giant (*Columbia/CBS*)
Manhattan Symphonie (*Columbia/CBS*)
The Bethlehem Years (*Bethlehem/—*)

Stephane Grappelli

Stephane Grappelli (originally surname was spelled with a 'y') would have earned himself a place in jazz history books if only for his important role in the Quintette of the Hot Club of France, featuring the dazzling virtuosity of Django Reinhardt (♦). Grappelli's violin was perfect foil to Reinhardt's guitar in this pianoless group. The tonal quality of his playing – with its unashamedly romantic overtones and a formidable technique that indicated a previous classical background – and an infectious swing were obvious elements of his musical make-up during his Reinhardt period. Grappelli's enthusiastic playing opposite the guitarist never did match the latter's fire and drive. But there was little doubt (especially in the earlier days of their association) that Grappelli understood the language of jazz.

Fired by Reinhardt's tremendous rhythmic powers, Grappelli's contributions to recordings by the Quintette like **Limehouse Blues, China Boy** and **It Don't Mean A Thing** (all 1935) and **Them There Eyes, Three Little Words** and **Swing '39** (these latter three tracks from 1938–9) (all **Swing '35-'39**) were admirable in their execution.

Occasionally, Grappelli would play piano, as when harmonica virtuoso Larry Adler recorded with the group in 1939, the year when Reinhardt and Grappelli, violin, recorded (with delightful results) as a duo (all **Django Reinhardt**). Grappelli, born and raised in Paris (1908), was involved with music from a very early age. By 12 years, he had acquired first violin – just one of several instruments he learned to play. Began professionally with theatre bands,

Above: Dexter Gordon, the biggest tenor sound around.

STEPHANE GRAPPELLI
meets the rhythm section
ROLAND HANNA · JIRI MRAZ · MEL LEWIS

*Stephane Grappelli Meets The Rhythm Section (Black Lion).
Great violinist, with Messrs. Hanna, Mraz, Lewis.*

eventually being introduced to jazz music. A French jazz musician, Philippe Brun, introduced Grappelli to Reinhardt. Soon after that meeting, they put the idea of the Quintette into practice.

When World War II hostilities commenced, Grappelli and the band were touring Britain. While the others returned to Paris, Grappelli opted to stay. During next six years, he became a popular figure in London to habitués of nightlife in general and musical entertainment in particular (such as it was), working with local musicians in various clubs. 1946: returned to Paris, renewed association with Reinhardt, but the magic of pre-war days did not re-appear too often. Between 1948–55, worked in Club St Germain, Paris, and in latter year played nine-month residency in St Tropez.

During past 20 years has played throughout Europe, in clubs, at concerts and festivals, broadcast, televised extensively, and been a regular visitor to recording studio. His popularity during past decade has been extraordinary: he cannot have been as respected, or as widely known during the halcyon days of the Quintette of the Hot Club of France. It is true, however, that the principal reason has been his astonishing consistency, in all areas of the music scene with which he has been associated. Moreover, he has taken on fresh dimensions of brilliance; his attack has become more fierce, his phrasing more audacious, and his improvisations have tended to be more interesting. In 1966, Grappelli was recorded in concert, in Switzerland, together with fellow jazz violinists Jean-Luc Ponty, Stuff Smith (♦), and Svend Asmussen **(Violin Summit)**. His solo on **Pennies From Heaven** is fine, and he graciously allows the extraordinary Ponty to do the leading during their duet on **Pent-Up House**. But excellently though he plays on a tearaway **It Don't Mean A Thing,** he is no match for either Ponty or Smith. Since then Grappelli has recorded fre-

quently in London (where he has become perennial favorite with audiences at Ronnie Scott's Club) using local musicians. Of London-made studio albums **(Stephane Grappelly & Friends** and **Stephane Grappelli 1971)** are particularly fine examples of his latterday rejuvenation. A live date at the Queen Elizabeth Hall **(Stephane Grappelli 1972)** finds him responding to an enthusiastic audience. (The same thing occurs during another in-person recording, **Just One Of Those Things!**, this one taped at the 1973 Montreux Jazz Festival.) Using British Diz Disley Trio as a kind of contemporary Quintette was a predictable, yet in the event excellent, idea **(Stephane Grappelli With The Hot Club Of London** and **Violinspiration)** but today it is Stephane Grappelli, and not Django Reinhardt, who takes a firm, incisive lead.

Elsewhere he has recorded with much success, with Americans Gary Burton (♦) **(Paris Encounter),** Bill Coleman (♦) **(Stephane Grappelli - Bill Coleman),** Roland Hanna **(Stephane Grappelli Meets The Rhythm Section)** and Barney Kessel (♦) **(I Remember Django).** Not once during any of these albums was Grappelli lacking in inspiration or fire. Only a mid-1960s get-together between the Frenchman and fellow jazz violinist great Stuff Smith failed to ignite **(Stuff & Steff).** This youthful near-septuagenarian, who has recorded and appeared alongside classical violin virtuoso Yehudi Menuhin, is one jazz musician who does get better as the years go by.

Recordings:
Django Reinhardt, Swing '35-'39
(—/Decca/Eclipse)
Django Reinhardt & Stephane Grappelli With The Quintet Of The Hot Club Of France
(GNP Crescendo/—)
Django Reinhardt, Parisian Swing (GNP Crescendo/—)
Django Reinhardt
(Columbia – Germany)
Various (Including Stephane

Grappelli), Violin Summit
(Saba/Polydor)
Stephane Grappelly & Friends
(—/Philips)
Stephane Grappelli 1971
(—/Pye)
Stephane Grappelli 1972
(—/Pye)
Stephane Grappelli, Just One Of Those Things (Black Lion)
Stephane Grappelli, I Got Rhythm (Black Lion)
Stephane Grappelli, Violinspiration (MPS/BASF)
Stephane Grappelli/Gary Burton, Paris Encounter
(Atlantic/Atlantic)
Stephane Grappelli - Bill Coleman (Inner City)
Jean-Luc Ponty - Stephane Grappelli (Inner City)
Stephane Grappelli Meets The Rhythm Section (Black Lion)
Stephane Grappelli/Barney Kessel, I Remember Django
(Black Lion)
Stephane Grappelli/Stuff Smith, Stuff & Steff (Barclay)

Milford Graves

Free drummer Milford Graves first unveiled his concept of non-metrical playing on an all-percussion album **(Milford Graves Percussion Ensemble)** with Sunny Morgan, revealing a wide dynamic range, lightning reflexes, and a total re-thinking of the traditional roles of the components of the kit. How this could be applied within the group context was revealed by Graves' work with the New York Art Quartet **(New York Art Quartet)** where his fast, crisp, darting drumming contributes much to the success of contrapuntal sections between Roswell Rudd and John Tchicai. A partnership begun in the Giuseppi Logan group between pianist Don Pullen and Graves, developed into amazing free interplay and dissonant structures. Two albums recorded live at Yale University on the artists' own label are unfortunately difficult to come by **(Nommo** and **In Concert).** Graves' eruptive work on an Albert Ayler session

Below: Drum innovator Milford Graves. His work with the percussion ensemble extends the frontiers.

Nommo (SRP): two of the giants of free music on their own label.

(Love Cry) seems to add density to the simple, melodic approach of the horns. Subsequently, Graves seems to have returned to the all-drum concept, and with Andrew Cyrille, summons up a percussion choir of drums, bells, voice, gongs, whistles etc **(Dialogue Of The Drums).**

Recordings:
Milford Graves Percussion Ensemble (ESP/ESP)
New York Art Quartet
(ESP/ESP)
Don Pullen - Milford Graves, Nommo (SRP/—)
Don Pullen - Milford Graves, In Concert (SRP/—)
Albert Ayler, Love Cry
(Impulse/Impulse)
Dialogue Of The Drums
(Institute of Percussive Studies/—)
Milford Graves & Babi Music
(Institute of Percussive Studies/—)

Wardell Gray

Tenorman Wardell Gray was born in 1921 in Oklahoma City, his parents moving to Detroit while he was young. Proficient on clarinet and alto, he switched to the bigger horn during his tenure with Earl Hines' big band 1943–5. Settling in Los Angeles, he played with local Beboppers along Central Avenue, jamming with Dexter Gordon, Sonny Criss and Teddy Edwards. Fine examples of two-tenor chases between Gray and Gordon can be found on several albums, with

Gray at his best in the four-bar exchanges (**The Chase, Jazz Concert - West Coast** and **Central Avenue**). This was one of the most exciting partnerships in jazz, each player gleefully challenging the other to combat.

A highly consistent player, Gray's style was rooted in Lester Young with a later overlay of Charlie Parker, following a studio session with the great altoist (**Charlie Parker On Dial, Vol 3**). A relaxed, on-the-beat swing, great mobility and a positive, rounded tone were the hallmarks of his tenor, which generated an atmosphere of great good humor in a period characterized by neurotic intensity. There is an even flow to his choruses, and extended performances like **Blue Lou** avoid crowd-raising climaxes (**Jazz Scene USA**) despite the presence of a Gene Norman **Just Jazz** audience. The double-album memorial (**Central Avenue**) gives a good idea of his range, from the ballad **Easy Living** to the fast blues of **Farmer's Market**. His solo on **Twisted** was popularized in Annie Ross's vocal version.

He played with the big bands of

The Chase And The Steeple chase (MCA): Bebop fashions.

Billy Eckstine, Count Basie and Benny Goodman, easily riding over the massed attack of the Basie trumpet section on numbers like **The King (Wardell Gray - Stan Hasselgard)** or pile-drivers like **Little Dog**. Even the King Of Swing, Benny Goodman, found the complex harmonies of Gray, and Charlie Christian, acceptable. Wardell Gray's death, possibly due to an overdose, in 1955, left jazz the poorer.

Recordings:
Charlie Parker On Dial, Vol 3
(—/Spotlite)
Central Avenue
(Prestige/Prestige)
The Chase (—/Spotlite)
The Hunt (Savoy/Savoy)
Jazz Scene USA
(—/Vogue – France)
Wardell Gray - Stan Hasselgard
(—/Spotlight)
The Foremost!
(Onyx/Polydor)
Live In Hollywood (Xanadu/—)
Jam Session 101 & 103
(Jam Session Records/—)

Freddie Green
♦ *Count Basie*

Sonny Greer

William 'Sonny' Greer (born Long Branch, New Jersey, 1903) is not, it has been said, as supremely

Above: Freddie Green, finest rhythm guitarist of all and heartbeat of the Count Basie band for four decades.

accomplished a drummer as Louis Bellson (♦), and did not lay down as solid a beat as Sam Woodyard – two of his successors in Duke Ellington (♦) Orchestra. Yet Greer, who made his musical debut with band of Harry Yerek during World War I, was, without question, good enough to sit behind his extraordinarily large and varied drum kit, as a member of the Ellington organization, from very beginning of the Ellington story until beginning of 1950s. In all, Greer was with Ellington for period 1923–51. (His actual playing experience, in Ellington's company, dates back to 1920.) To some, Greer's unflashy drumming might be considered to be stiff and not as rhythmically stimulating in comparison with some other big-band drummers. But his was a light, subtle beat that was absolutely right for Ellington during his long tenure.

Despite his lengthy career, Greer has made comparatively few records outside of the Ellington circle. Best of these probably comprise several items with one of the numerous all-star bands put together by Lionel Hampton (♦) between 1937–40 (**The Complete Lionel Hampton/Lionel Hampton's Best Records, Vols 1, 2, 5**) plus dates with Al Sears (♦) (**Greatest Of The Small Bands, Vol 5**) and Johnny Hodges (♦) (**The Jeep Is Jumpin'**); he was a member of the latter band for six months after both left Ellington in '51. Since then, with time off for recuperation from shoulder injury in 1960, has gigged in and around New York area with many name musicians, although in more recent times he has been virtually in semi-retirement.

Recordings:
Duke Ellington, Early Duke
(Jazz Panorama)
Duke Ellington, The Beginning (1928-1929) (MCA – Germany)
Duke Ellington, Hot In Harlem (1928-1929) (MCA – Germany)
Duke Ellington, Rockin' In Rhythm (1929-1931)
(MCA – Germany)
Duke Ellington, Toodle-oo

(—/Vocalion)
Duke Ellington, The Ellington Era, 1927-1940, Vols 1, 2
(Columbia/CBS)
Duke Ellington, The Works Of Duke, Vols 1-18
(RCA Victor – France)
Duke Ellington, The Duke 1940
(Jazz Society)
Duke Ellington, The Jimmy Blanton Years
(Queen Disc – Italy)
Duke Ellington, 'Black, Brown & Beige' (Ariston – Italy)
Duke Ellington, Ellington In Concert, Vols 1, 2
(—/World Record Club)
Duke Ellington, Braggin' In Brass 1936-1939
(Tax – Sweden)
Duke Ellington, Rockin' In Rhythm (—/Parlophone)
The Complete Lionel Hampton
(Bluebird)/
Lionel Hampton's Best Records, Vols 1, 2, 5
(RCA Victor – France)
Johnny Hodges, The Jeep Is Jumpin' (—/Verve)
Various (Including Al Sears), The Greatest Of The Small Bands, Vol 5
(RCA Victor – France)

Johnny Griffin

Born 1928, the Chicago tenorman is undoubtedly one of the fastest players in the history of the saxophone, and in Griffin's case, this is no empty, facile display. His imagination streaks ahead of his flying fingers, throwing out ideas in prodigal handfuls. Obviously not a master of the extended structure (few jazzmen are) his solos are a string of great breaks, cliff-hanging climaxes and startling tonal devices, the whole held together by his colossal drive. Johnny Griffin is the proto-typical Hard Bopper.

His early experience with the wild Lionel Hampton band set the pattern. Few of his early Blue Note albums remain in the catalogue (**Chicago Calling, Introducing Johnny Griffin** and **The Congre-**

The Congregation (Blue Note): cover by Andy Warhol.

gation) and they are well worth tracking down in the second-hand bins for their sheer youthful ebullience. Griffin's meeting with Coltrane and Mobley is available and catches the newcomer to the New York scene at his most competitive, calling the breakneck tempos and generally proving his superiority in this context (**Blowin' Sessions**).

He proved an ideal member of Art Blakey's hard-hitting Jazz Messengers, his short fuse flaring into hysterical excitement as the drummer bore down. The only easily available album (**Art Blakey's Jazz Messengers With Thelonious Monk**) is excellent, though a-typical. Griffin's association with Monk continues on a pair of deleted quartet albums (**Thelonious In Action** and **Misterioso**) but, though exciting, the tenorist's interpretation of Monk's themes lacks the weight that a thematic player like Rollins could muster. Nevertheless, Griffin is clearly attracted by the challenge, and returns time and again to this material on subsequent albums (**The Toughest Tenors**).

In the late '50s, early '60s, a fashion for 'Soul' redirected the thrust of Hard Bop away from the sensurround drumming to a baptist backbeat. Predictability soon crept in, and the only player to resist formula was Johnny Griffin. **Wade In The Water** is a classic in this genre (**Big Soul**). Forming a two-tenor unit with Eddie 'Lockjaw' Davis, a swinging, partying

Above: possibly the fastest tenorman ever, little Johnny Griffin. With Lockjaw Davis, ran a two-tenor unit of note.

player, Griffin cut a series of hard-driving albums that recall the great tenor partnerships of Dexter Gordon and Wardell Gray, or Sonny Stitt and Gene Ammons.

In 1962, Griffin moved to Europe, joined the Kenny Clarke–Francy Boland Big Band, and also toured extensively, using pick-up rhythm sections. Two of the best albums **(Blues For Harvey** and **The Man I Love)** are fueled by expatriate American drummers, Ed Thigpen and Albert Heath, who supply the strong direct beat that Griffin needs.

The tone is light and mobile, shooting up to the tip-toe top of the register in moments of overheating, or blasting suddenly from the depths. He's a witty player, projecting the most convoluted phrases from his horn with evident enjoyment.

Recordings:
Blowin' Sessions
(Blue Note/Blue Note)
Art Blakey's Jazz Messengers With Thelonious Monk
(Atlantic/Atlantic)
The Toughest Tenors
(Milestone/Milestone)
Big Soul *(Milestone/Milestone)*
Blues For Harvey
(—/Steeplechase)
The Man I Love *(—/Polydor)*

Tiny Grimes

Lloyd 'Tiny' Grimes (born Newport News, Virginia, 1916) always has been a capable soloist, with particularly biting, blues-based style, without ever aspiring to a position amongst acknowledged greats of jazz guitar. Originally a drummer, became pianist, dancer in Washington, DC area (1935). Performed similarly at Rhythm Club, NYC, three years later. Bought amplified guitar, taught himself to play, and by end of 1939 was working with combo known as The Cats & A Fiddle. Left group in 1941, moved to California. There, he met Art Tatum

(♦), became member of Tatum's Trio (completed by bassist Leroy 'Slam' Stewart), remaining until 1944. Being member of any Tatum rhythm section was no easy occupation, but Grimes managed task commendably, keeping out of pianist's way and contributing mostly excellent solos **(Art Tatum Masterpieces, Art Tatum** and **Masters Of Jazz, Vol 3: Art Tatum).**

After leaving Tatum, fronted own trio, then band he called the Rocking Highlanders (disbanded in '47). Fronted recording quintet including up-coming altoist Charlie Parker (♦) **(Bird/The Savoy Recordings: Master Takes** and **Charlie Parker Encores/The Savoy Sessions).** Grimes was hardly in Parker's class, harmonically or rhythmically, or indeed as improviser, but he contributed solid guitar solos to session, plus a couple of innocuous, harmless vocals. After break-up of Highlanders, moved to Cleveland. Did much touring in mid-west during first half of 1950s, music often reflecting strong, not unpleasant, R&B influence. Grimes Sextet provided accompaniment for Billie Holiday (♦) record date in '51 which produced, amongst four titles, a beautiful **Detour Ahead.**

During late-1950s, recorded series of hard-swinging, blues-laden albums for Prestige's Swingville label. Typical of all-star personnel involved were names like Coleman Hawkins (♦), Charlie Shavers (♦), Ray Bryant (♦) **(Hawk Eyes),** J. C. Higginbotham (♦), Eddie 'Lockjaw' Davis (♦) **(Callin' The Blues)** and Jerome Richardson, Art Taylor, Bryant **(Tiny In Swingville).** Continued to lead own bands during early-1960s. Off scene through ill-health for long spell. Made comeback in 1966, made tour of France in '68, and since then has continued to be more or less active with his own brand of uncomplicated guitar playing, including guest appearances with top jazzmen like Earl Hines (♦) **(An Evening With Earl Hines).**

Recordings:
Masters Of Jazz, Vol 3: Art Tatum *(Capitol – Germany)*
Art Tatum Masterpieces *(MCA/—)*
Art Tatum, Art Of Tatum, Vols 1, 2 *(MCA – Germany)*
Ike Quebec, Mellow Moods *(Blue Note/—)*
Charlie Parker, Bird/The Savoy Recordings (Master Takes) *(Savoy/—)*
Roy Eldridge/Tiny Grimes, Never Too Old To Swing *(—/Sonet)*
Coleman Hawkins, Hawk Eyes *(Prestige – Swingville/Xtra)*
Tiny Grimes, Callin' The Blues *(Prestige – Swingville/Esquire)*
Tiny Grimes, Tiny In Swingville *(Prestige – Swingville/—)*
Various, Jam Session At Swingville *(Prestige/Prestige)*
An Evening With Earl Hines *(Chiaroscuro/Vogue)*

Johnny Guarnieri

John A. Guarnieri (born New York City, 1917) has been, for more than four decades as a professional musician, a gifted keyboard practitioner whose origins and influences stem basically from the stylistic approaches of Fats Waller (♦), Teddy Wilson (♦) and, to a lesser extent, Count Basie (♦). With a surname like Guarnieri, it is hardly a surprise to learn his was a musical upbringing – his father was violinist and violin-maker, his brother Leo a bass player – or that Johnny Guarnieri studied classical piano from the age often. Eight years later, though, he was gigging with local dance bands, including those of Mike Riley and George Hall.

First important position – job of pianist with Benny Goodman (♦), with whom Guarnieri worked for approximately six months (1939–1940). Guarnieri appeared on such Goodman big-band recordings of the period as **Fiesta In Blue** and **Scarecrow (Benny Goodman Plays Solid Gold Instrumental Hits)** and on sundry Goodman Sextet/Septet dates of the period – **Solo Flight - The Genius Of Charlie Christian/Solo Flight, Charlie Christian With The Benny Goodman Sextet & Orchestra** and **Charlie Christian With Benny Goodman & The Sextet.** Left Goodman in July 1940 to join Artie Shaw (♦) Orchestra and Shaw's small-group offshoot he called his Gramercy Five **(Artie Shaw & His Gramercy Five).** With latter band, Guarnieri attained unexpected individual acclaim for his use of harpsichord. For in-person performances and for recordings of such as **Special Delivery Stomp, Summit Ridge Drive** and **My Blue Heaven,** Guarnieri's harpsichord gave Gramercy Five a distinctive sound – and although the idea might have been looked upon as some kind of gimmick, Guarnieri succeeded in eliciting from this most unjazzlike instrument solos which swung with undeniable strength. By early 1941, Guarnieri was back with Goodman for another six-month stint – then it was back to Shaw for an even shorter period. After which he spent just over a year with Jimmy

Dorsey (♦) (1942–43), before becoming session musician at CBS with Raymond Scott, taking time off for jazz club dates and record sessions. Typical of latter was a 1944 date in company with Lester Young (♦) **(Pres/The Complete Savoy Recordings)** for which the pianist wrote all but one of the selections, including a brace of tributes to a couple of his major influences – **Basie English** and **Salute To Fats.**

Continued to freelance during 1940s/1950s, with much studio work involved. Regularly featured within media of radio and TV, Guarnieri worked with own band at various times. Moved to West Coast in early 1960s, obtaining lengthy residency at Plaza Hotel, Hollywood (1963–66), then featured infrequently at other venues. A prolific composer, Guarnieri also has continued to record intermittently since mid-1960s. Typical of his offerings on disc are the pleasant **Jazz Lab Vol 6: The Duke Again,** a relaxed **Johnny Guarnieri Plays Harry Warren,** an intriguing **Breakthrough** with all items played in 5/4, and, best of all, a splendidly conceived **Superstride.**

Recordings:
Buddy Tate, Jive At Five *(Mahogany/—)*
Charlie Christian/Benny Goodman, Solo Flight - The Genius Of Charlie Christian *(Columbia)/*
Solo Flight *(CBS)*
Charlie Christian With Benny Goodman & The Sextet *(Jazz Archives/—)*
Charlie Christian With The Benny Goodman Sextet & Orchestra *(Columbia/CBS – Realm)*
Artie Shaw & His Gramercy Five *(RCA Victor/RCA Victor)*
Lester Willis Young, Pres/The Complete Savoy Recordings *(Savoy)*
Johnny Guarnieri, Jazz Lab Vol 6: The Duke Again *(MCA Coral – Germany)*
Johnny Guarnieri Plays Harry Warren *(Jim Taylor Presents/—)*
Johnny Guarnieri, Breakthrough *(Bet/—)*
Johnny Guarnieri, Superstride *(Taz-Jaz/—)*

Bobby Hackett

Robert Leo 'Bobby' Hackett (born Providence, Rhode Island, 1915) commanded much respect amongst musicians of all persuasions – jazz and otherwise. His fellow trumpeters of the past 45 years (Louis Armstrong (♦), Roy Eldridge (♦), Dizzy Gillespie (♦), Miles Davis (♦), and Ruby Braff (♦) can be safely included in any list of Hackett admirers) have been unstinting in their praise for his superbly lyrical and flowing style on cornet and trumpet. Of the above, Gillespie has recorded with Hackett **(Giants/The Great Modern Jazz Trumpet)** and Hackett worked with Armstrong's All Stars during 1947, supplying marvellously lyrical obbligatos during a celebrated concert appearance at New York's Town Hall **(Satchmo's Greatest, Vols 4, 5).**

Bobby Hackett played guitar, violin and cornet at school, leaving latter at 14 to play guitar in local Chinese restaurant. During late-1920s, early-1930s, gigged locally and elsewhere. Played guitar, cornet with Herb Marsh at Theatrical Club, Boston (1936), eventually leading own band at same venue. 1937: to New York, his horn being heard in several different settings before his Bix Beiderbecke (♦)-influenced cornet, and guitar, were heard, most effectively, with fine band which Joe Marsala (♦) fronted at Hickory House. Took own band into Nick's, then guest at all-star Benny Goodman (♦) 1938 Carnegie Hall Concert, re-creating, with customary meticulous care, Beiderbecke's immortal solo on I'm Coming Virginia. Took part in legendary Commodore record date which took place some hours after Carnegie Hall concert (Commodore Condon, Vol 1) contributing series of beautifully sculptured solos. Also during '38, Hackett's lyrical horn enriched record dates by Jack Teagarden (♦) and Miff Mole (♦) (both Trombone Scene); Teddy Wilson (♦) (The Teddy Wilson), and an all-star band which included Joe Marsala and Pete Brown (♦) (Swingin' Clarinets).

Hackett toured with own big band (1939), before disbanding to join Horace Heidt Orchestra. Joined Glenn Miller band as guitarist (1941–2), occasionally taking cornet solos, as on popular Miller recordings of A String Of Pearls and Serenade In Blue. Became staffman at NBC (1942–3), toured with Katherine Dunham Revue, rejoined Marsala at Hickory House for several weeks, then stayed with Casa Loma Orchestra for almost two years, until fall of 1946. Became immersed in session work, taking time off to play jazz gigs with others and with own band. Made series of non-jazz mood albums during 1950s, with Jackie

Gleason, on whose TV show Hackett made regular appearances. That he had lost little or nothing of his jazz abilities was demonstrated when old friend and colleague, Eddie Condon (♦) (Hacket had participated in scores of record dates and live appearances, including the war-time Town Hall concert series) invited him to take the cornet solos during an organized studio jam session (The Golden Days Of Jazz: Eddie Condon). When re-united on two separate occasions during 1950s with Jack Teagarden (Coast To Coast and Bobby Hackett: Jazz Ultimate) the Hackett lyricism and warmth was amply displayed. His work throughout both albums ranks with his very best – on a par, for instance, with his exquisite versions of Ghost Of A Chance and Embraceable You (Bobby Hackett Horn) from almost 20 years before.

Fronted own band for lengthy residences at Henry Hudson Hotel, New York (1956–7), followed by more involvement as studio musician. With Benny Goodman (1962–3); joined entourage of Tony Bennett, visiting Europe with singer in 1965 and 1966 as featured musician in accompanying band.

Between 1970–6, produced playing of astonishingly resilient quality, his horn being applauded in clubs, at concerts and major festivals, and on record. In latter category, albums like that with Gillespie (see above), with Zoot Sims (♦) (Strike Up The Band) and with Vic Dickenson (♦) (Bobby Hackett Live At The Roosevelt Grill/A String Of Pearls) provide idyllic memories of the last years of a distinguished musician. Bobby Hackett died in West Chatham, Massachusetts, in 1976.

Recordings:
Bobby Hackett Horn (Epic/—)

Benny Goodman, 1938 Carnegie Hall Jazz Concert (Columbia/CBS)
Eddie Condon, Commodore Condon, Vol 1 (—/London)
Various (Including Jack Teagarden/Miff Mole), Trombone Scene (—/London)
The Teddy Wilson (CBS/Sony – Japan)
Various (Including Bobby Hackett), Swingin' Clarinets (—/London)
Louis Armstrong, Satchmo's Greatest, Vols 4, 5 (RCA Victor — France)
The Golden Days Of Jazz: Eddie Condon (Columbia/CBS)
Bobby Hackett, Coast To Coast (Capitol/Regal)
Bobby Hackett/Jack Teagarden, Jazz Ultimate (Capitol/Capitol)
Bobby Hackett Live At The Roosevelt Grill With Vic Dickenson (Chiaroscuro)/ A String Of Pearls (Vogue)
Bobby Hackett/Dizzy Gillespie, Giants (Perception)/ The Great Modern Jazz Trumpet (Festival – France)

Charlie Haden

Missouri-born bassist, Charlie Haden, first came to prominence in the Ornette Coleman quartet in the late '50s. The first and best of a succession of white bassists to play with the great innovator, Haden had to find a way of responding to the free flow of melodic and rhythmic invention. The established role of the bass – Blanton, Pettiford and Ray Brown – was unsuitable, and Haden evolved a way of playing a roving line that sometimes complemented the soloist, sometimes moved independently. 'Forget about the changes in key and just play within the range of the idea' was the leader's instruction, and Haden was imaginative and intuitive enough to handle this freedom. Most of Ornette Coleman's Atlantic albums show how far the success of the music was due to the great bassist's contribution. Ramblin (Change Of The Century) shows the propulsive power of Haden's near-sitar sound, his uncannily apt use of suspensions and accelerations around the soloist, the use of double stops in his solo.

The contrast between Haden and the late Scott La Faro is well-illustrated on Ornette's great collective album Free Jazz. La Faro, technically brilliant and, in Bill Evans' trio, fulfilling a similarly independent role, comes out as over-decorative by contrast with the sheer taste and restraint and ability to listen shown by Haden.

Since leaving Ornette, Haden has played with many fine musicians, most notably in the Keith Jarrett group for a series of fine Impulse recordings. He is a fine composer, Song For Che (Crisis), and in 1969 drew upon the resources of the JCOA for a large musico-political work (Liberation Music Orchestra). Arranged by Carla Bley, the work ranges from the Spanish Civil War to the Chicago Convention, using both Spanish songs and expressionist devices.

Left: Charlie Haden, great bassist and composer of haunting themes dedicated to the socialist cause.

Most recently, Haden has released an album of duets with old friends Ornette Coleman, Keith Jarrett and Alice Coltrane (Closeness). The result is magnificent.

Recordings:
Ornette Coleman's Atlantic Albums (Atlantic/Atlantic)
Keith Jarrett's Impulse Albums (Impulse/Impulse)
Liberation Music Orchestra (Impulse/Impulse)
Closeness (A&M/A&M)
The Golden Number (A&M/A&M)

Al Haig

Pianist Al Haig was born in New Jersey in 1924. One of the earliest and best of the Bebop pianists, Haig was influenced originally by Nat King Cole and Teddy Wilson, influencing in his turn Hank Jones, Tommy Flanagan, Henri Renaud and Bill Evans. Charlie Parker's and Stan Getz's favourite accompanist, he was the pianist in Bird's classic 1945 quintet, which included Dizzy Gillespie, Tommy Potter on bass and Max Roach on drums, playing at the Three Deuces on 52nd Street. His second engagement with Bird lasted from 1948–50 (Bird On 52nd Street/ Bird At St Nicks). He also played with Gillespie's small combos in the mid-40s (The Greatest Of Dizzy Gillespie and In The Beginning) and with tenorman Wardell Gray (Central Avenue).

One of the few albums under his own name resulted from a trip to Paris with Bird (Al Haig Trio & Quintet) with James Moody depping for Bird. Great Bebop resulted, with all of Haig's characteristic logic and precision on display even at fast tempos like Maximum. The B side is trio recordings from 1954, including a version of Round Midnight which effectively distinguishes Haig's approach from Bud Powell's or the composer's, Thelonious Monk – cooler, smoother; in fact all of Haig's work is elegant and graceful. In the early '50s he played with Stan Getz, perfectly matching Getz's currently cool approach on numbers like There's A Small Hotel and eclipsing the leader on Indian Summer (Stan Getz).

A more virile spirit is to be found on a live recording of 1951 (Stan Getz At Storyville) a classic, unfortunately difficult to obtain. Al Haig's career throughout the '50s and '60s suffered from public neglect, and not until 1974 did he record an album of his choice (Invitation) his fourth in thirty years. On the evidence, he has lost none of his brilliance.

Recordings:
Al Haig Trio & Quintet (Prestige/Prestige)
Invitation (Spotlite/Spotlite)

Edmond Hall

Edmond Hall carved out a career which, stylistically, encompassed New Orleans, Dixieland and mainstream jazz. As with all New Orleans clarinettists, there was considerable warmth in his playing, even though his undoubted ability to swing hard at all times reflected much of the work of the Swing Era players. Tonally, too, he

AL HAIG
Trio and Quintet!
with Max Roach
Kenny Dorham, James Moody and others.

PR 7841

PRESTIGE HISTORICAL SERIES
Original **1949-54** Recordings

Al Haig (Prestige): one of Bebop's finest pianists, still under-recorded, still at the height of his powers.

differed from, say, Albert Nicholas (♦) or Barney Bigard (♦), eschewing the supple, liquid sound for a curiously effective astringency; certainly, his hot, piping clarinet could cut through any kind of jazz ensemble, large or small, with consummate ease.

However, Hall's allegiance to the Albert system was in keeping with New Orleans clarinet tradition. It was as guitarist that Hall started his career, playing instrument for two years before turning to clarinet, at 17. Hall (born New Orleans, 1901) first played clarinet professionally in 1919, with band of Bud Roussell. Worked with other local bands, including Jack Carey, Buddie Petit, before joining Eagle-Eye Shields in Jacksonville (1924-6). Played soprano-sax with Alonzo Ross (with whom he debuted on record), visiting New York. Worked with other bands, in New York and elsewhere, before joining Charlie Skeets. Stayed on when, in 1929, band's leadership passed to Claude Hopkins (♦). Played clarinet, baritone-sax and, occasionally, alto-sax with Hopkins. Typical of Hall's consistently fine clarinet work with Hopkins are his solos during **Washington Squabble** and **Chasing My Blues Away** (both **The Golden Swing Years**). With Lucky Millinder (1936, and again in '37), also with Zutty Singleton Trio (1939), then with fine Joe Sullivan Cafe Society Orchestra (**Cafe Society Swing & The Boogie Woogie**) which included two clarinettists: Hall, and Danny Polo (also tenor-sax). Joined equally superb Red Allen (♦) Sextet (**The Very Great Henry Red Allen**) from 1940-1, before moving on to Teddy Wilson's (♦) Quintet (1942-4).

During early 1940s, became strongly associated with Blue Note record label. Probably most famous of Hall's Blue Note recordings were those in which he led his

Right: Edmond Hall, whose piping hot clarinet reflected both New Orleans and mainstream influences.

Celeste Quartet (**Celestial Express**) completed by Charlie Christian (♦), Meade Lux Lewis (celeste), and Israel Crosby (♦). Hall rarely played better, anywhere; certainly, on tracks like **Profoundly Blue No. 2** and **Edmond Hall Blues**, his work was unusually mellifluous. Further date, this time by Edmond Hall's All Star Quintet (including Red Norvo (♦) and Teddy Wilson) (**Celestial Express**) resulted in clarinet solos almost as fine. Other Blue Note all-star dates (featuring Hall's Blue Note Jazzmen: Art Hodes (♦)) (**Blue Note Jazzmen**) juxtaposed Hall's clarinet with such as Max Kaminsky (♦), Sidney De Paris (♦), Vic Dickenson (♦) and Hodes (**Original Blue Note Jazz, Vol 1**) with mutually profitable results. Worked with own band in New York (1944-6), then spent several years in Boston.

Commenced five-year residency at Eddie Condon Club (1950), and participated with usual fervour in Condon jam-session record dates of period (**The Golden Days Of Jazz: Eddie Condon**). Hall's clarinet spiced proceedings at two classic 1950s mainstream sessions (**Vic Dickenson Septet**) contributing trenchant solo to **Suspension Blues** on second date. Edmond

Hall never sounded completely at ease during tenure with Louis Armstrong (♦) All Stars (1955-8), his individual contributions being mostly adequate rather than inspired. His solo work on tracks contained within **Louis Armstrong Memorial** bear testimony to this.

1959: moved to Ghana, with plans to settle there, but returned at end of year. Continued to be active during 1960s – also finding time to visit Europe on more than one occasion. Featured at all-star Carnegie Hall concert (1967), one month after which he died after heart attack at home in Boston. During his career, Edmond Hall also recorded with Jonah Jones (♦), Wild Bill Davison (♦), Bud Freeman (♦) and Jimmy McPartland. Younger brother Herbie Hall also jazz clarinettist/saxist.

Recordings:
Claude Hopkins, The Golden Swing (—/Polydor)
Various (Including Joe Sullivan), Cafe Society Swing & The Boogie Woogie (Swingfan – Germany)
The Very Great Red Allen (Rarities/—)
Edmond Hall/Art Hodes, Original Blue Note Jazz, Vol 1 (Blue Note/—)
Edmond Hall, Celestial Express (Blue Note/—)
Sidney DeParis, DeParis Dixie (Blue Note/—)
The Golden Days Of Jazz: Eddie Condon (CBS)
Vic Dickenson Septet (Vanguard/Vanguard)
Louis Armstrong Memorial (CBS – France)

Jim Hall

Guitarist Jim Hall was born in Buffalo in 1930, and, like most modern guitarists, first influenced by Charlie Christian. In 1955, he joined the Chico Hamilton Quintet, moving on to the Jimmy Giuffre Trio (**The Train & The River**). Following a tour of South America with Ella Fitzgerald, Hall became interested in the bossa nova; he joined Sonny Rollins' Quartet in 1961, his often contrapuntal lines alongside the tenorist casting a strong spell on the moving **Where Are You**, and driving on **John S** (**The Bridge**).

Hall has recorded with a vast number of musicians, always fitting in, always inventive. One of the best meetings was with pianist Bill Evans (**Interplay**) both players specializing in subtle shadings and gentle lyricism. A duo with bassist Ron Carter (**Alone Together**) results in the expected sensitivity, and on numbers like Rollins' **St Thomas** and **Whose Blues** shows a virile drive. Hall has played with John Lewis, Sonny Stitt, Zoot Sims, Paul Desmond and Lee Konitz in the '60s, and in recent years recorded with his own trio (**Jim Hall Live**).

Recordings:
Jimmy Giuffre, The Train & The River (Atlantic/Atlantic)
Sonny Rollins, The Bridge (RCA/RCA)
Bill Evans, Interplay (United Artists/United Artists)
Alone Together (Milestone/Milestone)
Jim Hall Live (A&M/A&M)
Concierto (CTI/CTI)

Above: drummer Chico Hamilton, master of brushes, leader of '50s quintet which included a cellist.

Above: Jimmy Hamilton – cool clarinettist, raunchy tenorist, and an invaluable Ellingtonian for 25 years . . .

Chico Hamilton

Drummer Chico Hamilton is probably best known for his crisp, tasteful time in the famous Gerry Mulligan Quartet (**Mulligan/Baker**) and for his own quintets which included the then oddball choice of cello. The original group, Buddy Collette, reeds, Jim Hall, guitar and Fred Katz, cello, played an often swinging jazz chamber-music that seemed to typify much of West Coast jazz in the '50s. The best album, long-deleted (**The Chico Hamilton Quintet**) included **Walking Carson Blues** and **The Sage**, which the group featured effectively in an excellent film, *Sweet Smell Of Success*. A compilation of later quintets includes early performances by Eric Dolphy and Charles Lloyd (**Chico Hamilton**). Various albums including Lloyd and Hungarian guitarist Gabor Szabo followed, marking a more aggressive outlook (**Passin' Thru** and **Man From Two Worlds**). A master of the brushes, Hamilton's drumming is a marvel of flexibility and drive.

Recordings:
Gerry Mulligan/Chet Baker
(Prestige/Prestige)
Chico Hamilton
(Atlantic/Atlantic)
Passin' Thru *(Impulse/Impulse)*
Man From Two Worlds
(Impulse/Impulse)
Chic Chic Chico
(Impulse/Impulse)
The Dealer *(Impulse/Impulse)*

Jimmy Hamilton

The fluent, smooth-as-glass, elegantly swinging clarinet playing of James 'Jimmy' Hamilton (born Dillon, South Carolina, 1917) was amply featured with the Duke Ellington(♦) Orchestra for approximately 25 years, from the time he joined the Duke in May 1943, after previous experience with, amongst others, Lucky Millinder (♦), Jimmy Mundy, then Teddy Wilson (♦) (1939–41), Benny Carter (♦) (1941–2), and Eddie Heywood (♦) (1943).

In terms of sheer technique, Hamilton lacks absolutely nothing. But his cool, detached style never achieved with Ellington the warmth and depth of Barney Bigard (♦), his most famous predecessor. Nevertheless, he was a decided asset to the band from 1943 onwards. For one thing, his academic background, which had included playing trombone, trumpet with bands in Philadelphia, city where he was raised as youngster, enabled him to produce more than adequate compositions and arrangements (**Dankworth Castle, Little John's Tune, Jamaica Tomboy** and **Moonstone**: all **Ellington '59**) are excellent examples of his abilities in this direction. And his skilled solo work on such musical Elling-

Clarinet (Jazz Kings). One of his few solo efforts.

tonia as **The Nutcracker Suite, Flippant Flurry (It's Duke Ellington); The Tattooed Bride (Masterpieces By Ellington)** and **Liberian Suite/A Tone Parallel To Harlem, Red Shoes** and **Red Carpet (Jazz At The Plaza, Vol 2)** was delivered with nothing less than complete professionalism, a technical accomplishment of the highest quality, and a brand of cool, mellifluous swing that owed much to the influence of Benny Goodman (♦), perhaps even more to Buddy De Franco (♦).

His Swing Era-type clarinet playing (with slight 'modern' overtones) was especially appropriate, and excellently showcased, on Ducal tributes to big-band favorites of 1930s/1940s like **Stompin' At The Savoy, In The Mood, One O'Clock Jump, Honeysuckle Rose,** and Ellington's own **Happy-Go-Lucky Local** (all **Ellington '55/Toast To The Duke); and For Dancers Only, Cherokee, Chant Of The Weed** (all **Recollections Of The Big Band Era**).

In complete contrast to his smooth, supple clarinet work, Hamilton's R&B-influenced tenor-saxophone playing likewise registered strongly with Ellington (as well as on record dates with others) from around late-1940s. His booting, rough-toned tenor expressed itself guttily on Ellington discs like **Smada, Bensonality, Come On Home** and **Rock City Rock (The World Of Duke Ellington, Vol 3/ The World Of Duke Ellington, Vol 2)** and **Gone & Crazy** and **Little Rabbit Blues (Johnny Hodges & The Ellington Men).** Outside of Ellington, on record at least, Jimmy Hamilton's clarinet solos, although always polished and immaculate, never did register with any degree of importance.

His role as totally disciplined sideman – always most useful to have on hand, for numerous obvious reasons – is much in evidence on albums by Johnny Hodges (♦), such as **Duke's In Bed/Johnny Hodges & The Ellington All Stars** and **Everybody Knows Johnny Hodges,** as well as those by Earl Hines (♦) (**Once Upon A Time**) and on the comparatively few recordings under his own name, like **Jimmy Hamilton – Clarinet.** But in any final assessment of Hamilton's career, it is his contributions whilst a member of the Duke Ellington orchestra, and on special projects like **The Far East Suite, Such Sweet Thunder, . . . And His Mother Called Him Bill,** and variously throughout **Souvenirs,** which count for most.

Recordings:
Duke Ellington 1943-1946
(Jazz Society)
Duke Ellington, Ellington In Concert, Vols 1, 2
(—/World Record Club)

The World Of Duke Ellington, Vol 2 *(Columbia)/*
The World Of Duke Ellington *(CBS)*
The World Of Duke Ellington, Vol 3 *(Columbia)/*
The World Of Duke Ellington, Vol 2 *(CBS)*
Duke Ellington, Ellington Presents *(Bethlehem/Bethlehem)*
Duke Ellington, Ellington '55 *(Capitol)/*
Toast To The Duke
(World Record Club)
Duke Ellington, Pretty Woman *(RCA Victor/RCA Victor)*
Duke Ellington, Ellington Indigos *(Columbia)*
Duke Ellington, Masterpieces By Ellington *(CBS – Holland)*
Duke Ellington At Carnegie Hall 1946 *(Queen Disc – Italy)*
Duke Ellington, Such Sweet Thunder
(Columbia/CBS – Realm)
Duke Ellington, Ellington Jazz Party *(Columbia/Philips)*
Duke Ellington, The Nutcracker Suite *(Columbia/CBS)*
Duke Ellington, Liberian Suite/ A Tone Parallel To Harlem *(Columbia/CBS – France)*
Duke Ellington, Jazz At The Plaza, Vol 2 *(Columbia/CBS)*
Duke Ellington, Recollections Of The Big Band Era
(Atlantic/ —)
Duke Ellington, The Far East Suite
(RCA Victor/RCA Victor)
Duke Ellington, . . . And His Mother Called Him Bill *(RCA Victor/RCA Victor)*
Duke Ellington, Souvenirs *(Reprise)*
Duke Ellington, It's Duke Ellington *(Allegro/Ember)*
Johnny Hodges, & The Ellington Men *(—/Verve)*
Johnny Hodges, Duke's In Bed *(Verve)/*
Johnny Hodges & The Ellington All Stars *(Columbia – Clef)*
Everybody Knows Johnny Hodges *(Impulse/Impulse)*
Earl Hines, Once Upon A Time *(Impulse/Impulse)*
Various (Including Duke Ellington), The Greatest Jazz Concert In The World *(Pablo/Pablo)*
Jimmy Hamilton – Clarinet *(Jazz Kings/—)*

Lionel Hampton

Lionel Hampton (born Louisville, Kentucky, 1913) is the kind of jazz musician whose very name conjugates the verb 'to swing'. He is also one of jazz's great catalysts, always in the thick of all kinds of musical events – especially the jam-session kind of get-togethers involving musicians who just want to blow. Hampton seems to have a personal obligation basically to provide exciting, essentially extrovert music-making, whether this is achieved by flailing away at the vibraphone (his premier instrument), thundering around – even jumping on and off – a drumkit, hammering away, two-finger style, at a piano keyboard, or taking the occasional high-pitch vocal. Hampton's own brand of jazz is basically representative of what is sometimes called 'mainstream' jazz – which means it has roots in more traditional forms of jazz, the big-band/Swing Era, a touch of bebop, and injected with a healthy dose of R&B. Apart from Milt Jackson (♦), Lionel Hampton's pre-eminence as the most celebrated exponent of vibes in jazz which he plays, like his other instruments, with unremitting swing and power and an almost fanatical adherence to the beat, has long since become part of jazz lore. No surprise, therefore, to learn that Hampton's first love was drums, which he first played in a 'Chicago Defender' Newsboys' Band, after he and his mother had moved from Louisville to, first, Wisconsin, then Chicago. Received tuition on xylophone from one-time Erskine Tate percussionist Jimmy Bertrand. Worked with several Chicago bands, then joined orchestra of Paul Howard, with whom he made debut on records. Next, came jobs with Vernon Elkins and Les Hite. With Hite, recorded in company of Louis Armstrong (♦) (both on drums and vibes); first recorded solo, using latter instrument, **Memories Of You (V.S.O.P. (Very Special Old Phono-**

ing is represented here by reflective, almost low-key dexterity on **Man I Love**. During his term with Goodman, which lasted until 1940, Hampton took time off to organize series of the most remarkable organized jam-session recordings to emanate from inside a studio. Not only were Hampton's multi-talents amply on display, including composing, arranging, but he proved himself impeccable assembler of major talents, borrowed mainly from important big bands of the day (viz Ellington (♦), Basie (♦), Goodman, Kirk (♦), Calloway (♦)) together with other top-notch instrumentalists like Nat Cole (♦), Benny Carter (♦), Coleman Hawkins (♦), and John Kirby (♦). Typical of the miniature Who's Who of Jazz personnel Hampton assembled for such dates was that which participated in session (like all the others, for Victor) in September '39 **(The Complete Lionel Hampton/Lionel Hampton's Best Records, Vol 3: 1939-1940)** which boasted sax section of Hawkins, Webster (♦), Chu Berry (♦), and Carter, plus Dizzy Gillespie (♦), trumpet, Hampton, Charlie Christian (♦), Milt Hinton, Clyde Hart, Cozy Cole (♦). And the music resulting therefrom was in keeping with the line-up. Put together own big band after leaving Goodman, first of long line of Hampton big bands that sold musical excitement in most blatantly extrovert way. Music from these bands was basic, dynamic, often uplifting; Hampton's playing was cast in apposite mold. Apart from which a string of talented soloists passed through ranks of succession of Hampton bands, including following: Quincy Jones, Wes Montgomery (♦), Clifford Brown (♦), Art Farmer (♦), Jimmy Cleveland, Alan Dawson, Milt Buckner, Dexter Gordon (♦), Illinois Jacquet (♦), Arnett Cobb (♦), Chico Hamilton (♦), Shadow Wilson, Cat Anderson, Gigi Gryce, Al Grey, Earl Bostic (♦), Johnny Griffin (♦), and Dinah Washington (♦). At the same time, Hampton never completely deserted small-group setting which helped make him famous, although, from time to time, has led galvanic orchestras **(Newport Uproar!** and **The Exciting Hamp In Europe)**, often with devastating effect.

But in small-group context, there have been more clearly defined

Above: Lionel Hampton – the fountainhead for all vibes players. Innovator, catalyst, extrovert. A Giant of Jazz.

graphy), Vols 7 & 8).** Studied music at University of Southern California early-1930s; appeared in films featuring Hite and Armstrong (played masked drummer in *Pennies From Heaven*) and own band. 1936: fronted big band at Paradise Cafe, Hollywood, occasionally guesting as member of Benny Goodman (♦) Quartet. Joined Goodman full-time, November of same year, playing vibes as important ingredient of Goodman Quartet (later with Quintet, Sextet, Septet too), and on occasion deputizing as drummer with big band. (Was one of several replacements for Gene Krupa (♦) when latter left Goodman in '38.) With Goodman, Hampton's reputation as major soloist realized. In turn, gave various Goodman units in which he appeared extra fire and dynamism. His recordings with Quartet are legion.

Most memorable moments originate from **1938 Carnegie Hall Jazz Concert** wherein his indefatigable, good-humored playing inspired his colleagues in Quartet to real heights of inspiration. He is particularly outstanding on exhilarating performances of Quartet favorites like **Stompin' At The Savoy, Dizzy Spells** and **Avalon**. Other side of his play-

examples of his vibraphone playing, even though there have been times (parts of **The Jazz Ambassadors, Vols 1, 2)** when his solos have tended to ramble on for longer than his creative powers have been able to sustain real interest. Nevertheless, Hampton rarely fails to spark a record session. For example, he succeeded in inspiring tenorist Stan Getz (♦) into producing harder swinging solos than was usual at the time (1955) during a Hollywood date involving both men **(Hamp & Getz)**. And during live date **(Memorable Concerts, Part 1)** inspired basically extrovert musicians like Charlie Shavers (♦) and Willie Smith (♦) to play at their passionate best. Conversely, at same concert **(Memorable Concerts, Part 2)** Hampton himself, during a ballad performance of some duration, proved that his finest work is not always at fast, hard-swinging tempos.

His lengthy, dazzling work-out on **Stardust** stands as testimony of his true greatness; certainly, his statement here remains as vital and inspiring as his countless up-tempo offerings, but it contains also elements of real creativity not always readily apparent in his more extrovert moments. Hampton remains perfect catalyst, able to fire the kind of premeditated studio jam session of which so often he has been an integral part. Like the many in which he participated that were produced by Norman Granz;

whatever the personnel, whatever the situation, Hampton fits. Situations like his own all-star date of July '55 which featured, Hampton apart, Art Tatum (♦), Buddy Rich (♦), Barney Kessel (♦), Harry Edison (♦), and others. Everyone soloed splendidly, with Hampton inspiring all and sundry in typical fashion. On this and another date from the day before which featured Hampton, Tatum and Rich, he refused to be overawed or even intimidated by Tatum's totally individualistic playing throughout (both **The Tatum Group Masterpieces**).

Two years before those two meetings of the giants, Hampton, in Paris as part of European tour with his then big band, was again a catalytic figurehead, accompanied by small contingent from his band, plus Mezz Mezzrow, and two local musicians. At this date, Hampton produced one more extraordinary ballad performance, **September In The Rain (The Complete 1953 Paris Sessions)**. More recently Hampton has been victim of ill-health (he has been hospitalized on more than one occasion), and his appearances – both on record and in concert – have been less than prolific. In 1955, he was seen and heard in *The Benny Goodman Story*. During time he spent with Goodman was also featured in several films. During early-1960s, Hampton recorded for Glad-Hamp, label started by late wife Gladyse Hampton (who also acted as manager). During his career, has composed number of durable jazz standards, best-known

Lionel Hampton's Best Records, Vol 5 (RCA Victor).   *The Best Of Lionel Hampton (MCA Coral, Germany).*

of which are: **Hamp's Boogie Woogie, Midnight Sun, Gin For Christmas, 'Till Tom Special** and the perennial **Flying Home** (which Hampton must have played a million times).

Recordings:
Louis Armstrong, V.S.O.P. (Very Special Old Phonography, 1931-1932), Vols 7 & 8 *(CBS – France)*
The Complete Benny Goodman, Vols 1-3 *(RCA Victor/—)*
Benny Goodman, Vols 1-3 *(RCA Victor – France)*
Benny Goodman Trio & Quartet Live (1937-1938), Vols 1, 2 *(CBS – France)*
Various (Including Benny Goodman), 1938 Carnegie Hall Jazz Concert *(Columbia/CBS)*
The Genius Of Charlie Christian *(Columbia)/***Solo Flight** *(CBS)*
The Complete Lionel Hampton (1937-1941) *(Bluebird)/*
  Lionel Hampton's Best Records, Vols 1-6 *(RCA Victor – France)*
Lionel Hampton, Steppin' Out (1942-1944) *(MCA – Germany)*
The Best Of Lionel Hampton *(MCA Coral – Germany)*
Lionel Hampton, Slide Hamp Slide (1945-1946) *(MCA – Germany)*
Lionel Hampton, Sweatin' With Hamp (1945-1950) *(MCA – Germany)*
Various (Including Lionel Hampton), Gene Norman Presents 'Just Jazz' *(Decca/Coral)*
Lionel Hampton, The Exciting Hamp In Europe *(Ember)*
Lionel Hampton, Memorable Concerts *(Vogue)*
Lionel Hampton, The Complete 1953 Paris Sessions *(Vogue)*
The Big Band Sound Of Lionel Hampton & His Orchestra *(—/Verve)*
Various (Including Lionel Hampton), The Jazz Ambassadors, Vols 1, 2 *(—/Verve)*
Various, Kings Of Swing *(—/Verve)*
Lionel Hampton/Stan Getz, Hamp & Getz *(Verve/Verve)*
Lionel Hampton, Hamp! *(Verve/Music For Pleasure)*
Art Tatum, The Tatum Group Masterpieces *(Pablo/Pablo)*
Lionel Hampton, Live! *(Fontana)*
Lionel Hampton, Newport Uproar! *(RCA Victor/RCA Victor)*
Lionel Hampton/Svend Asmussen, As Time Goes By *(—/Sonet)*

Herbie Hancock

Pianist Herbie Hancock was a child prodigy, performing Mozart Piano Concertos with the Chicago Symphony Orchestra at the age of 11. Born Chicago, 1940, he went to New York as a protégé of trumpeter Donald Byrd, and soon established himself as a recording artist for Blue Note. His debut album **(Takin' Off)**, with sidemen Freddie Hubbard and Dexter Gordon demonstrated his compositional gifts, from the gospel-funk of the hit number, **Watermelon Man**, to the rhythmically adventurous **The Maze. Blind Man, Blind Man** proved his talent for catchy tunes **(My Point Of View)** while a further album without horns spotlighted his keyboard technique **(Succotash)** which, while owing something to Bill Evans, Red Garland and Wynton Kelly, showed a graceful balance between single-note runs and texturally thick chord passages.

In the early '60s, Blue Note artists like Sam Rivers, Wayne Shorter, Grachan Moncur III, Andrew Hill, Bobby Hutcherson and Anthony Williams involved themselves in experiments with modes, free rhythms and tone colors, and Hancock proved a useful sideman, shaking rocks in a box for Bobby Hutcherson's **The Omen (Happenings)** and helping in the arrangements on Anthony Williams' first album **(Life Time)**. His finest work as a composer comes from this fertile period **(Maiden Voyage** and **Empyrean Isles)** both using Freddie Hubbard, Ron Carter and Anthony Williams. There is a litheness and melodic charm about tunes like **Dolphin Dance** that is worlds away from Hancock's current output. Miles Davis picked his new quintet from this stable of talent, Herbie Hancock, Wayne Shorter, Ron Carter and Anthony Williams, aiming at a unit capable of great rhythmic mobility and free of harmonic restrictions.

Miles' subsequent exploration of modes, unison playing, suspended and multiple rhythms was well-served by Hancock's and Shorter's writing talents. **Sorcerer, Madness** and **Riot** are typical Hancock scalar pieces built on shifting rhythms, while the pianist's role on his own **Little One** shows how important his atmospheric chording could be for the horns **(ESP)**. Within the rhythm section, his lightly lyrical lines fit into the intricate web of support from bass and drums. Switching to electric piano at Miles' suggestion, Hancock became part of an electric keyboard choir for the trailblazing jazz-rock album **(In A Silent Way)**, a role which continued throughout subsequent releases.

In 1968, Hancock left Miles Davis to form his own band, a sextet with tenorman Joe Henderson. **Fat Mama**, a near-R&B original, gives an indication of what was to come **(Fat Albert Rotunda)**, though the next group with saxophonist Bennie Maupin saw Hancock once more experimenting, this time with percussion and electronic voicings **(Crossings)**. **Ostinato** is mainly an exercise in riff, using 15 beats on 4/4 and 7/8 **(Mwandishi)**. **Hidden Shadows (Sextant)** continues this pre-occupation. The commercial turning point came in 1973, thanks to the overwhelming bass riff **(Headhunters)**. Except for the short, sneaky re-vamp of **Watermelon Man**, the entire album is dominated by rhythmic riff, **Chameleon** for example motoring on for fifteen minutes with little solo top-dressing. On a par with Donald Byrd's **Black Byrd** album for jazz-rock sales, Herbie Hancock was established as a superstar.

From this point on, the minimum quantity of jazz interest comes mainly from Bennie Maupin, and Hancock's main influences are Sly Stone and James Brown. Apart from the steady stream of best-sellers, he has also composed for the movies, most notably **Blow-up** and **Death Wish**. A convert to Shoshu Buddhism, Hancock believes now 'the whole thing is making people happy'.

Recordings:
Takin' Off *(Blue Note/Blue Note)*
My Point Of View *(Blue Note/Blue Note)*
Succotash *(Blue Note/Blue Note)*
Maiden Voyage *(Blue Note/Blue Note)*
Empyrean Isles *(Blue Note/Blue Note)*
Miles Davis:
  ESP *(Columbia/CBS)*
  Miles Smiles *(Columbia/CBS)*
  Sorcerer *(Columbia/CBS)*
  Filles De Kilimanjaro *(Columbia/CBS)*
  In A Silent Way *(Columbia/CBS)*
  On The Corner *(Columbia/CBS)*
Herbie Hancock:
  Fat Albert Rotunda *(Atlantic/Atlantic)*
  Crossings *(Warner/Warner)*
  Mwandishi *(Warner/Warner)*
  Sextant *(Columbia/CBS)*
  Headhunters *(Columbia/CBS)*
  Thrust *(Columbia/CBS)*
  Death Wish *(Columbia/CBS)*
  Man-Child *(Columbia/CBS)*
  Secrets *(Columbia/CBS)*

W. C. Handy

W. C. Handy, 'The Father Of The Blues', was a composer of stature, a bandleader and music publisher, but by no means the source of the blues. One of the first to recognize the commercial potential of Afro-American folk music, Handy incorporated the form into over-formal orchestrations for his nine-piece orchestra. Chiefly remembered as the composer of **St Louis Blues**, Handy also wrote **Aunt Hagar's Blues, Beale Street Blues, Memphis Blues** and many others.

Toby Hardwicke

Otto 'Toby' Hardwicke (born Washington, DC, 1904) was a suave, dapper figure of a man with sophisticated name (and nickname) to match. More important, he was an invaluable asset to orchestra of Duke Ellington (♦) during two periods he spent as member of its reeds section (1923–8, and 1932–6).

A founder-member of the Ellington band, Hardwicke provided immaculate lead to saxes and, prior to arrival of Johnny Hodges (♦), took most of the alto-sax solos. Typical of these: **Birmingham Breakdown, Black & Tan Fantasy (The Beginning: 1926-1928); Black & Tan Fantasy** (different version), **Jubilee Stomp (The Works Of Duke, Vol 1);** and **Got Everything But You (The Works Of Duke, Vol 2)**. Two of his finest solos come from two separate recordings of **In A Sentimental Mood (The Ellington Era, Vol 2** and **The Works Of Duke, Vol 18)** recorded, respectively, in 1935, 1945. Hardwicke's all-round abilities enabled him to be featured as soloist on soprano-sax **(Blues I Love To Sing)**, and baritone-sax **(Blue Bubbles)** (both **The Works Of Duke, Vol 1)**. Compositionally, the most famous (and indisputably the best) Hardwicke original is the elegant **Sophisticated Lady**.

Basically, Otto Hardwicke was a most gifted sideman, whose multi-instrumental accomplishments – he also played bass-saxophone, clarinet with the fluency that marked his work on the other instruments – never were in doubt.

Hardwicke, who had started his involvement with music by playing bass and C-melody sax, later violin, worked with both Elmer Snowden and Wilbur Sweatman before taking his place in first-ever Ellington band. Upon leaving Ellington on first occasion, worked in Paris, then with own and other bands (including Chick Webb (♦), Noble Sissle, et al). When he exited from the ranks, finally, in 1946, it was to retire from music altogether.

Recordings:
Duke Ellington, The Beginning (1926-1928) (MCA – Germany)
Duke Ellington, Hot In Harlem (1928-1929) (MCA – Germany)
Duke Ellington, Rockin' In Rhythm (1929-1931) (MCA – Germany)
Duke Ellington, Toodle-oo (—/Vocalion)
Duke Ellington, The Works Of Duke, Vols 1, 2, 8-12, 14-18 (RCA Victor – France)
Duke Ellington, The Ellington Era, Vols 1, 2 (Columbia/CBS)
Rex Stewart Memorial (CBS – Realm)

Joe Harriott

Born in the West Indies, 1928, alto-man Joe Harriott came to Britain in 1951. Initially a Hard Bopper, Harriott's naturally adventurous mind led him independently, into many of the free areas that Ornette Coleman was exploring. Dispensing with bar lines, set harmony and predetermined structure, Harriott led a fine combo with trumpeter Shake Keane, pianist Pat Smythe, bassist Coleridge Goode and drummer Phil Seaman on a successful album (**Free Form**). In the mid-60s, he collaborated with Indian musician John Mayer on a fusion of Indian music and jazz, using both modes and free jazz techniques. With a five-piece jazz unit and four Indian musicians, violin, sitar, tabla, tambura, Harriott and Mayer recorded the compositions of Mayer (**Indo-Jazz Suite**). Joe Harriott died in 1972.

Recordings:
Free Form (Jazzland/—)
Indo-Jazz Suite (Columbia/Columbia)

Bill Harris

Willard Palmer 'Bill' Harris (born Philadelphia, Pennsylvania, 1916) was one of the great individual voices on jazz trombone; a player of tremendous fire, real depth, and an eccentric style that made him totally unclassifiable. In the latter, Harris' playing was comparable to clarinettist Pee Wee Russell (♦), another of jazz's great eccentrics, whose own individualism offered no guidance to those who insist on pigeon-holing jazz musicians and putting them in dubious categories. His huge sound, formidable drive, and unpredictable phrasing was showcased for many years within the framework of the First and subsequent Woody Herman (♦) Herds, covering three different spells with the band.

During first of those periods (1944-6), name became household word in most jazz circles when the powerhouse First Herd burst on the scene. Harris soon became

Above: Alto innovator Joe Harriott. His experiments in free playing and fusions with Indian music were prophetic.

one of its most important individual sounds, producing series of classic solos, including those on **Bijou, I Wonder** and **Welcome To My Dream,** and two numbers written by Harris himself, **Your Father's Mustache** and **Everywhere** (all **The Thundering Herds**); last-named, a ballad performance, beautifully defined his approach to that genre (more straight-forward, softer in approach, but with much warmth).

In actual live performance, Harris' up-tempo features, like **Bijou** and **Your Father's Mustache,** took on even more electrifying proportions; similarly, his ballad-playing, in person, acquired even greater depth, as illustrated during **Woody Herman At Carnegie Hall, One Night Stand With Woody Herman** and **Woody Herman & His Orchestra & His Woodchoppers, Vols 1, 2.** After leaving Herman, in '46, worked with own band, then toured, recorded with Charlie Ventura, with whom he was allocated a regular feature with title requiring no elucidation whatsoever, **Characteristically B.H. (Charlie Ventura's Carnegie Hall Concert).**

Back with Herman's Second Herd (1948-50), and now oldest of the sidemen, Harris shared principal trombone solo duties with newcomer Earl Swope, being featured on fresh items like **More Moon, Tenderly, Music To Dance To, Keeper Of The Flame** (all **Early Autumn**). Leaving Herman again, became more or less regular member of Jazz At The Philharmonic touring units (he had worked previously with JATP in '47 (**JATP: New Volumes, 4, 5, 6**) with much acclaim). Although his best work was not always to be found in this context, Harris' assertive trom-

bone helped generate much of the typical JATP excitement. Visited Japan with JATP in 1953 (**JATP In Tokyo**) acquitting himself splendidly in customary all-star company. The duality of his style contrasted intriguingly between his 15 barking choruses during the pulsing **Jam Session Blues** and the sensitivity of his ballad feature, **The Nearness Of You.**

Worked with several bands, including Sauter-Finegan (1953), then back with Woody Herman (1956-8). His work throughout (**Pre-Herds**) taped in live performance, retains all its explosiveness of First Herd days (particularly **Natchel Blues,** and **At The Woodchopper's Ball),** and his ballad playing (**Body & Soul**) leaves nothing to be desired. Last real involvement with Herman in 1959, going to Europe as part of a specially-assembled Anglo-American Herd. Also in '59, worked with Benny Goodman (♦), with whose band he had been previously in in early-1940s. With Goodman, Harris came to Europe for second time in same year ('59).

Moved to Florida to live and work (including gigs with Red Norvo (♦), and several own bands) before joining Charlie Teagarden (♦) for two years (1962-4). Then, another year with Norvo (1965-6). Became member of Tropicana Hotel, Miami, houseband. Before taking up trombone, Bill Harris played saxophone, trumpet. First professional jobs were in Philadelphia area during early-1930s, before Harris signed for two years with Merchant Navy (1934). Resumed career in music in 1938, working briefly with Gene Krupa (♦), Ray McKinley, Buddy Williams, Bob Chester. Then came first spell with Goodman.

Outside his big-band work and his association with JATP, Harris' recording career has not been exactly prolific, at least not recordings under his own name. But there have been numerous superior recordings, demonstrating his vitality and his sometimes bizarre approach to his instrument, including an exceptional live date from 1947, with Harris assisted admirably by Herman associates Flip Phillips (♦) and Chubby Jackson, and with pianist Lennie Tristano (♦) member of rhythm section (**Bill Harris All Stars).** Also recorded variously for Norman Granz labels, including his own bands and those of Ralph Burns (♦), Phillips, and as co-leader of Jackson-Harris Herd (all **Kings Of Swing, Vol 2).** Added extra body to already hard-swinging Gene Krupa session (**The Exciting Gene Krupa).**

Best of all Harris recordings under own name must be **Bill Harris & Friends,** marvellously warm collaboration between Harris and tenorist Ben Webster (♦), both supported by a stimulating rhythm trio, and during which trombonist produces one of his most satisfying balladic statements on **It Might As Well Be Spring.** Bill Harris, the great individualist, died in 1974, mourned by almost anyone genuinely interested in jazz trombone development, and most of all by his fellow trombonists.

Recordings:
Woody Herman, The Thundering Herds (Columbia/—)
Woody Herman, His Orchestra & His Woodchoppers, Vols 1, 2 (First Heard/—)
Woody Herman At Carnegie Hall (MGM/Verve)
Woody Herman, Early Autumn (Capitol/Capitol – Holland)
Woody Herman, Pre-Herds (Ember)
One Night Stand With Woody Herman (Joyce/—)
Ralph Burns Amongst the JATPs (Verve/—)
Various (Including Ralph Burns/Bill Harris/Flip Phillips/Jackson-Harris), Kings Of Swing, Vol 2 (—/Verve)
Bill Harris & Serge Chaloff & Woody Herman (Alto/—)
Various (Including Bill Harris), The Herdsmen (—/Mercury)
Charlie Ventura's Carnegie Hall Concert (Verve/Columbia – Clef)
Terry Gibbs & Bill Harris (Premier/—)
Various (Including Bill Harris), Saturday Night Jazz Session (Everest)
Various (Including Bill Harris), Jazz At The Philharmonic: New Vols 4, 5, 6 (Verve/Columbia – Clef)
Various, JATP In Tokyo (Pablo/Pablo)
Bill Harris All Stars (Jazz Showcase/—)
The Exciting Gene Krupa (Verve/Verve – Germany)
Various, The Gillespie Jam Sessions (—/Verve)
Bill Harris & Friends (Fantasy/Vocalion)

Jimmy Harrison

James Henry 'Jimmy' Harrison (born Louisville, Kentucky, 1900) was trombonist of great warmth and feeling, and one of the first really great stylists on his instrument. Together with Jack Teagarden (♦), J. C. Higginbotham (♦) and Miff Mole (♦), helped move jazz trombone away from strictly New Orleans style, with its emphasis on ensemble playing.

After family had moved to Detroit, teen-ager Harrison first took up trombone. Played locally, then helped father run family restaurant in Toledo, Ohio. Toured with minstrel shows, before settling in Atlantic City. Worked with various orchestras, including those of Charlie Johnson, Sam Wooding, Hank Duncan (♦), latter engagement bringing him back to Detroit.

Moved once again to Toledo, playing there with, amongst others, James P. Johnson (♦). Toured with show bands, then to New York, working with Fess Williams, June Clark, et al. With Billy Fowler (1925–6); briefly with Duke Ellington (♦); also played with Elmer Snowden band. 1927: joined orchestra of Fletcher Henderson (♦), with whom was featured on record, soloing with great aplomb and with emotion on titles like **Hop Off, Feeling Good, I'm Feeling Devilish (The Fletcher Henderson Story, Vol 2)**. Often with Charlie Johnson during 1928, his solos on Johnson recordings like **The Boy In The Boat (Charlie Johnson/Lloyd Scott-Cecil Scott)** demonstrating marvellous relaxation in swing, and singing warm tone.

Rejoined Henderson, again taking recorded solos of quality on **Wang Wang Blues, Come On Baby,** and singing in engaging manner on **Somebody Loves Me (The Fletcher Henderson Story, Vol 3)**. Was taken ill while band was on location in Harrisburg, Pennsylvania (1930). Recovered to rejoin band, then worked for a few months in '31 with Chick Webb (♦) Orchestra. His few recordings with Webb, and particularly his solos on **Soft & Sweet** and **Heebie Jeebies (A Legend 1929-1936)** showed that even just prior to his death, his talent was still in the process of growing.

Recordings:
The Fletcher Henderson Story (Columbia)/
The Fletcher Henderson Story, Vols 2, 3 (CBS)
Charlie Johnson/Lloyd - Cecil Scott (RCA Victor – France)
The Chocolate Dandies (—/Parlophone)
Chick Webb, A Legend (1929-1936) (Decca/MCA – Germany)

Hampton Hawes

The son of a preacher, pianist Hampton Hawes was born in Los Angeles in 1928. At the age of 19 he was playing in trumpeter Howard McGhee's combo with Charlie

Hampton Hawes Trio (Contemporary): early piano.

Parker **(Lullaby In Rhythm)** and the Bird influence never left his playing. Bebop bands were everywhere in LA in the late '40s and early '50s, and Hawes played with many of the giants, Dexter Gordon, Teddy Edwards and Wardell Gray **(Jazz Concert - West Coast** and **Wardell Gray - Central Avenue)**.

In 1955 he landed a contract with Contemporary, and his debut album **(The Trio)** displayed his characteristic surging attack and deep feeling for the blues. All of his subsequent output swings with great inventiveness and vigor,

and the three albums cut at one session **(All Night Session)** with guitarist Jim Hall, bassist Red Mitchell and drummer Bruz Freeman, show an inexhaustible drive and jubilation.

The meeting with two members of the Curtis Counce group, tenorman Harold Land and the phenomenal Frank Butler on drums, plus the innovative bassist Scott La Faro, produced an album of surging power. Hawes' later work is rigorously controlled, with a greater emphasis laid on structure, and **The Green Leaves Of Summer** represents the high point.

Addiction and prison sentences have left his talent undiminished – in fact his autobiography *Raise Up*

Off Me gives a revealing picture of the Bebop hothouse. His recent work on an Art Pepper album **(Living Legend)** must remain his swansong, as he died on May 24, 1977.

Recordings:
The Trio (Contemporary/Contemporary)
All Night Session (Contemporary/Contemporary)
For Real (Contemporary/Contemporary)
The Green Leaves Of Summer (Contemporary/Contemporary)
Seance (Contemporary/Contemporary)
Live At The Monmartre (Arista Freedom/—)

Above: Bebop meets Beefeater. The late piano giant Hampton Hawes visiting the Tower of London.

Coleman Hawkins

To say that Coleman Hawkins (born St Joseph, Missouri, 1904) virtually single-handedly brought the saxophone into prominence as a solo instrument of individuality and believability, is not so far from being the truth. Before Hawkins wrought his miracle, some time during late-1920s (and indeed, progressively, for several years thereafter), the saxophone had been looked upon as something almost akin to a musical joke. Not only was Hawkins to pioneer (along with Sidney Bechet (♦), on soprano) the jazz saxophone in general, but he also became first and undisputed master of the tenor-sax. Indeed, apart from Lester Young (♦), Ben Webster (♦), John Coltrane (♦), and Sonny Rollins (♦), he remains the instrument's principal voice. A situation which is hardly likely to change.

Although his blues-playing often left something to be desired (his prowess in this genre really only blossomed during last 15–20 years of his life) Hawkins never lacked in any other department during a career which commenced as sideman with singer Mamie Smith's Jazz Hounds (with whom he made his record debut, in 1923), continued through an important developmental period as premier soloist (apart from Louis Armstrong (♦), for short spell) with orchestra of Fletcher Henderson (♦) (1923–34), passing on to his first acclaim as one of jazz's greatest solo virtuosi (1934–9).

The career which progressed with initial experience as leader of his own big band (1940); thence, through the Bebop era (1943–9); his involvement with touring jazz packages such as Jazz At The Philharmonic (1946–68), as well as with an amazing variety of small-combos, and literally hundreds of record dates which found his indomitable horn showing the way to such bands and fellow instrumentalists as the Mound City Blue Blowers **(The Complete Coleman Hawkins, Vol 1 (1924-1940/Body & Soul)** in 1929; Lionel Hampton (♦) **(The Complete Lionel Hampton/Lionel Hampton's Best Records, Vols 3, 6)** from 1939; Duke

Ellington (♦) **(Duke Ellington Meets Coleman Hawkins)** 1962; Sonny Rollins **(The Bridge/Sonny Meets Hawk)** 1963; Django Reinhardt (♦), **(Django Reinhardt & The American Jazz Giants/Django & His American Friends, Vol 1)** 1937; and his closest rival, Lester Young **(Coleman Hawkins/Lester Young)**. Juxtaposition of tenor-saxes of Young and Hawkins on latter album makes for absolutely fascinating listening, if for no other reason than the different approaches of the pair to the same instrument are brought dramatically into focus; Young's lazy-sounding, legato playing, with its great rhythmic subtlety and occasional penchant for riff-type honks in the lower region of the tenor, contrasting with Hawkins' rich, rhapsodic and more roco style – big-toned, with reliance on eighth note-dotted sixteenth patterns.

Hawkins' first recordings provide evidence that even he had to learn to get rid of the obligatory slap-tongue style prevalent amongst early-jazz saxophonists **(The Fletcher Henderson Story, Vol 1)**. Yet even in those early days, Hawkins' adventurous spirit asserted itself, as an **Old Black Joe's Blues (The Henderson Pathés)** from '23.

Apart from his recordings with Mamie Smith, Hawkins also took part in sessions involving Bessie Smith (♦) **(The Empress** and **Nobody's Blues But Mine)**; and Ma Rainey (♦) **(Ma Rainey)**, last-named finding Hawkins sounding stiff, uncomfortable on bass-saxophone, an instrument which, like clarinet, he occasionally played with Henderson, although he forsook both when leaving band. With Henderson, his reputation as tenorist was built on feature items such as **The Stampede (Fletcher Henderson Story, Vol 1); Whiteman Stomp, Hop Off** and **Feeling Good (Vol 2); Freeze An' Melt, Blazin', Sweet & Hot** and **Hot & Anxious (Vol 3)**. An intriguing, look-ahead solo with Henderson, also featuring another 'progressive' of late-1920s, Henry 'Red' Allen (♦), was **Queer Notions** (a Hawkins composition). Hawkins re-recorded number (with Henderson, with Allen again soloing on trumpet) a month later. Both versions still sound avant-garde for the time (1933).

Hawkins left Henderson in 1934 to accept invitation to become featured soloist with British dance band-leader Jack Hylton. With Hylton, toured Britain, France, during which time he recorded at regular intervals.

The mixed company Hawkins kept during his European sojourn can be judged from records he made during period: with fellow American Benny Carter (♦) and Dutch jazz band (**Benny Carter With The Ramblers & His Orchestra**); Django Reinhardt, Carter, plus sundry French musicians (**Django Reinhardt & The American Jazz Giants/Django & His American Friends, Vol 1**); British pianist Stanley Black and rhythm section (**Jazz Pioneers - 1933-36/Ridin' In Rhythm**); the aforementioned Dutch band, the Ramblers (**The Hawk In Holland**); and, with the Hylton Orchestra (**Ridin' In Rhythm**).

With World War II imminent, Hawkins returned to the US. There, in October 1939, he recorded what was to become the single most celebrated track with which to identify the unique artistry of Coleman Hawkins, **Body & Soul** (**The Complete Coleman Hawkins, Vol 1: 1924-1940: 'Body & Soul'**); a recording which soon after its release was to pass into jazz immortality. **Body & Soul** was, in many ways, a new beginning, for during next decade, Hawkins was to produce probably his consistently finest playing (certainly on record) of his career.

Despite inherent problems presented by a world war, and in spite of two major musicians' union bans, involving recording, Hawkins spent more time than most inside recording studios. Typical of awesome consistency in performance during this period is his irresistibly brilliant playing during first-ever concert sponsored by *Esquire* magazine (**The First Esquire Concert, Vols 1, 2**) and for Hawkins' and Leonard Feather's Esquire All Stars year before, in 1943 (**The Big Sounds Of**

and has been credited to at least two other composers, under different titles).

Monk was to be reunited with Hawkins at a Riverside record date in '57 (**Thelonious Monk & John Coltrane**), once again sounding neither out of place nor an anachronism. Made numerous tours as member of Jazz At the Philharmonic, and whatever selection of other musicians was available, Hawkins roared like proverbial lion (**Jazz At The Philharmonic 1946, Vol 2** and **Jazz At The Philharmonic In Europe, Vols 1, 3**). During late-1940s, continued to work with extraordinary variety of jazzmen, young and old, and including the boppers (**Greatest Of The Small Bands, Vol 2, The Hawk Flies** and **Essen Jazz Festival All Stars With Bud Powell/Hawk In Germany**) as well as the then more contemporary mainstreamers like the trumpeters Henry 'Red' Allen (**Henry 'Red' Allen & His All Stars, Vol 5**); Roy Eldridge (**The Moods Of Coleman Hawkins**); Buck Clayton (**The High & Mighty Hawk**); and Clark Terry (♦) (**Giants Of The Tenor Saxophone: The Genius Of Ben Webster & Coleman Hawkins**). And amongst a clutch of veterans, as with **Jam Session At Swingville, The Big Challenge, Henry 'Red' Allen, Vols 4, 5, The Big Reunion** and **Hawk Eyes** as well as with sympathetic mainstream-modernists, as with **Sittin' In** and **The Greatest Jazz Concert In The World**, Hawkins inevitably rose to any challenge, with a majestic drive and bristling passion that bordered on the angry. One out-of-the-ordinary challenge involved a 1963 record date, with Hawkins locking horns with Sonny Rollins (**The Bridge/Sonny Meets**

The Big Sounds Of Coleman Hawkins & Chu Berry (London). Boss tenor sounds from the 1930s and 1940s.

The Many Faces Of Jazz, Vol 52: Coleman Hawkins (Mode, France). Hawk, enjoying himself with some protoboppers.

Coleman Hawkins & Chu Berry) both containing typical rhapsodic Hawkins interpretations of the ballad, **My Ideal**. Tenorist recorded exclusively during 1943–4, particularly for Signature (**Classic Tenors**) and Keynote (**Cattin'** and **Swing!**). Colleagues on these dates included trumpeters Buck Clayton (♦), Charlie Shavers (♦), Roy Eldridge (♦); saxists Tab Smith, Don Byas (♦), Harry Carney (♦); pianists Teddy Wilson (♦), Johnny Guarnieri (♦); and drummers Cozy Cole (♦) and Big Sid Catlett (♦).

Most important recordings during 1940s, however, took place between years 1944–6. First – and most important – were two Apollo sessions from February '44. With trumpeter Dizzy Gillespie (♦) and saxist-composer-arranger Budd Johnson (♦) figuring prominently in 11-piece band, this is generally recognized as being first Bebop record date (**The Many Faces Of Jazz Vol 52: Coleman Hawkins**).

Although Hawkins' basic style has not undergone any drastic metamorphosis, he fits in with the young boppers with obvious enthusiasm, as on Gillespie's **Woodyn You** or **Bu-De-Dah** (composed by Johnson and pianist Clyde Hart). In actual fact, Hawkins never was a proto-bopper, but as subsequent recordings demonstrated, again he was very much en rapport with the younger musicians' ideas even though some critics have tried to minimise this period in Hawkins' career. Soon after this historical date, another bop figurehead, Thelonious Monk (♦), was hired by Hawkins to work with him on 52nd Street; the two recorded together for the short-lived Joe Davis label (**The Hawk Flies**). At end of same year, Hawkins put together bop-tinged band, featuring trumpet of Howard McGhee (♦) for California trip. This fine band, with 'extras' like Vic Dickenson (♦), trombone, Allan Reuss, guitar, and John Simmons, bass, added at one or more of three sessions, resulted in one of Hawkins most eminently satisfying of all albums (**Hollywood Stampede**) with sumptuous ballad playing (**What Is There To Say ?, I'm Thru With Love, April In Paris**, etc) being matched by Hawkins' fiercely-blown, exciting and beautifully etched solos on the swingers, of which **Rifftide** is most interesting. A Hawkins bop original (using chord sequence of **Lady Be Good**, it was recorded nine years later by Monk under title **Hackensack**

Hawk), the two vitally important musicians generally interacting in most productive fashion.

There is a story that towards the end of his life Hawkins was a bitter, frustrated man. Apocryphal or not, his playing certainly evinced new-found ferocity after he had passed 55, continuing right through to his death from bronchial pneumonia in May '69 in New York City. This was especially true of his live performances during early-1960s, handsomely documented by airshots like those from 1962, 1969 (**Centerpiece**), as well as with numerous record dates, such as the friendly-yet-combative get-together with fellow tenorist Ben Webster (**Blue Saxophones**); a far cry, in time at least, from his virtuoso performances on classic Hawkins features like **It's The Talk Of The Town (The Big Bands - 1933/Ridin' In Rhythm); The Man I Love, How Deep Is The Ocean ? (Classic Tenors); Georgia On My Mind (Recordings Made Between 1930 & 1941); I Can't Believe That You're In Love With Me (Coleman Hawkins Memorial - 1940); Chicago (Coleman Hawkins At The Savoy 1940**); or the marvellously inventive, superbly evocative, unaccompanied **Picasso (The Moods Of Coleman Hawkins**). But then, Coleman Hawkins always was a leader amongst jazz virtuosi, keeping a watchful eye (and ear) on the more important stylistic changes and developments that occurred in jazz during his lifetime yet going his own majestic way to the very end.

In his personal life, often he kept much to himself, acknowledging very few close friends. During last years, it has been reported that some of those friends helped keep him alive – literally – by insisting he supplement his daily intake of brandy by consuming at least one meal per week (he would accept Chinese food only). One of Hawkins' last important engagements took place a few weeks before his death when, together with long-time musical associate and friend Roy Eldridge, he appeared on a Chicago-originated TV show.

Recordings:
The Complete Fletcher Henderson (RCA Victor/—)
Fletcher Henderson, Vols 1-3 (RCA Victor – France)

The Fletcher Henderson Story *(Columbia)/*
  The Fletcher Henderson Story, Vols 1-4 *(CBS)*
Fletcher Henderson, The Henderson Pathés *(—/VJM)*
Ma Rainey, Ma Rainey *(Milestone)*
Bessie Smith, The Empress *(Columbia/CBS)*
Bessie Smith, Nobody's Blues But Mine *(Columbia/CBS)*
Coleman Hawkins, Recordings Made Between 1930 & 1941
  (CBS – France)
Spike Hughes & His All American Orchestra *(London/Ace of Clubs)*
The Chocolate Dandies *(Parlophone)*
Various, The Big Bands - 1933 *(Prestige)/*
  Ridin' In Rhythm *(World Records)*
Various, Django Reinhardt & The American Jazz Giants *(Prestige)/*
  Django & His American Friends *(HMV)*
The Complete Coleman Hawkins, Vol 1 (1924-1940): 'Body & Soul'
  (RCA Victor – France)
Coleman Hawkins, Swing! *(Fontana)*
Coleman Hawkins, Cattin' *(Fontana)*
Coleman Hawkins Memorial - 1940 *(Jazz Society)*
Coleman Hawkins At The Savoy 1940 *(Sunbeam)*
Coleman Hawkins, The Hawk In Holland *(—/Ace of Clubs)*
Benny Carter With The Ramblers & His Orchestra *(Decca – France)*
The Complete Lionel Hampton *(Bluebird)/*
  Lionel Hampton's Best Records, Vols 3, 6 *(RCA Victor – France)*
Coleman Hawkins, The Many Faces Of Jazz, Vol 52 *(Mode – France)*
Coleman Hawkins, The Hawk Flies *(Milestone/—)*
Various, Jazz At The Philharmonic, Vols 1, 2 *(Verve)*
Coleman Hawkins - Lester Young *(Spotlite)*
Coleman Hawkins/Lester Young, Classic Tenors
  (Contact/Philips – International)
Coleman Hawkins, Hawk Eyes *(Prestige/Xtra)*
Various (Including Coleman Hawkins), The Big Three

(Bob Thiele Music/RCA Victor)
Coleman Hawkins, Hollywood Stampede *(Capitol/Capitol – Holland)*
Various (Including Coleman Hawkins), In Concert *(Phoenix)*
The Moods Of Coleman Hawkins *(—/Verve)*
Coleman Hawkins, The Real Thing *(Prestige/—)*
Various (Including Coleman Hawkins), The Tenor Sax Album
  (Savoy/Savoy)
The Big Sounds Of Coleman Hawkins & Chu Berry *(—/London)*
Coleman Hawkins, The High & Mighty Hawk *(Felsted/Vocalion)*
Coleman Hawkins All Stars *(Prestige – Swingville)*
Coleman Hawkins, Centerpiece *(Phoenix)*
Coleman Hawkins/Ben Webster, Blue Saxophones *(Verve/Verve)*
Coleman Hawkins/Bud Powell, Essen Jazz Festival All-Stars With
  Bud Powell *(Fantasy)/*Hawk In Germany *(Black Lion)*
Giants Of The Tenor Saxophone: The Genius Of Ben Webster &
  Coleman Hawkins *(Columbia/CBS)*
Duke Ellington Meets Coleman Hawkins *(Impulse/Impulse)*
Various, The Greatest Jazz Concert In The World *(Pablo/Pablo)*
Sonny Rollins, The Bridge/Sonny Meets Hawk
  (RCA Victor – France)
Various, Jazz At The Philharmonic In Europe, Vols 1, 3
  (Verve/Verve)
Thelonious Monk & John Coltrane *(Milestone)*
Various, Sittin' In *(Verve/Columbia – Clef)*
Various, Jam Session At Swingville *(Prestige/Prestige)*
Various, The Big Challenge *(Jazztone/Concert Hall)*
Various, The Big Reunion *(Jazztone/—)*
Coleman Hawkins/Roy Eldridge, Hawk & Roy *(Phoenix)*
Henry 'Red' Allen, Vols 4, 5 *(RCA Victor – France)*
Various, The First Esquire Concert, Vols 1, 2 *(—/Saga)*
Various (Including Coleman Hawkins), The Greatest Of The
  Small Bands, Vol 2 *(RCA Victor – France)*

Above: The phenomenally-gifted Tubby Hayes, co-leader of the two-tenor Jazz Couriers and vibist of distinction.

Tubby Hayes

Born in London, 1935, multi-instrumentalist Tubby Hayes died in 1973. He played tenor with the Kenny Baker Sextet, and spent four years with the big bands of Vic Lewis, Ambrose and Jack Parnell before forming his own shortlived Octet in 1955. In 1957 he joined up with fellow tenorman Ronnie Scott to form the Jazz Couriers, a popular Hard Bop outfit which lasted for two-and-a-half years. Hayes, apart from his charging, high-speed tenor, played excellent vibes: **Whisper Not (The Message From Britain)** and **Some Of My Best Friends Are Blues (Jazz Couriers In Concert)**; while **If This Isn't Love** and **What Is This Thing Called Love** are typical Courier tear-ups. The Tubby Hayes Big Band featured many of Britain's finest musicians, including saxophonists Pete King and Bobby Wellins and trumpeter Jimmy Deuchar **(Tubbs Tours),** while the Hayes Quartet of 1967 had Mike Pyne on piano, Ron Mathewson bass and Tony Levin drums. The definitive album **(Mexican Green)** includes a brilliant, lengthy, open-ended title track, which shows that Hayes was aware of the possibilities of post-Coltrane/Coleman improvizing.

The finest talent to emerge in Britain in the '50s, Hayes' premature death dealt a severe blow to modern jazz.

Recordings:
**The Jazz Couriers, The
  Message From Britain**
  (Jazzland/—)
The Jazz Couriers, In Concert
  (—/Music For Pleasure)
Tubbs Tours *(—/Fontana)*
Mexican Green *(—/Fontana)*

Fletcher Henderson

A four-disc reissue set of important recordings by the Fletcher Henderson Orchestra (1923–38) and released many years ago was subtitled **A Study In Frustration.** Reason was because Henderson, one of three great pioneers of big-band jazz, never did gain full recognition and all-round acclaim that fell to Benny Goodman (♦) during Swing Era when Goodman used many of the original arrangements for his orchestra Henderson had written for his own trailblazing aggregation in previous years, not forgetting Goodman's use of kind of big-band structure which the older man had innovated during 1920s/1930s. Although perhaps too much has been made of this over the years, it is true that Fletcher Hamilton Henderson (born Cuthbert, Georgia, 1898) did not receive the kudos his pioneering work in this field so richly deserved.

His very early bands, in comparison with later versions, sound primitive, stiff-swinging, and not especially exciting, but by the time 1930s had arrived, Henderson had established an individual style that was at least as influential as Duke Ellington (♦) during same period.

Henderson himself came from well-to-do family; father was principal of a Macon, Georgia, training school; and he attended college as well as graduating from Atlanta University. Played piano at school dance dates. 1920: after receiving AB degree from University, Henderson came to New York, ostensibly to enrol at Columbia University. Instead took job as song demonstrator for Pace & Handy Music Co. Left next year to assemble band to accompany singer Ethel Waters (♦) and her troupe with whom he toured for a year. Recorded with Waters on regular basis **(Oh Daddy!** and **Jazzin' Babies' Blues).**

Back in New York, became house pianist for record companies, accompanying many noted blues singers, including Bessie Smith (♦) **(Nobody's**

Blues But Mine and **The World's Greatest Blues Singer**); Mamie Smith, Alberta Hunter, Trixie Smith and Ma Rainey (**Ma Rainey**).

Frankly, Henderson was competent rather than inspired accompanist – his work behind Bessie Smith, for instance, compares very unfavourably with that of James P. Johnson (♦). 1924: appointed leader of recently put-together band to play two lengthy residences in New York's Club Alabam and Roseland Ballroom, plus gigs at further New York venues and in other major cities. Probably first important recordings by this band made for Pathé (**The Henderson Pathés**) during which time several important contributors to Hendersonia emerged, notably arranger-composer-saxist-clarinettist Don Redman (♦), trombonist Charlie Green, clarinettist-saxist Buster Bailey (♦), drummer Kaiser Marshall, and, most significant of all, saxist-clarinettist Coleman Hawkins (♦). These early recordings more important for the respective solo contributions rather than the sometimes pedestrian arrangements and sloppy ensemble playing. First real significant solos, however, were provided by Louis Armstrong (♦), who worked with Henderson for around 14 months (1924–5). Armstrong's electrifying playing on such titles as **Go 'Long Mule, Shanghai Shuffle, Copenhagen, Everybody Loves My Baby, How Come You Do Me Like You Do?, Sugarfoot Stomp** and **T.N.T.** (**The Fletcher Henderson Story/The Fletcher Henderson Story, Vol 1**); and **Tell Me Dreamy, My Rose Marie** and **Twelfth Street Blues** (**The Henderson Pathés**) tend to relegate rest of his surroundings to another league. Redman was responsible for many of the earliest arrangements – certainly the better ones. (Difference between the wellnigh aridity of earlier efforts like **Dicty Blues** and a later score like that for **Dippermouth Blues** is interesting and marked.)

Fletcher Henderson did not come into his own in this area until 1933–4, and even then he was wise enough to invest in arranging talents of others, most notably Benny Carter (♦), and his own younger brother Horace Henderson (♦). Both latter produced superior charts for band. Henderson also used stock arrangements, **Singin' The Blues, My Gal Sal** (**The Fletcher Henderson Story/The Fletcher Henderson Story, Vol 3**). Amongst Fletcher Henderson's own most memorable arrangements were **Blue Moments, Sing You Sinners, Moten Stomp, Can You Take It** (**The Fletcher Henderson Story/The Fletcher Henderson Story, Vol 4**); **Shanghai Shuffle** (**First Impressions 1924-1931**); **Down South Camp Meetin', Wrappin' It Up, Hotter Than 'Ell** (**Swing's The Thing 1931-1934**).

1935: Henderson had no band at all. Accepted an offer to become chief arranger for up-and-coming Benny Goodman Orchestra. (There is illuminating chapter on Fletcher Henderson and his early big-band associate Don Redman in Richard Hadlock's book *Jazz of the 20's*. And for comprehensive fact-documentation on Henderson, his bands, sidemen, etc, one need go no further than Walter C. Allen's *Hendersonia: The Music Of Fletcher Henderson & His Musicians*, a bio-discography of monumental proportions).

The Goodman-Henderson association was mutually profitable and for Henderson it meant that, in 1936, he was able to re-start own orchestra that contained exceptional musicians of calibre of Chu Berry (♦), Big Sid Catlett (♦), Hilton Jefferson (♦), Eddie Barefield, and two former alumni, Buster Bailey and John Kirby (♦). Rejuvenated band got off to fine start with hit record (**Christopher Columbus** – its first disc) but it could not follow through.

Finally, in mid-1939, Henderson gave up again, to rejoin Goodman. Perhaps surprisingly, Goodman also made Henderson band pianist, in place of far superior Jess Stacy (♦), as well as with various small groups (taking over from departed Teddy Wilson (♦)). This situation lasted only until March 1940, when Johnny Guarnieri (♦) took his place; (Henderson had been given tough time by many critics for his keyboard inadequacies with Goodman. As arranger, composer, he was to stay until following January when he left again, to form another big band.

For Goodman, he had helped immeasurably in making clarinettist King of Swing and his band immensely popular, supplying superior charts to such items as **Remember, Three Little Words, When Buddha Smiles, Honeysuckle Rose** (**The Big Band Sound Of Benny Goodman**); **Down South Camp Meetin', Sugarfoot Stomp, Bugle Call Rag, Sometimes I'm Happy, Blue Skies, King Porter Stomp** (**The Complete Benny Goodman, Vols 1-3/Benny Goodman, Vol 5 1935-1938**); **Changes, Wrappin' It Up, Please Be Kind, Get Happy** and **I Can't Give You Anything But Love** (**The Complete Benny Goodman, Vols 1-3/Benny Goodman, Vol 6 (1935-1938): The Fletcher Henderson Arrangements**). Arrangements which, for Henderson's own bands, never gained for him any King-of-Swing type of accolade but which, to be fair to Goodman & Co, were played by latter with more collective skill and, at times, a fair degree of excitement. (More interesting background on Goodman-Henderson relationship to be found in *The Kingdom of Swing*, by Benny Goodman, Irving Kolodin.)

With Goodman's blessing, Henderson tried again (in 1941) to lead own band. But things never really worked out. Although this and subsequent line-ups included, between 1941-5, many promising instrumentalists – amongst these were Art Blakey (♦), Dexter Gordon (♦), Sahib Shihab, Vic Dickenson (♦) and Emmett Berry (♦) – Henderson never was able to revive the magic of earlier times.

During 1947: back again as staff arranger with Goodman. Between 1948-49, was re-united with Ethel Waters, with whom he toured. Together with pianist-composer J. C. Johnson, wrote revue called *Jazz Train*, assembling special band for the show at Bop City, NYC. Fronted sextet at Cafe Society Downtown, including Lucky Thompson (♦) and Jimmy Crawford (♦); engagement cut short in December, '50 when Henderson suffered stroke. Special radio show involving original Goodman Trio and guests like Buck Clayton (♦), Johnny Smith and Lou McGarity. Results released on record (**Benny Goodman Trio For The Fletcher Henderson Fund**), proceeds going to ailing musician.

Heart attack, followed by another (in '52) was too much, and in December 1952 Fletcher Henderson died in Harlem Hospital. Following re-union by Fletcher Henderson All Stars in 1957 Great South Bay Jazz Festival, Long Island, New York, participants (including past Henderson sidesmen like Rex Stewart (♦), Benny Morton (♦), J. C. Higginbotham (♦), Buster Bailey, Dicky Wells (♦), and Coleman Hawkins) recorded for Jazztone (**The Big Reunion**) using original charts of some of the most famous numbers. And unlike many such reunions, music produced by this illustrious line-up was exceptional; something which, although it came too late for him to appreciate during his lifetime, undoubtedly would have pleased Fletcher Henderson immensely.

During his career Henderson also contributed arrangements to bands of Count Basie (♦), Casa Loma Orchestra, Teddy Hill, Jack Hylton, Isham Jones, Dorsey Bros., and Will Bradley.

Recordings:
Ethel Waters, Oh Daddy! *(Biograph/—)*
Ethel Waters, Jazzin' Babies' Blues *(Biograph/—)*
Bessie Smith, Nobody's Blues But Mine *(Columbia/CBS)*
Bessie Smith, The World's Greatest Blues Singer *(Columbia/CBS)*
Trixie Smith *(Collector's Classics)*
Ma Rainey, Ma Rainey *(Milestone)*
Fletcher Henderson, The Henderson Pathés - Fletcher Henderson & His Orchestra (1923-1925) *(—/Fountain)*
The Fletcher Henderson Story *(Columbia)/*
The Fletcher Henderson Story, Vols 1-4 *(CBS)*
Fletcher Henderson, First Impressions (1924-1931) *(—/MCA – Germany)*
Fletcher Henderson, Swing's The Thing *(Decca/MCA – Germany)*
Fletcher Henderson Orchestra 1923-1927 *(Riverside)*
The Complete Fletcher Henderson *(RCA Victor)/*
Fletcher Henderson, Vols 1-3 *(RCA Victor – France)*
Fletcher Henderson & His Orchestra, Vols 1, 2 *(Collector's Classics)*
Various (Including Fletcher Henderson), The Big Bands *(Prestige)/*
Ridin' In Rhythm *(World Records)*
Benny Goodman, Vols 5, 6 (1935-1938): The Fletcher Henderson Arrangements *(RCA Victor – France)*
The Big Band Sound Of Benny Goodman *(—/Verve)*
Various, 1938 Carnegie Hall Jazz Concert *(Columbia/CBS)*
Benny Goodman Trio For The Fletcher Henderson Fund *(Columbia/Fontana)*
Fletcher Henderson All Stars, The Big Reunion *(Jazztone/—)*
Rex Stewart/Henderson All Stars, Henderson Homecoming *(United Artists)*

Horace Henderson

Horace Henderson (born Cuthbert, Georgia, 1904) too often during his career had to take a backseat to elder brother Fletcher Henderson (♦), which was unfortunate, in many ways. For one thing, Horace Henderson, although never in the front rank of jazz keyboard performers, was a far better soloist than Fletcher, and some of Horace Henderson's writing was as good as his brother's, sometimes even better.

After piano tuition, starting at 14, and education at Atlanta University, Henderson spent three years at Wilberforce College, where he gained AB degree. Formed own student band there which, apart from initial off-campus engagements, commenced regular club appearances, plus tours.

As the Dixie Stompers it continued these activities between 1928–9 apart from break (late-1928) when its leader left to work for short period with another band. Put together own band again, in 1929, for New York dates for next two years. Brief list of students who worked with Henderson-led outfits (including the Collegians) during this period includes: Benny Carter (♦), Rex Stewart (♦), Freddie Jenkins, Bill Beason, Tiny Bradshaw (♦), Shelton Hemphill, Roy Eldridge (♦), and Sandy Williams. Sometimes bands used name of Fletcher Henderson (eg Fletcher Henderson's Stompers).

In 1931 Horace Henderson handed over leadership to Don Redman (♦), although Henderson continued to work with Redman until 1933. With brother's orchestra for one-and-a-half years (1933–4), before putting together another band. 1936: back with Fletcher. Next year, it was back with yet another of his own bands, a situation which lasted until 1938. 1939: another Horace Henderson big-band venture, utilizing personnel of Nat Towles Orchestra.

Served in US Army for just under a year (1942–3), then back again with Fletcher Henderson. 1944: became accompanist for Lena Horne, before forming another band, in 1945. Cut down to small-combo size in 1949; continued to lead various aggregations during 1950s.

Following decade found Horace Henderson based primarily in Denver. During his career, Henderson has penned a host of arrangements for other bandleaders. For Fletcher Henderson, these included **Hot & Anxious, Comin' & Goin'** (**The Fletcher Henderson Story/The Fletcher Henderson Story, Vol 3**); **Yeah Man!, Queer Notions, Christopher Columbus, Blue Lou, Chris & His Gang** (**The Fletcher Henderson Story/The Fletcher Henderson Story, Vol 4**). For Benny Goodman too provided fine charts, like those for **Japanese Sandman** (**Benny Goodman, Vol 4**); **Dear Old Southland, I've Found A New Baby, Walk, Jennie, Walk** (**Benny Goodman, Vol 7**). Horace Henderson's superb **Big John's Special** (**Benny Goodman, Vol 5**) was favorite item in the Goodman book, although this was arranged for Goodman by Fletcher Henderson. For Charlie Barnet (♦), Horace Henderson scored **Charleston Alley** (**Charlie Barnet, Vol 1**) and **Little John Ordinary**. Also contributed to repertoire of Don Redman Orchestra (**Don Redman**) with particularly first-rate arrangement for **Hot & Anxious**. He produced one of his best piano solos for Redman, on **Nagasaki**.

His abilities as band pianist are heard to good advantage with Chocolate Dandies **(The Chocolate Dandies)** as well as with own orchestras **(Horace Henderson 1940** and **The Big Bands/Ridin' In Rhythm)**. Henderson, who also worked as accompanist for Billie Holiday (♦), wrote for bands of Tommy Dorsey (♦), Jimmie Lunceford (♦), Earl Hines (♦), and the Casa Loma Orchestra.

Recordings:
The Fletcher Henderson Story
  (Columbia)/
  The Fletcher Henderson Story, Vols 3, 4 (CBS)
Coleman Hawkins, Recordings Made Between 1930 & 1941
  (CBS – France)
Various (Including Horace Henderson), The Big Bands
  (Prestige)/
  Ridin' In Rhythm
  (World Records)
The Chocolate Dandies
  (—/Parlophone)
Benny Goodman, Vols 4, 7
  (RCA Victor – France)
Don Redman (—/CBS – Realm)
Charlie Barnet, Vol 1
  (RCA Victor/RCA Victor)
Horace Henderson 1940
  (Tax – Sweden)

Joe Henderson

Born in Ohio in 1937, tenorman Joe Henderson got his musical schooling in Detroit. His earliest influences were the Jazz at the Phil albums and R&B, but the Coltrane-Rollins dominance of the tenor shaped his approach. He seemed to turn up as a sideman on scores of Blue Note sessions in the '60s, always reliable, trenchant. Like many professionals in his age group, he has incorporated the newer approaches – modes, free playing – into a basically Bebop

Above: Joe Henderson, driving tenorman, recently ploughing a profitable furrow in the easy-listening field.

outlook, and he is flexible enough to accommodate the difficult challenge of Andrew Hill's music **Refuge (Point Of Departure)** or the basic bluesiness of Lee Morgan's **Sidewinder (Sidewinder)**. His collaboration with trumpeter Kenny Dorham, particularly in the field of Latin rhythms – **Blue Bossa, Recorda-Me (Page One); Trompeta Toccata, Mamacita (Trompeta Toccata)** – produced a series of workmanlike albums **(In 'N' Out, Our Thing** and **Una Mas)**.

The contract with Milestone, too, has produced solid work. An exciting, beefy player, his mannerisms include a furious, circular stirring that can sound repetitive or mesmerizing depending on

Joe Henderson In Japan (Milestone): a Japanese rhythm section spurs Henderson on to the heights. Coverwork Katsuji Abe.

taste and context. One of his most successful exercises in controlled freedom occurs on **The Bead Game (Tetragon)** where momentum alone seems to advance the piece. Live performances usually bring out the best in Joe Henderson, and both albums cut at The Lighthouse Cafe in 1970 are excellent **(If You're Not Part Of The Solution, You're Part Of The Problem** and **In Pursuit Of Blackness)**. Using his regular group, he reworks old material like **A Shade Of Jade, Dorham's Blue Bossa**, jazz classics like Monk's **Round Midnight**, as well as free mood pieces like **Mind Over Matter**. An album cut in Tokyo the following year, using a Japanese rhythm section **(Joe Henderson In Japan)** catches him at his peak. Some of his most recent output has been in the funky, easy-listening bag **(Canyon Lady)** but on the evidence of his latest work **(Black Narcissus)** he still functions as a committed player.

Recordings:
Page One (Blue Note/Blue Note)
In 'N' Out (Blue Note/Blue Note)
Our Thing (Blue Note/Blue Note)
Mode For Joe
  (Blue Note/Blue Note)
Inner Urge (Blue Note/Blue Note)
Tetragon (Milestone/Milestone)
If You're Not Part Of The Solution (Milestone/Milestone)
In Pursuit Of Blackness
  (Milestone/Milestone)
Joe Henderson In Japan
  (Milestone/Milestone)
Power To The People
  (Milestone/Milestone)
Black Narcissus
  (Milestone/Milestone)

Ernie Henry

Born 1926, died 1958, altoman Ernie Henry played in eminent company. A member of Tadd Dameron's Septet, he took fine solos on **The Squirrel** and **Dameronia**, also recording with the Howard McGhee–Fats Navarro

Boptet, **Double Talk, Boperation, The Skunk (Prime Source)**. Henry was in Thelonious Monk's Quartet in 1956, and played one of his finest solos on the blowing vehicle, **Ba-Lue Bolivar Ba-Lues-Are (Brilliance)** in company with Sonny Rollins. After several years of scuffling in R&B bands, Henry cut a series of albums for Riverside, all of which are unobtainable, although his work with Kenny Dorham in 1957 – his last session – carries considerable emotional impact **(But Beautiful)**. Eric Dolphy may have been influenced by Henry's vocalized sound, which was very distinctive.

Recordings:
Fats Navarro, Prime Source
  (Blue Note/Blue Note)
Thelonious Monk, Brilliance
  (Milestone/Milestone)
Kenny Dorham, But Beautiful
  (Milestone/Milestone)
Presenting Ernie Henry
  (—/Victor – Japan)

Woody Herman

Bandleader Woody Herman was born Woodrow Wilson Herman in 1913, starting in vaudeville with his parents at the age of 9, where he was billed as 'Boy Wonder Of The Clarinet'. By 1936, he had taken over the Isham Jones Orchestra, **The Band That Plays The Blues (The Best Of Woody Herman)** and was featured extensively on clarinet and alto in arrangements that fluctuated between Dixieland and Swing. In 1939, the band recorded the million-selling **Woodchopper's Ball** and popularity was assured. The First Herd was recruited in 1944, a glittering array of outsize personalities like trombonist Bill Harris, tenorman Flip Phillips, drummer Dave Tough, trumpet prodigy Sonny Berman and arranger-pianist Ralph Burns. It was a band of enthusiasts, and it still sounds like it on record. The good-humored vocal on **Cale-**

Live At Basin Street West (Philips): late Herd in great voice.

donia capped by the wildly exciting trumpet unison, Phillips' booting solo on **The Good Earth,** Harris' idiosyncratic brilliance on **Bijou**, all remain classics of the period **(The Best Of Woody Herman, CBS)** while the sheer exuberance of the band on **Apple Honey, Wild Root** or **Your Father's Mustache** has seldom been equalled. With arrangements by Neal Hefti, Burns and Shorty Rogers, the First Herd scored a radio show sponsored by Wildroot Cream Oil, hosted by Wildroot Cream Oil Charlie, that took the sound into a million homes. Airshots capture the spontaneity of the band better than studio dates, and a recent trio of releases are worth hunting down (**The Great Herd 1946** and **Woody Herman - His Orchestra & The Woodchoppers, Vols 1 & 2**).

Personnel changes occurred before the band broke up in 1946, Don Lamond replaced Tough at the drums, Shorty Rogers replaced Hefti and vibraphonist Red Norvo replaced Marjorie Hyams. The Second Herd, despite pessimistic predictions, proved every bit as good. The sax section comprised Stan Getz, Zoot Sims, Herbie Steward and Serge Chaloff, three tenors and a baritone. Jimmy Giuffre scored the famous **Four Brothers** to spotlight the section, and the smooth, low, close-formation ensemble became a trademark: Bebop out of Lester Young (**The Best Of Woody Herman, CBS**). The Ralph Burns feature for Getz, **Early Autumn**, made the tenorman's cool lyricism famous overnight. Bebop began to show in the trumpet section with the arrival of Red Rodney, while Shorty Rogers wrote Bebop numbers like **Keeper Of The Flame** and **Lollypop**, the latter a follow-up to George Wallington's famous **Lemon Drop** (**Early Autumn**). Again, airshots are worth a listen (**Boiled In Earl**) particularly as the recording ban kept the Second Herd out of the studios for a year.

At the end of 1949, Herman disbanded the Herd, formed another, but due to the decline of the big band market, he was forced to follow a more conservative line. The Third Herd is a blurred category, covering a multitude of personnel changes, though the arrangements remained the province of Burns and Giuffre. 1959 saw the reassembly of many of the Herman stalwarts, Zoot Sims, Conte Candoli, Bill Perkins, Urbie Green, for the Monterey Jazz Festival. With Mel Lewis on drums, the band tears into **Four Brothers (Live At Monterey)** while **Monterey Apple Tree** is the classic **Apple Honey**. An album from 1963 (**Live At Basin Street West**) reveals a vigorous, hard-hitting band of young talent; high-note specialist, trumpeter Bill Chase, lifting the trumpet section for the exciting **Caldonia**, the fast, driving tenorman Sal Nistico on **El Toro Grande**, or trombonist Phil Wilson on **Body & Soul**. With Nat Pierce writing the arrangements, this version of the Herd was a fine mixture of tradition and innovation. An album from the late '60s (**Jazz Hoot**) showcases the flaring trumpet section of Bill Chase, Dusko Goykovitch, Don Rader, Bob Shew and Gerald Lamy, as well as belting solos by Nistico.

Woody Herman's own playing has remained consistently excellent over the decades, still indebted to Frank Trumbauer, The Glissando Kid, for his alto sound, and still apposite on the unfashionable clarinet. Currently, the Herd's sax section hews close to Coltrane, and the electric piano has appeared, but the identity of the band seems indestructible.

Above: Woody Herman, leader of countless Herds over 30-odd years. Almost anyone of note has played with Woody.

The Best Of Woody Herman (CBS): first and second Herds. Herman has had the pick of jazz's giants for three decades.

Recordings:
The Best Of Woody Herman
(MCA/MCA)
The Best Of Woody Herman
(Columbia/CBS Realm)
Early Autumn (Capitol)
The Great Herd, 1946
(Swing Treasury/Swing Treasury)
Woody Herman - His Orchestra & The Woodchoppers, Vols 1 & 2
(First Heard/First Heard)
Boiled In Earl (Swing Treasury/Swing Treasury)
Live At Monterey
(Atlantic/Atlantic)
Live At Basin Street West
(Phillips/Phillips)
Jazz Hoot (Columbia/CBS)
The Kings Of Swing, Vol 2
(Verve/Verve)

Eddie Heywood

Edward 'Eddie' Heywood, Jr (born Atlanta, Georgia, 1915) was taught basic piano lessons by his father, Eddie Heywood, Sr (well-known bandleader, pianist in 1920s, '30s). A neat, economic jazz player, with no pretensions to virtuosic or innovatory greatness, Heywood perhaps was more gifted as accompanist than as solo performer.

By 1929 was playing in local theatre orchestra. Joined Wayman Carver (♦), early-1930s; then, with Clarence Love (1934). To New York (with Love), in '37. Freelanced, mostly in Harlem, before joining Benny Carter (♦) Orchestra (1939–40). Briefly with Don Redman (♦). Took band into Village Vanguard (1941). Eddie Heywood Sextet played lengthy, popular residences at Cafe Society and Three Deuces (1943-4).

During this period he recorded, with Edmond Hall (♦) as leader, for Commodore (**Eddie Heywood**) with fine playing from all concerned (band also included Emmett Berry (♦), Vic Dickenson (♦), Big Sid Catlett (♦)), particularly on **Downtown Cafe Boogie**. Presence of Coleman Hawkins (♦), in top form, inspired Heywood into producing what might be his finest solos during a record date, which, like Hall's, took place in '43 (**Shelly Manne & Co** and **Classic Tenors**). Obvious influence of Teddy Wilson (♦) throughout sparkling piano solos at this session, most notably on **Crazy Rhythm** and, best of all, **Man I Love**. Recorded own sextet (including Adolphus 'Doc' Cheatham (♦), Vic Dickenson, Lem Davis) early-1944 (**Eddie Heywood**) including distinctive treatment of **Begin The Beguine** (with its repetitive left-hand vamp). Heywood's **Begin The Beguine** caused widespread reaction, ending up as pop hit of million-selling proportions.

Heywood's band provided sympathetic accompaniments for Billie Holiday (♦) at three separate record dates in March, April '44 (**Strange Fruit/The 'Commodore' Days**) with Heywood's piano standing out on all tracks, including trio take of **On The Sunny Side Of The Street**. (Heywood had accompanied Holiday during latter's legendary second residency at New York's Cafe Society in early-1940s).

Played to enthusiastic response on West Coast during mid-1940s (he and sextet appearing in two movies). 1947: after further, successful, appearances in California, suffered partial paralysis of both hands, resulting in retirement until 1950–1. Resumed playing with trio, a format he continued to use over subsequent years. 1956: Eddie Heywood again high in pop charts (accompanied by Hugo Winterhalter Orchestra) with styling of composition, **Canadian Sunset**, similar to **Begin The Beguine**. Most of Heywood's recordings from 1950s and thereafter were of minimal jazz content (and therefore not of interest to jazz fans).

Recordings:
Eddie Heywood, Begin The Beguine (*Mainstream/Fontana*)
Shelly Manne & Co (*Flying Dutchman/—*)
Various (Including Cole Hawkins), Classic Tenors (*Contact/Philips International*)
Billie Holiday, Strange Fruit (*Atlantic*)/
The 'Commodore' Days (*Ace of Hearts*)

J. C. Higginbotham

The colorful career of J. C. Higginbotham (born Social Circle, nr Atlanta, Georgia, 1906) lasted from 1920 until the 1972 Newport Jazz Festival – his last major appearance. It was a career during which Higginbotham had played his own brand of gutsy, stomping trombone in all manner of jazz settings, large and small, and in company with acknowledged jazz giants such as Louis Armstrong (♦), Luis Russell (♦), Fletcher Henderson (♦), Benny Carter, Coleman Hawkins (♦), Red Allen (♦), and Sidney Bechet (♦).

First instrument was bugle, which he never used again after a sister had bought him trombone. After work with local bands, moved to

Cincinnati, Ohio, where he learned tailoring, then became motor mechanic. Back to music, in 1924, with Wes Helvey. Between 1924–8, led own band and worked in others before sitting in bands of Chick Webb (♦), Willie Lynch. Joined Luis Russell Orchestra (1928), staying four years.

It was with Russell that Higginbotham's huge sound and generally extrovert style made him one of leading trombone players in jazz. With Russell, he roared out solos on items like **Jersey Lightning** and **Doctor Blues** (both **Luis Russell & His Louisiana Swing Orchestra/The Luis Russell Story**). When Louis Armstrong used Russell orchestra as backing unit, Armstrong-influenced Higginbotham received opportunities to solo (excellently) on **Bessie Couldn't Help It, Mahogany Hall Stomp** and **St Louis Blues** (all **V.S.O.P., Very Special Old Phonography, 1928-1930, Vols 5 & 6**). With another great trumpeter, Red Allen, Higginbotham had long and happy associations. Both were major soloists in same Russell bands, and Higginbotham turned up, on record, in various Allen-led bands; for example, in 1929–30 (**Henry 'Red' Allen, Vols 1-3**); in 1935 (**Henry Allen & His Orchestra 1934-1935**); in 1946 (**Henry 'Red' Allen, Vol 4**); and in 1957 (**The Very Great Henry Red Allen, Vol 2**).

After working briefly – on two occasions – with Chick Webb (♦), joined Fletcher Henderson (1932), for one-and-a-half year period, getting chance to solo on **Underneath The Harlem Moon, Honeysuckle Rose, King Porter Stomp** (**The Fletcher Henderson Story/The Fletcher Henderson Story, Vol 4**). Then he worked with Benny Carter, and around the same time recorded with Coleman Hawkins (♦) (**Jazz Pioneers, 1933-36/Ridin' In Rhythm**). With Mills Blue Rhythm Band (1934–6) and after short spell once again with Henderson, became member of Louis Armstrong big-band (1937-40).

Because Armstrong admired his playing, was given solo space (viz **On The Sunny Side Of The Street, I Double Dare You, Let That Be A Lesson To You** (**Complete Recorded Works 1935-1945**)). Whilst with Armstrong, recorded with Lil Armstrong (**Harlem On Saturday Night**) and James P. Johnson (♦) (**Swing Combos 1935-1941**). Co-led sextet with Red Allen, from December 1940, start of an association which would continue through 1940s.

Worked mainly in Boston during late-1950s; spent long period in New York. Took part in Fletcher Henderson Reunion Band (1957) (**The Big Reunion**), visited Europe (1958). Active less frequently in 1960s, although sounded in splendid shape during 1961 (**Jam Session At Swingville**) with Hawkins, Hilton Jefferson (♦), Joe Newman, etc. Worked many times with trumpeter Joe Thomas during this period. Twice – in 1962, 1965 – played, recorded in Denmark. In hospital for several months in '71. Then came his final important engagement – at Newport Jazz Festival following year.

During his long involvement with jazz, this most exciting of trombonists also recorded with King Oliver (♦) (**King Oliver's Dixie Syncopators 1926-1928**); the

The Chocolate Dandies 1928-33. (EMI). Featuring J.C.

Chocolate Dandies (**The Chocolate Dandies**); trumpeter Jack Purvis (**Recordings Made Between 1930 & 1941**) and a late-1950s all-star band nominally led by Ellingtonians Cootie Williams (♦) and Rex Stewart (♦) (**The Big Challenge**). Because of his all-round versatility in either organized or impromptu jam-session situations, it is no surprise that Lionel Hampton (♦) called upon his services in 1939 (**The Complete Lionel Hampton/Lionel Hampton's Best Records, Vol 2**).

Recordings:
King Oliver's Dixie Syncopators (*MCA Coral – Germany*)
Luis Russell & His Louisiana Swing Orchestra (*Columbia/—*)
The Luis Russell Story (*—/Parlophone*)
The Chocolate Dandies (*Parlophone*)
Louis Armstrong, V.S.O.P. (Very Special Old Phonography, 1928-1930), Vols 5 & 6 (*CBS – France*)
Henry 'Red' Allen, Vols 1-4 (*RCA Victor – France*)
Various (Including Jack Purvis), Recordings Made Between 1930 & 1941 (*CBS – France*)

The Fletcher Henderson Story (*Columbia*)/
The Fletcher Henderson Story, Vol 4 (*CBS*)
Various (Including Coleman Hawkins), Jazz Pioneers, 1933-36 (*Prestige*)/
Ridin' In Rhythm (*World Records*)
Louis Armstrong, Complete Recorded Works 1935-1945 (*MCA – France*)
Henry Allen & His Orchestra 1934-1935 (*Collector's Classics – Denmark*)
Various (Including Lil Armstrong), Harlem On Saturday Night (*Ace of Hearts*)
Various (Including James P. Johnson), Swing Combos 1935-1941 (*Swingfan – Germany*)
The Very Great Henry 'Red' Allen, Vol 2 (*Rarities – Denmark*)
Fletcher Henderson Reunion Band, The Big Reunion (*Jazztone/—*)
Cootie Williams/Rex Stewart, The Big Challenge (*Jazztone/Concert Hall*)
Various, Jam Session At Swingville (*Prestige/Prestige*)

Andrew Hill

Pianist Andrew Hill was born in Haiti in 1936, and brought up in Chicago. His early influences were Tatum, Monk and Powell, and his interests remain within the harmonic framework despite the avant-garde label. As a result of his work as a sideman on Joe Henderson's **Our Thing** album, he landed a contract with Blue Note during the heady days of that label's patronage of experiment. Andrew Hill's work as composer and pianist remains the most natural-sounding of the sometimes

Below: pianist-composer Andrew Hill whose highly-original Blue Note albums place him near the summit.

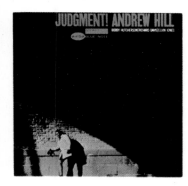

Judgment (Blue Note): ominous covershot by Francis Wolff.

self-conscious Blue Note school, which included Herbie Hancock, Anthony Williams and Bobby Hutcherson, and he is the only one to have stayed the course.

His debut album **Black Fire** displayed a mobile concept of trio, with Roy Haynes and bassist Richard Davis – an habitual collaborator – tugging the rhythms this way and that. Intense music, oblique, the leader's piano characterized by unusual intervals and a percussive drive that cloaks the lyricism of **Subterfuge** with sinew. Adding vibraphonist Bobby Hutcherson, Hill's next album **(Judgement)** was again an object lesson in combining freedom and discipline. The interaction over the basic vamp figure on **Siete Ocho** is fascinating, and the scurrying yet powerful piano on **Yokada Yokada** gives an idea of Hill's originality. With the great album **(Point Of Departure)** he gave notice of his arrival in the front

rank, deploying the talents of trumpeter Kenny Dorham, multi-instrumentalist Eric Dolphy and tenorman Joe Henderson like a master of colour and texture. The compositions, again originals, revolve around tonal centres, and seem to have been written for these specific sidemen. **Dedication,** a slow and beautiful piece, is a haunting choreography of stately movements. Using an expanded rhythm section, drums, African drums, conga, the pianist-composer recorded a work in four movements **(Compulsion)** to express 'the legacy of the Negro tradition'. From the opening – the dark, threshing drums, the jab of the horns, the rumbling, percussive piano and bass – the sheer power of Hill's conception is overwhelming. The consistency of his output **(Andrew!** and **One For One)** makes Blue Note's shelving of this artist a tragedy. After a three-year hiatus in his recording career, he again reappeared with a trio for Steeplechase **(Invitation)** and also cut an album of quintets, quartets and a duo with Lee Konitz **(Spiral)** which proved that he has lost none of his brilliance.

Recordings:
Black Fire *(Blue Note/Blue Note)*
Judgement *(Blue Note/Blue Note)*
Point Of Departure
 (Blue Note/Blue Note)
Compulsion
 (Blue Note/Blue Note)
Andrew! *(Blue Note/Blue Note)*
One For One
 (Blue Note/Blue Note)
Invitation
 (Steeplechase/Steeplechase)
Spiral *(Freedom/Freedom)*

Earl Hines

Although the mortality rate amongst jazz musicians is unnaturally high, there are some who seem to have found the elixir of life, and have a sense of indestructibility that is not always easy to explain. Some too, like Earl Kenneth 'Fatha' Hines (born Duquesne, District of Pittsburgh, Pennsylvania, 1905), not only are indestructible physically, but their musical talents remain completely untouched and undimmed, by the passing of the years. And when the talent is as out-of-the-ordinary as Hines', one should be grateful for any longevity of life.

Hines has been seminal figure amongst jazz keyboard players for over 50 years – fashions and new styles come and go, but Hines continues to reproduce technically astonishing performances of great rhythmic, harmonic and improvizational strengths which few, if any, can match, even today. It is simply untrue that every jazzman gets better with passing of the years especially when he reaches the age of 60 and over, yet Hines continues to convince even the stoutest disbeliever that his playing these days is at least as good as at any time during his lengthy career, sometimes unquestionably better than in previous years. Indeed, Hines, in his 70's, is as dexterous, as technically dazzling, as 99 per cent of all other living pianists, most of whom must be half his age; and his rhythmic powers are second to none.

Earl Hines comes from musical family: father played cornet in brass bands, sister was pianist-bandleader during 1930s. Started on cornet, but quickly switched to piano, commencing with lessons and studies at nine. Majored in music at Schenley High School.

First professional jobs with singer Lois B. Deppe. After undertaking first job as leader of own band, worked with Carroll Dickerson, Erskine Tate, and others. In 1927: worked as member of Louis Armstrong's (♦) band at Chicago's Sunset Cafe: during same year, Armstrong, Hines and Zutty Singleton (♦) ran own Chicago club, but venture did not last long. Late in '27, joined forces with Jimmie Noone (♦), their five- or six-piece (trumpetless) band producing some of the finest small-group jazz to be heard in the Windy City (at Apex Club, to be precise), or indeed anywhere, at that time. Titles like **Apex Blues, Sweet Lorraine, I Know That You Know** and **My Monday Date** (one of Hines' most popular compositions) derive from the Apex Club engagement, especially the recordings of same **(Jimmie Noone & Earl Hines At The Apex Club, Vol 1: 1928).** By which time, it had become blatantly obvious to musicians and fans alike that Earl Hines was in the process of taking story of jazz piano-playing several steps forward, adding extra dimensions even to the pioneering contributions from the likes of Fats Waller (♦), Willie 'The Lion' Smith (♦) and James P. Johnson (♦).

Hines' so-called 'trumpet style' had evolved from his deep admira-

Once Upon A Time (Impulse). The inimitable Earl Hines makes fine music, with Hodges, Pee Wee, Gonsalves & Co.

tion for the instrumental genius of Louis Armstrong. Hines even managed to recapture the essence of the Armstrong vibrato in his playing: his right-hand use of octaves and tremolo effects, his freeing of the left hand from a more or less obligatory heavy chording and use of unrelieved bass patterns by Waller-Smith-Johnson school, and his startling single-note right-hand attack, together made him jazz's most outstanding technician and most important keyboard innovator of 1920s. His trumpet style was never more admirably showcased than in tandem with Armstrong for the first time. **Weather Bird (The Louis Armstrong Legend)** moved forward creative processes of jazz about a decade when it was first issued, in 1929.

Hines' first recorded solos **(Earl 'Fatha' Hines)** confirm he was, without a doubt, jazz's first virtuoso of keyboard. His playing on tracks like **Caution Blues, My Monday Date** and the appropriately-titled **Fifty-Seven Varieties** shows an overall conception that had been barely hinted at by other jazz pianists of the decade, each solo containing myriad ideas that sound as fresh today as when first committed to disc.

Hines' first recorded solos **(Earl 'Fatha' Hines)** confirm he was, without spot said to have been part-owned by Capone) at tail-end of '28. During succeeding decade, Hines and band played so many regular engage-

Above: Earl 'Fatha' Hines – first of the great keyboard virtuosi. After half a century, still a jazz marvel.

ments at Grand Terrace that his became known as Grand Terrace Band. Recordings by same from 1930s, apart from further showcasing the sustained brilliance of its leader's playing, were models of consistency, both in solos as well as in ensemble playing. Hines apart, solo department was catered for by reliable musicians like clarinettists Omer Simeon (♦), Darnell Howard (♦); trombonists Trummy Young, John Ewing, Ed Burke; trumpeters Walter Fuller, Edward Sims, George Dixon; and saxophonists Jimmy Mundy, Budd Johnson (both regular and excellent contributors to band's book), Robert Crowder. (Both clarinettists doubled – Howard on violin and sax; Simeon on alto.)

Rhythm was strong point of various Grand Terrace bands, and it never sounded more dynamic than when Alvin Burroughs, drums, joined from Horace Henderson's orchestra. Although Hines disbanded, temporarily, at beginning of 1940, he had re-formed by end of same year.

Band led by Hines 1942–3 is of historic importance – although it was never to record, due to prolonged musicians' union ban. At various times this band contained Charlie Parker (♦) (playing tenor-, not alto-sax); Jerry Valentine, arranger, trombone; trumpeters Freddie Webster, Shorts McConnell, and Bennie Harris; trombonist Bennie Green; and singers Sarah Vaughan (♦) and Billy Eckstine (♦); soon all to become important contributors to burgeoning Bebop revolution. Only the rear portion of Hines' association with bop and some of its protagonists was documented, via gramophone records, and then its total output was minimal; two Extended-play discs (**Earl Hines Orchestra (1)** and **Earl Hines Orchestra (2)**), give something less than thorough examples. On these records, Green was still member of the trombones, and tenorist Wardell Gray (♦) is to be heard taking several typically first-class solos.

Hines disbanded, finally, in 1947 and, once again, became Chicago club-owner. But by beginning of following year he was once more on the road (and in the recording studios), this time as member of Louis Armstrong's All Stars (**Louis Armstrong, Vols 2, 3** and **Satchmo At Symphony Hall, Vols 1, 2**), a situation which lasted until 1951, when Hines put together own sextet.

Long residency at Hangover Club, San Francisco, with quartet, starting fall of '55. 1957: to Europe, as member of Jack Teagarden – Earl Hines All Stars, although during 1950s, for some inexplicable reason, Hines' playing went out of fashion, and he fell into totally unwarranted neglect.

Situation changed dramatically early-1960s. Suddenly, he was back in favor with a vengeance. Appeared at special concerts, to rapturous applause from critics and public alike. And, whereas his recorded output during previous decade had been less than prolific, new recording projects came thick and fast. What is more, the standard of performance to be found on the newer recordings was infinitely superior to those from the 1950s. Perhaps a major reason for their superiority has been a tendency often to record Hines as solo artist. And like his once greatest rival (and friend) Art Tatum (♦), Hines invariably is at his magical best when performing alone. Probably first of these exceptional albums to appear was that which Hines made for Contact (**Earl Hines At Home**) in 1964, with pianist's dazzling technique sounding at least as superb as in his younger days. Further solo albums of similar brilliance have included **Hines '65, Tea For Two, Earl Hines At Home, Hines Does Hoagy, Dinah, Tour De Force** and **Earl Hines Plays Duke Ellington,** each containing substantial quantities of awesome piano-playing.

Just how tremendous Hines remains as live performer can be gauged by the keyboard pyrotechnics he produced throughout his appearance, unaccompanied, at the 1974 Montreux Jazz Festival (**West Side Story**) nowhere better illustrated than during a torrid **Why Do I Love You?** And if comparisons need to be made, Hines' reworkings of old favorites such as **Down Among The Sheltering Palms, Love Me Tonight** and

Deep Forest (his old Grand Terrace theme) (**Quintessential Continued**) recorded in early-1970s, tend to overshadow even the classic original versions (**Earl 'Fatha' Hines**).

Apart from a tiresome gimmick of sustaining a right-hand tremolo for four or five minutes during concert performances, as with **Don't Get Around Much Anymore (West Side Story)**, Fatha Hines still is the greatest living jazz pianist and possibly, overall, the greatest pianist in the entire history of jazz.

Recordings:
Louis Armstrong, The Louis Armstrong Legend (World Records)
Louis Armstrong, V.S.O.P. (Very Special Old Phonography, 1928-1930), Vols 5 & 6 (CBS – France)
Louis Armstrong/Earl Hines, Armstrong & Hines (Smithsonian Collection/—)
Jimmie Noone & Earl Hines At The Apex Club, Vol 1 (1928) (MCA – Germany)
Earl 'Fatha' Hines (Columbia/Philips)
The Young Earl Hines (RCA Victor – France)
The Indispensable Earl Hines, Vols 1-3 (RCA Victor – France)
Hines Rhythm (Epic/—)
South Side Swing (Decca)/**Swinging In Chicago** (Coral)
Earl Hines, Fire Works (RCA Victor – France)
Earl Hines, RCA Masters (RCA Victor – France)
Earl Hines Orchestra (1) (Vogue) (EP)
Earl Hines Orchestra (2) (Vogue) (EP)
Louis Armstrong, Vols 2, 3 (RCA Victor – France)
Louis Armstrong, Satchmo At Symphony Hall (Decca/Coral)
The Father Jumps: Earl Hines & His Orchestra Featuring Billy Eckstine (1940-1942) (Bandstand)
Earl Hines, Fatha Blows Best (Decca/—)
Earl Hines/Johnny Hodges, Stride Right (Verve/Verve)
Earl Hines/Jimmy Rushing (Master Jazz Recordings/World Record Club)
Earl Hines, Spontaneous Explorations (Contact/Stateside)
Earl Hines, Once Upon A Time (Impulse/Impulse)
Earl Hines, A Monday Date: 1928 (Milestone)
Earl Hines, Quintessential Recording Sessions (Chiaroscuro/—)
Earl Hines, Quintessential Continued (Chiaroscuro/—)
Earl Hines, Hines '65 (Master Jazz Recordings/World Record Club)
Earl Hines At Home (Delmark)
Earl Hines, Hines Does Hoagy (Audiophile/—)
Earl Hines, Tea For Two (Black Lion/Black Lion)
Earl Hines Plays Duke Ellington (Master Jazz Recordings/Parlophone)
Earl Hines, West Side Story (Black Lion/Black Lion)
Earl Hines, Dinah (RCA Victor – France)
Earl Hines Plays George Gershwin (Festival – France)
Earl Hines/Maxine Sullivan, Live At The Overseas Press Club (Chiaroscuro/—)
Earl Hines, My Tribute To Louis (Audiophile/—)
The Incomparable Earl Hines (Fantasy/—)
Earl Hines/Budd Johnson, The Dirty Old Men (Black & White – France)
Earl Hines, Hits He Missed (Real Time/—)

Milt Hinton
♦ Cab Calloway

Art Hodes

Chicagoan pianist Art Hodes was a member of 'The White School' who remained faithful to the tenets of New Orleans, playing an exuberant brand of Dixieland music well into the 1940s. Influenced by Jelly Roll Morton, Hodes plays fine blues piano, though his most typical work is to be found away from the solo spotlight as a group player. Along with trumpeter Max Kaminsky, and various personnel, Rod Cless, Mezz Mezzrow, Vic Dickenson, Edmond Hall, Omer Simeon and Danny Alvin, Hodes led several excellent sessions for Blue Note between 1944 and 1945.

Recordings:
Original Blue Note Jazz, Vol 1 (Blue Note/Blue Note)
The Funky Piano Of Art Hodes (Blue Note/Blue Note)
Sittin' In (Blue Note/Blue Note)
Sidney Bechet (Blue Note/Blue Note)

Above: Milt Hinton, widely-respected bassist.

The Funky Piano Of Art Hodes (Blue Note).

Johnny Hodges

One of jazz's greatest solo instrumentalists, and without question one of the three most important alto-saxophonists in the history of the music, John Cornelius 'Rabbit' Hodges (born Cambridge, Massachusetts, 1906) was a supreme individualist whose playing (especially his vibrato) was reminiscent only of Sidney Bechet (♦), his sole admitted influence. (Not surpris-

ingly, Hodges' involvement with the soprano-sax, an instrument he played for some time during the 1930s, was an even more perfect corollary to Bechet.)

In all probability, Hodges was greatest of the many extraordinarily gifted soloists to grace the ranks of the Duke Ellington (♦) Orchestra. Although he had played with several different bands prior to his inception into Ellingtonia, including shortish spells with Willie 'The Lion' Smith (♦), Chick Webb (♦), and Luckey Roberts, it was not until Hodges joined Ellington, in May 1928, that he found the most idyllic setting for possibly the most ravishing saxophone tone to be heard thus far in the jazz world.

Hodges, who had studied for a time with his idol, Bechet, (he is also reported to have actually played live dates with Bechet, in 1925) contributed an unbelievably large number of classic alto-sax solos to the Ellington discography. His matchless tone, together with powerful yet always subtle approach to the rhythmic aspect of his art, and a passionate though never histrionic way of conveying emotion, soon established him as the major voice on his premier instrument. A situation which lasted until the emergence of the genius

*West Side Story
(Black Lion).*

of Charlie Parker (♦) at beginning of 1940s, and despite periodic challenges from Benny Carter (♦), Pete Brown (♦), and Willie Smith (♦).

It would be true to say that during the last period of his association with Ellington, 1955–70, Hodges often affected a seemingly total disinterest in his solos during concert performances; and his recordings with band during this period tended to range from absolutely brilliant (**The Far East Suite, Duke Ellington's 70th Birthday Concert** and **... And His Mother Called Him Bill**) to the merely average. In many cases, best work Hodges recorded during latter part of his career took place within context of the kind of small-group settings that had further helped him sustain his reputation during late-1930s/early-1940s (**Hodge Podge** and **The Works Of Duke, Vols 12, 16/17**). These later recordings (**Ellingtonia '56, Duke's In Bed/Johnny Hodges & The Ellington All Stars** and **Everybody Knows Johnny Hodges**) are admirably representative of the kind of invariably satisfying, unpretentious, always swinging record dates which, not at all surprising, usually involved fellow members of the then contemporary Ellington orchestra.

Elsewhere on record, Hodges' mellifluous, persuasive alto was an obvious major asset. Whatever the company, Hodges – like all truly great performers – inevitably stood out. Thus he contributed handsomely to sessions involving Billie Holiday (♦) (**The Golden Years, Vol 2** and **The Original Recordings**); Teddy Wilson (♦) (**The Teddy Wilson** and **Teddy Wilson & His All Stars**); Earl Hines (♦) (**Stride Right**); Shelly Manne (♦) (**Shelly Manne & Co.**) and Gerry Mulligan (♦) (**Gerry Mulligan Meets The Sax Giants, Vols 1-3**). Of even more importance – and achieving even greater artistic and musical success – was a rare session with Billy Strayhorn (♦) as leader (**Cue For Saxophone**). Although, for contractual reasons, Hodges masqueraded under pseudonym of 'Cue Porter', there was no chance of mistaking his glorious sound which dominated entire musical proceedings. Of special interest to aficionados of the alto-saxophone was a highly memorable record session (**The Charlie Parker Sides/The Parker Jam Session**) wherein Hodges locked altos with his two major rivals, Parker and Carter. If the overall results were something less than sensational (although standard overall of music produced by all three plus others was excellent) fact that such a summit meeting actually took place engenders some kind of stirring in the loins. Major triumph of organization for producer Norman Granz.

Granz it was who put together another remarkable studio session, this one involving Hodges, his then boss Ellington at the piano, Harry Edison trumpet, and a rhythm section which included Jo Jones (♦). The music which resulted therefrom was outstanding, even by the highest standards achieved previously (or indeed since) by those involved. Hodges' contributions were little short of magnificent – glorious, soaring alto which breathed freshness and vitality into fine old warhorses such as **Loveless Love, Weary Blues, Wabash Blues** and **Beale**

*Hodge Podge (CBS-Realm) –
Johnny Hodges at his best.*

Street Blues (Blues Summit/Back To Back - Side By Side).

Hodges equally beguiling work on soprano-sax is, of course, much less apparent on record than is his alto, but amongst his finest recordings on the straight saxophone, following can be said to represent impeccable performances: **Good Gal Blues, Jeep's Blues, Empty Ballroom Blues, Wanderlust** (all **Hodge Podge**); **Harmony In Harlem** (**The Ellington Era, Vol 1**); **Dear Old Southland** (**The Works Of Duke, Vol 8**); **Live & Love Tonight** (**The Works of Duke, Vol 9**) and **Blue Goose** (**The Works Of Duke, Vol 10**).

Apart from brief spells away from Ellington band during last portion of his career, Hodges' only lengthy absence was between 1951–5 when he left to form own band. Personnel included, at various times, Lawrence Brown (♦) (who left Ellington same time as Hodges, and Sonny Greer (♦), Ellington's drummer), Emmett Berry (♦), and, for a while, a youthful John Coltrane (♦) (**The Jeep Is Jumpin'**).

John Cornelius Hodges was indeed one of jazz's great irreplaceables, a fact which became stark reality when he died suddenly, following a heart attack, in May 1970.

Recordings:
Duke Ellington, The Beginning (1926-1928)
(Decca/MCA – Germany)

Duke Ellington, Hot In Harlem (1928-1929)
(Decca/MCA – Germany)
Duke Ellington, Rockin' In Rhythm (1929-1931)
(Decca/MCA – Germany)
Duke Ellington, The Works Of Duke Ellington, Vols 2-18
(RCA Victor – France)
The Complete Duke Ellington, Vols 1-7 *(CBS – France)*
Duke Ellington, In A Mellotone
(RCA Victor/RCA Victor – France)
Duke Ellington, Black, Brown & Beige *(Ariston – Italy)*
Duke Ellington, Such Sweet Thunder
(Columbia/CBS – Realm)
Duke Ellington, Ellington At Newport *(Columbia)*
Duke Ellington, The Far East Suite *(RCA Victor/RCA Victor)*
Duke Ellington, ... And His Mother Called Him Bill
(RCA Victor/RCA Victor)
Duke Ellington's 70th Birthday Concert
(Solid State/United Artists)
Duke Ellington, Souvenirs *(Reprise)*
Johnny Hodges, Hodge Podge *(CBS – Realm)*
Johnny Hodges, Ellingtonia '56 *(Norgran/Columbia – Clef)*
Johnny Hodges, Duke's In Bed *(Verve)/*
Johnny Hodges & The Ellington All Stars *(Columbia – Clef)*
Johnny Hodges & The Ellington All Stars *(—/Verve)*
Johnny Hodges *(Verve/—)*
Everybody Knows Johnny Hodges *(Impulse/Impulse)*
Earl Hines/Johnny Hodges, Stride Right *(Verve/Verve)*
Billy Strayhorn, Cue For Saxophone
(Master Jazz Recordings/Vocalion)
Billie Holiday, The Golden Years, Vol 2 *(Columbia/CBS)*
Billie Holiday: The Original Recordings *(Columbia/CBS)*
Gerry Mulligan Meets The Sax Giants, Vols 1-3 *(—/Verve)*
The Teddy Wilson *(CBS/Sony – Japan)*
Teddy Wilson & His All-Stars *(Columbia/CBS)*
Johnny Hodges, The Jeep Is Jumpin' *(—/Verve)*

Above: Johnny Hodges, peerless altoist, arguably the finest soloist from the ranks of Ellingtonia ...

Billie Holiday

The Voice Of Jazz proclaims title of a series of her recordings. For once it is not hyperbole. For Billie Holiday (born Baltimore, Maryland, 1915) was (and most certainly on record remains) the voice of jazz. Apart from Louis Armstrong (♦), and with possible exception of Sarah Vaughan (♦), there never has been a jazz vocalist whose unique abilities have approached those of Billie Holiday. Her timing, for example, was as impeccable as the finest jazz instrumental players (many of whom she worked with during her career). She phrased in a definitely instrumental fashion, although her instrumental-like, horn-influenced singing never was less than music, distorting neither melodic line nor interfering with matchless way in which she lived a lyric. The feeling she communicated through a song, whether it be in live performance or on record, could be devastating, and very real.

At time when Billie's talent was emerging – during early 1930s – it was fashionable often for black singers to sound white, to appeal to a wider audience. Billie Holiday always was a black singer; curiously, she ended up probably appealing more to a white audience. She had some of the basic earthiness, sexuality and real-life qualities that marked the best of Bessie Smith's (♦) work. However, Holiday was not a blues singer per se, using comparatively few actual blues items in her repertoire. Yet everything she sang was tinged with a blues feel – even pop banalities (viz **These 'N' That 'N' Those, Your Mother's Son-In-Law, Yankee Doodle Never Went To Town** and **Under A Jungle Moon**).

It is not at all surprising she could produce singing of such searing, gut-level quality. For Billie Holiday's life-story reads like something that even the most cruelly inventive Hollywood scriptwriter could scarcely dredge up. Born of unmarried teen-age parents, Sadie Fagan and Clarence Holiday, latter guitarist, banjoist who worked with Fletcher

Above: Billie Holiday (pictured with Jimmy Davis, co-composer of Lover Man) was the most gifted of all singers.

Henderson (♦), McKinney's Cotton Pickers, etc; was raped at 10, and went into prostitution a couple of years later. Apart from experiencing more than a fair share of racialist problems, she later sought solace in alcohol, marijuana, then finally, heroin. In fact, she died in hospital, under police guard, where she was incarcerated on what now seems to have been a trumped-up charge of narcotics possession.

For Billie Holiday, it was almost a logical ending to a career (and lifetime) that were constantly pock-marked with tragedy, despair, frustration and heartache. She did have her happier moments and there were lengthy periods during her career when she was an extremely well-paid artist. Most of those happy moments occurred during earlier part of her career, especially when she was in company of sympathetic jazzmen. After moving from Baltimore to New York with her mother in 1929, commenced singing engagements in Harlem clubs. At one of these, was heard by John Hammond who tried, unsuccessfully, to persuade Benny Goodman (♦) to sign her as singer with his band. Goodman did play at her initial record dates (in November, December '33), sessions that produced just two Holiday items; **Your Mother's Son-In-Law** and **Riffin' The Scotch (The Billie Holiday Story, Vol 1)**. Even at this time it was obvious that a teen-age Billie Holiday had both style and sound all her own, even though singing itself was raw and lacked later confidence.

In between her debut record dates and the next occasion she was to

The Golden Years, Vol 1 (CBS). Billie Holiday – her record dates in the 1930s became 'legendary events'.

appear inside a studio came unexpected chance to appear, briefly, in film featuring Duke Ellington (♦) Orchestra: *Symphony In Black*. She sang **Big City Blues (Saddest Tale)** with astonishing maturity, looking stunningly beautiful. Next recording date, organized by pianist Teddy Wilson (♦) (for several years he became Holiday's A&R man, bandleader, arranger) took place in July 1935. Session also involved, Wilson and Goodman apart, Roy Eldridge (♦), Ben Webster (♦). Recordings from this date finally established her reputation amongst jazz aficionados. Both singing and instrumental work were given equal prominence, a procedure that was to continue until the 1940s.

Billie Holiday recording sessions became almost legendary events during 1930s, involving always cream of musicians of the day, especially those featured with bands of Ellington, Fletcher Henderson, Benny Goodman, Chick Webb (♦), John Kirby (♦), and Count Basie (♦). It was in company with various members of latter band that Billie Holiday made many of the sides which rank with her very best – musicians like Freddie Green, Walter Page, Jo Jones (♦), and of even more importance, Buck Clayton (♦) and Lester Young (♦). With Young, she established almost unbelievable rapport, tenorist providing sublime intros, obbligatos, as well as solos of superlative quality, each complementing, enhancing vocal lines to perfection.

There is not one example of Holiday-Young collaboration on record between 1937–40 which can be said in any way to be less than good. Typical of kind of music produced by this unsurpassed partnership can be found on tracks like **This Year's Kisses, Why Was I Born?, I Must Have That Man, Mean To Me, Fooling Myself, Easy Living, Me, Myself & I, A Sailboat In The Moonlight** (all **The Lester Young Story, Vol 1**); **He's Funny That Way, My First Impression Of You, Now They Call It Swing** (all **The Golden Years, Vol 2**); **Getting Some Fun Out Of Life, If Dreams Come True, On The Sentimental Side, When A Woman Loves A Man** (all **The Golden Years, Vol 1**). And those items cover just one year: 1937. Other Holiday-Young masterpieces include: **Back In Your Own Backyard, The Very Thought Of You (The Billie Holiday Story, Vol 1); The Man I Love, All Of Me (The Original Recordings)**.

Billie Holiday's role as singer with big bands was limited, although she did work with Count Basie for just over a year (1937–8). Due to contractual reasons, she never did get a chance to record with Basie, although three fine airshot performances of singer in this setting **Swing! Brother, Swing!, They Can't Take That Away From Me** (both datelined 30/6/37), and **I Can't Get Started** (3/11/37) subsequently have come to light, courtesy John Hammond **(Billie Holiday, Vol 2)**. Billie also worked with Artie Shaw (♦) for nine months (1938). Again, her opportunity to record was negated by her Brunswick contract. She made just one side, **Any Old Time**, with Shaw **(Concerto For Clarinet)** but originally this was withdrawn because of objections by label to which she was signed.

She broadcast – apparently once only – with Benny Goodman band in 1939; **I Cried For You (BG. His Stars & His Guests)** certainly was a superior example of her rhythmic powers.

For rest of career, was usually to be found in small-combo setting – the kind of situation in which invariably she was to be found at her best – although she did make isolated big-band appearances as, for instance, with Duke Ellington **(Concert At Carnegie Hall)**. After leaving Shaw, the Holiday solo career blossomed when she became resident singer at New York's Cafe Society, accompanied by Frankie Newton's (♦) orchestra. During same year, together with Newton and band, recorded for Milt Gabler's Commodore label, session that produced three numbers which forever thereafter were to be identified with Billie Holiday alone; the macabre **Strange Fruit** (with lyric by poet Lewis Allan), terrifyingly sad **Yesterday's,** and a magnificent (and rare) blues performance and composition called **Fine & Mellow** (written by Holiday) **(Strange Fruit/The Commodore Years)**. From around that time, Billie Holiday's recordings, whilst still featuring solos and obbligatos from top jazzmen like Eldridge and Young, tended to become more arranged, less spontaneous.

But 1940s arrived with Billie Holiday singing as well as (sometimes even better than) before. There were more superb vocals to be found within recordings of **Georgia On My Mind, Body & Soul, Solitude, Jim** and **God Bless The Child** (all **God Bless The Child**); last-named most familiar of Billie Holiday's own lyrics and probably best. There was also the suicidal **Gloomy Sunday (The Golden Years, Vol 1)** sung inimitably by Holiday. Further sessions with Commodore followed termination of her association with Vocalion label.

By mid-1940s, she had moved on to Decca where strings, reeds, et al, were utilized on her records, presumably to make her art accessible to a wider audience. Very first Decca title – a poignant version of **Lover Man** (written by jazz pianist-organist Ram Ramirez) – became another of her most famous songs. **Don't Explain,** from third session, was blessed with another sensitive Holiday lyric. **Porgy,** from two years later, received definitive reading; **Ain't Nobody's Business** (1949) was a rare, but satisfying, blues performance (all Decca titles mentioned – **The Billie Holiday Story**).

Already, though, there were tell-tale signs of ennui creeping into Billie Holiday's work, and by 1950s it was obvious too that her personal excesses were beginning to take their toll of what writer-broadcaster Charles Fox once called 'a certain neutrality of timbre'. During last period of her lifetime, recorded extensively for various Norman Granz-owned labels **(The Voice Of Jazz, Vols 1-10)**. Singing ranged from very good to pitifully inadequate, the latter exemplified in two live recordings, from 1946 **(Vol 1)** and 1957 **(Vol 9)**. But there were times, especially when she was accompanied by old friends like Ben Webster, Harry Edison (♦), Benny Carter (♦), Charlie Shavers (♦), and younger musicians like Oscar Peterson (♦), Barney Kessel (♦), and Tony Scott, when temporarily she all but scaled previous peaks of performance.

One of the comparatively few occasions (on record at least) when she recaptured some of the magic of the past occurred during a four-session

THE GOLDEN YEARS

The Golden Years (CBS). Billie Holiday was probably the greatest – of either sex – of all the jazz singers . . .

Vol 1) accompanied by a really all-star band, including Young, Coleman Hawkins (♦), Eldridge, Gerry Mulligan (♦) and Vic Dickenson (♦). Holiday's penultimate studio album **Lady In Satin** harrowingly encapsulates the last tragic years of her life, with all its inherent bitterness and despair. By which time (1958), her voice was but a rasping parody of her peak years; but the mood and depth she sustains throughout (never better illustrated than on the prophetic **For All We Know**) rarely, if ever, has been surpassed – even by Billie Holiday herself.

Billie Holiday, who previously had served prison sentence for narcotics offence (1948), and had been acquitted on similar charge (also '48), died at Metropolitan Hospital, New York City, July 1959, where she was detained, prior to her being charged with possession of drugs.

During her career she appeared in following movies: *Symphony In Black* (1935), *New Orleans* (1947 – with Louis Armstrong All Stars, Woody Herman (♦) Orchestra), plus superior film short with Count Basie Sextet (1950) (*Hot Jazz On Film, Vol 2*).

Winner of various readers'/critics' jazz polls, she wrote (in collaboration with William Dufty) *Lady Sings The Blues*, her autobiography. *Billie's Blues*, biography by John Chilton, has been published in more recent times (1975), and there is an illuminating chapter on the singer in Ralph J. Gleason's *Celebrating the Duke & Louis, Bessie, Billie, Bird, Carmen, Miles, Dizzy & Other Heroes* (1975). Despite fine acting-singing performance by Diana Ross, 1973 movie, *Lady Sings the Blues*, purporting to be based on Billie Holiday's life story, was nothing more than a travesty.

record project which took place in January 1957 **(Vols 7-9)**. With admirable assistance from Edison, Webster, Kessel, et al, she imbued standard songs like **Just One Of Those Things, Day In, Day Out, Comes Love,** and **One For My Baby,** with a depth and meaning they have not received, before or since.

Not surprisingly, her in-person appearances tended to become even more erratic than her records. Again, though, there were those times when the adrenalin flowed as of old – or almost. Typical of the happier occasions are **The Lady Lives, Radio & TV Broadcasts, Vol 2, 1953-1956** and **The Real Lady Sings The Blues.** There is more fine singing to be found from recordings emanating from a season at Storyville Club, Boston, in 1951 **(Gallant Lady** and **Billie Holiday),** latter having additional interest with presence of Stan Getz (♦), a disciple of Billie's erstwhile partner, Lester Young.

Appeared on special CBS/TV programme, *The World of Jazz*, in 1957, singing a painful, moving version of **Fine & Mellow (Billie Holiday,**

Recordings:
The Billie Holiday Story, Vol 1 (*Columbia/CBS*)
Billie Holiday, God Bless The Child (*Columbia/CBS*)
Billie Holiday: The Original Recordings (*Columbia/CBS*)
Billie Holiday, The Golden Years, Vols 1, 2 (*Columbia/CBS*)
Billie Holiday, Strange Fruit (*Atlantic*)/
The 'Commodore' Days (*Ace of Hearts*)
Billie Holiday, The Real Lady Sings The Blues (*—/Boulevard*)
The Billie Holiday Story (*Decca/MCA – Germany*)
The 'Real' Lady Sings The Blues (*—/Coral*)
Billie Holiday, Vols 1-3 (*—/Saga*)
Billie Holiday, Gallant Lady (*Monmouth–Evergreen/One-Up*)
Various (Including Billie Holiday), The First Esquire Concert, Vol 1 (*—/Saga*)
The Teddy Wilson (*CBS/Sony – Japan*)
Teddy Wilson & His All Stars (*Columbia/CBS*)
The Lester Young Story, Vols 1-3 (*Columbia/CBS*)
Billie Holiday, The Voice Of Jazz, Vols 1-10 (*—/Verve*)
Various (Including Billie Holiday), Jazz At The Philharmonic: The Historic Recordings (*Verve/—*)
Billie Holiday, The First Verve Sessions (*Verve/—*)
Billie Holiday, Lady In Satin (*Columbia/CBS – Realm*)
Artie Shaw, Concerto For Clarinet (*RCA Victor/RCA Victor*)
Benny Goodman, BG, His Stars & His Guests (*Queen Disc – Italy*)
Various (Including Billie Holiday), Concert At Carnegie Hall (*DJM*)
For A Lady Named Billie (*Giants of Jazz*)

John Lee Hooker

Bluesman John Lee Hooker was born in Clarksdale, Mississippi in 1917, and like most post-war blues recording artists, soon learned to adapt to the amplified urban sound. Like most Delta bluesmen, Hooker's city style is merely an intensification of the drones, moans, repetitions and raw power of the original. Based in Detroit, he began recording in 1948 and sold phenomenally well in the R&B market, **Boogie Chillen'** selling a million copies. His voice has a menacing weight, heavy and bruising, the lyrics often violent and obsessive. The chopping of word-endings carries a primitive dramatic charge which is hammered home by the guitar in rhythmic unison. Hooker's guitar technique is functional, making the most of a rudimentary stock of devices. A more restricted artist than Lightnin' Hopkins, Hooker nevertheless triumphs in terms of impact. Moving between R&B and the more purist blues, his main audience today is the generation of young whites who first heard the blues secondhand from the Rolling Stones.

Recordings:
The Blues (*Crown/—*)

Slim's Stomp
  (*—/Polydor – Juke Blues*)
House Of The Blues
  (*Chess/Marble Arch*)
How Long Blues
  (*Riverside/Fontana*)
I Want To Shout The Blues
  (*Vee-Jay/Stateside*)
Don't Turn Me From Your Door/Drifting Blues
  (*Atco/Atlantic*)

Elmo Hope

Born 1923, Hope was dismissed at the outset as a Bud Powell imitator, though in fact his piano style developed a quirky, elusive quality

Hope-Full (Riverside): rare album of the late pianist.

that was all his own. His move to the West Coast shunted his career up the siding of public disinterest: back East, fashion decreed, was where the vigor and pace-setting occurred. Hope had proved himself in a Hard Bop blowing context **(All-Star Session)** with John Coltrane and Hank Mobley, though the trio section of the album gives him more room to show the startling elasticity of his concept. Notes are held until their edges puddle like spilled ink; bright treble runs hunch and buckle into dissonance. Scurry, tremolo, blur – time seems to stretch at his bidding. The definitive trio album is **Elmo Hope** with the perfect West Coast drummer, Frank Butler, whose inventiveness matches his own. Other sympathetic interpreters of his compositions are tenorist Harold Land **(The Fox)** and the Curtis Counce Quintet **(Exploring The Future)**, both albums fuelled by Butler. There is a quiet, off-centre lyricism in Elmo Hope's work, **Barfly, Eejah, Eyes So Beautiful** that is haunting.

Recordings:
The All-Star Sessions
  (*Milestone*)
Elmo Hope
  (*Contemporary/Vocalion*)
Harold Land, The Fox
  (*Contemporary*)
Curtis Counce, Exploring The Future (*Dooto*)

Claude Hopkins

A most accomplished all-round musician, Claude D. Hopkins (born Alexandria, Virginia, 1903), has been acclaimed throughout a lengthy career as bandleader, pianist, composer, arranger. Yet his obvious talents in each area somehow fell short of absolute greatness. For example, various big bands he has led over the years, whilst not lacking style or reasonable solo strength, never really offered a challenge to the real giants of that genre. Hopkins' arrangements – like his compositions – have been at all times clean-cut, professional, good to play or hear . . . but almost always lacking in real originality. As a pianist, Hopkins' earliest contemporaries were the likes of James P. Johnson (♦), Fats Waller (♦) and Willie 'The Lion' Smith (♦) – and he never really matched their virtuosity and individual brilliance. Starting piano at seven, Hopkins, studied both music and medicine at Howard University, gaining an AB degree. After further study at Washington Conservatory, worked in various college bands, then fronting own band in Atlantic City. In 1924 he went to New York (for work with Wilbur Sweatman), before travelling to Europe as musical director for cabaret artiste Josephine Baker. Also led own band

(1926) in Italy, Spain. Returned to New York, to take first of numerous residencies, in both Washington and Harlem.

Took own bands into Roseland Ballroom (1931–5) and Cotton Club (1935–6) for lengthy residencies. Hopkins band – which at various times included such musical talents as Vic Dickenson (◊), Jabbo Smith, Edmond Hall (◊), Herman Autrey, Snub Mosley and arranger-trombonist Fred Norman – attained enviable popularity during 1930s, through its live appearances as well as via radio, films and records (**The Golden Swing Years** and **Big Bands Uptown 1931-1940**). Hopkins disbanded, finally, in 1940. Worked as arranger for various jazz-tinged dancebands. Commenced band-leading again in '44 (up until 1947); led what has been described as novelty small combo (1948–9); then fronted a more jazz-orientated outfit at New York's Club Zanzibar (1950–1).

After gigging in Boston for a couple of years, worked regularly at Metropole, NYC, together with Henry 'Red' Allen (◊) ('54). Continued to work with various small-combo leaders from 1950s, as well as leading own units from time to time. It is a situation which continues (less frequently) today: Claude Hopkins' solo piano sometimes is to be heard at intermission at various New York night-spots.

His playing today, in his 70s, sounds not at all the work of an old man. During the past quarter-century, Hopkins has continued to be heard on record, invariably in mainstream context (**Swing Time!**, **Let's Jam** and **Yes Indeed!**) and in 1974 the Chiaroscuro label issued a fine Claude Hopkins solo album, **Crazy Fingers**.

Recordings:
Ma Rainey (Milestone)
Singin' In The Rain (Jazz Archives/—)
Big Bands Uptown (1931-1940) Various (Including Claude Hopkins) (MCA – Germany)
The Golden Swing Years (—/Polydor)
Coleman Hawkins/Pee Wee Russell, Jam Session In Swingville (Prestige/Prestige)
Swingtime (Swingville)
Let's Jam (Swingville)
Yes Indeed! (Swingville)
Crazy Fingers (Chiaroscuro/—)

Sam 'Lightnin' Hopkins

Born 1912, near Houston, Texas, Lightnin' Hopkins is one of the last of the old country bluesmen. He gained early experience with Blind Lemon Jefferson and with his cousin, Texas Alexander, acquiring his nickname through a partnership with barrelhouse pianist Thunder Smith. His first recordings from 1946 made an immediate impact, revealing a major artist. Much of his best and freshest work was done for Bill Quinn's now rare Gold Star label; the voice harsh and direct, and the guitar accompaniment quirkily irregular. A uniquely subjective performer, Hopkins is usually at his most expressive when dealing with episodes from his own life, but also invests that common pool of blues tradition with his own sense of immediacy

Above: Sam ('Lightnin') Hopkins, seminal figure – as guitarist, singer, composer – of post-war blues.

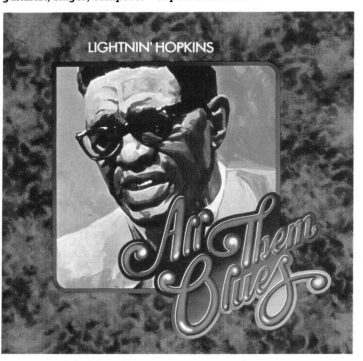

All Them Blues (DJM): Lightnin' Hopkins, best of the post-war Texans. Unchanging, eternal, the authentic country artist.

and drama. A prolific recording artist, Hopkins' talents have often been in danger of over exposure, though the mid-50s saw a slump in the country blues market in favor of Chicago blues bands. In 1959, he found acceptance among the folk audiences of the concert hall and campus.

Recordings:
Lightnin' Hopkins Strums The Blues (Score/—)
Lightnin' Hopkins Early Recordings (Arhoolie/Fontana)
Lightnin' Hopkins Sings The Blues (Time/Realm)
Lightnin' Hopkins Sings Dirty House Blues (Time/Realm)
Sam Lightnin' Hopkins (—/77)
Autobiography In Blues (Tradition/—)
Country Blues (Tradition/—)
The Roots Of Lightnin' Hopkins (Verve – Forecast/ Verve – Folkways)
Lightnin' Strikes (—/Stateside)
Lightnin' Hopkins, The Legacy Of The Blues, Vol 12 (Sonet/Sonet)

Darnell Howard
◊ *Earl Hines*
◊ *Jelly Roll Morton*

Noah Howard

Born 1943 in New Orleans, alto-man Noah Howard is stylistically in the second generation of the New Wave. After childhood exposure to Dixieland and gospel, Howard's major influence was Ornette Coleman. He studied with Sonny Simmons and Dewey Redman in San Francisco before moving to New York. After experience with Sun Ra, Albert Ayler, Pharoah Sanders and Archie Shepp (**Black Gipsy**), he formed his own groups, often in company with tenorman Frank Wright (**One For John** and **Space**

Live At The Swing Club (Altsax): New Orleans, new style.

Dimension). The music rages and soars, the locomotive and heavy onrush of Wright's tenor an excellent foil for the achingly lyrical alto. A group with the English trumpeter, Ric Colbeck, produced some of Howard's finest music (**Noah Howard At Judson Hall**) and the very Eastern interplay between bass and cello on **Homage To Coltrane** shows the composer's interest in other ethnic musics.

These days, the altoist alternates between Europe and America, and runs his own label, Altosax Records. A recent performance

(**Live At The Swing Club**) shows a refinement in group approach, away from collective improvizing in favor of space and simplicity. **Mardi Gras** is pure song, each instrument in the quartet taking unaccompanied solo space before coming together for the triumphal melody statement.

Recordings:
Archie Shepp, Black Gipsy
  (Prestige/America)
Frank Wright, One For John
  (Byg/Byg)
Space Dimension
  (Prestige/America)
Noah Howard At Judson Hall
  (ESP/ESP)
Live At The Swing Club
  (Altsax/Altsax)
Live In Europe *(—/Sun)*

Freddie Hubbard

Trumpeter Freddie Hubbard was born in Indianapolis in 1938 into a musical family, arriving in New York in 1958. He built up considerable experience with Jay Jay Johnson's Sextet, Max Roach, Sonny Rollins and Slide Hampton, before getting an ideal showcase with Art Blakey's Messengers in 1961. With Wayne Shorter sharing the front-line, this was arguably Blakey's finest unit since the Horace Silver days, and Hubbard's playing and writing were generously featured (**Mosaic, Free For All, Buhaina's Delight** and **Thermo**). Sounding completely poised over the leader's furious drumming, the young trumpeter often recalled the warmth, strength and prettiness of Clifford Brown, an early influence.

The same period saw Hubbard as a sideman on numerous Blue Note dates, playing with Dexter Gordon, Herbie Hancock, Jackie McLean and Wayne Shorter, as well as heading his own series of albums (**Open Sesame, Ready For Freddie** and **Breaking Point**). His romantic, rich approach to the ballad is well illustrated on **I Wish I Knew (Goin' Up)** and **But Beautiful (Open Sesame)**, while the schizophrenic approach, some chord change material, some Free Jazz, was exemplified on the album **Breaking Point**. Hubbard was flexible enough to play free with Ornette Coleman (**Free Jazz**) and with Dolphy (**Out To Lunch**) but his long, legato phrases and orthodox delivery made him better suited to an harmonic base. Vibrato, half-valve effects and growls played a very sparing role in his improvisation, which has a classic purity.

Having been hailed by some critics as the successor to Clifford Brown, and winning the *Downbeat* New Star Award in 1961, Hubbard's subsequent work for Atlantic began to show commercial tendencies. The debut album **Backlash** features a couple of soul tracks, the title track and **The Return Of The Prodigal Son,** while a later release, **High Blues Pressure,** showed a backbeat and riff on **Can't Let Her Go** that was more than a nod towards Lee Morgan's hit, **The Sidewinder.** On the jazz credit side, the two tracks fuelled by master drummer Louis Hayes, **True Colors** and **For B.P.,** are excellent examples of Hubbard's clean articulation at speed. The

Above: Altoman Noah Howard. In the background: Juma Sultan, Frank Lowe, Rashied Ali, Bob Bruno and Earl Freeman.

anti-war concept album composed by Ilhan Mimaroglu (**Sing Me A Song Of Songmy**) featured the lyrical, emotional trumpet.

In 1971 Hubbard signed to CTI, a label that had popularized the Creed Taylor A&R approach, and produced a series of big-selling albums (**Red Clay, Straight Life, First Light, Sky Dive** and **Polar Arc**) in which few chances are taken, or surprises sprung, and the emphasis is on the seamless and the glossy. He has since signed to Columbia, where his output has moved from disco material, choirs, violins and a regular amplified thud of drums (**Windjammer**) to the regular jazz setting again (**Super Blue**).

Recordings:
Art Blakey's Jazz Messengers:
  Mosaic *(Blue Note/Blue Note)*
Free For All
  (Blue Note/Blue Note)
Buhaina's Delight
  (Blue Note/Blue Note)
Thermo *(Milestone/Milestone)*
Open Sesame
  (Blue Note/Blue Note)
Ready For Freddie
  (Blue Note/Blue Note)
Breaking Point
  (Blue Note/Blue Note)
Goin' Up *(Blue Note/Blue Note)*
Here To Stay
  (Blue Note/Blue Note)
Backlash *(Atlantic/Atlantic)*
High Blues Pressure
  (Atlantic/Atlantic)
Sing Me A Song Of Songmy
  (Atlantic/Atlantic)
Red Clay *(CTI/CTI)*
Straight Life *(CTI/CTI)*
First Light *(CTI/CTI)*
Sky Dive *(CTI/CTI)*
Polar Arc *(CTI/CTI)*
Windjammer *(Columbia/CBS)*
Super Blue *(Columbia/CBS)*

Bobby Hutcherson

Vibraphone player Bobby Hutcherson was born in Los Angeles in 1941, playing with Curtis Amy and Charles Lloyd on the West Coast before moving to New York in 1961. Usually associated with the Blue Note school of experimentation – musicians like Andrew Hill, Anthony Williams, Herbie Hancock, fastidiously combining some of the freedoms of the New Thing within a basically harmonic outlook – Hutcherson's flexible approach to the vibraphone made him a useful voice in the more adventurous ensembles. His chiming, atmospheric sound graces the

Below: Trumpeter Freddie Hubbard. After a striking debut, his career followed more commercial paths.

Above: Vibist Bobby Hutcherson, the most original concept since Milt Jackson.

Above: Trombonist Quentin Jackson – he carried on the plunger-mute 'jungle' traditions of Tricky Sam Nanton.

textures on many excellent sessions: Eric Dolphy's **Out To Lunch;** Andrew Hill's **Andrew** and **Judgement;** Anthony Williams' **Lifetime;** Jackie McLean's **One Step Beyond** and Grachan Moncur III's **Evolution.** A Newport performance by Archie Shepp, **Scag (New Thing At Newport),** has Hutcherson playing a mesmerizing vamp that exemplifies the prison of heroin addiction.

His own early Blue Note albums cover a wide variety of approaches from the delicacy of **Bouquet** to the expressionistic **The Omen (Happenings).** Using a larger group **(Components)** Hutcherson shares the composer's credits with Joe Chambers, his most compatible drummer. A funkier version of Ornette Coleman's **Una Muy Bonita** is to be found on what was arguably his last challenging album **(Stick-Up!).** His later work has been in line with Blue Note's more popular and commercial orientation **(Linger Lane** and **Natural Illusions),** though there are indications that he is returning to his old form **(The View From The Inside).**

Recordings:
Dialogue (Blue Note/Blue Note)
Happenings
  (Blue Note/Blue Note)
Components
  (Blue Note/Blue Note)
San Francisco
  (Blue Note/Blue Note)
Stick-Up!
  (Blue Note/Blue Note)
The View From The Inside
  (Blue Note/Blue Note)

Components (Blue Note): free music's wizard of the vibes.

The JCOA
♦ *Carla Bley*
♦ *Mike Mantler*

Milt Jackson
♦ *Modern Jazz Quartet*

Opus De Funk (Prestige) from Milt Jackson.

Quentin Jackson

When Quentin 'Butter' Jackson took over from Tyree Glenn (♦) as trombone soloist and section man with Duke Ellington (♦) Orchestra in 1948, already he had chalked up a wealth of playing experience in big-band field. That experience included work with Gerald Hopson (1927–8), Wesley Helvy (1929–30), McKinney's Cotton Pickers (1930–2) **(McKinney's Cotton Pickers, Vols 4, 5)** and Don Redman (♦) (1932–40) **(Don Redman** and **Don Redman (1938–1940): The Little Giant Of Jazz).** Jackson had also worked again with Redman in 1946 – including a tour of Europe – apart from which his career prior to joining Ellington had been spent mostly with Cab Calloway (♦).

Joined Calloway's organization for six-year first spell in 1940 **(16 Cab Calloway Classics** and **Chu Berry Featured With Cab Calloway: 'Penguin Swing')** and rejoined after completing second stint with Redman (1947–8).

When Jackson joined Ellington he had, like his predecessor, the unenviable task of taking over mantle of plunger-mute trombone soloist established, more or less definitively, by Joseph 'Tricky Sam' Nanton (♦). That Jackson succeeded in carrying on that unique tradition in magnificent fashion is in itself testimony to his abilities (although, of course, it was an impossibility to expect anyone really to equal, let alone better, Nanton's work with the band).

Jackson (born Springfield, Ohio, 1909) studied trombone with private teachers and a brother-in-law, Claude Jones (also a trombonest who, amongst others, worked with McKinney's Cotton Pickers, Redman, and Ellington).

Sometimes employed as vocalist, bassist in earlier days, Quentin Jackson's expressive trombone playing only was strongly featured by Ellington on all kinds of material, including **The Mooche (Ellington Uptown); Fancy Dan (Duke Ellington); Black & Tan Fantasy (Ellington '55/Toast To The Duke); My Funny Valentine (Ellington Presents); Red Carpet (Ellington Jazz Party)** and even **Donkey Serenade (At The Bal Masque).** His pungent work also relayed the Nanton message with conviction on **Rockin' In Rhythm (Ellington '55/Toast To The Duke).** With Johnny Hodges (♦) Jackson flared brightly too **(Johnny Hodges & The Ellington Me/The Big Band Sound Of Johnny Hodges** and **Duke's In Bed/Johnny Hodges & The Ellington All Stars)** and especially throughout **Cue For Saxophone.**

More recently, Jackson has worked with Count Basie (full-time, after at first working freelance), then as featured soloist with Thad Jones-Mel Lewis Jazz Orchestra **(Suite For Pops** and **Potpourri).** And just to prove, once again, just how versatile Butter Jackson could be, it is worth remembering that Charles Mingus (♦) used his services on several occasions during 1963, as on the album **(Mingus, Mingus, Mingus, Mingus, Mingus).** And his unaccompanied solo on **Hearts' Beat,** from Mingus' totally memorable **The Black Saint & The Sinner Lady,** must rank as one of his most telling individual statements. Tricky Sam no doubt would have approved.

After leaving Ellington, in 1959, Jackson toured Europe with all-star Quincy Jones band (1960). With Basie (1961–2), Mingus then returned to the Ellington fold for short spell in '63. Studio and freelance work took him through the remainder of 1960s and into 1970s – including special big-band calls from Jones-Lewis, Louis Bellson (♦) and Gerald Wilson – but career was interrupted by major surgery. After which he was hoping for major comeback, had already joined pit band of revival of *Guys & Dolls,* but a heart attack took him in the fall of 1976.

Recordings:
McKinney's Cotton Pickers, Vols 4, 5 (RCA Victor – France)
Don Redman (CBS – Realm)
Don Redman (1938–1940): The Little Giant Of Jazz
  (RCA Victor – France)
16 Cab Calloway Classics
  (CBS – France)
Chu Berry Featured With Cab Calloway: 'Penguin Swing'
  (Jazz Archives)
Masterpieces By Duke Ellington And His Orchestra
  (Columbia/CBS – Holland)
The World Of Duke Ellington, Vol 2 (Columbia)/
The World Of Duke Ellington
  (CBS)
The World Of Duke Ellington, Vol 3 (Columbia)/

The World Of Duke Ellington, Vol 2 (CBS)

Duke Ellington, Liberian Suite/ A Tone Parallel to Harlem (CBS – France)

Duke Ellington, Ellington '55 (Capitol)/
Toast To The Duke (World Record Club)

Duke Ellington, Historically Speaking, The Duke (Bethlehem/—)

Duke Ellington, Such Sweet Thunder (Columbia/CBS – Realm)

Duke Ellington, Ellington Indigos (Columbia/CBS – France)

Duke Ellington, Ellington Jazz Party (Columbia)

Johnny Hodges, Mellow Tone (Vogue)

Johnny Hodges, Duke's In Bed (Verve)

Johnny Hodges & The Ellington All Stars (Columbia – Clef)

Johnny Hodges & The Ellington Men (Verve)/
The Big Band Sound Of Johnny Hodges (Verve)

Billy Strayhorn, Cue For Saxophone (Master Jazz Recordings/ Felsted)

Thad Jones – Mel Lewis, Suite For Pops (A&M Horizon/A&M Horizon)

Thad Jones – Mel Lewis, Potpourri (Philadelphia International/ Philadelphia International)

Charles Mingus, Mingus, Mingus, Mingus, Mingus, Mingus (Impulse)

Charles Mingus, The Black Saint & The Sinner Lady (Impulse/Impulse)

Illinois Jacquet

Illinois Battiste Jacquet was born Broussard, Louisiana, 1922, but his father, bass player with railroad company band, moved family to Houston, Texas, before Illinois was one year. Jacquet will be best remembered for the extraordinary potency of his swing – and an ability to build excitement in performance by use of freak high-note effects. But Jacquet – brother of Russell Jacquet, a trumpeter, singer, bandleader – is more than an eccentric, exhibitionist tenor-saxophonist. In fact, he has successfully outlived his somewhat dubious reputation, acquired with the wildly-swinging big band which Lionel Hampton (♦) put together when leaving Benny Goodman (♦).

With Hampton, Jacquet was featured soloist, whose special feature was the immensely exciting and grossly overused **Flying Home (The Best Of Lionel Hampton)**. Jazz At The Philharmonic impresario Norman Granz also utilized Jacquet's ability to stir jazz audiences into the kind of frenzy pitch rock concerts have engendered during past 20–25 years **(Concert Contrasts/Jazz At The Philharmonic 1944-46)**. And Jacquet's honking, booting tenor has been a welcome addition to organized studio jam sessions **(The Gillespie Jam Sessions)** where his playing generally has been, of necessity, free of gallery-fetching excesses with which he made his name in live performance.

Illinois Jacquet (Epic, Holland) – Jumpin' With Jacquet.

Began on soprano-, alto-saxes, playing with territory R&B bands (including Lionel Proctor, Bob Cooper, Milton Larkins). Joined Hampton from Floyd Ray Orchestra, after which the little man with the huge tone enlivened bands of Cab Calloway (♦) (1943–4), Count Basie (♦) (1945–6) and various JATP troupes. With Basie, his solo features included **Mutton Leg (One O'Clock Jump)**; and **The King (Count Basie Classics)**. During post-Basie period, Illinois Jacquet also led own bands, often including trumpet-playing brother Russell **(Illinois Jacquet** – Epic and **King Jacquet)**.

Since then, has toured with further outfits of which he has been leader, as well as with package shows such as Newport All Stars, or as featured soloist at concerts and in clubs, in the US and abroad. From 1960s, Jacquet, who had concentrated almost exclusively on tenor-sax during his halcyon big-band days, recommenced playing both alto- and soprano-sax. In addition, he added bassoon to his armory **(The King!)**, an instrument he plays with fair degree of fluency and expertise.

Below: The Tearaway of the Tenor Sax, Illinois Jacquet ... comprehensive swinger, archetypal JATP 'honker'.

During his career, Jacquet has locked horns with some of the greatest names in jazz. In 1944, for example, was seen and heard in jazz movie *Jammin' The Blues* **(Jammin' With Lester)** together with Lester Young (♦), one of his major influences, along with Coleman Hawkins (♦) and, most notably, Herschel Evans (♦).

Outside of big-band set-up, has worked with Count Basie **(Port Of Rico)**; Edison **(Groovin' With Jacquet)**; Nat Cole (♦) **(Nat Cole Meets The Master Saxes)** and Wynton Kelly **(The Blues: That's Me!)**.

In more recent years, Jacquet's blistering tenor work often has been heard in friendly, mutually inspiring dialogue with drummer Jo Jones (♦) and organist Milt Buckner **(Genius At Work!)** with trio sometimes affecting powerhouse storm of an extrovert big band.

Jacquet's presence at all-star gatherings, like Newport Jazz Festival, continues to give more than adequate demonstrations of his undiminished blowing powers, both as uplifting, fiery purveyor of ballads like **Misty (Newport In New York '72, Vol 3)**, **The Man I Love (Newport In New York '72, Vol 5)** and **Stardust (Here Comes Freddy)**. But for most fans, Illinois Jacquet remains the archetypal JATP honker whose extrovert outpourings at in-person dates **(Jazz At Town Hall, Vol 1)** are only marginally more combustible than those emanating from recording studios, especially when complemented by other tempestuous soloists like Roy Eldridge (♦) **(Illinois Jacquet** – Epic), Eddie 'Lockjaw' Davis **(The Angry Tenors)**, Fats Navarro (♦) **(Illinois Jacquet** – Imperial), Buddy Tate (♦) **(Buddy Tate & His Buddies)**, and Howard McGhee (♦) **(Here Comes Freddy)**.

Recordings:
The Best Of Lionel Hampton (MCA – Coral – Germany)
Nat Cole Meets The Master Saxes (Including Illinois

Jacquet) (Phoenix/Spotlite)

Lester Young, Jammin' With Lester (Jazz Archives/—)

Various (Including Illinois Jacquet), JATP New Volume Five-Concert Contrasts (Verve)/
Jazz At The Philharmonic 1944-46 (Verve)

Illinois Jacquet/Eddie 'Lockjaw' Davis, The Angry Tenors (Savoy/Realm)

Illinois Jacquet, Groovin' With Jacquet (Verve/Columbia – Clef)

Dizzy Gillespie, The Gillespie Jam Sessions (Verve)

Illinois Jacquet (Imperial)

Illinois Jacquet (Epic/Epic – Holland)

Illinois Jacquet, The King! (Prestige/—)

Illinois Jacquet, Bottoms Up (Prestige/—)

Illinois Jacquet, The Blues: That's Me (Prestige/—)

Illinois Jacquet/Arnett Cobb, Jazz At Town Hall, Vol 1 (JRC/—)

Various, Newport At New York '72, Vols 3, 5 (Atlantic/Atlantic)

Illinois Jacquet, Genius At Work (Black Lion/Black Lion)

Buddy Tate & His Buddies (Chiaroscuro/—)

Howard McGhee/Illinois Jacquet, Here Comes Freddy (—/Sonet)

Illinois Jacquet, King Jacquet (—/RCA – France)

Various (Including Illinois Jacquet), The Tenor Sax Album (Savoy/Savoy)

Various (Including Illinois Jacquet), The Changing Face Of Harlem, Vol 2 (Savoy/Savoy)

Harry James

Some jazz buffs never have forgiven Harry Haag James (born Albany, Georgia, 1916) for leaving Benny Goodman (♦), starting his own big band and playing schmaltzy trumpet on tunes like **Ciribiribin, You Made Me Love You** and **Carnival In Venice**. To the jazz lovers, it seemed that James had sold out and, to add insult to injury, he went and married a lady from Hollywood with the world's most famous legs. Thereafter, James was removed from any self-respecting list of 'real' jazz musicians. Which was sad, for in spite of the obvious commercial slantings of bands James has led since then, he has continued to show, from time to time, he can still play heated jazz with a technical expertise that is a byword amongst trumpet players throughout the

Harry James & His Orchestra 1936-1938 (The Old Masters).

Harry James & His New Swingin' Bands (MGM). Impact of Basie Band on James outfit can be gauged from this album.

through one smash-hit after another. Or almost.

Recordings:
The Complete Benny Goodman, Vols 1-3 *(RCA)/*
Benny Goodman, Vols 4-7 *(RCA Victor – France)*
Benny Goodman, 1938
Carnegie Hall Jazz Concert *(Columbia/CBS)*
Harry James & His Orchestra 1936-1938 *(The Old Masters/—)*
Teddy Wilson & His All Stars *(Columbia/CBS)*
Various (Including Harry James/Pete Johnson/Albert Ammons), Cafe Society Swing & The Boogie Woogie (1938-1940) *(Swingfan – Germany)*
Various (Including Harry James), Great Swing Jam Sessions, Vol 1 *(—/Saga)*
Swinging With Harry James *(Joker – Italy)*
The Big Band Sound Of Harry James, Vols 1-3 *(—/Verve)*

Joseph Jarman
♦ *Art Ensemble of Chicago*

Keith Jarrett

Pennsylvania-born pianist Keith Jarrett first established his reputation in the popular Charles Lloyd group **(Dream Weaver)** where he proved himself to be a dazzlingly gifted player. A period with Miles Davis in the early '70s **(Live/Evil and At Fillmore)** did not lead, as with pianists Chick Corea, Joe

The Koln Concert (ECM): the return of solo acoustic piano.

world. They forgot too, the string of superbly executed solos James had taken as a principal soloist with the most famous of Benny Goodman bands.

James had joined the clarinettist in January 1937, remaining as No 1 trumpet soloist until December 1938. During which time, his – and Goodman's – reputation had been established worldwide, through his personal contributions to such Goodman favorites as **Make Believe (The Complete Benny Goodman, Vols 1-3/Benny Goodman, Vol 4); Sugar Foot Stomp, Big John's Special (The Complete Benny Goodman, Vols 1-3/ Benny Goodman, Vol 5); Peckin'** and **Life Goes To A Party**, both composed-arranged by James **(The Complete Benny Goodman, Vols 1-3/Benny Goodman, Vol 7).** And, indeed, James' splendid blowing at the famous **1938 Carnegie Hall Jazz Concert** on numbers like **Sing, Sing, Sing, Blue Skies, Honeysuckle Rose** and, again, **Life Goes To A Party.**

Before his productive stay with Goodman, James had worked his way quietly to the forefront of the jazz-swing scene. Began on drums, then at ten took trumpet lessons from father. Family moved to Beaumont, Texas, and young James began working in various bands operating within that State. First major break came when he joined orchestra of Ben Pollack (♦) (1935–6) **(Harry James & His Orchestra 1936-1938).** During his time with

Goodman, James participated in one of Teddy Wilson's (♦) studio get-togethers, including one date at which James and Wilson were joined by Red Norvo (♦), xylophone, and John Simmons, bass. James' solos on **Ain't Misbehavin'** and **Just A Mood**, both from this session **(Teddy Wilson & His All Stars)** are as impeccable as those with Wilson at other similar occasions.

James himself fronted an impressive, hard-swinging nine-piece band inside recording studios in 1937 and 1938. Band, comprising seven members of then Basie (♦) outfit, James and pianist Jess Stacy (♦) from Goodman, plus Basie's singer, Helen Humes, laid down some fine tracks, with James' trumpet sparkling throughout both sessions **(Harry James & His Orchestra 1936-1938).** Even more impressive – surprisingly so – was James' superb, crackling trumpet work on all four titles emanating from an early-1939 record date in company with boogie-woogie piano giants Albert Ammons (♦) and Pete Johnson (♦) (sharing two numbers apiece). James immersed himself into the boogie woogie idiom with commendable application, with immensely satisfying results **(Cafe Society Swing & The Boogie Woogie 1938-1940).** With own big band became tremendous box office success, including **Ciribiribin, You Made Me Love You, I've Heard That Song**

Before, I Had The Craziest Dream, I Don't Want To Walk Without You, I'm Beginning To See The Light, Music Makers, etc. Popularity enhanced by appearances in many Hollywood movies, including *Private Buckaroo, Syncopation, Springtime In The Rockies* and *If I'm Lucky.*

For last 30 years, James has continued to lead big bands, based mostly in Nevada. And mostly has continued to take a fairly middle-of-the-road approach to his music. A welcome change of direction, jazz-wise, took place during late-1950s when James invited top jazz writers like Ernie Wilkins and Neal Hefti to write a brand new library for band. Jazz content was dramatically increased, and although the Harry James bands since then have rather closely mirrored the powerhouse sound and style of post-1950s Count Basie outfits **(The Big Band Sound Of Harry James, Vols 1-3)** the change has been greeted with widespread approval. And concomitant with the renascence of his band, James' trumpet playing flared more brightly than in years. Harry James, it seemed, had returned to jazz fold (if he ever completely left it).

Now in his sixties, James' trumpet-playing powers seem to be as formidable as ever. And the music produced by Harry James & His Music Makers today – old and new, jazz and pop – attracts the attention of a healthy number of admirers. Just like it was in the days when James shone with Goodman, and when he led his own bands

Zawinul and Herbie Hancock, to subsequent formation of a jazz-rock outfit.

Jarrett's career is remarkably diverse, operating in three separate fields. In 1971, he recorded a solo piano album for ECM, Manfred Eicher's quality label which has established new standards of freedom for the artist and brilliant sound reproduction. Jarrett's talents, his melodic inventiveness, sense of time, technical virtuosity, stand out with a new clarity **(Facing You).** Continuing the fruitful association with ECM, he has recorded hours of live, unaccompanied, acoustic piano **(The Koln Concert and Solo-Concerts, Bremen & Lausanne),** a project which, at that point in time, seemed sure commercial disaster. In fact, Jarrett's sheer approachability, romanticism and dedication to beauty, have won him a popularity beyond that of a coterie jazz following.

Impossible to categorize, his rushing stream of improvisation ransacks the classical, baroque, gospel, country and boogie bags, rolling them all together over ostinato rhythms that hypnotize the senses. Not restricted to theme and variations, Jarrett's longer pieces, untitled, treat form as a verb rather than a noun. He has also produced several albums as an orchestral composer (**In The Light, Luminescence** and **Arbour Zena**) which have a brooding, neo-classical feel. Saxophonist Jan Garbarek's contribution leavens the over-all tristesse and dolorousness of the string sections.

Keith Jarrett's American albums are different again. Using two of Ornette Coleman's sidemen, saxophonist Dewey Redman and bassist Charlie Haden, plus the flexible drummer, Paul Motian, Jarrett displays his ensemble talents. The music is vigorous, driving, and the interaction between the players – particularly between Haden and Jarrett – phenomenal. There is a great variety of approach towards Jarrett's compositions, from the simultaneous soloing on **Great Bird,** the rapt duet for bass and piano on **Prayer (Death & The Flower)** to tapestry of percussive effects on **Kuum (Backhand),** where all the musicians double on maracas, drums, etc.

In the great debate about the return of acoustic music, the names of Jarrett and Eicher are regularly cited. There is no doubt that Jarrett's solo concert albums have created a market for the sound of the grand piano again, and his eclectic approach and lyrical gifts have converted many who were baffled by the avant-garde dissonances of Cecil Taylor.

Recordings:
Charles Lloyd, Dream Weaver
(Atlantic/Atlantic)
Miles Davis, Live/Evil
(Columbia/CBS)
Miles Davis, At Fillmore
(Columbia/CBS)
Facing You *(ECM/ECM)*
The Koln Concert *(ECM/ECM)*
**Solo – Concerts, Bremen &
Lausanne** *(ECM/ECM)*
In The Light *(ECM/ECM)*
Luminescence *(ECM/ECM)*
Arbour Zena *(ECM/ECM)*
Ruta & Daitya *(ECM/ECM)*
Belonging *(ECM/ECM)*
Expectations *(Columbia/CBS)*
Fort Yawuh *(Impulse/Impulse)*
Treasure Island
(Impulse/Impulse)
Birth *(Atlantic/Atlantic)*
Death And The Flower
(Impulse/Impulse)
Backhand *(Impulse/Impulse)*
Mysteries *(Impulse/Impulse)*
Shades *(Impulse/Impulse)*
Staircase *(ECM/ECM)*

Jazz Messengers
♦ *Art Blakey*

Blind Lemon Jefferson

Lemon 'Blind Lemon' Jefferson (born near Couchman, Texas, 1897)

Above: Keith Jarrett. His solo acoustic piano recitals have attracted a cult following. A virtuoso.

remains not only one of the most important and influential country-blues artists of the period immediately following World War I and right up until his premature death in 1930, but a seminal figure in blues history. Blind from birth, Jefferson took up guitar and began singing blues at an early age, his career as a blues singer, guitarist and composer shaped by friendly association with established Texas (and touring) bluesmen. Alec Jefferson, his father, has told blues authority Sam Charters of how his son, barely into his teens, would sing and play at local country clubs from 'about eight and go on until four in the morning'.

At 17, the itinerant Jefferson had moved on to Dallas where he was to stay – singing and playing his own blues – for about a decade. During this period he met and deeply influenced Huddie 'Leadbelly' Led-

better (♦). Pair worked regularly as duo, Leadbelly acting as the blind man's guide, and supporting Jefferson's guitar work with his own mandolin playing. During 1920s, Jefferson recorded for Paramount and Okeh. His distinctive, high-pitched, never unmelodic vocals, his astonishing fluency and originality as guitarist-accompanist, and the extraordinary imagery and potency of his lyrics, made him a truly unforgettable contributor to the blues genre . . . and one of its most exceptional personalities. As a blues writer, his lyrics appear to have inspired innumerable composers, both during his lifetime and later, for they contain phrases which recurred in lyrics of countless other blues. Amongst Jefferson's most memorable recordings – all made between 1926–1929 – following are exceptional, even by his own high standards – **Black**

Snake Moan, Rabbit Foot Blues, Rising High Water Blues, Prison Cell Blues, Low Down Mojo Blues, Pneumonia Blues, Blind Lemon's Penitentiary Blues, Hangman's Blues and **Match Box Blues** (all **Blind Lemon Jefferson**). Last-named title remains his most popular blues, being recorded by various other blues artists, as well as by the late Elvis Presley and the Beatles. Leadbelly later attained much success with **Jack o'Diamonds,** which Jefferson himself had recorded in 1926. Jefferson's lyrics, on whatever subject, retain a quality of almost unsurpassed expressivity. Other notable Jefferson recordings include his **Lemon's Worried Blues, Bootin' Me 'bout** and **Black Horse Blues** (all on **The Immortal Blind Lemon Jefferson**), **Long Lonesome Blues** and **Got The Blues** (both on **The Country Blues - Texas),** and the spine-tingling **'Lectric Chair Blues.** Blind Lemon Jefferson, bluesman extraordinary, died, aged 33, in a snowstorm in 1930.

Recordings:
Blind Lemon Jefferson
(Milestone)
The Immortal Blind Lemon Jefferson *(Milestone/CBS)*
American Folk Music, Vol 3 Songs *(Folkways/—)*
The Country Blues - Texas
(—/Heritage)

Hilton Jefferson

Hilton Jefferson (born Danberry, Connecticut, 1903) was something of a reluctant soloist in a professional career which lasted for almost 30 years. But his presence as section leader in important big bands with whom he was associated, ensured that the respective sax sections had a distinctive sound.

First played banjo, in 1925, in a Philadelphia theatre orchestra, leaving for a spell to study alto-sax, then returned to work under same bandleader (Julian Arthur), this time as saxist only. To New York with Arthur, working with variety of top bands (as well as lesser-known outfits), including Claude Hopkins (♦) (1926–8); Chick Webb (1929–30); King Oliver (♦) (**King Oliver, Vols 1, 3**) (1930–1); Webb, again (1931); McKinney's Cotton Pickers (1931); and back with Claude Hopkins (1932). Jefferson starred both as section man and soloist during his two years with Fletcher Henderson (♦), taking impressive solo during **Can You Take It? (The Fletcher Henderson Story/The Fletcher Henderson Story, Vol 4)** at a 1933 record session. Also in '33, recorded with Henderson band under leadership of Benny Carter (♦) (**Benny Carter, 1933/Ridin' In Rhythm).** After leaving Henderson, spent most of following six years moving in and out of Henderson, Hopkins and Webb big bands. In 1940 joined Cab Calloway (♦), with whom he stayed until end of 1940s.

During this long period, Jefferson recorded (with Calloway, in 1941) his single most famous solo (**16 Cab Calloway Classics),** a beautifully poised reading of **Willow, Weep For Me;** warm, and

Above: Leroy Jenkins, the avant garde's foremost violinist, and founder member of The Revolutionary Ensemble.

showing how much he was indebted to Benny Carter (principally) and Frankie Trumbauer (♦) in terms of tone, vibrato and control. Spent eight-month spell with Duke Ellington (♦) (1952–3), and worked with Don Redman (♦) and Pearl Bailey (1953). After which he left music full time, taking job as guard at New York bank. Did not stop playing regular engagements, in clubs and on record, including membership of Fletcher Henderson Reunion Band (**Henderson Homecoming** and **The Big Reunion**) taking typically elegant solo on **Round Midnight**, during latter album. Other Jefferson solos, with Oliver, **Mule Face Blues (King Oliver, Vol 2)**; with Red Allen (♦), **Rug Cutter Swing (Henry Allen & His Orchestra 1934-1935)** and with Jimmy Witherspoon (♦), **Gee Baby, Ain't I Good To You (Blue Moods In The Shade Of Kansas City)'**

Hilton Jefferson died in New York's Sydenham Hospital, November 1968, following long illness.

Recordings:
King Oliver, Vols 1, 3
   (RCA Victor – France)
The Fletcher Henderson Story
   (Columbia)/
The Fletcher Henderson Story, Vol 4 *(CBS)*
Various, Benny Carter, 1933
   (Prestige)/
Ridin' In Rhythm
   (World Records)
Henry Allen & His Orchestra 1934-1935
   (Collector's Classics – Denmark)
16 Cab Calloway Classics
   (CBS – France)
Cab Calloway/Chu Berry,

Penguin Swing: 1937-1941
   (Jazz Archives/—)
Fletcher Henderson Reunion Band, Henderson Homecoming *(United Artists)*
Fletcher Henderson Reunion Band, The Big Reunion
   (Jazztone)
Coleman Hawkins, Recordings Made Between 1930 & 1941
   (CBS – France)
(Count Basie)/Jimmy Witherspoon, Blue Moods In The Shade Of Kansas City
   (—/RCA Victor – France)
Various, Jam Session At Swingville *(Prestige/Prestige)*

Leroy Jenkins

Violinist Leroy Jenkins, born Chicago, 1932, was part of that city's AACM and involved in sessions with Muhal Richard Abrams **(Levels & Degrees Of Light)** and Anthony Braxton **(Three Compositions Of New Jazz** and **New York, Fall, 1974).** In 1970 he formed the Revolutionary Ensemble with bassist Sirone and percussionist Jerome Cooper. To date they have made four albums, the first three live, and all embracing the collective principle. The impact of the first **(Vietnam)** is arguably the greater, though the level of intensity is high throughout their output. Jenkins states that he is 'carrying on the tradition of Stuff Smith and Eddie South', though clearly with vocabulary of today.

Classically-trained, his work avoids tonal distortion and concentrates on a sinuous projection

of melody. Sirone's bass lines plait with the violin, supplying textures, and on numbers like **New York (The People's Republic)** rising in arco duet. The music swirls and soars with a passion that is a far cry from chamber music, and through the use of gongs and voices, covers a wide spectrum. An extended work **(For Players Only)** uses the resources of an orchestra.

Recordings:
Muhal Richard Abrams, Levels & Degrees Of Light
   (Delmark/Delmark)
Anthony Braxton, Three Compositions Of New Jazz
   (Delmark/Delmark)
New York, Fall, 1974
   (Arista/Arista)
Revolutionary Ensemble, Vietnam *(ESP/ESP)*
Manhattan Cycles
   (India Navigation/—)
The Psyche
   (RE Records/—)
The People's Republic
   (A&M/A&M)
Leroy Jenkins, For Players Only *(JCOA/JCOA – Virgin)*
Swift Are The Winds Of Life
   (Survival/—)
Solo Concert
   (India Navigation)
The Legend Of Ai Glatsen
   (—/Black Saint)

Budd Johnson

By any yardstick, the career of Albert J. 'Budd' Johnson (born Dallas, Texas, 1910) has been an overall astonishing as well as a personally rewarding one. Apart from fact he is supremely gifted performer on all four of most familiar saxophones, and clarinet, Johnson's gifts as composer, arranger are considerable. Moreover, his lengthy career – first touring experience, as drummer, in 1924 – has found him rubbing shoulders with more significant jazz soloists and innovators than practically any other one living jazzman. More important, Johnson's impressive musical flexibility and obvious catholicity in taste has enabled him to blend his own talents within practically any framework, not as a passive sideman, but a meaningful contributor, both as instrumentalist and/or writer.

Budd Johnson and his trombone-playing brother Frederic H. 'Keg' Johnson (1908–67) received initial music tuition from father, a cornetist, organist. Both also studied with daughter of Booker T. Washington. At first, younger Johnson played piano, then drums, before switching to tenor-saxophone (today, still his premier instrument). Played, toured with local Texas bands, also for Jesse Stone, in Kansas City and other Missouri venues. After moving to Chicago, in '32, joined George E. Lee, followed by work with other sundry bands. 1933: became member of sax section of big band then accompanying Louis Armstrong (♦) **(Louis Armstrong: July 4, 1900 - July 6, 1971).** When Armstrong disbanded (in July, '33), Johnson gigged with various outfits, including Earl Hines (♦) Grand Terrace Orchestra, which he joined on full-time basis in 1935, on death of Hines' featured tenor-saxist Cecil Irwin. Remained with Hines, as reedman and staff

arranger, composer, until 1942, except one year (1936–7), as staff arranger with Gus Arnheim, and brief periods as lead altoist with bands of Fletcher Henderson (♦) (1937), Horace Henderson (♦) (1938), and Johnny Long (1940). With Hines, worked as lead alto, then as tenor soloist, and musical director (1938–42).

Immediate post-Hines work included employment with Don Redman (♦), Al Sears (♦), Georgie Auld (♦) as staff arranger. 1944: worked with Dizzy Gillespie (♦) on 52nd Street, and same year helped Gillespie and Coleman Hawkins (♦) put together very first Bebop record date **(The Many Faces Of Jazz, Vol 52: Coleman Hawkins),** during which he played baritone-sax, contributed to arrangements, and, together with pianist Clyde Hart, wrote **Bu De Dah,** one of the tunes recorded at this historically important session. Had worked with Gillespie previously when both were members of trail-blazing Hines band of 1942–3, band which included, Gillespie and Johnson apart, Charlie Parker (♦), Bennie Green, Sarah Vaughan (♦). During mid-1940s, also played for and contributed to libraries of other forward-looking aggregations like those led by Woody Herman (♦) **(The Turning Point)** and Gillespie.

Stylistically, Johnson's tenor-saxophone playing of this period in his career reflected still a perhaps unusual, but satisfying, blend of two formative influences, Hawkins and Lester Young (♦), although the music of Parker & Co. was also making its mark; this was especially true of his alto playing, which showed a definite ornithological bent, as on 1946 recording, **Jumpin' For Jane (The Greatest Of The Small Bands, Vol 2).** Played tenor during bootleg recording of live jam session (circa '48), with Parker as focal point **(Evening At Home With Charlie Parker** and **Charlie Parker Memorial Album, Vol 6)** although here the basic influence was focused on Young. Following the Eckstine-Raeburn-Herman-Gillespie period, Johnson worked with J. C. Heard (1946); Sy Oliver (♦) (1947); Machito (1949); Bennie Green (1951); Snub Mosley ('52 – USO European tour); Cab Calloway (♦) (1953).

During rest of 1950s, fronted variety of small combos, toured Asia with Benny Goodman (♦) as part of 15-month stint with Goodman orchestra (1956–7), then worked with Quincy Jones (1960); Count Basie (1961–2); Earl Hines (1965); Gerald Wilson and the Tommy Dorsey (♦) 'ghost' band (both '66). Linked up, again, with Hines for European package tour, returning following year as member of Hines Quartet **(Blues & Things).** Began to feature soprano-sax full-time, along with tenor, and yet again proved himself superbly equipped for task, using vaguely Bechet-ish vibrato and general approach evoking both Lester Young and Johnny Hodges (♦).

In 1969 formed JPJ Quartet (founder members: Johnson, Bill Pemberton, Dill Jones). 1970: visited Europe again, this time with Charlie Shavers (♦). Amongst innumerable recording dates not noted thus far – either made under own name or for other leaders – his timeless sax work can be heard to excellent advantage with Gil Evans (♦) **(Paci-**

fic Standard Time); Ben Webster (♦) (Ben Webster & Associates/ Ben Webster & Friends); Buck Clayton (♦) (Buck Clayton Jam Sessions); Roy Eldridge (♦) (The Nifty Cat); Al Sears (The Greatest Of The Small Bands, Vol 5) and, under own name (Blues A La Mode and Four Brass Giants), with Johnson writing splendidly for trumpet team of Harry Edison (♦), Nat Adderley, Ray Nance (♦), and Clark Terry (♦), and Let's Swing, latter with brother Keg co-featured.

Probably best recorded illustration of JPJ Quartet was stimulating live date (Montreux '71) with Johnson, not for the first time, in irresistible form. In so many ways, Budd Johnson remains an absolutely indefatigable, multi-talented and truly priceless musician.

Recordings:
Louis Armstrong: July 4, 1900 - July 6, 1971
(RCA Victor/RCA Victor)
The Indispensable Earl Hines, Vols 1-5 *(RCA Victor – France)*
Coleman Hawkins, The Many Faces Of Jazz, Vol 52
(Mode/Vogue – France)
Various (Including J. C. Heard), Jazz 44 *(Black & Blue – France)*
Billy Eckstine & His Orchestra
(Spotlite)
Billy Eckstine, Mister B & The Band *(Savoy/—)*
J. C. Heard, Cafe Society
(Onyx/—)
Various (Including Coleman Hawkins), The Greatest Of The Small Bands, Vol 2
(RCA Victor – France)
Woody Herman, The Turning Point (1943-1944)
(MCA/Coral)
Various (Including Al Sears), The Greatest Of The Small Bands, Vol 5
(RCA Victor – France)
Various (Including Sarah Vaughan), The New York Scene In The '40s: From Be-bop To Cool
(CBS – France)
Budd Johnson, Four Brass Giants *(Riverside)*
Budd Johnson, Let's Swing
(Prestige – Swingville/—)
Budd Johnson/Keg Johnson, Blues A La Mode
(Felsted/Felsted)
Gil Evans, Pacific Standard Time *(Blue Note)*
Earl Hines/Jimmy Rushing, Blues & Things
(Master Jazz Recordings/ World Record Club)
Various, USA Jazz Live
(MPS/BASF – Germany)
Roy Eldridge, The Nifty Cat
(Master Jazz Recordings/—)
A Buck Clayton Jam Session *(Chiaroscuro)/*
Buck Clayton Jam Session, Vol 2 *(Chiaroscuro)/*
Buck Clayton Jam Sessions *(Vogue)**
Budd Johnson/JPJ Quartet, Montreux '71
(Master Jazz Recordings/—)
Various (Including Budd Johnson), Newport In New York '72: The Jam Sessions, Vol 3 *(Atlantic/Atlantic)*
Ben Webster & Associates
(Verve)/
 Ben Webster & Friends
(Verve)
Dizzy Gillespie, Dee Gee Days/ The Savoy Sessions *(Savoy/—)*
*UK double album of both US releases.

Above: Budd Johnson – a decided asset on any occasion, and multiple threat as reedman, writer and enthusiast.

Bunk Johnson

William Geary 'Bunk' Johnson (born New Orleans, Louisiana, 1879) had worked with legendary Buddy Bolden before arrival of 1900. In early-1900s, had worked in minstrel shows, at a circus, on liners en route to and from the Orient, Australia and Europe; and had visited both East and West Coast of the US. By 1930, had played in more circus bands, minstrel shows, theatres, had worked extensively in New Orleans (1910-14); taught and played in Mandeville; played with variety of bands throughout Louisiana. But for all this vast playing/ touring experience, name Bunk Johnson was just a legend amongst New Orleans/Louisiana jazzmen. It was not until researchers Frederic Ramsey, Jr and William Russell re-discovered Johnson that anything but minimal information pertaining to his background was unearthed. By which time had retired to New Iberia (following fracas at Rayne, Louisiana, dancehall where bandleader Evan Thomas was murdered on stage, and his second cornettist lost all his teeth); had worked as caretaker, fairground worker (as professional whistler) and truck driver and was currently (in '37) teaching trumpet, trombone, courtesy Workers' Programme Association scheme. A plan to record Johnson, in 1940, alongside Earl Hines (♦), Sidney Bechet (♦), failed to materialize because of his (Johnson's) continued involvement in project.

Music-wise, it was not until 1942, with first of now legendary 'New Orleans-revival' recordings (chronologically, for Jazz Man, Jazz

Below: The Bunk Johnson Band, Classic NO combo, including Jim Robinson, George Lewis, Baby Dodds and Bunk Johnson.

Above: Gus Johnson – hard-swinging yet subtle, the perfect drummer for all occasions, big band or small.

Above: Jay Jay Johnson, the most polished of performers. The man who taught the trombone the complexities of Bebop.

Information, American Music, etc.), that Bunk Johnson, 63-year-old legend, was to be heard on record. Johnson had begun his comeback by playing local dates in New Iberia, following acquisition (courtesy of Bechet's dentist brother) of a brand new set of false teeth. Since their first appearance, controversy has reigned over John son's comeback records, mostly about Johnson himself. There are those who believe his playing is, in the main, sublime and of extraordinary importance, musically and historically, in helping not only to recapture the essence of what Johnson must have sounded during all the years he went unrecorded but also as a vital document of the beginnings of New Orleans jazz. Others take the view that, new teeth notwithstanding, Johnson's long absence away from his horn, plus his age, had resulted in woefully inadequate trumpet playing. In fact, there is probably much truth in both viewpoints.

Johnson's playing did lack certain technical requirements, and compared with work of other New Orleans trumpet giants he seemed inadequate. But whatever technical deficiencies there might have been, there was no doubting the warmth, or passion, in his work on these records. And his ensemble playing, in company with what was to become the obligatory Johnson front-line – George Lewis (◊), Big Jim Robinson (◊) – was absolutely right; in many ways, not typical New Orleans trumpet as had been recognized with numerous other players and bands, but right in the context of various Johnson-led bands (including Bunk Johnson's Jazz Band, Bunk Johnson's Street Paraders, and, on first record date, Bunk Johnson's Original Superior Band).

In contrast to the pedestrian-plus supporting band, Johnson's playing in front of the Yerba Buena Band (**Bunk & Lu**) sounds fine, in every way. The American Music records come off best, with **Sugar Foot Stomp, Sister Kate, Careless Love** (Bunk Johnson's Band 1944); **'827 Blues, All The Whores Like The Way I Ride** (Bunk Johnson's Band 1945); **Weary Blues** and **See See Rider** (Bunk Johnson) probably best. With Sidney Bechet, in 1945, Johnson proved an eminently suitable ensemble player, whilst solo-wise his contributions to titles like **Days Beyond Recall** (Sidney Bechet Jazz Classics, Vol 1) and **Up In Sidney's Flat** (Sidney Bechet Jazz Classics, Vol 2) are, in the event, most moving. 1945: Johnson worked with Bechet, in New York and Boston, but soon returned to Louisiana.

Put together own band for two lengthy seasons at Stuyvesant Casino, NYC, which disbanded in 1946. Returned to Stuyvesant following year, recorded for last time in December, then went into self-imposed retirement in New Iberia.

In 1948 suffered stroke which paralysed left arm. For rest of his life – Johnson died in 1949 – was semi-invalid.

Recordings:
Bunk Johnson's Band 1944 (*Storyville*)
Bunk Johnson's Band 1945 (*Storyville*)
Bunk Johnson/Lu Watters, Bunk & Lu (*Good Time Jazz/ Good Time Jazz*)
Bunk Johnson (*Storyville*)
Sidney Bechet Jazz Classics, Vols 1, 2 (*Blue Note/—*)

Gus Johnson
◊ *Count Basie*

J. J. Johnson

Recent years have seen a reaction against the J. J. Johnson (b. 1924) style of trombone playing which dominated the '40s and '50s. Dispensing with the growls and slurs of Swing and Dixieland players, Johnson used the instrument to play the fast, agile lines of the Bebop saxophonists, concentrating on its linear possibilities rather than old-style – and currently, new style – brass band expressionism. Technically perfect, Johnson's work within the idiom has never been equalled. As a sideman with Sonny Stitt's group (**Genesis**) he contributed three fine originals, **Blue Mode, Teapot** and **Elora**, as well as displaying a rare melodic gift on John Lewis' **Afternoon In Paris.** Leading a sextet that included the great trumpeter Clifford Brown, Johnson cut an album that was virtually a definition of Bebop trombone, the tone consistent, the turn of speed on numbers like **Get Happy** phenomenal (**The Eminent J. J. Johnson**).

In 1954 he teamed up with fellow trombonist Kai Winding, but none of their albums remains in catalogue. A meeting with tenorman Sonny Rollins (**Sonny Rollins, Volume 2**) results in some of the most exciting trombone on record, the lines complex, poised yet driving. Another off-the-cuff meeting with a tenorman, Stan Getz (**Getz & J.J. 'Live'**) finds Johnson in peak form, matching the lyrical Getz on the ballad features, and producing a magnificent **Yesterdays** and **I Waited For You.**

Increasingly, he concentrated on writing works like **El Camino Real, Sketch For Trombone & Orchestra** and the six-part composition, **Perceptions,** for Gunther Schuller's Third Stream orchestra, which attempted a marriage between jazz and classical music. Three pieces for this orchestra by John Lewis, Jimmy Giuffre and J. J. Johnson (**Music For Brass**) use classical forms such as the fugue in Johnson's **Poem For Brass.** Currently, he seems to have settled into film and studio work.

Recordings:
Sonny Stitt, Genesis (*Prestige/Prestige*)
The Eminent J. J. Johnson (*Blue Note/Blue Note*)
Miles Davis (*Blue Note/Blue Note*)
Sonny Rollins, Volume 2 (*BluI Note/Blue Note*)
Getz & J. J. 'Live' (*Verve/Verve*)
Music For Brass (*Columbia/—*)

James P. Johnson

James Price 'James P.' Johnson (born Brunswick, New Jersey, 1891) was a well-nigh perfect link between ragtime and early jazz. Moreover, he was finest musician to merge from the so-called stride school of piano-players – pianists with large hands and powerful wrists whose exciting, percussive style depended as much on physical strength and endurance as technical skills. Johnson though, was, like his pupil Thomas 'Fats' Waller (♦), a notch above the rest of the stride pianists in that he possessed a fine all-round technique, no doubt a legacy of his youth, when his mother and an Italian piano teacher ensured he received a thorough schooling in classical keyboard techniques.

The combination of several important musical influences – ragtime, blues, classical – resulted in jazz playing that was to give Johnson a position of omnipotence amongst early-jazz pianists before the arrival of 1920s. Johnson family moved to Jersey, then to New York (the home of stride piano – or to be more specific, Harlem in New York).

First public appearances were at numerous of the celebrated rent parties, before he was 21. 1912: played first professional gigs at Coney Island, after which he became a familiar figure, playing solo in clubs in New York and Atlantic City. Toured Southern vaudeville circuit, then back to New York for further seasons in variety of clubs. Made series of piano rolls for Aeolian Co, then QRS **(James P. Johnson 1917-21)** and in 1921 made debut on records. Played with James Europe's Hell Fighters Band (1920–21), fronted a band onstage during a Broadway show, also working in two revues, *Black Sensations* and *Smart Set*. Played with Harmony Seven band in New York (1922). Composed music for *Plantation Days*, which Johnson took to UK in 1923.

During 1920s became highly suc-

Fats & Me (1944) (MCA, Germany). At the piano: James P.

cessful composer of songs which long since have become standards, in both jazz and pop worlds. Amongst his most popular numbers are **If I Could Be With You (One Hour Tonight), Charleston, Runnin' Wild, Old Fashioned Love, A Porter's Love Song.** 1925: orchestrated own *Running Wild* revue, and three years later **Yamecraw**, an extended composition, received its première at Carnegie Hall. Johnson's most famous piano piece, **Carolina Shout**, received first recording by its composer in 1921 **(James P. Johnson: Piano Solos).** Other Johnson solo recordings of 1920s, all of which demonstrate his all-round superiority as Harlem-style pianist, include **Arkansas Blues, Eccentricity** (both 1921), **Ole Miss Blues** (1922), a four-song **Runnin' Wild** medley (including **Old Fashioned Love, Charleston**) (1924), and **Sugar,** and **Harlem Choc'late Babies On Parade** (both 1926) (all **James P. Johnson Piano Solos**). Further proof of his superb adaptability is contained in recordings he made (1927, 1929)

with blues singer Bessie Smith (♦). His superbly confident, yet totally sympathetic accompaniments for Smith on tracks like **Backwater Blues (Nobody's Blues But Mine); Blue Spirit Blues, Wasted Life Blues** and **Worn Out Papa Blues (Any Woman's Blues)** could not have been bettered. And just how good a band pianist he was, all through his career, can be judged from records by Mezz Mezzrow **(The Complete Ladnier-Mezzrow-Bechet)**, Frankie Newton (♦) **(The Big Apple)**, Pee Wee Russell (♦) **(Jack Teagarden/Pee Wee Russell)**, Edmond Hall (♦) **(Edmond Hall's Blue Note Jazzmen)** and Eddie Condon (♦) **(The Eddie Condon Concerts, Vol 2).**

In this context can be cited records made by Johnson himself, best of which was 1939 date, with Red Allen (♦), J. C. Higginbotham (♦), Big Sid Catlett (♦) and others **(Father Of The Stride Piano** and **Swing Combos 1935-1941).** In 1932 wrote four-movement *Symphony Harlem*, presented onstage as ballet music. During 1930s concentrated on composing, and also collaborated with poet Langston Hughes on one-act *De Organizer*, although he continued to record and play live gigs.

Apart from illness in 1940, continued to work regularly, with own bands and others. Suffered stroke in 1946, but was playing again following year. 1949: took part in production of his *Sugar Hill* revue. Suffered severe stroke on return to New York (1951), which left him bedridden and unable to speak until he died, in New York City, 1955.

Recordings:
Various (Including James P. Johnson), Rare Piano Rags 1920-23
(Jazz Anthology – France)
James P. Johnson, 1917-21
(Biograph/—)

James P. Johnson: Piano Solos
(Joker – Italy)
Bessie Smith, Nobody's Blues But Mine *(Columbia/CBS)*
Bessie Smith, Any Woman's Blues *(Columbia/CBS)*
Various (Including James P. Johnson), The Complete Ladnier-Mezzrow-Bechet *(RCA Victor – France)*
(Mezz Mezzrow)/Frankie Newton, The Big Apple *(RCA Victor – France)*
Jack Teagarden/Pee Wee Russell *(Byg – France)*
Edmond Hall's Blue Note Jazzmen *(Blue Note/—)*
The Eddie Condon Concerts, Vol 2 *(Chiaroscuro/—)*
Various (Including James P. Johnson), 'This Is Jazz', Vols 1, 2 *(Rarities/—)*
James P. Johnson, Father Of The Stride Piano *(Columbia/—)*
Various (Including James P. Johnson), Swing Combos 1935-1941 *(Swingfan – Germany)*
James P. Johnson, Fats & Me (1944) *(MCA – Germany)*
James P. Johnson *(—/Xtra)*

Lonnie Johnson

Alonzo 'Lonnie' Johnson (born New Orleans, Louisiana around 1889) was an exceptionally gifted and certainly most versatile bluesman, one who seemed as happy singing or playing pop ballads as more profound, moving blues. One of the most technically assured of all blues guitarists, and a wholly individualistic performer, Johnson nevertheless seldom lacked the essential blues feel. Less impressive, at times, as singer, occasionally lapsing into excesses of sentimentality. Little doubt, though, he could sing blues – it was when he featured pop-type ballads that he was less effective.

Above: Lonnie Johnson – whether alone or with Eddie Lang, Duke or Louis, one of the giants of the blues.

Played both violin and piano in New Orleans before going to London to various revues (1917), returning to New Orleans c. 1921-2. Moved to St Louis beginning of 1920s. Played with bands like those of Charlie Creath, Fate Marable (again, using mostly violin, piano), and worked in foundry for two years, playing only part-time. As result of winning OKeh Records talent contest, commenced lengthy association with label in 1925. Recorded with Louis Armstrong (♦) Hot Five in December 1927, producing typically fine solos on **Savoy Blues, I'm Not Rough,** and providing superb rhythmic support for Armstrong scat vocal on **Hotter Than That (V.S.O.P. (Very Special Old Phonography, 1927-1928), Vols 3 & 4).**

In 1928, recorded with Duke Ellington (♦) Orchestra – one of comparatively rare examples of guest soloists featured with Ellington. As with Hot Five recordings, Johnson adapted himself with skill and taste to this context. With Ellington, featured on **The Mooche, Hot & Bothered (The Ellington Era, Vol 1/The Ellington Era, Vol 1 – Part 1)** and **Move Over, Misty Morning (The Ellington Era, Vol 2).** Also in '28, recorded blues guitar solos, **Playing With The Strings, Stompin' 'Em Along Slow, Away Down The Alley, Blues, Blues In G,** all originals of infinite beauty, emotionally as well as technically. Same year, the extraordinary two-guitar partnership of Johnson and Eddie Lang (♦) entered recording studios for first time. The total empathy between the pair never was anything less than exceptional, at times achieving the musical sublime, as with **Bull Frog**

Moan, **A Handful Of Riffs, Two Tone Stomp**, and **Guitar Blues** (The Golden Days Of Jazz: Eddie Lang & Joe Venuti - Stringing The Blues). Duo also provided sympathetic accompaniment for blues singer Texas Alexander and cornettist King Oliver (♦). Johnson, alone, also soloed most efficiently with **The Chocolate Dandies** and, during late-1920s and early-1930s played guitar with, and occasionally supplied extra vocals for, singers Texas Alexander, Victoria Spivey, Katherine Baker, etc (**Mr Johnson's Blues**).

To Cleveland in 1932, worked for Putney Dandridge, also did much radio work. Went to Chicago 1937, becoming resident at Three Deuces (including work with Johnny Dodds (♦)) until 1939. During 1940s, concentrated mostly on singing, playing amplified guitar in accompaniment. To Britain in 1952, for concert, then back to US to live in Cincinatti; then, to Philadelphia (1958–62), where he worked as chef in leading hotel. Toured Europe in blues package show in 1963. From mid-1960s, was heard mostly in Toronto, Canada. Suffered stroke, after serious accident in '69. During '63 European tour recorded in Copenhagen, in company with pianist Otis Spann (**See See Rider**), playing, singing, almost as brilliantly as during his earlier peak years, including excellent guitar on **Swingin' With Lonnie**, and fine re-working of **Tomorrow Night**, original version of which resulted in huge-selling single disc (1948).

Of other records made in last 10–15 years of his life, probably best are **Lonnie Johnson**** and parts of **Blues By Lonnie Johnson**. Aficionados, however, probably would prefer his earlier work with Lang, Armstrong, including his superb solo on 1929 **Mahogany Hall Stomp** (V.S.O.P. (Very Special Old Phonography, 1928-1930), Vols 5 & 6) the Johnson solos mentioned above, plus 'mid-period' recordings like **Lonnie Johnson*** and **Bluebird Blues**.

Lonnie Johnson died in 1970.

Recordings:
Louis Armstrong, V.S.O.P. (Very Special Old Phonography, 1927-1928), Vols 3 & 4) (CBS – France)
Louis Armstrong, V.S.O.P. (Very Special Old Phonography, 1928-1930), Vols 5 & 6 (CBS – France)
Duke Ellington, The Ellington Era (1927-1940), Vol 1 (Columbia)
The Ellington Era (1927-1940), Vol 1 - Part 1 (CBS)
Duke Ellington, The Ellington Era (1927-1940), Vol 2 (Columbia)/
The Golden Days Of Jazz: Eddie Lang & Joe Venuti - Stringing The Blues (CBS)
The Chocolate Dandies (—/Parlophone)
Lonnie Johnson, Mr Johnson's Blues (Mamlish/—)
Lonnie Johnson* (—/Brunswick – Germany)
Lonnie Johnson** (—/Xtra)
Various (Including Lonnie Johnson), Bluebird Blues (RCA Victor/RCA Victor)
Blues By Lonnie Johnson (Prestige – Bluesville/—)
Lonnie Johnson, See See Rider (—/Storyville)
*and **two separate, and different, recordings.

Pete Johnson

During a career which lasted 45 years, Pete Johnson (born 1904) established enviable reputation as superior two-handed pianist whose basic style encompassed blues, jazz, barrelhouse and boogie woogie. Kansas City (his birthplace) and New York were two most important cities in respect of geographical location of his peak musical achievements. Started professional career in Kansas (in 1926), where he had spent part of his childhood in orphanage; then, worked initially as drummer (1922–6), accompanying various piano-players. After taking piano lessons, switched from drums to keyboard, full-time in '26. Soon, his reputation as powerful exponent of rolling blues established in KC, where he was to spend 12 years as solo act.

During this time, first met blues singer Joe Turner (♦), working as bartender at Piney Brown's Sunset Cafe, and pair played occasional gigs together. Combination of singer and pianist was to re-appear on numerous occasions throughout next 30-odd years. 1938: pair invited to New York to appear on Benny Goodman (♦) radio show as well as at Apollo, Harlem. After returning to KC, duo was recalled by John Hammond to appear at his December '38 Spirituals To Swing concert (**John Hammond's Spirituals To Swing**).

Johnson stayed on in New York, teamed up with fellow pianists Meade Lux Lewis (♦), Albert Ammons (♦), at times augmented by voice of Turner and became seminal participant in widespread popularity of boogie woogie. Focal point of impact was Cafe Society where all three played long residencies, from 1939 until early-1940s. Three recorded together extensively (again, with Turner adding his own unique brand of blues vocalism). And like Ammons, Johnson collaborated on record with Harry James (♦) in strictly

Master Of Blues & Boogie Woogie (Oldie Blues - Holland)

boogie woogie vein, most successfully on **Cafe Society Swing & The Boogie Woogie**. Later same year (1939), also successfully integrated his piano style with trumpet of Hot Lips Page (♦) and own Boogie Woogie Boys at record date. Also recorded extensively in solo capacity: fine Blue Note date (**Pete Johnson**) gives ample evidence of his capabilities when left to own devices, notably on **Barrelhouse Breakdown** and **You Don't Know My Mind**.

Following split between Lewis and Turner, Ammons, Johnson

stayed on together at Cafe Society. Johnson also took part in film, *Boogie Woogie Dream*. During 1940s, continued to make appearance throughout US, and to record at fairly frequent intervals (**Pete Johnson: Master Of Blues & Boogie Woogie, Vols 1, 2**), either alone or as part of quartet, or with additional instrumentalists, like Hot Lips Page, Budd Johnson (♦), Clyde Bernhardt. Perhaps his finest recorded work during this decade was in 1944 (**Vol 1**) when he cut eight titles for Brunswick, of which **Dive Bomber, Zero Hour** (an especially potent example of his blues-playing), **Rock It Boogie** and **Rock & Roll Boogie** are exceptional.

Johnson-Ammons recorded again in 1949 (**Boogie Woogie Man**) but then they, too, parted company. Three trips to California in 1947 resulted in further fine Johnson recordings. 1949: appeared at one of Blues Jubilee Concerts promoted by Gene Norman and Frank Bull (**Vol 1**) but by this time pianist's repertoire tended to drop in quality (viz **Swanee River Boogie**). Active 1949–52, playing major US cities. In latter year took part (with Erroll Garner (♦), Art Tatum (♦)) in Piano Parade tour. At conclusion of tour, Johnson lost part of little finger, whilst changing car tyre – a loss which, curiously, he shared with erstwhile keyboard companion, Ammons.

Was forced to leave music business full-time in 1953, playing only at week-ends. By following year, was employed as janitor. Was invited, in 1955, to take part in recording session, featuring singer Jimmy Rushing (♦) (**Listen To The Blues**) proving he had lost little of his old skills. Better still was 1956 date re-uniting Johnson with old friend Joe Turner (**Boss Of The Blues**). Two had last recorded together in late-1940s, but the '56 get-together sparked both men into producing of their exceptional best. Johnson's accompaniments throughout are absolutely first-rate; same can be said for his solos. Of particular potency – vocally and instrumentally – is comprehensive work-out on **Roll 'Em Pete**, Johnson's most famous composition. (Johnson had previously worked, briefly, as accompanist to Turner, in 1955; he performed in similar capacity for Rushing).

Toured Europe in 1958, as member of JATP (with Turner), played Newport Jazz Festival, but was stricken with serious illness towards end of year. Was to suffer from recurring ill-health for rest of his life, working and recording infrequently. Made poignant appearance at Carnegie Hall, as member of Joe Turner's Cafe Society All Stars (**Spirituals To Swing - 1967**) just before he died in 1967, although it was obvious by his appearance that he was gravely ill.

Much interesting information to be found in *The Pete Johnson Story*, compiled and edited by Hans J. Mauerer.

Recordings:
Various, John Hammond's Spirituals To Swing (Vanguard/Vogue)
Various, Cafe Society Swing & Boogie Woogie (Swingfan – Germany)
Meade Lux Lewis/Albert Ammons/Peter Johnson, The
Complete Library Of Congress Boogie Woogie Recordings (Jazz Piano/—)
Meade Lux Lewis/Albert Ammons/Pete Johnson, Giants Of Boogie Woogie (Storyville)
Pete Johnson (Blue Note)
Pete Johnson/Albert Ammons/Jimmy Yancey (Boogie Woogie Man) (RCA Victor – France)
Various, 29 Boogie Woogie Originaux (RCA Victor – France)
Pete Johnson, Master Of Blues & Boogie Woogie 1904-1967, Vols 1, 2 (Oldie Blues – Holland)
Jumpin' With Pete Johnson (Riverside/London)
Have No Fear, Big Joe Turner Is Here (Savoy/Savoy)
Various (Including Pete Johnson), Barrelhouse, Boogie Woogie & Blues (—/Fontana)
Joe Turner & Pete Johnson (EmArcy/—)
Jimmy Rushing, The Essential Jimmy Rushing (—/Vogue)
Joe Turner, Boss Of The Blues (Atlantic/Atlantic)
Various (Including Pete Johnson/Joe Turner), Spirituals To Swing - 1967 (Columbia/—)

Robert Johnson

Robert Johnson (born near Clarksdale, Mississippi, c. 1913) died at a tragically young age – he was not quite 24 years old when he was poisoned in a San Antonio, Texas, hotel by, it is said, a jealous girl friend. Robert Johnson's death was tragic insofar as his was one of the most extraordinary talents to emerge from any era of the history of the blues. Johnson, in a period of only a few years, established a powerful reputation as a bluesman whose music often was terrifyingly real and unbearably intense. The Johnson legend has been maintained in the years following his death, in 1937, with the fairly frequent re-appearance of 30-plus discs he cut between 1936–7. Not too much is known about his background but, personality-wise, he seems to have been something of a schizophrenic, a condition worsened by his persistent hard drinking. Said by some to be extremely shy, by all accounts he was far from being introverted or retiring in company of women – his fascination for opposite sex proved in the end to be the reason for his early demise. Certainly, women figured prominently in many of his blues – like **Kindhearted Women Blues**, whose two separate takes make intriguing contrast (**King Of The Delta Blues Singers, Vol 1** and **King Of The Delta Blues Singers, Vol 2**) and **Walking Blues (Vol 1)**, which finds him in inconsolable mood, after being ripped off by a woman. Other recordings, such as **Hellbound On My Trail, Preaching Blues, Me & The Devil** (all **Vol 1**) are formidable demonstrations of his pre-occupation with inner nightmares and fantasies of terror, no doubt induced by his alcoholic extravagances. Often, his vocals – sometimes using falsetto to a maximum dramatic effect – were imbued with a genuinely frightening intensity. Johnson ranks with the greatest of all blues poetry – afore-mentioned items typify his best work. Other classics include **Phonograph Blues, Drunken Hearted Man, Rambling On My Mind (Vol 2)** and **Crossroads Blues, Walkin' Blues, Come On In My Kitchen (Vol 1)**. And Johnson's pungent guitar lines, executed with the same passion as his singing, were the perfect corollary to his lyrics and their vocal projection. As a guitarist, Johnson was also influential – his unique walking bass line was copied by numerous other bluesmen (including many latterday blues-conscious rock guitarists); similarly, his bottleneck playing was exceptional.

Recordings:
King Of The Delta Blues Singers, Vol 1 *(Columbia/CBS)*
King Of The Delta Blues Singers, Vol 2 *(Columbia/CBS)*

Elvin Jones

Best known for his classic partnership with John Coltrane, Elvin Jones is one of the major innovators on drums. Born 1927, brother to trumpeter Thad and pianist Hank, Elvin Jones' conception of a freer accompaniment was a logical extension of post-Bop drumming. Breaking away from the regular cymbal beat, he launched a barrage of accents and rhythmic patterns that offered endless possibilities to the soloist. An early example of his polyrhythmic accompaniment can be found with the classic Sonny Rollins trio **(A Night At The Village Vanguard)** where the concepts of drummer and tenor-man, though not always compatible, strike sparks.

Coltrane's legato attack, the longer lines, was eminently suited to Jones' multiple pulse which moved out into freer areas as the solo developed. Any of the many Coltrane Impulse albums illustrate the partnership at work, the two men stretched to the utmost and transcending the traditional idea of solo and accompaniment.

Above: Elvin Jones, the master drummer who fueled Coltrane's finest flights. Leads his own groups.

The Drum Thing (Crescent) is a fine example of Jones' solo strength and ability to combine complexity with forward momentum, while **Africa (Africa Brass)** is structured from thematic elements. **Chasin' The Trane,** a classic and headlong tenor solo, fuels on the drummer's endless strength **(Live At The Village Vanguard)** while the addition of drummer Rashied Ali, an extremely loose worker, marked the beginning of the dis-

solution of the partnership **(Meditations)**.

Jones' own groups, though lacking the front-line distinction of a Coltrane, have been characterized by fine musicianship and great drumming. The first trios with saxophonist Joe Farrell and bassist Jimmy Garrison **(The Ultimate** and **Puttin' It Together)** are beautifully paced and show Jones' ability to vary the intensity of his work to complement the soloist.

Recordings:
Sonny Rollins, A Night At The Village Vanguard *(Blue Note/Blue Note)*
John Coltrane:
Crescent *(Impulse/Impulse)*
Africa Brass *(Impulse/Impulse)*
Live At The Village Vanguard *(Impulse/Impulse)*
Meditations *(Impulse/Impulse)*
Elvin Jones:
The Ultimate *(Blue Note/Blue Note)*
Puttin' It Together *(Blue Note/Blue Note)*
Heavy Sounds *(Impulse/Impulse)*
Live At The Vanguard *(Enja/Enja)*

Hank Jones

Henry ('Hank') Jones (born Pontiac, Michigan, 1918), and the eldest of three noted jazz brothers – Thad Jones (♦) and Elvin Jones (♦) are the other two – has worked with practically all the major jazz figureheads (pre-avant garde) of the past 30-odd years, including Coleman Hawkins (♦) **(The High & Mighty**

Hawk), Stan Getz (♦) **(Opus De Bop/The Savoy Sessions)**, Charlie Parker (♦) **(The Definitive Charlie Parker, Vols 1-3, 6)**, Milt Jackson (♦) **(Second Nature/The Savoy Sessions)** and Lester Young (♦) **(Lester Swings)**. Reasons for his popularity as pianist are obvious: a wholly distinctive touch – delicate, yet firm; his sensitivity as accompanist; his beautifully understated invention and constant rhythmic approach as soloist; and a brand of rare all-round musicianship that is without equal.

Jones, who as a youth studied with Carlotta Franzell, has worked with singers of the calibre of Ella Fitzgerald (♦) and Billy Eckstine (♦). His innate musical catholicity, coupled with a rare ability to operate within practically any given jazz framework, made him an obvious selection for numerous Jazz At The Philharmonic concert tours **(Norman Granz' JATP - Carnegie Hall Concert 1952, Record 3)**. And during 1950s Jones featured on literally hundreds of album dates, mostly for Savoy for whom he became, together with drummer Kenny Clarke (♦) and bassist Wendell Marshall, a member of house rhythm section. Jones recorded for Savoy alone **(Have You Met Hank Jones?** – one of his finest personal recorded statements), as well as together with his colleagues Clarke, and Marshall **(The Trio)** – and the same piano, bass and drums offered choice accompaniments to numerous Savoy artists. Jones also has worked many times in a quartet setting (together with bassist Milt Hinton, drummer Osie Johnson, and guitarist Barry

The Ultimate (Blue Note): one of the best of Elvin Jones' post-Coltrane units. His wife, Keiko, tunes the drum kit.

Above: Hank (eldest of the musical Jones brothers). As adroit a soloist as he is sensitive an accompanist.

Galbraith), providing ideal backings for further top-class instrumentalists. Jones also has spent periods undertaking commercial work, where his talents have been all but buried. Not in the very front rank of jazz piano soloists, Hank Jones' individual capabilities are exceptional nevertheless. His style might be described as basically mainstream-modern, with influences of Art Tatum (♦), Teddy Wilson (♦), Al Haig (♦) Bud Powell (♦), and Nat Cole (♦) being clearly discernible. Not all the albums made under his own name have done his talents full justice – Jones is one of those players who seems to produce his best work when working as sideman in someone else's band. But the two Savoy albums cited above, plus **Keeping Up With The Joneses** – a 1958 date in company with brothers Thad and Elvin and bassist Eddie Jones – contain much excellent piano playing. Earliest portion of Jones' career found him working mainly in Ohio and Michigan, before he moved to New York (1944). There, he worked with such as Hot Lips Page (♦), John Kirby (♦), Coleman Hawkins (♦) and Howard McGhee (♦). Was accompanist for Ella Fitzgerald (♦) between 1948 and 1953 (including a European tour). Has worked for Benny Goodman (♦) on several occasions (first time: 1956). Because of the extraordinary number of recordings which featured

Hank Jones' keyboard artistry the discography below is of necessity very selective.

Recordings:
Stan Getz Opus De Bop/The Savoy Sessions (Savoy)
Norman Granz' JATP – Carnegie Concert 1952 (Gene Krupa Trio), Record 3 (Clef/Columbia – Clef)
Milt Jackson, Second Nature/ The Savoy Sessions (Savoy)
Donald Byrd, Long Green/The Savoy Sessions (Savoy)
Ernie Wilkins, Top Brass (Savoy/London)
Milt Jackson, Big Band Bags (Milestone)
The Definitive Charlie Parker, Vols 1-3, 6 (Verve/Verve)
Coleman Hawkins, The High & Mighty Hawk (Felsted/Vocalion)
Flip Phillips, Flip (—/Verve)
Lester Young, Lester Swings (—/Verve)
Lucky Thompson, Lucky Strikes (Prestige/—)
Kenny Dorham, But Beautiful (Milestone)
Ray Brown/Milt Jackson, Much In Common (Verve/Verve)
The Jones Bros, Keeping Up With The Joneses (MetroJazz)
Have You Met Hank Jones (Savoy/London)
Hank Jones/Kenny Clarke/ Wendell Marshall, The Trio (Savoy/London)

Jo Jones
♦ Count Basie

Jonah Jones

For between 45 and 50 years Robert Elliott 'Jonah' Jones (born Louisville, Kentucky, 1909) has been a first-rate trumpet player in a basically mainstream bag, always a reliable soloist and section man. He has played with a variety of

The Jo Jones Special (Vanguard) – superior mainstream.

bands – his own as well as others – and can rarely have given a poor performance. Somehow, though, Jonah Jones lacks that something extra which, long ago, would surely have elevated him to the ranks of giants of the trumpet. Started playing trumpet in public during his teens, then took first professional job with Booker T. Wallace Bryant band aboard a Mississippi river boat (1929). Worked with Horace Henderson (♦) and other lesser-known bands until joining Jimmie Lunceford (♦) (1931). Linked up with Stuff Smith (♦), with whom he was to experience some degree of widespread popularity a few years hence, first working with the violinist between 1932–4. Rejoined Smith after being member of McKinney's Cotton Pickers for brief spell. Smith and Jones were members of a fine jumping band which enjoyed much success during a long residency at Onyx Club, 52nd Street, New York, drawing large crowds to venue. Jones played excellent trumpet with band **(Stuff Smith & His Onyx Club Orchestra),** helped Smith out with vocal chores and contributed to the overall humorous approach which was vital ingredient in its make-up. Stayed with Smith until moving on to Benny Carter (♦) Orchestra (1940–1).

His joyful solo outing on **Babalu (Benny Carter & His Orchestra 1940-1)** was typical of his playing of the period, showing off a warm, melodic approach and an undeniable ability to swing in relaxed fashion. After short stay with

Fletcher Henderson (♦), Jones began a lengthy association (1941–51) with orchestra of Cab Calloway (♦), an event which was celebrated by bandleader Calloway who wrote **Jonah Joins The Cab (16 Cab Calloway Classics)** as a kind of introductory showcase for trumpeter who responded with admirable, fiercely-blown solo. In 1944, Jones produced some of his finest playing at any time of his career **(Lowdown Blues),** first as member of Pete Brown's (♦) Jump Band, then leading his own studio band (including Tyree Glenn (♦), Ike Quebec, and J. C. Heard).

Influence of Louis Armstrong (♦) on his playing much in evidence on tracks like **I Can't Give You Anything But Love** and **You Can Depend On Me** (both with own band). Worked with pianist Joe Bushkin's Quartet at Embers (1952), then toured with Earl Hines (♦) Sextet for two years. Worked in pit band for show *Porgy & Bess* (1953), following year going to Europe as solo act. From 1955, led quartet which gained wide following, although its jazz content was not especially high. Leader played quiet, restrained trumpet, band played mostly pop standards, and combination helped to sell thousands of Jonah Jones records, like **I Dig Chicks,** probably best of the many that were released. Quartet visited Monaco (1959) and toured Australia (1960).

Earlier in his career, Jones' trumpet was heard in top form at one of Lionel Hampton's famous

Above: Thad Jones, co-leader of the Thad Jones-Mel Lewis big band, trumpeter and brother of pianist Hank and drummer Elvin.

late-1930s record dates **(The Complete Lionel Hampton/Lionel Hampton's Best Records, Vol 1)**, contributing splendid solos to **Drum Stomp** and **Confessin'**. Also participated in sessions with Billie Holiday (♦) **(The Billie Holiday Story, Vol 1)** producing passionate playing (both open and muted) on **That's Life I Guess**. Of later recordings, two from his '54 visit to Europe – both made in Paris – are more than adequate examples of his work of that period. With Sidney Bechet (♦) **(Refreshing Tracks, Vol 2)** he is not in the least over-awed; and as leader of an all-French pick-up band **(Jonah Jones Sextet)** his playing commands attention throughout.

Recordings:
Stuff Smith & His Onyx Club Orchestra
(Collector's – Switzerland)
Benny Carter & His Orchestra (1940-1941)
(RCA Victor – France)
16 Cab Calloway Classics
(CBS – France)
Jonah Jones/Pete Brown, Lowdown Blues
(Jazz Showcase/—)
The Complete Lionel Hampton
(Bluebird)/
Lionel Hampton's Best Records, Vol 1
(RCA Victor – France)
The Billie Holiday Story, Vol 1
(Columbia/CBS)
Sidney Bechet, Refreshing Tracks, Vol 2 *(—/Vogue)*
Jonah Jones Sextet
(HMV – France)
Jonah Jones, I Dig Chicks
(Capitol/Music For Pleasure)

Thad Jones

One of the famous Jones brothers – drummer Elvin, pianist Hank – Thad was born 1923 in Michigan. His initial impact as trumpeter with the Basie band in 1954 was considerable, but it was his own Blue Note releases which established

his reputation. His attack and accuracy at tempo, his hot, blatant tone balanced by a concept of musical architecture that is both weird and logical, made Jones a man to watch in the Hard Bop '50s.

His performance of **April In Paris**, a frequent ballad choice, illustrates his virtues **(The Magnificent Thad Jones)**. A meeting with Thelonious Monk struck creative sparks, both men highly individual in their use of intervals and far-fetched figures **(Brilliance)**, while an album with baritonist Pepper Adams **(Mean What You Say)** has the two men making intelligent use of the new harmonic freedom. With the fine drummer, Mel Lewis, Jones formed a big band in the mid-60s, and a series of hard-swinging, straight-ahead albums followed, featuring the leader's trumpet, cornet and flugelhorn. Consistently musically, there is little to choose between their albums.

Recordings:
The Magnificent Thad Jones
(Blue Note/Blue Note)
Thelonious Monk, Brilliance
(Milestone/Milestone)
Thad Jones-Pepper Adams, Mean What You Say
(Milestone/Milestone)
Thad Jones & Mel Lewis: Monday Night At The Village Vanguard *(Solid State/—)*
Central Park North
(Solid State/—)
Consummation
(Blue Note/Blue Note)
Potpourri
(Philadelphia International/—)
Thad Jones-Mel Lewis
(Blue Note/Blue Note)
Suite For Pops
(Horizon/A&M Horizon)
New Life
(Horizon/A&M Horizon

Scott Joplin Rags (Sonet). Ragtime was the music that preceded jazz, first in favor from the 1890s until the early 1900s, more recently in the 1970s.

Scott Joplin

Ragtime pianist-composer Scott Joplin was born in 1868 in Texarkana, the son of an ex-slave, and died in a mental institution in 1917. The origins of ragtime are difficult to pinpoint, but the songs and dances of the plantation, European popular dances like the waltz, mazurka, quadrille and polka, minstrel banjo music and marches all contributed to the genre. Ragtime is a written piano music, pre-dating gramophone records, and it gained its popularity through the sale of sheet music and piano rolls. Harmonically uncomplicated, ragtime is usually rhythmically in 2/4, the left hand maintaining a bass beat, while the melodic content is derived from folk music and dances like the jig or cakewalk.

The great pioneers, Joseph Lamb, Tom Turpin, James Scott and Louis Chauvin established the form, but Joplin's genius stretched it to its limits. He dreamed of moving ragtime from the saloons and sporting houses of St Louis into the concert halls, and his finest compositions aspire to the stature of Chopin or Strauss. Tragically, Joplin's dream of a respectable Afro-American art form was ignored, and his rags became the diversion of the hour. His opera,

The Magnificent Thad Jones (Blue Note): '50s cover by Francis Wolff. Today, Thad co-leads the Jones-Mel Lewis band.

Treemonisha, an extended work dealing with the black predicament, was a failure and Joplin sank into a depression which led to the final insanity.

There is a charming insouciance and primness about his best work, an avoidance of the robust displays of technique associated with ragtime. 'Do Not Play Fast' is the habitual instruction on the sheet music. His earliest compositions, **Original Rags** and **The Favorite,** are fairly thin in comparison with the late masterpieces like **Magnetic Rag.** His most popular number, **Maple Leaf Rag,** bought by music publisher John Stark, established Joplin as 'King Of Ragtime' from 1899, though he benefited little from the later ragtime boom-period with its commercial dilution and Tin Pan Alley exploitation. Among his large output of 50 or so rags, **The Entertainer, Elite Syncopations, Weeping Willow, Palm Leaf Rag, The Chrysanthemum, The Cascade, The Sycamore, Nonpareil, Gladiolus** and **Rose Leaf Rag** are outstanding in their combination of strains, melody and harmony cohering exquisitely.

Joplin influenced Jelly Roll Morton and the Harlem Stride School of Fats Waller, James P. Johnson and Willie 'The Lion' Smith, and ragtime in general has enjoyed resurgences of popularity in the '40s and '70s, the most recent attributable to the movie, *The Sting.* The best book on the subject remains *They All Played Ragtime* by Rudi Blesh and Harriet Janis.

Best-selling versions of Joplin favorites have been recorded by Joshua Rifkin **(The Scott Joplin Golden Gift Box);** these are distinguished by his authentic and scholarly approach. There are numerous piano rolls on record, though the sound quality is often poor.

Recordings:
The Scott Joplin Golden Gift Box *(Nonesuch/Nonesuch)*
Keith Nichols Plays Scott Joplin & The Classic Rag Masters *(—/One-Up)*
Heliotrope Bouquet, William Bolcom *(Nonesuch/Nonesuch)*
Ragtime Piano Roll Classics *(—/BYG)*

Louis Jordan

Louis Jordan (born Brinkley, Arkansas, 1908) is best remembered as leader of an R&B-based jazz combo which achieved considerable popularity throughout most of 1940s, playing before large audiences and selling impressive quantities of records. Its leader played basically swinging alto-sax and sang in blues-inflected style; both Jordan's playing and singing, like music produced by his Tympany Five, reflected appealing sense of humor and immense vitality. Jordan & His Tympany Five recorded prolifically for Decca between 1938–55, during which time it notched up string of hit records, including **Knock Me A Kiss, Choo Choo Ch'boogie, Caldonia, Beware, Brother, Beware, Saturday Night Fish Fry** and **Let The Good Times Roll** (all **The Best Of Louis Jordan**). During this period, Jordan also recorded with Louis Armstrong (♦), Bing Crosby (♦), Ella Fitzgerald (♦).

Repertoire of Tympany Five comprised mostly blues, R&B, jazz, novelty items and pops of the day – for millions, the combination was irresistible.

However, Jordan's career did not begin with his highly successful Tympany Five. Originally had studied clarinet and started professional career (in 1929) with Jimmy Pryor's Imperial Serenaders. Worked through various bands between 1930–6, latter year joining orchestra of Chick Webb (♦), playing alto-, soprano-sax, and taking occasional vocals. During his two years with Webb, Jordan's solo opportunities tended to be limited **(Mayor Of Alabam,** on soprano was one of his rare outings). On break-up of Tympany Five, Jordan signed as solo artist with Mercury. Not surprisingly, company asked him to re-record some of the old hits, like **Caldonia, Choo Choo Ch'boogie, I'm Gonna Move To The Outskirts Of Town, Is You Is Or Is You Ain't My Baby?** and **Let The Good Times Roll (Choo Choo Ch'boogie).** With arrangements by Quincy Jones, and with pick-up band including such as Budd Johnson (♦), Ernie Royal, Sam 'The Man' Taylor, and Jimmy Cleveland, results were better than comparable 'revival' records, with Jordan, instrumentally and vocally, as irrepressible as ever.

Choo Choo Ch'Boogie **(Philips International).**

Above: Louis Jordan – one of the early cross-over personalities to conquer jazz, R&B and pop

Tried his hand at leading big band in 1951 **(Silver Star Swing Series Present Louis Jordan & His Orchestra)** and although music this outfit produced was fine, it lacked a distinctive sound of its own. After a couple of years touring and recording, Jordan disbanded the larger unit and reverted to Tympany Five format. During early-1950s, suffered several bouts of ill-health, often preferring to stay in his Phoenix, Arizona, home. Moved to Los Angeles in early-1960s, after making something of a comeback during late-1950s. Visited UK in 1962, signed with Ray Charles' Tangerine label in '64 (after one LP, unsuccessful sales-wise, association was terminated), and toured Asia in two consecutive years (1967–8).

Formed own label, Pzazz, in '68, making at least one fine LP, with big band conducted-arranged by tenorist Teddy Edwards **(Santa Claus, Santa Claus/Sakatumi).** Recorded also in 1960s, with Chris Barber Band **(Louis Jordan Swings),** although generally results were less than inspiring.

Much more successful was **Great Rhythm & Blues Oldies, Vol 1** with Jordan, once again, revisiting trusted-and-true repertoire of the past, this time in company with Shuggie Otis (guitar, bass, piano, organ), Johnny Otis (drums, piano), and others. Recorded in 1974, year before his death, it is a healthy reminder of just how appealing – and vital – Louis Jordan and his music remained until the very end of a successful and colorful career.

Recordings:
Chick Webb, King Of The Savoy (1937-1939) *(Decca/MCA – Germany)*
Chick Webb, Strictly Jive (1936-1938) *(Decca/MCA – Germany)*
Louis Jordan, Let The Good Times Roll *(Decca/—)*

Louis Jordan, The Best Of . . . *(—/MCA)*
Louis Jordan, Choo Choo Ch'Boogie *(Philips International)*
Silver Star Series Present Louis Jordan & His Orchestra *(MCA/Coral – Germany)*
Louis Jordan/Chris Barber, Louis Jordan Swings *(Black Lion)*
Louis Jordan, Santa Claus, Santa Claus/Sakatumi *(Pzazz/—)*
Louis Jordan, Prime Cuts *(Swing House/—)*

Max Kaminsky

Max Kaminsky (born Brockton, Massachusetts, 1908) has demonstrated a remarkable consistency in performance during a professional career that dates back to to 1920s. In fact, led own band for first time at 12, in Boston. Worked with variety of bands during 1920s, including Art Karle and George Wettling. To New York (1929), and tour with Red Nichols (♦). During 1930s worked with many prominent jazz men and bands, as well as with commercial dance bands.

Recorded with Chocolate Dandies **(The Chocolate Dandies)** in 1933, soloing to advantage on **Krazy Kapers.** Joined Tommy Dorsey (♦) Orchestra (1936), returning two years later. During first spell, produced typically fine solos on items like **Maple Leaf Rag, Royal Garden Blues, Rhythm Saved The World (The Best Of Tommy Dorsey, Vol 4, 1935-1937)** and in '38, played with excellent control on **Hawaiian War Chant** and **Davenport Blues** (both **Tommy Dorsey & His Orchestra).** Spent two periods also with Artie Shaw (♦), 1938, 1941-2. Produced superb obbligato to vocal by Hot Lips Page (♦) during 1941 recording by Shaw

(**Artie Shaw & His Orchestra, Vol 2**) of **St James Infirmary**. With Alvino Rey, Joe Marsala (♦) before military service with US Navy during which he played in Shaw-led Naval Band, touring Pacific area.

Honorably discharged March 1944. Back in New York, fronted own bands, then worked with Art Hodes (♦). Recorded often with Hodes during 1944-5 (**The Funky Piano Of Art Hodes**) with beautifully unruffled solos, played with rare feeling, on **M.K. Blues, Slow 'Em Down Blues, KMH (Draggin' The Blues)**, and **Chicago Gal**. Equally superior Kaminsky emanated from same Hodes session which produced **Slow 'Em Down Blues (Art Hodes Blue Note Chicagoans)**, especially on **She's Crying For Me**. Continued to lead own bands through 1940s, also working regularly with Eddie Condon (♦). Took part in many of legendary Condon Town Hall concerts (**The Eddie Condon Concerts 1944-1945 Featuring Pee Wee Russell**) and during 1930s, 1940s, often was to be found in line-ups on Condon record dates (**Commodore Condon, Vol 1** and **We Called It Music**). Also participated in rewarding Sidney Bechet (♦) record date in '45 (**Sidney Bechet Jazz Classics, Vols 1, 2**) acquitting himself, as always, in handsome fashion.

During 1950s, combined jazz work with periodic submersion in glossy, jazzless society orchestras. Toured Europe in '57 with Earl Hines (♦), Jack Teagarden (♦), and to Far East following year with trombonist. From 1960s, has continued to work regularly, mostly at established Dixieland clubs, taking time off, for instance, to visit and work in London (1970). Kaminsky, still a terribly under-appreciated player in some quarters, will also be fondly remembered for his sterling lead and excellent solo work as member of Bud Freeman's (♦) Summa Cum Laude Orchestra (**Chicagoans In New York** and **Chicago Styled**). *My Life In Jazz*, Max Kaminsky's autobiography, was published in 1963.

Recordings:
The Chocolate Dandies
   (—/*Parlophone*)
The Best Of Tommy Dorsey, Vol 4 (1935-1937)
   (*RCA Victor – France*)
Tommy Dorsey & His Orchestra (*RCA Victor*)
Artie Shaw & His Orchestra, Vol 2 (*RCA Victor*)
The Funky Piano Of Art Hodes (*Blue Note*/—)
Art Hodes Blue Note Chicagoans (*Blue Note*/—)
The Eddie Condon Concerts 1944-45 Featuring Pee Wee Russell (*Chiaroscuro*/—)
Eddie Condon, We Called It Music (*Decca*/*Ace of Hearts*)
Eddie Condon, Commodore Condon, Vol 1 (—/*London*)
Sidney Bechet Jazz Classics, Vols 1, 2 (*Blue Note*/—)
Bud Freeman, Chicagoans In New York (*Dawn Club*/—)
Bud Freeman, Chicago Styled (*Swaggie – Australia*)

Stan Kenton

Bandleader Stanley Newcomb Kenton was born in Kansas in 1912,

Above: Bandleader Stan Kenton coaxes up a crescendo. His concertos and opuses gave rise to Progressive Jazz.

forming his first band in 1940 with a thirteen-piece group to play a residency at the Rendezvous Restaurant in Balboa, California. This was the jitterbug era, and Kenton's predilection for experimental classical music had to be tempered by the more straightforward demands of his audience. In fact, although Kenton is usually associated with grandiose cathedrals of sound, he has always played a varied book; dance music, pop, jazz and neo-classical. **Opus In Pastels (Artistry In Rhythm)** arranged and composed by the leader in 1941, gives a fair idea of his aspirations, while **Artistry In Rhythm** from 1943 has a strong flavor of the movie concerto, with romantic Kenton piano, punching brass, thumping drums.

Numbers like **Eager Beaver, Painted Rhythm** and the June Christy vocal on **Tampico** are typical early '40s Kenton, and went out over the airwaves three times a week, gaining him a considerable following.

In 1945, arranger Pete Rugolo started working for the band, contributing numbers like the impressionistic **Interlude, Unison Riff (Greatest Hits)**; the Stravinsky-influenced **Artistry In Percussion** and the Ravel-influenced **Artistry In Bolero (Artistry In**

Stan Kenton's Greatest Hits (Capitol): '40s nostalgia.

Rhythm), while Kenton wrote **Intermission Riff, Artistry In Rhythm** and **Eager Beaver**.

In 1947 Kenton organized his second orchestra with musicians like drummer Shelly Manne, guitarist Laurindo Almeido, tenorman Bob Cooper and trombonist Milt Bernhardt. Playing 'Progressive Jazz' which utilized dissonance and atonality, Kenton drew on the composing and arranging talents of Bob Graettinger, Neil Hefti, Gene Roland and Shorty Rogers. The sheer volume of the music, the screaming trumpet section, immensely structured works that slam in by section on schedule, intimidated the critics who declared Kenton's music empty and pretentious. Nevertheless, the Kenton Orchestra played the poshest venues, the classical concert halls and colleges.

His interest in Latin American music gave him his biggest hit of the period in **The Peanut Vendor (Greatest Hits)**. During 1950-1 he gave a series of concerts under the heading **Innovations In Modern Music** using a 43-piece orchestra including strings and woodwinds, and concentrating on neo-classical works like Graettinger's **City Of Glass**. In the early '50s the orchestra reverted to a jazz policy, employing a host of excellent soloists like altoist Art Pepper (♦) on **Blues In Riff**, altoist Lee Konitz on **Of All Things**, trumpeter Shorty Rogers on **Riff Rhapsody (Artistry In Jazz)**.

The list of talent that has been through the Kenton ranks is staggering – Vido Musso, Boots Mussulli, Jimmy Giuffre, Eddie Safranski, Frank Rosolino, Stan Getz, Bud Shank, Richie Kamuca, Bill Perkins, Charlie Mariano, Pepper Adams, Lennie Niehaus, Stan Levey, etc. The economics of maintaining a big band through 37 years without pandering to fashion indicates Stan Kenton's great organizational skills, as well as great artistic conviction. Throughout the '60s and

'70s, orchestra has succeeded orchestra – the Mellophonium Orchestra, the Neophonic Orchestra – and their output can be sampled via a late Kenton compilation, **Artistry In Jazz**, as well as on Kenton's own Creative World label.

Recordings:
Stan Kenton's Greatest Hits (*Capitol*/*Capitol*)
Artistry In Rhythm (*Capitol*/—)
Artistry In Jazz (*Capitol*/—)
Live At Redlands University (*Creative World*/—)
Adventures In Jazz (*Creative World*/—)
Kenton/Wagner (*Creative World*/—)
National Anthems Of The World (*Creative World*/—)
Viva Kenton (*Creative World*/—)
7.5 On The Richter Scale (*Creative World*/—)

Barney Kessel

A prolific recording artist, guitarist Barney Kessel, born 1923, was originally influenced by Charlie Christian. During the '40s, he played with both Charlie Parker (**Charlie Parker On Dial, Volume Three**) and Lester Young (**Jammin' With Lester**).

Born in 1924 in Oklahoma, Kessel was based in Los Angeles in the '40s and '50s, cutting an excellent, swinging series of albums for the West Coast Contemporary label in company with Ray Brown and Shelly Manne (**The Pollwinners** and **Pollwinners Three**). Oscar Peterson chose him for his JATP trio with bassist Ray Brown (**In Concert**), a demanding role for an accompanist. Kessel subsequently worked in Hollywood, re-emerging from time to time to cut a jazz album.

Using a British rhythm section of Brian Lemon, piano, Kenny Baldock, bass, and Johnny Richardson, drums, Kessel played an excellent set at the 1973 Montreux Jazz Festival (**Summertime In**

Above: Barney Kessel, a modern swinger in the Charlie Christian tradition. A prolific recording artist.

Montreux), with the outstanding numbers being the phenomenally dexterous **Laura** and the unaccompanied Lennon-McCartney **Yesterday**. Again using a British rhythm section, Kessel recorded the beautiful **Autumn Leaves** and the roisteringly bluesy **Watch The Birds Go By (Swinging Easy)**. Barney Kessel is obviously an artist of broad tastes, capable of playing in most idioms from rock 'n' roll, **One Mint Julep (Slow Burn)**, to the modern musical *Hair*, **Frank Mills (Blue Soul)**.

Recordings:
Charlie Parker On Dial, Volume Three
(Spotlite/Spotlite)
Lester Young, Jammin' With Lester *(Jazz Archives/—)*
The Pollwinners
(Contemporary/—)
Pollwinners Three
(Contemporary/—)
Oscar Peterson In Concert
(Verve/Verve)
Summertime In Montreux
(Black Lion/Black Lion)
Swinging Easy
(Black Lion/Black Lion)
Slow Burn
(Phil Spector/Phil Spector)
Blue Soul
(Black Lion/Black Lion)

Al Killian
♦ *Count Basie*

B. B. King

Together with Sam (Lightnin') Hopkins (♦), John Lee Hooker (♦), and Muddy Waters (♦), Riley 'B.B.' King remains the most important post-war blues guitar player. Certainly, from an all-round standpoint, he is the most gifted blues guitarist extant. Which makes it no surprise at all to learn that his basic influences include guitarists Django Reinhardt (♦), Elmore James, Charlie Christian (♦), Oscar Moore, Johnny Moore, and T-Bone Walker (♦).

King, and his beloved 'Lucille', have, in turn, exerted tremendous influence on other players since the early 1950s – guitarists from the areas of blues, R&B, jazz, rock; even C&W. In more recent years, B.B. ('Blues Boy') King (born Itta Bena, Mississippi, 1925) has tended often to alarm blues purists by straying outside a more or less defined blues bag; in truth, although blues remains King's first and most important love, he has been interested in many forms of music, right from a very early age. His singing, for instance, shows an obvious respect for and knowledge of the Big Joe Turner (♦), Jimmy Witherspoon (♦) and Jimmy Rushing (♦) syndrome of hard-shouting blues vocalism. In 1966, he recorded items from blues-shouters' repertoire like **Confessin' The Blues, Cherry Red, Please Send Me Someone To Love, I'm Gonna Move To The Outskirts Of Town, Goin' To Chicago Blues** (all on **Confessin' The Blues**). King regularly includes in his concert repertoire the Count Basie (♦)-Joe Williams hit, **Every Day I Have The Blues**, a number which he recorded in 1959 with what was, to all intents and purposes, the full Basie band (**B.B. King's Greatest Hits**). And his most familiar single recording, **The Thrill Is Gone (Completely Well)**, found the guitar and voice of King within unusual context (for blues performances) of strings, et al – a combination which worked admirably. First recordings, in 1949, were for Nashville label, Bullet (including **Miss Martha King**), with a 17-years-old Phineas Newborn on piano. King, cousin of another famous bluesman, Bukka White, had left his home town two years before for Memphis where he became, for three years, a resident disc jockey, following meeting with Sonny Boy Williamson II. 1950: commenced recording for Modern's RPM label – King's **Three O'Clock Blues**, for RPM, first major hit. This, and other subsequent recordings like **Woke Up This Morning** and **Sweet Little Angel** figured high on US R&B charts.

Continued to record prolifically during 1950s, although some discs from latter part of decade – obviously beamed at rock 'n' roll audiences – do not compare with his best, before and since that time. 1961: signed by ABC-Paramount, commencing lengthy relationship between artist and company. With ABC, genuine excitement engendered at typical King live performance recaptured on record in superb albums like – **Live At The Regal, Live In Cook County Jail** and one side of **Live & Well**. Both King's warm, unhistrionic vocals and melismatic guitar solos register richly and vividly throughout his live LPs – a situation which remains constant throughout his concert performances today. The deep impression King has made on countless rock musicians has resulted, perhaps inevitably, in recordings featuring King and Lucille in company with rockers like Hugh McCracken, Al Kooper (who both appear on the other – non-live – side of **Live & Well**); Carole King and Leon Russell (both featured on **Indianola Mississippi**) and Pete Green, Stevie Marriott (**B.B. King In London**). Although of general interest, these liaisons did not in truth result in superior playing by King himself. Away from his usual concert, recording ventures – wherein King's abiding love for big-band jazz finds him continuing to be supported by solid-swinging bands redolent of that genre – B.B. King's instrumental luminosity occasionally turns up, delightfully if a trifle unexpectedly, in somewhat out-of-the-ordinary places. One such rare event took place at 1972 Newport/New York Jazz Festival (**Newport In New York '72: The Jimmy Smith Jam, Vol 5**) during which time the contrasting guitar virtuosity of King and Kenny Burrell (♦) produced mutually stimulating music during an all-star jam session performance of Percy Mayfield's **Please Send Me Someone To Love**.

Recordings:
Confessin' The Blues
(ABC – Paramount/HMV)
The B.B. King Story, Chapter Two *(—/Blue Horizon)*
B.B. King, 1949-1950 *(Kent/—)*

B.B. King Sings Spirituals
(Crown/—)
Blues In My Heart *(Crown/—)*
The Jungle *(Kent/—)*
B.B. King's Greatest Hits
(America – France)
To Know You Is To Love You
(ABC – Paramount/Probe)
The Best Of B.B. King *(ABC/—)*
Completely Well
(ABC – Bluesway/Stateside)
Live At The Regal
(ABC/HMV)
Live & Well
(ABC/Stateside)
Live In Cook County Jail
(ABC/Probe)
Indianola Mississippi Seeds
(ABC/Probe)
Guess Who *(ABC/Probe)*
B.B. King/Bobby Bland, Together, Live . . . For The First Time
(ABC – Impulse/ABC – Impulse)
Various, Newport In New York '72: The Jimmy Smith Jam, Vol 5 *(Atlantic/Atlantic)*

John Kirby

Before the arrival of Jimmy Blanton (♦) in the late-1930s, John Kirby (born Baltimore, Maryland, 1908) was, without question, the most accomplished bassist on the jazz scene; George 'Pops' Foster, who was the finest of the early slap-bass players and, possibly, Artie Bernstein, were his only rivals.

Kirby, who took lessons from Foster and Duke Ellington's then bass player Wellman Braud, started on trombone, then moved to tuba. Played the latter instrument with almost the same remarkable facility he applied to bass. Played both tuba and bass with Fletcher Henderson (♦) (**The Fletcher Henderson Story/The Fletcher Henderson Story, Vol 4** and **Recordings Made Between 1930 & 1941**), also with Chick Webb (♦), (**Spinning The Webb 1934-39** and **A Legend 1929-1936**), although before he left Henderson was playing string bass only. During 1930s his lighter, subtler sound and generally superior technique meant he was in constant demand, from bandleaders, singers and, of course, for record dates.

Not surprisingly, he got to work with the very best, including Billie Holiday (♦) (**The Golden Years, Vol 2** and **The Billie Holiday Story, Vol 1**); Teddy Wilson (♦) (**The Teddy Wilson** and **Teddy Wilson & His All Stars**); Lionel Hampton (♦) (**The Complete Lionel Hampton/The Best Of Lionel Hampton, Vols 1, 2, 6**); Red Allen (♦) (**Henry Allen & His Orchestra 1934-1935**); and Lucky Millinder (♦), Frankie Newton (♦), Maxine Sullivan (♦), Mildred Bailey (♦), and Charlie Barnet (♦) (all **Boss Of The Bass**). Kirby rejoined both Henderson and Webb (1935, 1936, respectively), before joining Millinder, for approximately one year, late-1936.

Took over leadership of sextet which was playing residency at Onyx Club, 52nd Street (1937). Membership varied at first but eventually resolved into: Charlie Shavers (♦), trumpet; Russell Procope (♦), alto-sax; Buster Bailey (♦), clarinet; Billy Kyle (♦), piano; Kirby, and O'Neil Spencer (♦), drums. Thus was born the John Kirby Sextet, which became the epitome of the term 'chamber-group jazz'.

STEREO/BLS 6037

COMPLETELY WELL
B.B. KING

BluesWay
IS WHERE IT'S AT!

Completely Well (Bluesway). 'This album will show you . . . just why B. B. King is King of the Blues . . .'

Arrangements (mostly by Shavers) laid emphasis on superlative ensemble playing, with trumpet muted (or when open playing unusually softly) to accentuate the 'quiet' approach. The blending of the front-line horns was achieved brilliantly by tightness of the arrangements, and everything was discreetly, but firmly, underpinned by flexibility and restrained power of the rhythm section, including, of course, the ultra-subtle bass playing of Kirby. Repertoire was mixture of standards, originals and adaptations, a typical set by The Biggest Little Band In The Land (as it was sometimes billed) comprising **The Birth Of The Blues, Sextette From 'Lucia Di Lammermor', Tunisian Trail, Blue Skies, It Feels So Good, The Duke's Idea** and **Old Fashioned Love (The Biggest Little Band In The Land)**. Other memorable sides by a unique band, whose peak period was 1938–40, included: **I Love You Truly, Blues Petite, Front & Center, Royal Garden Blues, Jumping In The Pump Room (The Boss Of The Bass); It's Only A Paper Moon, Move Over, Close Shave, St Louis Blues (John Kirby & His Orchestra 1941-1942).**

Band disintegrated by mid-1940s, due to personnel leaving or being drafted (Spencer left due to illness, returned, collapsed during gig at Apollo, and died); also due to the fact that its very format had become outmoded (and, possibly,

because its emotional output was at a constant low-key level). A pathetic attempt at resuscitating the band, at Carnegie Hall concert in December 1950, received pitiful support. Kirby gave up, worked briefly in New York with other bands, then settled in California, in '52. Played occasional gigs with Benny Carter (♦), commenced plans to put together another John Kirby Sextet, but had to abandon project because of ill-health. Died in Los Angeles, from diabetes, in 1952. Was married to singer Maxine Sullivan (♦) between 1938 and 1941.

Recordings:
The Fletcher Henderson Story *(Columbia)/*
The Fletcher Henderson Story, Vol 4 *(CBS)*
Various (Including Red Allen-Coleman Hawkins) Recordings Made Between 1930 & 1941 *(CBS – France)*
Chick Webb, Spinning The Webb 1934-39 *(Decca/Coral)*
Chick Webb, A Legend 1929-1936 *(Decca/MCA – Germany)*
The Billie Holiday Story, Vol 1 *(Columbia/CBS)*
Billie Holiday, The Golden Years, Vol 2 *(Columbia/CBS)*
The Teddy Wilson *(CBS/Sony – Japan)*
Teddy Wilson & His All Stars *(Columbia/CBS)*
The Complete Lionel Hampton *(Bluebird)/*
Lionel Hampton's Best

Records, Vols 1, 2, 6 *(RCA Victor – France)*
Henry Allen & His Orchestra 1934-1935 *(Collector's Classics/—)*
Frankie Newton At The Onyx Club *(Tax – Sweden)*
John Kirby, Boss Of The Bass *(Columbia/—)*
John Kirby, The Biggest Little Band In The Land *(Trip/DJM)*
John Kirby & His Orchestra 1941-1942 *(—/RCA Victor – Germany)*

Andy Kirk

Andrew Dewey 'Andy' Kirk (born Newport, Kentucky, 1898) played saxophone and tuba. More important, though, he was leader of big-band which came to be known as Andy Kirk & His 12 Clouds of Joy. A band that was closely identified with term 'Kansas City jazz'.

Basically, it was a good band – with fine soloists in Dick Wilson, tenor-sax; Ted Donnelly, trombone; Floyd Smith, guitar; Harold 'Shorty' Baker (♦), Howard McGhee, trumpets; and Mary Lou Williams (♦), piano; all of whom played with Clouds of Joy at various times between 1929, when Kirk became leader, and 1948, when it disbanded. Two principal soloists of importance were Wilson (who died in 1941), whose persuasive, big-toned tenor sounded like a satisfying cross between Herschel Evans (♦) and Chu Berry (♦), two of his contemporaries,

both of whom shared Wilson's fate of premature death.

Williams, though, was the real instrumental star, her piano-playing reflecting variety of influences, including ragtime, boogie woogie and a more Hines (♦)-like approach. Just as important, though, were her contributions as composer and arranger; **Walkin' & Swingin', Froggy Bottom, Bearcat Shuffle, Moten Swing** and **Steppin' Pretty** (all **Andy Kirk & His 12 Clouds Of Joy - March 1936)**, all written and/or arranged by Mary Lou Williams, give some idea of how essential was her part in the overall structure of the band, from 1931–42. **Floyd's Guitar Blues (Instrumentally Speaking (1936-1942)** was a popular disc for band, featuring Floyd Smith, using amplified guitar at a time when such practice was not the norm.

McGhee, who worked with band in 1942, soloed impressively on his feature, **McGee Special (Instrumentally Speaking 1936-1942)**.

Biggest hit record for Clouds of Joy was **Until The Real Thing Comes Along** (1936) **(Andy Kirk & His 12 Clouds Of Joy - March 1936)** featuring Pha Terrell, band vocalist between 1933–41, whose style was something of an acquired taste. Generally, the band played fine music, although during its existence it acquired something of a dubious reputation for inconsistency. Kirk himself was hardly major threat as soloist (on bass-sax), but as leader earned respect and admiration from his sidemen.

During childhood, moved with his family to Denver, Colorado. Played mostly tuba, bass-sax with George Morrison (late-1920s), then joined Texas band calling itself Dark Clouds of Joy. When its leader left (1929), Kirk was appointed leader. At first he played sax and band was fronted by singers Billy Massey, then Terrell. Later, Kirk gave up his instrumental duties to conduct. After disbanding, Kirk moved to West Coast, tried – unsuccessfully – to keep another brand new band going, then settled in New York.

Became involved in real estate business at beginning of 1950s; in 1958, appointed manager of Hotel Theresa. Periodically, up to early-1960s, assembled big bands for special appearances. Amongst other jazz instrumentalists of note who were members of Kirk's Clouds of Joy were trumpeter Fats Navarro (♦), (1943-4), and tenorist Don Byas (♦) (1939-40).

Recordings:
Clouds Of Joy *(Ace of Hearts)*
Andy Kirk & His 12 Clouds Of Joy *(Parlophone)*
Instrumentally Speaking (1936-1942) *(Decca/MCA – Germany)*
Twelve Clouds Of Joy *(Ace of Hearts)*
'Live' From The Trianon Ballroom, Cleveland *(Jazz Society/—)*

Rahsaan Roland Kirk

Born 1936 in Ohio, Rahsaan Roland Kirk was playing with R&B bands at 11, and fronting his own unit at 14. His talents as a performer are extravagant: not only can he play three horns at once, but the result is usually creative music rather than vaudeville; not only can he blow continuously throughout a number (many instrumentalists can hold a note) but he can move all over the horn. In fact, he has developed a method of changing his airstream, so that simultaneous inhalation and exhalation take place, **Saxophone Concerto (Prepare Thyself To Deal With A Miracle)**. His aim is to produce an unbroken carpet of sound, to 'catch the sound of the sun'. Basically a tenorman, his armoury of outlandish instruments includes the stritch, manzello, flute, nose flute, clarinet, police whistle and siren. Blind, he wears the lot on a complex network of straps and adhesive tape while performing, a street buskerish image.

Rahsaan's early association with Charlie Mingus **(Oh Yeah)** reinforced his own sense of tradition, for both men pay musical respects to New Orleans and figures like Duke Ellington and Fats Waller – **Eat That Chicken (Oh Yeah)** and subsequent dedications on Rahsaan's own albums **Creole Love Call, The Seeker (The Art Of Rahsaan Roland Kirk)**. His clarinet approaches the genuine sound of New Orleans, but his flute playing – a mixture of humming, gasping and note-production – is all his own and has been widely imitated: **You Did It, You Did It (We Free Kings)**. Fine examples of his multiple horn playing are scattered throughout his albums, most notably on **A Sack Full Of Soul (We Free Kings); The Inflated Tear (The Inflated Tear)**. A fairly comprehensive idea of his range is caught live in a club on a double album **(Bright Moments)**. Critics usually put him down as an eclectic, an arid judgement on a man whose creativity ransacks black music to such good purpose.

A jam session re-union with Mingus **(Mingus At Carnegie Hall)** saw Rahsaan picking up the challenge of the formidable tenorman, George Adams, and producing solos of superhuman drive. In 1976, he experienced a stroke, continued to perform one-handed, and recaptured his old facility. Throughout his illness, he was showered with messages from all over the world, a tribute to his immense popularity; he died on December 6, 1977.

Recordings:
Charles Mingus, Oh Yeah
(Atlantic/Atlantic)
We Free Kings *(Trip/Mercury)*
The Inflated Tear
(Atlantic/Atlantic)
The Art Of Rahsaan Roland Kirk *(Atlantic/Atlantic)*
Bright Moments
(Atlantic/Atlantic)
Prepare Thyself To Deal With A Miracle *(Atlantic/Atlantic)*
Mingus At Carnegie Hall
(Atlantic/Atlantic)

Lee Konitz

Born 1927 in Chicago, altoman Lee Konitz is the most famous disciple of pianist-teacher Lennie Tristano, and the only one – apart from bassist Peter Ind – to play with musicians outside the 'Cool School' coterie. The long, thin-spun and serpentine lines of his alto mesh with those of tenorist Warne Marsh on Tristano's

historic Capitol album **(Crosscurrents)**; Baroque counterpoint quite at variance to the prevailing emotionalism of Bebop. Critics have pointed out that Konitz's approach to alto represented the only alternative to Parker's, but usually drew unfair comparisons between their expressivity. In fact, Konitz has never been interested in expressing his ego, aiming rather at the anonymity of Pre-Renaissance art: 'just music', as he says. Early Konitz solos trace patterns like a seismograph, undulating without reliance on climactic peaks, the tone pure and sharp, the movement sinuous. A deleted album from 1949 **(Subconscious-Lee)** shows all the typical Tristano school characteristics, and on **Rebecca** Konitz duets with guitarist Billy Bauer. His work with Claude Thornhill's orchestra, which used Gil Evans' arrangements, led to his inclusion in Miles Davis' classic sonnet **(Birth Of The Cool)** and Konitz solos on several tracks, most notably **Move** and **Israel**. Miles and Konitz, sharing similar emotional terrain, again worked together **(Ezz-thetic!)** which featured two of George Russell's compositions, **Ezz-thetic** and **Odjenar**, avant-garde and less successful than **Yesterdays** and **Hi Beck** which are moving performances of great unity. The rest of the album comprises material cut in Paris in 1953 with several takes of **I'll Remember April** and **These Foolish Things**. Throughout his career, the altoman has returned to his favorite standards, uncovering new subtleties and possibilities within the chord changes.

In 1952, Konitz joined Stan Kenton's orchestra, an unlikely environment for the introverted stylist, but one which stripped away much of the ethereal quality in his tone, and strengthened his attack. His collaboration with baritonist Gerry Mulligan the following year **(Gerry Mulligan-Lee Konitz)** showed how far he had developed, and **Too Marvellous For Words** is a classic performance. A Lennie Tristano album from 1955 **(Lines)** features a masterly live club date with Konitz, the altoist positively robust on **All The Things You Are**. Relaxation and swing are characteristics of Konitz's re-union with Warne Marsh **(Lee Konitz & Warne Marsh)** fuelled by the driving rhythm section of Oscar Pettiford and Kenny Clarke. The interplay between the two horns is phenomenally precise and adroit, adding up to one long, continuous melody line. Much of Konitz's best work from the late '50s is currently unavailable **(The Real Lee Konitz, Very Cool** and **Inside Hi Fi)**, the latter showing a surprisingly rugged Konitz on tenor, the Mr Hyde within the fastidious Dr Jekyll. In 1961, the altoman startled the jazz world by recording a trio album with drummer Elvin Jones, a freer and more tigerish player than the usual Tristanoite choice of timekeeper **(Motion)**. Clearly, Konitz's horizons had widened considerably, for the teaming produces some of his most driving and emotional work.

The late '60s saw a revival of interest in the great original, and a Milestone contract. Characteristically, Konitz has explored the contemporary avant-garde, finding some of it incompatible and

some – the pianists Bill Evans, Paul Bley and Andrew Bill – rewarding. **Invitation**, a duet by Hill and Konitz **(Spiral)** shows their spontaneous, one-take rapport. Konitz's own albums cover a variety of settings, from the alto and bass duo **(I Concentrate On You)** to a series of duos with guitarist Jim Hall, tenors Richie Kamuca and Joe Henderson and trombonist Marshall Brown **(The Lee Konitz Duets)**, to a solo album **(Lone-Lee)**. More conventional groups continue to elicit excellent playing – **Spirits, Satori** and **Oleo** – and show a growing interest in the soprano saxophone.

Lee Konitz is one of the greatest stylists in jazz. All stages of his development are unique from the airy lyricism and icily etched tone of his late '40s work to the fully rounded musical architecture of his maturity.

Recordings:
Lennie Tristano, Crosscurrents
(Capitol/Capitol)
Subconscious-Lee *(Prestige/—)*
Miles Davis, Birth Of The Cool
(Capitol/Capitol)
Ezz-thetic! *(Prestige/—)*
Gerry Mulligan – Lee Konitz
(Blue Note/Blue Note)
Lennie Tristano, Lines
(Atlantic/Atlantic)
Lee Konitz & Warne Marsh
(Atlantic/—)
Notion *(Verve/Verve)*
Andrew Hill, Spiral
(Arista Freedom/ Arista Freedom)
I Concentrate On You
(Steeplechase/Steeplechase)
The Lee Konitz Duets
(Milestone/Milestone)
Spirits *(Milestone/Milestone)*
Satori *(Milestone/Milestone)*
Oleo *(Sonet/Sonet)*
Lone Lee
(Steeplechase/Steeplechase)

Gene Krupa

Gene Krupa (born Chicago, Illinois, 1909) was the archetypal showman-drummer, the man who brought the drummer to the public's notice in a way which hitherto had not been accomplished. Krupa, though, was not the best drummer – showmanship or otherwise. His basic style was an exciting one, with accent on supplying non-stop powerful beat, using all the tricks of the drummer's trade to do so. But for all his undoubted skills and ability to lift a band, Krupa was hardly the equal of drummers like Big Sid Catlett (♦), Jo Jones (♦), or his own percussion idol, Chick Webb (♦). Nor did he possess, even during his peak years (1935–45), the speed of Buddy Rich, or the subtlety of Davey Tough; no matter. Whilst an integral member of the Benny Goodman (♦) Orchestra (and sundry small groups), from 1934–8, Krupa made the jazz drummer into a real front-row personality: a hero to be worshipped every bit as much as, say, Goodman or Harry James (♦). Better drummers there might have been during the period, and his drumming tended to sound a trifle heavy-handed and flashy with the Trio and Quartet, but the Goodman big band sounded better for his presence **(Benny Goodman, Vols 4-11)**. Krupa's speciality number with Goodman was Sing, Sing, Sing **(Benny Goodman, Vol 8)**, which hundreds of would-be Krupas attempted (unsuccessfully) to emulate. The gum-chewing, wisecracking Krupa reprised and extended Sing, Sing, Sing devastatingly during the legendary **1938 Carnegie Hall Jazz Concert** with an enraptured audience virtually applauding his every break during entire proceedings.

Although Krupa gained a Hollywood film star kind of popularity (and, apparently, the following) during the five years he spent with Benny Goodman, his playing career did not begin when he joined the clarinet-tist. For Krupa, a jazz enthusiast from a very youthful age, had spent nearly all the 1920s in his home town playing drums with as many of the leading Chicago jazzmen as possible. Indeed, he had participated at an important Chicago record date (1927), featuring McKenzie & Condon's Chicagoans **(That Toddlin' Town - Chicago 1926-28)** which first brought his name to attention of record-buyers. 1929: moved to New York, spending most of next two years in various bands (including theatre jobs) fronted by Red Nichols (♦), and recording with cornettist's Five Pennies **(J.T.)**. Played with mostly pop dancebands during early-1930s, although he managed to make jazz record dates at frequent intervals. Recorded with Goodman and Jack Teagarden (♦) in 1933 **(Benny Goodman & The Giants Of Swing/Jazz In The Thirties)** and with Goodman again following year **(Recordings Made Between 1930 & 1941)**, latter date also featuring Mildred Bailey (♦).

After joining Goodman (in December '34), occasionally recorded in other company, as with New Orleans Rhythm Kings **(Kings Of Jazz)** – in February, '35. Drummed especially well at Chicago record session under own name **(Gene Krupa & His Chicagoans)**, using personnel from Goodman band (including leader); also rhythm section colleagues Jess Stacy (♦) and Israel Crosby (♦) on further three titles **(Benny Goodman & The Giants Of Swing/Jazz In The Thirties** and **Swing Classics, 1935/Jazz In The Thirties)**. Gene Krupa's Swing Band (including also Roy Eldridge (♦), Chu Berry (♦) and Goodman) produced superb recorded jazz early in 1936 **(Benny Goodman, Vol 4, 1935-1939)** with drummer-leader supplying relentless beat throughout.

Left Goodman to start own big band, venture which proved most successful until forced to disband, for personal reasons, in 1943. The 1938–41 unit was first-class, benefiting enormously by its leader's personality and drumming which seemed to be improving all the time. Additional plus factors were Roy Eldridge and singer Anita O'Day. **Drummin' Man** was hit for band; **Rockin' Chair**, thanks to Eldridge, was a popular favorite with fans; and Eldridge and O'Day were jointly featured on **Let Me Off Uptown**, another successful number (all **Drummin' Man)**. Krupa returned to Goodman during part of 1943, moving on to Tommy Dorsey (♦) (1943–4).

Own big band, again, from 1944–51, with Krupa sympathetic to the newer jazz sounds to emerge from Bebop revolution (although Krupa himself did not make transition from swing to bop). **Disc Jockey Jump** (composed, arranged by youthful Gerry Mulligan (♦) who also produced numerous other superior charts for band), **Leave Us Leap, How High The Moon, Lemon Drop** and **Stardust** (all **Drummin' Man**) were representative of band's high-quality output. Decade later, Krupa was to re-record most of these, plus others, with all-star studio bands (**The Big Band Sound Of Gene Krupa** and **The Second Big Band Sound Of Gene Krupa**).

Disbanding in '51, Krupa joined Jazz At The Philharmonic, sometimes featuring own Trio (**Norman Granz' JATP Carnegie Hall Concert 1952** and **J.A.T.P. In Tokyo**) and often pitching Krupa and Buddy Rich into a crowd-baiting gladiatorial situations. When not touring with JATP, led own trios. Started drum school, with Cozy Cole (♦), in '54. Played on soundtrack of movie *The Gene Krupa Story* (alleged to be biography), in 1959. Active through 1960s, although laid off through heart problems on at least one occasion. Died of leukemia, in October, 1973.

Recordings:
Various (Including McKenzie & Condon's Chicagoans), That Toddlin' Town - Chicago (1926-1928) (—/Parlophone)
Red Nichols/Jack Teagarden, 'JT' (Ace of Hearts)
Benny Goodman & The Giants Of Swing (Prestige)/
Jazz In The Thirties (World Records)
Various (Including Benny Goodman), Recordings Made Between 1930 & 1941 (CBS – France)
Various (Including New Orleans Rhythm Kings), Kings Of Jazz (Swaggie – Australia)
Various (Including Jess Stacy), Swing Classics, 1935 (Prestige)/
Jazz In The Thirties (World Records)
Benny Goodman, Vols 4-11 (RCA Victor – Records)
Benny Goodman, 1938 Carnegie Hall Jazz Concert (Columbia/CBS)
Gene Krupa, Drummin' Man (Columbia/CBS)
The Big Band Sound Of Gene Krupa (—/Verve)
The Second Big Band Sound Of Gene Krupa (—/Verve)
Various (Including Gene Krupa), Norman Granz' Jazz At The Philharmonic Carnegie Hall Concert 1952, Record 3 (Verve/Columbia – Clef)
Various (Including Gene Krupa), J.A.T.P. In Tokyo (Pablo Live/Pablo Live)
The Exciting Gene Krupa (Verve – Germany)

Street, Vol 1) both in solo and accompanying roles. His rather self-effacing style works to advantage during one of Buck Clayton's (♦) legendary jam-session record dates (**The Golden Days Of Jazz: Buck Clayton**), this one from '54; and he was an obvious choice for one of Lionel Hampton's (♦) equally famous studio jams (**The Complete Lionel Hampton/Lionel Hampton's Best Records, Vol 2 - 1938-1939**). And his presence is felt more than heard during sessions involving Jack Teagarden (♦) (**Jack Teagarden/Pee Wee Russell**); Frankie Newton (♦) (**Frankie Newton At The Onyx**); and singers Mildred Bailey (♦) and Maxine Sullivan (♦) (**Boss Of The Bass**).

Billy Kyle was taken ill while on tour with Armstrong in 1966 and died a week after being admitted to a New York hospital.

Recordings:
Various (Including Billy Kyle), Swing Street, Vol 1 (Tax – Sweden)
John Kirby & His Orchestra 1941-1942 (—/RCA Victor – Germany)
John Kirby, Boss Of The Bass (Columbia/—)
The Golden Days Of Jazz: Buck Clayton (CBS)
The Complete Lionel Hampton (Bluebird)/

Lionel Hampton's Best Records, Vol 2 - 1938-1939 (RCA Victor – France)
Jack Teagarden/(Pee Wee Russell) (Byg – France)
Louis Armstrong Joue W. C. Handy/Ambassador Satch/Satch Plays Fats (CBS – France)

Steve Lacy

There's something in the siren song sound of the soprano saxophone that makes strong men strap themselves to the mast. These days, most saxophonists double on soprano instead of clarinet. It has a plangent brass bite that cuts through electric bass and thunderous drumming, but it tends to fly out of tune. Ironically, the man who has pioneered the use of the instrument in modern music, Steve Lacy, the man who showed Coltrane the way and thus caused its mass acceptance, remains unrewarded and underrated. Born in 1934, Lacy was originally inspired by the great Sidney Bechet, and continued to play in the New New Orleans–Dixieland tradition until he met Cecil Taylor. He played on and off with the avant-garde pianist over the next six years, more-or-less by-passing the complex harmonies of Bebop. A couple of deleted albums (**Cecil Taylor**

Steve Lacy Solo (Emanem): the Samuel Beckett of soprano.

& Donald Byrd At Newport and **New York City R&B**) are worth looking out for as examples of his sheer intelligence in dealing with the new music. Happily Blue Note have reissued some early Lacy (**In Transition/Cecil Taylor**) which shows him wisely avoiding that pianistic volcano with his long, tonally pure notes.

After Taylor, he fell under the influence of another piano giant, Thelonious Monk, and spent some twelve years concentrating on the Monk repertoire. He formed a quartet with another ex-Dixielander, trombonist Roswell Rudd, and together they explored those angular harmonies and rhythms (**School Days**). In the early '60s, arranger Gil Evans made frequent use of the soprano in his orchestral voicings, giving Lacy a chance to show his paces in performances like **Straight No Chaser (Pacific Standard Time)**.

In 1965, Lacy went to Europe, falling in with the US new music expatriates there, and showing up on various sessions with Don Cherry. He has been based in Paris for some years, and has gradually put together a group of like-minded players, bassist Kent

Billy Kyle

William Osborne 'Billy' Kyle (born Philadelphia, Pennsylvania, 1914) was a neat, precise pianist, whose touch and drive were reminiscent of Teddy Wilson (♦). Often a reluctant soloist, his reputation as a reliable, thoroughly professional musician was attained as much because of his undoubted qualities as a band pianist as solo performer. In many ways he was just about the most ideal choice for John Kirby (♦) Sextet, for whom he played a vital role (1938–42) and, briefly, on two further occasions, in mid-1940s. His solos usually were short and to the point and his interaction with front-line players and his colleagues in rhythm section was of seminal importance to band's highly-developed ensemble playing.

Started on piano at eight, later organ, and played in West Philadelphia High School's symphony orchestra. First professional work, locally, at 15. Put together own band, in 1936, after spell with Tiny Bradshaw (♦). Later same year, joined Lucky Millinder (♦), with whom he stayed until becoming member of Kirby group. With US Army, 1942–5, mostly in Pacific area, and after his first return to Kirby, on demobilization, went on tour with Sy Oliver (♦) Orchestra. Before fronting own small combos (1947–8), played for two years in pit band of Broadway production of *Guys & Dolls*. Freelanced extensively during 1950s, before accepting an offer to tour with Louis Armstrong (♦) All Stars. Solo-wise, opportunities were infrequent, but as ever Kyle performed his task with relish and total professionalism.

Of the small amount of own record dates, his playing registers particularly strongly throughout four tracks recorded in 1937 (**Swing**

Above: Band pianist with such as John Kirby, Louis Armstrong, Billy Kyle had touch like Teddy Wilson's.

Carter, for example, and established his own music.

Following a totally free and themeless period of improvisation, Lacy has returned to using tunes that restrict him to given areas of exploration. **The New Duke** from a solo album (**Steve Lacy Solo**) uses a controlled farmyard squawk as its point of departure, while **Stations** uses a randomly selected radio station as inspiration. His soprano covers an astonishing four octaves, and his tone in all registers is an ice maiden of purity. His approach over the years has been towards essences, so that his recent work has a concentration and rigor of thought miles removed from the current crop of dervish dancers.

Recordings:
In Transition/Cecil Taylor
(Blue Note/Blue Note)
School Days *(Emanem/Emanem)*
Pacific Standard Time, Gil Evans
(Blue Note/Blue Note)
Steve Lacy Solo
(Emanem/Emanem)
The Crust *(Emanem/Emanem)*
Saxophone Special
(Emanem/Emanem)
Trickles *(—/Black Saint)*
Flakes *(—/Vista)*

Tommy Ladnier

Thomas 'Tommy' Ladnier (born Mandeville, Louisiana, 1900) was one of jazz's all-time great blues instrumentalists. Blessed with only average technique (he was not a noted technician like, for example, Louis Armstrong (♦) or King Oliver (♦)), Ladnier made up for any mechanical deficiencies by the moving quality of his playing, especially in respect of blues, a genre of which he was a master. In this respect, he was an obvious (and ideal) choice to support singers Ma Rainey (♦) (**Mother Of The Blues, Vol 1**); Bessie Smith (♦) (**The Empress**); and Ida Cox (**Ida Cox, Vols 1, 2**), his work with latter artist being of exceptional standard. As member of Lovie Austin's Blues Serenaders (**Lovie Austin & Her Blues Serenaders**), Ladnier's cornet was at its most beseeching, exemplified best of all on **Steppin' On The Blues, Charleston, South Carolina, Peepin' Blues** and **Mojo Blues**.

After moving to Chicago (before 1920) he worked with numerous name bands, including Charlie Creath, Ollie Powers (**Blues & Stomps, Vol 1**), Fate Marable, King Oliver, and Sam Wooding. With Wooding, visited Europe in 1925 and left band in Germany, going on to Poland with touring Louis Douglas' revue (1926). Joined Fletcher Henderson (♦) (late '26), with whom he recorded several fine solos, including **Snag It, The Chant, Henderson Stomp (The Fletcher Henderson Story, Vol 1)**; and **St Louis Shuffle, I'm Coming Virginia** and **Goose Pimples (The Fletcher Henderson Story, Vol 2)**. To Europe in 1928, again with Sam Wooding, followed by further tour of continent (after leaving Wooding in France) with Benton E. Peyton. Played in Spain and France (again, this time with own band), and worked in Paris and London with Noble Sissle Orchestra. With Sid-

ney Bechet (♦), formed New Orleans Feetwarmers. Combination of Bechet's totally uninhibited soprano-sax, clarinet and Ladnier's more restrained passion resulted in glorious music, immortalized in recordings by band like **Maple Leaf Rag, Sweetie Dear, Shag** and **I've Found A New Baby** (all **Sidney Bechet, Vol 2**); and **Lay Your Racket** and **I Want You Tonight** (both **Sidney Bechet, Vol 1**).

Tommy Ladnier's most powerful, poignant playing (on record at least) was produced in year before he died (1938). At famous record sessions organized by French jazz critic Hugues Panassie (**The Complete Ladnier-Mezzrow-Bechet**) Ladnier's blues playing reached its peak of expression, gloriously so on **Revolutionary Blues, Weary Blues, Really The Blues** and **If You See Me Comin'** (even if presence of fellow trumpeter Sidney De Paris (♦) tended to clash with front-line ideas on first date). During same month as final Panassie session, Bechet and Ladnier reprised **Weary Blues** at John Hammond-promoted concert at Carnegie Hall (**John Hammond's Spirituals To Swing**) supported powerfully by James P. Johnson (♦), and Basie-ites Jo Jones, Walter Page and Dan Minor. Suffered illness after this, and in June 1939, died of a heart attack in New York.

Recordings:
Ma Rainey, Mother Of The Blues, Vol 1 *(Riverside)*
Tommy Ladnier, Blues & Stomps, Vol 1
(Riverside/London)
Ida Cox, Vols 1, 2 *(—/Fountain)*
Bessie Smith, The Empress
(Columbia/CBS)
Lovie Austin & Her Blues Serenaders
(Riverside/Fountain)
The Fletcher Henderson Story
(Columbia)/
The Fletcher Henderson Story,

Vols 1, 2 *(CBS)*
Sidney Bechet, Vols 1, 2
(RCA Victor – France)
The Complete Ladnier-Mezzrow-Bechet
(RCA Victor – France)
Various (Including Sidney Bechet/Tommy Ladnier), John Hammond's Spirituals To Swing *(Vanguard/Vanguard)*

Cleo Laine
♦ *Johnny Dankworth*

Harold Land

Born Houston, Texas, 1928, tenorman Harold Land got his first major break with the Max Roach–Clifford Brown group in 1954, staying two years and improving immensely in terms of dramatic power (**I Remember Clifford**). Initially influenced by Coleman Hawkins, Lucky Thompson and Charlie Parker, he gradually developed an extremely individual approach to rhythm, and his solos with the excellent Curtis Counce Group have a real sense of the shaping mind. Solos like **Sarah** or **Landslide (Landslide)** grow in a serpentine fashion before the logical arrival at long-held notes. His warm, round sound is well illustrated by the ballad, **I Can't Get Started (Carl's Blues)**, a sinuous mixture of the oblique and the declamatory. Land cut two albums under his own name, collaborating fruitfully with pianist-composer Elmo Hope (**Harold In The Land Of Jazz** and **The Fox**), the latter being a classic. The title track is taken at a great clip, but Land still shows his habitual mastery of dynamics and structure.

A meeting with Thelonious Monk (**In Person**) resulted in some

unusually committed examination of Monk's themes, and **Round Midnight** shows Land playing comfortably within this demanding field. Subsequent collaboration with vibes player, Bobby Hutcherson (**San Francisco, Total Eclipse** and **Now!**) showed Land's increasing allegiance to the Coltrane sound.

Recordings:
Max Roach-Clifford Brown, Remember Clifford
(Trip/Mercury)
Curtis Counce:
Landslide
(Contemporary/Contemporary)
Counceltation
(Contemporary/Contemporary)
Carl's Blues
(Contemporary/Contemporary)
Exploring The Future
(Dooto/—)
Harold In The Land Of Jazz
(Contemporary/Contemporary)
The Fox
(Contemporary/Contemporary)
Thelonious Monk, In Person
(Milestone/Milestone)
Bobby Hutcherson:
San Francisco
(Blue Note/Blue Note)
Total Eclipse
(Blue Note/Blue Note)
Now!
(Blue Note/Blue Note)
Dolo Coker, Dolo!
(Xanadu/Xanadu)

The Fox (Contemporary): best of the West Coast.

Eddie Lang

There is little doubt that Eddie Lang (born Philadelphia, Pennsylvania, 1904; real name Salvatore Massaro) was jazz's first real virtuoso guitar performer. His elegantly picked single-string work complemented by precise, warm chord patterns, and effortlessly rhythmic playing made him much in demand from early-1920s until his untimely death (complications resulting from tonsillectomy) in 1933.

During his all-too-short playing career he recorded prodigiously: consistency of his playing on record, whether solo or as accompanist, is testimony to his greatness. Possessed extraordinarily keen ear and seemingly unlimited powers of invention. Studied violin from seven and at 13 met Joe Venuti (♦), then aged 12, whilst both were in grade school. Had to read music for school concerts, but had no need to read music for guitar or banjo (which he played at beginning of his career in music) – his keen ear took care of that 'deficiency'. Played banjo, then

Above: pioneer of the soprano saxophone in post-Bop jazz, Steve Lacy. His career is a model of logic and integrity.

guitar, on first professional engagement with Venuti in 1921, after previously making debut at L'Aiglon Restaurant, Philadelphia, using violin, followed by short spell with Charlie Kerr Orchestra, this time using banjo. Continued to work prolifically with Venuti, the pair playing residencies in Atlantic City. After working with Billy Lustig's Scranton Sirens, became member of Mound City Blue Blowers, in '24, visiting London with band (1924-5).

Settled in New York from mid-1920s, becoming involved with what would today be called session work (ie radio, records). Worked with Roger Wolfe Kahn Orchestra (Venuti also in line-up) (1926-7), as well as in big band fronted by Adrian Rollini (♦). Spent year with Paul Whiteman (♦) Orchestra (1929-30); again, Venuti was at his elbow. Appeared in Whiteman movie *The King of Jazz*, then back again with Roger Wolfe Kahn (1932). During year before he died, was employed as personal accompanist to Bing Crosby (♦), whose admiration for his playing bordered on the idolatrous. Recorded with Red Nichols (♦) (**Red Nichols & His Five Pennies, 1926-9**) soloing expressively on **That's No Bargain**. Played both banjo and guitar on classic Bix Beiderbecke (♦) recording **Singin' The Blues**, and assumed important role in intriguing versions of **For No Reason At All In C** and **Wringin' & Twistin'**, as part of Frankie Trumbauer (♦)-Beiderbecke-Lang trio (all **The Golden Days Of Jazz: Bix Beiderbecke**). Had shared solo duties with Beiderbecke on 1927 recording of **Clementine (The Bix Beiderbecke Legend)** when both were members of Jean Goldkette Orchestra. And it was Lang who laid down an elegant rhythmic texture behind some of Tommy Dorsey's (♦) finest trumpet playing on record (**Tommy, Jimmy & Eddie, 1928-29**).

Lang was one-half of two of the most famous jazz partnerships.

With boyhood friend Venuti, invariably he was heard in optimum form, and there is scarcely one Lang solo during any one of their impressively large number of recordings which is not of an impeccable standard, as evinced by content matter of **Stringing The Blues, Venuti-Lang 1927-8** and **The Sounds Of New York, Vol 2: 'Hot Strings'**. Lang's partnership with fellow guitarist Lonnie Johnson (♦) was, if anything, even more en rapport than that with Venuti.

Listening to combination of Johnson's essentially blues-based sound and Lang's more sophisticated guitar working in unison surely is one of the greatest experiences in jazz appreciation. The sheer beauty of the Johnson-Lang duo on such as **Midnight Call Blues, Blue Guitars, Blues In G, Hot Fingers (Blue Guitars)**; and **Two Tone Stomp, Bull Frog Moan** and **Perfect (Blue Guitars, Vol II)** is unsurpassed in field of jazz guitar. Without Johnson or Venuti, Lang seemed less inspired, but still managed to produce delightful little cameos, like **Eddie's Twister, Add A Little Wiggle (Blue Guitars)**, even though the material was not always of comparable quality to the playing. **Church Street Sobbin' Blues (Blue Guitars, Vol II, The Golden Age Of Jazz: Eddie Lang-Joe Venuti/Stringing The Blues)** merely emphasizes that Lonnie Johnson was a far more natural blues player than Lang. Yet his solo on **In The Bottle Blues (The Golden Age Of Jazz: Eddie Lang-Joe Venuti/Stringing The Blues)** is masterful. Something which can also be said for his contribution to **Knockin' A Jug (Blue Guitars)** in company, this time, with Jack Teagarden (♦) and Louis Armstrong (♦). With Venuti, the Teagarden brothers, and Benny Goodman (♦) in support, Lang's playing on a 1931 record date by Eddie Lang-Joe Venuti All Star Orchestra (**Nothing But Notes**) was especially fluent, and fierier than

usual. At a Venuti-Lang Blue Five session the month before he died, Eddie Lang played as superbly as always (**Ridin' In Rhythm**).

Recordings:
Red Nichols & His Five Pennies
(MCA-Coral – Germany)
The Golden Days Of Jazz: Bix Beiderbecke *(CBS)*
The Golden Days Of Jazz: Eddie Lang-Joe Venuti/ Stringing The Blues *(CBS)*
The Bix Beiderbecke Legend
(RCA Victor – France)
Tommy Dorsey/Jimmy Dorsey/ Eddie Lang, Tommy, Jimmy & Eddie 1928-29
(—/Parlophone)
Joe Venuti/Eddie Lang, Venuti-Lang 1927-8 *(—/Parlophone)*
Joe Venuti/Eddie Lang, The Sounds Of New York, Vol 2: 'Hot Strings'
(RCA Victor – France)
Blue Guitars, Vols 1, 2
(—/Parlophone)
Joe Venuti (Including Eddie Lang), Nothing But Notes
(MCA Coral – Germany)
Various, Ridin' In Rhythm
(—/World Records)

Yusef Lateef

Born Bill Evans, 1921, multi-instrumentalist Yusef Lateef was one of the first jazzmen to incorporate Middle Eastern and Asian influences into his work. His early infatuation for the East led him to take up instruments like the argol and various ethnic flutes, pre-dating the general jazz interest by a decade or more. A Detroit musician, many of his early groups included fellow citizens like Donald Byrd and Barry Harris. Lateef is featured on tenor, flute and oboe on an excellent album (**Eastern Sounds**) which has the bass player, Ernie Farrow doubling on the rabat. **Blues For The Orient** is an outstanding display of oboe, while a later album (**The Golden Flute**) shows his sensitivity as a composer and flautist.

Exoticism aside, Lateef is an ex-

The Many Faces Of Yusef Lateef (Milestone): versatility.

Above: multi-instrumentalist Yusef Lateef. His experiments with Eastern instruments pre-date '60s universalism.

Jazz In The Thirties (World Records). Featuring Lang, Venuti, Sullivan, Freeman, Goodman, Berigan, et al.

cellent tenor player, with a hard, driving tone and a strong sense of the blues. **Rosetta** is a booting performance **(The Golden Flute)** and so is **Goin' Home,** despite tambourine and arco bass opening **(The Many Faces Of Yusef Lateef).** Two albums recorded live **(Live At Pep's** and **Club Date)** catch the player at his peak with a fine quintet including the excellent trumpeter, Richard Williams.

Lateef has recorded very little as a sideman, and the period with Cannonball Adderley proved that he was rather more intense than his employer **(The Japanese Concerts).**

Recordings:
Eastern Sounds
  (Prestige/—)
The Golden Flute *(Impulse)*
The Many Faces Of Yusef Lateef *(Milestone/Milestone)*
Live At Pep's *(Impulse/Impulse)*
Club Date *(Impulse/Impulse)*

Yank Lawson

Yank Lawson (real name, John R. Lausen), born Trenton, Missouri, 1911, established a reputation as strong-blowing, hard-hitting trumpet player, first with orchestra of Ben Pollack (♦) **(Ben Pollack & His Orchestra 1933-1934)** then with Bob Crosby (♦) **(South Rampart Street Parade** and **Big Noise From Winnetka).** Previously, Lawson worked with various musical outfits at University of Missouri; also in Shreveport, Louisiana.

Until the arrival in 1937 of Billy Butterfield (♦) he was responsible for trumpet solo work with Crosby, a task he executed with fine craftsmanship and enviable professionalism – if little real originality. In 1938 he accepted offer to join Tommy Dorsey (♦), with whom he was to remain 15 months. Soloed with typical impact on such Dorsey recordings as **Tin Roof Blues, Milenberg Joys** (both **Tommy Dorsey & His Orchestra)** and **Tea For Two, Lonesome Road** (both **Tommy Dorsey, Vol II).**

After leaving Dorsey, gigged with several dance-band aggregations before spending six months in pit orchestra for show *Louisiana Purchase.* Returned to Crosby in spring of '41, remaining this time until December of following year. Solo on **Chain Gang (South Rampart Street Parade)** demonstrated he had lost none of his previous potency with band, being also fine example of his ability with plunger mute. With Benny Goodman for few months in '42, then became comprehensively involved with radio studio work, taking time off periodically to record with such as Eddie Condon (♦) **(Jazz Concert)** and to appear, together with trombonist Bobby Byrne, on Steve Allen TV show (1953–1954). Association – musical and social – with Bob Haggart, dating from early days with Bob Crosby, continued in shape of Lawson–Haggart Jazz Band. This unit recorded at regular intervals between 1951–1960 **(The Best Of Dixieland).**

World's Greatest Jazz Band, co-led by Lawson and bassist-composer Haggart, and which came into being in 1968, was logical outcome of Lawson-Haggart Jazz Band. With Haggart and Lawson currently the only two original members, the band has continued to grow in stature and international acceptance. Lawson himself carries on producing basically same kind of effective solos, as exemplified by those for WGJB on **Love Is Blue, Do You Know The Way To San José? (Extra!); Five Point Blues, Dogtown Blues (WGJB Of Yank Lawson & Bob Haggart); Lawrenceville Blues (In Concert); California, Here I Come, South (At Massey Hall)** and several individual statements to be found within both **In Concert, Vol 2, At Carnegie Hall** and **Century Plaza.**

Recordings:
Ben Pollack & His Orchestra, 1933-1934 *(—/ VJM)*

The World's Greatest Jazz Band of Yank Lawson and Bob Haggart. ". . . has continued to grow in stature."

The Radio Years: Bob Crosby & His Orchestra 1937
  (—/London)
Bob Crosby, South Rampart Street Parade *(—/MCA)*
Bob Crosby, Big Noise From Winnetka *(—/MCA)*
The Bob Cats: Bob Crosby's Bob Cats 1938-1942
  (Swaggie – Australia)
Tommy Dorsey & His Orchestra *(RCA Victor)*
Tommy Dorsey, Vol II *(RCA Victor)*
Eddie Condon Jazz Concert *(Decca/Brunswick)*
Lawson-Haggart Jazz Band, The Best Of Dixieland *(MCA Coral – Germany)*
The World's Greatest Jazzband Of Yank Lawson & Bob Haggart *(Project 3/World Record Club)*
Extra! Enoch Light Presents WGJB Of Yank Lawson & Bob Haggart *(Project 3/Parlophone)*
WGJB Of Yank Lawson & Bob Haggart *(Atlantic/—)*
WGJB Of Yank Lawson & Bob Haggart *(Atlantic)/*
  Live At The Roosevelt Grill *(—/Atlantic)*
WGJB Of Yank Lawson & Bob Haggart Plays Duke Ellington *(World Jazz/—)*
WGJB Of Yank Lawson & Bob Haggart, At Massey Hall *(World Jazz/—)*
WGJB Of Yank Lawson & Bob Haggart, In Concert, Vol 2, At Carnegie Hall *(World Jazz/—)*
WGJB Of Yank Lawson & Bob Haggart, Century Plaza *(World Pacific/—)*

Above: Leadbelly – a law unto himself. His musical genre encompassed jazz, blues and folk . . .

Huddie 'Leadbelly' Ledbetter

Bluesman Huddie Ledbetter was born in Louisiana in 1885, spending much of his youth there and in Texas, though his musical influences pre-date the regional blues. A great maverick artist, Leadbelly's songs include folk material, reels, cowboy songs, spirituals and prison songs. He served two lengthy jail sentences for murder and intent to murder, and was discovered by the Lomax father-and-son team who were collecting recordings of folk music for the Library of Congress, and recorded at the Angola Penitentiary.

The Leadbelly Set (Xtra): King of the twelve-string guitar.

An indispensable repository of the vanishing musical heritage, Leadbelly travelled with the Lomaxes on their field-recording expeditions, and established himself as a night-club and concert hall performer. His powerful voice and driving accompaniment on 12-string guitar produced many classic interpretations, **Good Night Irene, Rock Island Line, John Henry, Good Morning Blues** and **Ella Speed,** being among the best-known. Since his death in 1949, his reputation has fluctuated. A legend to the white folklorists, his music was seldom popular among the black community.

Recordings:
Leadbelly: The Library Of Congress Recordings
(Elektra/Elektra)
Leadbelly's Legacy
(Folkways/—)
The Leadbelly Box (—/Xtra)
Leadbelly (Stinson/Melodisc)
Leadbelly Sings & Plays
(—/Saga)
Blues Songs By The Lonesome Blues Singer (Royale/—)
Good Morning Blues
(—/RCA Victor)
Leadbelly, His Guitar, His Voice, His Piano
(Capitol/Capitol)
Leadbelly – Keep Your Hands Off Her (Verve – Forecast/Verve – Folkways)
Take This Hammer
(Verve – Forecast/Verve – Folkways)
Rock Island Line (Folkways/—)
Leadbelly – Last Session
(Folkways/—)

Peggy Lee

Peggy Lee (real name: Norma Deloris Egstrom, born Jamestown, North Dakota, 1922) is superbly representative of the kind of vocalist who, whilst operating in a basically pop field (Mel Torme (♦) is another) most definitely is strongly influenced by jazz; indeed, often performs in a manner which can only be described as 'jazz singing'. In Peggy Lee's singing one can hear traces of Billie Holiday (♦), Mildred Bailey (♦), and Lee Wiley (♦), but she is a supreme individualist who can handle all types of pop songs and conventional jazz material with sensitivity and a highly-developed awareness of the message contained within lyric that contrives to make some sense. Ballads are delivered with a smoky voice that sometimes drops to a husky whisper. On non-ballad material, she swings with a delicious sense of rhythmic under-statement, her timing being both subtle and impeccable.

She came from family of six children, began singing at 14 with semi-professional bands (broadcasting over local radio station), finally joining up with vocal-instrumental outfit called The Four Of Us. Benny Goodman (♦) caught the group in Chicago, was impressed by lead singer, and asked her to join his band (as replacement for Helen Forrest, who had just given notice). He also gave her a new,

King of New Orleans – Live In Concert: George Lewis And His New Orleans All Stars *(Telefunken).*

professional, name: Peggy Lee. Stayed with Goodman almost three years during which time she built a healthy reputation amongst Goodman fans even though many jazz/swing critics remained unimpressed. It is true to say that mostly those early efforts with Goodman **(We'll Meet Again)** tended often to sound routine, at times even uninspired. Only real commercial success came with a July 1942 recording of **Why Don't You Do Right?** (arranged by band's pianist Mel Powell). But in March 1943 gave notice to quit. Had already married Goodman's guitarist Dave Barbour (they were to divorce in 1952), and she retired from music business for a couple of years. Made several record dates for Capitol (mostly directed-arranged by Barbour) during period of retirement, then re-established herself in 1946, winning as top female singer in that year's *Down Beat* readers' poll. Became successful single act, with hit recordings like **Manana, It's A Good Day, Don't Smoke In Bed** then, later, **Mr Wonderful, Fever** (a marvelous example of her rhythmic abilities with instrumental support consummately vided by just two jazz musicians, Shelly Manne (♦), drums, and Joe Mondragon, bass), and **Is That All There Is?** From more basic jazz standpoint a 1953 album date, **Black Coffee,** in company with trumpeter Pate Candoli, drummer Ed Shaughnessy, pianist Jimmy Rowles, and bassist Max Wayne, produced superlative jazz singing on titles like **Easy Living** (much

influenced by Billie Holiday's version), **Love Me Or Leave Me, I Didn't Know What Time It Was,** and a whirlwind **My Heart Belongs To Daddy;** it is representative of her very best work.

Other notable jazz-based recordings include sessions with Quincy Jones **(Blues Cross Country),** Benny Carter (♦), Max Bennett and Jack Sheldon (as featured trumpet soloist) **(Mink Jazz)** and a live recording, in company with George Shearing (♦) Quintet **(Beauty & The Beat).**

Peggy Lee has appeared in but a handful of films – *Mr Music* (1950), *The Jazz Singer* (1953), and *Pete Kelly's Blues* **(Pete Kelly's Blues),** last-named for which she was nominated for Academy Award as best supporting actress.

Talented songwriter, has written lyrics for successful full-length Walt Disney movie *The Lady & The Tramp* (she also did soundtrack vocals), as well as string of first-rate pop songs, including **It's A Good Day, What More Can A Woman Do, I Don't Know Enough About You** (all with Barbour), **Where Can I Go Without You?, I'm Gonna Get It, There'll Be Another Spring, Then Was Then (And Now Is Now).**

During early-1970s, over 35 years after she changed from Norma Deloris Egstrom into Peggy Lee, she remains one of precious few singers (Dinah Washington (♦) was of a similar breed, Ray Charles (♦) is another) who can handle practically any kind of song: pop, ballad, gospel, R&B, country, blues, Afro-Cuban or jazz.

Recordings:
We'll Meet Again (Hallmark)
The Very Best Of Peggy Lee
(—/Capitol)
Black Coffee (MCA/Coral)
Bewitching-Lee
(Capitol/Capitol)
Blues Cross Country
(Capitol/Capitol)
Things Are Swingin'
(Capitol/Capitol)
Mink Jazz (Capitol/Capitol)
Peggy Lee/George Shearing, Beauty & The Beat
(Capitol/Capitol)
If You Go
(Capitol/World Record Club)
Peggy (Polydor/Polydor)

George Lewis

George Lewis (born New Orleans, 1900) remains, for many purists, the archetypal New Orleans clarinettist. Self-taught, Lewis possessed all the customary attributes of the classic NO players (other than a disconcerting habit of going out of tune, frequently, during his solos): a tremendous feeling for blues; warm, mahogany tone; ample use of both lower and upper registers of his instrument; and a typical New Orleansian basic rhythmic concept.

Outside New Orleans, Lewis was not a household word until invited to take part in recordings by Bunk Johnson (♦) in '42, recordings usually credited with being in vanguard of great traditional jazz revival of 1940s. His singing and passionate playing alongside Johnson

KING OF NEW ORLEANS

Live In Concert:
GEORGE LEWIS
And His New Orleans All Stars

was a prime reason for success of the trumpeter's American Music discs of period. His sensitive dovetailing with Johnson's horn on **Sobbin' Blues** and **When I Leave The World** (**Bunk Johnson & His New Orleans Band**) ranks with finest NO traditions of front-line interplay. And his contribution to ensemble of **Lowdown Blues** (**Bunk Johnson's Band 1944**) was masterful. As a boy, Lewis' involvement with music began with his learning to play a toy fife; acquired his first clarinet at 16.

Between 1917–23, worked with many legendary New Orleans names, including Buddie Petit, Henry 'Kid' Rena, Kid Ory (♦), Chris Kelly. After leading own band in 1923 (Henry 'Red' Allen (♦) played trumpet), joined Eureka Brass Band, working with them for several years. Did not play in 1928 because of a broken leg. Joined Evan Thomas Band in 1932, based in Crowley, Louisiana (Bunk Johnson also worked in same band). Worked as stevedore in New Orleans, plus regular work as member of Eureka Brass Band. During a season at Harmony Inn, New Orleans, he played more alto-sax than clarinet.

After Johnson-American Music recording sessions, returned to New Orleans for work with own bands. To New York with Bunk Johnson Band (1945–6), then back to New Orleans where he continued his bandleading activities. Worked in San Francisco with singer Lizzie Miles (1952), after which embarked on regular tours with own band (occasionally also as soloist). Visited Europe in 1957, 1959, to rapturous applause from fans – even though the playing of Lewis and fellow New Orleans veterans tended to be erratic. Received even wilder acclamation in Japan (1964) (**King Of New Orleans: George Lewis & His New Orleans All Stars Live In Concert**) with one of his best post-1940s bands, including 'Kid Punch' Miller (♦), Louis 'Big Eye' Nelson and Joe Robichaux. His playing during concert at Tokyo's Kosai-Nenkin Hall was excellent, particularly on old Lewis favorites like **Just A Closer Walk With Thee**, **Ice Cream** and **Burgundy Street Blues**, although Japanese version of latter, like others before and since, could not compare with original recorded version which has depth and poignancy of almost unsurpassed quality (**George Lewis**).

During his career, Lewis made other classic recordings, including results of 1943 date which contains superb Lewis clarinet on **See See Rider Blues, Lord, Lord You Sure Been Good To Me** (**George Lewis & His New Orleans Stompers, Vol 1**); and **Just A Closer Walk With Thee, Deep Bayou Blues** and **Two Jim Blues** (**George Lewis & His New Orleans Stompers, Vol 2**), last-named title constituting realization of a totally supreme blues performance. Lewis (real name: George Louis Francis Zeno) had to contend with continued poor health during his final years. Died in 1968, fittingly in the city whose music he had helped perpetuate so movingly, for so long.

Recordings:
Bunk Johnson's Band 1944
(Storyville/Storyville)
Bunk Johnson & His New

Orleans Band
(Commodore/Melodisc)
George Lewis *(American Music/ American Music)*
George Lewis & His New Orleans Stompers, Vols 1, 2
(Blue Note/Blue Note)
George Lewis: Classic New Orleans Traditions
(Riverside/Riverside)
George Lewis With Kid Shots
(American Music/—)
George Lewis Jam Session 1950
(Alamac/—)
George Lewis, On Parade
(Delmark/Delmark)
George Lewis Memorial Album
(Delmark/Delmark)
George Lewis Jam Session
(Jazz Unlimited/—)

John Lewis
♦ Modern Jazz Quartet

Meade Lux Lewis

Meade 'Lux' Anderson Lewis (born Chicago, Illinois, 1905) spent part of his childhood in Louisville, Kentucky, where he learned to play violin, before turning to piano. Established reputation in and around Chicago as fine bluesman who could also adapt himself to play in several styles. Lewis (nickname 'Lux' apparently derived from fact that as child he was

Ridin' In Rhythm (World Records) – top-class 1930s jazz.

often called Duke of Luxembourg), recorded a remarkable train blues for Paramount Records, in 1929. **Honky Tonk Train Blues** was later to become one of the most familiar tunes during late-1930s/early-1940s boogie woogie craze. But for some time during early-1930s, Lewis found work in the world of music hard to find, having to take employment as taxi driver, member of a shovel gang, and car-wash attendant. It was while working in latter capacity that John Hammond discovered him, late in 1935. And it was Hammond who persuaded Lewis to re-record **Honky Tonk Train Blues**, specifically for release in Britain (**Ridin' In Rhythm**); by following year Lewis was again involved with music, leading own band in Chicago and by end of 1936 had recorded **Honky Tonk Train Blues** on two further occasions.

After moving to New York, teamed up with Albert Ammons (♦) and Pete Johnson (♦) to form formid-

able boogie woogie trio. Apart from recording as a threesome (**Cafe Society Swing & The Boogie Woogie** and **The Complete Library Of Congress Boogie Woogie Recordings**) and a live **Boogie Woogie Trio**, all three recorded in solo capacity. Lewis laid down series of sparkling tracks for Decca (**Kings & Queens Of Ivory, 1935–1940**), and for Victor (**29 Boogie Woogie Originaux**). Also recorded for Blue Note (**Blue Note's Three Decades Of Jazz - 1939-1949, Vol 1**) as solo pianist; as member of Edmond Hall's (♦) **Celeste Quartet** (**Celestial Express**); and with Sidney Bechet (♦) (**Sidney Bechet Jazz Classics, Vol 1**) to whom he gave sensitive support, on celeste, during sopranoist's classic version of **Summertime**. (At Lewis' first Blue Note solo date, he cut yet another version of his most famous composition!).

Lewis, whilst not as mightily percussive as his two boogie woogie associates, was more elegant pianist. Split from Ammons and Johnson in 1941, leaving New York too, to settle on West Coast (Los Angeles, to be precise). From whence he continued to tour, as solo act, and to record for variety of labels. Apart from a live date for Norman Granz's Clef label in 1946 (**Boogie At The Philharmonic**) and a further studio session for same label in 1954 (**Yancey's Last Ride**) Lewis' playing was heard on Tops (**Barrel House Piano**), Verve (again, for Granz), (**Cat House Piano**) and Stinson (**Meade Lux Lewis**).

As well as with Bechet and Hall, Lewis used celeste on at least one other occasion, with delightful results. This was his own recording date (**Piano Jazz - Boogie Woogie Style**) which produced an eloquent **I'm In The Mood For Love** and self-explanatory **Celeste Blues**. However, his final recordings tended to sound clichéd; the boogie-woogie fad had, of course, long since expired, probably the victim of over-exposure. Still, it was a sad occasion indeed when Lewis was killed in car crash when returning from a gig in Minneapolis.

Recordings:
Various, John Hammond's Spirituals To Swing
(Vanguard/Vanguard)
Various, Kings & Queens Of Ivory (1935-1940)
(MCA – Germany)
Meade Lux Lewis/Albert Ammons/Pete Johnson, The Complete Library Of Congress Boogie Woogie Recordings *(Jazz Piano/—)*
Various (Including Meade Lux Lewis (Ridin' In Rhythm)
(World Records)
Various, Blue Note's Three Decades Of Jazz - 1939-1949, Vol 1 *(Blue Note)*
Various, Barrel-house, Blues & Boogie Woogie, Vol 1
(—/Storyville)
Various, 29 Boogie Woogie Originaux
(RCA Victor – France)
Various, Cafe Society Swing & The Boogie Woogie
(Swingfan – Germany)
Various, Honky Tonk Train
(Riverside/—)
Meade Lux Lewis/Albert Ammons/Pete Johnson, Boogie Woogie Trio
(—/Storyville)

Meade Lux Lewis *(Stinson/—)*
Meade Lux Lewis, Boogie At The Philharmonic
(Clef/Columbia – Clef)
Meade Lux Lewis, Yancey's Last Ride
(Verve/Columbia – Clef)
Meade Lux Lewis, Piano Jazz - Boogie Woogie Style
(Swaggie – Australia)
Various, Giants Of Boogie Woogie *(Riverside/—)*
Meade Luxe Lewis, Barrel House Piano
(Tops/Storyville – Denmark)
Meade Lux Lewis, Cat House Piano *(Verve/—)*

Ramsey Lewis

Ramsey E. Lewis, Jr (born Chicago, Illinois, 1935) has been one of the most successful crossover artists to have risen to international prominence since tail end of 1950s and through 1960s. A pianist, composer, leader whose approach to conventional jazz gradually became synthesized with various other musical elements: soul, R&B, gospel, pop – even classical. A hybrid which has not, on the whole, endeared itself to pure-at-heart jazzers but which has enabled various Lewis-led combos (mostly trios) to attain popularity, acclaim of (literally) Hit Parade proportions starting with mid 1960s No 1 hit disc, **The In Crowd (Solid Ivory)** followed by other successful single releases, like **Hang On, Sloopy, Wade In The Water**, and **Uptight** (all on **Solid Ivory**).

Up to date, Lewis has been recipient of no less than seven Gold Discs, three Grammy Awards. Remains sell-out artist at festivals, concerts and club dates. Put together the first of his piano trios in '56 (it featured, Lewis apart, Eldee Young, bass; and Red Holt, drums). Combo gigged in and around Chicago until 1958, during which time Lewis also recorded with other top-rated jazzmen (Clark Terry (♦), Max Roach (♦)). First trio lasted ten years. Since then Lewis-led small combos – their basic sound and concept pivoting on leader's frankly unconvincing funky approach to piano – have continued to attract widespread attention from a majority audience, especially by way of their string of album releases, such as **Down To Earth, Back To The Roots, Tobacco Road, Upendo Ni Pamoja, Funky Serenity, Sun Goddess, Salongo** and **Love Notes**.

Since 1976, Lewis often has worked with six-piece band (including flute, clarinet, guitar, vocals) although, in truth, as with majority of his bands through the years, his music remains approachable to general public but of little interest to those concerned with more genuine manifestations of continued story of top-flight jazz and its most worthy practitioners.

Recordings:
Down To Earth
(EmArcy/Fontana)
Tobacco Road *(Chess/Checker)*
The Groover *(Chess/Checker)*
Solid Ivory *(Chess/Checker)*
Back To The Roots
(Chess/Checker)
Upendo Ni Pamoja
(Columbia/CBS)
Funky Serenity *(Columbia/CBS)*

Sun Goddess (Columbia/CBS)
Salongo (Columbia/CBS)
Love Notes (Columbia/CBS)

Booker Little

Born 1938, Tennessee, Booker Little died of uraemia at the age of 23 in 1961, another of jazz's tragically shortlived trumpet giants. His early promise was clear enough for Max Roach to hire him in 1958, along with his Memphis blowing partner, tenorman George Coleman (**Deeds Not Words**). The association continued through Roach's magnificent political albums, with Little excellent on **Tears For Johannesburg (We Insist! - Freedom Now Suite)** and **Garvey's Ghost** and **Praise For A Martyr (Percussion Bitter Sweet)**. Like Eric Dolphy, with whom Little produced much of his best work, the trumpeter was constantly searching beyond the chord changes: 'The more dissonance, the bigger the sound.' In fact, it is Little's lyricism that strikes the listener, the clean, sweet trumpet lines of **Ode To Charlie Parker (Far Cry)** or the soaring accuracy of **Life's A Little Blue** with Scott La Faro's brilliant bass below (**The Legendary Quartet Album**), while **The Grand Valse** invites comparison with the Roach–Clifford Brown waltzes. The collaboration with Dolphy is illustrated by the mammoth recording session from New York's Five Spot (**The Great Concert Of Eric Dolphy**) both players hitting a peak on **The Prophet** and **Fire Waltz**. Little's arranging skills are promi-

Booker Little: The Legendary Quartet Album (Island).

nent on singer Abbey Lincoln's album **Straight Ahead** and the rare Candid **Out Front**.

Recordings:
Max Roach
Deeds Not Words
(Riverside/Riverside)
We Insist! Freedom Now Suite
(Candid/—)
Percussion Bitter Sweet
(Impulse/Impulse)
Eric Dolphy:
Far Cry (Prestige New Jazz/—)
The Great Concert Of Eric Dolphy (Prestige/—)
Abbey Lincoln, Straight Ahead
(Candid/—)
Out Front (Candid/—)
The Legendary Quartet Album
(Island/Island)
Victory & Sorrow (Bethlehem/—)

Charles Lloyd

After a background in blues and R&B, multi-reedman Charles Lloyd first came to prominence as musical director of the Chico Hamilton Quintet in 1960, taking over Eric Dolphy's place in the group. Both editions can be heard on one album (**Chico Hamilton**) the later unit dispensing with the cello, and tracks like **Sun Yen Sen** putting the Rollins–Coltrane influenced Lloyd tenor through its paces. Following a period with the Cannonball Adderley Sextet, Lloyd branched out as a leader. With guitarist Gabor Szabo and Miles Davis' rhythm section of Ron Carter and Tony Williams, he showed his range from the Coltrane-derived **Apex** to the prettily piping flute on the Guiffre-ish composition **OfCourse, OfCourse** (on album of same name). An eclectic performer, Lloyd's commercial success led swiftly to formula. In 1966, he took his group to Europe on three rapturously received tours.

That period is typified by an album (**Charles Lloyd**) that ranges from the catchiness of **Sombrero Sam** to the exoticism of **Dream Weaver**. With pianist Keith Jarrett's flashy facility and the excellent Jack De Johnette on drums (the whole group colorfully kitted out in beads and kaftans) Charles Lloyd was a festival favorite (**Forest Flower**). It didn't last.

Recordings:
Chico Hamilton
(Atlantic/Atlantic)
Of Course, Of Course
(Columbia/CBS)
Dream Weaver
(Atlantic/Atlantic)
Forest Flower
(Atlantic/Atlantic)

Frank Lowe

Memphis-born tenorman Frank Lowe was influenced by Stax Soul as well as the more usual idols like John Coltrane. His early involvement with Sun Ra in 1966, and his studies in San Francisco with Donald Garrett and Sonny Simmons, resulted in enormously strong, assured playing. His work with ex-Coltrane drummer, Rashied Ali, in the exposed duo situation (**Duo Exchange**) is wildly exciting, screams, over-blowings and honks used to devastating effect. Less coherent is the meeting with AACM saxophonist Joseph Jarman (**Black Beings**) which tends towards the unrelieved energy blast. His contribution to a recent Don Cherry album (**Don Cherry**) adds short, fiery dabs to the transcendental atmosphere. His best work so far – and he does give promise of becoming a major voice – is with trombonist Joseph Bowie and trumpeter Leo Smith (**The Flam**), a major achievement of group playing. Much more spacious and occasionally desultory, is the treatment of Monk themes, **Epistrophy** and **Mysterioso (Fresh)** while **Chu's Blues** has Lowe accompanied by the Memphis Four.

Recordings:
Rashied Ali - Frank Lowe, Duo Exchange (Survival/—)
Black Beings (ESP/ESP)
Don Cherry (A&M/A&M)
The Flam
(Black Saint – Italy)
Fresh (Arista – Freedom/ Arista – Freedom)
Doctor Too Much (Kharma/—)

The Flam (Black Saint): free playing, fine music.

Duo Exchange (Survival). Ferocious brilliance.

Above: Frank Lowe with Rashied Ali, with whom he recorded the exhilarating Duo Exchange on Ali's Survival label.

Jimmie Lunceford

Jimmie Lunceford's orchestra was, along with Duke Ellington's and Count Basie's, one of the greatest of the '30s. Less emotionally expressive than Ellington's, less unswervingly dedicated to swing than Basie's, it was superior to either in terms of virtuosity. Lunceford's band was all things to all men; it was a great dance band; it was a visual treat, with the musicians wearing different uniforms for each show, sections standing up to point their trumpets at the ceiling, or rotating the trombones in circles, an expert showmanship that Glenn Miller copied; above all, it was a high-precision jazz outfit executing wildly original charts, and earning the description, 'the trained seals' from rival bands.

Lunceford was born in 1902 in Missouri, receiving musical tuition from Paul Whiteman's father and going on to get a BA from Fisk University in 1926. His orchestra opened at Harlem's Cotton Club in 1933. The distinctive character came mainly from Sy Oliver's arrangements which were bril-

Takin' Off With Jimmie (Tax). Lunceford and his Orchestra.

127

Above: Jimmie Lunceford – for 20 years he fronted a tremendously exciting, superbly drilled jazz orchestra.

Humphrey Lyttelton

Since the mid-1940s, Humphrey Lyttelton (born Windsor, England) has been a catalytic figure on British jazz scene, as a trumpet player (and occasionally clarinettist), bandleader, broadcaster and writer. At beginning of his career, Lyttelton was staunch traditionalist, his own playing showing obvious affection for Louis Armstrong (♦). With George Webb's Dixielanders, Lyttelton became a focal point in the great interest in traditional jazz in UK which followed World War II. The ex-public school boy assembled first band in 1948, containing other bastions of traditional jazz in Britain, including Webb, clarinettist Wally Fawkes, joined later by brothers Keith Christie, trombone, and Ian Christie, clarinet. Music produced by these early Lyttelton bands tried faithfully to recapture that of famous US bands within the genre. It was not always the best kind of jazz to be heard and there were times when comparisons between the originals and the efforts of Lyttelton & Co were decidedly in favor of former. But some of the bands recordings, including **Careless Love, Trouble In Mind, Trog's Blues** and **Original Jelly-Roll Blues** (all **The Best Of Humph 1949-56**) register with moderate conviction even today. And a 1956 recording of Lyttelton's own **Bad Penny Blues (The Best Of Humph 1949-56)** reached Top Twenty of UK pop charts. Other Lyttelton recordings (from 1950–1) which bring back fond memories for British fans are **Tom Cat Blues, Get Out Of Here** and **Cake Walkin' Babies Back Home** (all **Humphrey Lyttelton Jazz Concert**). Lyttelton's jazz horizons broadened during 1950s, music of his band moving more into a 'mainstream' groove. At same time, Lyttelton's trumpet playing evoked Buck Clayton (♦) as much as Armstrong. Presence of saxophonist/clarinettist Bruce Turner (♦) was significant in overall change in policy at this time. Other musicians to work with Lyttelton during 1950s were saxist-clarinettist Tony Coe, tenorist Kathleen Stobart, baritonist Joe Temperley. Temperley, Coe and Jimmy Skidmore, tenor-sax, worked with Lyttelton when **Triple Exposure** was recorded, in 1959; likewise, with **Blues In The Night** from following year.

Lyttelton band's repertoire on latter album was interesting: included were **Creole Love Call, Blues In Thirds** and **The Champ**. Buck Clayton recorded with Lyttelton band for first time in Switzerland, '63, and his presence inspired the band to give of its collective best (**Me & Buck**). Clayton recorded on two further occasions with band (**Le Vrai Buck Clayton** and **Le Vrai Buck Clayton, Vol 2**) with overall results even more mutually rewarding.

Just how much musical progress (in best sense) Humphrey Lyttelton made in over 20 years as a jazzman, can be found within the grooves of **Duke Ellington Classics** with Lyttelton's trumpet most impressive as part of superb nine-piece band, including Ray Warleigh, alto-sax, flute; Temperley; and John Surman (♦). Lyttelton has recorded live on several occasions, probably best of all at London's Queen Elizabeth Hall, in '73 (**South Bank Swing Session**) which includes a Turner–Lyttelton clarinet duet (**Blues At Dawn**) rather in the manner of Mezzrow-Bechet (♦). And Lyttelton's trumpet work during 1975-recorded **Take It From The Top** was as good as at any other time of his career.

Lyttelton, perennial catalyst, retains ability to lift proceedings during someone else's gig. As he did, as guest, during an early-1970s concert by Alex Welsh Band (**An Evening With Alex Welsh, Parts 1, 2**). A witty, perceptive writer, Lyttelton has authored three books: *I Play As I Please, Second Chorus* and *Take It From The Top.* Humphrey Lyttelton Band made its first visit to US in 1959.

Recordings:
Humphrey Lyttelton, **The Best Of Humph 1949-1956** (—/Parlophone)
Humphrey Lyttelton **Jazz Concert** (—/Parlophone)
Humphrey Lyttelton, **Triple Exposure** (—/Parlophone)
Buck Clayton/Humphrey Lyttelton, **Me & Buck** (—/World Record Club)
Buck Clayton/Humphrey Lyttelton, **Le Vrai Buck Clayton** (—/77)
Buck Clayton/Humphrey Lyttelton, **Le Vrai Buck Clayton, Vol 2** (—/77)
Humphrey Lyttelton, **Duke Ellington Classics** (Black Lion/—)
Humphrey Lyttelton, **South Bank Swing** (Black Lion/—)
Humphrey Lyttelton, **Take It From The Top** (Black Lion/—)
Various (Including Humphrey Lyttelton), **An Evening With Alex Welsh, Parts 1, 2** (Black Lion/—)

liantly unpredictable and showed a great feeling for dramatic contrast and dynamics. His range of approach – the simplicity of **Dream Of You** or **On The Beach At Bali-Bali**; the startling complexity of the section work on **My Blue Heaven**; the inspired absurdities of **Organ Grinder Swing**; the tongue-in-cheek deployment of sentimental vocals amid instrumental tours de force like **Charmaine** – shows that Oliver was one of the greatest arrangers in jazz history (**Harlem Shout, Harlem Express** and **For Dancers Only**). His scores for **Swinging Uptown, Annie Laurie, Swanee River** (Jimmie Lunceford), **Muddy Water, Slumming On Park Avenue** and **Stomp It Off** (**Rhythm Is Our Business**) are classics, and when Oliver left to join Tommy Dorsey in 1939, he achieved the same miraculous blend of the straightforward and the staggering. Other Lunceford arrangers like pianist Ed Wilcox or altoist Willie Smith contributed fine scores, most notably for the unrivalled sax section which was dominated by the exuberant lead alto of Smith. **Sleepy Time Gal (For Dancers Only)** or **I'm Nuts About Screwy Music** (Jimmie Lunceford) show Wilcox's skill, while the sheer punch of guitarist Eddie Durham's **Harlem Shout** and **Avalon** rival the impact of Basie (**Harlem Shout**).

Lunceford had two major soloists in Smith and trombonist Trummy Young, who joined in 1937, but tenorman Joe Thomas, trumpeter Eddie Tomkins and Durham all made significant contributions. The rhythm section, with the resourceful Jimmy Crawford on drums, functioned mainly in a two-beat style, a decision of Sy Oliver's which was hotly disputed by other members of the band, but which lends the band a distinctive springi-

Jazz Star Series (RCA Victor). Featuring Jimmie Lunceford.

ness. Humor was a strong feature of the vocals, with Dan Grissom, Sy Oliver or the vocal trio featuring a light-hearted nod to commercial viability.

The peak years were 1933–43, with low salaries a big factor in the band's decline. Lunceford's perfectionism and the genius of his arrangers elevated the slightest material into great music.

Recordings:
Harlem Shout (MCA/MCA)
Harlem Express (—/Coral)
For Dancers Only (Decca/Brunswick)
Jimmie Lunceford (—/Brunswick)
Rhythm Is Our Business (—/Ace of Hearts)
Lunceford Special (Columbia/Philips)
Lunceford Special (Columbia/Realm)
Jimmie Lunceford & His Orchestra (—/DJM)
Blues In The Night (MCA/MCA)
Jimmie's Legacy (MCA/MCA)
The Last Sparks (MCA/MCA)

Howard McGhee

Born 1918 in Tulsa, Oklahoma, trumpeter Howard McGhee was brought up in Detroit. Originally influenced by Louis Armstrong and Roy Eldridge, he subsequently broadened his harmonic scope after hearing Dizzy Gillespie, and became one of the leading Bebop trumpeters. He gained experience between 1936–40, joined Lionel Hampton briefly, and then Andy Kirk and Charlie Barnet. He was clearly a modernist during his tenure with

Coleman Hawkins' quintet, 1944–5, and a later album gives an opportunity to compare versions of **Disorder At The Border** by McGhee and his mentor, Roy Eldridge (**Disorder At The Border**).

He led his own groups in Los Angeles from the mid-40s, using sidemen like James Moody, Milt Jackson, Dodo Marmarosa and Teddy Edwards. Two of his best performances, **Trumpet At Tempo** and **Thermodynamics** (**Trumpet At Tempo**) show phenomenal speed, clean articulation and a flood of ideas. The remainder of the session (**Charlie Parker On Dial, Vol 1**) had featured the group with Charlie Parker, an ill-

Above: (left to right) Humphrey Lyttelton, Joe Temperley and blues singer Big Joe Turner in friendly pose.

Together Again
(*Contemporary/Contemporary*)
Maggie's Back In Town
(*Contemporary/Contemporary*)
Here Comes Freddy
(*Sonet/Sonet*)

Chris McGregor

At a time when political developments in America lent an added significance to the African heritage of jazz, there emerged from South Africa a band that combined cultures in a natural, unselfconscious way. Chris McGregor's Blue Notes – a racially-mixed unit and therefore subject to apartheid laws – played at the Antibes Jazz Festival and then, through the good offices of South African pianist, Dollar Brand, settled to regular gigs in Switzerland before reaching London in 1965. Their impact on the British scene was enormous, a force of nature. The leader's antecedents place him uniquely at the roots of jazz – the son of a Scottish mission teacher, raised in South Africa, McGregor soaked up both the tin-roof Moody & Sankey hymnal and the music of Xhosan tribesmen. At the Capetown College of Music he fell under the influence of Schoenberg, Bartok and Webern, but spent his evenings improvising in the native Township bands. The Blue Notes – Dudu Pukwana, alto; Montezi Feza, trumpet; Johnny Dyani, bass; and Louis Moholo, drums – moved away from their highly original version of Hard Bop, into freer areas following a residency at Copenhagen's Montmartre, scene of recent gigs by Cecil Taylor, Albert Ayler and Don Cherry.

In 1970, McGregor organized the Brotherhood of Breath, a big band that moved easily between Kwela, New Orleans, Swing and the New Wave. The proportion of writing to improvising is blurred, and a wild, often ragged ensemble fever will abruptly sweep the band. Moholo

omened affair kept from total breakdown largely due to the efforts of McGhee on numbers like **Max Is Making Wax.** A later session with Bird **(Charlie Parker On Dial, Vol 3)** featured the writing of the trumpeter on **Stupendous, Carvin' The Bird** and **Cheers.** McGhee also played with another Bebop giant, Fats Navarro, and numbers like **Double Talk** and

Below: Howard McGhee, one of the great survivors of the Bebop era. Much of his best work was with Parker and Navarro.

Boperation show his mastery of the middle register **(Fats Navarro).** Quite the opposite was true of his numerous JATP performances which tended to display his pyrotechnics at speed in the upper register **(JATP, Vols 1 & 2), Blues For Norman** and **After You've Gone.** In 1949 he topped the *Down Beat* poll, but the '50s saw his career collapse due to addiction. He returned in the early '60s, a less blazing but still splendid soloist on albums like the reunion with Teddy Edwards **(Together Again)** and the fleet Phineas

Newborn **(Maggie's Back In Town).**

A recent meeting with tenorman Illinois Jacquet **(Here Comes Freddy)** shows that he has retained his imagination and bite.

Recordings:
Coleman Hawkins, Disorder At The Border (—/Spotlite)
Trumpet At Tempo (—/Spotlite)
Charlie Parker On Dial, Vols 1 & 3 (—/Spotlite)
Fats Navarro (Blue Note/Blue Note)
Jazz At The Philharmonic, Vols 1 & 2 (Verve/Verve)

Trumpet At Tempo (Spotlite): Maggie back in the Bebop era. The long-unavailable classic, Thermodynamics, is included.

Brotherhood (RCA Victor): Multi-racialism in action.

is a great big-band drummer, playing with an iron and irreduceable simplicity, and there is no shortage of fine soloists, many of whom lead their own units. Dudu Pukwana's alto has the temperament of a burst fire hydrant and his own albums (**In The Townships** and **Flute Music**) are both explosive and danceable. Mongezi Feza, who died in 1975, was a rapidly developing trumpeter, moving away from the early Don Cherry influence into a personal style (**Music For Xaba**). Harry Miller's unit, Isipingo shows his lyrical writing and fine bass-playing.

Recordings:
Brotherhood Of Breath
  (—/RCA Victor)
Brotherhood Of Breath Live At Willisau (—/Ogun)
Dudu Pukwana & Spear, In The Townships (—/Caroline)
Dudu Pukwana & Spear, Flute Music (—/Caroline)
Mongezi Feza, Music For Xaba (Sonet/Sonet)
Blue Notes For Mongezi (—/Ogun)
Procession (—/Ogun)

Mahavishnu John McLaughlin

British-born guitarist John McLaughlin worked with Georgie Fame and the Graham Bond Band before a period of experimentation with free music in company with baritonist John Surman and bassist Dave Holland. In 1969, he crossed the Atlantic and joined Miles Davis' drummer, Anthony Williams, in his new Lifetime unit. Through Williams, he was included on Miles Davis' influential new direction album (**In A Silent Way**) and the association continued with McLaughlin growing in confidence and a new economy (**Bitches Brew**).

In 1971, the guitarist, by now a disciple of Sri Chinmoy, formed the Mahavishnu Orchestra with bassist Rick Laird, keyboard player Jan Hammer, violinist Jerry Goodman and drummer Billy Cobham. Mountains of equipment appeared on stage to project the colossal volume, and the eclecticism of approach ransacked the globe. Playing a double-barreled guitar, McLaughlin's rhythmic playing is usually closer to a fusion of Indian music and rock, and the group's impetus is based upon lengthy riff-figures, often used in multiples. The first orchestra (**Inner Mounting Flame, Birds Of Fire, Between Nothingness & Eternity**)

Above: Chris McGregor, South African pianist, whose Brotherhood of Breath did so much to enliven jazz in the UK.

was characterized by non-stop virtuosity by all members, and consequent confusion as to who was doing what, particularly on the opening of **Trilogy (Between Nothingness & Eternity)** while **Dreams** misses trance for monotony.

Clash of egos resulted in the break-up of the orchestra, members like Cobham and Hammer making their own bids for stardom. The second Mahavishnu Orchestra launched out with electric violinist Jean-Luc Ponty and the London Symphony Orchestra (**Apocalypse**) in 1974, followed by a return to the earlier format (**Visions Of The Emerald Beyond**). A meeting with fellow Chinmoy-disciple, Carlos Santana resulted in an album (**Love, Devotion & Surrender**). Currently, McLaughlin has gone deeper into Indian music with his new quartet, Shakti (**Shakti**) featuring an Indian line-up, L. Shankar on violin, Zakir Hussain, tabla, T. H. Vinayakram on percussion.

Recordings:
Devotion (Douglas/—)
Miles Davis:
  In A Silent Way
  (Columbia/CBS)
  Bitches Brew
  (Columbia/CBS)
Anthony Williams' Lifetime:
  Emergency (Polydor/Polydor)
  Turn It Over
  (Polydor/Polydor)
Mahavishnu Orchestra:
  Inner Mounting Flame
  (Columbia/CBS)
Birds Of Fire
  (Columbia/CBS)

Between Nothingness & Eternity (Columbia/CBS)
Apocalypse (Columbia/CBS)
Visions Of The Emerald Beyond (Columbia/CBS)
Inner Worlds (Columbia/CBS)
McLaughlin & Santana, Love, Devotion & Surrender (Columbia/CBS)
Shakti (Columbia/CBS)
Electric Guitarist (Columbia/CBS)
Natural Elements (Columbia/CBS)

Jackie McLean

Born 1931, altoist Jackie McLean had the early advantage of 'Keepin' heavy company'. At 17, he was playing with giants like Charlie Parker, Bud Powell and Thelonious Monk, Bebop's toughest forcing house. His earliest recordings with Miles Davis (**Dig**) catch both McLean and a young Sonny Rollins still under the Parker influence. A period with Charlie Mingus developed his tonal strength and exposed him to a freer climate in expressionist pieces like **Pithecanthropus Erectus (Pithecanthropus Erectus)** and raging blues like **Moanin' (Blues & Roots)**.

He spent nearly three years with Art Blakey's Jazz Messengers in the mid-1950s, sharing the front line with trumpeter Bill Hardman, and adding a sharp cutting edge to the unit which has subsequently utilized the beefier attack of tenor players. McLean's work on **Little Melonae** and **Stanley's Stiff Chickens (Art Blakey With The Jazz Messengers)** shows how successfully he could ride the leader's furious battery. Numerous Hard Bop sessions of the middle and late '50s feature the altoist (**House Of Byrd**) but it is with Blue Note's series under his own name that his full maturity blossomed. McLean's development had been steady, his tone becoming more expressive of emotional extremes – harsh, strident, relentless. His phrasing was angular and often unpredictable in its sidesaddle relationship to the beat. No longer at pains to deliver the multi-note passages of a Parker, McLean's work was stark and economic. All these characteristics cohere around the turn of the decade (**Swing Swang Swingin', Bluesnik, Capuchin Swing, New Soil** and **A Fickle Sonance**). **Bluesnik** contains a bursting solo, massive drive with passages of wildly effective tonal distortion. **Francisco (Capuchin Swing)** is searing in its intensity. All his best work is driven by great drumming; Pete La Rocca, Art Taylor, Billy Higgins; the atmosphere at its most demanding. These dates showed evidence of careful preparation, both in McLean's compositions and in the interaction of the various groups. The New York staging of the Jack Gelber play, *The Connection*, featured McLean as an actor as well as within the band, and the music is recreated on an excellent Freddie Redd album (**The Connection**).

In 1963, influenced by Free Music developments from Ornette Coleman and John Coltrane, McLean announced a change of direction: 'the search is on'. The first album to display his freer approach (**Let Freedom Ring**) had all the old qualities of drive and inventiveness plus a more intensely vocalized sound ranging from oboe-like low notes to a high, searing whistle. Collaboration with the Blue Note school of young experimenters, Grachan Moncur III, Anthony Williams and Bobby Hutcherson, produced several excellent albums (**Destination Out, One Step Beyond** and **Evolution**). 'The new breed has inspired me all over again,' wrote McLean, and formed a band with the talented young trumpeter, Charles Tolliver, which was distinguished by fine writing from both of them (**Action, It's Time** and **Jacknife**).

A meeting in 1967 with Ornette Coleman, featured on trumpet, showed that McLean's new direction was less radical and more rooted in conventional harmony than his iconoclastic sideman's, but that both men could work together fruitfully (**New And Old Gospel**). Currently, the altoist's work for Steeplechase with veteran tenorman, Dexter Gordon (**The Meeting**) and with fellow alto Gary Bartz (**Ode To Super**) find him in inventive form, and, in company with The Cosmic Brotherhood, sharing the front line with his son Rene (**New York Calling**).

Recordings:
Miles Davis, Dig
  (Prestige/Prestige)
Charlie Mingus:
  Pithecanthropus Erectus
  (Atlantic/Atlantic)
  Blues & Roots
  (Atlantic/Atlantic)
Art Blakey & The Jazz Messengers (CBS – France)

Donald Byrd, House Of Byrd
(Prestige/Prestige)
Swing, Swang, Swingin'
(Blue Note/Blue Note)
Bluesnik *(Blue Note/Blue Note)*
Capuchin Swing
(Blue Note/Blue Note)
New Soil *(Blue Note/Blue Note)*
A Fickle Sonance
(Blue Note/Blue Note)
Freddie Redd, The Connection
(Blue Note/Blue Note)
Let Freedom Ring
(Blue Note/Blue Note)
Destination Out
(Blue Note/Blue Note)
One Step Beyond
(Blue Note/Blue Note)
Grachan Moncur III, Evolution
(Blue Note/Blue Note)
Action *(Blue Note/Blue Note)*
It's Time *(Blue Note/Blue Note)*
Jacknife *(Blue Note/Blue Note)*
New & Old Gospel
(Blue Note/Blue Note)
The Meeting
(Steeplechase/Steeplechase)
Ode To Super
(Steeplechase/Steeplechase)
New York Calling
(Steeplechase/Steeplechase)

Capuchin Swing (Blue Note):
the altoist with Mr. Jones.

Joe McPhee

Trumpet and tenorman Joe McPhee
is an interesting avant-garde musician, pretty on his first instrument
(his father was a trumpeter too) and
darkly turbulent on the tenor. Both
can be heard within one number,
Scorpio's Dance (Nation Time),
the character of the piece changing
radically with the different horns.
The title track, dedicated to play-
wright and poet LeRoi Jones, is a
long, churning free outing fuelled
by two drummers, Bruce Thompson and Ernest Bostic. **Shakey
Jake** is probably the most approachable track, with attractive
counterpoint and a danceable
rhythm. An earlier album **(Underground Railroad)** takes its title
from the routes used by runaway
slaves, and opens with a long drum
solo – Bostic again – before the
horns take over, McPhee on trumpet, Reggie Marks tenor, then the
leader for a blistering tenor solo.
Based mainly in the Poughkeepsie
area, McPhee has played in New
York with Dewey Redman and
Clifford Thornton, and teaches at
Vassar College.

Recordings:
Nation Time *(CJR/—)*
Underground Railroad *(CJR/—)*
Trinity *(CJR/—)*
Pieces Of Light *(CJR/—)*

Jay McShann

Jay McShann (born Muskogee,
Oklahoma, 1909) is an accomplished blues pianist with a reputation for leading variety of blues-
based bands, large and small.
From late 1930s until compara-

Above: pianist-composer Jay McShann, from Muskogee, Okl.
Charlie Parker worked with his fine early-1940s band.

Above: altoman Jackie McLean, '50s Hard Bop giant and one of
the few of his generation to explore Ornette's territory.

tively recent times, McShann has
continued to lead variety of bands,
each representative of what usually
is known as 'Kansas City Jazz'. It
was after he commenced working
in that city (mid-1930s) that his
reputation was established, both
as pianist and leader. By 1937, had
played, and toured with various
bands.
Same year, put together first
combo (quintet), including bassist
Gene Ramey and altoist Charlie
Parker (♦).
By 1940 the band had increased to
eight pieces and was touring and
broadcasting regularly, building
up a healthy reputation. Parker, together with leader, was star soloist
(Early Bird). McShann Orchestra
made first records in 1941 **(The
Jumping Blues)**, by which time
it was of big-band size. Blues
shouter Walter Brown, an average
vocalist, appeared on many of
initial sides, but there was always
room for solos by Parker, McShann,
trumpeters Orville Minor, Bernard 'Buddy' Anderson, lead
altoist John Jackson. Discs like
Swingmatism, Hootie Blues (co-
authored by Parker, McShann)
and **One Woman's Man** achieved
some degree of real popularity –
Confessin' The Blues, written by
Brown, probably was most popular of all. 1942: band more widely
respected, thanks in part to records like **The Jumpin' Blues,
Get Me On Your Mind** (vocal, Al
Hibbler), **Sepian Bounce** (all **The
Jumping Blues**), but by 1943,
Parker, its principal soloist, had
left. Following band's New York

*The Jumping Blues (Coral
Decca) – Jay McShann & Band.*

debut, McShann was called up for
Army service (1943). A year later,
though, he re-formed, with subsequent McShann combos being
seven or eight strong then spent
1945 and 1946 based in Kansas
City, leading own combos.
Recorded for Swing Time (1947-
1949), with sidemen such as trumpeter Art Farmer (♦), guitarists
Louis Speigiter or Tiny Webb,
tenorists Maxwell Davis, Pete
Peterson or Charles Thomas. There
were generally superior blues
vocals, especially those by Jimmy
Witherspoon (♦) and solid instrumentals **(The Band That Jumps
The Blues!** and **Ain't Nobody's
Business!)** 1957: McShann assembled two all-star bands to support
his ex-singer Witherspoon for
Victor sessions, which produced
mostly first-rate music, vocally as
well as instrumentally – **Blue**

Early Bird (Spotlite) – Charlie Parker with Jay McShann.

Moods In The Shade Of Kansas City and **A Spoonful Of Blues.** 1969: first European trip, appearing at Jazz Expo festival, London. Since then, has continued to tour, mostly as soloist, and been recorded at fairly frequent intervals. One such latter occasion took place during 1975 Montreux Jazz Festival **(Vine Street Boogie)** where McShann's solidly-swinging piano-playing (and, on occasion, vocals) created favorable impression, with McShann saluting Ellington on **I'm Beginning To See The Light** and **Satin Doll**, recalling personal successes of the past on **Hootie Blues** and **Confessin' The Blues**, and paying respects to his most famous band alumnus on **Yardbird Waltz**.

In 1976 Sam Charters selected McShann to play piano at recording date **(Kansas City Joys)**, co-starring Buddy Tate (♦), Paul Quinichette (another former McShann sideman) and Claude Williams on violin, during which the spirit of KC jazz was evoked, superbly and rewardingly.

Recordings:
Jay McShann/Charlie Parker, Early Bird (1940-1943)
(—/Spotlite)
Jay McShann, New York - 1208 Miles (Decca)/
The Jumpin Blues (Coral)
Various (Including Jay McShann), History Of Jazz, Vols 3, 4 (Capitol/Capitol)
Count Basie/Jimmy Witherspoon, Blue Moods In The Shade Of Kansas City (RCA Victor – France)
Jimmy Witherspoon, A Spoonful Of Blues (RCA Victor – France)
Jay McShann, Vine Street Boogie (Black Lion)
Buddy Tate/Paul Quinichette/Jay McShann, Kansas City Joys (—/Sonet)
Jimmy Witherspoon/Jay McShann, The Band That Jumps The Blues! (Black Lion)

Mahavishnu Orchestra
♦ *Mahavishnu John McLaughlin*

Wingy Manone, Volume 1 (RCA Victor). Joseph 'Wingy' Manone, one-arm trumpeter, led a series of fine jumping bands in the 1930s.

Wingy Manone

Joseph 'Wingy' Manone (born New Orleans, Louisiana, 1904) took up trumpet as teenager – despite fact that several years before he had lost right arm in auto accident. From musical family, Manone worked on riverboats, embarking first at Chicago then, in 1924, New York. Gigged around NYC, then joined Crescent City Jazzers with whom he moved to St Louis. Subsequently, worked with other bands (including own), in Texas, California, New Mexico. 1926: own band in Biloxi, Mississippi; also made first – and abortive – record date for Columbia. Finally, recorded with own Harmony Kings in New Orleans the following year **(New Orleans Stomp)** before working once again in Chicago. First musician to record a riff tune – **Tar Paper Stomp**, 1929 – later to become famous as **In The Mood (Barbecue Joe & His Hot Dogs).**

Recorded in New York with Benny Goodman (♦) **(Benny Goodman's Boys 1928-1929).** Gained prominence in early 1930s after becoming resident, once again, in NYC; a familiar figure on 52nd Street. His Armstrong-inspired playing and singing, whilst never in same league as object of inspiration, endeared him to a wide audience, helped not a little by hit disc for Vocalion, **Isle Of Capri (Swing Street, Vol 1)** and previous reputation he had acquired through fine recordings as member of New Orleans Rhythm Kings.

Of lesser import, but no less helpful, were recordings with own orchestra, featuring Jack Teagarden (♦), Johnny Mercer et al, for Vocalion **(The Great Soloists Featuring Jack Teagarden)**, including **You Are My Lucky Star** and **I've Got A Note.** During successful, widely-publicized Hickory House engagement, in 1936, Manone cut several sides for RCA's Bluebird label **(Wingy Manone, Vol 1)** together with Eddie Miller (♦), Ray Bauduc, Joe Marsala (♦). More recordings, also for RCA, followed in 1937 and 1939 – including **Chew, Choo, Chu & Co** – which benefited tremendously by presence of tenorist Chu Berry (♦). Manone, apart from amusing vocal stylings of such Scottish airs as **Annie Laurie** and **Loch Lomond**, produced excellent trumpet solos on such as **Jumpy Nerves, Limehouse Blues, My Money's Lovin' Arms**, inspired, no doubt, by Berry's magnificent tenor work. After NYC successes, moved to Florida; then, later, to Hollywood where he appeared as guest on Bing Crosby (♦) radio series, also in latter's film *Rhythm On The River* (1940).

Remained on West Coast until mid-1950s, working in variety of clubs, occasionally taking time out to make appearances outside California. 1954: resident permanently in Las Vegas, since which time has led own combos in vicinity, or – on rare occasions – played NYC, principal US jazz festivals. In '66, toured Europe. Biography *Trumpet On The Wing* written with Paul Vandervoort, published 1948.

Recordings:
Wingy Manone, Barbecue Joe & His Hot Dogs (Swaggie – Australia)
New Orleans Rhythm Kings 1934-1935 (MCA Coral – Germany)
Benny Goodman's Boys (1928-1929) (MCA Coral – Germany)
Various (Including Wingy Manone), New Orleans Stomp (—/VJM)
The Great Soloists, 1929-1936, Featuring Jack Teagarden (Biograph/—)
Various (Including Wingy Manone), Swing Street, Vol 1 (Epic/Columbia)
Wingy Manone, Vol 1 (RCA Victor/RCA Victor)
Chu Berry/Wingy Manone, Chew, Choo, Chu & Co (RCA Victor – France)
Papa Blue's Viking Jazzband With Wingy Manone & Edmond Hall (Storyville/—)

Mike Mantler

Composer Mike Mantler, married to Carla Bley, established his reputation with the avant-garde of the '60s both musically and as a moving force behind the Jazz Composers Orchestra Association which produces its own albums and pools its musical resources. Mantler's writing is chiefly structured to highlight the soloist, and he is brilliantly served by Don Cherry, Gato Barbieri, Roswell Rudd, Pharoah Sanders and Cecil Taylor

The Jazz Composer's Orchestra (JCOA Virgin): massed giants.

on a series of **Communications** (Jazz Composers Orchestra). The characteristically slow, even swell of orchestral harmonies tends to evoke a somber mood, and subsequent works based on the Samuel Becket monolog, **How It Is (No Answer)**; Edward Gorey's writing and drawing (**The Hapless Child**); or Harold Pinter (**Silence**) are increasingly bleak. Using eerie, sustained chords and liturgical singers like Jack Bruce or Robert Wyatt, Mantler seems to be moving towards terminal beach. A competent trumpeter, he turns up on several JCOA productions.

Recordings:
Jazz Composers Orchestra
(JCOA/JCOA – Virgin)
No Answer *(Watt/Watt)*
The Hapless Child *(Watt/Watt)*
Silence *(Watt/Watt)*
Mike Mantler & Carla Bley,
13 & 3/4 *(Watt/Watt)*

Dodo Marmarosa

Bebop pianist Dodo Marmarosa, born 1926, settled on the West Coast and was chosen by Charlie Parker – following the departure of Joe Albany – as the group pianist. A brilliant technician capable of great speed and variety, Marmarosa's work won him a *Downbeat* New Star Award in 1946. The nickname came from his physical appearance, with his large head and short body. He can be heard on a couple of albums – **Charlie Parker On Dial, Volume One**, on tracks **Moose The Mooche**, **Yardbird Suite**, **Ornithology**, **Night In Tunisia**; and **Charlie Parker On Dial, Volume Three**, on **Relaxin' At Camarillo**, **Cheers**, **Carvin' The Bird**, **Stupendous**. A group led by trumpeter Howard McGhee (**Trumpet At Tempo**) featured excellent solo work by the pianist on **Up In Dodo's Room** and a cascading up-tempo outing on **Dilated Pupils**. A recently issued collection (**Dodo Marmarosa**) contains solo and trio performances. Like so many of the white Bebop pianists, Marmarosa disappeared from the scene after the '40s, turning up on record again in 1961 (**Dodo's Back!**) with all his old facility, though less so with Gene Ammons (**Jug & Dodo**) the following year.

Recordings:
Charlie Parker On Dial,
Volume One *(Spotlite/Spotlite)*
Charlie Parker On Dial,
Volume Three
(Spotlite/Spotlite)
Howard McGhee, Trumpet At

Tempo *(Spotlite/Spotlite)*
Dodo's Back! *(Argo/—)*
Jug & Dodo
(Prestige/Prestige)

Joe Marsala

Joseph Francis 'Joe' Marsala (born Chicago, Illinois, 1907) never has ranked amongst the most important stylists, either on clarinet or alto-saxophone, but has been respected as a gifted, reliable musician since his professional career began in mid-1920s.

Brother of trumpeter Mario Salvatore 'Marty' Marsala (1909–75), and husband of harpist Adele Girard, Joe Marsala was for many years associated with trumpeter Wingy Manone, with whom he had first worked in 1929. Manone Quartet (with Marsala) attracted much attention during engagement at multi-instrumentalist Adrian Rollini's Tap Room club, New York (1935). With Rollini and others, Manone-Marsala recorded some fine sides for Victor in 1935, under title of Adrian's Tap Room Gang (**Adrian Rollini & His Friends, Vol 1: 'Tap Room Special'**) and later same year singer-songwriter Johnny Mercer joined Jack Teagarden (♦) and Manone to produce more excellent recorded jazz, for Vocalion (**The Great Soloists Featuring Jack Teagarden**).

In 1936, with Eddie Condon (♦), he co-led one of the first bands to work regularly with multi-racial line-up. Was often associated with Condon in subsequent years; played opening engagement at Eddie Condon Club, 1945 – and recorded on numerous occasions in variety of Condon-led groups, including recording such as **Jam Sessions At Commodore** and **The Eddie Condon Concerts: Town Hall 1944-45 Featuring Pee Wee Russell**. Recorded with his Chicagoans (including brother Marty, Buddy Rich (♦), and violinist Ray Biondi) (**Swing Street, Vol 1**) day before opening for first time at Hickory House, New York, where he was to become something of an institution, performing regularly for almost a decade. Recorded again with Manone (in 1938) whose band also included tenorist Leon 'Chu' Berry (♦) (**Chew, Choo, Chu & Co.**) and played clarinet during historic trans-Atlantic radio link-up featuring live jam sessions in New York (**Great Swing Jam Sessions, Vol 1**), in 1938, 1939.

Booked to play clarinet at a 1940 record date under leadership of drummer George Wettling, switched instruments with tenorist for date, Danny Polo, and produced some of his best recorded work on any saxophone (**Chicago Jazz**). Same year, this time using clarinet only, Marsala & His Delta Four (**Swingin' Clarinets**) recorded one of his finest solos, during Leonard Feather's **Reunion In Harlem**. Tried his hand at leading a big band in 1939, but venture did not last for more than a few months. After tour of Canada in 1948, retired from music on full-time basis, settling in Colorado (1949–53). Back to New York in '54, to start own music publishing firm; Marsala had successes as pop songwriter, with **And So To Sleep Again**, **Little Sir Echo**, and, particularly, **Don't Cry, Joe**. To Chicago, 1962, as vice-president of Seeburg Music Corporation, position he held for

six years. To California in 1967, led Joe Marsala's All Stars band between 1969–70.

Virtually inactive during past decade, but has been known to make surprise – if rare – appearances; at which time he has demonstrated that his obvious talents as clarinettist and saxophonist have not been diminished by passing of the years.

Recordings:
Adrian Rollini & His Friends,
Vol 1: 'Tap Room Special'
(RCA Victor – France)
Jack Teagarden, The Great
Soloists Featuring Jack
Teagarden *(Biograph/—)*
Eddie Condon, Jam Sessions
At Commodore *(Ace of Hearts)*
The Eddie Condon Concerts:
Town Hall 1944-45 Featuring
Pee Wee Russell
(Chiaroscuro/—)
Various (Including Joe
Marsala), Swing Street, Vol 1
(Tax – Sweden)
Various (Including Joe
Marsala), Great Swing Jam
Sessions, Vols 1, 2 *(—/Saga)*
Various (Including George
Wettling), Chicago Jazz
(Decca/Coral)
Wingy Manone, Vol 1
(RCA Victor/RCA Victor)
Chu Berry, Chew, Choo, Chu &
Co *(RCA Victor – France)*
Various (Including Joe
Marsala), Swingin' Clarinets
(—/London)

Warne Marsh *Jazz From the East Village*
ronnie ball, eddie de haas, bob minnicucci, peter ind

Warne Marsh

Born 1927 in Los Angeles, tenorman Warne Marsh is a disciple of Lennie Tristano's 'Cool School'. Making his debut with altoist Lee Konitz and leader Tristano on the celebrated Capitol session of 1949 (**Crosscurrents**). Marsh's work is characterized by great rhythmic subtlety, a pale sound and long, looping lines that plait with those of Konitz. For many years, he recorded solely with other Tristanoites, preferring – like his mentor – to perfect his playing in isolation rather than compromise with the commercial world of the jazz club.

A session from 1955 finds him sharing a recording with Konitz (**Lee Konitz & Warne Marsh**) in which counterpoint and the interplay of serpentine lines generate considerable heat and tension. This is Baroque music, full of odd accents and unpredictable shapes. Marsh's work with fellow tenor, Ted Brown, and alto Art Pepper is largely deleted (**Jazz Of Two Cities** and **Free Wheeling**), but Art Pepper's belated release (**The Way It Was!**) catches the two men in a homage to their main influence, Lester Young, on **Tickle Toe**.

Marsh and pianist Joe Albany got together informally for a classic one-off session (**The Right Combination**) which contradicted all the critical brickbats about the tenorman's frigidity. **All The Things You Are** shows a rare melodic imagination at work while Marsh cooks like a peat fire. Bassist Peter Ind's Wave label has examples of the mature Marsh (**Release Record - Send Tape** and **Jazz From The East Village**) with a compatible rhythm section, which shows that he is one of the most original players around. He bumps along close to the ground, his tone a relentlessly pruned and buffed edge that breaks upwards into squawks at the end of a phrase like a yard fowl fleeing a broom. A master of inflexion, his curiously-wrought lines seem to challenge every convention while exhibiting

Jazz From The East Village (Wave): Peter Ind's recordings of the master.

a highly personal sense of balance. Sinuous, never declamatory in the currently fashionable style, Warne Marsh has yet to receive the recognition he deserves. In 1969 he led a quartet of second generation Tristano followers through the familiar steeplechase tempos of **Lennie's Pennies** and **Subconscious-Lee** (**Ne Plus Ultra**). In 1976 he came to Europe, teaming up again after ten years with Konitz, and the resulting music was a triumph of integrity, and a vindication of twenty-five years of obscurity (**The London Concert**).

Recordings:
Lennie Tristano,
Crosscurrents *(Capitol/Capitol)*
Lee Konitz & Warne Marsh
(Atlantic/—)
Art Pepper, The Way It Was!
(Contemporary/Contemporary)
Joe Albany, The Right
Combination *(Riverside/—)*
Release Record - Send Tape
(Wave/Wave)
Jazz From The East Village
(Wave/Wave)
Ne Plus Ultra *(Revelation/—)*
Lee Konitz+Warne Marsh
The London Concert *(—/Wave)*

George Melly

George Melly, author, art expert, film and television critic, cartoon collaborator and entertainer is a difficult man to classify. Influenced by Bessie Smith, Melly first came to prominence as a singer during the Trad boom of the early '50s. His re-emergence in 1974 with John Chilton's Feetwarmers has proved immensely successful, and although he is an all-round entertainer rather than a blues singer, he has feeling for the form.

Recordings:
Nuts *(Warner/Warner)*
Son Of Nuts *(Warner/Warner)*
It's George *(Warner/Warner)*
At It Again *(Reprise/Reprise)*

Memphis Slim

Memphis Slim (real name: Peter Chatman), born Memphis, Tennessee, 1915, has become, since 1950s, one of the most popular of all blues performers. Has fine vocal style – rarely intense or chilling like, say, Blind Lemon Jefferson (♦), or profound like Big Bill Broonzy (♦) – but convincing nevertheless. His rolling piano-playing is living proof of continued validity of the barrelhouse-cum-boogie-woogie school. Compositionally, too, is one of the most accomplished writers – his most famous number, **Every Day I Have The Blues** – indeed a modern blues standard – achieved international acclaim following recording by singer Joe Williams and orchestra of Count Basie (♦) **(Count Basie Swings, Joe Williams Sings).** Same combination brought Slim's **The Comeback** before a wide audience.

Memphis Slim began career in 1934, deputizing for one of his early blues idols, Roosevelt Sykes. It really began, though, after moving to Chicago in 1939. He jammed with top artists there, including Sonny Boy Williamson, Big Bill Broonzy (♦), Washboard Sam. Became regular pianist for Broonzy following year. Also in 1940 made record debut for Bluebird. Slim's humorous **Beer Drinking Woman (Memphis Slim)** helped establish his name almost immediately. Other fine early-Slim recordings (1940-1) – **Grinder Man Blues, You Didn't Mean Me No Good, Maybe I'll Lend You A Dime, Two Of A Kind, I Believe I'll Settle Down** (all **Memphis Slim**). Accompanied Broonzy on record **(Big Bill's Blues)** – but left to go solo in 1944, forming own accompanying unit, the House Rockers. For some years worked mainly in

Chicago. After prestigious appearances at Carnegie Hall and Newport Jazz Festival (both '59), moved to Paris two years later, city that has been his home since then.

Toured Europe extensively on numerous occasions, with occasional trips back home. Since 1950s, has recorded prolifically. Played piano behind Washboard Sam, Broonzy, in 1953 **(Genesis: The Beginnings Of Rock)** – and cut numerous records under own name, with or without House Rockers **(The Real Boogie Woogie, Memphis Slim & The Real Honky Tonk)** or with bassist Willie Dixon **(The Blues Every Which Way).** Year prior to becoming Parisian citizen, recorded in London for first time **(Chicago Boogie).**

Although not all subsequent recordings have been comparable to his greatest work inside studio, there have been other occasions when his talents have been heard at, or near to, his best. Such examples include **Memphis Slim - Matthew Murphy; The Legacy Of The Blues, Vol 7: Memphis Slim; No Strain; Rock Me Baby!** and **Raining The Blues.**

Like B. B. King (♦), Memphis Slim has tended to irritate blues purists by his periodic forays outside basic blues field. Whilst these attempts at extending his musical vocabulary, like **Going Back To Memphis,** have not always shown him in best light, like King, he has demonstrated an ability to relate musically to more than one area of expression.

Recordings:
Memphis Slim *(RCA Victor/Bluebird – France)*
Big Bill Broonzy, Big Bill's Blues *(—/CBS – Realm)*
Various (Including Memphis Slim), Genesis: The Beginnings Of Rock Vol 1 *(Chess/Chess)*
Travelling With The Blues *(—/Storyville)*
Bad Luck & Troubles *(Barnaby/—)*
The Real Boogie Woogie *(Folkways/—)*

The Blues Every Which Way *(Verve/—)*
'Frisco Bay Blues *(—/Fontana)*
Matt Murphy, Memphis Slim - Matthew Murphy *(Black & White – France)*
All Them Blues *(DJM)*
The Legacy Of The Blues: Vol 7 *(—/Sonet)*
Raining The Blues *(Fantasy/—)*
Chicago Boogie *(Black Lion/Black Lion)*
Various (Including Memphis Slim), Barrel-house Blues & Boogie Woogie, Vol 1 *(Storyville)*
Rock Me Baby *(Black Lion/Black Lion)*
No Strain *(Prestige – Blues/Fontana)*
Memphis Slim & The Real Honky Tonk *(Folkways/—)*

Bubber Miley

James 'Bubber' Miley (born Aiken, South Carolina, 1903) perhaps was the first trumpet player to gain widespread acclaim – within the context of a big band – for his adroit use of trumpet and mute. Miley specialized in 'growl' solos, moving plunger mute in and out of the bell of the instrument with left hand while depressing the trumpet's valves, in normal fashion, with the other. Miley was not, however, first trumpeter/cornettist to use mutes in successful, individual manner; Johnny Dunn (1897–1937), Chris Kelly, Tommy Ladnier (♦), Mutt Carey (1891–1948), and King Oliver (♦), were others who preceded him, but Miley's playing (emotion-filled, and like trombonist Tricky Sam Nanton (♦), a colleague for a while in Duke Ellington (♦) Orchestra, close to the cry of a human voice) was one of the earliest examples of American jazz instrumental playing at its most basic and expressive.

Coming from musical family, Miley served 18 months with US Navy before entering music, as trumpeter first, with Carolina Five

then, successively, with Willie Gant, Mamie Smith, Elmer Snowden before Snowden's Washingtonians were taken over by Duke Ellington. In between two spells with Mamie Smith, also toured as part of Sunny South revue, as well as undertaking cabaret, dance band work in New York. Left Ellington in 1929, visited Paris with Noble Sissle, then back to New York for various jobs, including leading own band (1931) which appeared in *Sweet & Low* revue. Band project was, however, short-lived. Miley contracted tuberculosis and died in hospital in 1932. Miley's major contributions are all too little documented on record. He recorded, briefly, with Jelly Roll Morton (♦) **(Jelly Roll Morton & His Red Hot Peppers, Vol 1, 1927-1930)** and, interestingly, alongside another of the great trumpet stylists of the 1920s, Bix Beiderbecke (♦), as member of Hoagy Carmichael's Orchestra, in 1930 **(The Bix Beiderbecke Legend)** although little of consequence happens from either Beiderbecke or Miley.

But Miley will be remembered best for his solo work with Ellington. Classic, biting offerings like those on **Black & Tan Fantasy, East St Louis Toodle-oo** (Miley was co-author of this, Ellington's first signature tune), **Tishomingo Blues, Immigration Blues, Yellow Dog Blues** (all **The Beginning 1926-1928); The Mooche, Louisiana (Hot In Harlem 1928-1929); Bandanna Babies, I Must Have That Man, St Louis Blues (The Works Of Duke, Vol 2); Creole Love Call, East St Louis Toodle-oo** (different version than before), **Black & Tan Fantasy** (ditto) **(The Works Of Duke, Vol 1);** and **Take It Easy, Hot & Bothered, Blues With A Feeling (The Ellington Era, 1927-1940, Vol 1).**

Miley's immediate post-Ellington work is documented intriguingly on **Bubber Miley & His Friends 1929-1931** through recordings of his playing with his own Mileage Makers as well as with orchestra of Joe Steele, Leo Reisman, and King Oliver (♦). It is especially interesting to hear him alongside Oliver (already in de-

Above: Memphis Slim – for once not singing and playing the blues, caught in horizontal off-stand repose.

cline), on **St James Infirmary** and **When You're Smiling**.

Recordings:
Duke Ellington In Harlem
(*Jazz Panorama/—*)
Duke Ellington, Toodle-oo
(*—/Vocalion*)
Duke Ellington, The Works Of Duke, Vols 1, 2
(*RCA Victor – France*)
Duke Ellington, The Beginning 1926-1928 (*MCA – Germany*)
Duke Ellington, The Ellington Era, 1927-1940, Vol 1
(*Columbia/CBS*)
Duke Ellington, Hot In Harlem (1928-1929) (*MCA – Germany*)
Jelly Roll Morton & His Red Hot Peppers, Vol 1 (1927-1930)
(*RCA Victor – France*)
The Bix Beiderbecke Legend
(*RCA Victor – France*)
Bubber Miley & His Friends (1929-1931)
(*RCA Victor – France*)

Eddie Miller

Eddie Miller (born New Orleans, Louisiana, 1911) always has retained the unmistakable sound of the Crescent City within his playing, whether it be on tenor-saxophone or clarinet, both of which he has played with great proficiency since his teens. His clarinet has that warm-and-woody sound that all the great New Orleans clarinettists possess. His playing in the low register, as personified by his recordings in 1942 with Muggsy Spanier (♦) (**Kings Of Jazz**) is most appealing, and is notable for its warmth. As a tenor-saxophonist, Miller is, if anything, even more impressive. Again, there is New Orleans-type fluency and passion; his playing on this latter instrument is never lacking in basic drive, although his rhythm patterns are far from being simple and uninteresting.

Worked professionally before he was 20, first in New Orleans, then in New York (where he played alto-sax for several bands). Changed to tenor when joining Ben Pollack (♦) Orchestra (1930), remaining four years (**Ben Pollack & His Orchestra 1933-1934**). During this period recorded, on tenor, with New Orleans Ramblers (**J.T.**) and, on tenor and clarinet, with Bunny Berigan (♦) (**Swing Classics, 1935/Jazz In The Thirties**). When Pollack band dispersed, Miller became founder-member of what was to become Bob Crosby (♦) Orchestra. Remained with Crosby 1935–42 (when Crosby likewise disbanded). Attained widespread reputation with Crosby as double-threat principal soloist, although his arrival into band (in '38) of Irving Fazola (♦) enabled him to concentrate mainly on tenor. On latter instrument, Miller was featured with big band on items such as **Panama, I'm Prayin' Humble, Stomp Off, Let's Go** and **Black Surreal** (all **South Rampart Street Parade**) and with Bob Cats, on items like **Can't We Be Friends?, Slow Mood** (own composition), **I Hear You Talking, Call Me A Taxi, Hindustan, Mournin' Blues** and **Till We Meet Again** (**Big Noise From Winnetka**). Miller's clarinet was showcased on **South Rampart Street Parade, Wolverine Blues** (**South Rampart Street Parade**).

With break-up of Crosby outfit, stayed on West Coast, and formed own big band (containing several former Crosby colleagues). Spent short period in US Army (1944), then became session musician. Appeared with own band in film *You Can't Ration Love* (1943). Worked regularly in California area with former Crosby guitarist-singer Nappy Lamare (1945–7). During 1950s, often worked with Bob Crosby in reunion bands; likewise, in 1960s, including engagements in Las Vegas, New York, and a trip to Japan (1964). Played in final band led by Red Nichols (♦), before latter's death in June, '65. Made successful solo tour of Britain in 1967.

During past 10 years has played regularly in city of his birth, often in bands fronted by clarinettist Pete Fountain. Of his many other recordings, his essentially melodic, always swinging tenor was featured expressively at fine 1936 record session under leadership of Wingy Manone (♦) (**Wingy Manone, Vol 1**) and as part of a special three-man Dixieland front line added to the main Harry James (♦) Orchestra (**The Second, Third, Big Band Sound Of Harry James**). There is more fine Miller tenor to be found on another big-band record date, this one produced under own name (**Eddie Miller Big Band**).

Recordings:
Ben Pollack & His Orchestra 1933-1934 (*—/VJM*)
Jack Teagarden (Including New Orleans Ramblers), 'J.T.'
(*Ace of Hearts/Ace of Hearts*)
Various (Including Bunny Berigan), Swing Classics, 1935
(*Prestige/World Records*)
Bob Crosby, South Rampart Street Parade (*—MCA*)
Bob Crosby, Big Noise From Winnetka (*—/MCA*)
Wingy Manone, Vol I
(*RCA Victor/RCA Victor*)
The Second, Third, Big Band Sound Of Harry James
(*—/Verve*)
Eddie Miller Big Band
(*Golden Era/—*)

Kid Punch Miller

Ernest 'Kid Punch' Miller (born Raceland, Louisiana, 1894) is a name that is sometimes overlooked in assessing the greatest trumpeters/cornettists of early jazz. In truth, Miller's playing during his peak years (1929–35) was on a par with that of Jabbo Smith, and on occasions all but matched the youthful virtuosity of Louis Armstrong (♦). Miller's tone was rich and hot, and his technique assured and articulate. His contributions to recordings by a bizarre blues singer known as Scare Crow in 1930 ('**Kid Punch' Miller Jazz Rarities 1929-1930**) are typical of his capabilities, and his strong and flowing solo on **High Society**, from 1944 (**Punch Miller/(Wild Bill Davison)**) is excellent, in every way. Miller, who played bass drum, then baritone-horn, trombone, before switching to cornet, also had an engaging, bluesy singing voice. From beginning of 1920s, played with such notables as Kid Ory (♦), Jack Carey, Fate Marable, Jelly Roll Morton (♦), Tiny Parham,

Freddie Keppard, and (for one night only) Earl Hines (♦).

From 1929 until 1935, worked on-and-off with Frankie Franko & His Louisianians. With Franko in 1930, recorded a tremendously exciting solo on **Somebody Stole My Girl** ('**Kid Punch' Miller Jazz Rarities 1929-1930**). Between 1935–45, he worked mainly in Chicago, often with own small groups. After which toured extensively in carnival shows. Although a trifle more inconsistent than in previous years, Miller often blew well on Rudi Blesh's 1947 *This Is Jazz* radio

'Kid' Punch Miller Jazz Rarities 1929-1930 (Herwin).

shows ('**This Is Jazz', Vol 1**). Returned to New Orleans in '56, after absence of almost 30 years, playing ing with local bands and musicians. Suffered serious illness in 1959, but was playing again next year. To Japan with George Lewis' band (1964) (**King Of New Orleans: George Lewis & His New Orleans All Stars Live In Concert**) and worked with Lewis, again, in New Orleans, following year.

Of his later records, few did him real justice. Only during part of **Music Of New Orleans, Vol 5** does an element of his peak-period shine through. Gigged in New Orleans through 1960s, although often dogged by poor health. It was following another, long, bout of illness that Miller died, in 1971, in New Orleans. Of his double-nickname: Miller was bestowed title of 'Punch' by twin sister Judy; fellow musicians added 'Kid' (a nickname indicating their admiration for his enviable gifts as trumpeter).

Recordings:
'**Kid Punch' Miller Jazz Rarities 1929-1930** (*Herwin/—*)
Various (Including Kid Punch Miller), 'This Is Jazz', Vol 1
(*Rarities/—*)
Punch Miller/(Wild Bill Davison) (*Paramount/—*)
Various (Including Kid Punch Miller), Music of New Orleans, Vol 5 (*Folkways/—*)
King of New Orleans: George Lewis & His New Orleans All Stars Live In Concert
(*Telefunken – Germany*)

Charles Mingus

Born Arizona, 1922, and raised in Los Angeles, bassist Charles Mingus started in the bands of Louis Armstrong and Kid Ory and later Lionel Hampton, but by 1953 was firmly in the modernists' camp, as the Massey Hall concert with Charlie Parker, Dizzy Gillespie,

Bud Powell, Mingus and Max Roach shows (**The Quintet Of The Year**). In fact, Mingus' career has always transcended categories, and his work as a bandleader-composer shows him to be one of the great innovators of jazz. Mingus workshops from the early '50s reveal, in rather academic terms, his embryonic interest in variable tempos, counterpoint and collective improvisation (**Jazz Composers' Workshop No 1**).

By 1955 he had made strides towards a more organic form of composition, and early drafts of **Love Chant** and **Foggy Day** with sidemen trombonist Eddie Bert and tenorman George Barrow are more than merely historically interesting. A duet with drummer Max Roach, **Percussion Discussion**, is very free and melodic (**Charles Mingus**). Successful, and highly influential, performances of his **Pithecanthropus Erectus** and **Foggy Day** make use of expressionistic devices and both horn men, Jackie McLean and J. R. Monterose, are driven into the extremes of register and pitch (**Pithecanthropus Erectus**). In 1956 Mingus was joined by Dannie Richmond, the ideal drummer for his music, and the association lasted over 20 years. The following year saw the first great plateau of achievement with a series of albums featuring the great trumpeter Clarence Shaw in performances like **Duke's Choice** (**Duke's Choice**) and exciting work from saxophonist Shafti Hadi and trombonist Jimmy Knepper. Both here and on a superior album (**Reincarnation Of A Lovebird**) Mingus uses a narrator in his compositions; the title track, based on fragments of Parker solos, and **Haitian Fight Song**, a more complex and developed version than on the **Charles Mingus** album, are outstanding tracks. A musical portrayal of a border town (**Tijuana Moods**) is a classic, with **Ysabel's Table Dance** raunchy and explosive, and **Tijuana Gift Shop** a masterpiece of texture.

Mingus' method of working without scores, rehearsing his team from the piano, shouting instructions during performances and allowing the soloists to develop the compositions in flight, accounted for the exhilarating sense of spontaneity. Unlike most composers, Mingus seldom had difficulty in reconciling the writing with the improvisation. Simultaneous soloing, cross riffs, collective playing and savage changes in tempo, stop-time, double-time, shaped the composion in the unique mold of this tempestuous leader. Volcanic climaxes erupted from his music, which, in its techniques and emotional climate, anticipated many of the features of the New Thing. Mingus had a great respect for tradition, for the music of Fats Waller (♦), **Eat That Chicken** (**Mingus Oh Yeah!**); for gospel, **Wednesday Night Prayer Meeting, Moanin'** (**Blues And Roots**); for Lester Young (♦), **Goodbye Pork Pie Hat** (**Mingus Ah-Um** and **The Great Concert Of Charles Mingus**); and Ellington (♦) on all of his longer works.

Brilliantly served by sidemen like tenorman Booker Ervin, trombonist Knepper and the preternaturally alert Dannie Richmond, Mingus' late '50s-early '60s output is crowded with fine solos. Multi-instrumentalist Roland Kirk's wild

Above: Charles Mingus in action, Holland 1977. A great bassist and composer, master of the molten ensemble.

Charles Mingus Presents Charles Mingus (Candid). Original Faubus Fables and other Mingus classics, circa 1960.

gifts find a compatible environment on **Hog Calling Blues (Mingus Oh Yeah)** while another great multi-instrumentalist, Eric Dolphy, pushes his bass clarinet technique to its limits in an expressionistic duet – a musical recreation of a quarrel – with the leader, **What Love (Charles Mingus Presents Charles Mingus)**. In the '60s, Mingus experimented with orchestral settings, using a 22-piece band **(Mingus Re-visited)** on several Ellingtonian pieces, and saw further compositions sabotaged by poor recording and incorrect juxtaposition **(Town Hall Concert)**. Two ambitious masterpieces **(Mingus Mingus Mingus Mingus Mingus** and **The Black Saint & The Sinner Lady)** are extended compositions of great complexity, built in layers of overlapping textures and using the talents of his regular team as well as brilliant contributions from altoist Charlie Mariano.

A concert in Paris in 1964 **(The Great Concert Of Charles Mingus)** was captured on a three-album set, with superb playing by the quartet, Dolphy, tenorman Clifford Jordan, Mingus and Richmond in lengthy performances of the leader's compositions. The next period is badly represented on record, but Mingus surfaced again in the '70s with a great group including the dynamic tenorman, George Adams, and the virtuoso pianist Don Pullen **(Mingus Moves, Changes One** and **Changes Two)**. A concert at Carnegie Hall in 1974 assembles Mingus, Richmond, Pullen, Adams, altoist Charles McPherson, trumpeter Jon Faddis, baritone saxist Hamiet Bluiett and the astoundingly extroverted Roland Kirk for a blowing session on **C Jam Blues** and **Perdido**.

Mingus wrote a brilliantly evocative score for the John Cassavetes film *Shadows* in the '50s, and an autobiography, *Beneath The Underdog*. He died in January 1979.

Recordings:
The Quintet Of The Year *(Debut/Vogue)*
Jazz Composers Workshop, No 1 *(Savoy/—)*
Charles Mingus *(Prestige/Prestige)*
Pithecanthropus Erectus *(Atlantic/—)*
Duke's Choice *(Bethlehem/Polydor)*
Re-incarnation Of A Lovebird *(Bethlehem/Polydor)*
East Coasting *(Bethlehem/Polydor)*
Tonight At Noon *(Atlantic/Atlantic)*
Tijuana Moods *(RCA/RCA)*
Mingus Oh Yeah *(Atlantic/Atlantic)*
Blues & Roots *(Atlantic/Atlantic)*
Mingus Ah-Um *(Columbia/CBS Realm)*
Mingus Dynasty *(Columbia/CBS)*
Charles Mingus Presents Charles Mingus *(Barnaby CBS/Barnaby CBS)*
Charles Mingus *(Barnaby CBS/Barnaby CBS)*
Mingus Re-Visited *(Trip/—)*
Town Hall Concert *(United Artists/—)*
Mingus Mingus Mingus Mingus Mingus *(Impulse/Impulse)*
The Black Saint & The Sinner Lady *(Impulse/Impulse)*
Mingus At Monterey *(Fantasy/—)*
The Great Concert Of Charles Mingus *(Prestige/America)*

Mingus Moves *(Atlantic/Atlantic)*
Changes One *(Atlantic/Atlantic)*
Changes Two *(Atlantic/Atlantic)*
Mingus At Carnegie Hall *(Atlantic/Atlantic)*
Cumbia & Jazz Fusion *(Atlantic/Atlantic)*

George Mitchell

George Mitchell (born Louisville, Kentucky, 1899) was a gifted trumpeter/cornettist whose sensitive, always heated, playing graced several 'name' bands of the 1920s and 1930s, earning him much respect amongst fans and fellow musicians. Only pity was he was contemporary of such superlative hornmen like King Oliver (♦), Louis Armstrong (♦), and Henry 'Red' Allen (♦). Started on trumpet at 12, toured with minstrel shows, revues. 1919: to Chicago, where he gigged with various local jazzmen, including Tony Jackson, Tubby Hall. On road approximately two years, before returning in late 1920s to work with Carroll Dickerson Orchestra, then with Doc Cook (on three separate occasions), Jimmie Noone (♦), Lil Armstrong and others. Joined first Earl Hines (♦) big band. Prior to this, had established enviable reputation as recording artist with New Orleans Wanderers and Bootblacks **(Johnny Dodds & Kid Ory)** on recordings such as **Perdido Street Blues, Papa Dip, Mad Dog** and **Gate Mouth;** also as member of Jelly Roll Morton's (♦) Red Hot Peppers **(Jelly Roll Morton, Vols 2, 3, 4)** wherein Mitchell's abilities both as lead trumpeter and soloist much in evidence particularly so on Morton classics like **The Pearls, Dead Man Blues, Grandpa's Spells, Steamboat Stomp**. Recorded with Hines (1929–31) **(The Indispensable Earl Hines, Vol 1)** – although solo opportunities surprisingly limited (on record, at least). After leaving Hines, played clubs, then left full time music to become bank

messenger. Played occasional gigs for local Chicago WPA Band. Final job – with Freddie Williams' Gold Coast Orchestra, 1934. During career, also recorded with Cookie's Ginger Snaps, Luis Russell (♦), Noone, Richard M. Jones. Died in Chicago in May 1972.

Recordings:
Jelly Roll Morton & His Red Hot Peppers/New Orleans Jazzmen, Vols 2-4 *(RCA Victor – France)*
Johnny Dodds & Kid Ory *(Columbia)/*
Johnny Dodds With Kid Ory *(Philips)*
The Indispensable Earl Hines, Vol 1 (1929-1939) *(RCA Victor – France)*

Roscoe Mitchell
♦ Art Ensemble of Chicago

Hank Mobley

Tenorman Hank Mobley, born 1930 in Georgia, is one of jazz's more under-rated figures, possibly because his great gifts ran counter to the prevailing climate. At the height of the Hard Bop era, with the declamatory approach at a premium, Mobley's tone was comparatively soft, a round sound capable of great subtlety. An early album **(Hank Mobley & His All Stars)** illustrates the problem, with Mobley's own contributions overshadowed by the more obviously driving work of Milt Jackson, Horace Silver and Art Blakey. His playing on the blues, **Lower Stratosphere,** is funky in a more relaxed and unpredictable way. After stints with Max Roach and Dizzy Gillespie, Mobley was in at the start of the Jazz Messengers in 1955. **Creepin' In (Horace Silver & The Jazz Messengers)** featured his best solo work to date, illustrating his unique, oblique rhythmic sense and complex ideas.

Ballad features like **Alone Together (The Jazz Messengers At The Cafe Bohemia)** or **Silver's Blue (Silver's Blue)** are tinged with melancholia. The typical hard-driving cutting contest **(Blowing Sessions)** with the supercharged Johnny Griffin and John Coltrane were not his forte, leaving no room for his thoughtful, restrained constructiveness.

By 1960, Mobley's own Blue Note albums had achieved a

Hank Mobley And His All Stars (Blue Note): early Hank.

balance of his unfashionable qualities, and the lyricism of **The More I See You (Roll Call)**, the elaborate attack of **This I Dig Of You (Soul Station)** represent a peak in his creativity.

A period with Miles Davis, replacing Coltrane in the quintet, produced the beautiful **I Thought About You (Someday My Prince Will Come)**, the imaginative **No Blues (Miles Davis At The Carnegie Hall)** and excellent, quirkily melodic solos on **Oleo** and **So What (Friday & Saturday Nights At The Blackhawk)**. Mobley seems to have recorded very little in the last decade, an expressionist period for saxophonists which would, yet again, have found him something of a loner.

Recordings:
Hank Mobley & His All Stars
(Blue Note/Blue Note)
Horace Silver & The Jazz Messengers
(Blue Note/Blue Note)
The Jazz Messengers At The Cafe Bohemia
(Blue Note/Blue Note)
Horace Silver, Silver's Blue
(—/Epic CBS)
Blowing Sessions
(Blue Note/Blue Note)
Roll Call
(Blue Note/Blue Note)
Soul Station
(Blue Note/Blue Note)
No Room For Squares
(Blue Note/Blue Note)
Miles Davis:
Someday My Prince Will Come *(Columbia/CBS)*
At The Carnegie Hall
(Columbia/CBS)
Friday & Saturday Nights At The Blackhawk
(Columbia/CBS)

The Modern Jazz Quartet

The MJQ's musical director, John Lewis, was born in Illinois, 1920, studying music and anthropology at the University of New Mexico.

His early work as a pianist in the Bebop '40s is usually forgotten, though he accompanied Charlie Parker on several sessions **(The Savoy Sessions** and **The Definitive Charlie Parker, Vol 5)**, played and arranged for Dizzy Gillespie's big band **(In The Beginning** and **The Greatest Of Dizzy Gillespie)** and contributed the beautiful composition **Afternoon In Paris** to the Sonny Stitt – J. J. Johnson date **(Genesis)**. His keyboard touch was extremely distinctive and, balancing his fastidious sense of structure, was the convincing emotionalism of his blues. The earliest quartet with Milt Jackson **(Milt Jackson)** from 1952 shows Lewis very much the accompanist, though by the time the group adopted its new collective name, he had taken over the direction.

Milt Jackson was born 1923, Detroit, and by 1945 was established as the pioneer Bebop vibraphone player. His early work with Dizzy Gillespie's small combos was badly recorded, the instrument sounding like a row of milk-bottles, but his mastery of the new idiom comes through loud and clear **(The Greatest Of Dizzy Gillespie** and **In The Beginning)**. Sessions with Thelonious Monk show him to be one of the few great interpreters of that idiosyncratic genius's music, **Genius of Modern Music, Eronel** and **Criss Cross** being particularly good, and **I Mean You** a masterpiece.

As the Modern Jazz Quartet, John Lewis, Milt Jackson, bassist Percy Heath and, initially, Kenny Clarke on drums, the group specialized in

The Last Concert (Atlantic): 22 years of sensitive music.

collective improvisation, fragmenting the melodies and reworking them in flexible interplay between the instruments. Lewis was the guiding hand, elegant and precise, vastly knowledgeable about European musical forms, preoccupied above all things with form. Most of the criticisms levelled at the MJQ centre on Lewis as too classical, not virile, miniaturist and effete, a straitjacket of respectability on the funky talents of Jackson, etc. In fact, during their 22 years together, the group achieved much of lasting merit, and comparison with a comparable chamber-jazz outfit, Chick Corea's Return To Forever, will show just how superior the MJQ were in exploiting a mood or combining swing and delicacy. The development of black militancy has tended to negate the MJQ's breakthrough in putting jazz into the Establishment's concert halls, the dark suits, sober manner, seriousness of presentation.

With the replacement of Clark by the quieter Connie Kay, a

percussionist more than a drummer, specializing in brushwork, tiny pinpoint cymbal sounds, the MJQ assumed its final form. Playing several versions of Lewis' compositions, fugues like **Vendome, Concorde** or the wonderfully structured **Django, Milano, Fontessa** and **Sun Dance**, the MJQ also extensively reworked standards like **Softly As In A Morning Sunrise, Night In Tunisia** and **How High The Moon**. Over the years, as technique and empathy has developed, their repertoire has been presented in increasingly polished form. More space has been given to Percy Heath as his tone has strengthened, while the effectiveness of Connie Kay is best judged in the ensemble rather than by brush features like **La Ronde** and **Drums (Night In Tunisia)**. The moving **Cortège (One Never Knows)** rises to its emotional peak on Kay's splendid command of dynamics, bursting in a shower of cymbals under Jackson's measured row of sombre chords; in fact, the entire album is a masterpiece of evocation and was written by Lewis for the Venice-based movie, *Sait-On Jamais*. **The Golden Striker** is a classic, while **Three Windows**, a triple fugue, works like a Swiss watch. Jackson's writing is best represented by **Bag's Groove (Modern Jazz Quartet, Night In Tunisia** and **The Last Concert)** and, outside the MJQ, with Miles Davis, Jackson and Monk **(Tallest Trees)**; while **The Martyr** shows his lyrical gifts at slow tempo **(The Legendary Profiel)**. In 1974, the vibesman's departure brought the group to an end, commemorated by one of their finest albums, which is in effect a summation of their achievements **(The Last Concert)**.

Recordings:
John Lewis, Charlie Parker:
The Savoy Sessions
(Savoy/Savoy)
The Definitive Charlie Parker, Vol 5 *(Verve/Metro)*
John Lewis, Dizzy Gillespie:
In The Beginning
(Prestige/Prestige)
The Greatest Of Dizzy Gillespie *(RCA/RCA)*
John Lewis, Sonny Stitt:
Genesis *(Prestige/Prestige)*
Improvised Meditations
(Atlantic/Atlantic)
Music For Brass *(Columbia/—)*
Milt Jackson:
Milt Jackson
(Blue Note/Blue Note)
Thelonious Monk, Genius Of Modern Music
(Blue Note/Blue Note)
Miles Davis, Tallest Trees
(Prestige/Prestige)
Second Nature *(Savoy/Savoy)*
Opus De Funk
(Prestige/Prestige)
Plenty, Plenty Soul
(Atlantic/Atlantic)
The Art Of Milt Jackson
(Atlantic/Atlantic)
Big Band Bags
(Milestone/Milestone)
Big 4 At Montreux
(Pablo/Pablo)
Big 3 *(Pablo/Pablo)*
Milt Jackson At The Kosei Nankin *(Pablo/Pablo)*
Modern Jazz Quartet:
First Recordings *(Prestige/—)*
Fontessa *(Atlantic/Atlantic)*
Pyramid *(Atlantic/Atlantic)*
One Never Knows
(Atlantic/Atlantic)

Lonely Woman
(Atlantic/Atlantic)
Night In Tunisia
(Atlantic/Atlantic)
At Music Inn
(Atlantic/Atlantic)
Blues At Carnegie Hall
(Atlantic/Atlantic)
Sheriff *(Atlantic/Atlantic)*
The Legendary Profile
(Atlantic/Atlantic)
Modern Jazz Quartet
(Atlantic/Atlantic)
The Art Of The Modern Jazz Quartet *(Atlantic/Atlantic)*
The Best Of The Modern Jazz Quartet *(Atlantic/Atlantic)*
The Last Concert
(Atlantic/Atlantic)

Miff Mole

Irving Milfred 'Miff' Mole (born Roosevelt, Long Island, New York, 1898) was one of the major influences on trombone during 1920s, a decade during which he, together with Jack Teagarden (♦), Jimmy Harrison (♦) and a few others, was responsible for helping the instrument to become a major solo voice in jazz, giving it more of an individuality than hitherto. Mole's was a major advance, in terms of sheer technical dexterity – less emphatic than some other trombonists, but superior to most in elegance of phrase and delivery.

Started on violin, age 11, studying that instrument for three years. Also played piano – indeed, first public performances were given on piano as accompanist to silent movies. First professional gig on trombone with Charlie Randall (with whom Mole studied). After two years with Randall, joined Original Memphis Five. Recorded with 'Ladd's Black Aces' **(Ladd's Black Aces, Vols 1-3)** between 1921–2. Ladd's Black Aces was pseudonym, used by OMF for recordings. Mole's playing on LBA titles like **Sister Kate, Two-Time Dan** and **All Wrong** demonstrate his all-round excellence and his ability to lift this and other bands. (OMF also recorded under other names, including Tennessee Tooters, Original Tampa 5). Mole left OMF temporarily, working with Abe Lyman Orchestra on West Coast, but rejoined former band for further period.

After work with various other bands, became closely associated with cornettist Red Nichols (♦). Contributed significantly to music produced by Nichols' Five Pennies **(Red Nichols & His Five Pennies 1926-1928)** and to yet another band which existed only inside a recording studio and of which both Nichols and Mole were seminal members **(The Charleston Chasers 1925-1928)**. Mole-Nichols partnership was heard at its best in 1928 recordings by Miff Mole & His Little Molers **(That Toddlin' Town - Chicago 1926-28)** with superb support from rest of band: Frank Teschemacher (♦), Joe Sullivan (♦), Eddie Condon (♦), Gene Krupa (♦). Mole worked with Roger Wolfe Kahn (1926-7), worked as staff trombonist with studio band at station WOR, then spent next nine years as session musician at NBC.

Joined Paul Whiteman (♦) Orchestra, 1938, staying two years. Recorded with Eddie Condon in '40 **(Jam Sessions At Commodore)** and his fine playing during four-part **A Good Man Is Hard To Find** proved his long involvement with session work had not taken the edge from his jazz-abilities. Left Whiteman due to ill-health, worked again for NBC, then became member of Benny Goodman (♦) Orchestra (1942–3). Participated in numerous Condon Town Hall concerts (**The Eddie Condon Concerts Town Hall 1944-45 Featuring Pee Wee Russell**) and recorded with his own Nicksieland Band (**Trombone Scene**) in '44; it transferred to Nick's, New York jazz spot, where Mole worked for four years (1943–7).

Spent several years in Chicago, underwent surgery on more than one occasion. Miff Mole, who died in New York in 1961, spent most of last years of his life in non-music activities.

Recordings:
Various (Including Miff Mole), Tresaurus Of Classics, Vol 2
(Columbia/CBS)
Ladd's Black Aces, Vols 1-3
(—/Fountain)
Red Nichols & His Five Pennies (1926-1928)
(MCA Coral – Germany)
The Charleston Chasers (1925-1928) (—/VJM)
Various (Including Miff Mole), That Toddlin' Town – Chicago (1926-28)
(—/Parlophone)
Eddie Condon, Jam Sessions At Commodore
(Commodore/Ace of Hearts)
The Eddie Condon Concerts Town Hall 1944-45 Featuring Pee Wee Russell
(Chiaroscuro/—)

Grachan Moncur III

Born in New York in 1937, Grachan Moncur III is the son of the bassist with the Savoy Sultans. After stints with Ray Charles and the Art Farmer–Benny Golson Jazztet, Moncur joined Jackie McLean, appearing on his change of direction album (**One Step Beyond**). Associated with the Blue Note school of young, second generation New Thing players, turns up as a sideman with Herbie Hancock (**My Point Of View**), taking a trenchant solo on **King Cobra**. His own album (**Evolution**) has a compatible band of McLean, Lee Morgan, Bobby Hutcherson and Anthony Williams, and the numbers – all by Moncur – cover a wide spectrum of approaches from the free and doomy title track to the more conventional **Monk In Wonderland**. He played a second trombone line with Roswell Rudd in Archie Shepp's combo in the late '60s, and was clearly more traditional than Rudd. Moncur's next album (**New Africa**) was strongly melodic, and the composition **When**, fueled by the amazing drumming of Andrew Cyrille, was a minor jazz hit. His most recent work with the Jazz Composers' Orchestra (**Echoes Of Prayers**) is a requiem for Luther King, Medger Evers and

Below: Grachan Moncur III, trombonist of the new school. Moncur II was bassist with Savoy Sultans back in the '30s.

Echoes Of Prayer (JCOA Virgin): the trombonist's turn.

Marcus Garvey, the atmosphere dark and the riffs overlapping. There are several movements, including a near-Township section and a chanted vocal. Moncur's trombone struts starkly at the beginning and end of this effective and homogeneous work.

Recordings:
Evolution
(Blue Note/Blue Note)
New Africa (—/BYG – France)
Echoes Of Prayers
(JCOA/JCOA Virgin

Thelonious Monk

Born 1920, the pianist and composer is one of the greatest seminal figures of Modern Jazz – and yet somehow remains at a tangent to every school. Along with Parker, Gillespie, Powell, Christian and Clarke, Monk was one of the pioneers of Bebop, but his originality was such that each new generation of musicians has found a different challenge in his concept of harmony, rhythm and structure. A reputation for eccentricity and a seemingly home-made keyboard technique kept him in comparative obscurity until the '50s, when the

Hard Bop movement discovered the exacting logic beneath the outlandish hats and deceptive hammerings. His angular, dissonant piano style omits the obvious and, like a scalpel, exposes basic structures. On a standard like **Sweet And Lovely (Thelonious Monk)** he will send up the sentimentality by introducing the sub-theme of **Tea For Two**, butting the tempo up and down, and plunging the close into a travesty of the romantic concerto as he searches for that final chord.

Sardonic towards the sugary, Monk's own compositions are virtually impregnable. Cunningly knotted, already stripped to essentials, they are an obstacle course to test the imagination and resourcefulness of the improviser. **Mysterioso** has the air of a walking bass line, but transposed for piano which makes it a very different animal. Interpretation of Monk's themes requires a thematic approach and few jazzmen have succeeded. Drummer Art Blakey and vibraphonist Milt Jackson are two of the earliest and most sympathetic sidemen (**Genius Of Modern Music**). Tenorman Sonny Rollins shares Monk's sense of humour, and thinks architecturally, so that their collaborations (**Brilliance** and **Sonny Rollins, Vol 2**) have a weight and unequivocal strength that Johnny Griffin's free-wheeling encounter lacks (**Thelonious In Action**).

During the '50s, Monk was signed to the now defunct Riverside label, and recorded prolifically. There are scores of versions of his **Epistrophy, Round Midnight, Blue Monk, Monk's Mood, Little Rootie Tootie, I Mean You** and **Off Minor** ranging from solo piano to big band. The Town Hall concert (**In Person**) features a 10-piece band handling the almost accidental harmonies in unison, and swinging like a trunk-to-tail Hannibal caravan. The solitary, unadorned artist can be found on **Pure Monk**.

Other notable encounters were

Monk's Music (Riverside): modern master complete with cap, shades and trolley. Hawkins and Coltrane are on hand.

Above: Thelonious Sphere Monk, one of the founders of Bebop, and one of jazz's greatest composers and piano stylists.

Above: Wes Montgomery, protégé of late great Cannonball Adderley. A legend.

Wes Montgomery

Born Indianapolis 1925, guitarist Wes Montgomery didn't leave his home town until the age of 34, when the success of his brothers Buddy and Monk, The Mastersounds, led him to enter the lists. In fact, Montgomery established his reputation from the first albums, which were rapturously received by the critics as the greatest guitar since Charlie Christian. The early, and best, work **(Beginnings)** shows all the hallmarks of his style, the octave-doubling runs on the amazing **Finger Pickin'**, the lyrical gifts allied to that glowing, bronze tone on **Old Folks.** Montgomery was unusual in that he didn't use a pick, preferring the tone he got with his thumb. Thanks to the enthusiasm of Cannonball Adderley, Montgomery secured a contract with Riverside, and much of his best work was recorded for that label. Many of his solos pursue a similar strategy in which single note runs build to chunky chord and octave passages that judder and crouch like a cavalry charge, **Airgun, Four On Six (While We're Young).** The unaccompanied title track is sumptuous, the rich, shot-silk tone at its most beautiful. Like most 'natural' jazzmen, the blues was his element, and he had a seemingly inexhaustible capacity for permu-

with John Coltrane **(Thelonious Monk & John Coltrane),** a stretching experience for the growing tenorman, and with Art Blakey's driving unit **(Art Blakey's Jazz Messengers With Thelonious Monk),** where the shifting metres and accents of the pianist find their perfect complement. In the late '50s, Monk formed a steady working quartet with Charlie Rouse on tenor, but the finest albums came with the addition of guest stars like Harold Land **(In Person)** and Thad Jones **(Brilliance).** Over-exposure has tended to sap the impact of Monk's music, but he is by no means a spent force, as the '70s recordings prove **(Something In Blue** and **The Man I Love).**

His influence on fellow pianists has been enormous – Randy Weston, Cecil Taylor, Stan Tracey – and continues to spread.

Recordings:
Genius Of Modern Music
(Blue Note/Blue Note)
Thelonious Monk (Prestige/
Prestige)
Pure Monk (Milestone/Milestone)
**Thelonious Monk & John
Coltrane** (Milestone/Milestone)
**Art Blakey's Jazz Messengers
With Thelonious Monk**
(Atlantic/Atlantic)
In Person (Milestone/Milestone)
Brilliance (Milestone/Milestone)
Something In Blue (Black Lion/
Black Lion)
The Man I Love (Black Lion/
Black Lion)

J. R. Monterose

Tenorman J. R. Monterose, born Detroit 1927, gained experience with Charles Mingus, Kenny Dorham and Horace Silver, but headed only three albums in 28 years. The only one still obtainable **(Straight Ahead)** is his best and a magnificent achievement by any standards. Basically a Rollins-derived Hard-Bopper, Monterose comes across from the opening notes of the title track with great authority, building to a climax with controlled power, and returning after Tommy Flanagan's piano solo for exchanges with the brilliant drummer, Pete La Roca. **Chafic,** a waltz, shows the leader's thrusting, angular figures intensifying over a call-and-response pattern, while **Green Street Scene** has him chopping away over a rocking rhythm section. Now domiciled in Belgium, Monterose has added the guitar to his skills.

Recordings:
Straight Ahead (Xanadu/—)

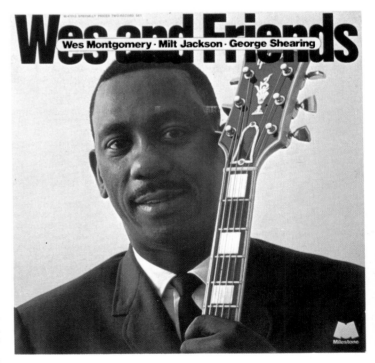

Wes And Friends (Milestone): the most influential guitarist since Charlie Christian, Montgomery died in 1968.

tating the obvious cadences in fresh ways, startling the expectations with an abruptly splayed chord. Later albums teamed the guitarist with Milt Jackson, George Shearing **(Wes & Friends)** to good effect, and with Johnny Griffin for a hard-driving blowing-session **(Movin')**.

Wes Montgomery's contract with Verve proved disastrous from the jazz point of view, featuring the guitarist in lush settings with strings, and removing him from the challenging small group context necessary to his most committed work. He died in 1968 at the age of 43.

Recordings:
Beginnings
(Blue Note/Blue Note)
While We're Young
(Milestone/Milestone)
Wes & Friends
(Milestone/Milestone)
Movin'
(Milestone/Milestone)

James Moody

Born 1925, the multi-instrumentalist's recording debut was with the Dizzy Gillespie big band. A reliable sideman throughout the Bebop era, Moody played with many of the giants, including Tadd Dameron, Al Haig, Howard McGhee and Milt Jackson, though in fact his playing has a straight ahead swing typical of an earlier period. In 1949, vocalist King Pleasure cut a version of his tenor solo on **I'm In The Mood For Love,** which turned out to be a hit, and Eddie Jefferson sang **Moody's Workshop** and **I've Got The Blues.**

Moody's history after that became picaresque; a lengthy sojourn in Europe; a physical collapse; a painful struggle back to professionalism with – along the way – expertise on alto and flute. By 1963, he was back with Gillespie. Never less than professional, Moody is a swinger on tenor and alto saxophones, and a fleet, sweet flautist – no mumbles, no phlegmy stunts.

Recordings:
James Moody *(Prestige/Prestige)*
Moody's Workshop
(Prestige/Xtra)
The Beginning & End Of Bop
(Blue Note/Blue Note)
Dizzy Gillespie, Trumpet Masters *(—/Vogue)*
Dizzy Gillespie, Something Old, Something New *(—/Philips)*
James Moody, Group Therapy
(—/DJM)

Moody And The Brass Figures (Milestone): tenor plus.

Above: James Moody, one of the most underrated and consistent players on flute, alto and tenor. Early convert to Bebop.

Lee Morgan

Born 1938, Philadelphia, trumpeter Lee Morgan was shot and killed outside Slugs, where he was working, in 1972, thus robbing jazz of one of its most delightful performers. Morgan turned professional before his 15th birthday, joining the Dizzy Gillespie big band at 17. His early albums for Blue Note show tremendous verve and high-spirited fireworks without a great deal of attention to structure. A session with John Coltrane from 1957 **(Blue Train)** shows his wildly spontaneous spirit and, on **I'm Old Fashioned,** indications of the deeper emotional impact to be created through restraint. In 1958, he joined Art Blakey's Jazz Messengers, remaining until 1961 and making great strides in that forcing house of talents.

His breadth of tonal variety, the vocalized half-valve effects and slurs, is shown on **It's Only A Paper Moon,** and his accuracy in the top register on **Lester Left Town (The Big Beat).** The search for concision continued through a series of excellent albums as leader and sideman with Jackie McLean **(Leeway)** and Wayne

Shorter **(Search For The New Land)**, all characterized by his bubbling wit and enthusiasm. In 1963 he made the charts **(The Sidewinder)** with the title track, a 24-bar blues that drives along on the drumming of Billy Higgins. In fact, every track packs a colossal rhythmic punch, with Morgan's solo on **Totem Pole,** his all-time best. Heading a quintet with multi-reedman Bennie Maupin **(Live At The Lighthouse)** he showed that constant growth was more important to him than repeating the commercial success of **The Sidewinder,** and over the four lengthy tracks displays his controlled inventiveness. The following year, another double album, with Billy Harper and Grachan Moncur III **(Lee Morgan),** showed considerable group organization with no loss of spontaneity in the solos, and an atmosphere of experimentation. Starting under the influence of Clifford Brown, Gillespie and Navarro, Lee Morgan found an individual voice. His death at 33 confirms the tragic dictum that good trumpeters die young.

Recordings:
John Coltrane, Blue Train
(Blue Note/Blue Note)
The Jazz Messengers, The Big Beat
(Blue Note/Blue Note)

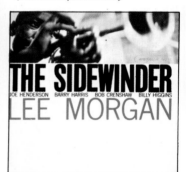

The Sidewinder (Blue Note): the trumpeter's biggest hit.

Above: the late Lee Morgan, bright young hope of modern trumpet, tragically murdered. Ex-Jazz Messenger and leader.

**The Jazz Messengers, The
Freedom Rider**
(Blue Note/Blue Note)
Leeway *(Blue Note/Blue Note)*
Search For The New Land
(Blue Note/Blue Note)
The Sidewinder
(Blue Note/Blue Note)
Live At The Lighthouse
(Blue Note/Blue Note)
Lee Morgan
(Blue Note/Blue Note)
Lee Morgan *(DJM/DJM)*

Benny Morton

During a professional career which
began in 1924 (with Billy Fowler's
Orchestra), Benny Morton has
earned and sustained a reputation
as one of the most consistent of
trombone soloists in jazz. His is not
a flashy, virtuosic style. 'Straight-
forward' might give the impression of a dull and uninteresting
player – which he most certainly is
not. Tonally warm and sensitive,
Morton manipulates his slide trombone with dexterity, phrasing with
elegance on ballads, operating
with restrained force on up-tempo
numbers. He is a player of great
taste, yet never lacking the ability
to produce uncontrived excitement, a quality basic to all good
'hot' jazz. Henry Sterling 'Benny'
Morton (born New York City,
1907) first played trombone with
school friends. After leaving
Fowler he joined Fletcher Henderson (♦) in 1926. Solo on **Jackass
Blues, 1926 (The Fletcher Henderson Story/The Fletcher Henderson Story, Vol 1)** is not typical
of his work in general (certainly
not in later years): blustery, hard-
hitting, with no frills. But Morton's
solo opportunities were not restricted during this two-year
period, even when the remarkable
Jimmy Harrison (♦) joined Henderson (1927).
 Worked with Chick Webb (♦)
(1930–1), but returned to Henderson in 1931, staying this time for
about one year as replacement for
ailing Harrison. By this time, Morton's style had taken shape, as
evinced in solos like **Clarinet
Marmalade** and **Sugarfoot Stomp
(The Fletcher Henderson Story/
The Fletcher Henderson Story,
Vol 3)**. Joined Don Redman (♦)
Orchestra, remaining from 1932–7.
His development as soloist of real
stature took place during this
period. Solos with Redman, in-
cluding **Exactly Like You, Tea
For Two** and **That Dallas Man
(Don Redman)** are beautifully
rounded, lyrical and rhythmically
buoyant. Whilst regular sideman
with Redman, also recorded with
Ben Pollack (♦) **(Ben Pollack & His
Orchestra 1933-1934)**; Coleman
Hawkins (♦) and Red Allen (♦)
**(Recordings Made Between 1930
& 1941)**; and Benny Carter (♦)
**(Benny Carter, 1933/Ridin' In
Rhythm)**. Next, with Count Basie
(♦) (1937–40). Solo-wise, **Out The
Window** represents Morton's only
individual contribution to Basie's
band **(The Best Of Basie)** on
record at least. His main contribution seems to have been as section
leader. Also appeared at some of
classic Billie Holiday (♦) sessions
arranged by Teddy Wilson (♦)
(The Golden Years, Vols 1, 2)
and other similar Wilson-led dates
(sans Holiday) **(Teddy Wilson
& His All Stars)** demonstrating usual
consistency during numerous,
albeit short, solo spots.

Joined jumping Joe Sullivan (♦)
Cafe Society band (1940), moving
on to Teddy Wilson for longer
spell (1940–3). At typical Eddie
Condon (♦) record date, in 1943
(Jam Sessions At Commodore)
Morton's versatility enabled him
to fit, with ease, at same time producing a beautifully controlled
statement on **O, Katharina**. Appeared at Condon's Town Hall
concerts during World War II.
With Edmond Hall (♦) after leaving
Wilson, before assembling own
band which lasted two years
(1944–6). Also worked with Raymond Scott orchestra at CBS, and
in pit bands of several well-known
Broadway musicals (including
Guys & Dolls, Silk Stockings and
Jamaica). Constantly in demand
for session work during 1950s,
1960s, with time off for jazz gigs and
recordings. In latter category,
produced what was his best-ever
ballad performance **(I Can't Get
Started)** at a mid-1950s record
date **(Buck Clayton's Band)** and
a rhythmically adroit solo on
**Wrapping It Up (The Big Re-
union)** for Fletcher Henderson
Reunion Band.
 Toured Europe late-1960s as
member of all-star 'Top Brass'
package. During 1968 worked
often with Wild Bill Davison (♦),
also participating in excellent recording date with Davison outfit
(The Jazz Giants), producing exquisite variations on **I Surrender,
Dear**. Has continued to be active
throughout the 1970s, including
memorable gigs with Bobby
Hackett (♦) (1970), Roy Eldridge
(♦), and World's Greatest Jazz
Band (as replacement for Vic
Dickenson (♦)). To date, Morton's
all-round consistency has served
him admirably. Amongst record
sessions in which his has been a
welcome sound, in addition to the
aforementioned, are those led by
Eldridge **(The Nifty Cate)**, Hot
Lips Page (♦) **(Swing Classics,
Vol 2)**, and Red Allen **(Harlem On
Saturday Night)**. His solos on
Allen date, particularly those on
King Porter Stomp, Shim-Me-

Sha-Wabble, plus that on **Limehouse Blues**, from session under
own leadership **(Blue Note's
Three Decades Of Jazz, Vol 1,
1939-1949)** together help define
Benny Morton's highly personal
approach to jazz trombone.

Recordings:
The Fletcher Henderson Story
(Columbia)/
 **The Fletcher Henderson Story,
Vols 1, 3** *(CBS)*
Don Redman *(—/CBS – Realm)*
**Ben Pollack & His Orchestra
1933-1934** *(—/VJM)*
**Coleman Hawkins, Recordings
Made Between 1930 & 1941**
(CBS – France)

*Above: gifted, consistent soloist, yet Benny Morton
remains one of jazz's most under-appreciated trombonists.*

Benny Carter, 1933 *(Prestige)/*
**Various (Including Benny
Carter), Ridin' In Rhythm**
(World Records)
Count Basie, The Best Of Basie
(Decca/MCA – Germany)
**Billie Holiday, The Golden
Years, Vols 1, 2**
(Columbia/CBS)
Teddy Wilson & His All-Stars
(Columbia/CBS)
**Various (Including Benny
Morton), Blue Note's Three
Decades Of Jazz, Vol 1 (1939-
1949** *(Blue Note/—)*
**Various (Including Red Allen),
Harlem On Saturday Night**
(—/Ace of Hearts)
**Eddie Condon, Jam Sessions
At Commodore**
(Decca/Ace of Hearts)
**Various (Including Hot Lips
Page), Swing Classics, Vol 2**
(Polydor/Polydor)
Buck Clayton's Band
(Vanguard/Vanguard)
**Fletcher Henderson All-Star
Reunion Band, The Big
Reunion** *(Jazztone/—)*
Roy Eldridge, The Nifty Cat
(Master Jazz Recordings/—)
**Wild Bill Davison, The Jazz
Giants** *(Sackville/Sackville)*

Jelly Roll
Morton

Pianist-composer Jelly Roll (Ferdinand Joseph La Menthe) Morton,
1885–1941, was one of the great
originals of jazz. His work is unclassifiable, combining elements
of ragtime, blues, opera, New
Orleans Brass Band, Spanish and
folksong. Influenced by Scott
Joplin, Morton's compositions are
multi-thematic, developing two or
three melodies within a number,
but his approach differs in important respects. Morton's use of
harmony is subtler, more complex, the rhythm surging over the
mechanical stop-go patterns of
ragtime. The interplay between
the hands is very different, the

*Jelly Roll Morton 1923-24 (Classic Jazz).
The great composer's earliest band recordings.*

Mr Jelly (Maestri del Jazz). Italian release.

left-hand in particular anticipating the beat and releasing octave runs of sixteen notes. The methods by which Morton transformed ragtime into jazz is well-illustrated on a late recording from 1939 on which he plays a selection of Joplin's Original Rags (**New Orleans Memories**). The reverse side of the album contains five classic blues, **Mamie's Blues, Michigan Water Blues, Don't You Leave Me Here, Buddy Bolden's Blues** and **Winin' Boy Blues**.

Morton's early experience playing in the Storyville sporting houses brought him into contact with the great piano 'professors' around the turn of the century. Some of his first recordings recall the tunes of that era, **Jelly Roll Blues, Big Fat Ham, New Orleans Joys, Perfect Rag (Jelly Roll Morton)**. The thirteen classic solos cut at the Gennett studios in 1923 and 1924 are included here, the version of 'King Porter' later taken up by Benny Goodman and turned into a Swing Era hit. Two devices originating with Morton, the break and the riff, became important features of big-band swing: 'If you can't have a decent break you haven't got a jazz band and you can't even play jazz. Without a break you have nothin'.' Morton consciously set out to increase the scope of the piano, using its voicings in ways suggestive of an orchestra: 'The piano should always be an imitation of a jazz band.'

In 1926, the pianist fronted the Red Hot Peppers, a small group including trumpeter George Mitchell and clarinettist Omer Simeon, and their recordings remain classics of New Orleans style. Morton's deployment of the three-horn front line, trumpet, clarinet and trombone, the polyphonic and the solo voice, the lithe rhythmic variety and the natural blending of improvisation and score show that Morton was a great composer.

Library of Congress Recordings (Classic Jazz Masters).

Versions of **Black Bottom Stomp, The Chant, Grandpa's Spells, Doctor Jazz** or **Jelly Roll Blues (King Of New Orleans Jazz)** include contributions from sidemen like Kid Ory, John St Cyr, while **Steamboat Stomp** and **Sidewalk Blues** add Darnell Howard and Barney Bigard to the unit. Apart from his work with the Red Hot Peppers, Morton recorded duo performances with cornettist King Oliver, **King Porter Stomp** and **Tom Cat Blues** in 1924, inspiring the later collaboration of Louis Armstrong and Earl Hines (**Louis Armstrong & King Oliver**). A collection by the New Orleans Rhythm Kings from 1923 has Morton on several tracks including **Clarinet Marmalade, Mr Jelly Lord, London Blues** and **Milenburg Joys**. A trio performance, **Mournful Serenade,** with Morton, Simeon and trombonist Geechy Fields, is a masterpiece of pastel lyricism, and contrasts with the lusty trio on **Shreveport Stomp** (Stomps & Joys) and **King Of New Orleans Jazz**).

With the onset of the Depression, Morton went to New York, touring for a while before finally fetching up in penury in a Washington club. Alan Lomax, who was collecting folk material for the Library of Congress archive, found him in 1938, and encouraged him to commit his reminiscences, verbal and musical, to record. Twelve albums (**The Library Of Congress Recordings**) contain Morton's often boastful version of jazz history, and examples of scat singing, blues singing, cabaret material and piano styles. His personality comes across forcefully; Jelly Roll Morton was a great dandy, a great pool player and womaniser, but, above all, a great musician. A fascinating album of piano rolls (**Jelly Roll Morton**) dating from 1924, captures the flavor of his compositions.

Recordings:
New Orleans Memories (Commodore/Fontana)
Jelly Roll Morton (Milestone/Milestone)
King Of New Orleans Jazz (RCA Victor/RCA Victor)
Louis Armstrong & King Oliver (Milestone/Milestone)
New Orleans Rhythm Kings (Milestone/Milestone)
Stomps & Joys (RCA Victor/—)
The Library Of Congress Recordings (Classic Jazz Masters/Classic Jazz Masters)
Jelly Roll Morton (—/DJM)

Bennie Moten

Bennie Moten (born Kansas City, Missouri, 1894) started on piano, switched to baritone-horn and, by 12, was playing latter instrument in youth brass band. After reverting to keyboard, started working in local Kansas City bands, before putting together own quintet – unit which had become six-piecer for its first records – **Elephant's Wobble, Crawdad Blues,** both Moten compositions (**Bennie Moten Kansas City Orchestra 1923-25**). Apart from leader's ragtime-influenced piano, Moten Sextet members included cornettist Iammar Wright, clarinettist Herman 'Woody' Walder, trombonist Thamon Hayes. Amongst band's recordings – most numbers

The Fabulous Gerry Mulligan Quartet (Vogue): the Salle Pleyel concert from 1954, Brookmeyer replacing Chet Baker.

composed by Moten – were fine sides like **Tulsa Blues, Vine Street Blues, Sister Honky Tonk** and **South,** last-named destined to become jazz standard. By time Moten band commenced recording for Victor (in 1926), its numbers had increased to 10 (personnel included saxists Harland Leonard, later to lead own fine jump band, and Jack Washington, and trumpeter Paul Webster). **White Lightin' Blues, Midnight Mama, Ding Dong Blues** and **Moten Stomp** (all **Bennie Moten's Kansas City Orchestra, Vol 1**) are fine examples of the Moten band during 1926–27. Nephew Ira ('Buster') Moten (1904–65) worked with band from around 1929, playing accordion and doubling on piano. Most important personnel arrival, also in '29, was pianist William 'Count' Basie (♦); guitarist-trombonist-composer-arranger Eddie Durham (♦) was another important addition to aggregation (both on **Bennie Moten's Kansas City Orchestra, Vol 3 (1929): Moten's Blues**). Subsequent key figures to join (both in '30): trumpeter Oran 'Hot Lips' Page (♦), singer Jimmy Rushing (♦) (both on **Bennie Moten's Kansas City Orchestra, Vol 4 (1929-1930): New Moten Stomp**). By time band made its final recordings (1932), notable newcomers included tenorist Ben Webster (♦), trombonist Dan Minor, saxist-clarinettist Eddie Barefield, bassist Walter Page. Bennie Moten Band, always improving, continued to spread message of big-band KC jazz music until leader's death in 1935, even though, by 1932, it had begun to feel effects of the Depression. First Count Basie Orchestra comprised, in the main, remnants of final Bennie Moten organization.

Recordings:
Bennie Moten's Kansas City Orchestra 1923-1925 (—/Parlophone)
Bennie Moten's Kansas City Orchestra, Vols 1-5 (RCA Victor – France)

Gerry Mulligan

Baritone saxophonist Gerry Mulligan was born in Long Island, 1927, writing arrangements for big bands like Elliot Lawrence, Claude Thornhill and Gene Krupa while still in his teens. He contributed tunes like **Jeru, Rocker** and **Venus De Milo,** as well as taking several good baritone solos, to the influential Miles Davis band of 1948 (**Birth Of The Cool**). 1951 saw him recording some of his finest compositions like **Bweebida Bobbida** and **Funhouse** with a tentet which included two baritones, George Wallington on piano and tenorman Allen Eager (**Gerry Mulligan & Chet Baker**). In 1952, his famous pianoless quartet with trumpeter Chet Baker, bassist Carson Smith and drummer Chico Hamilton, made its debut in Los Angeles. The lack of chord commentary from the piano gave the soloists great melodic freedom, and Mulligan and Baker played backing lines for each other. Interweaving counterpoint over a surging rhythm section gave the group an identifiable sound, and many of its characteristics were copied on the West Coast. In 1952, they recorded much of their standard repertoire for Prestige, including Mulligan compositions like **Line For Lyons, Bark For Barksdale, Turnstile,** as well as re-arrangements of standards like **Carioca, The Lady Is A Tramp** and their biggest hit, **My Funny Valentine** (**Gerry Mulligan & Chet Baker**). The following year, Mulligan added altoist Lee Konitz to the group for a classic version of **Too Marvellous For Words (Revelation),** and also led a tentet for a Capitol recording session which features some of Mulligan's arranger's piano, most of the solo work divided between the leader and Baker, and the odd instrumentation of two baritones, tuba and French horn (**Walking Shoes**). In 1954, with trombonist Bob Brookmeyer replacing Baker, the quartet

Above: Gerry Mulligan, whose pianoless quartet established a bold, new departure in the '50s. Still blowing the big baritone.

made a triumphant appearance at Salle Pleyel in Paris. Brookmeyer, like Mulligan, is a traditionalist despite great harmonic sophistication, and the two men made a highly compatible front line, with the great Red Mitchell bass, and Frank Isola drums (**The Fabulous Gerry Mulligan Quartet**). Various personnel changes occurred – Jon Eardlay on trumpet replacing Brookmeyer, Brookmeyer back with Zoot Sims added, and in 1957 Mulligan led an octet with Konitz, Sims, Al Cohn and Allen Eager through a set of Bill Holman arrangements (**Revelation**).

In 1958, the baritonist featured in the movie, *I Want To Live*, and several of the Johnny Mandel compositions from the score, including a great Mulligan solo on the theme, are included on the album made by his Concert Jazz Band (**Gerry Mulligan & The Concert Jazz Band Live**). Two versions of the ballad **Come Rain Or Come Shine** are presented, contrasting exercises in lyricism by Mulligan and Sims. Fuelled by drummer Mel Lewis, the band belts along, and **Blueport** has some of the most swinging Mulligan on record, especially in the exchange of fours and eights with Clark Terry. A musician who loves to jam, Mulligan has made numerous albums with Stan Getz, Paul Desmond and Thelonious Monk, all currently deleted. Contemporary Mulligan is best represented by an A&M album (**The Age Of Steam**), which bears a photo of the one-time prototypical modernist (crew-cut, shades) with long hair and a beard. A gruff, laconic player, Gerry Mulligan is the essence of relaxed swing.

Recordings:
Miles Davis, Birth Of The Cool (Capitol/Capitol)
Gerry Mulligan & Chet Baker (Prestige/Prestige)
Gerry Mulligan & Lee Konitz, Revelation (Blue Note/Blue Note)
The Gerry Mulligan Tentette, Walking Shoes (Capitol/—)

The Fabulous Gerry Mulligan Quartet (—/Vogue)
Gerry Mulligan & The Concert Jazz Band Live (Verve/Verve)
The Age Of Steam (A&M/A&M)

Jimmy Mundy
♦ Earl Hines

Sunny Murray

Free drummer Sunny Murray was born in Oklahoma, and gradually evolved a style of drumming to meet the needs of avant-garde leaders like Albert Ayler and Cecil Taylor. Using a very basic kit, cymbals, snare, bass drum and hi-hat, Murray avoided regular time-keeping duties altogether, building up layers of rhythm that ebbed and flowed dramatically between the continuous cymbal and the tripping snare runs. New Wave masterpieces like Ayler's ESP (**Spiritual Unity**) or Taylor's marathon **D. Trad That's What** (**Live At The Café Montmartre**) owe much to the drummer's unconfining momentum.

Albums under his own name revealed a gift for composition that incorporated characteristics of his former leaders, along with an advance and recede development that springs from his own style of playing. A great, original group player, he seldom solos, preferring to control the climate and dynamics of his bands within the ensemble. His first album (**Sunny Murray**) shows the rapport that existed with bassist Alan Silva, whose arco work in the upper register was equally pioneering. A session with Ayler and Don Cherry includes a LeRoi Jones poetry reading, **Black Art,** and a long Murray composition, **Justice** (**Sunny's Time Now**). In 1968 he left for France, recording three albums the following year with French and American

Above: ex-Ayler, ex-Taylor drummer Sunny Murray.

musicians. Using a septet, Murray's keening themes, like the outstanding **Angel Son**, owe much to the prescience of Alan Silva's violin (**Big Chief**). A long composition, **Suns Of Africa (Homage To Africa)** again uses dense ensemble textures and the large unit includes Archie Shepp, Lester Bowie, Roscoe Mitchell and Grachan Moncur III. A quartet (**An Even Break**) marks a return to comparatively straightforward performances, and has Murray reading his own poetry.

Recordings:
Albert Ayler:
  Spiritual Unity (ESP/ESP)
  Prophecy (ESP/ESP)
  Vibrations (Arista – Freedom/ Arista – Freedom)
  Witches & Devils (Arista – Freedom/Arista – Freedom)
  Spirits Rejoice (ESP/ESP)
Bells (ESP/ESP)
  New York Eye & Ear Control (ESP/ESP)
Cecil Taylor:
  Into The Hot (Impulse/Impulse)
  Live At The Café Montmartre (Fantasy/—)
  Nefertiti (Arista – Freedom/ Arista – Freedom)
Sunny Murray (ESP/ESP)
Sunny's Time Now (Jihad/—)
Big Chief (Pathé – France)
Homage To Africa (BYG/BYG)
An Even Break (BYG/BYG)
Wild Flowers, The New York Loft Sessions (Douglas/—)

Ray Nance

Raymond Willis Nance (born Chicago, 1913) was, like former Ellington colleagues Tyree Glenn (♦), Harry Carney (♦), and Otto Hardwicke (♦), something of a multi-talent. Primarily, he was a first-class Armstrong-influenced trumpet player, who could handle straight ballads as well as he could project blues or up-tempo swingers. He was no mean slouch either with plunger mute, carrying on the great tradition of Ellington trum-

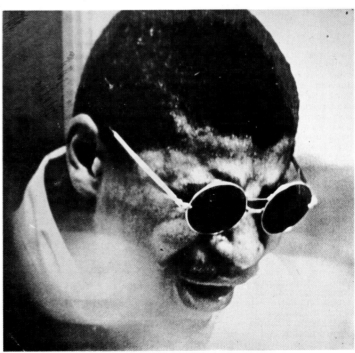

Sunny Murray Quintet (ESP): the pioneer of free drumming heading his own group which included bassist Alan Silva.

Above: triple threat Ray Nance – violinist, trumpeter and singer, for. many years associated with Duke Ellington.

peters, starting with Bubber Miley (♦). In addition, Nance had one of the most distinctive sounds of any jazz violinist – a somewhat curious hybrid of North American jazz and European gypsy-like music. And he was a reasonable singer and a jivey dancer (although his efforts in latter two areas tended, in live performance in particular, to border on the outrageously camp).

Nance, who died in 1976, started his career in music with college band, following tuition on piano, violin, trumpet. In 1932 played, sang in Chicago nightclubs, fronted own sextet, and gigged elsewhere, outside the Windy City. Joined Earl Hines (♦) big band (1937), staying for almost two years. Next, came period of just over one year (1939–40) with Horace Henderson (♦), followed by short interlude prior to joining Duke Ellington (end of 1940). First recorded solo in January, '41 (although track remained unissued until recently) when Ellington band recorded what was to become its longest-serving theme, **Take The 'A' Train.** (Version of number which did get released on original 78rpm disc was recorded month after the first.) At this second date, Nance's violin was heard for first time with Ellington (on Juan Tizol's **Bakiff**). Thereafter, Nance's trumpet, violin, voice were to be heard at regular intervals (especially between 1941–63) in Ducal surroundings. His trumpet contribution to **Pussy Willow (The Duke 1940)** was rather tentative – not at all surprising considering it was his first appearance with the legendary outfit. Certainly, though, there is no lack of assurance to be found in the innumerable other solos which Nance was to produce throughout the next 23 years (unbroken except for odd instances of his absence from band, in 1944, 1945, 1961).

The kind of unrivalled loyalty which kept so many musicians with Ellington for so many years, attracted Nance back into the fold, from time to time, from 1965 until

the end of 1960s. Whilst with Ellington first time round, Nance, together with Ellington and singer Kay Davis, toured British variety halls, in 1948. In 1966 toured Europe as solo act, and year later worked in Switzerland with band of Henri Chaix. During years 1966–9, teamed up at regular intervals with clarinettist Sol Yaged. Hospitalized in 1969. Of the many trumpet solos with Ellington, the following rank with the best: **Take The 'A' Train** (his first-ever statements on record with band) **(The Works Of Duke, Vols. 14, 15)**; another **'A' Train,** this one from Carnegie Hall concert, 1943 **(His Most Important Second War Concert)**; **Long, Strong & Consecutive,** with fine use of plunger mute **(Pretty Woman)**; **Black & Tan Fantasy, In The Mood (Ellington '55/Toast To The Duke)**; and **East St Louis Toodle-oo, Creole Love Call, Stompy Jones, In A Mellotone, Midriff** and **Stomp, Look & Listen (Historically Speaking, The Duke/Stomp, Look & Listen)**. His violin has been well to the fore on items like **Guitar Amor (Midnight In Paris); Autumn Leaves (Ellington Indigos)**; in tandem with Jimmy Hamilton (♦) on **Up & Down** and alone, on title track, (both from **Such Sweet Thunder**) and during last movement of **Suite Thursday**. As vocalist, he was featured on such as **My Honey's Lovin' Arms, Hey Baby, Just Squeeze Me** (all **Pretty Woman); Just A-Settin' & A-Rockin' (Duke Ellington, We Love You Madly)**; and **Tulip Or Turnip (The Golden Duke)**. Nance's violin playing has also figured interestingly on such diverse non-Ellington recordings as **Jazz For A Sunday Afternoon, Vol 1** in company with such as Dizzy Gillespie (♦), Elvin Jones (♦), Chick Corea (♦) – **Duke Ellington Jazz Violin Session** – pitting Nance's individualism against that of Stephane Grappelli (♦) and Svend Asmussen; and **Body & Soul,** probably finest, certainly most comprehensive, of Ray

Nance's jazz fiddle on record, this one under his own name. Elsewhere, both trumpet and violin were utilized at sessions involving musicians like Shelly Manne (♦) **(Shelly Manne & Co)**, Paul Gonsalves (♦), Harold Ashby **(Ellingtonians Play A Tribute To Duke Ellington)**, with Nance also playing trumpet, but not violin, on tracks by Harry Carney (♦); and Coleman Hawkins (♦) **(Duke Ellington Meets Coleman Hawkins)**.

Recordings:
Ray Nance, Body & Soul
(Solid State/—)
Ray Nance, Huffin' & Puffin'
(—/MPS/BASF)
Ray Nance/Stephane Grappelli/ Svend Asmussen, Duke Ellington's Jazz Violin Session *(Atlantic/—)*
Various (Including Ray Nance), Jazz For A Sunday Afternoon, Vol 1 *(Solid State/Solid State)*
Everybody Knows Johnny Hodges *(Impulse/Impulse)*
Duke Ellington Meets Coleman Hawkins *(Impulse/Impulse)*
Earl Hines, Once Upon A Time *(Impulse/Impulse)*
Various, Great Ellingtonians Play A Tribute to Duke Ellington *(—/Double-Up)*
Johnny Hodges, Ellingtonia '56 *(Norgran/Columbia – Clef)*
Shelly Manne & Co.
(Flying Dutchman/—)
Duke Ellington:
The Duke 1940 *(Jazz Society/—)*
The Works Of Duke Vols 14-20 *(RCA Victor – France)*
His Most Important Second War Concert *(—/Saga)*
Ellington '55 *(Capitol)/*
  Toast To The Duke
  (World Record Club)
Historically Speaking, The Duke *(Bethlehem)/*
  Stomp, Look & Listen
  (Ember)
Midnight In Paris
(Columbia/CBS)
Such Sweet Thunder
(Columbia/CBS – Realm)
Pretty Woman
(RCA Victor/RCA Victor)
We Love You Madly
(Capitol – Pickwick)

Duke Ellington Vol 2 *(—/Saga)*
(Peer Gynt Suites Nos 1, 2)/ Suite Thursday
(Columbia/CBS)
Ellington Indigos *(Columbia/—)*
The Golden Duke
(Prestige/Prestige)
Souvenirs *(Reprise – France)*

Joseph 'Tricky Sam' Nanton

Together with trumpeter Bubber Miley (♦), Joe Nanton provided Duke Ellington (♦) Orchestra with its first individual purveyors of the so-called 'jungle' style which Ellington pioneered in 1920s and thereafter. Nanton, not one of the great improvising musicians in the usual sense, nevertheless earned his place in the jazz pantheon by virtue of the inimitable way he manipulated a plunger mute in conjunction with his slide trombone. Nanton's ability in projecting a blues-filled, often poignant humanized 'cry', via trombone and plunger-mute, never has been surpassed. Even acknowledged plungerers like Quentin 'Butter' Jackson (♦), Tyree Glenn (♦) (both of whom were employed by Ellington to reproduce Nanton's highly personal, innovatory plunger work), Al Grey (♦) and Vic Dickenson (♦), could offer only first-rate reproductions of his style without ever truly embracing Nanton's depth of expression or the uniqueness of the sound he produced during 21 years in Ducal surroundings. Nanton's wah-wah plungering was integral ingredient of numerous Ellington recordings of **Black & Tan Fantasy** (where his trombone eccentricities provided its own totally individual evocation of the funereal atmosphere of an exceptional piece of Ellington creation), including the very first **(The Beginning)**. Nanton, who could also produce excellent, mute-less trombone solos of a more conventional nature, was one of most important individual contributors to work with Ellington from mid-1920s until mid-1940s.

Superb as his playing was during early days with band, he was especially rewarding during last decade of his lifetime. His were classic solos to add to the luster of acknowledged Ellington masterpieces during early 1940s, one of his most creative periods; **Ko Ko, A Portrait Of Bert Williams, Jack The Bear, Stompy Jones** and **Harlem Airshaft.** Joe Nanton (born New York, 1904, of West Indian parentage) began professional career with stride pianist Cliff Jackson (1921), then spent two years with Earl Frazier's Harmony Five (1923–5), before rejoining Jackson ('25). Prior to joining Ellington, worked with Elmer Snowden.

Suffered stroke in 1945, but recovered to resume work with band following year. Collapsed and died during band's 1946 West Coast tour. During his career, Joseph 'Tricky Sam' Nanton's trombone vocalism was one of the most easily recognizable individual sounds in jazz. As long-time member of Ellington trombone section, his almost bizarre solo style contrasted magnificently with those of colleagues Juan Tizol and Lawrence Brown (♦). His nickname was bestowed by fellow Ellingtonian Otto 'Toby' Hardwicke (♦).

Recordings:
The Complete Duke Ellington (1928-1937), Vols 1-7
(CBS – France)
The Works Of Duke Ellington, Vols 1-17 *(RCA Victor – France)*
Duke Ellington:
Masterpieces (1928-1930)
(RCA Victor – France)
Jungle Jamboree
(—/Parlophone)
The Beginning (1926-1928)
(Decca/MCA – Germany)
Hot In Harlem (1928-1929)
(Decca/MCA – Germany)
Rockin' In Rhythm (1929-1931)
(Decca/MCA – Germany)
At The Cotton Club, 1938, Vols 1, 2 *(Jazz Archives/—)*
Black, Brown & Beige
(Aristan – Italy)
His Most Important Second War Concert *(—/Saga)*
The Jimmy Blanton Years
(Queen Disc – Italy)

Fats Navarro

Born Key West, Florida, 1923, Theodore 'Fats' Navarro was Bebop's most perfect trumpeter. Never flamboyant like Dizzy Gillespie, Navarro's playing has a classical perfection and balance, the tone true and brassy, the articulation accurate at even the fastest tempos. Though he died of TB and addiction at the age of 26, his influence on later generations of trumpeters – Clifford Brown, Kenny Dorham, Lee Morgan – was paramount. Following experience with the big bands of Snookum Russell and Andy Kirk, he took over Dizzy Gillespie's chair in the legendary Billy Eckstine band from 1945, soloing brilliantly on **Long Long Journey** and **Tell Me Pretty Baby (Mister B & The Band).** Small group sessions for Savoy featured Navarro with baritonist Leo Parker, **Fat Girl, Ice Freezes Red;** with altoman Sonny Stitt and fellow trumpeter Kenny Dorham, **Boppin' A Riff;** with tenorman Eddie 'Lockjaw' Davis,

Good Bait (Riverside): classic Bebop combo.

Calling Dr. Jazz and, with pianist-composer Tadd Dameron's group, including Dexter Gordon and altoman Ernie Henry, **Bebop Caroll** and **Tadd Walk (Fat Girl).** The association with Dameron proved ideal, with the pianist's lyrical compositions providing a perfect setting for Navarro's beautiful sound and vaulting imagination. **Our Delight, The Squirrel, The Chase, Lady Bird, Dameronia, Jahbero** and **Symphonette (Prime Source)** show his poise at a variety of tempos, his harmonic ideas as sophisticated as Charlie Parker's and his improvisations as finished

as if they had been scored. Swapping choruses with trumpeter Howard McGhee on numbers like **Boperation, Double Talk** and **The Skunk,** conveys the soaring exhilaration of young musicians matching their gifts. The tracks with Bud Powell and a youthful Sonny Rollins **52nd Street Theme, Dance Of The Infidels, Wail** and **Bounding With Bud** show that no matter how turbulent the relationship between the trumpeter and the pianist, their music was a meeting of genius.

The Dameron band which was resident at The Royal Roost in 1948, including Navarro, tenorman Allen Eager and altoist Rudy Williams, made a stunning version of **Good Bait,** a headlong tour de force for the trumpeter **(Good Bait),** who somehow contrives to sound as relaxed as the laconic Eager. Recordings from Cafe Society with Charlie Parker and Bud Powell in the year of Navarro's death, 1950, proved a meeting of equals, the trumpeter's solos on **Street Beat, Ornithology** or **Move** hardly confirming the stories of physical deterioration.

Recordings:
Billy Eckstine, Mister B. & The Band *(Savoy/Savoy)*
Fat Girl *(Savoy/Savoy)*
Prime Source
(Blue Note/Blue Note)
Tadd Dameron, Fats Navarro, Good Bait *(Riverside/—)*
Saturday Night Swing Session
(—/GI Records)
Charlie Parker Historical Masterpieces *(Le Jazz Cool/—)*
Fats Navarro
(Milestone/Milestone)

Oliver Nelson

Before disappearing into Hollywood, Oliver Nelson – like Quincy Jones, Lalo Schifrin, Shorty Rogers – was an excellent jazz arranger and good saxophonist. A major suite in seven parts **(Afro-Ameri-**

The Blues And The Abstract Truth (Impulse): swinger.

can Sketches) uses a big band including cellos, French horns, a tuba and four rhythm for an imaginative re-working of ethnic sources. Typically here, as elsewhere, Nelson's alto is cast in the lead because of the purity and cutting edge of his upper register work. A lengthy collaboration with multi-instrumentalist Eric Dolphy resulted in some of Nelson's best work as arranger for combo and instrumentalist **(Images).** Some of his best known compositions like **Stolen Moments** and **Hoe-Down** came from the classic session with Dolphy, Freddie Hub-

bard and Bill Evans **(Blues & The Abstract Truth).** A big band session from 1967 **(Live From Los Angeles),** and a Montreux performance of his **Swiss Suite,** featuring Gato Barbieri and altoman Eddie 'Cleanhead' Vinson, prove that Nelson has the ability to give the most ad-hoc assembly a collective identity. Born 1932, St Louis, Nelson is also an expert in embalming and taxidermy.

Recordings:
Afro-American Sketches
(Prestige/—)
Images *(Prestige/Prestige)*
Blues & The Abstract Truth
(Impulse/Impulse)
Live From Los Angeles
(Impulse/Impulse)
Swiss Suite
(Flying Dutchman/Philips)

Frankie Newton

It was unfortunate for William Frank 'Frankie' Newton (born Emory, Virginia, 1906) that his most impressive work should fall during 1930s, when Newton's rivals included Louis Armstrong (♦), Henry 'Red' Allen (♦), Roy Eldridge (♦), and Bunny Berigan (♦); for Newton, whose first important gig was with Lloyd W. Scott's band in 1926, was indeed a gifted soloist whose warm tone and keen attention to dynamics ensured that his services constantly were in demand. And Newton got to play with some more impressive musicians and singers during his career. His trumpet was featured, in solo and accompanying roles, at Bessie Smith's (♦) final recording session **(The World's Greatest Blues Singer)** and it was Newton's band which provided sympathetic support for Billie Holiday (♦) during a 1939 Commodore date **(Strange Fruit/The 'Commodore' Days)** that resulted in four masterful examples of jazz singing. Newton seemed to have a penchant for offering the choicest of trumpet support to singers.

Apart from Smith and Holiday, he was present when Maxine Sullivan (♦) recorded her popular **Loch Lomond** disc, and he was on hand at slightly less superb session same year (1937) featuring Midge Williams & Her Jazz Jesters (both **Frankie Newton At The Onyx Club**). Newton first arrived in New York with Lloyd W. Scott, then moved through several bands into 1930s. At beginning of decade, played in trumpet sections of bands led by Chick Webb (♦), Charlie Johnson, Elmer Snowden (with whom he had worked previously in '27), and Sam Wooding. Rejoined Johnson (1933–5), with Teddy Hill for one year **(Teddy Hill & His Orchestra);** then with John Kirby (♦). Recorded with own Uptown Serenaders. Apart from leader's consistently fine playing, band also included Pete Brown (♦) and Edmond Hall (♦); music it produced **(Frankie Newton At The Onyx Club)** ranks with finest of the period, exemplified by individual titles like **You Showed Me The Way** and **The Onyx Hop.** Several of its members were in band which recorded with Willie 'The Lion' Smith (♦), also in '37, and apart from Smith's piano-playing both New and Brown were the standout soloists **(The Swinging Cub**

Men). With Lucky Millinder (1937–8). Participated in one of **The Panassie Sessions** during same period, together with Brown, James P. Johnson (♦), etc. Took own band into Cafe Society **(Frankie Newton At The Onyx Club)** to much acclaim. Continued to lead various bands through early-1940s, mostly appearing in New York. With James P. Johnson (1944–5), and with Big Sid Catlett (♦) ('47). Worked in Boston area 1947–50, occasionally taking jobs in New York. Between 1951 and his death, in 1954, mostly inactive.

Recordings:
Bessie Smith, The World's Greatest Blues Singer
(Columbia/CBS)
Teddy Hill & His Orchestra
(RCA Victor – France)
Frankie Newton At The Onyx Club *(Tax – Sweden)*
Willie 'The Lion' Smith, The Swinging Cub Men
(—/Ace of Hearts)
Various, The Panassie Sessions
(RCA Victor/RCA Victor)
Sidney Bechet Jazz Classics, Vol 2 *(Blue Note/—)*
Mary Lou Williams, Rehearsal
(Folkways/—)
Have No Fear, Big Joe Turner Is Here *(Savoy/Savoy)*

Albert Nicholas

Albert Nicholas (born New Orleans, Louisiana, 1900) was archetypal New Orleans clarinettist – warm, liquid tone, supple phrasing, attractive vibrato, subtle swing, blues-orientated. Nephew of cornettist/clarinettist Wooden Joe Nicholas (♦), Albert Nicholas took lessons from legendary Lorenzo Tio, Jnr, later playing with some of the other great New Orleans names: Buddie Petit, Manuel Perez, Kid Ory (♦), King Oliver (♦). Served in US Merchant Navy (1916–19). Returning to US, worked with various bands (including Perez) before fronting own band, in New Orleans (1923–4). In 1924: toured with King Oliver, leaving after two months to resume previous own gig **(King Oliver's Dixie Syncopators).** Returned with Oliver, staying this time almost two years (1924–6). With banjoist Frank Ethridge, went to Egypt, obtaining work both in Cairo and Alexandria (1927). Went from Egypt to Paris, briefly, before returning to US. Joined orchestra of Luis Russell (♦) (1928), staying over five years. With Russell, attained (at last) featured-soloist status, making memorable contributions to **Panama, Saratoga Shout** and others **(Luis Russell & His Louisiana Swing Orchestra/Luis Russell Story).** As brilliantly as he played with Russell, Nicholas' solos with Jelly Roll Morton (♦) in '39 were as good, if not better. Nicholas produced beautifully posed solos on **Climax Rag, Ballin' The Jack** and **West End Blues,** at second of two Morton record sessions, and partnered by soprano-sax of Sidney Bechet (♦), contributed significantly to the first (both **Jelly Roll Morton, Vol 2).**

In between Russell and Morton (with whom Nicholas had recorded previously, in '29), worked with Chick Webb (♦), Sam Wooding Orchestra and Bernard Addison (♦). Nicholas' contributions to series of recordings from 1935, involving bands led by Addison, Freddie Jenkins, Ward Pinkett (**Adrian Rollini & His Friends, Vol 1**) were wholly delightful, as demonstrated especially on **Tap-Room Special**. As with his stint with Addison band, Nicholas played Adrian Rollini's Tap Room with John Kirby (♦) and own group. Worked with band accompanying Louis Armstrong (♦) (1937–9) (Nicholas had fulfilled same task, with Luis Russell, in 1929) then with Zutty Singleton, for eight months (1939–40). Left music full-time, 1941, returning 1945. Reunited on record with Bechet in '46 (**Sidney Bechet Jazz Classics, Vols 1, 2**), Nicholas, if anything, seemed better than before. The rapport between pair on **Weary Way Blues, Blame In On The Blues** and **Old Stack O'Lee Blues** is masterful, and the sensitive, deeply-felt playing by both results in performances which, rightly, long since have been elevated to the pantheon of the greatest in record jazz. Nicholas' work with Wild Bill Davison (♦) & His Commodores, recorded one month before Bechet date (**The Davison-Brunis Sessions, Vol 3**) is not as emotionally involved, but produces fine clarinet solos nevertheless.

After working on West Coast with Kid Ory (♦), Nicholas started lengthy residency, with own trio, at Jimmy Ryan's, New York. Based mainly in Los Angeles and district, 1949–53, and after working season with Rex Stewart (♦), went to live in France (1953). Apart from occasional trips to States, lived in Europe (particularly France) for rest of his life. In Europe, was a highly respected musical personality for 20 years, playing numerous countries and at major European jazz festivals. Probably last visit to US was his visit to New Orleans (1969–70). Recorded during final portion of his career (**Let Me Tell You**) is a delightful retrospective survey by this Creole clarinettist of his career in music, with Nicholas' own reminiscences of important events along the way.

Supported with great sympathy at all times by group of British musicians (including Alan Branscombe, Dick Abel, Lennie Bush), Nicholas' playing is uniformly good, especially on **Albert's Blues, Memories Of You** and **How Long, How Long Blues**. Other Nicholas recordings emanating from period documenting his decision to live in Europe tended towards the disappointing but **Albert Nicholas Quartet**, recorded during Stateside trip, and **Albert's Blues** taped in London, have much to commend, not least the consistently rewarding clarinet playing. Apart from the Nicholas-Bechet classics on Blue Note, probably best example of Nicholas' recorded work in 1940s is to be found within **Creole Reeds**, with top-form clarinet on **Buddy Bolden's Blues** and **Albert's Blues**, supported only by Baby Dodds (♦) and Don Ewell, from 1946.

Albert Nicholas died in Basle, Switzerland, in 1973.

Recordings:
King Oliver's Dixie Syncopators
(*MCA Coral – Germany*)
Luis Russell & His Louisiana Swing Orchestra
(*Columbia/—*)

Above: Albert Nicholas, one of the classic New Orleans clarinet stylists. Died aged 73 in Switzerland.

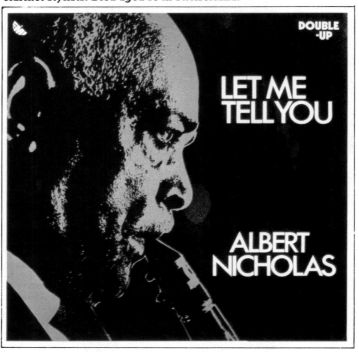

Let Me Tell You (Double-Up, EMI). Memories of a great clarinettist, talking as well as playing.

The Luis Russell Story
(*—/Parlophone*)
Jelly Roll Morton, Vol 2
(*RCA Victor – France*)
Adrian Rollini & His Friends, Vol 1 (*RCA Victor – France*)
Sidney Bechet Jazz Orchestra, Vols 1, 2 (*Blue Note/—*)
(Sidney Bechet)/Albert Nicholas, Creole
(*Riverside/London*)
Various (Including Wild Bill Davison), The Davison-Brunis Sessions, Vol 3 (*—/London*)
Albert Nicholas Quartet
(*Delmark/Esquire*)
Albert Nicholas, Albert's Blues (*—/77*)
Albert Nicholas, Let Me Tell You (*—/Double-Up*)

Wooden Joe Nicholas

Uncle of clarinettist Albert Nicholas (♦), 'Wooden Joe' Nicholas (born New Orleans, 1883) was said by William Russell, New Orleans historian, to have been 'the most powerful cornettist since King Bolden'. And much like Buddy Bolden, Nicholas was something of a legend as a superior horn man. For Wooden Joe made but a handful of records – and these, good as they are, give but a hint of his full capabilities during his peak years (say those who heard him in live performance during that time). Certainly, though, tracks that have been made available (**Wooden Joe's New Orleans Band: 1945-1949**) demonstrate he was more than capable of providing classic lead to typical New Orleans ensemble. Of available recordings, all made in Crescent City for American Music, earliest (1945) are best, especially from a solo standpoint. Nicholas' timing and strength are, even at 63, admirable, most notably on **Lead Me On, Eh-La-Bas, Shake It & Break It**. His ensemble playing is admirably evidenced on **Tiger Rag, Up Jumped The Devil**. Latter is trio number, with Nicholas receiving superb support from clarinettist Albert Burbank (who appears on all these sides; his presence was, in the event, vital) and banjoist Lawrence Marrero. On remainder of '45 tracks, additional presence of trombonist Jim Robinson (♦) and drummer Josiah Frazier completes well-nigh classic NO ensemble. Of two sides from '49, Nicholas joins Burbank on clarinet in one passage – Wooden Joe first worked with King Oliver (♦) in Storyville (circa 1917) as clarinettist, switching to cornet after practising with Oliver's instrument. And on **The Lord Will Make A Way Somehow**, playing both open and with plunger mute, Nicholas complements Ann Cook's vocal with tenderness and underlying strength – and good taste. In his youth, gained reputation for his stamina and power when participating in NO street parades. After working with Oliver, led own band (1918), known variously as Wooden Joe's Band or the Camelia Band. During Depression days, played only occasionally, concentrating on teaching music. Apart from American Music recordings (1945, 1949), Nicholas also recorded (in '44) with Creole Stompers.

Recordings:
Wooden Joe's New Orleans Band (American Music/—)
Wooden Joe's New Orleans Band (—/Storyville)

Herbie Nichols

The most moving study in A. B. Spellman's *Four Lives in the Bebop Business*, composer-pianist Herbie Nichols' career in jazz was destroyed by public indifference. Born 1919, New York, his style shows a Monk influence but overlaps most categories. All that remains in the catalog is a double album of trio performances with either Art Blakey or Max Roach on drums from 1955 and 1956, which happily represents his finest work. His evocative compositions, **House Party Starting, Chit-Chatting,** the justly famous **Lady Sings The Blues** which Billie Holiday picked up on, **(The Third World)**, reveal an encyclopaedic knowledge of jazz history from stride through Bop to the New Wave, and a rhythmic conception that demands considerable interaction with the drums. How his compositions would have sounded with a fuller instrumentation remains tragically unanswered. He died in 1963 at the age of 44.

Recordings:
The Third World
(Blue Note/Blue Note)

Herbie Nichols Trio (Blue Note): tragically underrated.

Red Nichols

Between 1925–30, Ernest Loring 'Red' Nichols (born Ogden, Utah, 1905) was classified by many as being closest rival to Bix Beiderbecke (♦) amongst white cornet/trumpet players of period. Which was rather a presumption in that Nichols had not the sensitivity, flair, or the superbly logical flow to his playing that was Beiderbecke's. In any case, Nichols' more-than-adequate playing followed a different pathway than Beiderbecke's. But Nichols was much involved in considerable amount of jazz activity which centered on New York during 1925–30. Was associated with numerous recording activities, working with bands with colorful names like Arkansas Travellers, Red Heads, Louisiana Rhythm Kings, Charleston Chasers, et al. His most famous name-association was with innumerable versions of own Red Nichols & His Five Pennies (containing, invariably, more members than that designated in

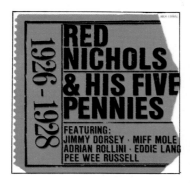

Red Nichols & His Five Pennies (1926-1928) (MCA Coral).

its title). Miff Mole (♦), Benny Goodman (♦), Jack Teagarden (♦), Jimmy Dorsey (♦), Fud Livingston, Pee Wee Russell (♦), Eddie Lang (♦) and Vic Berton were amongst those who played with Five Pennies of 1920s vintage. Personnel from Pennies' first record date (1926) did in fact comprise five players: Nichols, Dorsey, Berton, Lang, Arthur Schutt. From that session came **Washboard Blues** and **That's No Bargain (Red Nichols & His Five Pennies 1926-1928),** two perennial Five Pennies favorites. Trombonist Miff Mole (♦), added for second session, gave group extra dimension in overall sound as well as additional solo voice.

Nichols became director of Charleston Chasers in 1927. Basically, it comprised same (or similar) personnel as previously noted Five Pennies line-up. Again, Nichols' cornet was adequate in solo, but not more impressive than individual statements from, say, Mole, Jimmy Dorsey, or Russell **(The Charleston Chasers 1925-1928).**

Nichols' personal involvement with music began at 12, when he played cornet with family musical act, as well as father's brass band. Worked locally, before winning scholarship to Culver Military Academy (1919). At Academy, played cornet, violin, piano, before being dismissed in autumn of '20. Returned to Utah, again playing in local bands, before eventually heading for New York. From 1924, played with string of different bands, including those led by Sam Lanin, Bennie Kreuger, Vincent Lopez, as well as with California Ramblers. Two months with Paul Whiteman (♦), in '27. Fronted various bands for next two years, also directed theatre pit bands and studio orchestras for radio. Continued to be active as bandleader during 1930s.

Retired from music in 1942, moved to California, and took employment as shipyard worker. Back to playing, with five months as member of Casa Loma Orchestra (1944). Thereafter, continued to lead own Five Pennies bands, with three long residencies: El Morocco Club, Los Angeles (1945–8); Hangover Club, San Francisco (1948–51); Playroom, Los Angeles (1951–3). During 1950s, resided, played on West Coast (mostly). Also during this decade, film purporting to be based on Nichols' career was made: *The Five Pennies* **(Meet The Five Pennies/Masters Of Dixieland, Vol 5: Red Nichols & The Five Pennies).** Nichols appeared in another jazz biopic: *The Gene Krupa Story* **(Drum Crazy).** Interest engender-

ed by *Five Pennies* movie enabled Nichols to take further bands of same name on tour, including two overseas trips (1960, 1964). By then, of course, Red Nichols' greatest musical moments (such as they were) were 25–30 years behind when Red Nichols & His Orchestra, Red Nichols & His Five Pennies, and the Louisiana Rhythm Kings (to name but three titles with which his name was closely linked in those peak years) represented a handsome percentage of some of the best white jazz to emanate from New York (all bands featured on **J.T.**).

Ernest Loring 'Red' Nichols died, of a heart attack, in 1966.

Recordings:
Jack Teagarden/Red Nichols, J.T. (Ace of Hearts)
Benny Goodman, A Jazz Holiday (Decca/MCA)
Red Nichols & His Five Pennies 1926-1928 (MCA Coral - Germany)
The Charleston Chasers (—/VJM)
Meet The Five Pennies (Capitol)/
Masters Of Dixieland, Vol 5: Red Nichols & The Five Pennies (Capitol Electrola – Germany)

Jimmie Noone

One of the classic jazz clarinet players, Jimmie Noone (born Cutt-Off, Louisiana, 1895) first played guitar, switching to clarinet at 15. Tutored by Sidney Bechet (♦), first worked for band of trumpeter Freddie Keppard. Together with Buddie Petit assembled Young Olympia Band. Also worked with Papa Celestin, Kid Ory (♦). 1917: to Chicago, for debut on record and work with Keppard again. Following year, back to New Orleans – returning to Chicago for gigs with, amongst others, King Oliver (♦) **(West End Blues).** First recorded solo on **Play That Thing** with Tommy Ladnier (♦) **(Blues & Stomps).** With orchestra of Doc Cook (1920–6), played both clarinet, soprano-sax.

Fronted own combo at Chicago's Apex Club (1926–8), a superior little band which included pianist Earl Hines (♦), altoist Joe Poston (no trumpet, trombone in front line). Noone Apex Club Orchestra produced series of classic recordings, including **Sweet Lorraine, I Know That You Know, Four Or Five Times, Apex Blues, My Monday Date** and **Blues My Naughty Sweetie Gives To Me** (all *Jimmie Noone & Earl Hines* **At The Apex Club, Vol 1 (1928))**

Jimmie Noone: 1937-41 (Collector's Classics).

with Hines' forward-looking orchestral piano solos and accompaniments providing perfect complementary voice to Noone's limpid, warm, springy clarinet contributions. Even with eventual loss of Hines (replaced by Zinky Cohn), Noone's fine band continued to turn out further exquisite jazz discs, including **Delta Bound, I'd Do Anything For You, Liza** (all **Jimmie Noone 1931-1940).** Noone recorded with Louis Armstrong (♦) and singer Lillie Delk Christian – **(Armstrong & Hines, 1928)** – but here his quiet artistry had to take second place to Armstrong's incandescent brilliance. From 1928–31 he continued to front own groups in Chicago, where he remained until 1935, except for season at Savoy Ballroom, NYC (1931). 1935: to NYC, once more, for short residency before returning to Chicago. 1938: toured US, fronted (for radio) big band. Previous year had re-recorded selection of his old favorites, with all-star group, including Charlie Shavers (♦), Pete Brown (♦), Teddy Bunn (♦) **(Jimmie Noone 1937-41).** Continued touring, recording: in 1940, for instance, recorded with pick-up band that included Lonnie Johnson (♦), Richard M. Jones, Preston Jackson, Natty Dominique (♦) **(Jimmie Noone 1937-41).**

By beginning of 1940s, Jimmie Noone, though still a fine clarinet-tist, sometimes tended to sound less than inspired. A 1940 record date for Victor, helped not one bit by presence of nondescript singer Ed Thompson, had average-only Noone clarinet **(New Orleans, Vol 3).** 1943: to California, where he resided for rest of his life. Died of heart attack in Los Angeles 1944. Before his death, appeared with Kid Ory Creole Jazz Band **(Kid Ory & Jimmie Noone).** In latter environment, almost recaptured the relaxed brilliance of his greatest (Apex Club) days. Truly one of the great jazz performers on his instrument, cast in classic NO mould, Noone influenced many other first-rate players, including Irving Fazola (♦), Benny Goodman (♦), Jimmy Dorsey (♦), Omer Simeon (♦), Darnell Howard (♦).

Recordings:
Various (Including Tommy Ladnier), Blues & Stomps (Riverside/London)
King Oliver, West End Blues (CBS – France)
Jimmie Noone & Earl Hines: At The Apex Club, Vol 1 (1928) (Decca/—)
At The Apex Club (1928) (MCA – Germany)
Jimmie Noone, 1931-1940 (Queen-Disc – Italy)
Jimmie Noone/Johnny Dodds, Battle Of Jazz, Vol 8 (Brunswick/Vogue – Coral)
Louis Armstrong/Earl Hines, Armstrong & Hines, 1928 (Smithsonian Collection/—)
Jimmie Noone 1937-1941 (Collector's Classics – Denmark)
Various (Including Jimmie Noone), New Orleans, Vol 3 (RCA Victor – France)
Kid Ory & Jimmie Noone (—/Avenue – International)

Red Norvo

Red Norvo (real name: Kenneth Norville) single-handedly made the xylophone into a valid, respect-

achieved some popularity. (Tal Farlow, Charles Mingus (♦) were in first line-up; Jimmy Raney (♦), Red Mitchell, their replacements).

Although lacking in basic excitement, Red Norvo Trio (**The Red Norvo Trio/The Savoy Sessions**) did produce consistently fine music, the interplay between the respective musicians being the most notable attribute. Without ever changing his style, Norvo was very warmly disposed towards Bebop. In 1945, for example, he led an all-star sextet (including Charlie Parker (♦) and Dizzy Gillespie (♦)) through a generally satisfactory mainstream-bop record date (**Fabulous Jam Session**). For several years after this he was often to be found in presence of young bop-type musicians (Gerry Mulligan Tentet: **Walking Shoes (Plus Red Norvo & Stan Hasselgard)**) and during 1950s his combos tended to reflect much of the then prevalent cool West Coast sounds (**Ad Lib**).

First overseas trip, with Jazz Club USA unit, in 1954, then to Australia in '56. Red Norvo Quintet (as it was at the time) incorporated by Benny Goodman within a 10-piece band which toured Europe in '59. With Goodman again two years later. Subsequently has spent most of his working time in California (often working in bands accompanying Frank Sinatra). Has made very few records during past 20 years which might be called important, though some, like those in 1954 and 1957 respectively (**The Greatest Of The Small Bands, Vol 1**) contain music of excellent quality; especially the latter date, which benefits enormously from the presence of Ben Webster (♦) and Harry Edison (♦). Norvo's playing during a 1969 tour of Europe, as member of Newport All Stars is documented on **Tribute To Duke**, as is his appearance at a 1970 University of Pasadena concert (**The Complete 1970 Pasadena Jazz Party**). On both dates, Norvo performs in admirable fashion. Red Norvo is still active as a musician and he still plays as if he enjoys every moment . . .

Recordings:
Red Norvo & His All Stars
(Epic/Philips)
Mildred Bailey: Her Greatest Performances (1929-1946), Vols 1-3 *(Columbia/CBS)*
Benny Goodman 1945
(CBS – Holland)
Woody Herman, The Thundering Herds
(Columbia)
Various (Including Red Norvo), The Herdsmen *(Mercury)*
Red Norvo, Town Hall Concert, Vol 1 *(London)*
The Red Norvo Trio/The Savoy Sessions *(Savoy/—)*
Gerry Mulligan Tentette: Walking Shoes (Plus Red Norvo & Stan Hasselgard)
(Capitol/Capitol – Holland)
Red Norvo, Ad Lib
(Liberty/London)
Red Norvo, The Greatest Of The Small Bands, Vol 1
(RCA Victor – France)
Various (Including Red Norvo), Tribute To Duke *(MPS)*
Various (Including Red Norvo), The Complete 1970 Pasadena Jazz Party *(Blue Angel Jazz Club Presents/—)*
Red Norvo's Fabulous Jam Session *(Spotlite/Spotlite)*

King Oliver

Cornet player Joe 'King' Oliver was born in 1885, joining Kid Ory's Brownskin Babies in 1914 or 1915, and developing great expressive skills in the use of mutes. Oliver, like many New Orleans jazzmen, left for Chicago after the closure of Storyville in 1918, forming his own band, King Oliver's Creole Jazz Band. Various personnel changes occurred, with clarinettist Johnny Dodds replacing Jimmy Noone, Lil Hardin taking over piano from Lottie Taylor and Baby Dodds on drums in place of Minor Hall. In 1922, Oliver further cemented his dominance of the Chicago music scene by sending for the young Louis Armstrong, already a powerful contender for the cornet crown: 'As long as Louis is with me, he can't hurt me.' In 1923, the Creole Jazz Band became the first band to record in the New Orleans style, establishing a standard which was never to be surpassed. The loose counterpoint of the melody instruments, cornets balanced by trombone, clarinet weaving supple patterns between the brass, remains a model of symmetry. The intuitive understanding between the cornets in their brilliant breaks, the leader's mastery of the mute on the famous **Dippermouth Blues**, Armstrong's historic first recorded solo on **Chimes Blues**, or Dodds' work on **Riverside Blues**, all contribute to jazz's cornerstone collection (**Louis Armstrong & King Oliver** and **King Oliver's Jazz Band**). The former album also contains two duets between Oliver and Jelly Roll Morton, **King Porter Stomp** and **Tom Cat Blues**.

The strains of touring broke up the band by 1924, with Armstrong marrying Lil Hardin and the Dodds brothers and trombonist Honore

King Oliver's Jazz Band (EMI): legendary sessions.

Dutrey quitting. The following year, Oliver formed the Dixie Syncopators, usually a ten-piece band with three saxophones and tuba. Playing for dancers at the Plantation Cafe in Chicago between 1925-7, the band was commercially successful, and numbers like **Someday Sweetheart** and **Dead Man Blues** became King Oliver's best-selling records (**King Oliver's Dixie Syncopators**), though his playing on **Jackass Blues, Every Tub** and **Showboat Shuffle** is superior. Also included is Oliver's version of a number associated with Armstrong, **West End Blues**, a less dramatic rendering. From 1927 until his death in 1938, Oliver's decline was shown among scratch bands; pyorrhoea made playing

---

able solo jazz instrument, one which could safely take its place alongside sundry horns, keyboards, guitars, etc. Studied xylophone as a youth, but it was with the wooden marimba that Norvo made his first musical tour, in 1925 with The Collegians. Left band in Chicago, enrolled as mining student at University of Missouri (1926–7), then returned to music. Worked with own band at Station KSTP, and with Victor Young Orchestra. Moved on to Paul Whiteman (♦), where he met his future wife, Mildred Bailey (♦) (they were married 1933–45). Left Whiteman to settle in New York. Fronted an intriguing pianoless octet, with advanced-sounding arrangements by Eddie Sauter (♦). Enlarged band to dozen, employing Mildred Bailey as singer, and with Sauter as principal arranger. Records made by band (**Red Norvo & His All Stars**) are much sought after by aficionados of the period and those with a penchant for subtle, out-of-the-ordinary chamber-type music. Norvo's band (with Sauter often arranging) accompanied his wife regularly on recordings during 1930s (**Mildred Bailey: Her Greatest Performances (1929-1946), Vols 1-3**).

Worked regularly with various bands at all kinds of venues (mostly in New York), from 1935–44. Switched finally, in 1943, from xylophone to vibraphone. On latter instrument basic Red Norvo style

Above: vibraphonist Red Norvo, one of the veterans who has seen most of them come and go.

became even more apparent; little or no vibrato, subtle swing and fast technique (achieved by holding mallets close to the instrument). In 1944 disbanded sextet he was leading to become member of Benny Goodman (♦) aggregation (**Benny Goodman 1945**) and in June 1945, whilst still with Goodman, fronted nine-piece band at special New York concert, during which Norvo played vibes and xylophone (**Town Hall Concert, Vol 1**) producing a delicate, sensitive solo on **The Man I Love** with his first working instrument.

Joined Woody Herman (♦) in 1946, and although Norvo light vibes sound would seem to be totally unsuitable for deployment within the roaring First Herd ensemble, his presence gave the band an extra, if relatively unimportant, texture. And although his mid-period playing might have appeared at variance with the forward-looking Herd, his solos sounded fresh and hardly at all out of place (**The Thundering Herds**). Moved to California with second wife (Eva Rogers, sister of ex-Herman colleague Shorty Rogers (♦)), worked in freelance capacity and with own bands until returning to New York (1949) with sextet. Disbanded in '50, to front a vibes-guitar-bass trio which an agony, and his attempts to adapt to the changing musical climate were often ill-considered.

Pianist Clarence Williams used him on a fairly routine session with his Novelty Four in 1928, and Oliver plays well on **Blue Blood Blues** and **Jet Black Blues** the following year in an Eddie Lang group, Blind Willie Dunn's Gin Bottle Four **(Classic Jazz Masters: King Oliver)**. Occasional felicities are to be found among his late recordings for Victor **(King Oliver & His Orchestra** and **King Oliver In New York)**. At his death, he was working as a janitor.

Recordings:
Louis Armstrong & King Oliver
(Milestone/Milestone)
King Oliver's Jazz Band
(—/Parlophone)
King Oliver's Dixie Syncopators, Vols 1 & 2
(—/Ace of Hearts)
Classic Jazz Masters: King Oliver (Philips/Philips)
King Oliver & His Orchestra
(—/RCA Victor – France)
King Oliver In New York
(RCA Victor/—)

Original Dixieland Jazz Band

The Original Dixieland Jazz (originally spelled 'Jass') Band is of immense historical importance. For, in all probability, it was responsible for first recordings to be made by what truly can be said to be a *jazz* band – **Darktown Strutters' Ball, Indiana,** recorded January 1917. ODJB's next studio date (after being signed by Victor) produced **Livery Stable Blues** and **Original Dixieland One-Step** – which jointly became jazz's first big-selling disc. Most important of all, though, both ODJB's live appearances as well as its records together did more than any other one band or musician to spread the jazz word – first, in the US, thence to Europe and to other parts of the globe. Earliest ODJB comprised Dominic James ('Nick') La Rocca, cornet; Alcide Nunez, clarinet; 'Eddie' Edwards (Edwin Bransford), trombone; Henry Ragas, piano; Johnny Stein, drums. This quintet made its first live appearance at Schiller's Cafe, Chicago, in 1916. By the time band was making initial records, Nunez had been fired and replaced by Chicagoan Larry Shields (by concensus, ODJB's best soloist), and New Orleansian Tony Sbarbaro (Spargo) had joined in place of Stein. This personnel comprised lineup with which ODJB, for almost a decade, was to find fame and fortune. Band was given special boost by Al Jolson, whose influence enabled it to obtain prestigious gig at plush Reisenweber's, NYC (1917). ODJB's tremendous success at Reisenweber's, celebrated by band with its Aeolian recording of **Reisenweber Rag** (ODJB/ Louisiana Five), led to trip to UK where band appeared not only for London Palladium season but also – privately – for members of British Royal Family, by which time J. Russel Robinson had re-

Right: Edward 'Kid' Ory – the man who virtually single-handedly invented the jazz phrase 'tailgate trombone'.

placed Ragas (who died in 1918). Band recorded for Columbia whilst in London, during its lengthy stay in Britain. Continued to record for Victor on return to States. But by time 1920s had arrived its popularity began to wane – ODJB disbanded in 1925, Larry Shields having left in 1921. A revived ODJB recorded again in '35; the following year, Victor recorded **Nick La Rocca & His Original Dixieland Band** – this lineup included, La Rocca apart, Sbarbaro, and Robinson from ODJB's halcyon days in an otherwise ordinary-sounding big-band setting of dozen ODJB titles. La Rocca, Shields, Sbarbaro, Robinson, and Edwards (but minus altoist Benny Krueger, who had joined band in 1920) made final ODJB recordings in 1936 – again, efforts to rekindle spirit of earlier times resulted in music barely memorable. Finally, a six-piece outfit directed by Edwards recorded for Bluebird in 1938 – this time, only Shields, Sbarbaro remained of former ODJB colleagues. Later, in 1945 and 1946, Edwards recorded with own Original Dixieland Jazz Band **(Eddie Edwards & His Original Dixieland Jazz Band)** for Commodore. Once more drummer Sbarbaro was also present as representative of the past. Other musicians who took part in what were further re-creations of ODJB material included trumpeters Max Kaminsky (♦), Wild Bill Davison (♦), clarinettist Brad Gowans, guitarist Eddie

Condon (♦), and pianists Gene Schroeder, Teddy Roy. Ironically, these sides are far superior to efforts by the original band, certainly in terms of rhythmic flexibility and superior all-round solos (including those by ODJB veteran Edwards).

Amongst ODJB's most popular recordings from 1917–24 can be numbered: **Livery Stable Blues, Original Dixieland One-Step, At The Jazz Band Ball, Ostrich Walk, Tiger Rag, Sensation, Skeleton Jangle, Clarinet Marmalade** (composed jointly by Ragas, Shields: all on **Original Dixieland Jazz Band)**. From purely musical standpoint, the ODJB scarcely compares with classic black combos of early jazz – nor indeed with many of the superior white outfits like Original Memphis Five, McKenzie-Condon Chicagoans or those front-

ed by Miff Mole (♦), Eddie Lang (♦) and Joe Venuti (♦).

Rhythmically, band's records tend to make ODJB sound stiff and pedantic. Solo-wise, too, there is little about which to rave, apart from Shields' usual sprightly clarinet contributions and the firm lead and elegant cornet solos from La Rocca. Historically, however, the Original Dixieland Jazz Band was a first – and an important one. For literary reference – *The Story of The Original Dixieland Jazz Band*, by H. O. Brunn.

Recordings:
Original Dixieland Jazz Band (RCA Victor – France)
ODJB/Louisiana Five (—/Fountain)
Eddie Edwards & His Original Dixieland Jazz Band (London/ London)

Kid Ory

Edward 'Kid' Ory's major claim to jazz immortality is not as a solo player. Ory's greatness was in his unsurpassed trombone work as an ensemble player. As a soloist, often he was rhythmically stiff and his creative powers were minimal – both aspects magnified when he was matched alongside a musician of inestimable greatness like Louis Armstrong (♦), in whose recording band **(Hot Five)** Ory played during 1920s. But his enormously powerful and uplifting ensemble playing, especially in classic New Orleans format, with extensive use of glissandi, made him the king of so-called 'tailgate' trombone players of early jazz. Ory also played, at various times during a career which spanned over 50 years (c. 1910–71), clarinet, drums, string bass, cornet, alto-sax (which he played, briefly, with King Oliver (♦) in 1926), valve-trombone (which

he used prior to switching to the slide instrument in his younger days), and banjo (his first instrument which he played from ten).

After visiting New Orleans on several occasions, Ory (born La Place, Louisiana, 1886) moved to Crescent City from around 1912, staying seven years before, for reasons of health, he moved to California. Invited several New Orleans musicians with whom he had worked previously to join him on West Coast, in new band which played that area regularly for several years. In addition, it became first black small combo to make records (1922). Gave up leadership of band in 1925 to record with Armstrong in Chicago. Results of first and subsequent Hot Five sessions resulted in truly classic jazz, with Ory's driving trombone standing out in ensembles, especially in numbers like **Muskrat Ramble, Skid-Da-De-Dat, Gut Bucket Blues (The Louis Armstrong Legend)**. Even better, though, was Ory's playing on recordings from 1926 by his and Johnny Dodds' (◆) New Orleans Wanderers and Bootblacks (**Johnny Dodds & Kid Ory**). And his contributions to Jelly Roll Morton's **Doctor Jazz, Black Bottom Stomp** and **Grandpa's Spells (Jelly Roll Morton & His Red Hot Peppers, Vol 3)** were of infinite importance in helping to make these and other Morton tracks on which he appeared assume similar classic proportions. With King Oliver (1925–27) he performed a similar role in admirable fashion (**King Oliver's Dixie Syncopators 1926-1928).**

Before returning to Los Angeles in 1930, Ory had spent previous two years playing in both Chicago and New York. After gigging with several West Coast bands and touring with Leon Rene Orchestra, left music altogether to help brother on a chicken farm (1933). Resumed playing career during early 1940s and between 1943–4 played mostly bass or saxophone. After widespread acclaim following appearance on Orson Welles radio show (1944) put together own Kid Ory's Creole Jazz Band. With a rejuvenated Ory roaring away in ensembles/solos, it became finest band he was to lead, as indicated via its 1944–45 recordings, including **Tailgate! (Kid Ory's Creole Jazz Band)**. Personnel included Mutt Carey, trumpet, Omer Simeon (◆) or Darnell Howard, clarinet, and Minor Hall or Alton Redd, drums. Continued to lead own bands during 1940s through early 1950s. Disbanded in 1955 because of health problems, but recovered to tour abroad on several occasions. **Muskrat Ramble**, his most famous composition, became pop smash-hit in 1954 after it had been given lyrics.

Had acting/playing role in film *The Benny Goodman Story* in '55, after previously appearing in *New Orleans* and, together with own band, in *Crossfire, Mahogany Magic* and *Disneyland After Dawn*. Regular performer at own club On The Levee, San Francisco, between early 1950s and 1961. After recurring ill-health, settled in Hawaii, playing occasional gigs in Honolulu. His final trip to Europe had taken place in 1959.

Kid Ory died at beginning of 1973, of pneumonia and heart failure.

Recordings:
The Louis Armstrong Legend *(World Records)*
King Oliver's Dixie Syncopators *(MCA Coral – Germany)*
Johnny Dodds & King Ory *(Columbia/—)*
Tailgate! Kid Ory's Creole Jazz Band
(Good Time Jazz/Good Time Jazz)
Kid Ory, When The Saints *(Good Time Jazz/Good Time Jazz)*
Various (Including Kid Ory), New Orleans Memories
(Ace of Hearts)
Jelly Roll Morton & His Red Hot Peppers, Vol 3
(RCA Victor – France)

Mike Osborne

The finest alto saxophonist outside America, the British Mike Osborne plays with an intensity that slices deep into the emotions. From an early Jackie McLean influence, he has added the freedoms of Ornette Coleman, and gradually emerged with a style that is all his own. His tonal range covers the oboe-like lower register and the squalling upper, and his frame of reference covers Bop classics, folk songs and a near-medieval estampe. A volcanic player – indeed, there seems no distance between the sound and the emotion behind it – his best work has been with players of equal stature, bassist Harry Miller and the mighty Louis Moholo on drums (**Border Crossing** and **All Night Long**) or in duet with pianist Stan Tracey (**Original** and **Tandem**) and in the all-saxophone trio with John Surman and Alan Skidmore (**SOS**). He is also a featured soloist in the big bands of Mike Westbrook and The Brotherhood of Breath.

Recordings:

Mike Osborne Trio, **Border Crossing** (—/Ogun)
Mike Osborne Trio, **All Night Long** (—/Ogun)
Mike Osborne-Stan Tracey, **Original** (—/Cadillac)
Mike Osborne-Stan Tracey, **Tandem** (—/Ogun)
Osborne-Surman-Skidmore, **SOS** (—/Ogun)
Mike Westbrook, **Metropolis** (—/RCA Neon)
Brotherhood Of Breath, **Live At Willisau** (—/Ogun)

All Night Long (Ogun): Osborne in searing form.

Above: two of the UK's finest altomen, Mike Osborne (right) and Dudu Pukwana. Intensity, and then some.

Hot Lips Page

Oran Thaddeus 'Hot Lips' Page (born Dallas, Texas, 1908) ranks with the greatest blues players – vocally as well as instrumentally – jazz has produced. Much influenced by Louis Armstrong (◆), Page's fierce trumpet playing and warm hoarse-voiced singing seemed at home in most jazz surroundings, be it as guest in one of Eddie Condon's war-time Town Hall concerts, or showing youthful exuberance during his solos with Bennie Moten's Orchestra (**Bennie Moten's Kansas City Orchestra, Vol 5**) or scatting in his own highly individual way while jamming at Minton's (**Hot Lips Page After Hours In Harlem**) with Thelonious Monk (◆) and others.

Page took up trumpet after earlier efforts to master clarinet and alto-sax had not proved fruitful. Eventually, started music career proper as member of blues singer Ma Rainey's (◆) accompanying band, his first trip to New York was accomplished whilst working in this capacity. Also accompanied other blues artists, including Bessie Smith (◆) and Ida Cox (◆). Gigged with various Texas bands before joining Walter Page's Blue Devils (1928), leaving in 1930 to work with Bennie Moten. With Moten his blues-based playing was apposite; at the same time improved as all-round trumpeter. Following Moten's death, fronted own quintet in Kansas City. Worked with Count Basie (◆) at Reno Club, KC, in '36.

Moved to New York, where he had no difficulty in finding work. Assembled own band (1937) which lasted for about one year. About same time as his band was due to start residency at Plantation Club, it recorded for Victor. It was a healthy-sounding outfit with an admirable regard for blues, but resting on the horn and voice of Page – the former passionate and strong on **Skull Duggery, Feelin' High & Happy;** the latter featured warmly and humorously on **Small Fry, I'm Gonna Lock My Heart (And Throw Away The Key)** (all **Feelin' High & Happy/Big Sound Trumpets)**.

Toured with Bud Freeman (◆), Joe Marsala (◆), then re-united, briefly, with own big band, worked with small combo on 52nd Street, before joining Artie Shaw (◆) Orchestra for five months (1941–2). With Shaw, was given valuable solo space, his features including **St James Infirmary** (vocal too) (**Artie Shaw & His Orchestra, Vol 2)** and **Solid Sam, Deuces Wild, Blues In The Night** (vocal and trumpet), and **Sometimes I Feel Like A Motherless Child** (vocal only) (all **Concerto For Clarinet).**

Left Shaw in January '42 to resume touring with own big band, but by mid-1943 was back to smaller size. Between 1943–9, played major cities with mostly small combos, although did increase for specific engagements. Recorded prolifically for Commodore label in early-1940s, with Albert Ammons (◆) (**Commodore Jazz, Vol 1)** and own bands (**Sax Scene)**. Latter included, variously, Big Sid Catlett (◆), Lucky Thompson and Don Byas (◆). Page's playing was admirably consistent throughout all his Commodore dates. Apart from his regular appearances with Condon at Town Hall, also worked with Don Redman(◆) (1945), and backed Ethel Waters (◆) during New York engagement (1946). Although choice of Page for Mezzrow-Bechet (◆) Septet dates in '45 (**The Prodigious Sidney Bechet Quintet & Septet** and **Sidney Bechet-Mezz Mezzrow)** was an obvious one, in practice the relaxation that marked his best work was missing for most part.

Visited Europe for first time in 1949, scoring heavy applause at Paris Jazz Festival. Same year, record by Page and Pearl Bailey (**Baby, It's Cold Outside)** made pop charts. Made four-months

RCA
LPV-576

Feelin' High & Happy (RCA Victor). The blues-based trumpet and voice of 'Hot Lips' Page operating at optimum level.

European tour (1951), then back to US for touring and concerts, etc. To Europe, again, in '52. Before his death in November, 1954, following heart attack, Page had continued to work at frequent intervals. Amongst other superior recordings in which Page was involved during his career was a supremely relaxed session co-featuring Teddy Bunn (♦) **(Feelin' High & Happy)** with both musicians playing (and in Page's case, singing, too) at their best. Also made some fine music at sessions featuring stellar sidemen like Lucky Thompson (♦), Vic Dickenson (♦) (1944) **(Swing Classics, Vol 1, 1944/45)** and Buck Clayton (♦), J. C. Higginbotham (♦) (1945) **(Swing Classics, Vol 2, 1944-45).** At various times through the years, played mellophone as well as, or in place of, trumpet.

Recordings:
Bennie Moten's Kansas City Orchestra, Moten's Swing, Vol 5 (1929-1932) *(RCA Victor – France)*
Various, All Star Swing Groups *(Savoy/Savoy)*
Hot Lips Page/(Louis Jordan), Jumpin' Stuff *(Rarities/—)*
Hot Lips Page, Feelin' High & Happy *(RCA Victor)/*
The Big Sound Trumpets *(RCA Victor – France)*
Artie Shaw, Concerto For Clarinet *(RCA Victor/—)*
Artie Shaw & His Orchestra, Vol 2 *(RCA Victor/—)*

Various (Including Albert Ammons), Commodore Jazz, Vol 1 *(—/London)*
Various (Including Hot Lips Page) Sax Scene *(—/London)*
Chu Berry, Chu *(Epic – France)*
Sidney Bechet-Mezzrow *(Concert Hall/—)*
The Prodigious Sidney Bechet Quintet & Septet *(—/Festival – France)*
Various (Including Hot Lips Page), Swing Classics, Vols 1, 2 *(—/Polydor)*

Walter Page
♦ *Count Basie*

Tony Parenti

Anthony 'Tony' Parenti (born New Orleans, Louisiana, 1900), son of Sicilian parents, always evinced healthy regard for jazz traditions, and origins of the music. Which is why, at a time when it was considered unfashionable, Parenti's piping clarinet often was to be heard in a definite ragtime context **(Tony Parenti-Ragtime** and **Tony Parenti-Ragtime Jubilee).** Parenti, whose father was Italian Peasant Army musician, started on violin. Studied at New Orleans' St Philip's School, played in Italian Band of Prof Joseph Tavernor for almost two years. Deputized for

Alcide Nunez in Papa Laine's Band, also playing similar gigs with Nick LaRocca. After leading own or working with other outfits, moved to and worked in first, New Orleans (1925), then, New York (1927). Worked with several society bands, and as deputy for Benny Goodman (♦) with Ben Pollack (♦). Much experience as CBS staff musician (doubling on saxophones) – Parenti fronted saxophone quartet, for broadcasting purposes and to make film short.

Joined Ted Lewis' band in 1939, after four years as member of Radio City Symphony Orchestra, remaining until 1945. Thereafter, Parenti's jazz abilities underwent something of a renascence. First, he worked with band of Eddie Condon (♦) (1946); then, both in same year, was with Georg Brunis (♦), and fronted own band at Jimmy Ryan's, Nick's, in New York, before rejoining Condon. Was with Muggsy Spanier (♦) in 1947 before joining Miff Mole (♦), in Chicago (1948–9). Spent four-and-a-half years with Florida-based Preacher Rollo Laylan's Five Saints, but by 1954 was back in New York. Regular figure at Metropole (with Joe Sullivan (♦), Zutty Singleton (♦) and others) and Central Plaza. Deputized for George Lewis (♦) in fellow clarinettist's New Orleans band (1959), and worked at Eddie Condon's Club ('62). By far longest bandleading experience during latter part of his life occurred between 1963–9, when he returned to Jimmy Ryan's, leaving only to start his own short-lived jazz spot

after which he worked once again as a freelance.

Active right up until his death – at Mount Sinai Hospital, NYC, following brief illness – in April, '72. Was student of, and something of an expert on ragtime. Happiest when in company of musicians like Condon **(We Called It Music);** Brunis, Wild Bill Davison (♦) **(The Davison/Brunis Sessions, Vol 3);** and also managed to fit his New Orleans-styled clarinet into kind of setting arranged for singer Jimmy Rushing (♦) **(The Odyssey Of James Rushing Esq.).** Of own recordings, Parenti was especially well served by two afore-mentioned ragtime-based albums, as well as by **Happy Jazz,** this time making music with likes of Red Allen (♦), Tyree Glenn (♦), and Hank Duncan (♦); and a 1955 quartet date for Southland **(Tony Parenti & His New Orleans Quartet)** finds him in splendid form. Parenti could also present convincing blues performances, nowhere better perhaps than **Blues For Faz (Tony Parenti-Ragtime Jubilee),** a 1949 recorded tribute to fellow New Orleans clarinettist Irving Fazola (♦). And for a glimpse of what City of New Orleans must have been like in his younger days, Parenti's reminiscences **(Music Of New Orleans, Vol 5 – New Orleans Jazz, The Flowering)** make for absorbing listening. So too do some New Orleans-recorded tracks from Parenti's earlier days, including **New Crazy Blues** and **African Echoes.**

Recordings:
Tony Parenti *(—/VJM)*
Tony Parenti-Ragtime *(Riverside/London)*
Tony Parenti – Ragtime Jubilee *(Jazzology/—)*
Tony Parenti's All Stars *(Jazztone/—)*
Tony Parenti & His New Orleans Quartet *(Southland/—)*
Eddie Condon, We Called It Music *(—/Ace of Hearts)*
Wild Bill Davison/Georg Brunis, The Davison/Brunis Sessions, Vol 3 *(—/London)*
The Odyssey Of James Rushing Esq. *(Columbia/Philips)*
Various (Including Tony Parenti), Hot Clarinets *(Historical/—)*
Various (Including Tony Parenti), Music Of New Orleans, Vol 5 – New Orleans Jazz, The Flowering *(Folkways/—)*

Charlie Parker

Charlie Parker was born in Kansas City in 1920, and died in the apartment of Baroness Nica de Koenigswarter in 1955, prematurely worn out by narcotics and alcohol. The key figure in the Bebop revolution of the '40s, and – with Louis Armstrong – jazz's greatest soloist, Parker's innovations still determine much of the course of jazz today. The impetus of Kansas City and the Southwest had congealed by the mid-40s, and Parker, nicknamed 'Bird' or 'Yardbird', sought alternative musical directions. His earliest recordings with Jay McShann's Orchestra in 1940 show a debt to tenorman Lester Young on numbers like **Lady Be Good,**

The Immortal Charlie Parker (London): jazz's supreme artist at his peak. Note sartorial trends of the period.

and great technical fluency on up-tempo features like **Honeysuckle Rose (Early Bird)**. **Hootie Blues** and **The Jumpin' Blues** find the young altoist further into complex harmonic changes, grace notes, and an oblique relationship to the beat: 'I kept thinking there's bound to be something else, I could hear it sometimes but I couldn't play it.' His experiments provoked mockery and abuse among the older generation, but young musicians were spellbound. Parker's concept was radical, affecting every aspect of the music. Harmonically, he pointed the way out of the diatonic log-jam into the wider field of chromaticism, using progressions that were new to jazz and sounded angular and unsettling to contemporary ears. In fact, without commensurate breadth of imagination, a musician could run himself ragged among that plethora of choice like a rat in a maze. Rhythmically too, Parker was the most imaginative player that jazz has known, accents falling on heavy, weak and between the beats, yet still making the line swing. He cut clean across the old four and eight bar divisions, moving in an up-rush of semi-quavers that would abruptly skid back into line with a simple and perfect phrase. He brought a harder edge to the music, an emotional force and passion that held his super-technical dexterity in subordination and revealed the man. His sound on alto is unforgettable.

In New York, Parker found a handful of musicians who were working along similar lines, men like Dizzy Gillespie, Thelonious Monk, Charlie Christian and drummer Kenny Clarke who congregated at the after-hours clubs like Minton's Playhouse and Monroes. Parker's first small group recordings in 1944 found him in mixed company with Swing players like guitarist Tiny Grimes, and his solos on **Red Cross** and **Tiny's Tempo** sit oddly amidst the chugging jollity **(The Savoy Sessions)**. The Parker-Gillespie combo made its debut on record, unfortunately

saddled with Swing drummers like Cozy Cole and Big Sid Catlett, playing their own material like **Dizzy Atmosphere, Groovin' High, Salt Peanuts** and **Shaw 'Nuff** which, for speed and complexity and imagination, stand as a manifesto of modern music **(In The Beginning)**. In 1945, the definitive Bebop group recorded for Savoy. Parker, Gillespie, a young Miles Davis, pianist Argonne Thornton, bassist Curley Russell and drummer Max Roach laid a series of masterpieces like **Now's The Time, Ko Ko** and **Billie's Bounce (The Savoy Sessions)**. The altoist's three choruses on **Now's The Time** are a model of modern blues playing, the swoops and descents in the line touching subtly on the notes of the chord, the shape of the solo infinitely elastic, accommodating double-tempo runs and unfamiliar chords like the augmented 2nd and minor 7th. *Down Beat* magazine failed to recognize its quality, awarding the track a no-star rating. Over the next three years, Parker added **Cheryl, Buzzy, Bird Gets The Worm, Blue Bird, Another Hairdo, Barbados, Parker's Mood** and **Constellation** to his Savoy classics, quintet performances with Miles Davis, Bud Powell or John Lewis or Duke Jordan on piano, Russell or Tommy Potter on bass, and Max Roach on drums.

In 1945, Parker went with the Gillespie Sextet to California for an engagement at Billy Berg's club, staying on when the rest of the group returned to New York in 1946. Playing at the Finale Club with the young West Coast Be-boppers, he turned Los Angeles into a second centre for the new music. He signed a contract with Ross Russell for Dial, cutting six incredible albums over seven sessions **(Charlie Parker On Dial)**. The first date produced **Ornithology, Moose The Mooche** (dedicated to Emry Byrd, Parker's pusher), **Yardbird Suite** and **A Night In Tunisia**, but the second, four months later, found the genius in a desperate mental and physical

condition. Russell's book, *Bird Lives*, gives a detailed account of the session which produced the nightmarish beauty of **Loverman**, stark, strident and unparalleled in its exposure of the artist's emotional depths. Following **Bebop**, where Parker was too sick to play, the altoman returned to his hotel, somehow set his bed on fire, and was confined in Camarillo State Hospital for the next six months. Following his release, he recorded some sides with singer Earl Coleman, **Dark Shadows, This Is Always** and splendid instrumentals like **Cool Blues** and **Bird's Nest**. Subsequent classic performances include **Relaxin' At Camarillo, Cheers, Carvin' The Bird, Stupendous, Home Cooking, Dexterity, Bongo Bop, Dewey Square, The Hymn, Bird Of Paradise, Embraceable You, Drifting On A Reed, Quasimodo, Charlie's Wig, Bongo Beep, Crazeology, How Deep Is The Ocean, Bird Feathers, Klactoveesedstene, Scrapple From The Apple, My Old Flame, Out Of Nowhere** and **Don't Blame Me** following Parker's return to New York. Most of these are quintet performances with Davis, Jordan, Potter and Roach, the band that Parker was using around 52nd

Charlie Parker On Dial (Spotlite): cornerstones.

Street at clubs like the Three Deuces. Illegally recording for Savoy as well as Norman Granz's label, he showed an Olympian disregard for the niceties of business, as did the scores of amateur recordists who taped broadcasts, club performances and concerts. Away from the studios, Parker's work often rises to greater heights of imagination and daring; the meeting with Woody Herman's band **(Bird Flies With The Herd)**; the extended blowing session with Chet Baker and altoman Sonny Criss **(Bird On The Coast)**; the pairings with Navarro **(Historical Masterpieces)** and Gillespie **(Diz 'n' Bird In Concert** and **The Quintet Of The Year)**.

In 1949, Parker brought his quintet to Paris; Kenny Dorham, Al Haig, Potter and Roach **(Bird In Paris)**, visiting Sweden the following year and playing with local musicians **(Bird In Sweden)**. Back home, signed to Granz's Mercury label, Parker appeared in a great variety of contexts. He had already toured with Jazz At The Phil, playing with altoist Willie Smith and tenormen Lester Young and Coleman Hawkins **(Jazz At The Philharmonic, 1946, Vol 2)** an idea which later produced the historical jam session with Parker, Johnny Hodges and Benny Carter, three great altomen together on

Funky Blues (The Parker Jam Session). With an assortment of woodwinds and singers, Parker recorded the brilliant **Old Folks**, while a session with Machito's Afro-Cuban band produced **Mango Mangue** and **Okiedoke**. **Just Friends,** from an album with strings, is a classic performance, the contrast between the conservative and romantic setting and the passionate alto curiously moving. The best tracks are to be found in the small combo setting, **Now's The Time, Confirmation, I Remember You, Kin, Chi Chi, Cosmic Rays, Star Eyes, Si Si, Swedish Schnapps, Au Privave, She Rote, KC Blues (The Definitive Charlie Parker)**. A 1950 reunion with Gillespie, Monk and Russell, and the unsuitable Buddy Rich on drums, produced **Bloomdido, Mohawk** and **Leapfrog**. For Prestige, Parker cut several tracks on tenor with Sonny Rollins and Miles Davis, using the pseudonym Charlie Chan **(Collectors Items)**.

With the advent of Bebop, jazz lost much of its audience, leaving Parker in the limbo between pop and art. His music reflects his predicament, alternatively wooing and defiant, sardonic and anguished: without the sounding board of an audience, he anatomizes himself. Parker's blues were an anthem for the dispossessed, celebrations of the fleeing moment, and one of the most revealing portraits of our times.

Recordings:
Early Bird *(Spotlite/Spotlite)*
Jay McShann, Kansas City Memories *(Decca/Brunswick)*
The Savoy Sessions *(Savoy/Savoy)*
Alternative Takes *(Savoy/Savoy)*
Dizzy Gillespie, In The Beginning *(Prestige/Prestige)*
Charlie Parker On Dial, Vols 1-6 *(Spotlite/Spotlite)*
Anthropology *(Spotlite/Spotlite)*
Bird Flies With The Herd *(Main-Man/Main-Man)*
Bird On The Coast *(Jazz Showcase/Jazz Showcase)*
Bird On The Road *(Jazz Showcase/Jazz Showcase)*
Historical Masterpieces *(Le Jazz Cool/MGM)*
Bird On 52nd Street/Bird At St Nick's *(Prestige/Prestige)*
Hi Hat Broadcasts 1953 *(Phoenix/Phoenix)*
Charlie Parker *(Queen-Disc/Queen-Disc)*
Diz 'N' Bird In Concert *(—/Saga)*
The Quintet Of The Year *(Debut/Vogue)*
Lullaby In Rhythm *(Spotlite/Spotlite)*
Bird In Paris *(Spotlite/Spotlite)*
Bird In Sweden *(Spotlite/Spotlite)*
Jazz At The Philharmonic 1946, Vol 2 *(Verve/Verve)*
The Parker Jam Session *(Verve/Verve)*
The Definitive Charlie Parker, Vols 1-4 *(Verve/Metro)*
Miles Davis, Collectors' Items *(Prestige/Prestige)*
Birds Nest *(—/Vogue)*
Collections *(Japanese Odeon)*

Evan Parker

Saxophonist Evan Parker is, along with Phil Seaman, Stan Tracey and Derek Bailey, one of the most original jazzmen Britain has ever produced. A leading figure in the

European free music field, he has worked with Alexander von Schlippenbach's Quartet and the Globe Unity Orchestra, as well as the comparatively orthodox Brotherhood Of Breath. Associated in the '60s with John Stevens' Spontaneous Music Ensemble, Parker formed a duo with percussionist Paul Lytton in 1970 (**Collective Calls** and **Evan Parker & Paul Lytton At The Unity Theatre**) in which the two musicians extend sonic barriers and produce some very inventive lines and textures. The Music Improvisation Company, with Parker, Bailey, Hugh Davies and Jamie Muir proved to be another fertile arena for free playing (**Music Improvisation Company**), while the saxophonist's collaboration with guitarist Bailey has produced some of the most adventurous music of the decade (**The Topography Of The Lungs** and **London Concert**).

Parker's style, taking Coltrane and Pharoah Sanders as a starting point, has evolved over the years into a tonally rich and intensely emotional vehicle for his essentially logical imagination, the furiously scribbled lines contributing to a musical shape of great originality. A demonstration of his skills on soprano saxophone reveals total command of free music techniques (**Saxophone Solos**), circular breathing, slaps, snorts and overblowing used to symmetrical ends. Involvement in Company, a pool of international free musicians, demonstrates his ability for concentrated listening and response to the collective situation (**Company 1**).

Recordings:
Collective Calls (—/Incus)
Music Improvisation Company (—/Incus)
The Topography Of The Lungs (—/Incus)
London Concert (—/Incus)
Saxophone Solos (—/Incus)
Company 1 (—/Incus)
Globe Unity 73, Live In Wuppertal (—/FMP)
Manfred Schoof, European Echoes (—/FMP)
Peter Brotzmann, Machine Gun (—/FMP)
Monocerous (—/Incus)
Company 2 (—/Incus)
The Longest Night (—/Ogun)

Leo Parker

Originally a Bebopper, Washington baritone saxophonist Leo Parker was a featured sideman with Fats Navarro, **Ice Freezes Red** (**Fats Navarro Memorial**) and Dexter Gordon, **Settin' The Pace** (**Long Tall Dexter**). Usually a

Let Me Tell You 'Bout It (Blue Note): boisterous baritone.

driving, bellowing player, his sensitive side is shown on **Solitude** (**The Foremost!**). Born in 1925, Parker began on alto, switching to the bigger horn for the Billy Eckstine band as Charlie Parker had the alto chair (**Mr B & The Band**). His work with Gene Ammons (**Red Top**) shows the honking influence of Illinois Jacquet – in fact, Jacquet once warned him off his stylistic territory. After a long period with R&B bands, Parker made a short-lived comeback for Blue Note (**Let Me Tell You 'Bout It**) and died in 1962.

Recordings:
Fats Navarro Memorial (Savoy/—)
Dexter Gordon, Long Tall Dexter (Savoy/Savoy)
The Foremost! (Onyx/Polydor)
Billy Eckstine, Mr B & The Band (Savoy/Savoy)
Gene Ammons, Red Top (Savoy/Savoy)
Leo Parker, Let Me Tell You 'Bout It (Blue Note/—)

Joe Pass

Guitarist Joe Pass has been on the scene since the '40s, achieving widespread recognition in the '70s due to shrewd management by Norman Granz. A veteran of countless sessions with a wide selection of musicians – Chet Baker, Bud Shank, Gerald Wilson, Les McCann, Earl Bostic and Duke Ellington – Pass is a complete professional. Since signing to Pablo, he has made triumphant appearances at the Montreux Festival (**Joe Pass At Montreux**) and JATP tours with Oscar Peterson, Zoot Sims, etc. A sensitive, lyrical soloist with a warm and sonorous tone, Pass can also sound like a full rhythm section in accompaniment. An album with another veteran guitarist, Herb Ellis, finds the two men plaiting melody and countermelody, and showing great empathy in interplay on numbers like

Surf Ride (Savoy): early Art Pepper and friends. Cover artwork uncredited; small wonder.

Cherokee (**Two For The Road**). A duet with Ella Fitzgerald (**Ella Fitzgerald & Joe Pass**) is relaxed and melodic, while the collaboration with Oscar Peterson reaches a more demanding artistic peak (**Oscar Peterson Et Joe Pass A Salle Pleyel**) with both players at full stretch. A pretty album with Peterson on clavichord (**Porgy & Bess**) has Pass dispatching rhythm duties until his solo outing on **They Pass By Singing**. Recently, the guitarist has expressed a preference for solo performance, and two of his finest albums, **Joe Pass, Virtuoso 1 & 2**, project the sort of rapt inventiveness that Pass personifies in a club setting.

Recordings:
Joe Pass At Montreux (Pablo/Pablo)
Herb Ellis - Joe Pass, Two For The Road (Pablo/Pablo)
Portraits Of Duke Ellington (Pablo/Pablo)
Ella Fitzgerald & Joe Pass (Pablo/Pablo)
Oscar Peterson Et Joe Pass A Salle Pleyel (Pablo/Pablo)
Porgy & Bess (Pablo/Pablo)
Virtuoso 1 & 2 (Pablo/Pablo)

Art Pepper

Born 1925, Los Angeles, Art Pepper is one of the greatest altoists in post-Bebop jazz, ranking with Lee Konitz or Eric Dolphy, but less well-known for a variety of extra-musical factors. Influenced by Lester Young, Parker, Konitz and Zoot Sims, Pepper's best work is poised on the knife edge between raw emotion and form. His early work with Stan Kenton and Shorty Rogers (**Artistry In Jazz, Blues Express**) and with his own West Coast groups from the early '50s (**Discoveries**) shows great technical fluency and the makings of an original style. 1956 found him in great form with tenorman Warne Marsh on numbers like Lester Young's **Tickle Toe** (**The Way**

Living Legend (Contemporary): Pepper's first in 15 years.

It Was!) while a group with vibraphonist Red Norvo features his own Zootish tenor on **Tenor Blooz**, and with pianist Russ Freeman for numbers like **Mambo De La Pinta** dedicated to the various prisons his addition had introduced him to (**Early Act**).

Pepper's life, narcotics, ill-health, prison, is similar to Chet Baker's, and the survival of his talent miraculous. In 1957, he made an album with Miles Davis' rhythm section of Red Garland, Paul Chambers and Philly Joe Jones; the results make nonsense of much of the critical comparisons between East and West Coast. **Jazz Me Blues**, a Dixieland classic, shows the altoman's freedom from musical snobbery, while **Star Eyes** is a searingly emotional statement (**Art Pepper Meets The Rhythm Section**). A later session with another Davis rhythm section (**Gettin' Together**) is even better, with Pepper's rhythmic mastery feeding on Thelonious Monk's **Rhythm-a-ning**, and his passionate lyrical gifts in full spate on **Whims Of Chambers, Bijou The Poodle** and **Softly As In A Morning Sunrise**. A recently issued obscurity features Pepper and the great pianist Carl Perkins in almost an hour of magnificent invention (**The Omega Man**). **I Can't Believe That You're In Love With Me** shows all the characteristics of Pepper's style, the clear, concise articulation, the pure tone, the in-increasingly fragmented melody stretched tight over an alternating pattern of rests and squeezed notes until it yields up a deeper, more anguished emotion.

Between 1957 and 1961 he cut a series of classic albums for Contemporary (**Art Pepper Meets The Rhythm Section, Gettin' Together** and **Modern Jazz Classics**) which use an 11-piece band and Marty Paich's arrangements of numbers like **Walkin'**, a great Pepper tenor outing, and a clarinet version of **Anthropology**.

Two further albums made with the perfect rhythm team of Jimmy Bond, bass, and Frank Butler, drums, are even better. Ornette Coleman's **Tears Inside** proves a fine vehicle for the altoist's own brand of tonal variations (**Smack Up**), while a programme of ballads like **Long Ago & Far Away** and **Too Close For Comfort** (**Intensity**) results in moving interpretations.

Most of the '60s were a wasteland of imprisonment and illness, but an album from 1975 (**Living Legend**) finds Pepper with an ideal rhythm section, Hampton Hawes, piano; Charlie Haden, bass; Shelly Manne, drums; all in peak form. An original, **Lost Life**, is an overwhelming experience comparable to Billie Holiday's **For All We Know,** the alto harsh and crying.

Recordings:
Stan Kenton, Artistry In Jazz
(Capitol/ —)
Shorty Rogers, Blues Express
(RCA/RCA – France)
Art Pepper, Discoveries
(Savoy/Savoy)
The Way It Was
(Contemporary/Contemporary)
Early Art *(Blue Note/Blue Note)*
Art Pepper Meets The Rhythm Section
(Contemporary/Contemporary)
Gettin' Together
(Contemporary/Contemporary)
The Omega Man *(Onyx/—)*
Art Pepper 11, Modern Jazz Classics
(Contemporary/Contemporary)
Smack Up
(Contemporary/Contemporary)
Intensity
(Contemporary/Contemporary)
Living Legend
(Contemporary/Contemporary)
The Early Show
(Xanadu/Xanadu)
Dolo Coker, California Hard
(Xanadu/—)

Carl Perkins

Born Indiana, 1928, pianist Carl Perkins was self-taught and used an unorthodox technique with his left forearm parallel to the keyboard. Centred in Los Angeles, Perkins was one of the finest pianists of the '50s, direct, sinewy and totally convincing as a blues performer. His one featured album **(Introducing Carl Perkins)** shows a Bud Powell influence and a very personal emotionalism on ballads like **You Don't Know What Love Is.** He turns up on another Dooto album **(Dexter Blows Hot & Cool)** as a virile

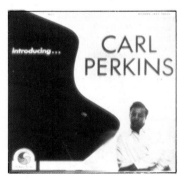

Introducing Carl Perkins (Dooto): collector's item.

accompanist for the driving tenor of Dexter Gordon. His work with the Curtis Counce group **(Landslide, Councelation** and **Carl's Blues)** featured some of his writing **(Mia, Carl's Blues)** and much of his finest playing. An album by practically the same personnel under Harold Land's leadership **(Harold In The Land Of Jazz)** contains Perkins' **Grooveyard,** a performance steeped in the blues tradition. Sadly, it was his swansong, for he died the same year, 1958.

Recordings:
Introducing Carl Perkins
(Dooto/—)
Dexter Gordon, Dexter Blows Hot & Cool *(Dooto/—)*

Curtis Counce Group:
Counceltation
(Contemporary/Contemporary
Landslide
(Contemporary/Contemporary)
Carl's Blues
(Contemporary/Contemporary)
Harold Land, Harold In The Land Of Jazz
(Contemporary/Contemporary)

Oscar Peterson

Oscar Peterson was born in Montreal, 1925, taken up by promoter Norman Granz in 1949 to make a startling debut at the Carnegie Hall Jazz At The Phil concert. Tatum-influenced, Peterson is a virtuoso pianist with an overwhelming command of everything from up-tempo numbers to ballads, great harmonic insight and a monumental swing. Not an innovator in the Bud Powell or Cecil Taylor sense, Peterson's style is securely anchored in the existing mainstream-modern tradition. A long-running favorite of JATP audiences, Peterson has worked with almost everybody throughout his career, contributing to the success of numerous Verve albums in the '50s **(Sittin' In, Soulville** and **The**

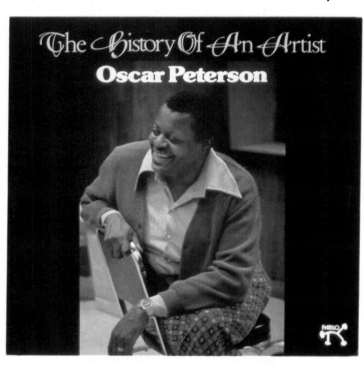

The History Of An Artist (Pablo): one of jazz' most prolific artists in a variety of trio settings.

Parker Jam Session) as well as heading his own groups. Starting as a duo with bassist Ray Brown, he has added guitarists Barney Kessel and Herb Ellis to form the famous trio, dropping the guitar in 1959 to take on a succession of drummers like Ed Thigpen, Louis Hayes and Bobby Durham. Two excellent albums map out his achievement in this area, one **(In Concert)** collecting highlights from 1950, including the famous **Tenderly** and **C-Jam Blues** and closing with the superb set from the 1956 Shakespeare Festival; the other **(History Of An Artist)** is a series of re-unions with past sidemen, recorded in the '70s.
Peterson's reputation, for years under attack as flashy, eclectic,

mechanical, reached a turning point with an undeniably great series of albums recorded at the home of a German recording engineer **(Exclusively For My Friends).** All four albums display his total commitment to the material, with the lengthy **I'm In The Mood For Love (Girl Talk); Satin Doll (The Way I Really Play); At Long Last Love (Action);** and the unaccompanied **Perdido (My Favorite Instrument)** outstanding. His recordings for Granz's Pablo label in the '70s have set the final seal on his emergence as a great solo performer, summoning vast orchestral textures from the piano. Two classic double albums of solo, duo and trio concert performances capture Peterson at his peak, with **Just Friends** a staggering display of artistic resources **(In Russia)** and the unaccompanied fireworks of **Indiana** and **Sweet Georgia Brown** rivalled only by the chases with guitarist Joe Pass on **Honeysuckle Rose (A Salle Pleyel).**
Five encounters with great trumpeters displayed Peterson's gifts as an accompanist, capable of varying his manner from stride for the older players **(Oscar Peterson & Roy Eldridge, Oscar Peterson & Clark Terry** and **Oscar Peterson & Harry Edison)** to the more harmonically complex backing on **Dizzy Atmosphere (Oscar Peterson & Dizzy Gillespie)** or waltz-time for **Take The A-Train (Oscar Peterson & Jon Faddis).** An album on clavichord with Joe Pass **(Porgy & Bess)** shows the same craftsmanship and lyrical imagination as his work on the piano. A meeting with Count Basie works splendidly, the two dissimilar styles – Basie economic, Peterson multi-fingered – respectfully deployed **(Satch & Josh).** Due to well-managed TV and concert appearances, Oscar Peterson is one of the best-known jazz names in the world today, and players like Joe Pass or bassist Niels Pedersen have achieved due re-

cognition by association with him in the trio.

Recordings:
Sonny Stitt, Sittin' In
(Verve/Verve)
Ben Webster, Soulville
(Verve/Verve)
Charlie Parker, The Parker Jam Session *(Verve/Verve)*
Oscar Peterson:
In Concert *(Verve/Verve)*
History Of An Artist
(Pablo/Pablo)
Exclusively For My Friends
(BASF/Polydor)
In Russia *(Pablo/Pablo)*
A Salle Pleyel *(Pablo/Pablo)*
Oscar Peterson & Roy Eldridge
(Pablo/Pablo)
Oscar Peterson & Clark Terry
(Pablo/Pablo)
Oscar Peterson & Harry Edison
(Pablo/Pablo)
Oscar Peterson & Dizzy Gillespie *(Pablo/Pablo)*
Oscar Peterson & Jon Faddis
(Pablo/Pablo)
Porgy & Bess *(Pablo/Pablo)*
Satch & Josh *(Pablo/Pablo)*
The Trio *(Pablo/Pablo)*
Peterson 6 *(Pablo/Pablo)*

Flip Phillips

'Flip' Phillips (real name Joseph Edward Filipelli, born Brooklyn, New York, 1915) is primarily remembered as one of the leading lights in the trail-blazing Woody Herman (♦) First Herd, with whom he stayed from 1944–6, and his ten-year gallery-fetching involvement with Jazz At The Philharmonic (1947–56). Basically, Phillips is a tenor-saxophonist who (still) plays consistently well in manner which suggests, though does not ape, elements of Ben Webster (♦) and Coleman Hawkins (♦), although there are occasions when a strong Lester Young (♦) influence prevails, very much so during a live recording as member of a Buddy Rich (♦) Quartet, recorded on location in Florida in 1957 **(Buddy Rich In Miami/Strike It Rich).** Originally, Phillips studied clarinet, theory with a cousin. As clarinettist, worked mainly at Schneider's Lobster House, Brooklyn, occasionally on alto-sax.
Joined Frankie Newton (♦) on 52nd Street (1940), playing clarinet; with same band at Lake George (1941). Switched to tenor-sax in '42 to work with Larry Bennett, in New York. Brief period with Benny Goodman (♦), then with Wingy Manone (♦), Red Norvo (♦), before joining Herman. With latter he established enviable reputation as warm ballad player on **With Someone New** (a Phillips original), **I Wonder, I Surrender Dear,** and perpetrator of exciting, hard-swinging tenor solos on flagwavers like **Caldonia, Apple Honey, Northwest Passage** (all **The Thundering Herds).** Apart from his work with the Woodchoppers (the Herman small combo used in conjunction with big band), Phillips recorded with colleagues Chubby Jackson and Bill Harris (♦), on separate occasions during 1945 **(The Herdsmen).** There was much

fine music to be heard too when Phillips, Jackson, Denzil Best, drums, and Lennie Tristano (♦), joined Harris for a typical 1947 New York club performance (**A Knight In The Village**).

Phillips' peak of popularity – exceeding his following with Herman in terms of fever-pitch response – came with his joining JATP. Basically, his employment called for Phillips to use all kinds of extreme devices (like Illinois Jacquet (♦) at his most extrovert), to raise JATP audiences to frenzies of excitement. **Perdido** (which for years he had to repeat ad nauseam) was the one number which brought Phillips his widespread following (**JATP: New Vol 6-Midnight At Carnegie Hall**) and it was something he had to try to live down for years after he left the Granz troupe.

Following his appearances with JATP in US (**Norman Granz, Jazz At The Philharmonic - Carnegie Hall Concert 1952**) Phillips (and JATP colleagues) made first of several trips the package were to make to Europe. Went to Japan with JATP (**JATP In Tokyo**) following year. As exciting as were Phillips' performances in this context, a better idea of his real abilities can be found in **Flip with Phillips** leading bands of varying sizes. Even though Phillips never crossed over into Bebop field, it is interesting (and, in the event, rewarding) to hear him inspire and be inspired by boppers like Howard McGhee (♦), Max Roach (♦), and Sonny Criss. Likewise, his playing on own 1950–1 tracks and others by an all-star Ralph Burns unit (**Kings Of Swing, Vol 2**) shows him in a more productive vein than all the honking and squealing effects of JATP days. Phillips was also to give a good account of himself at the legendary **The Charlie Parker Sides/The Parker Jam Session**, although not in the same league as participants such as Johnny Hodges (♦), Charlie Parker (♦), Benny Carter (♦) and Ben Webster. Was member of Gene Krupa (♦) Trio in 1952.

During late-1950s, settled in Florida, not emerging to play dates elsewhere. Co-led band with Bill Harris, who had also emigrated to Florida. Came out of Florida to tour Europe with Benny Goodman (♦) (1959). During 1960s, continued to prefer Florida climes, but started playing more dates elsewhere. That Phillips entered 1970s with talents undiminished can be gauged from his playing at two of the legendary US jazz parties. Indeed, during **The Complete 1970 Pasadena Jazz Party** his tenor appeared to have become more spring-heeled on the up-tempo numbers than in 25 years, and a re-working of his Herman ballad feature **Sweet & Lovely** is coated with a maturity that comes only from the wide experience in music of someone like Flip Phillips. And **USA Jazz Live** recorded in the Grand Ballroom, Broadmoor Hotel, Colorado Springs, as part of Dick Gibson's 1971 Colorado Jazz Party, finds him in equally fetching form, especially when paired with Clark Terry (♦).

Recordings:
Woody Herman, The Thundering Herds
(Columbia)
Woody Herman At Carnegie Hall *(Verve/Verve)*

Above: Flip Phillips, tenor-sax star of the first Herman Herd. Warm-toned Flip never fails to swing.

One Night Stand With Woody Herman *(Joyce/—)*
Various (Including Chubby Jackson/Bill Harris), The Herdsmen *(—/Mercury)*
Bill Harris, A Knight In The Village *(Jazz Showcase/—)*
Various (Including Flip Phillips), JATP: New Vol 6-Midnight At Carnegie Hall *(Verve/Columbia – Clef)*
Various (Including Flip Phillips), Norman Granz' Jazz At The Philharmonic - Carnegie Hall Concert, 1952, Vols 1-3 *(Verve/Columbia – Clef)*
Various (Including Flip Phillips), J.A.T.P. In Tokyo *(Pablo Live/Pablo Live)*
Flip Phillips, Flip *(—/Verve)*
Various (Including Flip Phillips), Kings Of Swing, Vol 2 *(—/Verve)*
Various (Including Flip Phillips), The Charlie Parker Sides *(Verve)/*
The Parker Jam Session *(Verve)*
Various (Including Flip Phillips), The Complete 1970 Pasadena Jazz Party *(Blue Angel Jazz Club Presents/—)*
Various (Including Flip Phillips), USA Jazz Live *(MPS – Germany)*

King Pleasure

Born Clarence Beeks, 1922, King Pleasure was one of the first vocalists to fit words to famous instrumental solos. Similar artists have been Eddie Jefferson, Lambert, Hendricks and Annie Ross. His biggest hits were **I'm In The Mood For Love** based on James Moody's tenor solo; **Parker's Mood, Little Boy, Don't Get Scared** from Stan Getz, **Sometimes I'm Happy** from Lester Young. His popularity lasted from 1952–6, with a come-back album in 1960 (**Golden Days**).

Recordings:
The Source *(Prestige/Prestige)*
Golden Days *(HiFi/Vogue)*

Ben Pollack

Ben Pollack (born Chicago, Illinois, 1903) was a good, if at times rather unimaginative, drummer who came into prominence at a time when Chicago was emerging as a major jazz centre. More important, though, Pollack fronted a succession of bands (first in 1926) into which came embryonic solo

talent, or instrumentalists in the process of acceptance as first-class contributors to jazz. Pollack himself played drums at school, and despite parental desires for him to enter fur trade, decided on career in music. After gigging in variety of bands in different parts of US, achieved breakthrough through association with New Orleans Rhythm Kings (Pollack made his first records with NORK (**New Orleans Rhythm Kings**) in 1922). Drums spiritedly on **Eccentric, Bugle Call Blues** and **Tiger Rag**).

Continued to find work with various bands – in Los Angeles, Chicago and New York – then, put together his first band (1926). Consolidated his bandleading activities during 1928, with prestige residency at Park Central Hotel, New York; plus an appearance by full orchestra in Broadway show *Hello Daddy*. At this time, Ray Bauduc was hired as temporary drummer whilst Pollack conducted. Pollack's idea of adding strings to line-up tended to lessen jazz impact, but when soloist of the calibre of Jack Teagarden (♦) was around to take care of that end of the business, music produced by Pollack outfits could not be all bad. **My Kinda Love (Jack Teagarden, Vol 1: 'Texas Tea Party')** is typical, with average band performance, dire vocal by Pollack and superlative trombone contribution from Teagarden. Pollack continued leading band through early-1930s until 1934, when he disbanded.

Many of the '34 band (including Eddie Miller (♦), Matty Matlock, Yank Lawson (♦), Gil Rodin, Ray Bauduc, and Gil Bowers) stayed together for inception of Bob Crosby (♦) band. Although he played less drums during 1930s, Pollack continued to lead various outfits, until 1942. Put together band in '42 for Chico Marx to lead. Following year, started own record label (Jewel) and booking agency. During 1960s, ran restaurant in Hollywood, with music supplied at various times by proprietor. Also played occasional gigs elsewhere. Appeared as himself in film *The Benny Goodman Story*. Apart from those mentioned above, musicians who worked with Pollack orchestras included: Irving Fazola (♦), Glenn Miller, Charlie Spivak, Benny Goodman (♦), Dean Kincaide, Benny Morton (♦), Dave Matthews, and Jimmy McPartland. And working with Pollack between 1935–6 was gifted young trumpeter named Harry James (♦) (**Harry James & His Orchestra 1936-1938**) destined to make huge name for himself when joining Benny Goodman in 1937.

Ben Pollack died at his Palm Springs, California, home, in 1971, by committing suicide.

Recordings:
New Orleans Rhythm Kings *(Milestone/—)*
Jack Teagarden, Vol 1: 'Texas Tea Party' *(RCA Victor – France)*
Ben Pollack & His Orchestra 1933-1934 *(—/VJM)*
Harry James & His Orchestra 1936-1938 *(The Old Masters/—)*

Jean-Luc Ponty

Born in a Normandy village, violinist Jean-Luc Ponty was the son of a violin professor, putting in six hours practice a day at the age of 13. A phenomenal technician, Ponty toured the USA in 1969, making a greater impact than most European jazzmen. A double-album from this period, with George Duke on keyboards (**Cantaloupe Island**) and a meeting of four of the foremost violinists, Stuff Smith, Svend Asmunssen, Stephane Grappelli and Ponty (**Violin Summit**) contains a good example of his jazz output. Ponty has gradually moved away into more popular areas; a period with the Mahavishnu Orchestra, a year with Frank Zappa and collaboration with Elton John have severed most of his links with jazz. Playing mainly electric violin these days with his own rock band (**Aurora** and **Upon The Wings Of Music**) Ponty's music has a romantic, often raga-like feel.

Recordings:
Cantaloupe Island
   (Blue Note/Blue Note)
Violin Summit *(BASF/BASF)*
Aurora *(Atlantic/Atlantic)*
Upon The Wings Of Music
   (Atlantic/Atlantic)

Bud Powell

Between 1947–53, Bud Powell was the most overwhelmingly creative piano player in the hothouse of Bebop. His drive – like Charlie Parker's – was a monstrous horse-power that shook the chassis apart, and Powell spent a good part of his life in mental institutions. There is nothing of the Joycean artist here, the creator paring his nails, indifferent. Powell is emotion in spate: ecstatic. The first piano album (**The Bud Powell Trio**) was a perfect translation of the Parker style on to the keyboard, and up-

tempo numbers like **Bud's Bubble** or **Indiana** show a speed of imagination and rhythmic variety that rival Tatum. The two Blue Note albums (**The Amazing Bud Powell**) give a broader picture of his genius. **Glass Enclosure** is a Powell composition in four distinct movements, opening ceremonially and quickly becoming angular and ominous before swerving again into the more familiar attack. It never settles for long on any mood, and its bewildering transpositions leave behind an impression of stasis. On bumpy, Bebop warhorses like **Ornithology** and **Reets & I,** the vertiginous flow of single-note, right-hand figures tugs solid chords from the left. Counterpoint and tension underpin the most fevered flights of imagination. Horn-like blast-offs abound in up-tempo numbers like **I Want To Be Happy,** the sudden dip followed by the plunging, high-velocity run in which every note is cleanly articulated. In Powell's music, off the ground and moving, the moment is everything. His treatment of ballads is deeply affecting, from the sombre, glowing **Polka Dots And Moonbeams** to the scampering **Somewhere Over The Rainbow.** The tracks with trumpeter Fats Navarro and tenorman Sonny Rollins, **Dance Of The Infidels, 52nd Street Theme, Wail** and **Bouncing With Bud** are classics of combo jazz.

Bud Powell's work with Charlie Parker is a meeting of giants, and the Massey Hall concert from 1953 (**The Quintet Of The Year**) has the unbeatable line-up of Parker, Dizzy Gillespie, Powell, Charlie Mingus and Max Roach, while the Cafe Society broadcasts find Parker and Powell joined by Fats Navarro (**Charlie Parker Historical Mas-**

The Amazing Bud Powell (Blue Note): Bebop's greatest pianist and one of the most emotional experiences in music.

terpieces). A meeting with Sonny Stitt (**Genesis**) found Powell at the height of his powers, sweeping through the session like a cavalry charge. From 1954 on, following a breakdown, Powell's work became inconsistent. Conflicting moods, misfingerings and loss of speed mark some of his playing, but the emotional and imaginative content remained unique. His interpretation of Thelonious Monk's **Round Midnight** (**Ups 'N' Downs**) is strangely disturbing in its massive chords and oblique timing, while a Blue Note date (**The Scene Changes**) finds him in good humour, funky on **Duid Deed,** simple and affecting on **Borderick** and confident on the up-tempo **Crossin' The Channel.**

In 1959 Powell settled in Paris, cutting an album with tenorman Dexter Gordon (**Our Man In Paris**) and with Coleman Hawkins (**Hawk In Germany**) both of which offer fine piano playing in accompaniment and solo. A meeting with the dynamic tenorman Johnny Griffin (**Hot House**) produced wildly exciting music, with **Straight No Chaser** outstanding. A trio album from the same year, 1964, has the ultra-fast **Little Willie Leaps** and the moving slow blues title track (**Blues For Bouffemont**). Great Bebop standards receive classic treatment on a live session from Paris' Blue Note Club (**Earl Bud Powell**) with the pianist in joyous command.

Powell returned to his hometown, New York, and died shortly afterwards in 1966. One of the most affecting players in all of jazz, comparable to Billie Holiday in terms of emotional impact, Bud Powell's technical innovations form the basis of modern jazz piano.

Recordings:
The Bud Powell Trio
   (Roost/Vocalion)
The Vintage Years

Left: the late, great Bud Powell, Bebop's foremost pianist. One of the most moving players in jazz.

(Verve/Verve)
The Amazing Bud Powell, Volumes 1 & 2
   (Blue Note/Blue Note)
The Quintet Of The Year
   (Debut/Vocalion)
Charlie Parker Historical Masterpieces
   (Le Jazz Cool – France)
Sonny Stitt, Genesis
   (Prestige/Prestige)
Ups 'N' Downs
   (Mainstream/Mainstream)
The Scene Changes
   (Blue Note/Blue Note)
Dexter Gordon, Our Man In Paris *(Blue Note/Blue Note)*
Coleman Hawkins, Hawk In Germany
   (Black Lion/Black Lion)
Hot House *(—/Fontana)*
Blues For Bouffemont
   (—/Fontana)
Earl Bud Powell
   (ESP/Fontana)

Sammy Price

Samuel Blythe ('Sammy') Price (born Honey Grove, Texas, 1908) is a blues-based pianist of some considerable accomplishment, both as soloist and accompanist. After early experience on alto-horn in local boys' band, Price and family moved in 1918 to Dallas and he switched to piano. But after winning talent contest as dancer (1923), toured in terpsichorean capacity with Alphonse Trent Orchestra. Began professional career as instrumentalist in 1925, in role of accompanist. Fronted own big band in Dallas, then toured theatres, moving to Oklahoma City (1929) where he helped pioneer jazz on radio. Following this, worked primarily in Kansas City between 1930–1933. Subsequently, switched to New York (1937), where he obtained post as house pianist and sometime A&R man at Decca Records. As pianist for company, Price provided accompaniments for many blues artists during 1930s, 1940s, including Cousin Joe, Trixie Smith and Cow Cow Davenport (**Out Came The**

Above: Russell Procope, big-band clarinettist, saxophonist (Webb, Henderson, Carter, Ellington) of distinction.

Blues, Vol 2). Recorded with own Texas Bluesicians, also for Decca; combo comprised, variously, musicians like trumpeters Herman Autrey, Emmett Berry (♦), altoist Don Stovall, drummer J. C. Heard. Perhaps finest examples of Price's Bluesicians, on record, are to be found on **Battle Of Jazz, Vol 7,** with Price's driving piano more than adequately complemented by altoist Joe Eldridge, bassist Oscar Pettiford, trumpeter Bill Coleman (♦), drummer Harold 'Doc' West, and tenorist Ike Quebec.

Price was familiar figure in 52nd Street during same decade. Also appeared in pit band for Tallulah Bankhead play *Clash By Night.* Starred at 1948 Nice Jazz Festival – first European visit – also recording in Paris, with Kenny Clarke (♦). Heard regularly in company with Sidney Bechet (♦), including historic Bechet-Mezzrow recording sessions of 1945, 1947 **(Bechet-Mezzrow Quintet** and **The Prodigious Sidney Bechet-Mezz Mezzrow Quintet & Septet)** which included solo features for Price like **Gully Low Blues** and **Cow Cow Blues,** plus fine duet between Price and drummer Big Sid Catlett (♦) – **Boogin' With Big Sid.** Ran two night-clubs in Dallas during early 1950s, but by '54 had moved back to NYC.

During latter year, recorded with Jimmy Rushing (♦) **(Going To Chicago).** Between December 1955 and spring of '56, toured Europe, leading own combo.

Worked in Switzerland for one month during following year, returning to tour Europe in 1958. Was regular at Metropole, New York – mostly with Henry 'Red' Allen (♦) during late 1950s, early 1960s. Also played residency (1962–1963), together with clarinettist Tony Parenti (♦), at Eddie Condon's club. To Europe, again, in 1969, taking time off from string of concerts and club appearances to record in London, with British musicians like Sandy Brown (♦), Keith Smith, Lennie Hastings. Result: a fine comprehensively-swinging album, **Barrelhouse &**

Blues. Other superior examples of Sammy Price's hard-swinging piano-playing can be found on **Swingin' The Berries** with Emmett Berry, Guy Lafitte, Pops Foster and Freddie More; the self-explanatory **Piano Solo** containing 16 titles recorded in Paris in 1956; and **Feeling Good** a memorable Red Allen date from '66, with Price offering stimulating support to some of the trumpeter's finest latterday work, and also acquitting himself admirably in own solos. Producing archetypal Sam Price pianistics – potent combination of barrelhouse, blues and boogie woogie.

Recordings:
Various, Out Came The Blues, Vol 1 *(Decca/Coral)*
Various, Out Came The Blues, Vol 2 *(Decca/Ace Of Hearts)*
Various, Battle Of Jazz, Vol 7 *(Brunswick/Vogue – Coral)*
Sidney Bechet/Mezz Mezzrow, Bechet-Mezzrow Quintet *(Concert Hall)*
The Prodigious Sidney Bechet-Mezz Mezzrow Quintet & Septet *(Festival – France)*
Jimmy Rushing, Going To Chicago *(Vanguard)/***The Essential Jimmy Rushing** *(Vogue)*
Piano Solo *(Musidisc – France)*
Swingin' Paris Style *(Mahogany/—)*
Swingin' The Berries *(Columbia)*
Henry 'Red' Allen, Feeling Good *(Columbia/CBS)*
The New Sammy Price 'King Of The Boogie Woogie' *(Mahogany/—)*
Fire *(Black & White – France)*

Russell Procope

The lengthy career of Russell Procope (born New York City, 1908) has been largely dominated by association with five major big bands, plus one celebrated small combo. First of the notable larger

aggregations was that led by drummer Chick Webb (♦), with whom the altoist-clarinettist worked during 1929–30. Then followed four-year period (1931–4) with Fletcher Henderson (♦), one of the most important jazz orchestras of late-1920s/early-1930s. During this time, Procope (who had studied violin, alto-sax, clarinet as youngster) was heard mostly as clarinettist.

Clarinet Marmalade (The Fletcher Henderson Story, Vol 3) and **Yeah Man!, King Porter Stomp (The Fletcher Henderson Story, Vol 4)** are those recordings perhaps best-remembered from Procope's Henderson period. Subsequently, this accomplished musician worked with Benny Carter (♦) (1934) then Teddy Hill (1934–8) before became constituent member of the highly musical John Kirby (♦) Sextet (1938–45), with whom he soloed exclusively on alto-sax. Also contributed neat, swinging, if unimportant solos to recordings by Mildred Bailey (♦), viz **I'm Forever Blowing Bubbles, The Little Man Who Wasn't There (Boss Of The Bass);** Frankie Newton (♦); Jelly Roll Morton (♦) **(Jelly Roll Morton, Vol 5);** Coleman Hawkins (♦); Red Allen (♦) **(Recordings Made Between 1930 & 1941);** and Clarence Williams (♦) **(Country Goes To Town).**

But it was after joining Duke Ellington (♦), as lead alto, that Procope, finally, established a real international reputation.

Procope, who worked with Ellington from 1945 until the Maestro's death, has been semi-active since that time. Ellington used twin instrumental talents to good effect, mostly as a reminder of earlier jazz influences. As clarinet soloist, his warm, woody New Orleans-influenced playing contrasted, on many occasions, with the studied, academic approach of Jimmy Hamilton (♦).

Amongst superior examples of Procope's clarinet with Ellington can be numbered **Creole Love Call (Historically Speaking, The Duke/Stomp, Look & Listen),** **Swamp Goo (The Greatest Jazz Concert In The World), Christopher Columbus (Recollections Of The Big Band Era), 4.30 Blues**

(Duke Ellington's 70th Birthday Concert), La Plus Belle Africaine (Togo Brava Suite/The English Concert), Mood Indigo (Masterpieces By Ellington), Red Carpet (Ellington Jazz Party) and Blues To Be There (Ellington At Newport). Procope also produced superior clarinet solos on record dates with Earl Hines (♦) (Black & Tan Fantasy and Once Upon A Time) and Johnny Hodges (♦) (Cue For Saxophone), his playing throughout last-named LP as good as anywhere else on record. On alto, features with Ellington included Things Ain't What They Used To Be (Dance To The Duke), Lady Mac and Up & Down (both Such Sweet Thunder), Festival Junction (Ellington At Newport) and In The Mood (Ellington '55/ Toast To The Duke).

Recordings:
The Fletcher Henderson Story *(Columbia)/*
The Fletcher Henderson Story, Vols 3, 4 *(CBS)*
Coleman Hawkins, Recordings Made Between 1930 & 1941 *(CBS – France)*
Jelly Roll Morton, Vol 5 *(RCA Victor – France)*
Various (Including Mildred Bailey, Frankie Newton, John Kirby), Boss Of The Bass *(Columbia/—)*
Clarence Williams, Country Goes To Town *(RCA Victor – France)*
Duke Ellington, Historically Speaking, The Duke *(Bethlehem)/*
Stomp, Look & Listen *(Ember)*
Duke Ellington, Dance To The Duke *(Capitol/Capitol – France)*
Duke Ellington, Ellington '55 *(Capitol)/*
Toast To The Duke *(World Record Club)*
Duke Ellington, Such Sweet Thunder *(Columbia/CBS – Realm)*
Duke Ellington, Ellington At Newport *(Columbia/—)*
Duke Ellington, Masterpieces By Ellington *(Columbia/Philips)*
Duke Ellington, Recollections Of The Big Band Era *(Atlantic/—)*
Duke Ellington's 70th Birthday Concert *(Solid State/United Artists)*
Duke Ellington, Togo Brava Suite *(United Artists)/*
The English Concert *(United Artists)*
Various (Including Duke Ellington), The Greatest Jazz Concert In The World *(Pablo/Pablo)*
Duke Ellington, Ellington Jazz Party *(Columbia/Philips)*
Earl Hines, Once Upon A Time *(Impulse/Impulse)*
Billy Strayhorn/Johnny Hodges, Cue For Saxophone *(Master Jazz Recordings/Vocalion)*
John Kirby, The Biggest Little Band In The Land *(Trip/DJM)*
John Kirby, John Kirby & His Orchestra 1941-1942 *(RCA Victor – Germany)*

Don Pullen

Avant-garde pianist Don Pullen's debut was with the Giuseppi Logan Quartet, where he and drummer Milford Graves supplied most of the interest. Their partnership continued through two duo albums recorded at Yale University in 1966 **(Nommo** and **In Concert)** which are something of a classic in Free Music. Their improvisations intersect and diverge in an ever-changing flow, the pianist's variety of keyboard device staggering in its complexity and inventiveness. Dissonant, scattering handfuls of tone clusters, the texture of Pullen's music is similar to Cecil Taylor's, but less abrupt and dramatic.

Having established a near-legendary reputation, Pullen disappeared for a decade into the anonymity of the accompanist, playing behind singers Arthur Prysock and Nina Simone. A period with the Charles Mingus Quintet revealed hitherto unimagined facility within the traditional forms. On **Black Bats And Poles** his solo moves from fleet, boppish, single-note runs into harmonic areas, and back into a funky vamp, while on **Free Cell Block F, 'Tis Nazi USA** his playing is rhapsodic. Mingus' sense of tradition breaks down most of the artificial classifications, and Pullen's work within the group showed a mastery of varied idioms **(Changes One** and **Changes Two).**

1975–6 was a productive period, with Pullen recording with Sam Rivers **(Capricorn Rising)** and ex-Mingus colleague George Adams **(Don Pullen, George Adams** and **Suite For Swingers)** as well as three solo albums. **Pain Inside** shows his sensitive and effective use of the inside of the piano and a delicate lyricism, while **Tracey's Blues (Healing Force)** and **Big Alice (Solo Piano Album)**

Healing Force (Black Saint). Pullen solo.

move the funkiest blues in and out of tonality without ever losing the emotion.

Recordings:
Don Pullen & Milford Graves:
 Nomo *(SRP/—)*
 In Concert *(SRP/—)*
Charles Mingus:
 Changes One
  (Atlantic/Atlantic)
 Changes Two
  (Atlantic/Atlantic)
George Adams:
 George Adams
  (Horo – Italy)
 Suite For Swingers
  (Horo – Italy)
Capricorn Rising *(Black Saint/—)*
Don Pullen *(Horo – Italy)*
Five To Go *(Horo – Italy)*
Solo Piano Album *(Sackville/—)*

Healing Force *(Black Saint/—)*
Warriors *(—/Black Saint)*
Montreux Concert
 (Atlantic/Atlantic)

Ma Rainey

If Bessie Smith (◆) was the Empress of the Blues, then certainly Ma Rainey was the Mother of the Blues. Rainey (real name Gertrude Malissa Pridgett, born Columbus, Ohio, 1886) begat a whole string of classic (or near-classic) female blues singers – straight blues and/or vaudevillian in style, of whom Bessie Smith undoubtedly was the most extraordinary. Bessie Smith apart, most self-respecting all-time blues lists would include Trixie Smith, Edith Wilson, Victoria Spivey, Lucille Hegamin, Ida Cox (◆), Sippie Wallace, Clara Smith, Mamie Smith and Sara Martin. Rainey's first public appearance came at 12 when she appeared in vaudeville show, *A Bunch of Blackberries* in Columbus. At 18, married William 'Pa' Rainey – a dancer, singer, comedian. Couple toured with Rabbit Foot Minstrels show, also with Tolliver's Circus & Musical Extravaganza (1914–16), billed as Rainey & Rainey, Assassinators of the Blues. Her first recordings were for Paramount label in December 1923, aged 37. Whether material was pure blues or vaudevillia did not matter; Ma Rainey's majestic vocal

powers always were equal to the occasion. And only Bessie Smith could surpass that extraordinary Rainey vibrancy. Over the years, her accompaniments varied. The backgrounds provided by 'Georgia Tom' Dorsey and Tampa Red left much to be desired (in terms of overall singer-band rapport) during magnificent examples of blues vocalism to be found on 1928–recorded titles like **Hear Me Talking To You, Deep Moanin' Blues, Sweet Rough Man, Tough Luck Blues** and **Leavin' This Morning** (all on **Ma Rainey).**

Better, by far, were backings from earlier sessions (1924, 1925) which featured such as Coleman Hawkins (◆), Joe Smith (◆), Louis Armstrong (◆), Fletcher Henderson (◆), Kaiser Marshall, Charlie Green. Armstrong's cornet was, as always, a major asset on **Jelly Bean Blues, See See Rider, Countin' The Blues** (all on **Ma Rainey)** – and Smith, also playing cornet, was equally prominent on **Titanic Man Blues, Stack O' Lee** (both **Ma Rainey, Vol 3); Wringin' & Twistin' Blues, Chain Gang Blues, Bessemer Bound Blues** (all on **Ma Rainey).** Tommy Ladnier (◆) was equally complementary to the Rainey declamatory style on other recordings, like **Ma Rainey's Mystery Record, Cell Bound Blues (Ma Rainey, Vol 1).** Even more basic accompaniments are provided for **Dead Drunk Blues** (Claude Hopkins), **Mountain Jack Blues** (Jimmy Blythe), **Trust No Man** (Lil Henderson) (all on **Ma Rainey)** – each having piano as sole support. Rainey's humour (**Ma Rainey's Black Bottom** on **Ma Rainey)** contrasts splendidly with the despair of tracks like **Wringin' & Twistin' Blues, Deep Moanin' Blues** and **Daddy, Goodbye Blues,** or the sensuality of **Slow Driving Moan** (all on **Ma Rainey)** – and **Shave 'Em Dry Blues (Ma Rainey, Vol 1).**

Toured tent-show and theatre circuits during 1920s, fronted own show *Arkansas Swift Foot* in 1930. Latter fell apart whilst Rainey was on the road and she became one of Boise De Legge's 'Bandana Babies' for three years. 1933: Ma Rainey's sister and mother died, so she retired to Rome, Georgia, where she also ran two theatres. Ma Rainey died in 1939, in the town of her birth and where she had spent last years of her life. Much interesting background material on Ma Rainey and those she influenced to be found within *Ma Rainey & The Classic Blues Singers*, by Derrick Stewart-Baxter (see companion record below).

Recordings:
Ma Rainey *(Milestone)*
Ma Rainey, Vols 1-8 *(—/Rarities)*
Various, Ma Rainey & The Classic Blues Singers
 (—/CBS)

Jimmy Raney

Born 1927, guitarist Jimmy Raney is a master of that cool brand of Bebop that falls halfway between Lester Young and Charlie Christian. An infrequent visitor to the recording studios, his best-known work remains the sides he cut with Stan Getz in 1951 **(At Storyville).** In the passages of counter-point with the tenorman

Ma Rainey (Milestone). Mother of the Blues; many classic recordings are to be found on this LP.

Above: Tenorman Dewey Redman, whose combination of voice and horn comes on like the down-homest Delta blues.

and on solos like **Move, Parker 51** and **The Song Is You**, he shows his subtle melodic invention, the unemphatic surface with the muscular strength below. Collaborations with fellow guitarist Jim Hall have been long out of print, but a recent concert appearance found him playing two-part Bach contentions with his guitarist son, Chuck. A couple of albums for Don Schlitten's Xanadu label **(Live In Tokyo** and **Influence)** with Sam Jones on bass and either Billy Higgins or Leroy Williams on drums, find the great guitarist in great form, rocketing through **Anthropology** and **Cherokee** and producing, in his judgment, his best ever solo on **Darn That Dream.** Another recent album finds him reunited with ex-Getz pianist, Al Haig, an ideal partner of similar temperament **(Special Brew).**

Recordings:
Stan Getz At Storyville
(Prestige/—)
Live In Tokyo (Xanadu/—)
Influence (Xanadu/—)
Special Brew (Spotlite/Spotlite)

Dewey Redman

Born Fort Worth, Texas, 1931, tenorman Dewey Redman cut his debut album, **Look For The Black Star**, in 1966, which showed him to be one of the more conservative avant-garde players. In 1968 he joined Ornette Coleman, where his strong regional feeling (both men are from Texas) and his stylistic similarity to Ornette's tenor playing made him a compatible member of that demanding group.

Redman takes good solos on several albums **(Ornette At 12, New York Is Now, Love Call, Crisis** and **Science Fiction)** showing considerable development so that by the time **Trouble In The East** was recorded **(Crisis)** Redman was confident enough to handle the free collective performance. A light-toned player, Redman literally vocalizes through his horn, moaning and exhorting down the mouthpiece in tandem with his playing. Subsequent albums made under his own name invariably work best on blues material; **Lop-O-Lop,** a trio performance with the great Ed Blackwell on drums and Malachi Favors on bass **(Tarik); Boody,** with the great bass support of Sirone **(The Ear Of The Behearer)** and **Qow (Coincide).** Whooping and moaning, Redman seems to reach all the way back to the field holler. He is also a member of pianist Keith Jarrett's group, along with Charlie Haden on bass and Paul Motian drums, where his taste for exotic instruments – musette, maracas – forms a part of the ensemble texture. Tenor solos like **Rotation** are well-controlled and close to the orthodox **(Mysteries)** while **Inflight (Backhand)** motors along comparatively evenly over a surging groundswell of percussive effects.

Recordings:
Ornette Coleman:
Ornette At 12
(Impulse/Impulse)
New York Is Now
(Blue Note/Blue Note)
Love Call
(Blue Note/Blue Note)
Crisis (Impulse/Impulse)
Science Fiction
(Columbia/CBS)

Look For The Black Star
(Arista – Freedom/—)
Tarik (BYG/BYG)
The Ear Of The Behearer
(Impulse/Impulse)
Coincide (Impulse/Impulse)
Keith Jarrett:
  Birth (Atlantic/Atlantic)
  El Juicio (Atlantic/Atlantic)
  Death & The Flower
  (Impulse/Impulse)
  Mysteries (Impulse/Impulse)
  Backhand (Impulse/Impulse)
  Shades (Impulse/Impulse)

Don Redman

Arranger Don Redman was the pioneer of big-band jazz and his innovations determined the course of the '30s, establishing the size and relationship of brass, reed and rhythm sections. Even reading techniques followed the Redman pattern, departing from legitimate methods to get that swing. Born in 1900 in Piedmont, West Virginia, Redman was an infant prodigy, playing cornet, piano, trombone and violin before settling for alto saxophone. He was conservatoire trained, arranging for Billy Paige's band in 1922, and then working for Fletcher Henderson from 1923-7. Aiming at a blend of writing and improvisation, Redman's writing improved as the band's soloists became more flexible, but the great leap forward came with the arrival of Louis Armstrong in the ranks in 1924.

The New Orleans influence was dominant, and a great source of inspiration to Redman in its use of riffs, blues feeling and elastic but precise ensemble playing. **Sugar Foot Stomp,** a re-working of the King Oliver – Louis Armstrong classic, **Dippermouth Blues,** features Armstrong over an eleven-man band, as does **Copenhagen (The Fletcher Henderson Story),** while on **Words** Redman uses sustained chords from the three-man sax section under the trumpet. The pioneering use of saxophones playing together in harmony was a constant feature of Redman's writing, as was the clarinet trio on **Alabamy Bound.** By 1925, with musicians like trombonist Charlie Green, tenorman Coleman Hawkins and clarinettist Buster Bailey (Armstrong was replaced by Tommy Ladnier in 1926) the Fletcher Henderson band was equal to Redman's increasingly sophisticated use of sectional counterpoint, advanced harmonies and abrupt changes of rhythm. **Henderson Stomp** and **Whiteman Stomp** – also recorded by Paul Whiteman – are very advanced pieces, well in advance of the public ear **(Smack** and **The Fletcher Henderson Story).**

In 1927 Redman left to take over McKinney's Cotton Pickers, a novelty band until he took over the book. He built up the sax section into a formidable unit by the following year, contrasting their sweetness with other voicings in a growing pre-occupation with texture. Vocal routines like **If I Could Be With You One Hour, Rocky Road** (McKinney's Cotton Pickers) and **Gee Baby, Ain't I Good To You** brought the band considerable commercial success, which enabled Redman to recruit Joe Smith, Coleman Hawkins and Benny Carter from the Henderson band.

In 1931 he took over the Horace Henderson band. With soloists like trombonist Benny Morton and clarinettist Edward Inge, Redman's first recording session saw the unveiling of masterpieces like **Shakin, The African** and **Chant Of The Weed (Harlem Jazz),** and some fine arrangements like **Got The Jitters,** while **Sophisticated Lady** gives an example of Redman's clarinet, and **Tea For Two** to his soprano **(Don Redman).** His use of a swing choir, much imitated, in which the band sing a unison counter-melody to the lyrics, is shown on **Exactly Like You** and **Sunny Side Of The Street. Sweet Sue** is the best of late-Redman.

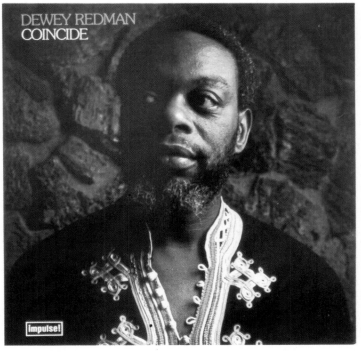

Coincide (Impulse): simultaneously moaning and playing tenor, Dewey Redman offers an updating of the blues.

In 1940 he gave up bandleading to freelance as an arranger, **Five O'Clock Whistle** for Count Basie, **Deep Purple** for Jimmy Dorsey, and numerous scores for Harry James, Jimmy Lunceford, Charlie Barnet, Ella Fitzgerald and Pearl Bailey. He took a big band overseas on a continental tour immediately after World War Two, and briefly directed Jay McShann's band in 1941. Don Redman died in 1964, one of jazz's most influential arrangers.

Recordings:
The Fletcher Henderson Story
(Columbia/CBS)
Smack (—/Ace of Hearts)
Fletcher Henderson & His Orchestra (—/Fountain)
McKinney's Cotton Pickers
(—/RCA Victor – France)
The Chocolate Dandies
(—/Parlophone)
Master Of The Big Band
(RCA Victor/RCA Victor)
Harlem Jazz
(Brunswick/Brunswick)
Don Redman (—/Realm)
**Louis Armstrong, V.S.O.P.,
Vol 5** (Columbia/CBS)
Bessie Smith (Columbia/CBS)

Django Reinhardt

One of jazz's most exotic legends, guitarist Django Reinhardt was the first non-American jazzman of originality. Born 1910 in a caravan in Belgium, Reinhardt was a gypsy, and his playing was a fusion of jazz and tzigane traditions. Forced to give up the violin after a caravan fire had mutilated his left hand (he retained the effective use of only two fingers) he concentrated on guitar and developed a highly individual technique.

His most famous unit, the all-string Quintet of the Hot Club de France, was founded in 1934 with Reinhardt and violinist Stephane Grappelli improvising over a rhythm section of two guitars and a string bass. Most of the interest centres around Reinhardt's lyrical and baroque contributions, his glittering single-string runs and occasional octave passages. The Quintet broke up in 1939 with the outbreak of war, leaving a legacy of fine recordings (**Django** and **Reinhardt- Stephane Grappelli**). Between 1935–9, the guitarist recorded with many of America's giants on tour in Europe, including Rex Stewart, Dicky Wells, Coleman Hawkins, Benny Carter, Barney Bigard, Eddie South and Bill Coleman (**Django Reinhardt & His American Friends, Vols 1 & 2**).

Django Reinhardt (RCA): a chance to study these figures.

Undeterred by the Occupation, Reinhardt soon recruited a new Quintet using a different instrumentation of clarinet and drums along with the second guitar and bass. The leader himself switched to amplified guitar, cutting down on his use of chords. A pair of albums from 1947 reflect the influence of Bebop on tracks like **Moppin' The Bride** and **Babik (Django Reinhardt)** though the habitual romanticism is evident on numbers like **Vendredi 13**. His inventiveness at tempo is illustrated by performances like **Lover** or **Apple Honey** which feature him with big bands, or by **Crazy Rhythm** with the re-united Hot Club from 1947 (**Django Reinhardt**). His best work tended to be at slow tempo, like the melancholy **Nuages** or **Crepuscule (Django Reinhardt)**.

Stories about Django Reinhardt are legion – his obsession with billiards, his obliviousness to time which led him to be late for one Carnegie Hall concert with Duke Ellington in 1946, and to miss the second; his restlessness, inability to read music, lavish spending. He died suddenly in 1953, a standard influence on subsequent guitarists. Composer-pianist John Lewis named a piece **Django** after him, acknowledging an affinity for the unique enchantment of his music.

Recordings:
Django (—/Oriole)
Django Reinhardt-Stephane Grappelly (—/Ace of Clubs)
Django Reinhardt & His American Friends (—/HMV)
Django Reinhardt (Everest/Xtra)
Django Reinhardt (—/DJM)
Django Reinhardt (—/Vogue)

Return To Forever
♦ *Chick Corea*

Buddy Rich

Born in New York, 1917, drummer Buddy Rich began in vaudeville at the age of 18 months, earning the nickname 'Baby Traps' by the time he was seven. He worked with the bands of Bunny Berigan, Artie Shaw and Tommy Dorsey, developing into one of the best big-band drummers of the swing period. In 1946, he formed his own big band with financial help from Frank Sinatra, with whom the belligerent drummer had stormy relations since their Dorsey days. With the decline of big bands, Rich joined Norman Granz's Jazz At The Phil unit and features on numerous albums from the tours (**Jazz At The Philharmonic, Vol 2**). The competitive, flamboyant atmosphere suited him well, better than the Bebop combo context with Charlie Parker, Dizzy Gillespie, Thelonious Monk and Curley Russell (**The Definitive Charlie Parker, Vol 2**). A typical Granz session pitted Rich against fellow drummer Gene Krupa, with the bristling Rich grabbing all the honours on **Bernie's Tune, The Drum Battle** and **Perdido (Drum Battle)**.

One of his best albums from the '50s remains the live session with Flip Phillips (**The Monster**) where

Drum Battle (Verve): Krupa and Rich slug it out.

his drumming combines with Peter Ind's masterly bass to drive the tenorman into some of his best performances. In 1966, Rich returned to fronting his own bands, with excellent arrangements but usually devoid of colorful soloists, apart from Rich. Two albums from 1968 represent the band's best work (**Take It Away** and **Mercy, Mercy**) the second including altoist Art Pepper. In 1971, Rich signed with RCA and recorded in the jazz-rock vein using an increased rhythm section (**A Different Drummer**).

Buddy Rich is a controversial figure. Some rate him as the greatest drummer of all time, others as insensitive and flashy. Technically, he is phenomenal; fast, accurate and endlessly driving.

Recordings:
Jazz At The Philharmonic, Vol 2
(Verve/Verve)
The Definitive Charlie Parker, Vol 2 (Verve/Metro)
Drum Battle (Verve/Verve)
The Monster (Verve/Verve)
Take It Away (Liberty/Liberty)
Mercy, Mercy (Liberty/Liberty)
A Different Drummer
(RCA/RCA)
Stick It (RCA/RCA)
The Roar Of '74
(Groove Merchant/Mooncrest)

Sam Rivers

Multi-reedman Sam Rivers was born in Oklahoma, 1930, of musical

parents both of whom were in The Silvertone Quartet, a spiritual outfit. Over the years, Rivers has developed fluency on six instruments: tenor, soprano, bass clarinet, flute, piano and viola, playing the latter at the Boston Conservatory of Music where he studied composition. In Boston he met drummer Anthony Williams who recommended him to Miles Davis, and Rivers went with Miles' group on the Japanese tour in 1964 (**Miles In Tokyo**) but left, finding the atmosphere too conservative. Together with his tenor replacement, Wayne Shorter, he appeared on Anthony Williams' date (**Spring**) and proved himself to be a dramatically powerful and original soloist; in fact, his work dominates this and the earlier Williams' session (**Life Time**). His own albums for Blue Note (**Fuschia Swing Song, Contours** and **A New Conception**) proclaim the essential logic behind his avant-garde stand. His compositions, like his playing, reflect a sense of jazz's continuing tradition, so that his forays into noise effects and sound clusters are never alien graftings. Unlike many of the Blue Note experimenters, Rivers stayed with it because it was a natural arena for his creativity. A performance like **Dance Of The Tripedal (Contours)** hangs together mainly due to the velocity of attack which effectively dismantles the theme. As a member of the Jazz Composers' Guild, he came to the attention of Cecil Taylor accompanying him to Europe (**Nuits De La Fondation Maeght**) and subsequently landing a contract with Impulse. At the Montreux Jazz Festival in 1973, Rivers led his trio, Cecil McBee, bass, and Norman Connors, drums, through an astonishing 50 minutes of music (**Streams**) playing tenor, flute, piano and soprano and sustaining the interest throughout the extended work. A collection of short pieces by the trio (**Hues**) was recorded the same year, and a big-band album showcasing his

Below: multi-instrumentalist Sam Rivers. His Studio Rivbea is one of the powerhouses of contemporary music.

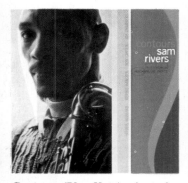

Contours (Blue Note): giant of free music plus house team.

unique writing talents **(Crystals)** followed.

Sam Rivers' development has been consistent, never aridly doctrinaire, always committed. He has run the Studio Rivbea for some years on a policy of open-house for experimentation, and is an established force on the New York scene.

Recordings:
Miles Davis, Miles In Tokyo
(CBS-Sony – Japan)
Anthony Williams, Spring
(Blue Note/Blue Note)
Anthony Williams, Life Time
(Blue Note/Blue Note)
Fuschia Swing Song
(Blue Note/Blue Note)
Contours *(Blue Note/Blue Note)*
A New Conception
(Blue Note/Blue Note)
Involution *(Blue Note/Blue Note)*
Cecil Taylor, Nuits De La
Fondation Maeght
(Shandar/Shandar)
Streams *(Impulse/Impulse)*
Hues *(Impulse/Impulse)*
Crystals *(Impulse/Impulse)*
Sizzle *(Impulse/Impulse)*
Wildflowers, The New York
Loft Sessions *(Douglas/—)*
Essence *(—/Circle Records)*
Black Africa *(—/Horo)*
Dave Holland – Sam Rivers
(Improvising Artists Inc/—)

Max Roach

Drummer Max Roach was born in 1925 in New York, and first came to prominence as Charlie Parker's drummer between 1946–8. Extending Kenny Clarke's concept of polyrhythmic accompaniment, Roach carried the beat on the cymbal and used the rest of the trap set for subsidiary rhythms which allowed greater mobility for the soloist. The Parker Savoys and some of the Dials furnish excellent examples of Roach's work **(The Savoy Recordings** and **On Dial, Vol 4).** Roach has recorded with most modernists of importance, including Thelonious Monk, Dizzy Gillespie and Bud Powell.

In 1954 Roach assembled a classic quintet with the great trumpeter Clifford Brown, and Harold Land or Sonny Rollins on tenor. Every album made by this unit represents an unbeatable peak within the Hard Bop idiom **(The Best Of Max Roach & Clifford Brown In Concert, At Basin Street, Study In Brown, Remember Clifford** and **Dahoud).** Sonny Rollins' **Valse Hot** was the first modern jazz composition in 3/4 time, and marks the beginning of Roach's interest in metric experiments **(Three Giants).**

Above: Max Roach; after thirty years, still jazz's greatest drummer. One of the Bebop pioneers.

In 1956, Brown and the group's pianist, Richie Powell, were killed in a car crash, and although Roach continued with Kenny Dorham and Ray Bryant, the unit eventually began to drift. Two good albums were produced; **Jazz In 3/4 Time** which includes an up-tempo and superior version of **Valse Hot;** and **Dr Free-Zee,** which is a drum solo

Speak, Brother, Speak! (America): the master drummer.

supplemented through multi-tracking with tympani **(Max Roach + 4).** In 1958, Roach was joined by another phenomenal young trumpeter, Booker Little, whose rhythmic confidence matched his own, and the collaboration produced some excellent albums. Dispensing with the piano, Roach's new instrumentation featured Little, George Coleman, tenor, and Ray Draper on tuba. At the same time, Max Roach's commitment to the growing movement towards racial equality gave a political significance to much of his writing, a fact which goes far in explaining the five-year blacklist from the studios in the '60s. The first of these

albums **(We Insist! Freedom Now Suite)** was the result of a collaboration with songwriter Oscar Brown Jr and features singer Abbey Lincoln. **Driva Man** opens starkly and violently with voice over tambourine, the lyrics describing the brutality of plantation life and giving way to a driving tenor solo by Coleman Hawkins. **Freedom Day** is fast and intense, while **Tears For Johannesburg** has a wordless vocal and a magnificent solo by Booker Little.

Roach's drumming style had undergone major alterations, and in place of the former crowded surface was a heightened and more ascetic style in which bar length was determined by the phrase. The finest album from this period **Percussion Bitter Sweet** featured Abbey Lincoln, Little and Eric Dolphy. Roach's playing here is very free and, as shown on **Mendacity,** carefully structured. **Tender Warriors** combines 3/4 and 6/8 without any of the self-consciousness of Dave Brubeck. Multiple meters and voices combine splendidly on **It's Time,** and an album from 1966, **Drums Unlimited,** has three solo drum tracks which display the breadth and logic of Roach's conception. **In The Red** has the leader playing very freely, and an excellent solo by James Spaulding on alto. A live album with tenorman Clifford Jordan, **Speak, Brother, Speak,** is one of the most exciting performances of recent years. Max Roach is the greatest drummer in modern jazz, and his style has influenced most drummers over the past three decades.

Recordings:
Charlie Parker, The Savoy
Recordings *(Savoy/Savoy)*

Charlie Parker, On Dial, Vol 4
(Spotlite/Spotlite)
The Best Of Max Roach &
Clifford Brown In Concert
(GNP/—)
At Basin Street
(EmArcy/Mercury)
Study In Brown
(EmArcy/Mercury)
Remember Clifford
(EmArcy/Mercury)
Dahoud
(Mainstream/Mainstream)
Sonny Rollins, Three Giants
(Prestige/—)
Jazz In 3/4 Time
(EmArcy/Mercury)
Max Roach + 4 *(Trip/—)*
Deeds Not Words *(Riverside/—)*
We Insist! Freedom Now Suite
(Candid/—)
Percussion Bitter Sweet
(Impulse/Impulse)
It's Time *(Impulse/Impulse)*
Drums Unlimited
(Atlantic/Atlantic)
Speak, Brother, Speak
(Fantasy/America – France)
Graz 1963 Concert
(—/Jazz Connoisseur)
The Loadstar *(—/Horo)*
Anthony Braxton – Max Roach,
Duo *(—/Black Saint)*

Jim Robinson

Nathan 'Big Jim' Robinson (born Deeringe, Louisiana, 1892) and Kid Ory (♦) were the finest – certainly the most important – trombonists from the area of New Orleans jazz. First instrument was guitar. Learned to play trombone whilst serving in US Army in France during World War I. Taught music theory by brother of bassist George 'Pops' Foster.

Returned to New Orleans after completing service, but did not play at all for several months. Then, deputized for absent trombonist in Kid Rena's Band. Worked part-time with Jessie Jackson's Golden Leaf Orchestra, Tuxedo Brass Band although full-time job was as longshoreman. Spent most of 1920s with Sam Morgan Orchestra **(The Sound Of New Orleans (1917-1947), Vol 1, Record 3).** During 1930s, with John Handy, Kid Howard (including dates with Howard's Brass Band), as well as leading own bands. Recorded with Kid Rena and Alphonse Picou (1940), although playing (Robinson excepted) was less than ordinary. Much better were those in 1942 with Bunk Johnson (♦) **(Bunk Johnson & His Superior Band, Bunk's Brass Band** and **Bunk Johnson)** with Robinson's powerful trombone anchoring the front-line in inimitable fashion. Robinson worked regularly with Johnson (1945–6) before returning to New Orleans to work in bands led by George Lewis (♦) and to resume playing in marching parades. With Lewis more often during 1950s, including overseas tours, and irregularly during 1960s. Recorded many times with the clarinettist, his sensitivity as well as his big sound being important in this context **(George Lewis & His New Orleans Jazz Band** and **Immortal Sessions: George Lewis & His Orchestra).** With Lewis, Robinson produced perhaps his greatest playing during the first recordings issued under former's name **(George Lewis & His New Orleans Stompers, Vols 1, 2)** which contain quintessence of trombonist's work

Above: Jim Robinson who learned trombone whilst serving in US Army in France during World War I.

as soloist and as contributor to classic New Orleans ensemble playing. His feature, **Two Jim Blues**, set against somber background of nephew Sidney Brown's tuba, is, in any language, profound blues-playing. Also much in evidence during recordings by Wooden Joe Nicholas (◊) **(Wooden Joe's New Orleans Band, 1945-1949)** and Sweet Emma Barrett **(New Orleans, The Living Legends: Sweet Emma Barrett – The Bell Gal & Her Dixieland Boys)**. Best of records issued under own name: **Jim Robinson & His New Orleans Band; New Orleans, The Living Legends: Jim Robinson Plays Spirituals & Blues** and **Jazz At Preservation Hall, Vol 2.**

Robinson toured with Billie & Dee Dee Pierce (1966–7) and with Preservation Hall Jazz Band (1969). Spent most of his remaining years in and around New Orleans. Died of cancer in 1976.

Recordings:
Various (Including Sam Morgan), The Sound Of New Orleans (1917-1947), Vol 1, Record 3 *(Columbia/CBS)*
Bunk Johnson *(Storyville/ Storyville)*
Bunk Johnson & His Superior Band *(Good Time Jazz/ Good Time Jazz)*
Bunk Johnson, Bunk's Brass Band *(Dixie/—)*
George Lewis Jam Session 1950 *(Alamac/—)*
Immortal Sessions: George Lewis & His Orchestra *(Saga/—)*
George Lewis & His New Orleans Stompers, Vols 1, 2 *(Blue Note/—)*
Wooden Joe Nicholas, Wooden Joe's New Orleans Band 1945-1949 *(Storyville/Storyville)*

New Orleans, The Living Legends: Sweet Emma Barrett – The Bell Gal & Her Dixieland Boys *(Riverside/—)*
Jim Robinson & His New Orleans Band *(Riverside/—)*
New Orleans, The Living Legends: Jim Robinson Plays Spirituals & Blues *(Riverside/—)*
Jim Robinson/(Billie & Dee Dee Pierce), Jazz At Preservation Hall, Vol 2 *(Atlantic/London)*

Red Rodney

Trumpeter Red Rodney, born Robert Chudnick, 1927, Philadelphia, worked extensively with the big bands of the '40s, including Jimmy Dorsey, Gene Krupa, Claude Thornhill and Woody Herman. Conversion to Bebop led him to association with the other modernists in Herman's Second Herd, most notably with baritonist Serge Chaloff **(Brother & Other Mothers)**. In 1949, his worship of Charlie Parker was rewarded by an offer to join the quintet. Ross Russell's book *Bird Lives*, describes how Bird beat the bigots by billing Rodney as Albino Red for a tour of the Southern States. He was an ideal foil for Parker, and in his eight-month stay recorded several excellent solos, **Si Si, Swedish Schnapps, Back Home Blues (The Definitive Charlie Parker, Vol 5)** and showed the same confidence and attack on the live sessions **(Bird At St Nick's)**. After Bird, he played with Charlie Ventura, but much of the '50s was written off to narcotics problems. In recent years, Rodney has made a convincing comeback, having lost none of his old bubbling viva-

Red Rodney: Yard's Pad (Sonet).

city and big sound. Currently based in Denmark, he cut an excellent album with the Scandinavians, altoist Arne Domnerus and pianist Bengt Hallberg **(Yard's Pad)** with driving trumpet on the title track and **Red Rod** and muted lyricism on **Informality**. During a British tour, Rodney recorded with the highly compatible Bebop Preservation Society, including altoist Pete King, trumpeter Hank Shaw and Bill Le Sage piano, a session which he declared his easiest and happiest ever **(Red Rodney With The Bebop Preservation Society).**

Recordings:
Brothers & Other Mothers *(Savoy/Savoy)*
The Definitive Charlie Parker, Vol 5 *(Verve/Metro)*
Bird On 52nd Street, Bird At St Nicks *(Prestige/Prestige)*
Yard's Pad *(Sonet/Sonet)*
Red Rodney With The Bebop Preservation Society *(Spotlite/Spotlite)*

Shorty Rogers

Born 1924 in Massachusetts as Milton M. Rajonsky, Shorty Rogers worked with Red Norvo and – most significantly – with the big bands of Woody Herman and Stan Kenton

as an arranger-composer-trumpeter. Leading his own groups from 1951 in the Los Angeles area, Rogers became the leader of the much-maligned West Coast movement. Critics have found the music rigid, emotionless and over-written, but the best of Roger's work – happily contained on the only two albums remaining in catalog – still sounds fresh two decades later. His 17-piece big-band boasted men like Art Pepper, Bob Cooper, Jimmy Giuffre, Bud Shank and Shelly Manne, and at least four tracks, the stomping **Short Stop**, the tenor-French horn chase **Coop De Graas, Sweetheart Of Sigmund Freud** and the moody **Infinity Promenade** are classics **(Blues Express)**. The original 10-inch album, **Cool & Crazy**, was a prized collectors' item fetching enormous prices, and the re-release has four extra tracks by a later outfit including Harry Edison. For sheer brass punch, the Rogers trumpet section with Maynard Ferguson screaming an octave above, takes some beating. His small group work with Giuffre, pianist Peter Jolly, bassist Curtis Counce and the driving drummer, Shelly Manne produced the fine **Not Really The Blues (West Coast Jazz)**.

Recordings:
Blues Express *(RCA – France)*
West Coast Jazz *(Atlantic/Atlantic)*
Clickin' With Clax *(Atlantic/Atlantic)*
Jam Session No 100 *(Jam Session/—)*

Adrian Rollini

Adrian Rollini (born New York City, 1904) was one of the most in-demand musicians during 1920s–1930s – not surprising, as he was an immensely gifted multi-instrumentalist, who could produce superior solos on bass-sax, vibraphone, xylophone, piano, drums, as well as two instruments

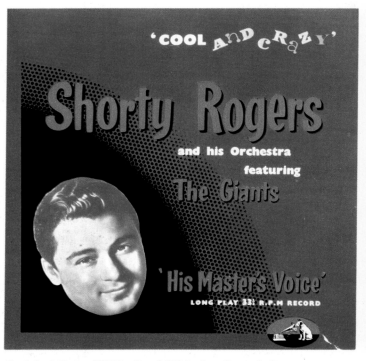

Cool And Crazy (HMV): the old 10-inch collector's item, available again. A big band classic from the West Coast.

he devised himself: a 'hot fountain pen' (miniature clarinet), and goofus (adapted from harmonica). Brother of saxist-clarinettist Arthur Rollini, Adrian Rollini was child prodigy on piano, giving Chopin recital at four, at Waldorf-Astoria, New York.

First professional work, in 1921, was playing xylophone in New York club. Joined California Ramblers, switching to bass-sax. Used this instrument in most intelligent fashion within ensembles of variety of bands with which he was associated, from California Ramblers until he gave up playing bass-sax during 1930s. Moreover, he became only jazz musician to master a basically cumbersome instrument and convert it into a convincing solo voice. Made notable solo contributions to recordings by Miff Mole (♦) (**Thesaurus Of Classic Jazz, Vol 2**); Red Nichols (♦) (**Red**

Adrian Rollini & His Friends Vol 1 (RCA Victor, France).

Nichols & His Five Pennies 1926-1928); Bix Beiderbecke (♦) (**The Golden Days Of Jazz: Bix Beiderbecke** and **The Early BG**); Jack Purvis (**Recordings Made Between 1930 & 1941**); and a myriad of recordings featuring Joe Venuti (♦) or Venuti and Eddie Lang (♦) (**The Golden Days Of Jazz: Stringing The Blues** and **Benny Goodman & The Giants Of Swing/Jazz In The Thirties**) and others. With Nichols, Rollini, mostly on bass-sax, was driving force behind recording band, Goofus Five (**The Goofus Five 1925-1926**) which produced charming, if lightweight, chamber-style jazz of the period.

Rollini was an average vibes player, accomplished technically, but rhythmically rather stilted. **Vibraphonia (Benny Goodman & The Giants of Swing/Jazz In The Thirties)** and **Vibraphonia No 2 (Nothing But Notes)** give adequate definitions of his style on this instrument. His efforts on hot fountain pen and goofus come into the novelty category, but like everything he attempted his solos on these instruments were musically impeccable. An average piano soloist, Rollini was an even better drummer, his crisp, tasteful brush-work on recordings by Freddie Jenkins and Bernard Addison (♦) (**Adrian Rollini & His Friends, Vol 1: 'Tap Room Special'**) being most impressive. Rollini managed to attract the interest of some of the best musicians available for his own record sessions, including Benny Goodman (♦), Bunny Berigan (♦), and brother Arthur, all of whom worked in studio under his leadership during 1933–4 (**Adrian Rollini & His Orchestra 1933-34**). Even better were recordings by Adrian's Tap Room Gang (music-

ally documenting own club he organized in 1935, at Hotel President, New York), as well as similar small-group sessions, also from 1935, featuring The Little Ramblers, Freddie Jenkins & His Harlem Seven, and Bernard Addison & His Rhythm (all **Adrian Rollini & His Friends, Vol 1: 'Tap Room Special'**).

Regrettably, from jazz standpoint, music produced by Rollini-led bands of post-1935 contained but minimal amount of jazz, leaning towards a more cocktail brand of music. Moved to Florida in 1950s, opening own hotel. Last-known job as musician was in Miami, in 1955. Died Homestead, Florida, 1956.

Recordings:
Miff Mole, Thesaurus Of Jazz, Vol 2 (*Columbia/Philips*)
Red Nichols & His Five Pennies 1926-1928
(*MCA Coral – Germany*)
The Golden Days Of Jazz: Bix Beiderbecke
(*CBS – Germany*)
The Golden Days Of Jazz: Eddie Lang-Joe Venuti (*CBS*)
Benny Goodman, The Early B.G. (*—/Vocalion*)
Coleman Hawkins/Jack Purvis, Recordings Made Between 1930 & 1941 (*CBS – France*)
Various (Including Joe Venuti/ Adrian Rollini), Benny Goodman & The Giants Of Swing (*Prestige*)/
Jazz In The Thirties (*World Records*)
The Goofus Five 1925-1926 (*—/Parlophone*)
Joe Venuti, Nothing But Notes (*MCA Coral – Germany*)
Adrian Rollini & His Friends, Vol 1: 'Tap Room Special' (*RCA Victor – France*)
Adrian Rollini & His Orchestra 1933-34 (*Sunbeam/—*)
Benny Goodman, A Jazz Holiday (*MCA/—*)

Sonny Rollins

Tenorman Sonny Rollins was born in New York, 1930, of a musical family. Coleman Hawkins was his first influence, although most of his direct aquaintances in the neighbourhood, Thelonious Monk, Bud Powell, Jackie McLean, were Beboppers. His earliest recorded gigs were with scat-singer Babs Gonzales (**Strictly Bebop**) and the Bud Powell – Fats Navarro combo (**The Amazing Bud Powell**) both from 1949 and revealing a strong Parker influence, ambitious but beset by technical lapses. Most of his pre-1954 work is like this, daring, driving, but the grand conception just out of reach. Early Rollins can be found in company with Miles Davis and Charlie Parker(**Collector's Items**) and on **Vierd Blues** he shows that his method of improvising was strongly based on thematic material, rather than merely running the chord changes. With the release of a 1954 album (**Moving Out**) Rollins gives notice of his arrival in the major league, charging through numbers like **Swinging For Bumsy** and **Solid** with massive confidence and vigor. Between 1956–7, he worked in the Max Roach – Clifford Brown unit, rising to the challenge of Roach's front-line drumming and unusual time signatures like the waltz-

time **Valse Hot (3 Giants)**. The fertile relationship with the drummer continued throughout Rollins' next albums, including his masterpiece **Saxophone Colossus**. Here, the tenorman's sense of architecture produced the great **Blue 7**, his improvised structure as formally perfect as a composition, yet losing none of the heat and immediacy of the moment. His tonal strength, muscular, declamatory, bites like an axe on a frosty morning, and his rhythmic mastery on his own calypso, **St Thomas**, is swaggeringly evident. Musicologist Gunther Schuller's analysis of the **Blue 7** performance probed so deeply into Rollins' creative processes that he vowed never to read the critics again. His output throughout 1957–8 showed that **Saxophone Colossus** had not been a fluke, and even a trio session with unfamiliar musicians on the West

The Cutting Edge (Milestone). Sonny in party mood.

Coast, bassist Ray Brown and drummer Shelly Manne (**Way Out West**) resulted in the magnificent **Come Gone** as well as demonstrating Rollins' penchant for odd material in **Wagon Wheels** and **I'm An Old Cowhand**.

A session with drummer Philly Jo Jones produced the incredible tenor-drums duo version of **The Surrey With The Fringe On Top (Newk's Time)** while a com-

pletely solo **Body & Soul** was intended as a homage to Coleman Hawkins who had cut the definitive version back in 1939 (**Meets The Big Brass**). Various sessions with Thelonious Monk (**Brilliance** and **Sonny Rollins, Vol 2**) showed the similarity of approach in structure. A live session with a trio, including the polyrhythmic drumming of Elvin Jones – subsequently Coltrane's partner – caught the tenorman in peak form on numbers like **Sonnymoon For Two (Live At The Village Vanguard** and **More From The Vanguard)**. In 1958 Rollins produced an extended composition of some nineteen minutes, with a dedication to the cause of Afro-American equality (**The Freedom Suite**), one of the earliest instances of the politico-musical statement that was to explode so forcefully in the '60s. Clearly a hot potato, for the record company deleted the dedication and re-issued it as **The Shadow Waltz**, the title of a short, noodling track on the reverse. There are superb performances by Rollins, bassist Oscar Pettiford and Max Roach, the interaction of the trio an outstanding feature.

In 1959 established as a jazz master, Rollins retired from public performance for two years. He needed time to re-think his playing in the light of new developments pioneered by John Coltrane, Ornette Coleman and Cecil Taylor, and he needed time to develop himself spiritually. A fan reported that Rollins had been seen playing high on the catwalk over the East River on the Williamsburg Bridge, and indeed his first album following the sabbatical takes its name from these al fresco sessions (**The Bridge**). Rollins states that he made the album because he needed the money for dental work, but the partnership with guitarist Jim Hall resulted in fine music, though little different from the pre-retirement period. The next album, apart from a couple of jolly bossa nova numbers, **Don't Stop The Carnival, Brownskin Girl**, does

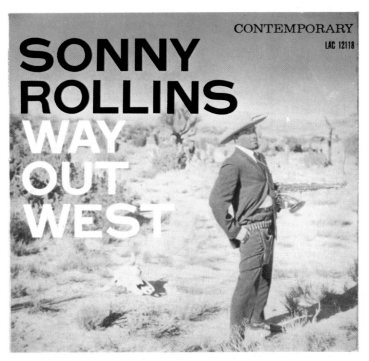

Way Out West (Contemporary): East Coast meets West in a masterpiece.

show some startling developments in tonal manipulation on **Jungoso** with the tenorman stuttering out the components of the theme in shifting accents, clipping notes, slurring, honking and sustaining notes for bar upon bar as he alters the pitching **(What's New)**. The long-awaited meeting with the New Thing occurred on his next album **(Our Man In Jazz)** with Don Cherry, bassist Bob Cranshaw and drummer Billy Higgins. Performances like **Oleo** illustrate that the great tenorman had a good deal in common with the younger musicians, for he had never belonged to the Hard Bop orthodoxy and many of his innovations – the tonal distortions, freedom from harmonic restriction, concern with sound as an expressive force – foreshadowed their revolution.

His experiments continued throughout the '60s. Rollins moved around as he played, angling his horn at the walls and ceiling, probing the environment for resonances. He worked out of doors, playing to streams and bluebell woods, and it came as a surprise to discover that he had recorded the soundtrack for that secular movie, *Alfie*. **Three Little Words (On Impulse)**, **Four (Now's The Time)** and **Blessing In Disguise (East Broadway Rundown)** show that the master was still at the height of his powers, though the oddly inconclusive treatment of **East Broadway Rundown** indicates deep-seated problems, and following this, he once again retired, this time for five years.

His output since his return has shown all his old supremacy of the tenor, but little of that intensity of spirit that characterized his work in the late '50s. His series of albums for Milestone are mainly very good, full of charging elation and beautifully played ballads like **To A Wild Rose (The Cutting**

Freedom Suite (Riverside):
Sonny's political statement.

Edge) or **Skylark**, while **Poinciana** showcases his soprano sax **(Next Album)**. Performances like **Playin' In The Yard** or **Swing Low, Sweet Chariot** with Rufus Harley on bagpipes are high-calibre funk **(Next Album** and **The Cutting Edge)** and subsequent releases show that Rollins is finding his energy in electric soul-beat contexts **(Nucleus** and **The Way I Feel)**.

Recordings:
Strictly Bebop *(Capitol/Capitol)*
The Amazing Bud Powell
(Blue Note/Blue Note)
Miles Davis, Collector's Items
(Prestige/Prestige)
Moving Out *(Prestige/—)*
Sonny Rollins *(Prestige/Prestige)*
3 Giants *(Prestige/—)*

Saxophone Colossus
(Prestige/Prestige)
Way Out West
(Contemporary/Contemporary)
Newk's Time
(Blue Note/Blue Note)
Sonny Rollins, Vols 1 & 2
(Blue Note/Blue Note)
Live At The Village Vanguard
(Blue Note/Blue Note)
More From The Vanguard
(Blue Note/Blue Note)
Meets The Big Brass *(MGM/—)*
Thelonious Monk, Brilliance
(Milestone/Milestone)
The Freedom Suite
(Milestone/Milestone)
The Bridge *(RCA/RCA)*
What's New *(RCA/RCA)*
Our Man In Jazz *(RCA/RCA)*
On Impulse *(Impulse/Impulse)*
Now's The Time *(RCA/RCA)*
East Broadway Rundown
(Impulse/Impulse)
Alfie *(Impulse/Impulse)*
Next Album
(Milestone/Milestone)
Horn Culture
(Milestone/Milestone)
The Cutting Edge
(Milestone/Milestone)
Nucleus *(Milestone/Milestone)*
The Way I Feel
(Milestone/Milestone)
Stuttgart 1963 Concert
(—/Jazz Connoisseur)
Graz 1963 Concert
(—/Jazz Connoisseur)
Don't Stop The Carnival
(Milestone/—)

Annie Ross

British singer Annie Ross has had considerable big band experience, working with Lionel Hampton and Jack Parnell in the '50s. Most usually associated with vocalese (fitting words to a jazz musician's solo, a technique pioneered by King Pleasure) Annie Ross recorded her interpretations of tenorman Wardell Gray's **Twisted** and **Farmer's Market** in 1952 **(Annie Ross Sings)**. As part of the vocal trio, Lambert, Hendricks & Ross, she appears on a couple of albums devoted to the Count Basie classics. The first of these **(Sing A Song Of Basie)** uses multi-taping to reproduce the sound of the entire band, with Miss Ross covering the trumpet section. Her version of Buck Clayton's **Fiesta In Blue** solo or **One O'Clock Jump** are gymnastic in the extreme, and later versions of **Jumpin' At The Woodside, Let Me See** and **Swingin' The Blues** show her phenomenal range and control **(Sing Along With Basie)**. Since her return to England, she has concentrated on stage revues and cabaret work.

Recordings:
Annie Ross Sings *(Prestige/—)*
Sing A Song Of Basie
(Impulse/HMV)
Sing Along With Basie
(Impulse/HMV)

Roswell Rudd

The finest trombonist of the New Wave, Roswell Rudd reintroduced many of the tonal qualities of that instrument which had been sacrificed for mobility during the Bebop period. Rudd's early background in Dixieland with Eddie Condon and subsequent move

Above: Roswell Rudd, the New Wave trombonist who moved the instrument away from glibness and back into brass truculence.

into the avant-garde meant that he bypassed the pervading Jay Jay Johnson influence, playing, as one critic remarked, 'tailgate on a spaceship'. With the shortlived New York Art Quartet, which he co-led with altoist John Tchichai **(New York Art Quartet** and **Mohawk)** all his characteristic brass, vocalized efforts are deployed in the interplay with the jagged, angular alto. **Rosmosis**, his finest performance with the group, utilizes plunger mute and long slurring lines that recall both the traditional blues and free music. With the magnificent Milford Graves on drums, the music interweaves in a loose counterpoint, free yet disciplined.

A period with tenorman Archie Shepp followed, starting with a sextet **(Four For Trane)** for which Rudd arranged **Niema**. Subsequent albums **(Live In San Francisco** and **Three For A Quarter,**

One For A Dime) gave more space to Rudd as a soloist and in duet with the leader, their declamatory styles well-suited. Shepp's interest in brass bands led to performances like **King Cotton (Mama Too Tight)** and textures for Rudd's trombone and Howard Johnson's tuba. **One For The Trane (Live At The Donaueschingen Festival)** added a second trombone, Grachan Moncur III.

Rudd's finest work to date has been on **Communications No. 10 (The Jazz Composers Orchestra)** where Michael Mantler's writing and Rudd's explosive, emotional playing reached a classic peak. Rudd's own album with the JCOA **(Numatik Swing Band)** shows his concern for textures, French horns rising over drum beat, piano and basses in unison, the scampering piccolo. Rudd himself plays well, but the star of the session is drummer Beaver Harris, tirelessly inventive.

Recordings:
New York Art Quartet
(ESP/ESP)
Mohawk (—/Fontana)
Archie Shepp:
  Four For Trane
  (Impulse/Impulse)
  Live In San Francisco
  (Impulse/Impulse)
  **Three For A Quarter, One For
  A Dime** (Impulse/Impulse)
  Mama Too Tight
  (Impulse/Impulse)
  **Live At The Donaueschingen
  Festival** (BASF/Saba)
The Jazz Composers Orchestra
(JCOA/JCOA – Virgin)
Numatik Swing Band
(JCOA/JCOA – Virgin)
The New Village On The Left
(—/Black Saint)
Trickles (—/Black Saint)

Jimmy Rushing

James Andrew 'Jimmy' Rushing (born Oklahoma City, Oklahoma, 1903), was, together with Joe Turner (♦) and Jimmy Witherspoon (♦), probably finest of the urban blues 'shouters'. But Rushing sang not only blues, which formed only part of his extensive repertoire, he could (and did) handle pop tunes of the day, standards, and even novelties. His forthright, high-pitched, always swinging vocal style made him ideal for big-band setting, which is where his enviable reputation first was established. It was with Walter Page's Blue Devils (1927) that Rushing began to make a name. But it was with orchestra of Bennie Moten (♦) that he grew in stature. Remained with Moten 1929–35. His earliest recordings with Moten show a not yet fully-developed singer, although Rushing sings well on average-to-good material, written mostly by Moten, Eddie Durham (♦), and occasionally Rushing himself. Typical of Rushing-Moten collaborations are **Won't You Be My Baby?, That Too, Do, When I'm Alone, As Long As I Have You** (all Bennie Moten's Kansas City Orchestra, Vol 4) and **New Orleans, Ya Got Love, I Wanna Be Around My Baby All The Time,** and **The Only Girl I Ever Love** (all Bennie Moten's Kansas City Orchestra, Vol 5).

On Moten's death, in 1935, Rushing sang briefly with brother Buster Moten, before joining newly-formed Count Basie (♦) band in Kansas City (1935). Was to remain as Basie's principal singer until 1948. During his long tenure with Basie, Rushing was involved with some of band's most popular items. Included in lengthy list are following: **Send For You Yesterday & Here You Come Today, Good Morning Blues, Blues In The Dark, The Blues I Like To Hear, Do You Wanna Jump Children?, Don't You Miss Your Baby, Evil Blues** (all **Blues I Love To Sing**); **Harvard Blues, Take Me Back, Baby, Blues (I Still Think Of Her), Nobody Knows, How Long Blues** (all **Blues By Basie**); and **Jimmy's Blues, Rusty Dusty Blues** (**Basie's Best**). The combination of Basie band and Rushing's declamatory singing – invariably augmented by choice obbligatos and/or solos from such as Lester Young (♦), Buck Clayton (♦) or Herschel Evans (♦) – was indeed a potent one, and

Blues I Love To Sing (Ace of Hearts) – Jimmy Rushing, Esq.

Above: singer Jimmy Rushing – 'Mr Five By Five' – belted out the blues and pop for 50 years.

resulted in recordings which with much justification have long since earned privilege of being called classics. **Harvard Blues**, especially, is something of a vocal-instrumental masterpiece. And just how potent the combination could be in live performance can be gauged from aural perusal of existing airshots. Even when faced with trivia such as **When My Dreamboat Comes In** and **Rhythm In My Nursery Rhymes** (both **Basie Live!**) Rushing's personality, rhythmic powers and sheer exuberance enabled him to produce eminently satisfying singing. Sang occasionally with Basie between 1949–50, but as from 1948 worked as solo act. Put together own septet to accompany him on gigs and for touring purposes.

Rushing and this band were regularly to be heard between 1950–2 at Savoy Ballroom. Disbanded in '52, to work as single act. During early-1950s, undeservedly went through period of neglect.

His 'comeback' coincided with mid-1950s surge of interest in 'mainstream' jazz. His first LP, **Going To Chicago,** was total success, with singer in magnificent form (with particular reference to **Boogie Woogie, Goin' To Chicago Blues** and **Sent For You Yesterday),** with inspired support from seven-piece, including Buddy Tate (♦). Follow-up album **Listen To The Blues** was every bit as good, with octet this time including Pete Johnson (♦), and a reunion for Rushing with former colleagues comprising most famous of all Basie rhythm sections; Freddie Green, Walter Page, Jo Jones. Third album, dating from late-1956 **(The Odyssey Of James Rushing, Esq)** sustained the high level of its predecessors with more fine singing and playing, particularly from Tate, again, and two other Basie alumni, Buck Clayton (♦), Vic Dickenson (♦).

Visited Europe in 1957, same year as he was reunited with Basie band (plus former colleagues Young, Illinois Jacquet (♦), Jones) for rousing reworkings of old Basie-Rushing favorites at Newport Jazz Festival **(The Newport Years, Vol 6)**. Worked with Benny Goodman (♦) at Brussels World Fair ('58), and back for more extensive

European tour with Clayton All Stars following year. By time mid-1960s arrived – with Rushing having made numerous other appearances with Basie and other bands – years of blues-shouting had coarsened the voice, and there were times when, vocally at least, he had begun to show his age. Could still produce the goods on record, though, as in 1963 **(Five Feet Of Soul)** together with all-star big band playing superior charts by Al Cohn (♦). Probably Rushing's last successful recordings emanated from same session **(Gee Baby, Ain't I Good To You** and **Who Was It Sang That Song?)** with singer responding nobly to sterling support from accompanying unit, including Clayton (a constant companion, musically and otherwise, during last 15 years of Rushing's life), Jo Jones, Sir Charles Thompson, and Dickie Wells (♦).

Final album date was, vocally, both excellent and sad in equal proportions. Rarely has Rushing evinced the kind of poignancy which permeates **The You & Me That Used To Be** but, sadly, the seemingly indestructible vocal cords could not reproduce another of jazz's inimitable sounds anywhere near as emphatically as before. Same year – 1971 – suffered heart attack, and in June 1972, James Rushing, Esq, died in Flower Fifth Avenue Hospital, NYC, of leukemia.

Recordings:
**Bennie Moten's Kansas City
  Orchestra: 'New Moten
  Stomp', Vol 4 (1929-1930)**
(RCA Victor – France)
**Bennie Moten's Kansas City
  Orchestra: 'Moten's Swing',
  Vol 5 (1929-1932)**
(RCA Victor – France)
**Jimmy Rushing/Count Basie,
  The Blues I Like To Sing**
(Decca/Ace of Hearts)
Count Basie, Blues By Basie
(Columbia/Philips)
Count Basie, Basie's Best
(CBS – France)
Count Basie, Basie Live
(Trip/DJM)
**Jimmy Rushing, Going To
  Chicago** (Vanguard)/**Listen To
  The Blues** (Vanguard)/**The
  Essential Jimmy Rushing**
(Vogue)
**The Odyssey Of James
  Rushing, Esq**
(Columbia/Philips)
**Count Basie, The Newport
  Years, Vol 6** (Verve/—)
**Jimmy Rushing, Five Feet Of
  Soul** (Colpix/Pye)
**Jimmy Rushing, Gee Baby,
  Ain't I Good To You**
(Master Jazz Recordings/—)
**Jimmy Rushing, Who Was It
  Sang That Song?**
(Master Jazz Recordings/—)
**Jimmy Rushing, The You & Me
  That Used To Be**
(RCA Victor/RCA Victor)

George Russell

Composer-pianist George Russell has a formidable reputation as a theorist, based on his massive work, *The Lydian Chromatic Concept of Tonal Organisation*, which was published in 1953. Devising a system of shifting key centres, Russell's theory extends the innovations of Bebop rather than bypassing them, as with the New Thing. Far from being clinical or

*Outer Thoughts (Milestone).
With Eric Dolphy.*

frigid, his music is full of guts and variety, and draws from all periods of jazz history. Born 1923, the son of a music professor, Russell started out as a drummer with Benny Carter, even being offered a gig with Charlie Parker which he turned down through ill-health. Early compositions like **Cubano Be, Cupano Bop** for the Dizzy Gillespie big band **(The Greatest Of Dizzy Gillespie)** and **Ezz-thetic** and **Odjenar**, recorded by Lee Konitz **(Ezz-thetic!)** established him in the avant-garde of his contemporaries, and a piece like **A Bird In Igor's Yard** which combined the concepts of Parker and Stravinsky, was so far ahead that it waited years for release **(Crosscurrents)**.

A brilliant album from 1956, unfortunately deleted, **The Jazz Workshop**, gives an idea of the breadth of his vision, particularly in the dazzling **Round Johnny Rondo**. A later album from 1960, **Jazz In The Space Age**, uses a larger ensemble, including piano duets by Paul Bley and Bill Evans. At the same time, Russell established his own working unit with ex-students of his, including Dave Baker, trombone and Don Ellis, trumpet. A compilation of his early **Riversides (Outer Thoughts)** also includes Eric Dolphy, outstanding on Thelonious Monk's **Round Midnight**, and singer Sheila Jordan on the classic arrangement of **You Are My Sunshine**. Russell left for Scandinavia in the mid-'60s, and experimented with electronic music which has dominated his subsequent output **(Living Time** and **Sonata For Souls)**.

Recordings:
The Greatest Of Dizzy Gillespie
   (RCA/RCA)
Ezz-thetic! (Prestige/—)
Lennie Tristano-Buddy De Franco, Crosscurrents
   (Capitol/Capitol)
Jazz In The Space Age (MCA/—)
Live At Beethoven Hall
   (BASF/BASF)
Outer Thoughts
   (Milestone/Milestone)
Living Time (Columbia/CBS)
Electronic Sonata For Souls Loved By Nature
   (Strata – East/—)

Luis Russell

Luis Russell (born Careening Clay, near Bocos Del Toro, Panama, 1902) was no teenage beginner in jazz when he joined Joseph 'King' Oliver (♦) in Chicago, in 1925. But his career really blossomed during time he spent with the great New Orleans trumpeter's band, both as

Above: George Russell, a leading theorist whose experiments with the Lydian Mode have produced unique jazz.

pianist and sometime composer, arranger. During next two years, also took time off from playing to study music. Recorded frequently with Oliver, including **King Oliver's Dixie Syncopators**, and was quiet, relatively anonymous force behind the activities of that band during 1925–8. Reluctant (and modest) soloist, nevertheless Russell was a fine pianist who held rhythm section together in admirable fashion, as he demonstrated on subsequent recordings by Oliver's Orchestra **(King Oliver & His Orchestra, Vol 1, 1928-1930)**, an Oliver orchestra which, eventually, was taken over by his trumpet-playing nephew Dave Nelson **(King Oliver/Dave Nel-**

*The Luis Russell Story
1929/30 (Parlophone).*

son, Vol 3, 1929-1931). During this latter period, Russell also supervised accompaniment for another of the era's greatest trumpet players; Henry 'Red' Allen (♦) **(Henry 'Red' Allen With Luis Russell, Vol 3, 1930-1931)** with Allen as featured soloist, vocalist, or as support for singers Victoria Spivey, Addie 'Sweet Pea' Spivey, and for the appalling vocalism, clarinet-playing of Wilton Crawley (all **Henry 'Red' Allen, Vol 2, 1929)**. Allen's pungent trumpet became integral part of Russell's own bands.

During 1929–30, Russell fronted superb ten-piece unit at Saratoga Club, Harlem. Along with Russell and Allen, important constituent members included bassist George 'Pops' Foster, trombonist J. C. Higginbotham (♦), drummer Paul Barbarin (♦), trumpeter Bill Coleman (♦), and saxists-clarinettists Albert Nicholas (♦) and Charlie Holmes. Some idea of just how exciting band must have sounded in person can be gauged from recordings like **Jersey Lightning, Song Of Swanee, Saratoga Shout, Feelin' The Spirit** and **Panama**, with emphatically rhythmic ensembles and expressive, characteristic solos from Allen, Higginbotham, Holmes, et al. More sedate **Doctor Blues** showed another side of this important jazz aggregation, as do **Call Of The Freaks** and **The New Call Of The Freaks**, same

tune made eight months apart, which must be considered strictly avant-garde for the period. Perhaps **Louisiana Swing** (in two takes) most clearly defines the quintessence of the Luis Russell Orchestra (all **Luis Russell & His Louisiana Swing Orchestra/The Luis Russell Story)**. Allen and Russell continued their mutually productive association through several years, especially on record **(Henry Allen & His Orchestra 1934-1935)**.

From 1935–43, Luis Russell's band became virtually an accompanying unit used as backdrop to trumpet artistry of Louis Armstrong (♦); it had first undertaken this project during part of 1929, touring with Armstrong as well as appearing on his records **(V.S.O.P. (Very Special Old Phonography, 1928-1930), Vols 5 & 6** and **Complete Recorded Works 1935-1945)**. After this arrangement ceased, Russell put together another big band which played lengthy residencies at top New York venues like the Apollo, and toured the US extensively. Russell retired from music business in 1948 to become shopkeeper, occasionally teaching piano, even less often playing live gigs. 1959: visited the country of his birth first time in 40 years. Worked as chauffeur in early-1960s, although continuing to teach. Died of cancer in New York, December 1963.

Recordings:
Luis Russell & His Louisiana Swing Orchestra (Columbia)/
The Luis Russell Story
   (Parlophone)
King Oliver's Dixie Syncopators (1926-1928)
   (MCA Coral – Germany)
King Oliver/Dave Nelson, Vol 3 (1929-1931)
   (RCA Victor – France)
Louis Armstrong, V.S.O.P. (Very Special Old Phonography, 1928-1930), Vols 5 & 6 (CBS – France)
Louis Armstrong, Complete Recorded Works 1935-1945 – 145 Titles In Chronological Order (MCA – France)
King Oliver & His Orchestra, Vol 1: 'New Orleans Shout' (1929-1930)
   (RCA Victor – France)
Henry 'Red' Allen, Vols 2, 3
   (RCA Victor – France)
Henry Allen & His Orchestra, 1934-1935 (Collector's Classics)

Pee Wee Russell

Charles Ellsworth 'Pee Wee' Russell (born St Louis, Missouri, 1906) had a way of playing clarinet which not only was unique, but the sounds which he coaxed from his instrument were those which could only have come from jazz. The croaky, strangulated tone which was Russell's had a kind of slightly abrasive beauty that was enhanced by his ability to communicate deep emotion, particularly when playing blues. Russell's technique, although influenced in part by Frank Teschemacher (♦) and Johnny Dodds (♦), bore no resemblance to that of any other jazz clarinettist. The difference between Russell's asthmatic outpourings indeed made extraordinary contrast with the more academic approach of Benny Goodman (♦) or Jimmy Hamilton (♦).

For most of his playing career – starting with Perkins Brothers Band, near Muskogee, before 1920, and ending with his death in Alexandria, Virginia, in 1969 – Russell was more or less pigeon-holed as a typical member of the white Dixieland school of jazz. And Russell himself for years did nothing to discourage the situation. From early-1930s right up until his last years, worked with likes of Bud Freeman (♦) (**Home Cooking** and **Chicagoans In New York**); Georg Brunis (♦) (**The Davison-Brunis**

bass-drums rhythm section seemed to help give his playing a lift. (Far from being successful, though, were the record dates which matched Russell's delightful eccentricities with Monk's equally individualistic approach and Jimmy Giuffre's (♦) strictly academic clarinet playing.) Undoubtedly, many of Russell's finest recordings were achieved in Dixieland context. Apart from the Condon Town Hall concerts, clarinettist seemed sublimely happy throughout (**Jam Session At Commodore, Condon A La Carte** and **Chicago & All That Jazz!**). With superb support

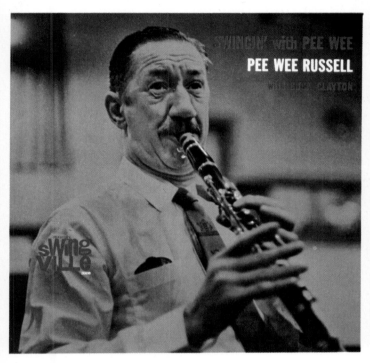

Swingin' With Pee Wee (Transatlantic). 1960 mainstream date.

Above: Pee Wee Russell. Once dubbed (with admirable perception) Poet of the Clarinet. Indeed he was.

called 'The Poet of the Clarinet'. There seems no better epitaph to his uniqueness. Pee Wee Russell died in 1969.

Sessions, Vol 1 and **Trombone Scene**) and, especially, the ubiquitous Eddie Condon (♦) (**Commodore Condon, Vol 1** and **The Commodore Years**). And Russell was a 'regular' at Condon's renowned World War II organized jam sessions (**The Eddie Condon Concerts: Town Hall 1944-45 Featuring Pee Wee Russell** and **The Eddie Condon Concerts, Vol 2**), his playing during these events being of a uniformly high standard and, of course, totally individual in execution. Often, though, Russell's playing tended to be even more adventurous, and interesting, outside a basic two-beat setting. Although he seems strangely subdued as guest in a typical Teddy Wilson (♦) all-star recording of **Don't Be That Way** (1938) (**Teddy Wilson & His All Stars**) he sounds happy and refreshed at two basically 'mainstream' dates from 1960 (**The Pee Wee Russell Memorial Album/ Swingin' With Pee Wee**) and 1961 (**Jam Session At Swingville**) respectively.

Late in his career, 1962, he was persuaded, temporarily at least, to give the old Dixie warhorses a rest and tackle 'foreign' material; John Coltrane's (♦) **Red Planet**, Thelonious Monk's (♦) **Round Midnight** and Tadd Dameron's (♦) **Good Bait**, could be said to have been successful (**New Groove**). Certainly, the more contemporary

from Jess Stacy (♦), quartet of 1944 tracks recorded by Russell's Hot Four (**Swingin' Clarinets**) contain playing by the leader that he rarely produced, before or later, including exquisite blues-playing on own **D.A. Blues.**

Russell's early career was as colorful as his clarinet playing. After taking lessons on violin, piano and drums, did likewise with clarinet. After initial introduction to music business, worked for a short time on Arkansas riverboat. Enrolled at Western Military Academy, Alton, Illinois (1920–1), also attended University of Missouri. Played with bewildering variety of bands during early-1920s, including work with legendary pianist Peck Kelley, in Houston. With Frankie Trumbauer (♦) Orchestra in St. Louis, in 1925, and after working with Jean Goldkette, joined Red Nichols (♦). Recorded with Nichols' variously titled bands, including **The Charleston Chasers 1925-1928** and **Red Nichols & His Five Pennies 1926-1928** and Louisiana Rhythm Kings ('JT').

Made superb contribution to 1929 recording by Mound City Blue Blowers of **If I Could Be With You One Hour Tonight (Body & Soul)** and his clarinet is at its most biting and exciting during the semi-legendary '32 recordings under singer Billy Banks' name (**Billy Banks & His Rhythm-**

makers) during which he also proved that he was a tenor-saxophonist of limited capabilities. During 1930s, continued to work in all manner of settings (often in company with Bobby Hackett (♦), with nationwide exposure as member of trumpeter Louis Prima's combo (1935–7).

Played with Bud Freeman's Summa Cum Laude Orchestra, also with Bobby Hackett big band, then became more or less regular at Nick's, NYC. Worked regularly during World War II, member of Condon band of '46, and for rest of 1940s spent most of his playing time either in New York or Chicago. Major operation end of 1950, after moving to San Francisco earlier that year. Back in New York in 1951, playing irregularly until 1951–2. Resident at Eddie Condon Club (1955–6). During late-1950s and through 1960s, played major jazz festivals, toured Europe with Newport All Stars (1961) (**Midnight In Paris**) then fronted clarinet-valve trombone-bass-drums quartet which recorded the **New Groove** album and played gigs in US and Canada. To Australasia and Japan in 1964 with Condon and Britain in different setting same year. Topped bill at special, 1968 New York concert, at Town Hall. Several times during his career, Pee Wee Russell was

Recordings:
The Bix Beiderbecke Legend (RCA Victor – France)
The Charleston Chasers (1925-1928) (—/VJM)
Red Nichols & His Five Pennies (1926-1928) (MCA Coral – Germany)
Coleman Hawkins (Including Mound City Blue Blowers), Body & Soul (RCA Victor/—)
Jack Teagarden (Including Red Nichols), 'JT' (Ace of Hearts)
Billy Banks & His Rhythmmakers (CBS – Realm)
Bud Freeman, Home Cooking (Tax – Sweden)
Bud Freeman, Chicagoans In New York (Dawn Club/—)
The Davison-Brunis Sessions, Vol 1 (—/London)
Various (Including Georg Brunis), Trombone Scene (—/London)
Eddie Condon/Bud Freeman, The Commodore Years (Atlantic/—)
Eddie Condon, Commodore Condon, Vol 1 (—/London)
The Eddie Condon Concerts: Town Hall 1944-45, Featuring Pee Wee Russell (Chiaroscuro/—)
The Eddie Condon Concerts, Vol 2 (Chiaroscuro/—)
Eddie Condon, Condon A La Carte (—/London)

Above: Johnny St Cyr (ex-Oliver, Armstrong, Morton et al) was first jazz banjoist to attain a reputation.

Eddie Condon, Chicago & All That Jazz! (—/Verve)
(Jack Teagarden)/Pee Wee Russell (Byg – France)
Teddy Wilson & His All Stars (Columbia/CBS)
The Pee Wee Russell Memorial Album (Prestige)/
Swingin' With Pee Wee (Transatlantic)
Various (Including Pee Wee Russell), Jam Session At Swingville (Prestige/Prestige)
Pee Wee Russell, New Groove (Columbia/CBS)
Various (Including Pee Wee Russell), Swingin' Clarinets (—/London)
Pee Wee Russell, Portrait Of Pee Wee (Counterpoint/Society)

Johnny St Cyr
◆ *Louis Armstrong*

Edgar Sampson

Edgar Melvin Sampson (born New York City, 1907) produced some of the finest compositions and arrangements to be first heard during 1930s, the decade which was his most productive, and during which he established an enviable reputation. Sampson was also an excellent alto-sax soloist. He can be heard in this capacity on records by Chick Webb (◆), with whom he spent two productive

years (1934–6), including **That Rhythm Man, Facts & Figures (A Legend 1929-1936).** Moreover, he was reasonable violinist, an instrument he played with Fletcher Henderson (◆) on that band's recording of **Sugar (The Fletcher Henderson Story/The Fletcher Henderson Story, Vol 3).** Sampson worked with Henderson between 1931–2. Even earlier, Sampson's violin playing had been featured with orchestra of Charlie Johnson, on **Hot Tempered Blues (Charlie Johnson/Lloyd Scott-Cecil Scott).** Sampson was a member of that band, between 1928–30. On a Bunny Berigan (◆) record date of December 1935, he switches to clarinet, on **Chicken & Waffles (Swing Classics, 1935/Jazz In The Thirties).** And Sampson's instrumental versatility enabled him to play more than reasonable baritone-sax on one of Lionel Hampton's famous studio jam sessions **(The Complete Lionel Hampton/Lionel Hampton's Best Records, Vols 1, 5).**

But it is as composer/arranger that Sampson is best remembered. Amongst his most memorable compositions can be numbered **Don't Be That Way, Stompin' At The Savoy, Blue Lou, If Dreams Come True,** all major items in the repertoire of first, Chick Webb, then Benny Goodman (◆), **Lullaby In Rhythm, Blue Minor** and **Light & Sweet.** Sampson's orchestrations were amongst the finest to be heard throughout the 1930s and on a par with his compositions in all-round excellence. In his younger days, Sampson had deputized with Duke Ellington (◆) Orchestra, worked with big band led by Rex

Stewart (◆); later, in 1939, became musical director for Ella Fitzgerald (◆) (when she became leader of Webb band, following drummer's death). For some time after leaving Webb, concentrated on writing to exclusion of his instrumental work. During this time, apart from Webb, Goodman, Sampson wrote for Teddy Wilson (◆), Red Norvo (◆), Artie Shaw (◆), Teddy Hill. Resumed playing during his spell with

Ella Fitzgerald, then played sax with Al Sears (◆) band (1943). Worked as instrumentalist on full-time basis during late-1940s, fronting own New York-based outfit 1949–51. Following this, played with and arranged for Afro-Cuban bands, Tito Puente, Marcellino Guerra, etc.

Led own small band during late-1950s/early-1960s, but from late-1960s was forced to retire from

Above: supersonic tenor of Pharoah Sanders, ex-Coltrane sideman of frightening power. On bass, Richard Davis.

playing completely through illness, culmination of which was amputation of a leg. Died at home in Englewood, New Jersey, in 1973.

Recordings:
Charlie Johnson/Lloyd Scott-Cecil Scott
(RCA Victor – France)
Chick Webb, A Legend (1929-1936)
(Decca/MCA – Germany)
The Fletcher Henderson Story (Columbia)/
The Fletcher Henderson Story, Vol 3 (CBS)
Various (Including Bunny Berigan), Swing Classics, 1935 (Prestige)/
Jazz In The Thirties
(World Records)
The Complete Lionel Hampton (Bluebird)/
Lionel Hampton's Best Records, Vols 1, 5
(RCA Victor – France)
Chick Webb, King Of The Savoy (1937-1939)
(Decca/MCA – Germany)

Pharoah Sanders

One of that second wave of New Thing tenor players – Shepp, Ayler – Sanders does not seem to have maintained his early promise. His recording debut was on the courageous ESP label (**Pharoah Sanders**) and showed a style that was composed entirely of extremes: overblowing, screaming

Jewels Of Thought (Impulse): high-tension tenor from Pharoah, but the best moments come from the two bassists.

ed a new direction for Coltrane's music, and the end of the great Quartet. As a foil for the leader's heavy, majestic passion, Sanders' raggedly scribbled outbursts offered the wildest contrast in trajectory; a writhing, tattooed Queequeg to the leader's iron-prowed obsession. **Meditations** remains the best album, the two horns plaiting and jostling over the dense rhythmic groundswell. On all albums, there are moments of incoherence, which is probably the price tag on free polyphony. Only **Naima (John Coltrane Live At The Village Vanguard Again)** catches Sanders in formal mood, the extremes of pitch and phrase pressed into service to tell a story, a twisted, volatile language of hieroglyphic and morse which nevertheless has its own symmetry. **Live In Seattle** has high peaks of excitement, but long stretches of tedium.

Pharoah Sanders is an excellent sideman under someone else's direction, thus his work with trumpeter Don Cherry (**Symphony For Improvisers** and **Where Is Brooklyn**) or set against the massive orchestration of Michael Mantler's **Preview (Jazz Composers Orchestra)** where he turns and twists through the pile-driving forest of chords, remains his best work.

His own albums as leader have grown progressively flabbier. The debut for Impulse (**Tauhid**) is interesting, but contains the seeds of later shortcomings, for example, the short weight tenor exposure. **Upper And Lower Egypt** takes

out clusters of notes, the line a furious supersonic scribbling. Traces of his influences remain, the usual Rollins-Coltrane axis. He next appears with John Coltrane, chosen for his strength and spirit to remain the multi-directional impetus of that legendary unit, and his work here is probably his best. The wild collective session of 1965 (**Ascension**) including Coltrane, Sanders and Shepp, herald-

bass duet between Cecil McBee and Richard Davis. Subsequent albums (**Karma, Thembi** and **Wisdom Through Music**) are dull affairs, endless chanting, rippling and swirling, music as embroidered as a matador's costume, and – very occasionally – the entrance of the bull. The energy seems to have fled, leaving an Eastern veal.

Recordings:
Pharoah Sanders (ESP/ESP)
John Coltrane, Ascension (Impulse/Impulse)
John Coltrane, Meditations (Impulse/Impulse)
John Coltrane, Live At The Village Vanguard Again (Impulse/Impulse)
John Coltrane, Live In Seattle (Impulse/Impulse)
Don Cherry, Symphony For Improvisers (Blue Note/Blue Note)
Don Cherry, Where Is Brooklyn (Blue Note/Blue Note)
Michael Mantler, The Jazz Composers Orchestra (JCOA/Virgin)
Tauhid (Impulse/Impulse)
Jewels Of Thought (Impulse/Impulse)
Pharoah (India Navigation/—)

Mongo Santamaria

Cuban drumming has often fascinated jazz musicians like Dizzy Gillespie (♦), who experimented with the genre in his Afro-Cuban big band recordings. Conga, bongo and percussion player, Mongo Santamaria came up through the more commercial Cuban bands like Perez Prado and Tito Puento, before joining with Cal Tjader. Much of his own output features a dense polyrhythmic surface supplemented by timbale and cowbell players, of whom Willie Bobo is the best-known. One of Santamaria's compositions, **Afro-Blue**, has been frequently recorded by jazzmen. Very much in the tradition of Gillespie's original Cuban conga player, Chano Pozo, he has dedicated a composition to that master drummer (**Afro-Roots**).

Recordings:
Afro Roots (Prestige/Prestige)
Skins (Milestone/Milestone)
Watermelon Man (Milestone/Milestone)
Greatest Hits (Columbia/—)

Eddie Sauter

Although Edward Ernest Sauter (born Brooklyn, New York, 1914) has proved himself many times over the years to be one of the most gifted and imaginative jazz writers, still he remains, in many circles, a grossly underappreciated talent. As a youth he played trumpet and drums. Graduate of Columbia University, Sauter played trumpet during summer vacations for bands booked by French Lines. After studying theory at Juilliard School of Music, joined orchestra of Archie Bleyer in 1932. First came into real prominence as member of Red Norvo's (♦) Orchestra (1935-1939), playing both trumpet, mellophone, and supplying arrange-

ments and/or compositions for band and its singer, Mildred Bailey (♦). Typical of subtle, tasteful, inventive and ahead-of-their-times charts Sauter produced for Bailey are **Rockin' Chair (Mildred Bailey: Her Greatest Performances, Vol 2)** and **Darn That Dream, Peace, Brother!, I'm Nobody's Baby (Vol 3)**. Worked as arranger-composer for Benny Goodman (♦) between 1939-1945 (although not all of that period). Together with Mel Powell (♦), helped rejuvenate a flagging Goodman orchestra. Prime amongst Sauter's often breathtaking arrangements for clarinet-tist-leader can be numbered **Superman** (superb showcase for Cootie Williams' (♦) trumpet), **Clarinet A La King** (ditto, for Goodman, of course), **Moonlight On The Ganges, Time On My Hands, Birth Of The Blues** and **Love Walked In** (all on **Benny Goodman Plays Solid Gold Instrumental Hits**). During 1940s, also wrote for bands of Ray McKinley, Artie Shaw (♦) (fine scores for *Summertime* and own *Maid With The Flaccid Hair* (**Reissued By Request**) and Woody Herman (♦).

Gained further widespread acclaim in collaboration with ex-Miller, T. Dorsey arranger-composer Bill Finegan. Sauter-Finegan Orchestra was part-jazz, part-classical, overall pop. The inventiveness, wit in writing by the two leaders resulted in sparkling musical hybrid. Venture started in 1952, firstly just as a recording studio idea, ending in '57 when Sauter moved to West Germany to take up two-year position as staff musical director with radio station Sudwestfunk in Baden-Baden. Amongst most popular Sauter-Finegan recordings are **Doodletown Fifers, Nina Never Knew** (featuring vocal by blind accordionist-pianist Joe Mooney), **April In Paris, Midnight Sleigh-ride**, and a reworked **Clarinet A La King** (with studio clarinettist Walt Levinsky re-creating Goodman's role) – all on **Sauter Finegan**.

After returning from Europe, Eddie Sauter became involved in variety of film, radio, TV and record work. 1961: made something of a comeback through series of remarkable orchestrations, compositions for an extraordinary Stan Getz (♦) LP **Focus On Stan Getz**. Without in any way diminishing Getz' own magnificent contributions, Sauter's work is of equal importance to the album's uniqueness. Compositionally, moods vary: for instance, a breathless **I'm Late, I'm Late**, a tender **Her**, a restless **Night Rider**, a ruminative **I Remember When**. Four years later, Getz and Sauter were reunited when latter was asked to supply music for soundtrack of film *Mickey One* (**Focus On Stan Getz**). Individual items for this were, of necessity, more fragmentary, but again it was a combination of two major talents made for music that never lacked for excitement or creativity. Whilst with Goodman, Sauter wrote several first-class arrangements for band's singer Peggy Lee (♦), including **That's The Way It Goes, That Did It, Marie, Not A Care In The World** (all on **We'll Meet Again**).

Recordings:
Mildred Bailey: Her Greatest Performances, Vols 2, 3
(Columbia/CBS)

forever to establish a climate for one of his Behemoth entrances, and the long haul – all ebb and flow and percussive textures – isn't greatly grabbing until the montuna section which triggers the Sanders blast off. A fatal liking for the Om-type mantra begins to take the foreground, with a romantic, anonymous lyricism. The best feature of his next album (**Jewels Of Thought**) is the incredible double

Benny Goodman Plays Solid
  Gold Instrumental Hits
  (Columbia/CBS)
Peggy Lee/Benny Goodman,
  We'll Meet Again (Hallmark)
Artie Shaw, Reissued By
  Request (RCA Victor/—)
Sauter Finegan (RCA Victor)
Focus On Stan Getz
  (Metro/Metro)
Various (Including Eddie
  Sauter), The Historic
  Donaueschingen Jazz Concert
  1957 (MPS)

Ronnie Scott

Tenorman Ronnie Scott was born
in London, 1927, working with the
bands of Ambrose, Tito Burns,
Cab Kaye, Ted Heath and Jack
Parnell before forming his own
band in 1952. Belonging to that
generation of British jazzmen who
worked on the liners crossing the
Atlantic for a chance to hear the
Bebop revolution for themselves,
Scott remains true to the chord
changes, although his style has
kept abreast of the newer developments, due to his ownership of an
internationally renowned jazz club
since 1959. Zoot Sims, Stan Getz,
Hank Mobley and Sonny Rollins –
all featured at his club – have had
an influence on his playing over the
years. An album of the early Scott
band has recently been re-issued
(Great Scott).

With tenorman Tubby Hayes, he
co-led the driving Jazz Couriers
(The Jazz Couriers) 1957-9,
was a featured soloist with the
Kenny Clarke-Francy Boland band
(At Her Majesty's Pleasure) and
led a young band of New Thing
players including John Surman
and drummer Tony Oxley (Ronnie
Scott & The Band). Currently, he
is playing better than ever with a
challenging quartet, the brilliant
guitarist Louis Stewart, bassist Ron
Matthewson and drummer Martin
Drew. The Grand Old Man of British
Jazz, Ronnie Scott's tenor and jazz
club have been a major force on the
scene for decades.

Recordings:
Great Scott (—/Esquire)
The Jazz Couriers
  (Jazzland/Jazzland)
Ronnie Scott & The Band
  (Columbia/CBS Realm)
Scott At Ronnie's (RCA/RCA)
The Kenny Clarke-Francy
  Boland Big Band, At Her
  Majesty's Pleasure
  (Black Lion/Black Lion)
Serious Gold (—/Pye)

Phil Seaman

Drummer Phil Seaman, who died
in 1972, was a legend in his own
lifetime, both as a world-class
musician and as a personality. He
came up through the big bands in
the late '40s – Nat Gonella, Jack
Parnell – and became a convert to
Bebop. Usually described as
Britain's greatest big-band drummer, his work with small combos is
equally distinguished, often anticipating developments that later
occurred in America. His driving,
aggressive playing can be heard
behind the two-tenor Jazz Couriers
(The Message From Britain)
while his gift for timbre and imaginative melodic improvisation within a free context is represented
with altoman Joe Harriott (Free

*Above: the late Phil Seaman, a legend in his own time, and
the most powerful and original drummer Britain produced.*

Form). A meeting with Bill Evans'
bassist, Eddie Gomez, further illustrates his openness and adaptability. Drum battles, starting with
Jack Parnell, continued throughout
his career, contestants including
Vic Feldman, Ginger Baker, a
student of his, and John Stevens. A
tribute album (The Phil Seaman
Story) includes his work with
American blues singer, Jimmy
Witherspoon, and great blues
tenorman, Dick Morrissey.

Recordings:
Jazz Couriers, The Message
  From Britain (Jazzland/—)

Joe Harriott, Free Form
  (Jazzland/—)
Phil Seaman Meets Eddie
  Gomez (—/Saga)
The Phil Seaman Story
  (—/Decibel)
A Jam Session At The Hide-
  Away (—/77 Jazz)

Al Sears

Albert Omega Sears (born
Macomb, Illinois) had had considerable playing experience with
his own and other bands, led by

such as Chick Webb (♦), Zack
Whyte, Elmer Snowden, before
joining Andy Kirk (♦) in 1941. Sears'
raw-toned, R&B-influenced tenor-
sax style subsequently was heard,
for a short period, with Lionel
Hampton (♦), and then, between
1944-9, as a featured solo player
with Duke Ellington (♦) Orchestra
as successor to the great Ben
Webster (♦). With Ellington, Sears
received more than adequate exposure. First important solo role
was during the 'Blues' section of
Victor recording of the prestigious
Black, Brown & Beige suite
(The Works Of Duke, Vol 19).

Ellington also used the Sears
tenor-sax during the Dance No 1
movement from the 1947 Liberian
Suite. Other Sears solos for Ellington included Hiawatha (The Golden Duke), St Louis Blues (Pretty
Woman), It Don't Mean A Thing
(Johnny Come Lately). On Suddenly It Jumped his basic style,
sinewy, hard-hitting, basic with
limited vocabulary, is recaptured
in variety of moods. He is raunchy
on A-Gatherin' In A Clearin';
not at all unlike Flip Phillips (♦) on
In A Mist and assured and easy-
swinging on The Suburbanite (a
Sears showcase).

Left Ellington in 1949; two years
later became partner/musical
director for Johnny Hodges (♦)
band, for which he also played
saxophone (The Jeep Is Jumpin').
During this time, wrote Castle
Rock, an R&B hit for the band. A
year after his association with
Hodges, Sears quit to become
music publisher in New York.
Since then his playing career has
been intermittent, but has included
occasional engagements with Duke
Ellington.

Is brother of bandleader Marion
Sears, also a saxophonist. Of comparatively few recordings issued
under Sears' name The Greatest
Of The Small Bands, Vol 5 contains work which ranks with his

*Below: big-toned Al Sears'
R&B-influenced tenor-sax was
featured with Duke Ellington
Orchestra during the 1940s.*

very best with Ellington. Included in a fine studio band are Budd Johnson (♦), Sonny Greer (♦), Harold Baker (♦), and Tyree Glenn (♦). There is also ample representation of Sears' composing-arranging gifts, with **Huffin' & Puffin'** and **Sear-iously** being of interest.

Recordings:
Duke Ellington, The Works Of Duke, Vols 19, 20
(RCA Victor – France)
Duke Ellington, Liberian Suite/ (A Tone Parallel To Harlem)
(Columbia/CBS – France)
Duke Ellington, Suddenly It Jumped *(Big Band Archives/—)*
Duke Ellington, The Golden Duke *(Prestige/Prestige)*
Duke Ellington, Johnny Come Lately *(RCA Victor/RCA Victor)*
Johnny Hodges, The Jeep Is Jumpin' *(—/Verve)*
Various (Including Al Sears), The Greatest Of The Small Bands, Vol 5
(RCA Victor – France)

Shakti
♦ *Mahavishnu John McLaughlin*

Bud Shank

Ohio-born multi-reedman Bud Shank worked mainly on the West Coast, playing in the big bands of Stan Kenton and Shorty Rogers, as well as numerous Californian combos. An excellent alto, heavily influenced by Art Pepper, he was also a sensitive flautist and a proficient tenor and baritone. Along with Brazilian guitarist Laurindo Almeida, he pioneered the Latin American and jazz fusion in the mid-'50s, eight years before Stan Getz's trendsetting **Jazz Samba** album. Performances like **Acertate Mas (Laurindo Almeida Quartet)** combine swing and lightness of touch. Shank's later work showed an increasing power, and solos like **Walkin'** or **Bag of Blues (Bud Shank Quartet)** and the later **White Lightnin' (New Groove)** catch him at his peak. After several years of commercial work, Shank has recently surfaced again **(Sunshine Express)'**

Recordings:
Laurindo Almeida Quartet
(Pacific Jazz/—)
Bud Shank Quartet
(Pacific Jazz/—)
New Groove *(Pacific Jazz/—)*
Sunshine Express *(Concord/—)*

Charlie Shavers

Charles James Shavers (born NYC, 1917) was one of the most dazzlingly gifted trumpeters produced by jazz thus far. Possessor of formidable technique, Shavers' natural exuberance and basically emotional approach to his music sometimes led him into producing the kind of tasteless, gallery-fetching blowing that has, from time to time, marred the work of other such acknowledged trumpet masters as

Above: Charlie Shavers, trumpeter of enviable technique and fire – and a composer of merit to boot.

Dizzy Gillespie (♦), Roy Eldridge (♦), and Maynard Ferguson (♦). This has been most noticeable when Shavers has toured with Jazz At The Philharmonic troupes **(Jazz At The Philharmonic: Carnegie Hall Concert – 1952, Record 1).** Although his playing tended too often to be under wraps, it benefited enormously by discipline imposed upon Shavers during his important tenure with John Kirby (♦) Sextet – Shavers' contributions to this combo, both as instrumentalist and writer, were significant. Amongst items recorded by Kirby Sextet, featuring Shavers in joint instrumentalist-writer role are: **It Feels So Good, Dawn On The Desert, Jumping In The Pump Room, Blues Petite** (all on **Boss Of The Bass**); **Close Shave** (written in collaboration with Kirby), **Comin' Back** and **Move Over** (all **John Kirby & His Orchestra 1941-1942**) and Shavers' bright, melodic trumpet playing provided major solo interest within **The Biggest Little Band In The Land.** Shavers, whose first instruments were banjo and piano, played firstly with New York pianist Willie Gant before appearing with Frankie Fairfax band in Philadelphia. Back in NYC he played with Tiny Bradshaw (♦) Orchestra.

1937: with Lucky Millinder, be-

fore replacing Frankie Newton (♦) in Kirby group. After leaving latter, worked for a while with Raymond Scott (as CBS session man) before commencing an almost five-year period with Tommy Dorsey (♦) Orchestra (he was to rejoin Dorsey subsequently on several occasions). Fine samples of Shavers' playing with Dorsey can be found within **Tommy Dorsey & His Orchestra** and **Tommy Dorsey, Vol II.** In 1950s, toured several times with JATP **(JATP In Tokyo/Live At The Nichigeki Theater, 1953)** and also led fine combo with Louis Bellson (♦) and Tommy Gibbs in 1950. Featured soloist with Benny Goodman (1954). Fronted own combos during 1960s, and toured on more than one occasion with Sam Donahue-led Tommy Dorsey Orchestra (including UK tour, '64). Also with Donahue for several years was Frank Sinatra Jr; Shavers worked in combos accompanying singer when Sinatra Jr went solo, including tours of Far East and South America. Toured Europe as soloist during 1969, 1970, before succumbing to heart attack in '71.

Among a host of other recordings which featured Charlie Shavers' exciting trumpet solos are those which conjoined his particular talents with other artists like Billie Holiday (♦) – **The Billy Holiday**

Story, Vol 1 and **The Voice Of Jazz, Vols 1, 2, 3, 5, 6;** Sidney Bechet (♦) **(Sleepy Time Down South);** Coleman Hawkins (♦) **(Swing);** Louis Bellson **(Kings Of Swing, Vol 2)** – *Flip Phillips (♦); an alto-sax triumvirate of Benny Carter (♦), Charlie Parker (♦) and Johnny Hodges (♦) (*The Charlie Parker Sides/The Parker Jam Session);** Billy Kyle (♦) **(Swing Street, Vol 1,** Charlie Ventura's Carnegie Hall Concert, Jimmie Noone 1937-1941 and **The Exciting Gene Krupa).** A 1945 session, also featuring Nat Cole (♦), Buddy Rich (♦) et al **(Anatomy Of A Jam Session)** and a live concert presented by Gene Norman **(Jazz Scene USA)** together contain much excellent trumpet, fully displaying Shavers' rich tone and exceptional technique. Of his numerous compositions, by far the most familiar is the perennial **Undecided,** first recorded by Kirby band in 1938.

Recordings:
John Kirby & His Orchestra, 1941-1942
(RCA Victor – Germany)
John Kirby, The Biggest Little Band In The Land *(Trip/DJM)*
John Kirby, Boss Of The Bass
(Columbia/—)
The Billie Holiday Story, Vol 1
(Columbia/CBS)
Various (Including Billy Kyle), Swing Street, Vol 1
(Tax – Sweden)
Jimmie Noone 1937-1941
(Collector's Classics – Denmark)
Coleman Hawkins, Swing!
(—/Fontana)
Tommy Dorsey & His Orchestra
(RCA Victor)
Tommy Dorsey, Vol II
(RCA Victor)
Various (Including Charlie Shavers), Jazz Scene USA
(Vogue – France)
Sidney Bechet, Sleepy Time Down South, Vol 1
(RCA Victor – France)
Various (Including Charlie Shavers), JATP Carnegie Hall Concert 1952, Record 1
(Verve/Columbia – Clef)
Various (Including Charlie Shavers), JATP In Tokyo/ Live At The Nichigeki Theater, 1953 *(Pablo Live/Pablo Live)*
Various (Including Louis Bellson), Kings Of Swing, Vol 2 *(—/Verve)*
Billie Holiday, The Voice Of Jazz, Vols 1, 2, 3, 5, 6
(—/Verve)
Billie Holiday, The First Sessions *(Verve/—)*
Various (Including Charlie Parker, Johnny Hodges, Benny Carter, *Flip Phillips)*
*The Charlie Parker Sides
(Verve)/
The Parker Jam Session
(Verve)
Various (Including Charlie Shavers), Anatomy Of A Jam Session *(Black Lion/Black Lion)*
*Tracks by Flip Phillips not on US release.

Artie Shaw

Artie Shaw (born New York City, 1910) brought to jazz one of the finest clarinet techniques. A superbly fluent player, with a pleasingly melodic approach, he lacked only the intensity and depth of expression that was such an integral part of the work of other jazz clarinettists like, for example,

Artie Shaw & His Gramercy Five (RCA). Artie Shaw's jazz was lightweight – but the Gramercy Five was best of all.

Sidney Bechet (♦), Barney Bigard (♦), Johnny Dodds (♦) and Jimmie Noone (♦). He swung in a subtle and effortless way (although not as emphatically as Benny Goodman (♦), for years his great rival, both as bandleader and clarinettist). And there were occasions when his improvisations tended to become little more than decoration. That Shaw could indeed play jazz with body, as well as great technical expertise, is evident in his solo from a recording by Billie Holiday (♦) of her own **Billie's Blues (Lady Day/Billie Holiday's Greatest Hits)** during which Shaw plays a remarkably authentic blues solo.

Raised in New Haven, Connecticut, Shaw (real name Arthur Jacob Arshawsky) played saxophone in local high school band. After gigging locally with quartet, made professional debut with Johnny Cavallaro, as saxophonist, clarinettist. Resident for three years in Cleveland, playing with various bands (including Irvin Aaronson's Commanders – this time featured on tenor-sax). Moved to New York, freelanced for CBS and on record; then, in 1934, left music completely for a year. Returned to New York and music following year, appearing in concert with clarinet-and-strings quintet. Recorded with Billie Holiday (see above) in 1936 and Bunny Berigan (♦), taking part in session which produced Berigan's first version of **I Can't Get Started With You (Bunny Berigan & His Boys)**, then put together first (and short-lived) big band with string section. Put together second, more conventional, big band (1937) which soon became one of the most popular outfits during so-called Swing Era. Band had tremendous hit with its recording of **Begin The Beguine (The Complete Artie Shaw/Concerto For Clarinet)** and its popularity became too much for its leader, who disbanded in December, '39, and lived for two months in Mexico. Reformed mid-1940, and before joining US Navy (1942), had disbanded at least once, and toured

with large band containing sizeable string section. Fronted Naval Band which toured Pacific area (1943–4).

Medically discharged in February 1944, formed another (civilian) band later that year, which included Roy Eldridge (♦) as star soloist, and youngsters like Dodo Marmarosa (♦), Herbie Steward, and Barney Kessel (♦) **(The Complete Artie Shaw/Concerto For Clarinet, Artie Shaw & His Orchestra, Vol 2)**. Often outspoken critic of commercial exploitation of music, Shaw disbanded orchestra for last time and retired to become writer. (His autobiography, *The Trouble With Cinderella*, caused much comment when first published in 1952.) Periodically, from late-1940s until late-1953, led small groups. Final band was updated version of his Gramercy Five, his band-within-a-band of the peak years of popularity. Much of basic jazz content of Shaw's music came from Gramercy Five, which first recorded in 1940 **(Artie Shaw & His Gramercy Five)** with fine solos from Billy Butterfield (♦), pianist Johnny Guarnieri (♦) (who also played harpsichord), and Shaw himself. Even here, though, jazz was, like that emanating from larger outfit, of low-key variety. Best of Gramercy Five tracks probably were **Special Delivery Stomp, Summit Ridge Drive** (recording of which sold over a million), **My Blue Heaven** and **The Grabtown Grapple** (from later Gramercy Five and featuring Eldridge).

Retired to run dairy farm, then to live in Spain (1955–60). Married (at last count) eight times, Shaw has resisted tempting offers to return to music business.

Recordings:
Bunny Berigan, Take It, Bunny! *(Epic/Philips)*
Billie Holiday, Lady Day *(Columbia)*
Billie Holiday's Greatest Hits *(CBS – Italy)*
The Complete Artie Shaw, Vols 1, 2 *(Bluebird)/*

Concerto For Clarinet *(RCA Victor)/*
Artie Shaw & His Orchestra, Vol 2 *(RCA Victor)*
Artie Shaw & His Orchestra (1937-1938), Vols 1-3 *(First Time Records/—)*
Artie Shaw & His Gramercy Five *(RCA Victor)*
Artie Shaw Featuring Roy Eldridge *(RCA Victor/—)*
Artie Shaw, Melody In Madness, Vols 1, 2 *(Jazz Guild/—)*
Dance To Artie Shaw *(Coral)*
Artie Shaw & His Gramercy Five *(Clef/Columbia – Clef)*

Archie Shepp

Tenorman Archie Shepp was born in Florida, 1937, and made his earliest recordings with Cecil Taylor **(Air** and **Into The Hot)** sounding at that time, 1960, like an amalgam of Rollins and Coltrane. By 1962 he had emerged as a highly original voice and his quartet with trumpeter Bill Dixon produced a classic solo on **Trio (Bill Dixon – Archie Shepp Quartet)**. With the New York Contemporary Five of the following year, Shepp picked up ideas about group voicings **(Archie Shepp & The New York Contemporary Five)** and although the free drumming of J. C. Moses suited him less well than Don Cherry or John Tchicai, the lessons of the NYC5 were fruitfully continued in a Shepp studio band with Tchicai, trumpeter Alan Shorter and trombonist Roswell Rudd **(Four For Trane)**. His arrangement of Coltrane's **Syeeda's Song Flute** and Rudd's of **Niema**

Archie Shepp Live At The Pan-African Festival (BYG).

are excellent small group writing. The links with Coltrane were reinforced on the massive collective work **Ascension** in 1965, featuring many of the New Thing musicians, including Shepp. The most readily approachable of that group, Shepp's tone is a fiercely exciting blend of hoarse cries, rasps, loose vibrato and cutting clarity, his dramatic control of dynamics similar to Ben Webster's. His feeling for the blues is intensely emotional, while his ballad playing – **In A Sentimental Mood (On This Night** and **Live In San Francisco)** or **Prelude To A Kiss (Fire Music** and **Mama Too Tight)** – is robustly romantic and recalls an earlier era. Shepp's second major involvement in group writing **(Fire Music)** produced two magnificent works, **Hambone** and **Los Olvidados**, and a deeply moving trio performance, **Malcolm, Malcolm – Semper Malcolm** on which the tenorman reads his own poem to

Malcolm X. Shepp's poetry, *The Wedding* **(Live In San Francisco)**, *Scag* **(New Thing At Newport)** or his later albums like **Things Have Got To Change** and **Attica Blues,** are aspects of his fervent political beliefs: 'I play of the death of me by you'. A period with vibraphonist Bobby Hutcherson in the group **(On This Night** and **New Thing At Newport)** gave way to the collaborations with trombonists like Roswell Rudd **(Live In San Francisco** and **Three For A Quarter)** and later, additionally, Grachan Moncur III **(One For The Trane** and **Mama Too Tight)**.

1966–7 saw Shepp experimenting with dense counterpoint, savage collective playing and straight-faced Sousa marches, the lengthy **Portrait Of Robert Johnson (Mama Too Tight)** being a fine example. The title track, an explosive tenor solo over a ragged R&B riff, is a genre in which Shepp reigns supreme, while **Damn If I Know (The Way Ahead)** follows a similar pattern. Eighteen minutes of tenor over assorted percussion **(The Magic Of Ju-Ju)** is either boring or mesmerizing depending on the listener's stamina, but the unaccompanied **Rain Forest** made during Shepp's stay in France, 1969–70, is an unqualified masterpiece, spinechillingly brutal and tender by turns **(Poem For Malcolm)**. A great deal of recording went on in 1969 as Paris was seething with expatriate New Thingers like the Art Ensemble Of Chicago and Sunny Murray, and most of the albums for BYG featured extensive sitting-in. Malachi Favors and Philly Joe Jones back the tenorman, as well as two bluesy harmonica players, on an album featuring the singer Jeanne Lee **(Blase)**, while Lester Bowie, Roscoe Mitchell, Hank Mobley, Leroy Jenkins, Anthony Braxton, Noah Howard, Clifford Thornton and Sunny Murray turn up variously on several excellent Shepp dates **(Yasmina, A Black Woman, Black Gipsy, Archie Shepp & Philly Joe Jones** and **Coral Rock)** and during an Algerian festival which also includes Tuareg musicians **(Live At The Panafrican Festival)**.

Returning to America in 1971, Shepp worked with singer Joe Lee Wilson **(Things Have Got To Change** and **Attica Blues)** using some of the practices of Tamla Motown to achieve a broad image of black culture. Recent Shepp releases from Europe reveal him to be in great form, and his current group, Charles Greenlea trombone, Dave Burrell piano, Cameron Brown bass and the habitual Beaver Harris on drums, played a magnificent set at the Massy Festival **(Shepp A Massy)**. Archie Shepp's piano playing is interesting, his soprano leaner than his tenor, which remains one of the most commanding sounds in jazz.

Recordings:
Cecil Taylor, Air *(CBS Barnaby/CBS Barnaby)*
Cecil Taylor, Into The Hot *(Impulse/Impulse)*
Bill Dixon-Archie Shepp Quartet *(Savoy/—)*
Archie Shepp & The New York Contemporary Five *(Sonet/Polydor)*
Archie Shepp, Four For Trane *(Impulse/Impulse)*

Quintet remains the heart of his music.

As a pianist, he has stripped away much of the multi-note complexity of Bop in favour of a more direct, blues based, percussive approach. Boogie figures rumble from the left hand, single note on the beat phrases alternating with locked hands chordal hammerings, the style seemingly simple but in fact inimitable. The cheeky quotes and immediately attractive lines generate a friendliness that has communicated to a wide audience over two decades.

Above: Archie Shepp, articulate spokesman for a people's music. Emotionally overwhelming tenor player.

John Coltrane, Ascension
(Impulse/Impulse)
On This Night *(Impulse/Impulse)*
Live In San Francisco
(Impulse/Impulse)
Fire Music *(Impulse/Impulse)*
Mama Too Tight
(Impulse/Impulse)
New Thing At Newport
(Impulse/Impulse)
Three For A Quarter
(Impulse/Impulse)
The Way Ahead
(Impulse/Impulse)
The Magic Of Ju-Ju
(Impulse/Impulse)
One For The Trane
(BASF/Saba)
Poem For Malcolm
(—/BYG – France)
Blase *(—/BYG – France)*
Yasmina, A Black Woman
(—/BYG – France)
Live At The Panafrican Festival
(—/BYG – France)
Black Gipsy *(Prestige/America)*
Archie Shepp & Philly Joe Jones
(Fantasy/America)
Coral Rock *(Prestige/America)*
Things Have Got To Change
(Impulse/Impulse)
Attica Blues *(Impulse/Impulse)*
Shepp A Massy
(—/Uniteledis – France)
Archie Shepp *(—/Horo – Italy)*
Steam *(Enja/Enja)*
A Sea Of Faces
(—/Black Saint – Italy)
There's A Trumpet In My Soul
(Arista Freedom/Arista Freedom)
Live At Montreux
(Arista Freedom/Arista Freedom)
Body & Soul *(—/Horo)*

Wayne Shorter
◆ *Weather Report*

Horace Silver

Born 1928, the pianist composer started out as a Bud Powell disciple like many of his generation, and following a stint with the Stan Getz Quartet began to develop into an influential stylist in his own right. With drummer Art Blakey, he co-founded The Jazz Messengers, which was – with its fire and brimstone attack – the most typical Hard Bop unit in the '50s. Silver's playing became increasingly percussive, so that accompaniment for the soloist – caught between the drums and piano, and forced to raise his game – was a barrage of rhythmic riffs, goadings and peremptory proddings.

Silver's themes for The Jazz Messengers **Quicksilver, Doodlin'**, and particularly **The Preacher**, set the pattern for much of the next decade. The fact that **The Preacher** started the trend for 'Soul', a back-to-the-roots mixture of gospel and blues over a simple backbeat, often featuring call and response patterns along the lines of the preacher and congregation, obscures the fact that the composer was responsible for many innovations. All the Messengers' albums from the early period are excellent **(A Night At Birdland, At The Cafe Bohemia** and **Horace Silver & The Jazz Messengers)**, but Silver left in 1956 to form his own Quintet.

Personnel over the years includes tenormen Junior Cook, Hank Mobley, Joe Henderson, trumpeters Joe Gordon, Carmell Jones, Woody Shaw, Blue Mitchell and Art Farmer, and drummers Louis Hayes, Roy Brooks and Roger Humphries. Silver's arrangements for the unit are seldom complex, but never predictable either. The horns state the theme – often a mixture of blues, gospel and latin influences, multi-layered,choppy and chock-a-block with contrasts – and the leader's piano figures slide slyly sideways as if begging to differ. Bars come in an odd assortment of remnant lengths, and alternative melodies emerge as the piece gets under way. Funky blues, **Home Cookin' (The Stylings Of Silver), Sweet Sweetie Dee** and **Let's Get To The Nitty Gritty (Silver's Serenade)**; hard-driving blues, **Filthy McNasty (Doin' The Thing)**; exotic blues, **Senor Blues (Six Pieces Of Silver), The Cape Verdean Blues (The Cape Verdean Blues), Song For My Father (Song For My Father)**; and hauntingly beautiful ballads like **Calcutta Cutie (Song For My Father)** seem to pour from Silver's fertile imagination.

His more recent output for Blue Note shows an attempt to broaden his palette **(Silver & Wood)** and write for larger ensembles, but the

The Stylings Of Silver (Blue Note): Fingerpoppa.

Recordings:
The Jazz Messengers, A Night At Birdland
(Blue Note/Blue Note)
The Jazz Messengers, At The Cafe Bohemia
(Blue Note/Blue Note)
Horace Silver & The Jazz Messengers
(Blue Note/Blue Note)

Above: pianist and leader, Horace Silver. Wrote The Preacher which started a funky trend in the '50s.

The Stylings Of Silver
(Blue Note/Blue Note)
Silver's Serenade
(Blue Note/Blue Note)
Doin' The Thing
(Blue Note/Blue Note)
Six Pieces Of Silver
(Blue Note/Blue Note)
Song For My Father
(Blue Note/Blue Note)
The Cape Verdean Blues
(Blue Note/Blue Note)
Silver & Wood
(Blue Note/Blue Note)

Omer Simeon

Omer Victor Simeon (born New Orleans, Louisiana, 1902) was one of a great dynasty of New Orleans clarinet players whose warmth and suppleness was equalled only by their ability to swing at all times. Fine ensemble player, Simeon's remained a major solo voice on his instrument for over three decades. Taught by legendary Lorenzo Tio Jr, Simeon grew up in Chicago (his family moved there when he was 12). 1920: debut as professional musician, with brother Al's band. Became mainstay of Charlie Elgar's Creole Band (1923–1927), before moving on to King Oliver's (♦) Dixie Syncopators, taking place of Darnell Howard (♦). With Oliver, played alto-sax as well as clarinet **(King Oliver's Dixie Syncopators 1926-1928)**, also soloing occasionally on soprano-sax **(Willie The Weeper** and **Every Tub).**

After reunion with Elgar, worked with Luis Russell (♦), Jelly Roll Morton (♦). Recorded with latter **(Jelly Roll Morton & His Red Hot Peppers, Vols 2-4)**, sounding superbly at ease within this environment. His contributions to

Georgia Swing, Shreveport Stomp, Mournful Serenade, The Chant and Dead Man Blues are most memorable. 1929: much-in-demand Simeon recorded with own group **(Beau Koo Jack** and **Smoke-House Blues)** as well as with Reuben Reeves, Dixie Rhythm Kings, Alex Hill (all on **Omer Simeon)** and with Erskine Tate, in whose orchestra Simeon played between 1928-1930. Apart from spells with Horace Henderson (♦), Fletcher Henderson (♦), Walter Fuller in '38, spent approximately 10 years with orchestra of Earl Hines (♦) **(The Indispensable Earl Hines, Vols 1-3)**, playing clarinet and alto- and baritone-sax. 1940: briefly with Coleman Hawkins (♦), then joined – in succession – Walter Fuller, Jimmie Lunceford (♦) **(Jimmie Lunceford & His Orchestra 1941-1943)**. Stayed with Lunceford aggregation until 1950, by which time its leader had died and band had been taken over by Eddie Wilcox. Freelanced in NYC during 1950–1951 before becoming member of Wilbur De Paris' New Orleans Band in latter year – remaining its most gifted and important soloist **(Marchin' & Swingin'** and **Wilbur De Paris & His New Orleans Jazz)** until his death, from throat cancer, in 1959. Simeon, who visited Africa with De Paris band in 1957, also recorded with other notable jazz-men during his distinguished career. Amongst record dates which resulted in work comparing with his finest elsewhere can be numbered those in company with Jabbo Smith **(The Ace Of Rhythm)**,

Below: Omer Simeon – 'one of a great dynasty of New Orleans clarinet players'. Fluent, warm and swinging.

Above: Zoot Sims, a living guarantee of taste, drive and imagination. Often in company with Al Cohn.

Kid Ory (♦) **(Tailgate!)** and Tiny Parham **(Tiny Parham & His Musicians).**

Recordings:
Omer Simeon *(—/Ace of Hearts)*
King Oliver's Dixie Syncopators 1926-1928 *(MCA Coral – Germany)*
King Oliver, Vols 1, 3 *(RCA Victor – France)*
Jabbo Smith, The Ace Of Rhythm *(—/Ace of Hearts)*
Jelly Roll Morton's Red Hot Peppers, Vols 2-4 *(RCA Victor – France)*
The Indispensable Earl Hines, Vol 1, 1929-1939 *(RCA Victor – France)*
Tiny Parham & His Musicians *(Pirate – Sweden)*
Jimmy (sic) Lunceford & His Orchestra (1941-43) *(First Time Records/—)*
Kid Ory, Tailgate! *(Good Time Jazz/Vogue)*
Wilbur De Paris, Marchin' & Swingin' *(Atlantic/Atlantic)*
Wilbur De Paris & His New Orleans Jazz *(Atlantic)*
Jimmy Witherspoon With Wilbur De Paris & His New Orleans Band *(Atlantic/London)*

Sonny Simmons

Born in Louisiana, 1933, altoman Sonny Simmons made his first record with flute and altoman Prince Lasha **(The Cry)**, an early friend of Ornette Coleman's, both men turning up on a five-night re-

cording session under Eric Dolphy **(Memorial Album** and **Iron Man)**. Ornette's influence is strongly felt in **A Distant Voice (Staying On The Watch)** a stately, sombre performance. Sidewoman on the date was trumpeter Barbara Donald, a continuing musical partnership. Both musicians sound considerably stronger by 1969, with Simmons fiercely attacking all over the horn **(Manhattan Egos)** which is possibly his finest work.

Recordings:
The Cry *(Contemporary/—)*
Eric Dolphy Memorial *(DJM/DJM)*
Eric Dolphy, Iron Man *(Douglas/—)*
Staying On The Watch *(ESP/ESP)*
Manhattan Egos *(Arhoolie/—)*
Rumasuma *(Contemporary/—)*
Burning Spirits *(Contemporary/—)*

Zoot Sims

Tenorman Zoot Sims is one of the most consistent musicians in jazz, unfailingly swinging and inventive on ballads and blues. Born in California, 1925, he joined Benny Goodman in the mid-40s, and then Woody Herman's Second Herd, where he made up the famous 'Four Brothers' saxophone line with Stan Getz, Herbie Steward and

ZOOT SIMS
Zootcase
With ART BLAKEY, JOHN LEWIS, AL COHN, PERCY HEATH

SPECIALLY PRICED
TWO-RECORD SET
PR 24061

Zootcase (Prestige): the long-playing album had just emerged, and Zoot took the opportunity to stretch out.

Serge Chaloff **(The Best Of Woody Herman).** Stylistically, Sims derives from Lester Young, but incorporates the wider harmonic practices of the early modernists. He stayed two years with Herman, 1947–9, before moving back to the West Coast where he gigged with a wide variety of players like Clifford Brown and Chet Baker.

He joined Stan Kenton in 1953, and the Gerry Mulligan Sextet in 1955, and recorded later with Mulligan's Concert Jazz Band. **Red Door, Apple Core** and **Come Rain Or Come Shine** are outstanding performances **(Gerry Mulligan & The Concert Jazz Band Live).** In 1950, Sims recorded Prestige's first long-playing album, taking advantage of the room to stretch out on **Zoot Swings The Blues (Zootcase).** The compilation also includes fine sessions from the early '50s with George Wallington and Al Cohn, a favorite blowing partner from the Herman days. Sims and Cohn have cut several albums together **(Body & Soul)** including the lyrical dovetailing on **Emily (Motoring Along** and **You 'N' Me)** with their compatibility illustrated by **Improvisation For Unaccompanied Saxophones.**

Another great partnership occurred with veteran violinist, Joe Venuti **(Joe & Zoot)** and numbers like **I Got Rhythm** are the epitome of swing. One of the best Sims albums, **Jive At Five,** from 1960,

is currently deleted, but recent years have seen a flood of Sims albums for Norman Granz. They are all excellent, and show his mature style with its warm, Ben Websterish tone **(Basie & Zoot, Zoot Sims & The Gershwin Brothers** and **Hawthorne Nights)** with a large ensemble and arrangements by Bill Holman, and an album featuring Sims, airy and elegant soprano saxophone **(Soprano Sax).**

Recordings:
The Best Of Woody Herman
(Columbia/CBS)
Gerry Mulligan & The Concert Jazz Band Live
(Verve/Verve)
Zootcase *(Prestige/Prestige)*
Body & Soul *(Muse/—)*
Motoring Along *(Sonet/Sonet)*
You 'N' Me *(Mercury/Mercury)*
Joe & Zoot *(Chiaroscuro/Vogue)*
Basie & Zoot *(Pablo/Pablo)*
Zoot Sims & The Gershwin Brothers *(Pablo/Pablo)*
Hawthorne Nights *(Pablo/Pablo)*
Soprano Sax *(Pablo/Pablo)*
Dream Dancing *(Choice/DJM)*
If I'm Lucky *(Pablo/Pablo)*

Zutty Singleton
♦ Louis Armstrong

Right: Zutty Singleton – he drummed splendidly with the giants, including Louis, Morton, Bird, et al.

Bessie Smith

The Empress of the Blues, Bessie Smith, was born in Chattanooga, Tennessee, at a date variously given as 1894 or 1898. Her voice, ringing and declamatory, retained the early influence of the black churches, and by the age of 14 she had become the protégé of blues singer Ma Rainey, touring with her Rabbit Foot Minstrels on the tent show circuit and learning the craft. Like Ma Rainey, she based her interpretations around secure center tones, returning to them time and again to produce a stark, incantatory effect, utilizing key changes to vary the impact. More sophisticated than her mentor, Bessie Smith's dramatic delivery employs bent notes, slurs and a rhythmically adventurous use of rests, which tends to place her stylistically at a midpoint between the rural blues and instrumental jazz.

Despite the blues vogue opened up by Mamie Smith's hit record, **Crazy Blues,** Bessie was passed over by the record companies as too rough-hewn until 1923, when she cut two commercially-successful sides, **Down Hearted Blues** and **Gulf Coast Blues,** for Columbia. These performances can be found on the first of a five-volume set **(The World's Greatest Blues Singer)** in a format which groups early and late recording sessions. Clarence Williams' piano accompaniment is easily outclassed by the Fletcher Henderson sides, while the singer's swansong, **Do Your Duty, Gimme A Pigfoot, Take Me For A Buggy Ride** and **Down In The Dumps** use a Swing Era instrumentation of Frankie Newton, Jack Teagarden, Benny

Goodman and Chu Berry.

The second volume (**Any Woman's Blues**) is a very mixed bag, offering popular and vaudeville material on **Sam Jones Blues** and **My Sweetie Went Away**, duets with the rival blues singer, Clara Smith, **Far Away Blues** and **I'm Going Back To My Used To Be**, the classic **Nobody Knows You When You're Down And Out** from 1929 and the magnificent partnership with pianist James P. Johnson. The third and fourth volumes contain examples of the singer with her ideal accompanists, trombonist Charlie Green and cornettist Joe Smith, the latter a simple and affecting foil on the great **Weeping Willow Blues**, while the trombonist provides a humorous commentary on **Empty Bed Blues (Empty Bed Blues)**. Both men with Fletcher Henderson on piano and a youthful Coleman Hawkins on tenor add greatly to the excitement on **Cake Walkin' Babies** and **Yellow Dog Blues**, while Louis Armstrong plays classic obbligatos on **St Louis Blues**, **Reckless Blues** and **Cold In Hand Blues (The Empress)**.

The final volume, **Nobody's Blues But Mine**, covers 1925–7, arguably her finest period, before drink and declining popularity overcame her talents. Competition from singer Ethel Waters and public boredom with the more elemental blues forced Bessie to include material like **Alexander's Ragtime Band** and **After You've Gone** along with the more appropriate and magnificent **Back Water Blues** and **Preachin' The Blues**.

The Depression saw the long decline of Bessie Smith, and her tragic death in a car accident in 1938. She had taken the blues from the tent shows and vaudeville circuits into the Northern theatres, and given the form its most majestic expression. Her power and emotional integrity transcended the often trivial lyrics, paring away prettiness to reveal an irreduceable structure. Her dramatic gifts found an outlet in revues like *Harlem Frolics*, *The Midnight Steppers*

and the two-reel movie, *St Louis Blues*. The definitive biography, *Bessie*, by Chris Albertson, clears away many of the baseless legends and rumors that have surrounded her turbulent life and death.

Recordings:
The World's Greatest Blues Singer *(Columbia/CBS)*
Any Woman's Blues *(Columbia/CBS)*
Empty Bed Blues *(Columbia/CBS)*
The Empress *(Columbia/CBS)*
Nobody's Blues But Mine *(Columbia/CBS)*

Jimmy Smith

Organist Jimmy Smith was responsible for transforming that much-reviled instrument into the ubiquitous and popular seller of the '60s. Born in Philadelphia, 1925, he started out as a pianist, formally training as a bassist after service in the navy. In the early '50s, he switched to organ, forming his first trio in 1955, and his early output for Blue Note remains the best. Adapting the Hard Bop style to the organ, and influenced by pianists Horace Silver and Bud Powell, Smith brought a crispness and speed of attack which effectively removed all associations with skat-

The Incredible Jimmy Smith (Blue Note)

Above: Jimmy Smith, jazz's best-known organist, a fine exponent of funky blues with several hits in the '60s.

ing rinks. Supplying his own bass line, the virtuoso spun endless variations; fast, single-note runs and sustained chords around which he embroidered his supercharged improvisations. By 1956, he was hailed as Metronome's New Star. Two volumes with Art Blakey (**The Incredible Jimmy Smith**) show what a dazzling performer he was, from the wildly exciting duet for drums and organ, **The Duel**, to the blues **All Day Long** or **Plum Nellie**. His endless inventiveness around the blues is well-illustrated on Silver's hit, **The Preacher (At Club 'Baby Grand')**. A series of blowing sessions produced the expected tear-up, and also showed Smith's gifts as an accompanist (**Open House, The Sermon** and **A Date With Jimmy Smith**) to players like Hank Mobley, Jackie McLean, Ike Quebec and Lou Donaldson.

Mid-period Smith tended to reflect the great popularity of **Midnight Special** and, with Stanley Rurrentine or Lou Donaldson, he recorded a string of medium tempo funky blues (**Back At The Chicken Shack, Rockin' The Boat** and **Prayer Meetin'**). Two of the best albums from this period return to the trio format (**Softly As A Summer Breeze** and **Crazy!**

Baby). Leaving Blue Note, he signed with Verve and increased his popularity with numbers like **A Walk On The Wild Side (Bashin')** on which he fronts a big band, and **Goldfinger (Monster)** an album which also contains the more interesting **Slaughter On Tenth Avenue** and **Bluesette**.

Success tended to produce formula playing and a rash of imitators like Jimmy McGriff and Jack McDuff, and the adoption of electric piano has seen the eclipse of the organ.

Recordings:
The Incredible Jimmy Smith *(Blue Note/Blue Note)*
At Club 'Baby' Grand *(Blue Note/Blue Note)*
Open House *(Blue Note/Blue Note)*
The Sermon *(Blue Note/Blue Note)*
A Date With Jimmy Smith *(Blue Note/Blue Note)*
Midnight Special *(Blue Note/Blue Note)*
Back At The Chicken Shack *(Blue Note/Blue Note)*
Rockin' The Boat *(Blue Note/Blue Note)*
Prayer Meetin' *(Blue Note/Blue Note)*

The World's Greatest Blues Singer (CBS). Never was an album more appropriately titled than this one . . .

Softly As A Summer Breeze
   (Blue Note/Blue Note)
Crazy! Baby
   (Blue Note/Blue Note)
Greatest Hits
   (Blue Note/Blue Note)
Bashin' *(Verve/Verve)*
The Monster *(Verve/Verve)*

Joe Smith

Joe Smith (born Ripley, Ohio, 1902) is alleged to have been favorite trumpet of Bessie Smith (♦). Certainly, the blues singer utilized Smith's services on numerous record dates, most notably on items like **Muddy Water, There'll Be A Hot Time In The Old Town Tonight, Send Me To The 'Lectric Chair** (all on **The Empress**); **Weeping Willow Blues, The Bye Bye Blues** (both on **Empty Bed Blues**); **Lost Your Head Blues, Hard Driving Papa, Alexander's Ragtime Band, Baby Doll,** and **Money Blues** (all on **Nobody's Blues But Mine**). Smith's soulful, sensitive trumpet provided the choicest obbligatos and/or solos that were the perfect complement to Bessie Smith's unsurpassed blues singing. Smith's uniqueness as accompanist-soloist has been documented on numerous recordings by other singers. Ethel Waters (♦), for example, had benefited from Smith's presence during 1922 recordings like **That Da Da Strain, Georgia Blues** (both on **Oh Daddy 1921-1924** and **Jazzin' Babies' Blues: 1921-1927, Vol 2**). Indeed, Smith was for a time (1922) member of Waters' Jazz Masters combo, touring in company with Fletcher Henderson (♦) as part of Black Swan Jazz Masters Show. He was present at further Waters recording sessions, including that which produced **Brother, You've Got Me Wrong,** and **Sweet Georgia Brown** (both on **Ethel Waters' Greatest Years**) in 1925.

Smith's melodic playing is superbly evidenced in recordings by Ma Rainey (♦), dating from '25, including **Wringin' Twistin' Blues, Slave To The Blues** (both on **Ma Rainey**).

Smith, who was taught trumpet by his father, was one of seven brothers – each of whom played trumpet. At first, worked locally then, in 1920, in New York, Pittsburgh. After Black Swan tour, worked with yet another singer – Mamie Smith – between 1922-1923. Freelanced extensively, including work as musical director for Sissle-Blake revue, *In Bramville*.

1925: started a three-and-a-half-year stint with Fletcher Henderson Orchestra (brother, Russell Smith, was Henderson's lead trumpet during this period). Smith's eloquent solo work was heard in Henderson recordings such as **What-Cha-Call-'Em Blues, The Stampede, Snag It (Fletcher Henderson Story, Vol 1)** and **Rocky Mountain Blues, Variety Stomp, St Louis Blues (Vol 2)**. Transferred to McKinney's Cotton Pickers (1929), and the Smith elegance of phrase and warmth of expression is to be found on recordings like **Gee, Baby, Ain't I Good To You, Plain Dirt (McKinney's Cotton Pickers: 1923-1929, Vol 2)** and **The Way I Feel Today (Vol 3)**.

Injured in car accident, Smith left McKCP end of 1930. Rejoined Fletcher Henderson for short period, worked also with Kaiser Marshall, then returned to McKCP (1931–1932). During this time, and afterwards, Smith's health deteriorated rapidly. Attempted comeback with Henderson but was taken to New York sanatorium. Died in Belle Vue Hospital end of '37 of paresis.

Recordings:
Bessie Smith, The Empress
   (Columbia/CBS)
Bessie Smith, Empty Bed Blues *(Columbia/CBS)*
Bessie Smith, Nobody's Blues But Mine *(Columbia/CBS)*
Ma Rainey *(Milestone)*
Fletcher Henderson, Henderson On Columbia *(—/VJM)*
Fletcher Henderson, The Fletcher Henderson Story, Vols 1-2 *(Columbia/CBS)*
McKinney's Cotton Pickers, Vols 2-4 *(RCA Victor – France)*
Ethel Waters, Oh Daddy! (1921-1924) *(Biograph/—)*
Ethel Waters, Jazzin' Babies' Blues (1921-1927), Vol 2 *(Biograph/—)*
Ethel Waters' Greatest Years *(Columbia/—)*

Stuff Smith

Hezekiah Leroy Gordon 'Stuff' Smith (born Portsmouth, Ohio, 1909) was, without a shade of doubt, the most basic jazz violinist of all. In many ways, he could well be termed the greatest jazz violinist. Even for those who still find violin unacceptable within a jazz context, usually there is to be found some little, even grudging, praise. Certainly, though, in various ways Smith was indeed a great jazz musician. He bowed his instrument with an unequalled ferocity and swung with tremendous unrelenting power. He had a genuine and readily-communicated feeling for the blues. And never, where Stuff Smith was concerned, was there a trace of the palm-court kind of playing which has marred attempts to play jazz by other violinists. Not that Smith was some kind of primitive savage with no technical skills, academically speaking, whatsoever. He was capable of the most astonishing flights of fancy, as his playing opposite another virtuoso, Dizzy Gillespie (♦), during their second get-together on record **(Dizzy Gillespie & Stuff Smith)** indicates superbly. And in company with fellow jazz violinists, there was little if anything they could teach him in terms of technique and, of course, swing; a fact illustrated graphically on **Violin Summit** wherein Smith is juxtaposed, in a concertized setting, with Jean-Luc Ponty, Stephane Grappelli (♦) and Svend Asmussen.

After Smith's father (himself a multi-instrumentalist) had made him his first violin at eight, had an early introduction to playing music by appearing with his father's band, aged twelve. Won musical scholarship to Johnson C. Smith University, North Carolina, but left in 1924 to tour with a revue band. Worked with Alphonse Trent (1926–9) except for a brief spell, in '27, as member of Jelly Roll Morton's band; he left to return to Trent because the loudness of the rest of the band drowned out his acoustic violin. Moved to Buffalo where he became a regular favorite in local clubs. Eventually he and small combo he was leading at the time went to New York (1936). Smith's reputation was established thereafter, mostly because of long residency at Onyx Club, on 52nd Street. It was during this engagement that Smith first used an amplifier with his violin. Stuff Smith's became one of the most popular bands on 52nd Street, with the leader's violin and hoarse vocals complemented splendidly by trumpet (and sometimes additional vocals) of Jonah Jones (♦) and driving drumming of Cozy Cole (♦). The accent was firmly on straight-ahead, no-nonsense swinging, laced with liberal doses of humor, which did not always go down too well with the more purist critics and fans. But the music by Stuff Smith & His Onyx Club Orchestra was good, always, as recordings like **I Hope Gabriel Likes My Music, Tain't No Use, After You've Gone, Serenade For A Wealthy Widow** (all **Stuff Smith & His Onyx Club Orchestra**) and **Twilight In Turkey, Upstairs** and **Onyx Club Spree** (all **The Swinging Small Bands 1 - 1937-1939**) indicate delightfully. A single record by the band, **I'se A-Muggin'**, a piece of infectious musical hokum, became a hit. Smith & Co also proved popular during 1937–8 in California.

There was a temporary halt to activities when Smith was forced to disband, due to union and financial problems. But with problems resolved, band continued until, with Jones (Cole having left), Smith took over leadership of Fats Waller's band on death of latter in 1943. After contracting pneumonia in Hollywood, he left. On recovery, put together own trio, playing regularly in Chicago where he settled for a while in 1940s. Moved again, to live in California. Spent most of 1950s on West Coast, mostly neglected by jazz buffs. Recorded in 1957, in company with Oscar Peterson (♦)-led quartet **(Stuff Smith)**; created favorable impression all over again. During the years, his playing had taken on fresh dimensions of excitement and creativity, at same time evincing a maturity that (sometimes) goes with age. Included in repertoire at this date were two fine Smith originals, **Desert Sands** and **Time & Again**. Two months later, recorded with Dizzy Gillespie (see above). (In 1951, Gillespie, Smith had recorded for Savoy **(Dee Gee Days/The Savoy Sessions)**, but the results, whilst not at all poor, did not compare with later meeting.) Recorded third album in '57 for same label as Peterson, Gillespie sessions, Verve, and standard again was first-rate **(Have Violin, Will Swing)**.

Below: Hezekiah Leroy Gordon 'Stuff' Smith - 'swung with tremendous unrelenting power . . .'

During rest of 1950s, and early-1960s, continued to lead own groups, as solo attraction, and with others (including highly successful season at Embers, New York, with Joe Bushkin Quartet, '64). Starting with well-received season in London, Smith was more or less permanently based in Europe from 1965. Proved immensely popular throughout the continent, especially in Denmark, where he recorded, in '65, the remarkable **Swingin' Stuff**, producing searing solos of almost unbelievable intensity. Probably his final recording, before he died in 1967 (in Munich, Germany), was **One O'Clock Jump**, from same year. As with his first recordings, so with his last; Stuff Smith was in dazzling form, technically superb and, of course, re-conjugating verb 'to swing' in own inimitable style.

Recordings:
Various (Including Stuff Smith), **The Swinging Small Bands 1 (1937-1939)** *(MCA – Germany)*
Stuff Smith & His Onyx Club Orchestra *(Collector's/—)*
Dizzy Gillespie, Dee Gee Days/ The Savoy Sessions *(Savoy/—)*
Stuff Smith *(Verve/Columbia – Clef)*
Dizzy Gillespie & Stuff Smith *(Verve/HMV)*
Stuff Smith, Swingin' Stuff *(EmArcy/Polydor)*
Various (Including Stuff Smith), **Violin Summit** *(Saba/Polydor)*
Stuff Smith, One O'Clock Jump *(Polydor)*
Stuff Smith, Have Violin, Will Swing *(Verve/—)*
Herb Ellis/Stuff Smith, Together *(Epic/—)*

Willie Smith

William McLeish 'Willie' Smith (born Charleston, South Carolina, 1910) was, without question, one of the great names of the jazz alto-saxophone. Certainly, his name is generally linked with those of Johnny Hodges (♦) and Benny Carter (♦) as being amongst the top three altoists prior to the emergence of Charlie Parker (♦) in the 1940s. Smith, who also was a fine clarinettist, played baritone-sax averagely and occasionally sang in a pleasant, if forgettable way; started on clarinet and played with Boston Serenaders during late-1920s. Attended both Case Technical College and Fisk University, Nashville. Whilst student at latter, first met Jimmie Lunceford (♦), whose band he was to join two years later (1929).
Thereafter, Smith became one of the foundations of Lunceford orchestra, soloing on alto and clarinet, taking the odd vocal, and providing strong, matchless, lead for saxes. He remained with band until 1942, when he left to work with Charlie Spivak. With Lunceford, contributed innumerable celebrated solo performances. On alto, his hard-swinging style, easily identified by impressively large and certainly distinctive tone, will be best remembered through recordings with band like **'Taint What You Do, Lunceford Special, Uptown Blues** (all **Lunceford Special**); **Rain, Shake Your Head, Rhapsody Junior** (all **Rhythm Is Our Business**); **Avalon, Me & The Moon** (**Harlem Shout**); **Stratosphere, The Melody Man, Teasin'**

Tessie Brown (Jimmie's Legacy) and **Lonesome Road (Lunceford Special)**. On clarinet, Smith's work was fluent, swinging, but if hardly as distinctive as on alto. Amongst best clarinet solos with Lunceford were **Rose Room, Bird Of Paradise, Black & Tan Fantasy, Rain** (all **Rhythm Is Our Business**); **Sophisticated Lady, Babs** (both **Jimmie's Legacy**); **On The Beach At Bali-Bali (Harlem Shouts)** and **What's Your Story Morning Glory Glory? (Lunceford Special)**. Willie Smith also contributed his share of arrangements for band, including **Runnin' Wild, Mood Indigo, Rose Room** (all **Rhythm Is Our Business**) and **Sophisticated Lady (Jimmie's Legacy)**.
After almost year with Spivak, enlisted with US Navy, in order to became musical director. On demobilization, in 1944, joined Harry James (♦) band, of which he was a principal featured soloist, section leader until 1951 (apart from one brief absence, in 1947). With James, Smith continued to produce kind of fiery playing that had marked his finest with Lunceford. At same time, Smith's alto was heard in variety of jam-session concert settings, most notably **Jazz At The Philharmonic 1944-46, Jazz At The Philharmonic, Vol 2, 1946** and **Memorable Concerts**; the latter, with Smith's also sharing solo honors with nominal leader Lionel Hampton (♦), took place during Gene Norman Presents 'Just Jazz' concert in 1947. Smith's playing on some of the JATP dates sometimes tended to be erratic, occasionally almost bizarre. Much better were his lucid, powerful contributions to two Norman Granz studio jam sessions **(Jam Sessions, Nos 2, 3)** where Smith's essentially 'mainstream' blowing sounds comfortably at home with younger players like Wardell Gray (♦), Stan Getz (♦) and Buddy De Franco (♦), as well as with contemporaries such as Count Basie (♦), Harry Edison (♦) and Carter.
Made comparatively few recordings under own name. One of the best dates from August 1965 **(The Best Of Willie Smith/Alto Saxophonist Supreme)** supported by interesting cross-section of younger musicians, including Stan Levey, Tommy Gumina, Jimmie Rowles or Johnny Guarnieri (♦), Bill Perkins. Smith's own **Willie's Blues** shows his ability in that idiom. Willie Smith always was kind of musician useful for conventional record dates, as Nat Cole (♦) **(After Midnight)**, Gene Krupa (♦) **(The Exciting Gene Krupa)** or producer Granz **(Jazz At The Philharmonic Carnegie Hall Concert 1952)** and others surely would testify. Yet in any final summation of Smith, there is little doubt that his major contributions were with big-band section of jazz. Apart from long stints with Lunceford and James, other big-band associations of note were with Duke Ellington (♦), with whom he worked for a year (1951–2) as replacement for Hodges, and Billy May, for whose studio orchestra Smith worked regularly during 1950s/1960s, as principal soloist and section leader. When Charlie Barnet (♦) assembled studio big band to rework numerous of his old hits, Willie Smith was present to lead saxes and take alto solos of distinction **(Big Band 1967)**. During last five years of his life, worked in Los Angeles–Las Vegas territories,

mostly with variety of local house bands.
Suffered prolonged illness after leaving Harry James for last time (in 1963), and died, in 1967, from cancer after spending several weeks in a Los Angeles hospital.

Recordings:
Jimmie Lunceford:
Rhythm Is Our Business (1934-1935) *(MCA – Germany)*
Harlem Shout (1935-1936) *(MCA – Germany)*
For Dancers Only (1936-1937) *(MCA – Germany)*
Blues In The Night (1938-1942) *(MCA – Germany)*
Jimmie's Legacy (1934-1937) *(MCA – Germany)*
The Last Sparks (1941-1944) *(MCA – Germany)*
Lunceford Special* *(Columbia/CBS – Realm)*
Lunceford Special* *(Columbia/Philips)*
Takin' Off With Jimmie *(Tax – Sweden)*
The World Of Duke Ellington *(Columbia)/*
The Duke: Edward Kennedy Ellington (1899-1974) *(CBS)*
The World Of Duke Ellington, Vol 2 *(Columbia)/*
The World Of Duke Ellington, Vol 1 *(CBS)*
Duke Ellington, The Liberian Suite/A Tone Parallel To Harlem *(Columbia/CBS – France)*

Swingin' With Harry James *(Joker – Italy)*
The Big Band Sound Of Harry James *(Verve)*
The Second/Third Big Band Sound(s) Of Harry James *(Verve)*
Various, **Jazz At The Philharmonic, 1944-46** *(—/Verve)*
Various, **Jazz At The Philharmonic, 1946, Vol 2** *(—/Verve)*
Various, **Norman Granz' Jazz At The Philharmonic Carnegie Hall Concert 1952** *(Verve/Columbia – Clef)*
Various, **Jammin' At Sunset, Vol 1** *(Black Lion/Black Lion)*
Various, **Memorable Concerts** *(Vogue/Vogue)*
Various (Including Louis Bellson/Willie Smith), **All Star Sessions** *(Capitol/Louis – Holland)*
Various, **Jam Sessions, Nos 2, 3** *(Verve/Columbia – Clef)*
The Best Of Willie Smith *(GNP – Crescendo)/*
Alto Saxophonist Supreme *(London)*
Nat King Cole, After Midnight *(Capitol/Capitol – Denmark)*
Charlie Barnet, Big Band 1967 *(Vault/Vocalion)*

Below: Willie 'The Lion' Smith, master of the Harlem Stride piano and an influence on Ellington.

Willie 'The Lion' Smith

Born William Henry Joseph Bonaparte Bertholoff Smith in 1897, Willie The Lion was one of the New York pioneers who adapted ragtime to the needs of jazz piano, establishing the style known as Harlem Stride. The Harlem pianists of the '20s, James P. Johnson, Willie The Lion, Luckey Roberts, Duke Ellington, Fats Waller, engaged in piano cutting-contests, interacting creatively at rent parties and clubs like the Clef Club, the Rhythm Club, The Rock and Leroy's. Willie The Lion, creator of scores of delicate, impressionistic melodies, is also an exciting performer with a rhythmically driving left hand and a jaunty and bombastic stage presence complete with bowler hat and cigar. Uneven on record, **Hallelujah (A Legend), Tango La Caprice** and **Relaxin',** his own compositions **(Harlem Piano), Contrary Motion (Jazz Piano - A Musical Exchange), Portrait Of The Duke,** the teacher's response to his famous student's tribute, **Portrait Of The Lion (Memorial),** and a keyboard partnership with Don Ewell **(Grand Piano),** represent a cross-section of his best work.

Recordings:
A Legend
(Mainstream/Fontana)
Harlem Piano, Willie The Lion Smith & Luckey Roberts
(Good Time Jazz/Good Time Jazz)
Jazz Piano - A Musical Exchange
(RCA Victor/RCA Victor)
Memorial *(—/Vogue)*
Grand Piano, Willie The Lion Smith & Don Ewell *(—/'77)*

Eddie South

Eddie South (born Louisiana, Missouri, 1906) received extensive private tuition as violinist from early age, in both 'straight' (classical) and jazz idioms. First professional work, at 16, in Chicago (his family had moved there from Louisiana shortly after South was born) when he was studying at Chicago College of Music. Not surprising, with his musical training, coupled with a natural flair and imagination, that South is usually considered to be the most technically skilful of all jazz violinists; truly, a virtuoso in the field. Tonally, there cannot have been a jazz violinist his equal and technically, his talents enabled him to execute the most dazzling flights of fancy. Perhaps his rhythmic powers were not as emphatic as those of Stuff Smith (♦) or Joe Venuti (♦), but there was no doubting his ability to swing at all times.

After leaving college, worked with various bands, including that of Erskine Tate. Took own band The Alabamians on tour of Europe (1930) during which time studied music in Paris and Budapest. Fronted own bands in Chicago, in California, then toured as accompanist to mostly vocal artists. Paid return visit to Europe, working for several months in Paris, 1937, then Holland (following year). Whilst in

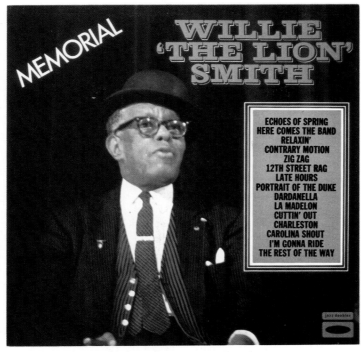

Memorial (Vogue). Willie 'The Lion' Smith was one of the great characters in jazz as well as a top performer.

French capital, recorded with Django Reinhardt (♦) **(Django Reinhardt & The American Jazz Giants/Django & His American Friends, Vol 2).** Pair established instant rapport during recording sessions of September, November '37. **I Can't Believe That You're In Love With Me,** from second session, has startlingly inventive South, with Reinhardt (who occupies non-solo role throughout both dates) supplying buoyant rhythmic backgrounds. **Eddie's Blues** provided good indication of his abilities in this area; in every way it was a masterful performance. Further title from first session, **Dinah (Eddie South & Stephane Grappelly)** contained more exceptional fiddle-playing from South with Stephane Grappelli (♦) adding second violin solo voice to proceedings. At second date, two violins (accompanied only by Reinhardt) soloed, then improvised together, during 'Swing interpretation' of, and 'Improvisation' on, opening movement of Bach's D Minor Concerto: an experiment which can be said to have been something of a success. Even more successful was **Fiddle Blues** (from a third session, two days after second), this number cast in more conventional jazz mould (both **Eddie South & Stephane Grappelly).**

After returning to US, South

The Great 16 (RCA Victor) – Muggsy's finest recordings?

continued to front own combos, of differing sizes, during next two decades. Starred in own radio series during 1940s; appeared in TV programmes from Chicago, 1950s. Poor health during last years. Died in Chicago in 1962.

Recordings:
Various (Including Eddie South/Django Reinhardt), Django Reinhardt & The American Jazz Giants *(Prestige)/*
Django & His American Friends, Vol 2 *(HMV)*
Eddie South & Stephane Grappelly *(—/HMV)*
Various (Including Eddie South), Swing Classics, Vol 1 (1944-45) *(Polydor)*

Muggsy Spanier

Francis Joseph 'Muggsy' Spanier (born Chicago, Illinois, 1906) never claimed to be the best technique among trumpeters/cornettists to emerge from beginning of 1920s. Always, though, right up until 1960s, he insisted on playing in a fiery, hard-hitting manner. His playing, at all times throughout his career, reflected a deep and abiding admiration for King Oliver (♦) and Louis Armstrong (♦). Started on drums, but at 13 had acquired cornet. Played semi-professionally with Elmer Schoebel (1921), then with a succession of varied bands through 1920s, culminating in his joining Ted Lewis Orchestra in 1929 (he was to remain until 1936). Made record debut 1924 with Bucktown Five **(Muggsy Spanier 1924-1928)** with 18-year-old cornettist acquitting himself well, as indeed he was to do on numerous subsequent recording dates during this decade, including those with Charles Pierce Orchestra and the Jungle Kings (particularly his hot, rhythmic playing on **Darktown Strutters' Ball (Muggsy Spanier 1924-1928).**

Visited Europe with Lewis (1930). With Ben Pollack (♦) Orchestra (1936-8). Suffered complete physical collapse which proved almost fatal and was confined in Touro Infirmary, New Orleans. To commemorate event – and his recovery – composed blues **Relaxin' At Touro,** which, together with 15 other titles, he recorded in 1939 with his Ragtimers. **Touro,** with marvellous use of plunger-mute, illustrates his greatness as blues-player, and remains probably his finest recorded solo. The Ragtimers tracks **(The Great 16)** collectively rank with finest-ever white Dixieland recordings, and playing throughout the leader is nothing less than impressive. Assembled in April, '39, Ragtimers lasted for less than one year. Spanier was back with Lewis (1939-40) for three months, later joining Bob Crosby (♦) Orchestra (1940-1). Left to put together own big band **(Muggsy Spanier)** which he fronted for two years (1941-3) until financial difficulties ended its life. Led own groups and worked with other bands before rejoining Ted Lewis a second time (1944). Between 1944-8, mostly led own small combos at Nick's, NYC, and until joining Earl Hines (♦) in '51, had worked in other major US cities as bandleader. Stayed with Hines, on and off, until 1959; late-1959, continued to make appearances in various parts of the States, plus trip to Germany (1960). Appeared at 1964 Newport Jazz Festival, but soon afterwards illness forced his retirement.

Died in Sausalito, California (the State in which he had settled, in '57), early in 1967. Amongst other notable Spanier recordings were those with Mound City Blue Blowers **(Recordings Made Between 1930 & 1941),** New Orleans Rhythm Kings **(New Orleans Rhythm Kings 1934-1935)** and Sidney Bechet (♦) **(Ragtime Jazz/Tribute To Bechet).** The tracks which Spanier made with Bechet with only Carmen Mastren, guitar, and Wellman Braud, bass, in support must be considered equal to, if not better than, anything he produced at any other period in his career. Even in the almost tranquil atmosphere which permeated the two sessions, there is an underlying passion that adds the final touch to some superb playing by the two horns (Spanier is particularly impressive on **Sweet Lorraine** and **Four Or Five Times)** with cornet counterpointing soprano-sax or clarinet magnificently. Spanier (and Bechet) also participated in numerous Rudi Blesh's WOR-Mutual Network programs, *This Is Jazz* ('**This Is Jazz': Muggsy Spanier and Sidney Bechet & Friends)** and, as always, his cornet flared, hotly and happily, to the satisfaction of all concerned.

Recordings:
Various (Including Bucktown Five), Bix Beiderbecke & The Chicago Cornets *(Milestone)*
Muggsy Spanier 1924-1928 *(—/Fountain)*
Various (Including Mound City Blue Blowers), Recordings Made Between 1930 & 1941 *(CBS – France)*
New Orleans Rhythm Kings (1934-1935) *(MCA Coral – Germany)*
Muggsy Spanier, The Great 16 *(RCA Victor/RCA Victor – France)*

Sidney Bechet/Muggsy Spanier,
Ragtime Jazz (Olympic)/
Tribute To Bechet (Ember)
Muggsy Spanier (Ace of Hearts)
Muggsy Spanier & His
Ragtimers (—/London)
'This Is Jazz': Muggsy Spanier
(Jazzology/—)
The Genius Of Sidney Bechet
(Jazzology/—)

Spontaneous Music Ensemble

All too often for the avant-garde,
the proof of the pudding has been
the recipe; toothsome theories,
indigestible works. The Spontaneous Music Ensemble has never
been concerned with abstractions,
but rather with shapes, relation-
ships and the organic growth of
musical conversation. Established
in 1966 by drummer John Stevens
and altoman Trevor Watts, SME
has had a shifting personnel –
Evan Parker, Kenny Wheeler,
Paul Rutherford, Derek Bailey,
Dave Holland – but since the music
is based on collective principles,
the texture remains the same. The
music might develop from a short
question and answer phrase between the instruments, advancing
in clipped, staccato bursts, flaring,
folding, overlapping and tugging
against itself like hands at iso-
metric exercise. 'Change is constant' says Stevens, and certainly
no other group has taken flux so
far, or subordinated the ego to such
an extent. There are no solos in
SME music, yet it has attracted star
soloists like Steve Lacy and Bobby
Bradford (Bobby Bradford + SME)
and, during SME's eight-year residency at the Little Theatre Club,
avant-gardists like Don Cherry,
Rashied Ali and Han Bennink sat in.
This English group is the finest
free collective in the world, and its
output reflects its steady growth
(Challenge, Karyobin, Oliv, The
Source, Birds Of A Feather, So
What Do You Think and Face To
Face). Trevor Watts' band Amalgam, with John Stevens on drums
and various bassists, gives a more
conventional setting to their talents
and shows both men to be magnificently inventive swingers
(Prayer For Peace, Amalgam
Play Blackwell & Higgins and
Innovation). Currently Stevens
and Watts are leading jazz-rock
outfits, Away and a re-vamped
Amalgam.

Recordings:
Challenge (—/Eyemark)
Karyobin (—/Island)
Oliv (—/Marmalade)

The Source – From And
Towards (Tangent).

The Source (—/Tangent)
Birds Of A Feather (BYG/BYG)
So What Do You Think
(—/Tangent)
Face To Face (Emanem/Emanem)
Amalgam:
Prayer For Peace
(—/Transatlantic)
Play Blackwell & Higgins
(—/A Records)
Innovation (—/Tangent)
John Stevens/Evan Parker, The
Longest Night (—/Ogun)
Chemistry (—/Vinyl)
Amalgam - Deep (—/Vinyl)

Jess Stacy

Jess Alexandria Stacy (born Cape
Girardeau, Missouri, 1904) never
has been accorded the kind of
recognition his pianistic talents
have deserved. His neat, melodic,
rhythmic piano style eschews
flashiness or the keyboard pyrotechnics of others. Showing traces
of the style pioneered by James P.
Johnson (♦), Stacy otherwise is an
individualist whose more unassuming approach to jazz piano too
often has led to his neglect. A
mostly self-taught player, Stacy
once played piano (and calliope)
on a steamship. During late-1920s
worked mostly in Chicago, managing to work with many of the famous
jazz names resident in or visiting
that city. Was still operating from
Chicago when, on John Hammond's
recommendation, he joined Benny
Goodman (♦) (1935).
In Chicago recorded, together
with Israel Crosby (♦) and Gene
Krupa (♦), remarkably fine session
resulting in excellent examples of
his playing on his own Barrelhouse (on World Is Waiting For
The Sunrise) and a beautifully conceived tribute to Bix Beiderbecke
(♦) in the form of a medley of
Flashes and In The Dark (all
Swing Classics, 1935/Jazz In The
Thirties). Three days later, Stacy
recorded with septet of Goodman
sidemen led by Krupa, again
showing the kind of unflurried,
crisp piano-playing that was to
make him the perfect band pianist
with the King of Swing's big band
until 1939 (Benny Goodman, Vols
4-10). Apart from commercial recordings, Stacy gave sterling service during the hundreds of live
performances band played during
his stay, including the long-running
CBS Camel Caravan radio shows
(Kings Of Swing and The Big
Band Sound Of Benny Goodman).
Perhaps the single most memorable example of Stacy's work with
Goodman came at the famous 1938
Carnegie Hall Jazz Concert.
Apart from his customary fine
band work, and excellent solo on
One O'clock Jump, it was his
almost impressionistic five-chorus
contribution to Sing, Sing, Sing – in
total contrast to the previous fiery
solos – that proved to be one of the
individual highlights of the evening. During late-1930s, Stacy also
recorded at more than one of the
legendary recordings put together
by Goodman colleague Lionel
Hampton (The Complete Lionel
Hampton/Lionel Hampton's Best
Records, Vols 1, 5, 6). His presence was felt during recording
dates fronted by another of Stacy's
associates with Goodman, Harry
James (Harry James & His Orchestra 1936-1938) from same period.
Stacy produced some of his most
eloquent playing under Eddie
Condon's (♦) supervision only

Above: Rex Stewart – his half-valve skills and fierce
blowing made him a real individualist on cornet.

hours after Carnegie Hall concert
with Goodman. His contribution to
two extended originals by assembled group, notably Carnegie
Drag, was masterful (Commodore Condon, Vol 1). Worked
often with Condon during the
1940s, on record (Jam Sessions
At Commodore) or during Condon's concert series in 1944-5
(Eddie Condon & His All Stars,
Vols 7, 8).
After leaving Goodman, returned
to his Missouri home. Then joined
Bob Crosby (♦) (1939-42) (South
Rampart Street Parade) leaving
to reclaim his role of pianist with
Benny Goodman, remaining until
1944 (during which time he married singer Lee Wiley (♦)). With
Tommy Dorsey (♦) (1944-5), leaving to form own band which folded
early 1946. Back with Goodman
(1946-7), an attempt at leading own
big band (1947-8), then a spell with
Billy Butterfield (♦). Since that time,
Stacy has worked as soloist and lead
of own small combos, although he
was reunited with Goodman,
briefly (1959-60). Recorded eight
titles in quartet setting early 1951
(Ralph Sutton & Jess Stacy)
providing further evidence of his
abilities. His solos on such as
Fascinating Rhythm, You Took
Advantage Of Me and If I Could
Be With You, show less of the
Johnson influence, but more than a
hint of Earl Hines (♦), a facet of his
playing which had become more
apparent since beginning of 1940s.
Still, there was no doubting the
individualism of Jess Stacy, a fact

confirmed by his playing on self-
explanatory Tribute To Benny
Goodman recorded during mid-
1950s. A more recent recording
(Jess Stacy Still Swings) sum-
marizes perfectly the continuing
art of Jess Stacy, the underrated
piano-player from Missouri.

Recordings:
Various (Including Jess Stacy/
Benny Goodman) Swing
Classics, 1935 (Prestige)/
Jazz In The Thirties
(World Records)
Benny Goodman, Vols 4-10
(RCA Victor – France)
Various (Including Benny
Goodman), Kings Of Swing
(—/Verve)
The Big Band Sound Of Benny
Goodman (—/Verve)
Various (1938 Carnegie Hall
Jazz Concert (Columbia/CBS)
The Complete Lionel Hampton
(Bluebird)/
Lionel Hampton's Best
Records, Vols 1, 5, 6
(RCA Victor – France)
Harry James & His Orchestra
1936-1938 (The Old Masters/—)
Eddie Condon, Commodore
Condon, Vol 1 (—/London)
Eddie Condon & His All Stars,
Vols 7, 8 (Jazum/—)
Bob Crosby, South Rampart
Street Parade (—/MCA)
(Ralph Sutton) & Jess Stacy
(Brunswick/Ace of Hearts)
Jess Stacy, Tribute To Benny
Goodman (Atlantic/London)
Jess Stacy Still Swings
(Chiaroscuro/—)

Jeremy Steig

An excellent technician, flautist Jeremy Steig has made Roland Kirk (♦)-style overblowings a central part of his aesthetic. He led one of the pioneering jazz-rock fusion outfits in the late '60s, the shortlived Jeremy & The Satyrs.

Recordings:
This Is (Solid/—)
Temple Of Birth (Columbia/—)
Wayfaring Stranger
  (Blue Note/Blue Note)

John Stevens
♦ *Spontaneous Music Ensemble*

Rex Stewart

At his best, Rex William Stewart (born Philadelphia, Pennsylvania, 1907) was one of the most expressive, and impressive, trumpeters/ cornettists thus far produced by jazz. Established an impressive reputation as prominent soloist with Duke Ellington (♦) between 1934–45, without doubt most productive, stimulating setting for his talents. With Ellington, Stewart was featured as cornet player of immense power and totally individual style – capable of projecting humor and pathos with equal ease and skill. Most distinctive quality of his playing was an ability to produce an instantly recognizable tonal effect by depressing valves of his instrument halfway (other trumpeters have attempted to reproduce this effect but only Clark Terry (♦) has succeeded in obtaining kind of originality in approach which Stewart pioneered with total success). Nowhere else but within the framework of Ellingtonia did Stewart sound as compelling and fulfilling, nor did he ever achieve elsewhere the heights he scaled with, say, **Boy Meets Horn**, heard first in a studio recording **(The Ellington Era, 1927-1940, Vol 1)** and then in a stunning live performance, **The Duke 1940**. Period when Stewart's cornet vied for solo honors with colleague Cootie Williams' (♦) trumpet – 1934–40 – was indeed a musically productive one, for Stewart and for Ellington. Both men were accorded equal share of solo space, and when the two were matched in friendly, but fierce, combat, musical sparks really flew, as exemplified in several versions of the exciting duets on **Tootin' Through The Roof**, best of which probably were on **The Ellington Era, 1927-1940, Vol 2** and **Duke Ellington/All That Jazz: Duke Ellington)**.
When Williams left Ellington for Benny Goodman (♦), Stewart (until arrival of Ray Nance (♦), Williams' replacement), shouldered responsibility of taking lion's share of trumpet solos, task he undertook with commendable fortitude and impressive results. Just how much he obviously relished this challenge can be judged from **The Duke, 1940**, recorded at dance

in North Dakota, during which Stewart unleashed a string of dazzling solos, running wide range of emotion, as well as taking in diverse moods, tempos, etc. There was the menacing **The Mooche**, with Stewart's magnificent growl trumpet preaching powerfully; joyful **Rumpus In Richmond**, with Stewart taking over Williams' original solo spot; lyrical **Warm Valley**, and passionate **Harlem Airshaft**. Other superlative Stewart performances with Ellington include **Morning Glory** (co-composed by Stewart and Ellington) **(The Works Of Duke, Vol 9)**; **Portrait Of Bert Williams, Conga Brava, Dusk** (all **The Works Of Duke, Vol 10**); **John Hardy's Wife** (**The Works Of Duke, Vols 14, 15** – two separate versions); **In A Sentimental Mood** (**The Complete Duke Ellington, Vol 6**); plus clutch of solos contained within **Duke Ellington 1943-1946**, including **Hayfoot Strawfoot, Blue Serge, Bugle Breaks** and **Between The Devil & The Deep Blue Sea**. Stewart figured prominently in several of the classic small-group recordings made by various contingents of Ellingtonians, including **Mobile Bay Blues, Linger Awhile, My Sunday Girl, Without A Song** (all **The Works Of Duke, Vol 13**); and **Some Saturday, Subtle Slough** (later known as **Just Squeeze Me**), **Poor Bubber** and **Menelik - The Lion Of Judah** (all **The Works Of Duke, Vol 16**). Last title is example of Stewart's 'talking trumpet' speciality, a take-it-or-leave-it device which fascinated some, appalled others.
With Fletcher Henderson (♦), Stewart first established himself as top-class soloist. With Henderson, he soloed impressively on **The Stampede** (**The Fletcher Henderson Story, Vol 1**); **Feeling Good, Old Black Joe Blues** (**Vol 2**); and **Wang Wang Blues, Sugar Foot Stomp** and **Singin' The Blues** (**Vol 3**). Most interesting of these is **Singin' The Blues** because it shows Stewart's obvious affection for and familiarity with Bix Beiderbecke's (♦) more famous solo on same. Stewart worked with Henderson several occasions between 1926–33. Before this, had been employed by several little-known bands as well as playing on Potomac riverboats.
First visit to New York in 1921, returning in 1925 to work with Elmer Snowden, Horace Henderson (♦) and others. Also worked with McKinney's Cotton Pickers (1931), Luis Russell (1934), and even led own big band in New York for over a year (1933–4). After leaving Ellington, fronted several small combos as well as guesting with others, including regular work, on and off, with Eddie Condon (♦) bands. Worked for radio stations as disc jockey and began to write regularly for leading jazz periodicals when he settled in California at end of 1950s. Worked sporadically during 1960s – including at least two trips to Europe – mostly as guest soloist, at jazz festivals and special events. Probably his best work on record, outside of Ellington, came when he was re-united with former big-band colleagues Coleman Hawkins (♦), Cootie Williams (♦) and others for a totally delightful **The Big Challenge**. Like some other ex-Ellingtonians, sometimes he found it difficult to recapture his consistency of performance when away

from Ducal surroundings. Made in 1960, **The Rex Stewart Memorial Album** contains much fine post-Ellington playing, but there are also occasions when his solos tend to become sloppy and uncreative, and his singing and kazoo-playing are of even less stature. A much more real picture of the true Rex Stewart, dating from 1934–9, and with numerous Ellington associates in support, is to be found within the grooves of **Rex Stewart Memorial**.

Recordings:
Luis Russell & His Louisiana Swing Orchestra (Columbia/—)
The Fletcher Henderson Story (Columbia)/
The Fletcher Henderson Story, Vols 1, 2, 3 (CBS)
The Complete Duke Ellington, Vols 6, 7 (CBS – France)
Duke Ellington, The Ellington Era, 1927-1940, Vols 1, 2 (Columbia/CBS)
Duke Ellington (Trip)/
All That Jazz: Duke Ellington (DJM)
If Dreams Come True: Duke Ellington - Cotton Club, 1938, Vol 1 (Jazz Archives)
The Works Of Duke, Vols 9-17 (RCA Victor – France)
Duke Ellington, Black, Brown & Beige (Ariston – Italy)
Duke Ellington 1943-1946 (Jazz Society/Jazz Society)
Django Reinhardt, Django & His American Friends, Vol 2 (—/HMV)
Various (Including Rex Stewart/Cootie Williams), The Big Challenge (Jazztone/Concert Hall)
Various, The Big Reunion (Jazztone/ —)
Rex Stewart Memorial (—/CBS – Realm)
The Rex Stewart Memorial Album (Prestige/—)

Sonny Stitt

Born 1924 in Boston, saxophonist Sonny Stitt had the misfortune to come up with a sound and style similar to Charlie Parker's, for, unlike the imitators, Stitt's had developed independently. To duck the Bird comparisons, he switched to tenor for a period after 1949, and in fact he has equal facility on alto, tenor and baritone. Like most of his generation, Stitt gained experience in the big bands, Tiny Bradshaw, Billy Eckstine, Dizzy Gillespie, and solos with a Gillespie small group on **Oo Bop Sh'Bam** and **That's Earl, Brother** in 1946 **(In The Beginning)**. He can be heard playing all three horns on a compilation of his own small groups, 1949–51, which included sidemen like Bud Powell, John Lewis, Jay Jay Johnson, Gene Ammons, Max Roach and Art Blakey. Stitt stretches throughout and the result is arguably his best work, from the stomping **All God's Chillun Got Rhythm** to the unique voicings of **Afternoon In Paris** **(Genesis)**.
An unlikely pairing of Stitt and trumpeter Roy Eldridge takes off, with both men attacking the blues programme with ferocity **(Sittin' In)**. The second album from this set features Stitt with Oscar Peterson (♦) and has excellent solos from the Stitt tenor on **Moten Swing, Blues For Pres, Sweets, Ben & All The Other Funky Ones** and **Easy Does It**. A meeting with fellow tenorman, Sonny Rollins, illustrates their different gifts – Rollins analytical and adventurous,

Below: Sonny Stitt, alto and tenor saxophones, and baritone on occasion. A faithful disciple of Charlie Parker.

Stitt lithe within the tradition (**Sonny Side Up**).

He has made scores of albums over the last two decades, the best being in company with contemporaries like Gene Ammons, two-tenor stormers (**Soul Summit, Together Again For The Last Time**) or Art Blakey's Messengers (**In Walked Sonny**), while a session from 1967 re-united him with Be-Bop giants Howard McGhee and Kenny Clarke (**Night Work**). In the '70s, he toured with the Giants of Jazz, in company with Gillespie, Monk, Blakey and Al McKibbon.

Recordings:
Dizzy Gillespie, In The Beginning (Prestige/Prestige)
Genesis (Prestige/Prestige)
Sittin' In (Verve/Verve)
Sonny Stitt-Gene Ammons, Soul Summitt (Prestige/Transatlantic)
Sonny Stitt-Gene Ammons, Together Again For The Last Time (Prestige/—)
Sonny Stitt, Art Blakey, In Walked Sonny (Sonet/Sonet)
Night Work (Black Lion/Black Lion)
The Bop Session (Sonet/Sonet)

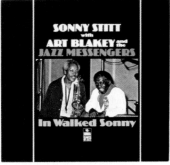

In Walked Sonny (Sonet): grey hair, youthful vigour.

Billy Strayhorn

Even as a teenager, Billy Strayhorn (born Dayton, Ohio, 1915) apparently was more or less fully developed as an impressionistic composer, orchestrator, lyricist, pianist. For a youngster, Strayhorn showed remarkable gifts of sophistication and maturity in writing complex melody for, and scholarly lyric to, songs like **Lush Life** – one of his finest of all songs (recorded by many top-notch artists, such as Stan Getz (♦), Nat King Cole (♦), Ella Fitzgerald (♦)). Strayhorn (also known as 'Swee' Pea', or 'Strays') played classical music in school orchestra in Pittsburgh (his parents had moved to Pennsylvania, via Hillsboro, North Carolina), after he had received private tuition.

Submitted composition (1938) to Duke Ellington (♦), who was impressed: **Something To Live For**, with vocal by Jean Eldridge and with Strayhorn at the piano, was first of his compositions recorded by Ellington (**The Ellington Era, 1927-1940, Vol 2**) by which time he had been welcomed as part of Ellington entourage. Was to remain thus employed until his death 29 years later. From '37 onwards, Strayhorn was to become Ellington's closest collaborator, an inseparable companion and friend (one of Ellington's precious few confidants) and a second pianist – alone or in duet with Ellington – in both big-band and small-group

settings. As pianist, Strayhorn was best-known as sensitive accompanist; as soloist, his style was spare, economic, but not especially distinctive. There was, however, a certain similarity in approach to keyboard by Strayhorn and his employer. Even more pronounced was the closeness in the writing by the pair. So close, in fact, that where it was known the two had collaborated on one particular project, it is difficult to tell which of them had composed what portions, where one ended and the other began, such as **Such Sweet Thunder, Toot Suite (Ellington Jazz Party), A Drum Is A Woman, The Far East Suite, The Queen's Suite (The Ellington Suites)** and **Suite Thursday**. On his own, Strayhorn was responsible for **Take The 'A' Train** which, following its initial recordings (**The Works Of Duke, Vols 14, 15**) was to become Ellington's longest-serving signature tune. Other Strayhorn creations which became part of the Ellington song book were: **I'm Checking Out, Goodbye** – feature for singer Ivie Anderson (♦) (**The Ellington Era, 1927-1940, Vol 2**); **Daydream** – first recorded by Ellington small group in 1940 (**The Works Of Duke, Vol 12**); **Rock Skippin' At The Blue Note (The World Of Duke Ellington, Vol 3/The World Of Duke Ellington, Vol 2**); **Johnny Come Lately (The Works Of Duke, Vol 18**); and **Passin' Flower, Raincheck, Clementine, Chelsea Bridge, Love Like This Can't Last, After All** (all **The Works Of**

Above: Billy Strayhorn, Duke's alter ego and right-hand man – composer, arranger, friend - from 1939-67.

Duke, Vol 17). **Chelsea Bridge**, which has been compared – favorably–to Ravel's **Valse Nobles Et Sentimentales**, is a firm clue as to one of Strayhorn's premier musical influences and inspirations.

Outside of Ellington, Strayhorn's output on record never was a large one. Best of all was a 1959 date (**Cue For Saxophone**) with leader-for-the-day Strayhorn's compositions and arrangements resulting in much exceptional music from a sextet including Johnny Hodges (♦) (for whom Strayhorn wrote and played piano on many occasions, before and later), Harold Baker (♦) and Strayhorn himself. Strayhorn also recorded several piano duets with his alma mater, best of which are divided more or less evenly between the 12 selections on **The Golden Duke**, four of which are more or less a showcase for the cello artistry of Oscar Pettiford (♦), then Ellington's bassist. Other albums that bear testimony to Strayhorn's musical sensitivity and eloquence include **Everybody Knows Johnny Hodges**; Ella Fitzgerald's (♦) **Ella At Duke's Place**; Hodges' **The Jeep Is Jumpin'** and **... And His Mother Called Him Bill**, last-named a deeply-felt salute by Ellington and his then (1967) orchestra, immediately following Strayhorn's death. There could be no

more poignant tribute to Billy Strayhorn than the unaccompanied piano solo (featuring Strayhorn's **Sweet Lotus Blossom**), recorded by Ellington after the session officially had ended.

Recordings:
Duke Ellington, The Ellington Era, 1927-1940, Vols 1, 2 (Columbia/CBS)
Duke Ellington, The Works Of Duke Vols 12-20 (RCA Victor – France)
Duke Ellington, The Golden Duke (Prestige/Prestige)
The World Of Duke Ellington, Vol 3 (Columbia)/
The World Of Duke Ellington, Vol 2 (CBS).
Duke Ellington & The Ellingtonians (Vogue – France)
Duke Ellington, Such Sweet Thunder (Columbia/CBS-Realm)
Duke Ellington, Ellington Jazz Party (Columbia/Philips)
Duke Ellington, A Drum Is A Woman (Columbia/Philips)
Duke Ellington (Peer Gynt Suites, Nos 1 & 2)/Suite Thursday (Columbia/CBS)
Duke Ellington, The Far East Suite (RCA Victor/RCA Victor)
Duke Ellington, The Ellington Suites (Pablo/Pablo)
Everybody Knows Johnny Hodges (Impulse/Impulse)
Ella Fitzgerald, Ella At Duke's Place (Verve/Verve)
Billy Strayhorn, Cue For Saxophone (Master Jazz Recordings/Vocalion)
Duke Ellington, ... And His Mother Called Him Bill (RCA Victor/RCA Victor)

Joe Sullivan

Joe Sullivan (real name, Dennis Patrick Terence Joseph O'Sullivan) was one of the first white pianists completely to understand – and play – the kind of hard-driving, two-fisted piano-playing produced by such great black keyboard artists as Fats Waller (♦), Willie 'The Lion' Smith (♦), Lucky Roberts, and Earl Hines (♦). His playing, whilst something of a compendium of the various styles of his major influences, curiously had its own individuality. Probably to be heard at his best alone, but Sullivan was a major asset in all kinds of jazz situations, especially with a hard-blowing small combo. His fine technique no doubt was helped by his initial studies at Chicago Conservatory of Music. Led own band, 1923, at 17, at Pine Point Resort, Indiana, followed by one-and-a-half years' work on vaudeville circuit.

During 1920 became closely associated, personally as well as musically, with Chicago fraternity personified by Bud Freeman (♦), Muggsy Spanier (♦), Gene Krupa (♦) and Eddie Condon (♦) as well as with commercial dance bands in the city; also undertook many broadcasts at various Chicago radio stations. Recorded (in Chicago) with McKenzie & Condon's Chicagoans (1927), and (in New York) with Miff Mole & His Little Molers (1928) (**That Toddlin' Town - Chicago 1926-28**) acquitting himself splendidly in company of such as Frank Teschemacher (♦), Bud Freeman, Jimmy McPartland and Mole. Also in Chicago in '28, recorded with

Jungle Kings (same as McKenzie-Condon Chicagoans, except Muggsy Spanier replaces McPartland, and Mezz Mezzrow is in for Freeman) **(Muggsy Spanier 1924-1928)**, showing how fine he was, always, as band pianist.

On record with Condon following February – under collective title of Eddie's Hot Shots – Sullivan plays spirited solo on **That's A Serious Thing**, although Condon's penetrative banjo all but obscures his fine band work on **I'm Gonna Stomp, Mr. Henry Lee (Prince Of The Bones)**. Same year recorded with Louisiana Rhythm Kings **(Jack Teagarden Classics)** including famous version of **Basin Street Blues ('JT')** containing peerless vocal from Jack Teagarden (♦) and admirable down-home piano from Sullivan. With Red Nichols (♦) (1929), followed by work with various other bands (even singer Russ Colombo, '32), and in 1933, recorded with Joe Venuti (♦) & His Blue Six, month after cutting quartet of superb solos (all **Swing Classics, 1935/Jazz In The Thirties**). Solos still are rightly looked upon as perfect definitions of Joe Sullivan's playing, demonstrating that for all the full-blooded approach to his art, he possessed an enviable subtlety in touch and use of dynamics. Tracks are: a deeply-felt **Gin Mill Blues**, a romping **Little Rock Getaway**, a finely structured **Onyx Bringdown** and a joyful **Honeysuckle Rose** (with Sullivan paying respects to, but not engaging in outright copying of, Fats Waller's playing). **Bringdown** documents solo residency at famous 52nd Street jazz club, same period, before moving to West Coast to work with George Stoll's studio orchestra and, on frequent occasions, Bing Crosby (♦). Continued to make jazz records before returning to New York to join for first time Bob Crosby (♦) band, for almost six months (1936).

Career interrupted for almost a year, from December, '36, entering sanitarium for almost a year, suffering from lung complaint. Resumed playing on record with Bing Crosby (1939) and mid-way through '39 returned to Bob Crosby, as featured pianist **(Big Noise From Winnetka)**. Latter engagement did not last for long and after returning to New York recorded with Eddie Condon **(Chicago Jazz)** he commenced a highly successful residency at Cafe Society with superb, tight-knit combo which included in its personnel trombonist Benny Morton (♦) and two clarinettists, Danny Polo and Edmond Hall (♦). Band laid down superior recordings in February, 1940 **(Cafe Society Swing & The Boogie Woogie 1938-1940)** with Big Joe Turner (♦) adding vocal excitement on **I Can't Give You Anything But Love** and **Low Down Dirty Shame**, Sullivan adding totally sympathetic accompaniment. Took band into Nick's (1940), Famous Door (1940-1), then trio back at Cafe Society, before going to California for two years (1943–5). Worked as duo with Meade Lux Lewis (♦), in Chicago, was regular at Eddie Condon's Club (1946–7), then settled on West Coast.

Brief period as member of Louis Armstrong's All Stars (1952) – Sullivan had recorded with Armstrong at famous **Knockin' A Jug** recording date in 1929 **(V.S.O.P.**

(Very Special Old Phonography, 1928-1930), Vols 5 & 6) but most of 1950s spent in California as solo pianist, especially in San Francisco. Starred at 1963 Monterey Jazz Festival but taken seriously ill at Newport Jazz Festival following year. Recovered, returned to West Coast to resume solo appearances. Had recorded previously ('61) in New York with Jack Teagarden, Condon, Krupa and other old friends **(Chicago & All That Jazz!)** showing all his old fire and skills on **China Boy** and **Chicago**. Played few engagements during latter half of 1960s, was seriously ill again in 1970, and died following year. Fondly remembered by musicians and fans alike as pianist who, despite his obvious gifts, never quite achieved the status that most thought he so richly deserved.

Recordings:
Various, That Toddlin' Town – Chicago (1926-28)
(—/Parlophone)
Muggsy Spanier 1924-1928
(—/Fountain)
Jack Teagarden, Vol 2 (1928-1957), 'Prince Of The Bone'
(RCA Victor – France)
Jack Teagarden Classics
(Family – Italy)
Jack Teagarden, 'J.T.'
(Ace of Hearts)
Louis Armstrong, V.S.O.P. (Very Special Old Phonography, 1928-1930), Vols 5 & 6 (CBS – France)
Various (Including Miff Mole), Chicago Jazz (1927-1928)
(Odeon – Italy)
Various (Including Joe Sullivan/Joe Venuti), Swing Classics, 1935 (Prestige)/
Jazz In The Thirties
(World Records)
Various (Including Eddie Condon), Chicago Jazz
(Decca/Coral)
Various (Including Joe Sullivan), Cafe Society Swing & The Boogie Woogie (1938-1940)
(Swingfan – Germany)
Bob Crosby, Big Noise From Winnetka (MCA)
Joe Sullivan, Piano
(Folkways/—)
Joe Sullivan, New Solos By An Old Master (Riverside/—)
Eddie Condon, Chicago & All That Jazz (—/Verve)
Coleman Hawkins/Roy Eldridge, Hawk & Roy
(Phoenix/—)

Maxine Sullivan

The owner of a remarkably pure, non-abrasive singing voice, Maxine Sullivan (née Marietta Williams) began her career during early-1930s on radio stations in Pittsburgh (she was born in Homestead, Pittsburgh, 1911) before she was introduced to bandleader-pianist-writer Claude Thornhill (♦). Thornhill supervised her recording debut, using his own band. Gained reputation with her fine singing at Onyx Club, New York, where she sang with musicians like John Kirby (♦), Frankie Newton (♦), Pete Brown (♦) and Buster Bailey (♦). Thornhill took these, himself, and two others into the studios in 1937 to make a series of records on which singer and band interacted beautifully. Sullivan's

delightfully subtle phrasing and admirable timing were present then – as indeed they remain today – and the obvious sincerity and sensitivity in lyric interpretation made her an outstanding singer, right from the beginning. Tonally and rhythmically, it is easy to understand why and how she influenced Ella Fitzgerald (♦).

Amongst tracks recorded with Onyx Club musicians in August, '37, were two traditional Scottish airs, **Loch Lomond** and **Annie Laurie**, which they had been featuring at the club. Recording of former became her first major hit record (and the biggest), **(Frankie Newton At The Onyx Club)** and for a while was prevailed upon to repeat process with other such material. Worked regularly in California during late-1930s, then toured and recorded with Benny Carter (♦) Orchestra **(Benny Carter & His Orchestra 1940-41)**.

Retired to live in Philadelphia (1942), but made comeback during mid-1940s, playing clubs and occasional concerts. Visited Europe for first time in '48, returning six years later. Once again, left music business, only to make second comeback in 1958. As before, there was no diminution of the bell-like clarity of her voice, and this time she added to her vocal performances by playing either valve-trombone or miniature trumpet or flugelhorn, instruments she had studied and learned to play – well – during her second 'retirement'. Since then, she has made numerous appearances in all media, singing with splendid consistency, and in particular making records that are joy to hear; such as two albums she made in close association with Bob Wilber (♦) **(Close As Pages In A Book)** and **The Music Of Hoagy Carmichael)** both showing, again, her obvious talents.

Has also worked in person/on record with pianist Earl Hines (♦) **(Earl Hines & Maxine Sullivan At The Overseas Press Club)** and has, on more than one occasion, further enhanced concerts by World's Greatest Jazz Band **(The World's Greatest Jazz Band Of Yank Lawson & Bob Haggart In Concert, Vol 2: At Carnegie Hall)**. Typical latterday Sullivan artistry is to be found within **Sullivan, Shakespeare, Hyman**, as she and pianist-arranger Dick Hyman work jazz-like wonders with Shakespearean lyrics to which Hyman set music. During her career, Maxine Sullivan has appeared in movies *St Louis Blues, Going Places, Swingin' The Dream* and *Take A Giant Step*. Is widow of pianist Cliff Jackson.

Recordings:
Frankie Newton At The Onyx Club (Tax – Sweden)
Benny Carter & His Orchestra (1940-41) (RCA Victor – France)
Maxine Sullivan/Bob Wilber, Close As Pages In A Book
(Monmouth-Evergreen/Parlophone)
Maxine Sullivan/Bob Wilber, The Music Of Hoagy Carmichael (Monmouth-Evergreen/Parlophone)
Various (Including Maxine Sullivan), Cafe Society
(Onyx/—)
Earl Hines & Maxine Sullivan Live At The Overseas Press Club (Chiaroscuro/—)
The World's Greatest Jazz Band Of Yank Lawson & Bob Haggart In Concert, Vol 2: At

Carnegie Hall (World Jazz/—)
Maxine Sullivan/Dick Hyman, Sullivan, Shakespeare, Hyman
(Monmouth-Evergreen)

Sun Ra

Bandleader Sun Ra was born Sonny Blount, 1928, and began as an arranger for Fletcher Henderson in the late '40s. The earliest records of his own band **(Sun Song** and **Sound Of Joy)** give few hints of his subsequent and logical development into the avant-garde, although his preoccupation with percussive textures is shown in the gongs and organ of **Sun Song** and massed tympani of **Street Named Hell**. Musicians like baritonist Pat Patrick and tenorman John Gilmore, featured here, were to remain with him for two decades. Based in Chicago, Sun Ra developed his ideas at a tangent to the prevailing Hard Bop idiom, exploring exotic voicings with his Solar Arkestra. A mystic, Sun Ra's image has always been other-worldly, but his music, though startlingly original in its combination of naivety and prediction, is always approachable. The great series of albums recorded on his own Saturn label – hand-painted, distributed by members of the Arkestra in their space-robes – were prized collectors' items throughout the '60s, and have since been re-issued by Impulse. In fact, the Arkestra scarcely worked at all in this period, the bizarre pairings, maverick borrowings, dense collectives and massive strike-force of percussion being light-years ahead of the market.

In the aftermath of the New Wave, it was realized that Sun Ra had anticipated many of the new directions, Gilmore in particular having had an influence on John Coltrane, and the Arkestra's reputation moved from the Underground into the mainstream. Atmospheric, often programmatic, his work on pieces like **Atlantis** (Atlantis) or **The Magic City** (The Magic City), **The Sun Myth** or **Cosmic Chaos** (The Heliocentric Worlds Of Sun Ra) offers an alternative to western methods of composition. In recent years, Sun Ra has added to his regular keyboards and once again sounds utterly unique on electric piano and Moog synthesizer **(The Solar-Myth Approach)** using the latter, that Fort Knox of sounds, to extend the textural variety of the Arkestra. On stage, Sun Ra's Arkestra are overwhelming both musically and visually, the musicians dressed in weird costumes with light-up hats, back-projected film, dancers and fire-eaters. Soloists like Sun Ra himself, Gilmore, Patrick and altoist Marshall Allen are brilliant improvisers, though it is the ensembles, developing the composer's themes in layered counterpoint, that are the most breathtaking.

Recordings:
Sun Song (Delmark/Delmark)
Sound Of Joy (Delmark/Delmark)
Angels & Demons At Play
(Impulse/Impulse)
Astro-Black (Impulse/Impulse)
The Magic City
(Impulse/Impulse)
Atlantis (Impulse/Impulse)
The Nubians Of Plutonia
(Impulse/Impulse)

Above: Sun Ra conducting his Arkestra. Startlingly visual, Sun Ra's band have been ahead of their time since the '50s.

The Heliocentric Worlds Of Sun Ra, Volumes 1 & 2 *(ESP/Fontana)*
Pictures Of Infinity *(Black Lion/Black Lion)*
The Solar-Myth Approach, Volumes 1& 2 *(BYG/BYG)*
Unity *(—/Horo)*
Other Voices, Other Times *(—/Horo)*
New Steps *(—/Horo)*
Sun Ra Solo Piano *(Improvising Artists Inc/—)*

John Surman

British-born baritone saxophonist, John Surman, is both a virtuoso and an innovator, extending the range of the big horn upwards into high harmonics, and freeing it of its lumbering tendencies while losing none of its weight. A Coltrane-disciple, Surman's early work was in the Mike Westbrook Orchestra, 1958–68. Over the years he has added soprano and bass clarinet. His finest work with Westbrook **(Citadel/Room 315)** sees him rising like Krakatoa through the section on **Outgoing,** echo effects and overblowings running like seismic faults, and soaring lyrically on soprano on **Tender Love.** In 1969, Surman established a trio with Americans Barre Phillips, bass and Stu Martin, drums **(John Surman)** playing with a scope and

Angels And Demons At Play (Impulse): the innovatory music of Sun Ra. Mystical and marvellous.

authority that established him as the foremost baritonist in the history of that instrument. The unaccompanied section of **Caractacus**, for example, has a range, flexibility and grandeur that has never been equalled. In 1973, Surman formed an all-saxophone trio (SOS) with altoist Mike Osborne and tenorman Alan Skidmore, each horn in turn falling back to provide a rhythmic figure. The music is like a strange, barbaric maypole dance. In recent years, he has concentrated on electronics with controversial results.

Recordings:
Mike Westbrook, Citadel/ Room 315 (*RCA/RCA*)
John Surman (*Vogue/Vogue*)
SOS (*—/Ogun*)

Ralph Sutton

Ralph Earl Sutton (born Hamburg, Missouri, 1922) plays the kind of robust, two-fisted piano that instantly evokes memories of James P. Johnson (♦), Fats Waller (♦), and the entire school of stride pianists. A complete keyboard practitioner, he has perfect touch, a predilection towards comprehensive swing, and an inventiveness not always apparent in this area of jazz piano-playing. His timing is faultless, and his accompaniments to others always have been tasteful, unobtrusive. Took piano lessons at nine, continued to play at high school where his interest in jazz was more or less formulated. 1941: sat in with Jack Teagarden (♦) who visited Northeast Missouri State Teachers' College, where Sutton was student. Impressed, Teagarden later offered youngster job with his band. This, Sutton's first important job, lasted only two months – in February, 1943, he was drafted. Medically discharged in '45, joined Joe Schirmer Trio in East St Louis. Rejoined Teagarden (1947), during which time participated in around dozen of weekly *This Is Jazz* radio shows **(The Genius Of Sidney Bechet** and **Sidney Bechet & Friends)**, playing with astonishing maturity, tremendous attack and dazzling technique. Apart from his prowess as a stride pianist, Sutton's playing impressed doubly because of his additional expertise in ragtime genre. 1948: worked in NYC, at Jimmy Ryan's, Village Vanguard, then as intermission pianist at Eddie Condon's Club (where he began lengthy residence during year). 1950: recorded with Condon (♦) on **We Called It Music** and Sidney Bechet on **Commodore Jazz, Vol 1**.
Visited UK at invitation of local National Federation of Jazz and, together with Lonnie Johnson (♦), appeared at London's Royal Festival Hall (1952). Following year recorded several sides for American Decca **(Ralph Sutton & Jess Stacy)**, including superb versions of **I Got Rhythm**, Willie 'The Lion' Smith's (♦) **Sneakaway** and **Fussin'**, and James P. Johnson's **Snowy Morning Blues**, accompanied by drummer Cliff Leeman. Substituted at San Francisco's Hangover Club for touring Earl Hines (♦). Paid tribute to mentor Fats Waller – Art Tatum (♦) is Sutton's other admitted influence – with **Salute To Fats** by recording selection of Waller tunes (1951).

Above: John Surman, the great British virtuoso of the baritone saxophone. He has recently been experimenting in electronics.

Moved with family to San Francisco (1956), obtaining gig as intermission pianist at Storyville (club owned by jazz trumpeter-bandleader Bob Scobey). Sutton recorded four albums with Scobey's 'Frisco Jazz Band and another with Bing Crosby (♦) plus band, during 1956–7. 1960: was guest on NBC/ TV's *Those Ragtime Years*, and worked again at Eddie Condon's (1960, 1961). Recorded together with cornettist Ruby Braff (♦), in quartet setting, at Sunnie's Rendezvous, Aspen, Colorado, once owned by Sutton's second wife **(On Sunnie's Side Of The Street)**. Same year became one of original members of World's Greatest Jazzband of Yank Lawson (♦) & Bob Haggart. Fitted admirably within WGJB framework, supplying perfect band-piano accompaniments and first-rate solos, including **Honky Tonk Train Blues (The WGJB Of Yank Lawson & Bob Haggart)** and **That's A-Plenty (Live At The Roosevelt Grill)**. Since leaving band, has continued to tour, with much acclaim, as solo act – he is a regular and warmly welcomed visitor to London. And he retains all his enviable fluency and powerful

Ralph Sutton & Jess Stacy (Ace of Hearts) - all piano.

drive. Biography, *Piano Man*, by James D. Schacter.

Recordings:
The Genius Of Sidney Bechet (*Jazzology/—*)
Sidney Bechet & Friends (*Ford Discriminating Collectors/—*)
Eddie Condon, We Called It Music (*Decca/Ace of Hearts*)
Tony Parenti, Ragtime (*Riverside/London*)
Ralph Sutton & Jess Stacy (*Ace of Hearts/—*)
Ragtime Piano (*Roulette/Vogue – France*)
Backroom Piano (*Verve/Columbia – Clef*)
Salute To Fats (*Harmony/Fontana*)
Ralph Sutton/Ruby Braff, On Sunnie's Side Of The Street (*Blue Angel Jazz Club/—*)
The Compleat Bud Freeman (*Monmouth-Evergreen/ Parlophone*)
The World's Greatest Jazzband Of Yank Lawson & Bob Haggart (*Project 3/ World Record Club*)
The WGJB Of Yank Lawson & Bob Haggart, Live At The Roosevelt Grill (*Atlantic/—*)
The WGJB Of Yank Lawson & Bob Haggart (*—/Atlantic*)
The WGJB Of Yank Lawson & Bob Haggart, Century Plaza (*World Pacific/—*)
The WGJB Of Yank Lawson & Bob Haggart, In Concert, Vol 1, At Massey Hall (*World Jazz/—*)
Various, The Chicago Jazz Giants Live (*MPS – Germany*)
Edmond Hall At The Club Hanover (*Storyville*)
Ralph Sutton Live (*—/Flywright*)

Above: Buddy Tate, veteran Texas tenorman. Ex-Basieite and leader of numerous swinging small combos.

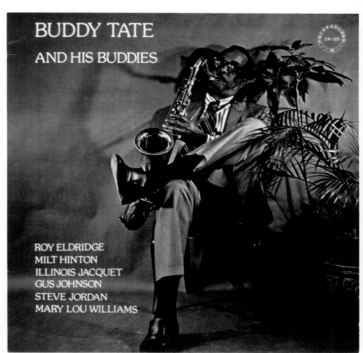

Buddy Tate And His Buddies (Chiaroscuro).
An exceptionally talented collection of buddies.

Buddy Tate

Born 1915, mainstream tenorman Buddy Tate is part of that T-bone dynasty of Texas tenors, Illinois Jacquet, Arnett Cobb, Herschel Evans, Budd Johnson, characterized by a big, meaty sound. He gained early experience in the territory bands, playing with Herschel Evans in Troy Floyd's band, then with Andy Kirk and Nat Towles. In 1939, he took over Evans' chair in the Basie band, and stayed until 1948, a featured soloist on '40s warhorses like **Rock-A-Bye Basie** and **Superchief**. Tate finally left the band and took up a 19-year incumbency at Harlem's Celebrity Club, fronting a fine septet. A straight-ahead swinger, beefily tender on ballads, Tate has been a thoroughly dependable recording artist and is usually at

his best with fellow ex-Basieites. **Teeny Weeny** from an album which has one side of Tate with Buck Clayton, Dicky Wells and Jo Jones, is a good example of his tenor style **(Swinging Like Tate),** while another session with Buck Clayton features his warm, relaxed clarinet on **Blue Creek (Kansas City Nights).** Albums with Clark Terry **(Tate-a-Tate)** and with Paul Quinichette and Jay McShann **(Kansas City Joys)** abound with his robust sense of enjoyment.

Recordings:
Swinging Like Tate
(Felsted/Felsted)
Kansas City Nights
(Prestige/Prestige)
Tate-a-Tate *(Prestige-Swingsville/Prestige-Swingsville)*
Kansas City Joys *(Sonet/Sonet)*
Groovin' With Buddy Tate
(Prestige-Swingsville/
Prestige-Swingsville)

Art Tatum

The truly great pianists of early jazz possessed superior techniques. No-one could pretend otherwise when listening to the playing of such acknowledged giants as James P. Johnson (◆), Fats Waller (◆), or Cliff Jackson. Yet it was not until the arrival of Earl Hines (◆) on the scene, with his orchestral approach to the subject, that jazz piano-playing truly entered the realms of the virtuoso. Hines carried the art of jazz piano a giant step forward.

The appearance of Arthur 'Art' Tatum (born Toledo, Ohio, 1910) represented even further astonishing progress. When Tatum first paraded his technical skills, he amazed musicians and non-musicians alike.

They marveled at his dazzling right-hand runs (executed often at frightening speed), whilst an ever-active left hand pumped out what was his own refinement of a stride beat; his command of the keyboard was total. Harmonically Tatum was advanced for the 1920s, indeed, despite all the technical developments which were to take place in subsequent decades, his harmonic sense was to cause a sense of wonderment amongst other pianists after his death in 1956. Tatum's predilection for sudden changes of key and tempo tended to baffle his listeners (even some musicians), but there was no denying his interest in retaining melodic interest in whatever piece of music he was playing. All in all, it is little wonder that classical piano virtuosi like Gieseking and Horowitz were to be seen in New York jazz clubs during late-1930s, 1940s, watching in apparent abject disbelief (and no little admiration) as Tatum unleashed his pyrotechnical skills. But even Tatum has had his critics. There are those still who maintain that whilst there was no doubting his ability to swing, others have swung (or swing) more profoundly, and with more power. Yet such criticisms seems absolutely ridiculous when listening to recorded performances at any time during the man's career: from the very beginning of his career as a solo pianist on record and in particular to a coruscating version of **Tiger Rag (Piano Starts Here)** from 1933; from the middle period – a devastating **I Got Rhythm (Masterpieces/ Here's Art Tatum);** or from the final year of his life – a breathtaking dissecting of **Too Marvellous For Words (Art Tatum In Person).** It is true to say, however, that for all Tatum's technical dexterity and harmonic ingenuity, his improvisations sometimes seemed superficial in direct comparison with those of Hines, as well as younger men like Bud Powell (◆), Thelonious Monk (◆), Herbie Nichols (◆), McCoy Tyner (◆), and Keith Jarrett (◆). And there were times when he was guilty of little more than fancy, tricksy embellishments which lacked real depth and substance. His penchant for certain clichéd runs – rightly termed by one US critic as being 'trick waterfall arpeggios' – could be irritating and tedious. For all this, Tatum was one of the few instrumental geniuses to emanate thus far from the world of jazz. A statement with which few, if any, other jazz pianists would disagree.

Like all supreme individualists (Tatum certainly was one), usually he was heard to best advantage when left to his own extraordinary devices. For in the role of accompanist, often he would continue to go his own way, irrespective of the needs – or indeed the presence – of others. Not that he was entirely incapable of supplying sympathetic accompaniments. His first recording session, in 1932, found him sharing the piano stool with Joe Turner, as accompanists for singer Adelaide Hall. And Adelaide Hall has said she had no complaints about his playing. (Tatum was heard by Hall's husband and Turner, who offered joint recommendation that he should work for her; Tatum left his native Toledo for New

York in pursuance of the job). Nine years later, Tatum was to provide accompaniments for blues shouter Big Joe Turner (♦) that not only were sympathetic, but indeed inspirational (**Masterpieces**), most notably the contrasting **Wee Baby Blues** and **Lonesome Graveyard Blues** (from two separate recording dates in '41).

Art Tatum was totally blind in one eye and suffered diminishing vision in the other. Started on piano at very young age, taking violin and guitar lessons at 13 (whilst attending a Columbus, Ohio, school for blind). Two years' study at Toledo School of Music, then worked with own band in Toledo and district. Worked with band of Speed Webb prior to taking residency on local radio station (WSPD). After spending one-and-a-half years with Adelaide Hall, worked for a while in New York, before spending next two years in Cleveland and Chicago. Moved to Hollywood in 1936 where he stayed for almost one year. Came to London in 1938 where he played at clubs and in variety. Back to California, where he worked for another period before returning to New York. After his first recording date, in 1933, Tatum continued to make discs (for Decca) which demonstrated, time and again, his highly-developed artistry. Stand-out items from a batch of uniformly superb recordings – all solo – included **Get Happy, Tiger Rag, Indiana** (**Masterpieces/Art Of Tatum 2**) and **Gone With The Wind** (**Masterpieces/Art Of Tatum**). There was fine Tatum too at a 1937 date with Tatum leading a six-piece band through a quartet of numbers, including a spirited **I've Got My Love To Keep Me Warm** (**Swing Combos 1935-1941**).

Switched from solo to trio format in 1943 (with Tiny Grimes, guitar; Slam Stewart, bass). It worked well, in live performance and on record (**Masterpieces/Art Of Tatum, 1, 2**) but by 1945, Tatum was again performing as solo artist. Remarkably fine concert performance taped by its promoter Gene Norman in 1949 (**Piano Starts Here/An Art Tatum Concert**) with Tatum, in joyous form throughout, showing incredible rhythmic flexibility on tracks like **The Man I Love** and **I Know That You Know**, and, on **Willow, Weep For Me**, evincing more feeling than was

The Tatum Solo Masterpieces (Pablo). '. . . Tatum, inexhaustible . . . producing one masterpiece after another.'

customary. Also in 1949, recorded three times for Capitol (**Solo Piano**) with **Aunt Hagar's Blues** proving that Tatum was no slouch when it came to playing basic blues. A further Capitol session, in 1952, had the pianist reverting, temporarily, to trio setting (Everett Barksdale replacing Grimes). Starting during last month of 1953, and completed probably in following April, Tatum recorded, alone, around 125 titles for Norman Granz, 121 of which eventually found their way on to **The Tatum Solo Masterpieces**. The standard of performance throughout what were marathon sessions – over 70 titles were cut during first two sessions – is unbelievably high, with Tatum, apparently inexhaustible throughout, producing one solo masterpiece after another. From the colossal list, following find Tatum (even for him) in incredible form: **The Man I Love, Jitterbug Waltz, Too Marvellous For Words, It's The Talk Of The Town, Stompin' At The Savoy, Caravan, You're Driving Me Crazy, This Can't Be Love, Fine & Dandy**, and **Ain't Misbehavin'**. But there is not one track that is less than excellent.

For Granz, Tatum also undertook a series of interesting dates which placed him in company of first-rate musicians (**The Tatum Group Masterpieces**) like Roy Eldridge (♦), Ben Webster (♦) and Lionel Hampton (♦). Overall, the collaborations worked well, excepting that with Eldridge, with trumpeter sounding inhibited by constant flurry of piano arpeggios Tatum furnished in accompaniment. The problems of total individualist Tatum being less than commendable accompanist were not (or could not be) resolved to satisfaction of all concerned, but, Eldridge apart, there were not too many; Benny Carter (♦) in particular seemed to thrive on challenge; although rather emotionless, Buddy DeFranco's (♦) mer-

curial clarinet proved a perfect foil for Tatum's own pyrotechnics; Hampton and Buddy Rich (♦) did not allow themselves to be overawed by Tatum's reputation, and Tatum–Hampton–Rich Trio produced superlative music (especially **How High The Moon** and **Perdido**); and these three, together with Harry Edison (♦), Barney Kessel and Red Callender, turned in similar results a month later. Tatum was star soloist of latter date, but meeting between pianist and Ben Webster, almost exactly a year later (1956), found Tatum, at times, having to take a back seat to tenorist's matchless playing. Webster, like Carter and Hampton, seemed unmoved by Tatum's background decorations – certainly, there is a continuity in his playing that gives no indication other than he was indeed stimulated by the presence of one of his own keyboard idols. Both men, in fact, were taped at an absolute peak of performance. To complete **The Tatum Group Masterpieces** Tatum achieved a wholly satisfactory trio date at beginning of '56 (with Callender and Jo Jones), repertoire including a convincing **Trio Blues**.

Tatum's final concert appearance was at Hollywood Bowl in August, '56. His last-known recordings (made at unspecified date(s), not too long before his death, in Los Angeles in November of same year) show not one iota of diminution of his immense talent. Indeed, there are tracks from these recordings (**Art Tatum In Person** and **Memories Of Art Tatum**) that rank with his finest recordings of the past.

Recordings:
Art Tatum, Piano Starts Here (Columbia/—)
Art Tatum, Art Of Tatum (MCA – Germany)
Art Tatum Masterpieces (MCA/—)
Various, Swing Combos (Including Art Tatum)
   (Swingfan – Germany)
Various (Including Art Tatum) First Esquire Concert, Vols 1, 2
   (—/Saga)
Various (Including Art Tatum), Second Esquire Concert, Vols 1, 2
   (—/Saga)
Art Tatum, Solo Piano (Capitol/Capitol – Holland)
Art Tatum, Masters Of Jazz, Vol 3 (Capitol/Electrola – Germany)
Art Tatum, Song Of The Vagabonds (Black Lion/Black Lion)
Art Tatum, The Genius (Black Lion/Black Lion)
Art Tatum, Get Happy (Black Lion/Black Lion)
Art Tatum, God Is In The House (Onyx/Polydor)
Art Tatum, At The Piano, Vols 1, 2 (GNP – Crescendo/—)
The Tatum Solo Masterpieces (Pablo/Pablo)
The Tatum Group Masterpieces (Pablo/Pablo)
Art Tatum In Person (20th Fox/Ember)
Memories Of Art Tatum (20th Fox/Ember)

Cecil Taylor

Born 1933, the pianist was not only the first of the New Thing players to record, but possessed such phenomenal technique that it was impossible for critics to dismiss him as a charlatan. Taylor's first album (**Jazz Advance**) combines atonality with a deep and abiding respect for the jazz tradition, for Waller, Ellington, Monk and Powell. Accusations of classical borrowings – Bartok, Stravinsky – are irrelevant in the light of the pianist's belief that all Western music began in Africa. Taylor's lineage becomes clear on numbers like **Excursion On A Wobbly Rail (Looking Ahead)** which continues the jazzman's fascination with train rhythms – Ellington's **Take The 'A' Train**, Monk's **Little Rootie Tootie**. Taylor's music is overwhelming, so that the newcomer might like the toehold of a familiar standard to begin with. **This Nearly Was Mine** displays clearly the chalkmarks and pins of the pianist's alterations, and a subversion of the original mood of the piece through tempo changes á la Monk (**Air**).

Naturally, the complexity of his music made it difficult for him to find suitable sidemen and steady employment. Sonny Murray's free drumming dovetailed beautifully with the abrupt, percussive keyboard, and altoman Jimmy Lyons has proved one of the few who can rise to the challenge of such tireless energy. One of Taylor's finest achievements, **D Trad, That's What (Café Montmartre)** features the trio without a bassist. A larger unit, including tenorist Archie Shepp gives a less torrential workout to three of Taylor's composi-

tions (**Into The Hot**) while a later composition, **Enter Evening (Unit Structures)**, explores gentler, more wistful moods than the New Thing usually gravitated towards. On this album, and the next (**Conquistador**) Taylor uses two bassists, including the pioneer of the bowed upper register, Alan Silva and Andrew Cyrille, a drummer with a less melodramatic, more agitated style than Murray, begins his long association with the pianist.

As Taylor's influence spread, he had the opportunity to record more frequently. The Jazz Composers' Orchestra assembled by Mike Mantler provides a massive backdrop for the virtuoso's headlong piano solo on **Communications 11**, which is literally overwhelming. Three albums resulted from an evening's recital in Europe (**Nuits De La Fondation Maeght**)

Nefertiti, The Beautiful One Has Come (Fontana): genius.

by the regular trio, Taylor, Lyons, Cyrille, supplemented by multi-instrumentalist Sam Rivers.

While there are changes of mood and dynamic level in the music of Cecil Taylor, the impression of

Above: Cecil Taylor, genius. A model of artistic integrity, his piano playing is the spearhead of free music.

superhuman energy dominates. It can be tiring to listen to, but it can be one of he most exhilarating and emotional experiences in all of jazz. It demands an open response and it imposes a total rhythm on audiences accustomed to more predictable patterns of tension and release that can be discharged through simple foot-tapping. Taylor's followers find catharsis by swaying the body back and forth in a variant of the Eastern chant.

Unrelentingly demanding within his groups, Taylor as a solo player (**Spring Of Two Blue J's, Silent Tongues** and **Indent**) proves a more tractable prospect to the average ear. He moves in and out of key register, ransacking past and future to feed his molten imagination. Arpeggios that sound as if he were zipping and unzipping the keyboard are abruptly coun-

Unit Structures
(Blue Note/Blue Note)
Conquistador
(Blue Note/Blue Note)
Nuits De La Fondation Maeght
(Shandar – France)
Spring Of Two Blue J's
(Unit Core/—)
Silent Tongues
(Arista Freedom/Arista Freedom)
Indent
(Arista Freedom/Arista Freedom)
Dark To Themselves
(Enja/Enja)
Air Above . . . Mountains Below
(—/Enja)

Charlie Teagarden

Charles ('Charlie') Teagarden (born Vernon, Texas, 1913) always

has been most reliable and pleasing trumpet soloist whose basically melodic, lyrical style has made him a much sought-after musician, both in small-combo and big-band contexts. Brother of trombonist-vocalist Jack Teagarden (♦), came to New York in 1929, after initial experience with local bands. Joined Ben Pollack (♦) same year (**Jack Teagarden, Vol 2 (1928-1957): Prince Of The Bone**) then worked with Red Nichols (♦) during 1930 (**The Early B.G.**). After spell with Roger Wolfe Kahn, joined aggregation of Paul Whiteman (♦). Never at all well-featured with Whiteman, nevertheless is fondly remembered for neat, Bixian solo on **Announcer's Blues (Paul Whiteman)**. Stayed with Whiteman from 1933–40, during which time he participated in recordings by orchestra and its offshoots, such as **My Reverie** and **Jeepers Creepers (Featuring Jack Teagarden)**. 1933: took part in Billie

Holiday's (♦) first recording sessions (**The Billie Holiday Story, Vol 1**). And in 1939, together with brother Jack, plus Chu Berry (♦), Harry James (♦) and others, was featured at live recording from Hickory House, NYC, broadcast beamed via airwaves to Britain (**Great Swing Jam Sessions, Vol 1**). 1940: was in good form during fine Dixieland record date by George Wettling's Chicago Rhythm Kings (**Chicago Jazz**) but in September left Paul Whiteman to join trumpet section of Jack Teagarden band. Did not stay long; then worked with 'Cabin In The Sky' pit orchestra.

After gigging in freelance capacity (plus spell of leading own combo), was drafted into US Ferry Command Service (1942). More freelance work in Los Angeles on release; then, briefly, with bands of Harry James; brother Jack (again); before starting three-year stint with Jimmy Dorsey (♦) (1948–51). Reunited with Ben Pollack for six months, he fronted his own trio (1951–2), then became involved with studio work. Regular with revived Bob Crosby (♦) bands during middle-to-late-1950s, also taking part in record dates like that of November 1953, featuring brother Jack and sister Norma (**Big T's Jazz**). Continued to freelance actively in Las Vegas, to which city he had moved. Was almost habitué of Cinderella's Club, LV, during 1960s. Became member of impressive Lionel Hampton (♦) Sextet which recorded in actual performance at Silver Slipper Club, LV, in '63 (**The Best Of Lionel Hampton**) showing Teagarden had lost nothing of his technical skills and sensitivity, especially during **Blues For Little T** (his long-standing nickname) and **Silver Slipper.** Earlier in career, Charlie Teagarden – too often in the shadow of a more famous brother – also had soloed with distinction (and sung a commendable blues) on **St James Infirmary** for Mills' Merry Makers (**The Great Soloists 1929-36 Featuring Jack Teagarden**) and had contributed handsomely to a classic 1931 Eddie Lang (♦)-Joe Venuti (♦) All-Star Orchestra record date (**Nothing But Notes**) which also featured Benny Goodman (♦) . . . and Jack Teagarden.

Recordings:
Jack Teagarden, Vol 2 (1928-1957): Prince Of The Bone
(RCA Victor – France)
Benny Goodman, The Early B.G. (—/Vocalion)
Joe Venuti, Nothing But Notes (MCA Coral – Germany)
Red Nichols, Tresaurus Of Classic Jazz, Vol 3 (Columbia/Philips)
Various, The Great Soloists 1929-36, Featuring Jack Teagarden (Biograph/—)
Paul Whiteman (RCA Victor)
The Billie Holiday Story, Vol 1 (Columbia/CBS)
Featuring Jack Teagarden (—/MCA)
Various (Including Charlie Teagarden), Great Swing Jam Sessions, Vol 1 (—/Saga)
Various (Including George Wettling), Chicago Jazz (Decca/Coral)
Jack Teagarden, Big T's Jazz (—/Ace of Hearts)
Charlie Teagarden (Coral/—)
The Best Of Lionel Hampton (MCA Coral – Germany)

Nuits De La Fondation Maeght (Shandar).

tered by rapid rumblings in the deep end. Dance and song are the disciplines that lie behind his art, so that there is – despite the avant-garde devices – a real sense of the Afro-American heritage.

Recordings:
In Transition
(Blue Note/Blue Note)
Looking Ahead
(Contemporary/—)
Air (CBS Barnaby/CBS Barnaby)
Cafe Montmartre
(Arista Freedom/Arista Freedom)
Into The Hot (Impulse/Impulse)

Silent Tongues (Arista Freedom): solo piano in spate, live at Montreux.

Jack Teagarden

John Weldon 'Jack' Teagarden (born Vernon, Texas, 1905) could well turn out to be the greatest trombone soloist in jazz history. He possessed a superb technique which he never overused or misused, complemented by a tremendous warmth, both tonally and in delivery. Particularly strong on blues and ballads, Teagarden further ranks with the greatest jazz vocalists – his mode of delivery and sound together were uncannily similar to his trombone playing. Because of his great flexibility, Teagarden's role in steering the trombone away from the rigid format of the established 'tailgate' style is of major importance. Altogether then, just about the perfect trombone stylist of any era, and it is the timelessness about his playing and all-round facility which have made him a special favorite amongst jazz trombonists of all persuasions.

Came from a musical family, with brothers Charlie on trumpet and Clois on drums, and sister Norma on piano. Jack Teagarden began on piano, age five, before he acquired a baritone-horn. By ten he was playing trombone, and first playing experience in public came in 1918, after Teagarden family had moved to Chappell, Nebraska; together with his mother at the piano, he worked at local theatres. Teagarden moved to Oklahoma City, then to San Angelo. There, he played with several local bands, also gigging in San Antonio and Shreveport. Worked with legendary Texan pianist Peck Kelley (1921–2). Then came work with succession of bands, including Doc Ross, Wingy Manone (♦), and singers Willard Robison and Elizabeth Brice. Worked (during 1928) with bands of Billy Lustig, Tommy Gott, before joining Ben Pollack (♦). Apart from brief periods away from this band, Teagarden remained with Pollack from 1928–33. Although its jazz content never was high, when Teagarden soloed or sang (sometimes both), or when a youthful Benny Goodman (♦) stepped forward to take a biting clarinet solo, the Ben Pollack band became – perhaps for half a chorus – a jazz unit. Fine examples of Teagarden's trombone injecting a much-needed jazz boost into the Pollack organization can be found in his work on such recordings as **Futuristic Rhythm, Song Of The Blues** and **Keep Your Undershirt On** (all **Jack**

Jack Teagarden, Vol 2 (1928-1957) (RCA Victor, France).

'J.T.' (Ace of Hearts) – or John Weldon Teagarden . . .

Teagarden, Vol 2 (1928-1957): 'Prince Of The Bone'). During his tenure with Pollack, Teagarden was involved in a large and varied number of recording dates, taking in the Mound City Blue Blowers, Eddie's (Condon) Hot Shots, commercial dance-band-leader Roger Wolfe Kahn (including magnificent Teagarden trombone on **She's A Great, Great Girl** (all **Texas T. Party**); Red Nichols (♦) (dozens of sides) (**J.T.** and **Jack Teagarden Classics**); Jimmy McHugh's Bostonians, Mills' Merry Makers; and Cornell & His Orchestra (all **The Greatest Soloists Featuring Jack Teagarden**). The overall standard of performance, vocal and instrumental, is very high. There was also much good jazz trombone in dates under his own name (including one with Fats Waller (♦) in line-up) (**King Of The Blues Trombone, Vols 1, 2**). And Teagarden and Louis Armstrong proved, not by any means for the last time, that they were a great front-line partnership during a memorable 1929 recording of **Knockin' A Jug** (**V.S.O.P. (Very Special Old Phonography, 1928-1930), Vols 5 & 6**).

Worked with Mal Hallett Orchestra during fall of 1933, then joined Paul Whiteman (♦) with whom he remained until 1938. To Whiteman's own brand of music, Teagarden added a definite warmth, and some real jazz. His solos with Whiteman, like those on **Announcer's Blues** and **Ain't Misbehavin'** (vocal too on this latter number) (**Paul Whiteman**) are gems, and emphasize, most strongly, the gulf between 'real' jazz and something which was only a pastiche. Teagarden recorded also with what was known as Paul Whiteman & His Swing (**Featuring Jack Teagarden**). Jazz-wise, it was an obvious consolation for Teagarden that at various times of his stay with Whiteman band contained jazzmen as talented as brother Charlie Teagarden, singer Johnny Mercer (a fine jazz singer as well as superb composer), George Wettling, and Frankie Trumbauer (♦) (**Featuring Jack Teagarden, Jack Teagarden, Vol 2 (1928-1957): 'Prince Of The Bone'** and **Jack Teagarden – Frankie Trumbauer**). Trumbauer and the Teagardens also were featured as the Three T's during special one-month engagement in New York, December 1936. Whilst with Whiteman, continued to record outside the band, a 1934 session with Adrian Rollini (♦) (**Featuring Jack Teagarden**) producing several fine solos. Between 1939 and 1947 Teagarden fronted series of own big bands. None of these produced music of any real importance – even though the leader's own playing and singing was as appealing as ever – but there were moments when it seemed capable of making an

impact; **Rompin' & Stompin', Jack Teagarden & His Orchestra 1944** and **It's Time For Teagarden** are representative of its basic swing-period sound and approach (with Dixieland influences). Much more of a compliment to Jack Teagarden's talents were record sessions like that by his Big Eight, in 1940 (**Jack Teagarden/Pee Wee Russell**) with the Texan undoubtedly stimulated by presence of such as Ben Webster (♦), Rex Stewart (♦), Barney Bigard (♦) and Dave Tough (♦).

Joined first of Louis Armstrong All Stars (1947–51) and pair forged one of the great partnerships in jazz, playing, singing of each seeming to stimulate the other to fresh heights of brilliance (**Satchmo At Symphony Hall** and **Louis Armstrong, Vols 1, 2**). Probably the peak of the partnership was reached at celebrated 1947 New York concert (**Satchmo's Greatest, Vols 4, 5** and **Town Hall Concert: The Unissued Part**) with rapport between both men resulting in absolutely unforgettable jazz. Teagarden sings, plays gloriously on **St James Infirmary** (something of a Teagarden speciality), demonstrating another important facet of his playing, his deep and natural affinity with blues. There is also a sublime vocal duet between Armstrong and Teagarden on **Rockin' Chair**, another regular feature for Armstrong All Stars (even after Teagarden had left).

After leaving Armstrong, Teagarden formed own small combo with which he toured and recorded. Accepted invitation to play with Ben Pollack in 1956, then put together another band, this one with Earl Hines (♦) as co-leader. This all-star band visited Europe (1957), to widespread acclaim. Toured Asia (1958–9) with own band, with subsidy granted by State Department. One of his last groups was that which contained, amongst others, trumpeter Don Goldie and pianist Don Ewell (**The Legendary Jack Teagarden**). It was a good group but nothing more – certainly not the stimulus needed to elicit from the leader playing that would rank with his very best, for by this time (1959, until his death, from bronchial pneumonia in 1964) Teagarden's work tended often towards blandness, even repetition.

Of records on which he played during last decade of his life, there were those that confirmed his stature as King of the Blues Trombone, including a brace of superb albums in company with Bobby Hackett (♦) (**Coast To Coast** and **Jazz Ultimate**); and another with Teagarden reworking old favorites like **St James Infirmary, Lover, Stars Fell On Alabama** and **A Hundred Years From Today (T For Trombone)** helped by fine band that included Lucky Thompson, Ruby Braff (♦) and Denzil Best. Even better were Teagarden's vocal-instrumental performances during a 1957 recording date featuring a reformed Bud Freeman-led Cum Laude Orchestra (**Jack Teagarden, Vols 1, 2**).

During his career, Teagarden acted as well as played and sang in movie *Birth of the Blues. Jack Teagarden*, a biography by Jay D. Smith & Len Gutteridge, first published 1960; *Jack Teagarden's Music*, by Howard J. Waters, Jr, first published in same year.

Recordings:
Benny Goodman, A Jazz Holiday (Decca – MCA/—)
Jack Teagarden, Texas T. Party (RCA Victor – France)
Jack Teagarden, Vol 2 (1928-1957): 'Prince Of The Bone' (RCA Victor – France)
Jack Teagarden/Red Nichols, 'JT' (Ace of Hearts)
The Great Soloists Featuring Jack Teagarden (Biograph/—)
Jack Teagarden Classics (Family – Italy)
Jack Teagarden, King Of The Blues Trombone, Vols 1-3 (Epic/Columbia)
Louis Armstrong, V.S.O.P. (Very Special Old Phonography, 1928-1930), Vols 5 & 6 (CBS – France)
Paul Whiteman (RCA Victor)
Featuring Jack Teagarden (—/MCA)
Jack Teagarden – Frankie Trumbauer (Totem – Canada)
Jack Teagarden & His Orchestra 1944 (Alamac/—)
Jack Teagarden, Rompin' & Stompin' (Swing Era/—)
Jack Teagarden, Sounds Of Swing (Sounds of Swing/—)
Jack Teagarden/(Pee Wee Russell) (Byg – France)
Louis Armstrong, Satchmo's Greatest, Vols 1, 2 (RCA Victor – France)
Louis Armstrong, Town Hall Concert (The Unissued Part) (RCA Victor – France)
Louis Armstrong, Satchmo At Symphony Hall, Vols 1, 2 (Decca/Coral)
Louis Armstrong, Vols 1, 2 (—/Saga)
The Legendary Jack Teagarden (Roulette)
Bobby Hackett/Jack Teagarden, Jazz Ultimate (Capitol/Capitol)
Bobby Hackett/Jack Teagarden, Coast To Coast (Capitol/Regal)
Jack Teagarden, T For Trombone (Jazztone/Society)

Clark Terry

Trumpeter Clark Terry was born in St Louis in 1920, the home of many trumpeters, and gained experience with Charlie Barnet, Charlie Ventura and Eddie 'Cleanhead' Vinson before a three-year stint with Count Basie. He joined Duke Ellington in 1951 and stayed for eight years (**The World Of Duke Ellington, Vol 2**). Probably his best known work was on **Up And Down, Up And Down** and **Lady Mac**, which Ellington wrote around his bubbling personality (**Such Sweet Thunder**). He spent

Clark Terry's Big Bad Band Live On 57th Street (Big Bear)

the next few years as a staff musician with NBC, also co-leading a group with trombonist Bob Brookmeyer **(Terry-Brookmeyer Quintet)**. Numerous small albums find Terry with Johnny Griffin and Thelonious Monk **(Cruisin')**; with Ben Webster **(The Happy Horns Of Clark Terry)** and with baritonist Cecil Payne in a set of Bebop standards **(Cool Blues)**. An exhilarating encounter between Oscar Peterson and Terry **(Oscar Peterson Trio With Clark Terry)** which includes the trumpeter's hilarious brand of blues mumbling, is outstanding. Most recently, Clark Terry has formed his own big band, which is a straight-ahead swinger using arrangements by Ernie Wilkins and Frank Wess **(Live On 57th Street)**. A highly distinctive stylist on trumpet and flugelhorn, Terry's work is witty and colored with half-valve effects and mutes.

Recordings:
The World Of Duke Ellington,
 Vol 2 (Columbia/CBS)

Above: Clark Terry; trumpet, flugelhorn and vocals. Ex-Ellington and currently leader of his own big band.

Duke Ellington, Such Sweet
 Thunder (Columbia/CBS)
The Terry-Brookmeyer Quintet
 (Mainstream/Mainstream)
Cruisin' (Milestone/Milestone)
Cool Blues (—/DJM)
Oscar Peterson Trio With Clark
 Terry (Mercury/Philips)
Clark Terry's Big Band Live On
 57th Street (—/Big Bear)
The Happy Horns Of Clark
 Terry (Impulse/Impulse)

Sonny Terry

'Sonny' Terry (real name: Saunders Terrell, born Durham, North Carolina, 1911) has few, if any, rivals as the most expressive blues harmonica practitioner of all. His great dexterity with the tiny instrument enables him to produce an inimitable array of sounds; often as near to a human cry as seems possible, sometimes of an inhuman variety. Terry can express grief, elation, misery, mirth . . . any kind of human emotion. As a singer, too, his gruff-voice style, whilst never approaching the electrifying quality of his 'mouth harp' work, often can be very effective. Terry – blind in one eye from age 11 and totally blind five years following the accident which precipitated the loss of sight – teamed up, to mutual advantage, with another sightless blues exponent, singer-guitarist-composer Blind Boy Fuller. Terry was still in his teens. The pair recorded numerous classic blues performances **(Blind Boy Fuller With Sonny Terry & Bull City Red)**. 1939: year after debuting on record with Fuller, took part in John Hammond's *Spirituals To Swing* concert **(John Hammond's Spirituals To Swing)** using his falsetto whoops, eerie cries and extraordinary technique with harmonica to superb advantage on own **Mountain Blues**; then, supported by Bull City Red,

wailing through a fast **John Henry.** 1940: first got together with guitarist - singer - composer Brownie McGhee – start of a most fruitful partnership, and one that lasts until today. Previously, had recorded with Leadbelly (♦) **(Keep Your Hands Off Her)**. Also, during '40, made first records under own name **(History Of Jazz - The Blues)** including **Harmonica & Washboard Breakdown.** With McGhee, has made countless recordings (see below for selective listing). Although duo has not made records which would be considered bad, often there has been too much repetition in repertoire and sameness in performance level. Same with many live performances by pair during past 10–15 years.

Alone, Terry's 'harp' has been heard to good advantage in front of washboard band **(Sonny Terry's Washboard Band)** together with guitarist-singer Alec Stewart **(Folk Blues)** – an album that includes the marvelously evocative **Fox Chase;** unaccompanied **(Harmonica Blues);** and accompanied only by Sticks McGhee (Brownie's brother), guitar, and J. C. Burris (Terry's nephew), bones **(On The Road).** Of Terry-McGhee LPs, amongst best are **Sonny Is King, Sonny's Story, Where The Blues Begin, Whoopin' The Blues, A Long Way From Home** and **Blues From Everywhere,** last named with additional assistance from Sticks McGhee, Burris, and with Terry playing jawharp on some tracks (eg **Shortnin' Bread, Skip To My Lou).** With McGhee, Terry has visited Europe on many occasions (also India, once). Apart from which he has appeared on Broadway in production of musical *Finian's Rainbow* (mid 1940s) and toured (together with Brownie McGhee) in Broadway production of *Cat On A Hot Tin Roof* (1955–1957).

Recordings:
Blind Boy Fuller With Sonny
 Terry & Bull City Red
 (Blues Classics/—)
Various (Including Sonny
 Terry), John Hammond's
 Spirituals To Swing
 (Vanguard/Vogue)
Leadbelly, Keep Your Hands
 Off Her (Verve–Forecast/
 Verve–Folkways)
Various (Including Sonny
 Terry), History Of Jazz - The
 Blues (Folkways/—)
Sonny Terry's Washboard Band
 (Folkways/—)
Folk Blues (Elektra/Vogue)
Harmonica Blues
 (Folkways/Topic)
On The Road (Folkways/Xtra)
Sonny Terry/Brownie McGhee,
 Sonny Is King
 (Prestige–Bluesville/—)
Sonny Terry/Brownie McGhee,
 Sonny's Story
 (Prestige–Bluesville/Xtra)
Sonny Terry/Brownie McGhee,
 Where The Blues Begin
 (Fontana)
Whoopin' The Blues (Capitol)
Sonny Terry/Brownie McGhee,
 At Sugar Hill (Fantasy/—)
The Best Of Sonny Terry &
 Brownie McGhee (Fantasy/—)
Sonny Terry/Brownie McGhee,
 Live! At The Fret (Fantasy/—)
Sonny Terry/Brownie McGhee,
 A Long Way From Home
 (ABC–Blues Way/Stateside)
Sonny Terry/Brownie McGhee,

Right: wailing the blues, with harmonica and voice, Sonny Terry produces the most extraordinary sounds.

Blues From Everywhere
(Folkways/Xtra)
Various (Including Sonny Terry), Penitentiary Blues
(Fontana)

Frank Teschemacher

Frank Teschemacher (born Kansas City, Missouri, 1906) was an important member of so-called Austin High School Gang. Raised in Chicago and primarily a clarinettist, Teschemacher could also play tenor- and alto-sax, banjo, violin. Played last-named instrument with Austin High School Orchestra: it was also first instrument he learned to play (at ten). Went with other Austin members into Husk O'Hare's Red Dragons (1924), working exclusively on alto. Switched to clarinet following year, then worked with various outfits (including Charlie Straight, Art Kassel; and, for two years, Floyd Town). Took part in historical, influential 1927 McKenzie-Condon Chicagoans recordings **(That Toddlin' Town – Chicago 1926-28)** – his piercing, angular clarinet solos (never lacking in warmth) providing that band's most distinctive solos. 1928: to New York for many and varied jobs, including recording dates with Ted Lewis, Miff Mole (♦) & His Little Molers and Eddie Condon's Quartet **(That Toddlin' Town – Chicago 1926-28)**; the Chocolate Dandies **(The Chocolate Dandies)**; the Jungle Kings, Charles Pierce's Orchestra (both on **Muggsy Spanier 1924-1928**) plus gigs with Ben Pollack (♦), Red Nichols (♦).

Back to New York in fall of '28, where his fine musicianship kept him in almost constant employ before his death – following automobile accident in Chicago, March 1932. Before he died, he had toured with big bands of Jan Garber and Wild Bill Davison (♦) – in whose car he received fatal injuries. Played mostly alto, violin during last two-three years of his life. Was originally influenced by black clarinet players like Jimmie Noone (♦), Omer Simeon (♦) and, most notably, Johnny Dodds (♦), yet forged an individual approach. In turn, influenced others, like Pee Wee Russell (♦), Ernie Caceres and, earlier in his career, Benny Goodman (♦). Another who died prematurely, the pitifully few recordings by Teschemacher, like his sparkling solo on **Indiana (Eddie Condon's World Of Jazz)** show him nevertheless to have developed into an important and influential clarinettist.

Recordings:
Various (Including McKenzie & Condon Chicagoans, Miff Mole & His Little Molers, Eddie Condon), That Toddlin' Town – Chicago (1926-28)
(—/Parlophone)
The Chocolate Dandies
(—/Parlophone)
Various (Including Frank Teschemacher), Eddie Condon's World Of Jazz
(Columbia/CBS)
Muggsy Spanier 1924-1928
(—/Fountain)

Art Themen
♦ *Stan Tracey*

Claude Thornhill

Claude Thornhill (born Terre Haute, Indiana, 1909) by the end of 1930s had established an enviable reputation as pianist-arranger. He had worked with various bands, including those of Hal Kemp, Paul Whiteman (♦), Benny Goodman (♦), Leo Reisman, Ray Noble, André Kostelantez, as well as working as singer Maxine Sullivan's (♦) musical director-pianist **(Frankie Newton At The Onyx Club)** arranging and producing **Loch Lomond,** her major hit record. Had recorded with another great singer, Billie Holiday (♦) **(The Golden Years/The Golden Years, Vol 2).** Also had worked in Hollywood, writing music for films, radio and record dates. After which Thornhill helped Skinnay Ennis to assemble a big band – which is where no doubt he first met arranger, composer Gil Evans (♦), a musician who was to play an important part in Thornhill's imminent future.

Claude Thornhill put together his own band in 1940. It was an orchestra with a sound all its own, with Thornhill and Bill Borden creating unique voicing, including unison clarinets, and a hitherto unsurpassed use of dynamics. And it was a quiet band – it might be said to have sold quiet excitement. Eventually this was to work against the Thornhill Orchestra and in part led to its demise. Repertoire comprised originals (Thornhill wrote the unusual **Portrait Of A Guinea Farm,** and the band's theme, **Snowfall,** which featured his piano – a distinctive feature of many recordings), pop material (old and new), and adaptations of classical pieces by such as Greig, Dvorak, Brahms **(Claude Thornhill At Glen Island Casino 1941).** Mostly, these were orchestrated by Thornhill. After a cool initial reception, the band broke into the big-time through a first-time appearance in 1941 at Glen Island Casino, which resulted in equally successful return visits to a venue popular with big-band aficionados of the time. Apart from the rich tonal textures of ensemble and its collective uniqueness, it also possessed first-class soloists in Irving Fazola, clarinet, Rusty Dedrick, trumpet, and Bob Jenny, trombone, with the much-respected Conrad Gozzo as leader of the trumpets. Other exceptional items in the Thornhill book between 1940-2 – when leader disbanded because called up to serve in US Navy – included exquisite re-workings of **I Don't Know Why, Where Or When** and further classical adaptations, **Traumerai, Hungarian Dance No 5** and Grieg's **Piano Concerto (all The Memorable Claude Thornhill).**

During his Naval service, Thornhill got to play with Artie Shaw's (♦) Naval Band, later leading own Service band. On demobilization in 1946, formed new band, which was even more remarkable than its predecessor. For one thing it was larger, and its instrumentation was, for the time, unusual insofar as it included a French-horn section – allowing for further development in producing even richer tonal tapestries. Gil Evans, who had supplied arrangements for the previous Thornhill orchestra, including **Buster's Last Stand, Where Or When, There's A Small Hotel** (all **The Memorable Claude Thornhill),** became the seminal figure with the new band. At Evans' instigation Thornhill, willingly, augmented its repertoire to acknowledge the importance of Bebop. As well as the more predictable pop-slanted items, like **A Sunday Kind Of Love** – a size-

The Memorable Claude Thornhill (Columbia).

able hit record for band and its singer Fran Warren – were included Evans' brilliant orchestrations of bop classics, **Anthropology, Yardbird Suite** and **Donna Lee**, featuring solos by up-and-coming young musicians like Lee Konitz (♦) and Red Rodney (♦) (all **The Memorable Claude Thornhill**). It was indeed a band ahead of its time, and one which was to prove influential in future musical developments, most important of all as guide-line and starting point for Miles Davis' (♦) 1948 'Birth of the Cool' band.

Then, suddenly, it was all over; Thornhill disbanded. He reformed again, in 1949, and although the third outfit produced much fine music (including records for Victor, 1949–50), the charisma of the first two never was quite recaptured. Kind of live performances of which this post-1949 band was capable are to be found within **One Night Stand With Claude Thornhill**. During 1950s, rarely was seen in front of big band, more often led small combos. Worked with Tony Bennett during this period. In following decade, toured occasionally with six-piece outfit, but mostly lived in retirement. Died suddenly from heart attack in 1965.

Recordings:
Frankie Newton At The Onyx Club *(Tax – Sweden)*
Billie Holiday, The Golden Years *(Columbia)*/
  The Golden Years, Vol 2 *(CBS)*
The Memorable Claude Thornhill *(Columbia/—)*
Claude Thornhill At Glen Island Casino 1941 *(Monmouth–Evergreen/—)*
The Early Cool: A Memory Of Claude Thornhill – On Stage 1946/1947 *(Monmouth–Evergreen/Ember)*
One Night Stand With Claude Thornhill *(Joyce/—)*

Charles Tolliver

The aim of trumpeter Charles Tolliver is to be able to take any song for 25 or 50 choruses, and every one of them is a new song. Born in Florida in 1942, an abiding influence has been Clifford Brown – in fact Tolliver is remarkable for his orthodox values which place him squarely in the mainstream of modern jazz. Like Woody Shaw, who shares his sense of tradition, he is a brilliant player capable of handling any tempo or mood. His debut as a sideman with altoist Jackie McLean **(It's Time** and

Live In Tokyo (Strata-East): blistering trumpet.

192

Above: Charles Tolliver, one of the most impressive of the younger trumpeters. Runs his own record company.

Action), featured some of his dramatic writing, **Plight,** as well as evocative ballads like **Truth.** He spent two useful years with drummer Max Roach **(Members Don't Git Weary)** and dedicated a later number, **Grand Max,** to the master **(Live At The Loosrechdt Jazz Festival).** In 1969, Tolliver established Music Inc with pianist Stanley Cowell, and their first recording was made on tour in Europe **(The Ringer)** featuring Tolliver compositions and excellent, lyrical, driving playing from the quartet. The finest single solo, **Drought,** was recorded by the trumpeter in 1973 **(Live In Tokyo),** and is on his own label, Strata-East, which he set up in the early '70s as 'a natural extension of wanting to be able to govern what I'm involved with'. Tolliver is one of the finest trumpeters on the scene today, and a practical businessman – a rare combination.

Recordings:
Jackie McLean, It's Time *(Blue Note/Blue Note)*
Jackie McLean, Action *(Blue Note/Blue Note)*
Jackie McLean, Jacknife *(Blue Note/Blue Note)*
Max Roach, Members Don't Git Weary *(Atlantic/Atlantic)*
Live At The Loosrechdt Jazz Festival *(Strata-East/Black Lion)*
The Ringer *(Arista/Black Lion)*
Live In Tokyo *(Strata-East/Strata-East)*
Live At Slugs *(Strata-East/Strata-East)*

Mel Tormé

Singer Mel Tormé, usually associated with the ritzier nightspot circuits, laid a series of classic jazz albums in the '50s, With his light voice and impeccable timing, he was *The* Cool School vocalist, approaching the material with all the lyricism and inventiveness of a Stan Getz. After paying dues with the Chico Marx Orchestra – Tormé's career began at the age of four – he collaborated with arranger Marty Paich, using his Dektette to duplicate the sound of the Miles Davis 'Birth of the Cool' band. With Tormé singing definitive versions of the better popular songs, **Old Devil Moon, Too Darn Hot (Mel Torme Swings Shubert Alley)** and **The Lady Is A Tramp**

Mel Tormé Swings Shubert Alley (HMV): the Velvet Fog.

(Lulu's Back In Town) and soloists like Art Pepper, Bud Shank, Bill Perkins, most of the albums are collector's items. The 'Velvet Fog' is a fine scat singer and all-round musician.

Recordings:
Mel Torme Swings Shubert Alley *(Verve/HMV)*
Lulu's Back In Town *(King/Polydor)*
Mel Torme Loves Fred Astaire *(Bethlehem/—)*

Dave Tough
♦ *Woody Herman*

Stan Tracey

The grand old man of British modern jazz, pianist Stan Tracey has been a vital force since 1950, playing with Roy Fox, Laurie Morgan, Kenny Baker, Ronnie Scott, Tony Crombie and Ted Heath before his tenure as house pianist at Ronnie Scott's Jazz Club from 1960–8, when he played behind legions of American guest artists. His original Duke Ellington-Thelonious Monk influence has born fruit in a highly idiosyncratic style of writing and playing that seems to bring out the ibex in each new generation of jazzmen. Most of his earlier work has been deleted, but his classic interpretations of Dylan Thomas **(Under Milk Wood)** aided by the highly original Scottish tenorman, Bobby Wellins, have been reissued.

Starless And Bible Black is a haunting piece, rigorously pared to cast its somber mood. A master of harmony, Tracey has put himself out to explore those areas of freedom that most of his generation dismiss as noise, and has been met halfway by the young musicians attracted to his structural wisdoms. His duets with altoist Mike Osborne (**Original** and **Tandem**) and his solo concert (**Alone At Wigmore Hall**) show how far he has incorporated New Wave techniques into his jolting, angular style. His current quartet (**Captain Adventure**) with the wildly imaginative tenor, Art Themen – a bone-surgeon by profession – the aggressively apt drummer, Bryan Spring, and the rock-steady bassist, Dave Green, is arguably the finest combo in Britain. Tracey's octet, recently recorded, plays his quirky charts with punch, and features two-tenor chases between Themen and the trenchant Don Weller.

In the climate of apathy towards British jazz that pervades the native scene, Stan Tracey's survival and continual growth is a tribute to his integrity.

Recordings:
Under Milk Wood (—/Steam)
Original (—/Cadillac)
Tandem (—/Ogun)
Alone At Wigmore Hall
 (—/Cadillac)
Captain Adventure (—/Steam)
The Bracknell Connection
 (—/Steam)
**Stan Tracey & Keith Tippett,
 TNT** (—/Steam)
The Salisbury Suite (—/Steam)
**Stan Tracey & John Surman,
 Sonatinas** (—/Steam)

Lennie Tristano

Born 1919 in Chicago, blind pianist and teacher Lennie Tristano attracted a small dedicated group of disciples in the '40s and '50s for what was popularly called 'The Cool School'. Running counter to the prevailing passion of Bebop, Tristano experimented in linear improvisation, long, undulating Bach-like lines, counterpoint, atonality, a low decibel count and intense and subtle rhythmic complexity. An example of his playing in the mid-'40s (**Lennie Tristano/ Red Rodney**) shows the piano lines interweaving with the guitar of Billy Bauer in an even flow. In 1949, the Lennie Tristano Sextet with altoist Lee Konitz, tenorman Warne Marsh, Billy Bauer, recorded a classic (**Crosscurrents**). Over a steady rhythm, the players wove in and out of each other's lines lightly and precisely. **Intuition** from this session dispensed with an harmonic base and is arguably the starting point of the New Thing – certainly free collective improvisation has never sounded so seamlessly beautiful.

Though his detractors have accused Tristano of sounding bloodless and academic, Charlie Parker respected his music and the two men played together on the All Star Metronome broadcast (**Anthropology**). Tristano's moving blues for Bird, **Requiem** (**Lines**) proves that the cerebral approach need not preclude feeling. Multi-tracking on **Turkish Mambo** so that the three lines

move in different times, **East 32nd Street** and **Line Up** caused a storm of controversy at the time, 1955, but would pass unnoticed in the technological '70s. In this case, the music justifies the means. Always a recluse, the great pianist did not choose to record again until 1962 (**The New Tristano**) which in terms of melodic invention, facility with complex time signatures and sheer technical mastery remains

Crosscurrents (Capitol): the foundations of Cool.

unsurpassed. An outspoken, uncompromising man, Tristano has remained aloof from the jazz world since, completely out of sympathy with the overt emotionalism of today's music – 'all emotion, no feeling'.

Recordings:
Lennie Tristano/Red Rodney
 (Mercury/Mercury)
Crosscurrents (Capitol/Capitol)
Charlie Parker, Anthropology
 (Spotlite/Spotlite)
Lines (Atlantic/Atlantic)
The New Tristano
 (Atlantic/Atlantic)

Frankie Trumbauer

Frankie Trumbauer (born Carbondale, Illinois, 1902) was a first-rate musician who performed impressively on a variety of instruments, including alto-sax, clarinet, bassoon. But it is his work as C-melody sax player that is best remembered. On this latter instrument – a now forgotten member of the saxophone family, pitched in key of C – Trumbauer produced an airy, limpid, cool-sounding tone, both distinctive and melodically pleasing. Hearing Trumbauer soloing on C-melody sax, it is not difficult to understand why he was a major influence on Lester Young (♦). Trumbauer, raised in St Louis, also studied violin, flute, trombone during his teens. Was leader of own band by the time he was 17, after which served in US Navy during World War I.

On demobilization, returned to St Louis to work with several bands, including Gene Rodemich (with whom he made record debut); then, in Chicago, with Ray Miller. First really important assignment (1925–6) was as musical director for Jean Goldkette Orchestra; he also fronted band at Arcadia Ballroom whose other principal soloist was Bix Beiderbecke (♦). Pair became well-nigh inseparable, working, next, with Goldkette (1926–7), then, with big band led by another multi-instrumentalist Adrian Rollini (♦) (1927). Trumbauer joined Paul Whiteman Orchestra in '27, staying five years.

Then, put together and toured with own orchestra (1932–3), rejoining Whiteman in '33. With Jack Teagarden (♦) and Charlie Teagarden (♦), co-led The Three T's (1936) before moving to West Coast, co-leading another band with trumpeter Manny Klein. Worked with Georgie Stoll, in 1938, before assembling another band (using name 'Trombar').

Left music for good in 1939, for job in civil aeronautics. But by following year was leading own band again. Was test pilot during World War II, returning to music scene in 1945, with Russ Case and NBC Studio Orchestra, in New York. After moving to California (1947), retired – full-time – again. Rejoined Civil Aeronautical Authority, in Kansas City, although from time to time played occasional gigs. Collapsed and died in Kansas City in June, 1956. Trumbauer's fine musicianship was heard mostly in three areas: (1) with the Paul Whiteman band (**The Bix Beiderbecke Legend** and **Paul Whiteman**); (2) with own bands, often with Beiderbecke as star soloist (**Bix & Tram, The Golden Days Of Jazz: Bix Beiderbecke** and **The Rare Bix**); (3) with own orchestra (sans Beiderbecke) (**Frankie Trumbauer & His Orchestra 1931-1932**). Invariably was heard on C-melody sax, including a justly celebrated solo on **Singin' The Blues (The Golden Days Of Jazz: Bix Beiderbecke)** although he also recorded on bassoon, **'Tain't So, Honey, 'Tain't So (The Rare Bix)** and **Running Ragged (The Golden Days Of Jazz: Eddie Lang-Joe Venuti: Stringing The Blues)**. One of his rare solos on alto-sax emanated from a recording session by the Chicago Loopers (**Chicago Loopers & Midway Garden Orchestra**).

Recordings:
**Frankie Trumbauer & His
 Orchestra 1931-1932**
 (The Old Masters/—)
**The Bix Beiderbecke Story,
 Vol II: Bix & Tram** (Columbia)/
 Bix & Tram 1927 (Parlophone)
**The Golden Days Of Jazz:
 Eddie Lang - Joe Venuti/
 Stringing The Blues**
 (CBS – Holland)
**The Golden Days of Jazz:
 Bix Beiderbecke**
 (CBS – Holland)
The Bix Beiderbecke Legend
 (—/RCA Victor – France)
**The Bix Beiderbecke Story,
 Vol III: Whiteman Days - In A
 Mist** (Columbia)/
 The Rare Bix (Parlophone)
Paul Whiteman (RCA Victor)
**Various, Chicago Loopers &
 Midway Garden Orchestra**
 (Audobon/—)

Bruce Turner

Bruce Turner (born Saltburn, Yorkshire, England, 1922) is living proof that Great Britain can produce totally original jazz players, who can compete on equal terms with American greats – something which, until the past one-and-a-half decades, could not have been said in earlier days. Turner, a confirmed 'mainstreamer' and influenced mostly by mid-period instrumentalists, spent childhood in India. Back to England for education at Dulwich College, London. Spent five years (1941–1946) in

RAF where from time to time managed to play jazz (an occupation he had commenced prior to call-up). Worked with various bands on demobilization, including one bop-styled outfit. Played alto sax, clarinet with bands of Roy Vaughan, Freddy Randall (1948–50), then took job in quartet making trans-Atlantic trips on liner *Queen Mary*. Eventually, together with QM colleagues pianist Ronnie Ball, bassist Peter Ind, took lessons in New York, first, from Lennie Tristano (♦), then with Lee Konitz (♦). Despite an obvious preference for altoists like Johnny Hodges (♦) and Benny Carter (♦), Turner today has retained a superficial element of Konitz in his own work. Worked with Ronnie Ball Quintet (1951), before rejoining Randall for two years. Accepted offer to work with Humphrey Lyttelton (♦) Band (in '53), playing clarinet, alto-, and, for a while, soprano-sax. Was in fine fettle when Lyttelton band recorded in live performance twice: at London venues Conway Hall (**Humph At The Conway**) and Royal Festival Hall (**Humphrey Lyttelton Jazz Concert**), both dating back to 1954.

Left Lyttelton in 1957 (also having worked during the 1953–7 period with Kenny Baker, and visiting US jazzmen Sidney Bechet (♦) and Eddie Condon (♦)). Formed first of his celebrated Bruce Turner Jump Bands – small combos specializing in hard-swinging mainstream jazz – which lasted from 1957–65. During its lifetime it supported touring Americans of the calibre of Bill Coleman (♦), Don Byas (♦), Ben Webster (♦), Ray Nance (♦).

Spent four years as member of Acker Bilk's Paramount Jazz Band (1966–70), visiting Far East, Middle East, Europe, and New Zealand and Fiji. Since then, has gigged with various British bands (including Lyttelton) and has fronted a revived Turner Jump Band. His recording activities have been frequent, including guest appearances at concerts headlined by trumpeter-bandleader Alex Welsh (**An Evening With Alex Welsh & His Friends, Parts 1 & 2** and **Salute To Satchmo**) plus splendid studio reunions with Lyttelton (**South Bank Swing Session** and **Take It From The Top**). His presence was felt throughout London-made album **Song Of The Tenor** showcasing tenor-saxophone artistry of Bud Freeman (♦) – Freeman calls Turner 'one of the greatest, most original saxophone players in the world' – and, together with Alex Welsh reedman Johnny Barnes, he turned in series of excellent solos on **Jazz Masters: Live At St Pancras Town Hall** during most rewarding 1976 London concert.

Recordings:
**Humphrey Lyttelton, The Best
 Of Humph 1949-56**
 (—/Parlophone)
**Humphrey Lyttelton, Jazz
 Concert** (—/Parlophone)
**Humphrey Lyttelton, Humph
 At The Conway**
 (—/Parlophone)
Accent On Swing
 (—/International Jazz Club)
Jumpin' For Joy, Nos 1, 2
 (—/Philips) (EPs)
Goin' Places (—/Philips)
**Wild Bill Davison With Freddy
 Randall & His Band**
 (—/Black Lion)

Big Joe Turner

Joseph 'Big Joe' Turner (born 1911) started a long, impressive career by singing blues whilst doubling as bartender in variety of clubs in home town of Kansas City. It was at this time that Turner first worked together with pianist Pete Johnson (♦). Couple stayed as team in city for several years before joint discovery by John Hammond resulted in sudden trip to New York to appear in concert at Carnegie Hall, as well as in 52nd Street clubs. After return trip to New York had gained Turner further recognition, was featured in Duke Ellington (♦) revue, *Jump For Joy*, in Hollywood (1941). When show closed, Turner chose to work locally on West Coast, together with pianists Meade Lux Lewis (♦) and Joe Sullivan (♦) and others. Turner previously had worked with Sullivan, on record, in 1940 **(Cafe Society Swing & The Boogie Woogie)** and also with an even more famous pianist, Art Tatum (♦) **(Swing Combos: 1935-1941** and **Swing Street, Vol 4)**. Each of these record dates found Turner singing at top of his game – a veritable definition of 'blues shouting'. The huge voice – warm, yet with steely masculinity – is very essence of this vital area of black American music. During 1940s, Turner-Johnson partnership continued to flourish, in concert and/or on record, usually in company with dynamic, rocking little band; another pianist, Albert Ammons (♦) also worked with Turner during this period. Results of their efforts are encapsulated, warmly and vitally, in **Have No Fear, Big Joe Turner Is Here** with Turner's hoarse, impassioned voice declaiming marvelously on titles such as **S.K. Blues (Parts I & II), Howlin' Winds, Hollywood Bed** (a re-styling of **Cherry Red**, a superb Turner-Johnson collaboration contained in **Swing Street, Vol 4** from several years before), and the self-explanatory **Johnson & Turner Blues**.

Toured with Ammons and Johnson, 1944, and with Luis Russell (♦), in 1945. Continued to record fairly frequently, including some electrifying sides for Arhoolie (Johnson, again, featured as pianist) **(Jumpin' The Blues)**. The 1950s found Turner attaining fresh popularity, mostly within an R&B frame-

The Boss Of The Blues (Atlantic) – Joe Turner, no less.

work. In many ways, his early-1950s recordings for Atlantic **(His Greatest Recordings)** were of great importance in the gradual emergence, then explosion, of rock 'n' roll, not the least of which were **TV Mama, Sweet Sixteen, Honey Hush, Chains Of Love, Teenage Letter** and **Shake, Rattle & Roll,** latter soon to become principal break-through for rock music, via bowdlerized version by Bill Haley & His Comets. But perhaps Turner's single most impressive contribution to vocal blues recordings came in 1956 when, together with jazz instrumentalists of the calibre of Pete Brown (♦), Lawrence Brown (♦), Freddie Green and re-united with his off-time musical associate and friend Pete Johnson, he laid down the tracks for what was to become probably the single most impressive definition of the urban blues shouter **(Boss Of The Blues)**. Turner sounded as indestructible as ever on 11 tried-and-trusted compositions of the genre (viz **Roll 'Em Pete, Cherry Red, How Long Blues, St Louis Blues, Wee Baby Blues)** along with a couple of pop standards **(Pennies From Heaven** and **You're Driving Me Crazy)**.

During 1950s visited Europe on several occasions; in 1962, played residency at La Calvados, a Parisian club. Although often troubled by arthritis in more recent years, Joe Turner continues to make records (albeit in an armchair). Often, though, the material has become hackneyed and in the case of **Summertime** and **I've Got The World On A String (In The Evening)** unsuitable. Yet there are times still when the big man can recall his peak years during 1930s–50s, especially when the musical company is congenial, as with Count Basie (♦), Eddie 'Lockjaw' Davis (♦) and Harry Edison (♦) **(The Bosses)**, or Milt Jackson (♦), Roy Eldridge (♦) and Pee Wee Crayton **(Nobody In Mind)** or maybe with a truly all-star trumpet section comprising Edison, Eldridge, Dizzy Gillespie (♦), and Clark Terry (♦) **(The Trumpet Kings Meet Joe Turner)**.

Recordings:
Various (Including Joe Turner), Cafe Society Swing & The Boogie Woogie 1938-1940 (Swingfan – Germany)
Various (Including Joe Turner), Swing Combos 1935-1941 (Swingfan – Germany)

Left: Joe Turner, the archetypal urban blues shouter who popularized Shake Rattle & Roll before Haley.

McCoy Tyner

Born Philadelphia, 1938, pianist McCoy Tyner came from a musical background, consolidated by later enrolment at music colleges. In 1959 he was playing with the Jazztet, a group led by Art Farmer and Benny Golson, and in 1960 he joined the John Coltrane Quartet within a fortnight of its inception. He was with Coltrane for the next five years, an integral part of that classic, innovative group. He owes his tireless strength to that period, often laying a series of vamping figures that drove Coltrane in a modal, scalar direction away from conventional harmony. Tyner's later work was foreshadowed by the creative climate within the Quartet – the intensity, the heightened rhythmic activity, the juggernaut drive. His keyboard style was largely formed in the '60s, fast, splashing arpeggios which leavened the sinew of percussive, massed chords.

Leaving Coltrane in 1965, Tyner had five bad years when work was scarce, even considering the alternative of taxi driving. Dissatisfied with his Impulse contract, he switched to Blue Note, working on other artists' sessions as well as heading his own. There is a remarkable consistency throughout Tyner's albums, and a direct line runs through the percussive themes of **African Village (Time For Tyner)**, **Vision (Expansions)**, **Message From The Nile (Extensions)** and on into his recent work for Milestone. His compositions reflect the universality of his – and Coltrane's – vision, drawing from ethnic origins other than the Afro-American, such as the rippling **Song Of Happiness (Expansions)** which is based upon Japanese scales.

Signing with Milestone in 1972, Tyner's career finally took off. The debut album **(Sahara)** brought all the ingredients into focus – the sulphurous percussive climate established before the storming entry of the piano, the thumping, hypnotic chord structures, the sense of a series of triumphal entries into the Capitol. **Rebirth** showcases the pianist's incredible technique, while **Valley Of Life**

Atlantis (Milestone): pianist McCoy Tyner, surmounting all obstacles. One of the most vital players on the scene.

has him trying the lighter voice of the koto; Tyner has experimented with various instruments, usually at the beginnings and ends of his compositions – harpsichord and celeste **(Trident)** – and dulcimer **(Focal Point).** Subsequent albums testify to his unswerving sense of purpose, and his freedom from fashion's dictates: 'When you remove yourself and just become a vehicle, that's when those moments happen.' A Moslem since the age of 18, McCoy Tyner stands four-square in his creativity – 'I play what I live'.

The value of having a steady, working band is illustrated by the live double albums **Enlightenment** and **Atlantis,** all the players hitting an exhilarating level of intensity from the start and staying there. Tenor and soprano Azar Lawrence, bassist Joony Booth and Tyner himself are overwhelming, and Alphonse Mouzon on **Enlightenment** was a powerhouse of invention. Tyner has made numerous changes in the drum department, kneading the difficult combination of fire and sensitivity to the dynamic level of acoustic piano. As if to temper the titanic breakers from keyboard and cymbals, he has added a free-ranging thread to the rhythmic fabric in the percussionist Guillerme Franco.

In a sincere and moving tribute to his late employer **(Echoes Of A Friend)** Tyner recorded an album of unaccompanied piano, includ-

ing some of Coltrane's most popular pieces, **Naima** and **My Favourite Things.** A trio album re-united him with Elvin Jones **(Trident)** and with Ron Carter on bass; this is a meeting of equals, a three-way exploration. Tyner's work with larger groups **(Sama Layuca, Song Of The New World** and **Fly With The Wind),** the last two including strings and woodwinds, are romantic in the full-blooded sense, orchestral textures parting for the catapulting rush of the piano. Indeed, there is a touch of the tail-coated piano concerto manner about Tyner's grand entries, and his touch is unmistakable.

One of the most vital creative forces on the scene today, McCoy Tyner's music is all of a piece. Hard work and commitment have earned him his reputation, and his entire output is excellent.

Recordings:
John Coltrane:
  A Love Supreme
    (Impulse/Impulse)
  Live At The Village Vanguard
    (Impulse/Impulse)
  Transition *(Impulse/Impulse)*
  Coltrane *(Impulse/Impulse)*
  Meditations *(Impulse/Impulse)*
Live At Newport
  (Impulse/Impulse)
Reaching Fourth
  (Impulse/Impulse)
The Real McCoy
  (Blue Note/Blue Note)
Time For Tyner
  (Blue Note/Blue Note)
Extensions
  (Blue Note/Blue Note)
Expansions
  (Blue Note/Blue Note)
Asante *(Blue Note/Blue Note)*
Sahara *(Milestone/Milestone)*
Trident *(Milestone/Milestone)*
Focal Point
  (Milestone/Milestone)
Enlightenment
  (Milestone/Milestone)
Atlantis *(Milestone/Milestone)*
Echoes Of A Friend
  (Milestone/Milestone)
Sama Layuca
  (Milestone/Milestone)
Song Of The New World
  (Milestone/Milestone)
Fly With The Wind
  (Milestone/Milestone)

Sarah Vaughan

Singer Sarah Vaughan's vocal style was formed by her early association with Bebop, singing with Billy Eckstine, Charlie Parker and Dizzy Gillespie in the Earl Hines and Billy Eckstine bands in the '40s. An early version of **Loverman** with Parker and Gillespie **(In The Beginning)** and **Everything I Have Is Yours** with Lennie Tristano **(Anthropology)** show the wide Eckstine-influenced vibrato and the gymnastic Bebop phrasing. Much of her subsequent output, like Ella Fitzgerald's, is not strictly jazz, though always jazz-inflected. An album from 1954 with Clifford Brown, Paul Quinichette and Herbie Mann contains some of her finest work, including the seldom-used verse to **I'm Glad There Is You,** definitive versions of **Lullaby Of Birdland** and **April In Paris (Sarah Vaughan).** Another session from the same year featured her trio, pianist Jimmy Jones, bassist Richard Davis and drummer Roy Haynes **(Swingin' Easy)**

Sarah Vaughan 'Live' In Japan (Mainstream).
Great songs from a highly successful Eastern tour.

Above: The divine Sarah Vaughan. After thirty-odd years, her voice and timing are a miracle. The best.

Sarah Vaughan In The Land Of Hi-Fi (Trip): the Divine One.

Swingin' Easy (Trip): good vintage Vaughan.

Venuti-Lang 1927-8 (Parlophone) – a perfect partnership.

and **Shulie A Bop** shows her mastery of scat-singing, while **Loverman** is altogether more mature and authoritative than the 1945 version. A date with the Basie band, minus Basie, resulted in a fine, swinging album (**No Count Sarah**). Always a superlative singer, Sarah Vaughan's more recent output often places her in strings-laden contexts.

Recordings:
**Dizzy Gillespie, In The
  Beginning** *(Prestige/Prestige)*
Charlie Parker, Anthropology
  (Spotlite/Spotlite)
Sarah Vaughan *(Trip/—)*
Swingin' Easy *(Trip/—)*
No Count Sarah *(Trip/—)*
Sarah Vaughan Live *(—/Pye)*

Joe Venuti

Giuseppe 'Joe' Venuti (born Lecco, near Milan, Italy, *c.* 1898/1903) is unusual among living jazzmen in that born just before opening of 20th century and a professional musician at opening of 1920s, he is still a musician of unquenchable fire, invention and vitality. Venuti was the great jazz violinist, totally individual in approach, an improviser of originality, and one who believed in jazz that swung, always. Even allowing for the presence today of a gifted player like Jean-Luc Ponty, Venuti remains a supremely gifted jazz violinist who takes second place to no-one. Something of an eccentric by nature, with a vast reputation for engaging in most outrageous pranks, Venuti is noted for his physical toughness (there is a story, apparently true, of Venuti, in Prohibition days, felling a Chicago gangster who was pestering him in a club – and living to tell the tale).

Raised by Italian immigrant parents in Philadelphia, he met guitarist Eddie Lang (♦) (*c.* 1920) and both worked in small-combo in Atlantic City in '21. Lang was to become important influence on Venuti's continued progress as jazzman during 1920s. Worked with Red Nichols (♦), Jean Goldkette, Roger Wolfe Kahn (both latter bands on more than one occasion), Red McKenzie **(That Toddlin Town – Chicago 1926-28)**, Adrian Rollini (♦) and, on numerous occasions, Lang, all during 1920s. Lang-Venuti partnership was prolific one on record – altogether, pair made over 70 sides, under Venuti's name, or using both their names. Inspired by Lang's intuitive promptings and filigree guitar solos, Venuti's playing throughout almost all these titles was constant joy, emphasizing his almost playful sense of humor, as well as his other attributes. Was particularly effective on **Beatin' The Dog, Wild Cat** (from first-ever Venuti-Lang session, playing as duo), **Goin' Places, Stringing The Blues, Dinah** and **Doin' Things** (all **Stringing The Blues); The Wild Dog** and remakes of **Doin' Things** and **Wild Cat** (all **The Sounds Of New York, Vol 2 (1927-1933): 'Hot Strings').**

During 1920s, Venuti also got to record with Bix Beiderbecke (♦) and Frankie Trumbauer (♦) **(The Golden Days Of Jazz: Bix Beiderbecke).** Joined Paul Whiteman (♦) in '29, staying until following spring (interrupted only by car crash mid-1929 in which he suffered injuries). With line-up including Benny Goodman (♦), Jack Teagarden (♦) and Charlie Teagarden (♦), Eddie Lang-Joe Venuti All Star Orchestra recorded some splendid music for American Decca in 1931 **(Nothing But Notes)** with Venuti's violin outstanding on **Farewell Blues** and **After You've Gone.** Recorded (with and without Lang who died in March) several titles for British market, with his Blue Five, Blue Six, and as member of Joe Venuti-Eddie Lang Blue Five **(Benny Goodman & The Giants of Swing/ Jazz In The Thirties)** all in 1933.

Following year visited London, recording with local musicians and working with own band. Continued to work throughout US, until being called up for service in US Forces in 1943. After moving to West Coast, in 1944, started work as MGM studio musician. From late-1940s to mid-1950s, toured on regular basis, making further trip to Europe in '53. Led own big band during mid-1940s, apparently without much success. Band did not record commercially, and only recorded evidence **(Joe Venuti & His Big Band)** suggests its output was mediocre and, surprisingly, featured miniscule amount of Venuti's violin. During 1950s-into-1960s, Venuti's became unfashionable name, violinist suffering unwarranted neglect. His 'comeback', as special guest at Newport Jazz Festival of '68 astounded all present; his playing was as vitally swinging and time-

Above: Joe Venuti – in terms of comprehensive swinging, this indomitable violinist takes second place to no-one.

less as ever – if anything, it had gained in terms of maturity and eloquence. Unanimously selected as most impressive soloist at Jazz Expo week in London (1969), despite opposition from other great names taking part in festival. Despite serious illness following spring, Venuti's career during 1970s has been truly a succession of triumphs. One such triumph took place at University Club of Pasadena **(The Complete 1970 Pasadena Jazz Party)** where Venuti effortlessly demolished solo opposition. And during which (on own **Four-String Blues)** he repeated an oft-used device of unfastening bow of his instrument and stringing it around the back of the violin before resuming playing, to devastating, and musical, effect. And in concert, in Switzerland, previous year **(Tribute To Duke)** Venuti had stolen the notices from fellow Newport All Stars like Kenny Burrell (◊), Ruby Braff (◊), and Barney Kessel (◊). In 1971 recorded in Holland with Dutch Swing College Band **(The Dutch Swing College Band Meets Joe Venuti)** to eminent satisfaction of both parties. Earlier same year, he had recorded yet another successful album in Europe – this time in Villingen, West Germany. Since then audiences have continued to receive his playing rapturously.

The records too have appeared,

Stringing The Blues (CBS). One of the great partnerships in jazz, forged in the Roaring Twenties.

Joe & Zoot (Vogue Pye) - top
tenor + vibrant violinist . . .

including albums for Ovation (The
Jazz Violin Of Joe Venuti),
Chiaroscuro and Concord Jazz.
Two Chiaroscuro recordings (Joe
& Zoot, The Joe Venuti Blue Four/
Joe & Zoot) are remarkable for
striking rapport between two principal participants. Here, age-dif-
ferences mean absolutely nothing
and time, musically at least, stands
still. It is safe to say that guitarist
George Barnes (♦) can rarely have
played better (certainly, never
with so much bite and gusto) than
on Joe Venuti & George Barnes -
Live At The Concord Summer
Festival; no further explanation
is necessary. The redoubtable
Venuti's sudden death, in August

1978, remains one of the most
unlikely single events of our
times.

Recordings:
**Various (Including Red
McKenzie), That Toddlin'
Town - Chicago 1926-28**
(—/Parlophone)
**The Golden Years Of Jazz:
Eddie Lang-Joe Venuti/
Stringing The Blues** (CBS)
**Eddie Lang/Joe Venuti, The
Sounds Of New York, Vol 2
(1927-1933): 'Hot Strings'**
(RCA Victor – France)
**The Golden Days Of Jazz: Bix
Beiderbecke** (CBS)
Joe Venuti, Nothing But Notes
(MCA Coral – Germany)
**Various (Including Joe Venuti),
Benny Goodman & The Giants
Of Swing** (Prestige)/
Jazz In The Thirties
(World Records)
Joe Venuti & His Big Band
(Big Band Archives/—)
**Newport All Stars (Including
Joe Venuti), Tribute To Duke**
(MPS)
**Various (Including Joe Venuti),
The Complete 1970 Pasadena
Jazz Party** (Blue Angel Jazz
Club Presents/—)
**The Dutch Swing College Band
Meets Joe Venuti** (Parlophone)
**The Jazz Violin Of Joe Venuti:
Once More With Feeling**
(Ovation/—)

**Joe Venuti/Zoot Sims, Joe &
Zoot** (Chiaroscuro)/
The Joe Venuti Blue Four
(Chiaroscuro)/
Joe & Zoot (Vogue)
**Joe Venuti & George Barnes -
Live At The Concord Summer
Festival** (Concord Jazz/—)

Eddie 'Cleanhead' Vinson

Eddie ('Cleanhead') Vinson (born
Houston, Texas, 1917) is a marvellously potent combination of
primitive bluesman and sophisticated jazzman. A vocal-instrumental performer who bridges most
successfully crossover areas of
jazz, blues, R&B, and who manages
to appeal to a wide (including rock)
audience. Prematurely bald (hence
nickname), Vinson's first important
engagement was as singer and
instrumentalist with orchestra of
Milt Larkins during 1930s. Then, he
took his impassioned blues-based
alto-sax and raucous blues singing
to band of Floyd Ray. 1942: to

*Below: preachin' the blues -
as altoist, singer, composer -
comes second nature to
Eddie 'Cleanhead' Vinson.*

New York, to join new Cootie
Williams (♦) big band. Remained
until call-up (1945) for US Army.
With Williams, became popular
and familiar figure, both in jazz and
R&B circles, a featured singer and
instrumentalist with full band and
sextet drawn from same.

Contributed numerous items to
Williams book, including **Floogie
Boo** and **I Don't Know**, taking
searing alto solos and humorous
blues vocals on these and other
numbers, like **Something's Gotta
Go** (all **Cootie Williams Sextet &
Orchestra**). On return from Army,
put together own 16-strong band
which attained national success
with **Kidney Stew Blues** and
Juice Head Baby. Played New
York in 1947, then toured with
same band following two years.
Cut back to six men because of
economic situation re big bands at
end of 1940s. Success came again
with King recording of **Queen
Bee Blues**. Disbanded early-1950s,
became solo act. Rejoined Williams
for few months in '54 (**Big Band
Bounce**). Co-leader, with tenorist
Arnett Cobb (♦), of hard-swinging
combo based in Houston.

Widespread popularity eluded
Vinson until 1969 when, thanks to
efforts of bandleader-drummer
Johnny Otis, undertook European
tour (in company with Jay McShann
(♦)). During same year, recorded
for Flying Dutchman label (**The
Original Cleanhead**) giving fresh
touch to old and new numbers
alike (viz **Juice Head Baby, Cleanhead Blues** and **Cleanhead Is
Back**). Vinson's re-emergence
continued into 1970s, with ecstatic-
ally-received performances at
Montreux Jazz Festival, as leader
of own combo (**You Can't Make
Love Alone**) or as featured soloist
with huge (26-piece) orchestra
assembled by Oliver Nelson (♦)
(**Swiss Suite**). Also on all-star
record dates like **Blue Rocks** in
company with blues giants Otis
Spann, Joe Turner (♦), T-Bone
Walker (♦). Perhaps single best
example of Eddie Vinson's continued potency as bluesman/jazz-
man – from both in-person and
recording standpoints – has been
Jamming The Blues, which documents yet another successful appearance (this one in '74) at Montreux. On this LP, his debt as
altoist to Charlie Parker (♦) is
saluted nicely on Parker's **Now's
The Time**, even though Vinson's
Parkerish approach to the ballad
Laura lacks the other man's total
mastery and sensitivity.

Recordings:
**Cootie Williams Sextet &
Orchestra** (Phoenix/—)
The Original Cleanhead
(Flying Dutchman/Philips)

*Jamming The Blues (Black
Lion) - with Cleanhead . . .*

Mal Waldron

New York-born pianist Mal Waldron started in the mid-'50s as part of the house rhythm section – along with bassist Doug Watkins and drummer Art Taylor – for Prestige, accompanying musicians like Jackie McLean, Phil Woods and Donald Byrd. He was with Charles Mingus on one of his most expressionistic ventures **(Pithecanthropus Erectus)** and also with Max Roach **(Percussion Bitter Sweet)**. He spent two-and-a-half years as Billie Holiday's accompanist, learning the use of space and shadings from her. His association with Eric Dolphy and Booker Little opened him to the new developments **(The Quest and At The Five Spot)** and **Fire Waltz** on the latter album is a typical Waldron composition. His writing, like his playing, is economic: 'really drain every drop out of the given notes before moving on to something new'. Now based in Munich, Waldron keeps up a regular output of solo and trio albums and is the biggest jazz seller in Japan. Over the years, his work has changed at a steady, controlled rate, never subject to fashion, always characterized by dark vamping figures of great rhythmic power.

Recordings:
Charles Mingus,
  Pithecanthropus Erectus
  (Atlantic/—)
Max Roach, Percussion Bitter
  Sweet *(Impulse/Impulse)*
Eric Dolphy, At The Five Spot
  (Prestige/Prestige)
The Quest *(Prestige/—)*
Black Glory *(Enja/Enja)*
Up Popped The Devil
  (Enja/Enja)
Free At Last *(ECM/ECM)*
The Call *(JAPO/JAPO)*
Mal Waldron Solo Piano
  (—/Horo)

T-Bone Walker

Aaron Thibaud 'T-Bone' Walker (born Linden, Texas, 1909) was, from 1940s, a major influence on blues and R&B guitar. Influenced deeply by such as Blind Lemon Jefferson (♦), Lonnie Johnson (♦) and Scrapper Blackwell, Walker evolved an individual style that, in turn, was to influence innumerable other electric guitarists. Technically, Walker always was an impressive performer, his lines showing influence of jazz more markedly than is customary with bluesmen. Also an exciting player, able to produce torrid blues solos of great intensity and containing genuine excitement, and who complemented his instrumental virtuosity with deep-throated, often friendly-sounding vocal style that could be most effective. Self-taught as musician, first came into prominence through Columbia

Above: T-bone Walker, a seminal figure in post-war blues as singer, composer, and (especially) guitarist.

disc, cut in 1929 **(Trinity River Blues** and **Wichita Falls Blues)** although it was released under pseudonym of 'Oak Cliff T-Bone'. Did not record again until decade later. Toured with 16-piece band of Lawson Brooks, through Texas and Oklahoma. When Walker left, replacement was teenaged Charlie Christian (♦). Pair had met in 1933, often jammed together. Moved to West Coast where he led own bands – around this time his horn-like technique really began to be put together. Came into focus with orchestra of Les Hite where his amplified guitar became familiar sound – Walker has claimed he was using electric instrument as early as 1935. With Hite, recorded **T-Bone Blues**, his first successful disc. Other successes on record during early-1940s included **Mean Bone Boogie** (1945 – with orchestra of Marl Young), and his most famous composition, **Call It Stormy Monday**. Latter (also

known as **Stormy Monday** and **Stormy Monday Blues)** Walker recorded first in 1947 and this, along with other items from 1940s –including **T-Bone Shuffle, Hypin' Woman Blues, I Want A Little Girl, Lonesome Woman Blues** – remain amongst his most celebrated vocal-instrumental performances. Recorded originally for either Black & White or Comet, these and other performances of period were subsequently issued on Capitol LP, **The Blues Of T-Bone Walker.**
Jazz musicians like Al Killian, Bumps Myers, Teddy Buckner and Jack McVea featured on these discs. Walker's association with Imperial label was equally productive **(Classics Of Modern Blues)** – as evinced by truly electrifying guitar playing on items such as **Strollin' With Bones, You Don't Love Me, Evil Hearted Woman** (all 1950); **Alimony Blues, I'm About To Lose My Mind, Blues Is A Woman** (all '51); **Blue Mood, Love Is A Gamble** ('52); and **Railroad Station Blues, Got No Use For You, Bye-Bye Baby** ('52 or '53). A fine LP for Atlantic,

recorded in 1955, and a few odd tracks for same label basically was all Walker recorded during latter half of 1950s. But during 1960s, and thence up to his death in 1975, continued to make regular club and concert appearances. His continued predilection for the company of jazzmen manifested itself in all media, including more than one European tour, and at concerts like a 1967 appearance for Norman Granz **(The Greatest Jazz Concert In The World)** – where, among others, he sang and played in company with Oscar Peterson (♦), Johnny Hodges (♦), Clark Terry (♦) and Paul Gonsalves (♦). In the recording studios, too, his talent remained virtually undimmed by time, with albums such as **Funky Town** (with Basie-type big band), and all-star sessions with bluesmen of the calibre of Joe Turner (♦), Otis Spann **(Super Black Blues)**, Eddie Vinson (♦), again with Spann and Turner **(Blue Rocks),** and top jazz instrumentalists like Gerry Mulligan (♦), Dizzy Gillespie (♦), Zoot Sims (♦), Al Cohn (♦) and Wilton Felder **(Very Rare).**

Recordings:
The Blues Of T-Bone Walker
(Capitol/Music For Pleasure)
Classics Of Modern Blues
(Blue Note)
Feeling The Blues
(Black & White – France)
Stormy Monday Blues
(Blues Way/—)
**Various (Including T-Bone
Walker), Texas Guitar - From
Dallas To LA**
(Atlantic/Atlantic)
Very Rare *(Reprise/Reprise)*
**Various (Including T-Bone
Walker), The Greatest Jazz
Concert In The World**
(Pablo/Pablo)
**Various (Including T-Bone
Walker), Blue Rocks**
(Blues Time/RCA Victor)
**Various (Including T-Bone
Walker), Super Black Blues**
(Blues Time/Philips)

Fats Waller

Thomas Wright 'Fats' Waller (born
New York City, 1904) was one of
jazz's most colorful personalities.
He was also a pianist, organist and
song-writer of much distinction,
and a singer of average ability who
laced every performance with his
own brand of irrepressible humor.
He remains, almost 35 years after
his death, one of the most popular
of all jazzmen – accessible even to
those who profess not to like jazz
music. As a songwriter his tunes
(often with lyrics added by Andy
Razaf), have become, in many
cases, part of standard-pop history;
amongst the best-known, **Honeysuckle Rose**, **Ain't Misbehavin'**,
Keepin' Out Of Mischief Now,
Black & Blue and **Blue Turning
Gray Over You**.

Waller's father was a church
minister; his mother played both
piano and organ, which makes it
not at all surprising that Waller
should occasionally desert his
piano to try his hand at pipe organ.
His earliest recordings on this
latter instrument are best **(Young
Fats At The Organ (1926-1927),
Vol 1)** with Waller managing to
coax a genuine jazz sound from an
instrument which, jazz-wise, has
defeated others who have tried.
Sugar and **Soothin' Syrup Stomp**
probably are best here, although
Messin' Around With The Blues
and **Loveless Love** are not far
behind. And Waller's accompaniments to singer Alberta Hunter on
Sugar and **Beale Street Blues**
are first-class. Of less interest are
the tracks he made during an extended visit to Britain during late-
1930s **(Ain't Misbehavin')** working both alone and with a pick-band
comprising local musicians. Here
the organ all but defeats his comprehensive rhythmic powers. Recorded on Hammond organ in
early-1940s.

Waller began on piano at six, received lessons from James P. Johnson (♦), sometimes known as the
King of the Stride Piano; he even
took instruction from Cal Bohm and
Leopold Godowsky. Began recording in 1922, at his debut session
cutting **Muscle Shoals Blues** and
**Birmingham Blues (Fats Plays,
Sings, Alone & With Various
Groups)**, both unaccompanied
solos. These tracks illustrate perfectly the Waller approach to jazz
piano (his basic style already fully
developed) which was a slightly
more flexible version of the school

of stride, epitomized at its finest by
James P. Johnson, usually described as Waller's mentor. As events
would prove, Waller's finest playing was either in an unaccompanied
role, or as catalyst in some all-star
gathering. In the former, Waller,
regrettably, recorded comparatively few solo tracks, which makes
Young Fats Waller something of
a rarity and an album to treasure.
Especially in view of the fact that it
contains gems like **Squeeze Me**
(another of his most famous tunes),
Laughin', Cryin' Blues, **18th
Street Strut** and **T'ain't Nobody's
Biz-ness If I Do**.

As a member of someone else's
band, Waller is heard most advan-
tageously under leadership of
Billy Banks **(Billy Banks & His
Rhythmmakers)**, Jack Teagarden
(♦) and Ted Lewis (both **Fats Plays,
Sings, Alone & With Various
Groups** and **The Chocolate
Dandies)**. On these Waller proved
himself not only a sparkling soloist
but also an exceptionally fine band
pianist. And in distinguished company of Louis Armstrong (♦), Teagarden and Bud Freeman (♦)
**(Louis Armstrong/All That Jazz:
Louis Armstrong)** Waller tended
to steal solo honors, as well as providing marvellous uplifting background support for the three other
instrumentalists. He also recorded,
with some success, with Fletcher
Henderson (♦) **(The Fletcher Henderson Story/The Fletcher Henderson Story, Vol 1)** and McKinney's Cotton Pickers **(McKinney's
Cotton Pickers, Vols 2, 3)**.

*Fats Waller Memorial, Vol 2
(RCA Victor, France).*

But Waller's meal-ticket for commercial success and international
fame commenced in 1934 with the
first of the Fats Waller & His Rhythm
bands. The 'Rhythm' was a five-
piece band with front-line of trumpet and saxophone (doubling clarinet). This format was to last until
late-1930s, and although it provided much good-natured jazz and
a perfect setting for leader's
singing, succeeded in all but
stifling Waller's pianistic skills
completely. Certainly, Waller &
Rhythm recorded prodigiously
(Fats Waller Memorial, Nos 1, 2
is just ten albums-worth of mostly
the quintet formula that has been
made available in recent years).
Occasionally there were performances which were comparable to
his pre-Rhythm days, as with **Fats
On The Air, Vols 1, 2**, and mostly
these were concerned with solo
piano performances. But for aficionados of Fats Waller's keyboard
talent, his huge legacy of recordings contains only a trace of his
greatness. His attempts at leading
own big band for touring and/or
recording purposes **(Fats Waller
& His Big Band 1938-1942)** were

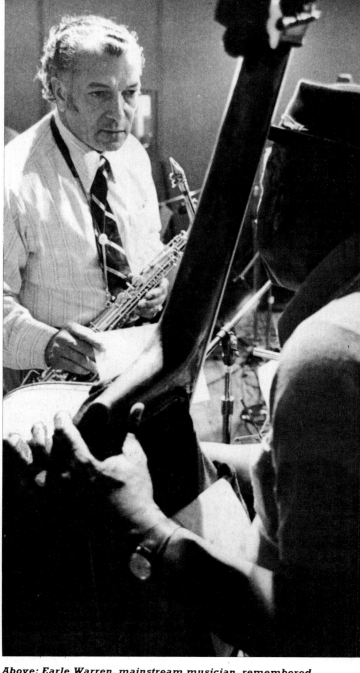

*Above: Earle Warren, mainstream musician, remembered
primarily as lead altoist with Basie for many years.*

not exactly successful. And during
last year had taken to working as
single act.

Appeared in Hollywood movies
like *Stormy Weather* and *Hooray
For Love* as well as in numerous
film shorts. *Ain't Misbehavin, The
Story Of Fats Waller*, a biography
by Ed Kirkeby, his manager, was
first published in 1966.

Recordings:
Young Fats Waller
(Joker – Italy)
**Various, Fats Plays, Sings,
Alone & With Various Groups**
(CBS – France)
**Young Fats At The Organ
(1926-1927), Vol 1**
(RCA Victor – France)
Fats Waller Memorial, Vols 1, 2
(RCA Victor – France)
Jack Teagarden
(RCA Victor/RCA Victor)
Louis Armstrong *(Trip)/*
**All That Jazz: Louis
Armstrong** *(DJM)*
Fats Waller, Ain't Misbehavin'
(—/Music For Pleasure)
**Fats Waller & His Big Band
1938-1942**
(RCA Victor – Germany)

**Billy Banks & His
Rhythmmakers** *(CBS – Realm)*
Fats Waller, Here 'Tis
(Jazz Archives/—)
Fats Waller Memorial Album
(—/Encore)
The Fletcher Henderson Story
(Columbia)/
**The Fletcher Henderson
Story, Vol 1** *(CBS)*
The Chocolate Dandies
(—/Parlophone)
Thomas 'Fats' Waller
(Biograph/—)

George
Wallington

Born in Palermo, Sicily, 1924, as
George Figlia, the pianist's parents
came to New York a year later. His
taste for elegant clothes earned
him the nickname 'Lord Wallington'. In the '40s, George Wallington was involved in the 52nd Street
scene, playing with Serge Chaloff,
Kai Winding and the Dizzy Gilles-
pie-Oscar Pettiford unit. His main
influence was Bud Powell and he

shared some of that giant's melodic inventiveness. Two of his compositions, **Godchild,** which was recorded by the Miles Davis 'Birth of the Cool' band, and **Lemon Drop,** recorded by Woody Herman, have become jazz classics. His album with Mingus and Max Roach **(George Wallington Trios)** is one of his finest, and the larger unit featuring trumpeter Dave Burns and tenorman Frank Foster with arrangements by Quincy Jones **(The Beginning & End Of Bop)** shows the muscularity of his style. The mid-'50s quintets with sidemen like Donald Byrd, Phil Woods and Teddy Kotick offer driving Hard Bop and on ballad performances like **Graduation Day (The New York Scene)** or **What's New (Jazz For The Carriage Trade)** sensitive and sinewy work from Wallington. Around the late '50s, George Wallington withdrew from the jazz world, reputedly in disgust at the growing commercial pressures.

Recordings:
George Wallington Trios
(Prestige/—)
The Beginning & End Of Bop
(Blue Note/Blue Note)
The New York Scene
(Prestige/—)
Jazz For The Carriage Trade
(Prestige/—)
Brothers & Other Mothers
(Savoy/Savoy)

Earle Warren
♦ *Count Basie*

Dinah Washington

Dinah Washington (real name; Ruth Jones, born Tuscaloosa, Alabama and raised in Chicago) was one of the great singers of her generation. Yet, curiously, in some quarters reaction to her talent remains lukewarm (in one or two otherwise reputable reference books she does not warrant even a miniscule entry). Such oversight cannot be because of any inability on Dinah Washington's part in the area of singing – possibly the reverse. For to some, hers was a talent that encompassed far too many musical fields. Hers was a unique vocal gift, one which enabled her to take in jazz, blues, R&B, pop and even gospel. And that, for those with a singular mentality, seems to preclude Washington's inclusion in the pantheon of jazz vocalism. All of which seems ridiculous when you hear her singing in the company of the kind of top-class jazzmen with whom she surrounded herself for so many years; jazzmen like Clark Terry (♦), Eddie 'Lockjaw' Davis (♦), Jimmy Cleveland, and Wynton Kelly, who accompanied her at one or both sessions covered by **The Jazz Sides** dating from 1954–5. And in an even more freewheeling studio record date like that encapsulated within **Dinah Jams** her jazz credentials are never in doubt.

Washington could sing the blues in a most comprehensive manner **(Bessie Smith Blues)** and they were blues delivered with more than a hint of gospel overtones. In

Above: Dinah Washington. One of the great individualists in jazz, she died, aged 39, in 1963. A great loss.

front of a wailing jazz big band, her declamatory vocal style registered strongly, as with **Dinah Washington Sings Fats Waller,** with band and singer, in turn, apparently inspiring each other to peaks of genuine, uncontrived excitement. And her natural flexibility allowed her to cross over from jazz to blues, to R&B with consummate ease, as demonstrated in just one of her numerous albums **(Best In Blues),** wherein she tackles blues and R&B material like **Baby, Get Lost, TV Is The Thing, Long John Blues** and **Gambler's Blues** with absolute conviction. That she could appeal to a wide public – a public outside of jazz or blues – was proved by the fact she notched up several hit records in the pop charts, including **What A Diff'rence A Day Made, September In The Rain, Where Are You?, A Rocking Good Way, Baby, You Got What It Takes** (last two duets with Brook Benton), and **Fly Me To The Moon.** In fact, majority of her later recordings – including some of the above hits – were made with string orchestra and other commercial trappings. Yet even the most treacly string section or undistinguished pop-slanted arrangement failed to prevent Dinah Washington from doing her thing in customary uninhibited, always professional, style. It is true, too, that often she was given first-class big-band backings from studio

orchestras which, whilst they were arranged with an eye on a non-jazz public, usually swung, and complemented the singer adequately, sometimes more than adequately **(Dinah Washington Sings The Standards** and **Dinah Washington Sings Blues & Things).**

Just how remarkably diversified her talent could be can be gauged by perusal of the contents of **Spotlight On Dinah Washington,** which includes **Mad About The Boy, Tears To Burn, Stormy Weather** and **On Green Dolphin Street;** and **The Very Best** which contains repertoire as different in

Very Best of Dinah Washington (Philips).

style and mood as **Teach Me Tonight, Trouble In Mind, There Is No Greater Love** and **This Bitter Earth.** Dinah Washington was an amateur talent contest winner at 15, in Chicago (where, as a girl, she had played piano in support of local church choir) and was heard by agent Joe Glaser. Apart from recommending her to bandleader Lionel Hampton (♦), Glaser suggested name-change, from Ruth Jones to Dinah Washington. With Hampton's big band from 1943–6, during which time she made debut on record (1943). Even at 19, Washington's singing at that first date was electrifying, particularly on **Salty Papa Blues** and **Evil Gal Blues.** Her accompaniment was supplied by a contingent from the Hampton band with its leader sitting in on piano, drums, for part of the session. Her next record date, a year later, was even more mature-sounding and rewarding, with sympathetic backing directed by and featuring tenor-sax of Lucky Thompson **(Dinah Washington Sings The Blues).** Her supreme assurance – musically and otherwise – and her undoubted talents made sure that when she left Hampton to go solo, success was hers for the taking. And so it proved. In 1958 she appeared at the Newport Jazz Festival, singing with all her power and conviction, even finding time to duet on vibes on one number with Terry Gibbs. Her performance at the '58 Festival was included (in part) in the much-praised film *Jazz On A Summer's Day.*

Dinah Washington, who influenced a host of other singers, died at end of 1963, the result of tragic mix-up with tranquilizing tablets. At 39 it was a major loss to music in general and a terribly sad way to end a life that was as colorful as her singing. Although she was influenced, as a singer, by both Billie Holiday (♦) and Bessie Smith and showed traces of both these other great singers in her own work, Dinah Washington never could be mistaken for anyone else.

Spotlight On Dinah Washington (Philips). 'The Queen' sang jazz, blues, gospel, R&B, pop . . . marvelously . . . !

Recordings:
Dinah Washington Sings The
Blues
(Grand Award/Golden Guinea)
Dinah Washington, The Very
Best *(—/Philips)*
Dinah Washington, Best In
Blues *(Mercury/Mercury)*
Spotlight On Dinah Washington
(—/Philips)
Dinah Washington, Dinah
(EmArcy/EmArcy)
Dinah Washington In The Land
Of Hi-Fi *(EmArcy/—)*
Dinah Washington Sings Fats
Waller *(Mercury/Wing)*
Dinah Washington, Dinah Jams
(EmArcy/EmArcy)
Dinah Washington, Bessie
Smith Blues *(EmArcy/EmArcy)*
Dinah Washington, The Jazz
Sides *(EmArcy/—)*
Dinah Washington Sings The
Standards *(Vogue/Vogue)*
Dinah Washington Sings Blues
& Things *(Roulette/Roulette)*

Ethel Waters

Ethel Waters (born Chester, Pennsylvania, 1900) proved herself, on numerous occasions, to be a fine jazz singer. But she was more than that. Like Dinah Washington (♦) and Peggy Lee (♦), her always flexible approach enabled her to encompass, more often than not with great success, blues, pop, novelty tunes and the area of stage and film musicals. She was a fine rhythmic singer whose work in this area compared with the best of the 1920s and thereafter. She used melody to the best advantage and – most important of all for singers of any genre – she knew how to extract the maximum from lyrics, especially those lyrics of a truly poetic and meaningful class.

Sang in church choirs as a youngster then, after winning talent contest, started to sing professionally in Baltimore and Philadelphia. Because of her exceptional height, accentuated by her thinness, earned nickname of 'Sweet Mama Stringbean'. Her reputation was strengthened by appearances at Lincoln Theatre, Harlem. Record debut took place in March, 1921, when she recorded **The New York Glide** and **At The New Jump Steady Ball**, accompanied, muddily, by Albury's Blues & Jazz Seven **(Jazzing' Babies' Blues: Ethel Waters (1921-1927) - Vol 2)**. Even then, it was obvious she had a distinctive, compelling way with a song. She always seemed more relaxed and at home in the company of jazz musicians, and during her recording career jazzmen like Tommy Dorsey (♦), Bunny Berigan (♦), Benny Carter (♦), Tyree Glenn (♦) and Fletcher Henderson (♦) often were to be found as sidemen. It was Henderson who played piano and was musical director of Black Swan Troubadours with which she made her first tour (1921–2).

Continued to record regularly for Paramount (with which label she had cut her first records), Black Swan and then Columbia. Her records for first two labels improved more than marginally between 1921–4, especially in respect of accompaniments. One particularly rewarding date found her responding enthusiastically to backing provided by Lovie Austin & Her Serenaders (including Tommy Ladnier (♦) cornet and, it is believed, Johnny Dodds (♦) clarinet) **(Oh, Daddy!: Ethel Waters 1921-1924)** and, on **Craving Blues,** producing some of her most convincing blues singing. First major success on records came in 1925, with **Dinah (Ethel Waters - On Stage & Screen 1925-1940)** which she had introduced at Plantation Club, Broadway, revue. Apart from **Dinah,** Waters recorded several songs to which she gave definitive interpretations. These included: **Am I Blue?, Memories Of You** (an obvious send-up of Jolson), **Stormy Weather, Heatwave, Takin' A Chance On Love** (which she introduced in movie *Cabin In The Sky*) (all **Ethel Waters - On Stage &**

Above: Muddy Waters, single most important figure in post-war Chicago blues; a compelling, gifted musician.

Jazzin' Babies' Blues (Biograph). Classic sides by one of the most influential singers, jazz or pop.

Screen 1925-1940); and **Porgy, You Brought A New Kind Of Love To Me** and **Don't Blame Me** (all **Ethel Waters Greatest Years 1924-1934)**. Apart from her successful appearances in Plantation Club revue, Waters appeared regularly at similar revues during 1920s, 1930s.

With Duke Ellington (♦) Orchestra in attendance, she introduced Harold Arlen's **Stormy Weather** to patrons of Cotton Club in 1933. She also recorded with the Ellington band in 1932, at session which produced **Porgy** and **I Can't Give You Anything But Love,** and also following year when she was featured during a **Blackbirds Medley.** And she recorded with orchestra of Benny Goodman (♦) at a 1933 session that produced **I Just Couldn't Take It, Baby,** and **A Hundred Years From Today (Ethel Waters Greatest Years 1924-1934).** Was principal attraction of her own touring show 1935–9 with accompaniment directed by her then husband Eddie Mallory. Mallory, a trumpet player, also fronted band with which Ethel Waters recorded for Victor in 1938–9 **(Ethel Waters 1938-1939).**

Became overnight success as dramatic actress in 1939 Broadway production *Mamba's Daughter*. She essayed other equally successful acting roles, including that of Berenice Sadie Brown in *The Member of the Wedding* (1950). At same time, she enjoyed recognition as screen actress in films like *Cabin In The Sky*, *Pinky* and *The Sound & The Fury*. Yet she never lost her ability to sing in a definitely jazz-influenced manner even though her accompaniments from 1950s onwards had very little to do with jazz and even allowing for a sad deterioration in vocal quality at 55 and thereafter. But proof that she could still, at turned 50, turn on the Waters magic is evidenced throughout **'Live' – Miss Ethel Waters,** wherein she sings 25 songs she had never recorded, including a recent composition of the period (c. 1954–5), **Young At Heart.**

In 1957 the singer gave up show business to undertake evangelical work with Billy Graham's Crusade. She wrote two autobiographies, *His Eye Is On The Sparrow* (title also of a song she introduced, inimitably, during *The Member of the Wedding*), and *To Me It's Wonderful.* Examples of latterday Waters involvement with religion, musically, can be found on Word label. She died, aged 80, on September 1, 1977. Ethel Waters was a major influence on many important singers of a younger generation, including Ella Fitzgerald (♦), Lena Horne, Mildred Bailey (♦). Connee Boswell, and even Billie Holiday (♦). No wonder Henry Pleasants, with his usual perception, wrote of her: 'Along with Bessie Smith and Louis Armstrong, she was a fountainhead of all that is finest and most distinctive in American popular singing' *(The Great American Popular Singers)*.

Recordings:
Ethel Waters, Oh, Daddy: Ethel Waters 1921-1924 *(Biograph/—)*
Jazzin' Babies' Blues: Ethel Waters (1921-1927) - Vol 2 *(Biograph/—)*
Ethel Waters - Greatest Years 1924-1934 *(Columbia/—)*
Ethel Waters - On Stage & Screen 1925-1940 *(Columbia/—)*
Ethel Waters (1938-1939) *(RCA Victor – France)*
'Live' - Miss Ethel Waters *(—/Garrafollo – Australia)*

Muddy Waters

Muddy Waters (real name: McKinley Morganfield, born Rolling Fork, Mississippi, 1915) is the epitome of the electric post-war blues scene – indeed, he remains its seminal figure. An immensely powerful, utterly compelling guitarist, a gifted harmonica player, a warm, convincing singer, and a writer of stature and character within the idiom. Taught himself to play harmonica, from ten years, but father gave him lessons on guitar. Mother died young so father sent him to be raised by a grand-mother on Stovall plantation near Clarksdale – it was she who gave him the nickname Muddy Waters. From a youthful age, became absorbed with Delta blues and was deeply influenced by Robert Johnson and Son House, both acknowledged masters of the art of bottleneck guitar playing. In time Waters too was to be revered for his own masterful use of the technique.

Began playing in early-1930s,

Hard Again (Blue Sky) – Muddy Waters, blues giant.

but first exposure of his burgeoning talents outside Mississippi locale came about when Alan Lomax and others from Library of Congress visited Stovall plantation to record Waters – alone and as member of Son Simms Four – in 1941 **(Down On Stovall's Plantation: The Celebrated 1941-42 Library Of Congress Recordings)**. Recordings showed Waters to be impressive country-blues guitarist-singer, although barely hinting at later developments. Waters himself continued to play at local dances, bars, picnics, etc, no doubt featuring fine blues origi-

nals like **Why Don't You Live So God Can Use You?** and **You're Gonna Miss Me When I'm Dead**, both numbers having been recorded by Lomax & Co. Moved to Chicago, 1943, worked in clubs and bars in Windy City. Commenced recording for Aristocrat in fall of 1947, and second single for this Chicago label, **I Feel Like Going Home** and **I Can't Be Satisfied (Genesis: The Beginnings Of Rock, Vol 1)** became a hit in 1948. **I Can't Be Satisfied**, a fine, basic Delta blues performance-composition, remains archetypal late-1940s Waters.

Success of disc was itself a signal event which helped the amplified blues scene to break through in Chicago. It was not, however, until 1951 when Waters was able to record full-time with what is now a classic line-up of harmonica, piano, drums, bass, rhythm guitar and, of course, Waters himself on lead guitar and vocals; by which time Aristocrat had metamorphosed into Chess. Sidemen to work in Muddy Waters blues bands from beginning of 1950s and thereafter include following: Little Walter, Walter Horton, James Cotton, Junior Wells, harmonica; Matt Murphy, Jimmy Rogers, Pat Hare, Buddy Guy, Sammy Lawhorn, guitar; Big Crawford, Willie Dixon, Luther Johnson, Luther Tucker, string bass or bass-guitar; Francey Clay, Fred Below, Clifton James, drums; and, most important of all, pianist-vocalist Otis Spann.

Apart from recording for Chess under his own name, Waters also played guitar on records for label made by Jimmy Rogers and Little Walter (both **Genesis: The Beginnings Of Rock, Vols 1, 2)**. Then came further hit records, **Louisiana Blues, Long Distance Call, Rollin' Stone, I'm Your Hoochie Coochie Man, I Want You To Love Me, I'm Ready, Just To be with You, Got My Mojo Working**, and **Trouble No More** (Waters' last hit record, up to the present). By this time, the music of Muddy Waters had had a profound effect on the whole development of popular music of 1950s/1960s, being of crucial importance in careers of such as Jimi Hendrix and Rolling Stones. Waters (and Cotton) appeared at Carnegie Hall in 1959, in band with Memphis Slim (Folk Song Festival) the year after he made his first-ever visit to UK. Muddy Waters Blues Band recorded for blues singer Victoria Spivey's label, Spivey (1966), with proprietress sitting in for two numbers. Made literally electrifying appearance at 1960 Newport Jazz Festival. A poll-winner in leading jazz/blues publications, Waters has been recipient of Grammy Awards for following records: **They Call Me Muddy Waters, The London Muddy Water Sessions** (recorded in company with top British rock stars, including Rory Gallagher, Stevie Winwood, Mitch Mitchell, et al), and has received Grammy Award nominations for others. Continues to tour with Blues Band, and visited Europe in 1976 as part of package show which also included jazz instrumental giants Sonny Rollins (♦), McCoy Tyner (♦).

Recordings:
Afro-American Songs *(Library of Congress/—)*
Down On Stovall's Plantation:

The Celebrated 1941-42 Library Of Congress Recordings *(Testament/Bounty)*
The Real Folk Blues *(Chess/Chess)*
After The Rain *(Cadet/—)*
Muddy Waters Sings 'Big Bill' *(Chess/Pye)*
Muddy Waters At Newport *(Chess/Checker)*
Muddy Waters In London *(Chess/Chess)*
McKinley Morganfield AKA Muddy Waters *(Chess/—)*
More Real Folk Blues *(Chess/—)*
Muddy Waters, Live At Mister Kelly's *(Chess/—)*
Can't Get No Grindin' *(Chess/Chess)*
Muddy Waters, Hard Again *(Blue Sky/Blue Sky)*
Various (Including Muddy Waters), Genesis: The Beginnings Of Rock, Vols 1, 3 *(Chess/Chess)*

Leo Watson
♦ *Teddy Bunn*

Weather Report

At the creative centre of Weather Report, jazz-rock's finest unit, are Wayne Shorter and Joe Zawinul, the

Above: Wayne Shorter, ex-Jazz Messenger, and today a vital component of the overall sound of Weather Report.

only constant members throughout the group's history. Shorter's work has always been impressive, from his period with Art Blakey's Jazz Messengers when he wrote **Lester Left Town (The Big Beat), Children Of The Night (Mosaic), This Is For Albert (Thermo)** and the title track, **Free For All**. At this time his tenor was a personal amalgam of Sonny Rollins and John Coltrane, a coarse-toned and unbelievably savage rip-saw, playing weirdly asymmetrical lines. It was a little like being knocked down by a chess-player. In the '60s, he joined Miles Davis and his style changed. He wrote meticulously precise structures, often modal, that swivelled and snaked to allow room for the drummer. Pieces like **Nefertiti (Nefertiti)** or **Orbits, Dolores (Miles Smiles)** avoid the old statement-solo-reprise format in favor of densely plaited unison statements that prowl like a wolfpack.

Zawinul came to New York in 1959 from Vienna and joined the popular Cannonball Adderley band, contributing numbers like **Mercy Mercy Mercy** to the book during his nine-year stay. The two men met in the Maynard Ferguson Orchestra, and then, more

I Sing The Body Electric (CBS): featuring the Rolls Royce of jazz-rock, the unit that continues to stretch.

significantly, in the Miles Davis group for the seminal album, **In A Silent Way,** the title track being a Zawinul composition. The combination of Zawinul's harmonically strong yet economic themes and Shorter's sinuous soprano saxophone were responsible for much of the success of Miles' new direction and with the departure of Zawinul after **Bitches Brew,** the group lost much of its flexibility.

In 1971, Shorter, Zawinul and Czech bassist, Miroslav Vitous, established their own band, Weather Report, to extend some of the implications of Miles Davis' fusion with rock. The role of the soloist was subordinated to an ensemble attack, a great premium was placed upon instrumental texture and group sound and great care was taken over the themes, which had to be strong enough to support fragmented interpretation. Adding drummer Alphonse Mouzon and percussionist Airto Moreira, Weather Report made their debut album, **Weather Report,** which remains one of their best. The sumptuous chiming effect on **Milky Way,** and the sheer beauty of Zawinul's **Orange Lady** showed that this was the Rolls Royce of fusion music. The next album, despite the substitution of Eric Gravatt and Dom Um Romao for Mouzon and Moreira, was even

The All Seeing Eye (Blue Note): Wayne in the laboratory.

better, especially on the choppily driving **Directions (I Sing The Body Electric)** while Zawinul's **Dr Honoris Causa** gets a shorter, sharper workout than on his own album, **Zawinul.** The third album proved to be their biggest seller **(Sweetnighter)** though artistically less successful and more riff-bound. Friction was already blowing up in the rhythm section – a common hazzard in jazz-rock outfits – and Gravatt's absence from three tracks was patched over with multiple percussion. Titled in honor of an anti-bed-wetting prescription, **Sweetnighter** is their least flexible work. Gravatt was briefly replaced by Gregg Errico, and then Ishmael Wilburn, a fast, light drummer well-suited to group needs. A great return to form resulted **(Mysterious Traveller)** and excellent themes like **American Tango** and **Blackthorn Rose** received imaginative treatment, the electronic effects from Zawinul's battery of keyboards, Moog synthesizer, electric piano, piano, always to the point. Two of the tunes, **Jungle Book** and **Nubian Sundance,** grew out of Zawinul's improvisations at home which he normally tapes as source material.

1973 saw the departure of a founder member, bassist Vitous, and problems in the drum department kept Weather Report from public performance for a year. By 1975, with Alphonso Johnson on bass, Ngudu drums and Alyrio Lima percussion, the group recorded an album **(Tail Spinnin')** which in many ways marks a return to solo routines. Shorter's tenor excursion on **Lusitanos** and the tenor-keyboard duets of **Five Short Stories** imply a reliance on the strength of the founders rather than on group interaction. The next album **(Black Market)** breaks no new ground, but has many of Weather Report's virtues – for example, the way that Zawinul establishes a change of tempo with one attacking chord after the introduction to **Gibraltar.**

New virtuoso bassist, Jaco Pasto-

rius, registers in the greatly improved group sound of a 1977 album **Heavy Weather,** and Alejandro Neciosup Acuna and Badrena make an extremely flexible rhythm section. Shorter dispenses with the showy lyricon to make a lyrical return to acoustic saxophones, while Zawinul's pen-and-ink and delicate gold leaf approach to synthesizer on the ballad **A Remark You Made,** exemplifies his sensitive economy. **Birdland** is a snappy hand-clap and hi-hat exercise in funk, while **The Juggler** is a marvel of rhythm and plaintive melody.

Recordings:
Wayne Shorter:
 Night Dreamer
  (Blue Note/Blue Note)
 Juju *(Blue Note/Blue Note)*
 Speak No Evil
 (Blue Note/Blue Note)
 All Seeing Eye
  (Blue Note/Blue Note)
 Adam's Apple
 (Blue Note/Blue Note)
 Schizophrenia
 (Blue Note/Blue Note)
 Super Nova
 (Blue Note/Blue Note)
 Odyssey Of Iska
  (Blue Note/Blue Note)
 Native Dancer *(Columbia/CBS)*
Joe Zawinul:
 Zawinul *(Atlantic/Atlantic)*
 Concerto *(Atlantic/Atlantic)*
Weather Report:
 Weather Report *(Columbia/CBS)*
 I Sing The Body Electric
  (Columbia/CBS)
 Sweetnighter *(Columbia/CBS)*
 Mysterious Traveller
  (Columbia/CBS)
 Tail Spinnin' *(Columbia/CBS)*
 Black Market *(Columbia/CBS)*
 Heavy Weather *(Columbia/CBS)*

Chick Webb

William 'Chick' Webb (born Baltimore, Maryland, probably 1907) was one of the greatest drummers, not only of 1920s/1930s, but indeed during entire history of jazz thus far. Despite physical deformity (caused by tuberculosis of spine), he emerged from mid-1920s as a superbly equipped percussionist who could drive a band – especially a big band – with almost superhuman strength and power, using all manner of dynamics and every part of his kit (most notably bass drum, cymbals) to maximum advantage. A major influence on drummers of 1930s – including Buddy Rich (♦) and Gene Krupa (♦) – his drumming on his own records still continues to amaze generations of young drummers. After playing with local Baltimore

Spinning The Webb (Coral) – Ella Fitzgerald, Chick Webb.

boys' band, age 11, Webb's first experiences were with pleasure steamer bands.

To New York, mid-1920s, and after working with Edgar Dowell Orchestra put together five-piece for lengthy residency at Black Bottom Club, NYC (1926). Led own Harlem Stompers (larger in size) from 1927 through 1930s. Although it played all leading New York ballrooms (including regular appearances at Savoy Ballroom, with which the band is forever associated), made regular tours, and even accompanied Louis Armstrong (♦) during tour of theatres, its impact did not come until 1934, when its records began to appeal to jazz fans in general, big-band aficionados in particular. Webb introduced 17-year old singing discovery, Ella Fitzgerald (♦), to band's audiences in 1935. It was at this time that Webb band (the Harlem Stompers title had long since been dropped) began to achieve enormous popularity, due as much to its singer as its own collective (and individual) efforts. Between 1935–9, its key men included Edgar Sampson (alto-, baritone-sax) (♦); Taft Jordan, Bobby Stark, trumpets; Wayman Carver (♦), flute, alto-sax; Hilton Jefferson (♦), alto-sax; Louis Jordan (♦), alto-sax, soprano-sax, vocals; Sandy

Midnite In Harlem (Ace of Hearts) with Chick Webb.

Williams, trombone; and, of course, Ella Fitzgerald and Chick Webb. Amongst Webb band's most popular and best numbers were: **Blue Lou, Stompin' At The Savoy, Don't Be That Way, If Dreams Come True** (all composed-arranged by Sampson), **Stardust, Liza, Who Ya' Hunchin', Undecided, Rock It For Me, Holiday In Harlem** and **I Got Rhythm** (latter by The Chicks, Webb's band-within-the-band). Ella Fitzgerald's contributions include **Sing Me A Swing Song, Ella, If You Can't Sing It (You'll Have To Swing It), Little White Lies, Vote For Mr Rhythm** and **A-Tisket, A-Tasket.** Last-named, unashamed novelty number, was most popular Webb disc of all, by 1950 it had qualified for Gold Disc status.

In 1938, at peak of band's popularity, Webb became ill. Was hospitalized twice – in '38, and again, in '39. Resumed playing in January 1939, but died five months later in a Baltimore hospital, following major operation. Band decided to continue its activities, under Ella Fitzgerald's leadership. This situation prevailed for two years, before singer went out as solo act.

Recordings:
Chick Webb, A Legend (1929-1936) *(Decca/MCA – Germany)*

**Chick Webb, King Of The Savoy
(1937-1939)**
(Decca/MCA – Germany)
**Chick Webb, Strictly Jive
(1936-1938)**
(Decca/MCA – Germany)
**Chick Webb/Ella Fitzgerald,
Ella Swings The Band
(1936-1939)**
(Decca/MCA – Germany)
**(Count Basie)/Chick Webb,
Swingmusic From The
Southland Cafe, Boston**
(Collector's Classics – Denmark)
**Chick Webb, Stompin' At The
Savoy** *(Columbia/CBS – Realm)*

Ben Webster

Benjamin Francis 'Ben' Webster
(born Kansas City, Mo, 1909) mostly
was self-taught as saxophonist; his
was one of the most gratifying of
all sounds to emanate from the
world of jazz saxophone playing. The Websterian sound was
one of almost schizophrenic
duality; on the up-tempo, more
overtly rhythmic numbers, the
tone was coarse, threatening and
fierce, the swing huge; on ballads,
the tonal quality became breathy,
tender and sumptuous – rather
like the muted roar of a contented
lion. Either way, it was a totally
individual voice. Basically influenced by Coleman Hawkins (♦),
then by Johnny Hodges (♦), Webster was one of the top three or four
tenor-saxophonists during 1930s,
and remained an influential and
rewarding soloist thereafter. Even
though towards the very end of
his career his solos were often
short and at times uneventful,
it was, nevertheless, always an
experience to hear, once again,
that ample sound and the depth of
expression, and to admire the
comprehensive drive. And on
ballads, varying in content and
origin, he remained, right to the
end, a masterful performer, capable of producing poignant readings of such as **Danny Boy, Love
Is Here To Stay** and **My Romance**
(all **Saturday Night At The Montmartre**).
    Played piano in Amarillo, Texas,
silent-movie house; Webster was
always interested in the school of
Harlem/stride piano and, in fact,
was himself an accomplished stride
pianist. Chronologically, Webster
worked with bands of W. H. Young
(father of Lester Young (♦)); Gene
Coy (playing alto as well as tenor);
Jap Allen, 1930; Blanche Calloway,
1931; Bennie Moten, 1931-3; Andy
Kirk (♦), 1933; Fletcher Henderson (♦); Benny Carter (♦), 1934;
Willie Bryant, 1935; Cab Calloway
(♦), 1936-7; Fletcher Henderson,
again, 1937; Stuff Smith (♦), Roy
Eldridge (♦), 1938; and Teddy
Wilson (♦), 1939-40.
    But Webster's reputation became
part of jazz legend when, in January
1940, he joined Duke Ellington (♦)
Orchestra as featured tenor-saxophonist. (Webster previously had
worked with and recorded for
Ellington in 1935, 1936 – briefly
on both occasions.) With Ellington,
Webster produced some of his
greatest recorded solos, including
those on **Cotton Tail** (a classic
showcase for his fierce up-tempo
playing), **All Too Soon, Conga
Brava, Bojangles** (all **The Works
Of Duke, Vol 10**); **Sepia Panorama**
(**The Works Of Duke, Vol 11**);
Just A-Settin' & A-Rockin' (**The
Works Of Duke, Vol 16***); **The**

*Above: Ben Webster's sumptuous tenor-saxophone was
one of the most unforgettable sounds in all jazz.*

**Girl In My Dreams (The Works
Of Duke, Vol 17); Chelsea Bridge
(The Works Of Duke, Vol 17*)
Blue Serge (The Works of Duke,
Vol 16*).**
    Webster's contribution to the
blues section of **Black, Brown
& Beige** at its Carnegie Hall pre-
miere in January, '43, was a major
one. And his was a comforting
presence on diverse recordings
by such as Billie Holiday (♦) **(The
Golden Years, Vol 1** and **The
Voice Of Jazz, Vols 6-9);** Jack
Teagarden (♦) **(Jack Teagarden/
Pee Wee Russell);** Dizzy Gillespie
(♦) **(The Gillespie Jam Sessions);**
Red Norvo (♦) **(The Greatest Of**

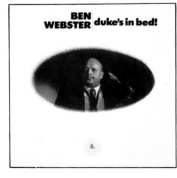

*Duke's In Bed! (Black Lion) . . .
Ben Webster's blowin'!*

The Small Bands, Vol 1); Benny
Carter (♦) **(Jazz Giant)** and Gerry
Mulligan (♦) **(. . . Meets The Sax
Giants, Vols 1-3).** His gentle-
raucous double-edged approach
to tenor-sax was ready-made for
Norman Granz' Jazz At The Philharmonic concerts **(JATP In
Tokyo)** as indeed it was for the less
frenetic atmosphere of the organized studio jam session, particularly when in the company of musicians he respected and with whom
he obviously felt happiest. Apart
from those mentioned also recorded productively with Don Byas (♦)
(Ben Webster Meets Don Byas);
Johnny Hodges **(Blues Summit/
Side By Side - Back To Back);**
Oscar Peterson (♦) **(Soulville);**
Coleman Hawkins (♦) **(Blue Saxophones);** and Harry Edison **(Walkin' With Sweets** and **Blues For
Basie).** Elsewhere, it was a case of
working with local rhythm section,
or using pick-up band, and doing
his own special things in sometimes superb fashion **(Ben Webster & Associates/Ben Webster &
Friends, Atmosphere For Lovers
& Thieves, Ben Webster At Ease,
John Lewis-Kenny Clarke-Ben
Webster-Milt Jackson, Duke's In
Bed** and **Days Of Wine & Roses).**
Probably most eminently satisfying of all Webster's studio dates
was that which Granz supervized
in 1955, juxtaposing his saxophone,

at its most relaxed, with the keyboard individualism of one of the
tenorist's idols, Art Tatum (♦). The
results **(The Tatum Group Masterpieces)** never were less than
glorious, with Tatum at peak form,
and Webster, ignoring pianist's
'solo-accompaniments', producing
one solo after another of great
warmth and beauty. Contrastingly,
his blues-playing abilities rarely
have been more graphically illustrated than during a live record
date, in support of Jimmy Witherspoon (♦) **(Witherspoon At The
Renaissance).** If **Jimmy Witherspoon & Ben Webster** has less
impact, then it is only because this
latter collaboration is devoid of the
live atmosphere of its predecessor.
    Webster, one of the true giants on
saxophone, lived in Denmark for
last nine years of his life. It was
in Europe, in Amsterdam this time,
that his majestic horn was silenced,
finally, for all time, in 1973.

Recordings:
**Bennie Moten, Moten's Swing,
Vol 5 (1929-1932)**
(RCA Victor – France)
**Willie Bryant/(Jimmy
Lunceford) & Their Orchestras**
(Bluebird/RCA Victor – France)
The Fletcher Henderson Story
(Columbia)/
**The Fletcher Henderson
Story, Vol 4** *(CBS)*
**Duke Ellington, The Works Of
Duke, Vols 9-18**
(RCA Victor – France)
**Duke Ellington, Black, Brown &
Beige** *(Ariston – Italy)*
**Billie Holiday, The Golden
Years, Vol 1** *(Columbia/CBS)*
**Billie Holiday, The Voice Of
Jazz, Vols 6-9** *(Verve/Verve)*
**Various, Jack Teagarden/Pee
Wee Russell** *(Byg – France)*
**Ben Webster - A Tribute To A
Great Jazzman**
(Jazz Archives/—)
**Various, The Charlie Parker
Sides** *(Verve)/*
The Parker Jam Session
(Verve)
**Various, The Gillespie Jam
Sessions** *(—/Verve)*
Various, JATP In Tokyo
(Pablo/Pablo)
**Red Norvo, The Greatest Of
The Small Bands, Vol 1**
(RCA Victor – France)
Benny Carter, Jazz Giant
(Contemporary/
Vogue – Contemporary)
**Coleman Hawkins/Ben
Webster, Blue Saxophones**
(Verve/Verve)
Barney Kessel, Let's Cook!
(Contemporary/
Vogue – Contemporary)
**Ben Webster/Oscar Peterson,
Soulville** *(Verve/Verve)*
**Jimmy Witherspoon, At The
Renaissance** *(HiFi/Ember)*
**Jimmy Witherspoon & Ben
Webster** *(Atlantic/Atlantic)*
**Giants Of The Tenor
Saxophone/The Genius Of Ben
Webster & Coleman Hawkins**
(Columbia/CBS)
**Various, Gerry Mulligan Meets
The Sax Giants, Vols 1-3**
(—/Verve)
**Duke Ellington/Johnny Hodges,
Blues Summit** *(Verve)/*
Side By Side - Back To Back
(Metro)
**John Lewis-Kenny Clarke-
Ben Webster-Milt Jackson**
(Ozone/—)
**Various (Including Ben
Webster), The Big Three**
(Bob Thiele Music/RCA Victor)

Bill Harris & Friends
(Fantasy/Vocalion)
Teddy Wilson & His Big Band
1939-40 *(Tax – Sweden)*
Art Tatum, The Tatum Group
Masterpieces *(Pablo/Pablo)*
Ben Webster & Associates
(Verve)/
Ben Webster & Friends
(Verve)
Ballads By Ben Webster
(Verve/Verve)
Harry Edison, Walkin' With
Sweets *(—/Verve)*
Harry Edison, Blues For Basie
(—/Verve)
Beb Webster, Atmosphere For
Lovers & Thieves
(Black Lion/Black Lion)
Ben Webster, Days Of Wine &
Roses *(Black Lion/Black Lion)*
Ben Webster, Duke's In Bed!
(Black Lion/Black Lion)
Ben Webster, Saturday Night
At The Montmartre
(Black Lion/Black Lion)
*There are two separate issues of
Volume 16 (has been withdrawn
in last year but nevertheless was
officially released by RCA Victor –
France). Same applies to at least
two other volumes in this series,
including Volume 17.

Dicky Wells

William 'Dicky' Wells (born Cen-
terville, Tennessee, 1909) has become, within the past decade or so,
something of a forgotten man of
jazz – shamefully neglected by
record companies, concert and
festival promoters, and the like.
Indeed, he has more often than not
been employed in menial tasks, in
a world far removed from the
music scene to which he was once
such an impressive and important
contributor. For Wells' reputation,
as one of the most totally expressive trombonists in jazz history, is
one which is indisputable. In practically any setting – big band or
small combo – his has been a voice
that stands out for its warmth, drive,
humor, pathos and individualism.
His earliest recordings, with the
band led by Charlie Johnson
**(Charlie Johnson/Lloyd Scott-
Cecil Scott)** demonstrate that as an
18–20 year old Wells had something vital to say on his instrument.
Subsequent recordings, with
Fletcher Henderson (♦) **(The Fletcher Henderson Story / The
Fletcher Henderson Story, Vol
4 and The Big Bands - 1933/
Ridin' In Rhythm)**, with whose
orchestra Wells spent part of
1933, offered further, even more
conclusive, evidence. Indeed, 1933
was a very good year for Wells,
particularly on record. A contingent from the Henderson band,
co-led by Coleman Hawkins (♦),
Red Allen (♦) **(Recordings Made
Between 1930 & 1941)** and including Wells, recorded during that
year, with the young trombonist
more than holding his own in such
impressive company. Even more
august was the line-up which
British arranger, composer Spike
Hughes assembled for a unique
all-star record date which took
place in New York during April,
May of '33. Wells, at that time
featured soloist with Benny Carter
(♦), was invited by Hughes to
participate. And it is safe to say that
his contributions – even though his
colleagues included Carter, Hawkins, Allen and Chu Berry (♦) –
were not surpassed by any other

*Above: the underrated Dicky Wells, whose best work has
undoubtedly been produced in partnership with Lester Young.*

soloist. On **Sweet Sorrow Blues**,
Wells' affinity with blues is amply
demonstrated; his exciting up-
tempo playing is at its most adventurous on **Bugle Call Rag** (full of
delightful rhythmic eccentricities);
and his playing on **How Come
You Do Me Like You Do?** is typical in its mixture of utter relaxation
and total commitment.
If Wells' playing throughout the
Hughes sessions **(Spike Hughes &
His All American Orchestra)** is
uniformly superb, then his performances during two recording
dates, held in Paris in 1937, are, if
possible, better. Although there
were fine contributions from others
present from the American–French
contingent (including Bill Coleman
(♦), trumpet and Django Reinhardt
(♦), guitar), Wells is omnipotent at
both sessions, taking one glorious
trombone solo after another. The
second of the two dates was, for
Wells anyway, the better, reaching
classic proportions during his
seven-chorus contribution to
Dicky Wells Blues (all **Dicky
Wells In Paris, 1937/Swing Sessions, Vol 1 (1937-1939))**. Wells
never again was able to equal his
playing in Paris, although there
was much fine trombone-playing
to come over the years.

In 1938 became member of trombone section of Count Basie (♦)
Orchestra. Although Basie did not
seem to care much for featuring his
trombonists during the first decade
of band's existence, obviously he
was mindful of Wells' expertise.
Excellent use was made of Wells'
ability to project poignancy, even
grief, on many Basie recordings
featuring blues vocals by Jimmy
Rushing (♦), either in supplying
sympathetic solos and/or obbligatos. The partnership was particularly effective on **London Bridge
Is Falling Down (You Can Depend On Basie); How Long Blues,
Harvard Blues, Take Me Back,
Baby, Nobody Knows (Blues By
Basie)** and **Jimmy's Blues
(Basie's Best)**. From a purely
instrumental stand-point, Wells
was heard to good effect on **Panassie Stomp, Jive At Five (You
Can Depend On .Basie); Texas
Shuffle (Jumpin' At The Wood-
side); Love Jumped Out (Super-
chief); Taxi War Dance (Lester
Young With Count Basie & His
Orchestra)** and **One O'Clock
Jump, Avenue C, Taps Miller
(Basie's Best)**. With Basie col-
league, Lester Young (♦), Wells
invariably produced his best work.
Indeed, he all but steals the show

from Young during a memorable
record date from 1939, featuring
the Count Basie Kansas City Seven
(Young Lester Young) with solos
on all known takes of **Dicky's
Dream** being marvellous evoca-
tions of his whole approach to jazz
trombone. There was more fine
Wells too **(Lester Young & The
Kansas City 5** and **Lester Leaps
Again!)** – both dating from 1944
Young record dates. And Wells'
trombone, as with his other recordings with the tenorist, was perfect
foil for Young during celebrated
jazz movie, *Jammin' The Blues*
(Jammin' With Lester).
Wells left Basie in 1946, working
with such bands as those led by
J. C. Heard, Willie Bryant and Sy
Oliver (♦). Back with Basie in 1947,
leaving for second, and final, time
in 1950. Joined band supporting
Jimmy Rushing for just under two
years, before leaving US for
France. Toured Europe as member
of trumpeter Bill Coleman's Swing
Stars. After his return to US, gigged
with several 'name' leaders, including ex-Basie colleague Buck
Clayton (♦) whose band he worked
with, on and off, between late-1950s
and 1961, including two European
tours (1959, 1961). Toured with Ray
Charles (♦) big band (1961–3);
revisited Europe twice (1965,
1968). Record-wise, Wells has not
been exactly over-used during

past 20 years. True, his services were used on several occasions by Buck Clayton, including **Swinging At The Copper Rail** and **Songs For Swingers**. And he registered fairly convincingly at a Buddy Tate (♦) session in 1958 **(Swinging Like . . . Tate!)** and during brace of Rushing album dates **(Who Was It Sang That Song?** and **Sent For You Yesterday)**. But although there were moments of sheer brilliance during the precious few recordings under his own name, including two for Felsted label **(Bones For The King** and **Trombones Four In Hand)**, not all did his great talent full justice. However, two LPs which find Wells at somewhere near his form of much earlier times are **Beauty & The Blues**, with Tate and Emmett Berry (♦) as co-leaders, and even better (for Wells), **Mainstream**, with companions this time including Joe Thomas, Buster Bailey (♦) and, again, Tate. Certainly, Wells produced his finest playing during this session since at least his first period with Basie. Of literary interest is book by Dicky Wells, *The Night People*, and an illuminating chapter in *Count Basie & His Orchestra*, by Raymond Horricks.

Recordings:
**Charlie Johnson/Lloyd Scott -
Cecil Scott**
(RCA Victor – France)
The Fletcher Henderson Story
(Columbia)/
**The Fletcher Henderson
Story, Vol 4** *(CBS)*
**Various (Including Fletcher
Henderson), The Big Bands –
1933** *(Prestige)/*
Ridin' In Rhythm
(World Records)
**Various (Including Coleman
Hawkins/Red Allen),
Recordings Made Between
1930 & 1941** *(CBS – France)*
Dicky Wells In Paris, 1937
(Prestige)/
**Swing Sessions, Vol 1
(1937-1939)** *(World Records)*
**Jimmy Rushing/Count Basie,
Blues I Like To Hear**
(MCA – Germany)
**Count Basie, You Can Depend
On Basie** *(Coral/—)*
**Count Basie, Jumpin' At The
Woodside** *(Coral/—)*
**Lester Young With Count
Basie & His Orchestra**
(Epic/Epic – France)
Count Basie, Superchief
(Columbia/CBS)
Count Basie, Blues By Basie
(Columbia/CBS)
**Spike Hughes & His All
American Orchestra**
(London/Ace of Clubs)
The Lester Young Story, Vol 1
(Columbia/CBS)
Count Basie, Basie's Best
(CBS – Holland)
Young Lester Young
(CBS – France)
**Lester Young, Jammin' The
Blues** *(Jazz Archives/—)*
**Lester Young & The Kansas
City 5 (sic)**
(Mainstream/Stateside)
**Lester Young, Lester Leaps
Again!** *(EmArcy/Fontana)*
**Buck Clayton, Songs For
Swingers** *(Columbia/Philips)*
**Buck Clayton, Swingin' At The
Copper Rail**
(Columbia/Philips)
**Buddy Tate, Swinging Like . . .
Tate!** *(Felsted/Felsted)*
**Jimmy Rushing, Sent For You
Yesterday** *(Blues Way/—)*
**Jimmy Rushing, Who Was It
Sang That Song?**
(Master Jazz Recordings/—)
**Dicky Wells, Trombones Four
In Hand** *(Felsted/Felsted)*
**Dicky Wells, Bones For The
King** *(Felsted/Felsted)*
**Emmett Berry/Buddy Tate,
Beauty & The Blues**
(Columbia/CBS)
Various, Mainstream
(Atlantic/London)

Dick Wellstood

Richard McQueen Wellstood (born Greenwich, Connecticut, 1927) has been a first-class Waller-inspired 'strider' since his professional career began in 1946, as a member of Bob Wilber's (♦) Wildcats. Yet today – and particularly since the beginning of 1970s – Wellstood has finally come of age, having taken his place amongst the world's best jazz keyboard practitioners. This has been achieved through his recordings – especially those on Jazzology, Chiaroscuro, 77 Records – and constant tours, especially those undertaken in solo capacity. Of the solo albums, **Dick Wellstood Alone, Walkin' With Wellstood** and **From Ragtime On** probably best show off his capabilities. Last-named gives admirable demonstration of his felicitous touch and unhackneyed approach to all kinds of material (from Lennon & McCartney's **Yesterday** to Scott Joplin's **New Rag**, to Zez Confrey's **Kitten On The Keys**, to Waller's **Keepin' Out Of Mischief Now** and **A Handful Of Keys)**. The Jazzology set is, if anything, better. His attack and joyful rhythmic approach to over-done pieces such as **Viper's Drag, Squeeze Me, Carolina Shout**, give these and other selections a freshness that would seem to be scarcely possible.

Walkin' With Wellstood is handsome momento of pianist's first-ever British tour, recorded with invited audience at London's Ronnie Scott Club. Included amongst a clutch of Wellstoodian performances of infinite quality are crackling versions of **If Dreams Come True**, and **Chantez Les Bas**, a nicely conceived Ellington medley, and his own **Walkin' With Watney's**. Of other more recent recordings, a duet album with Billy Butterfield (♦) **(Rapport)** is beyond reproach. Wellstood worked with Bob Wilber for five years (1946–1950). Then, following two years were with trombonist Jimmy Archey (touring Europe in '52). 1953: worked with various groups, and was house pianist at Lou Terazzi's, NYC. Worked with Roy Eldridge (♦) same year; also Pete Brown (♦), Charlie Shavers (♦) and others. Between 1953–9 played with Conrad Janis' Tailgaters (during which time also played with bands led by Eddie Condon (♦), Tony Parenti (♦). House piano player at Metropole, then Nick's, NYC, providing accompaniments for top musicians like Coleman Hawkins (♦), Henry 'Red' Allen (♦). Member of Gene Krupa (♦) Quartet between 1964–6. 1966: started three-year stint as member of Ferryboat, in Brielle, New Jersey. Since then has worked in solo capacity as well as guest with various small bands, has toured South Africa (1973–4), the UK (1974, and on subsequent occasions).

Above: Mike Westbrook, UK bandleader with a healthy gift for entertainment. Also heads a brass band.

Remarkably catholic in his jazz tastes, Wellstood is one of shrinking number of pianists carrying on stride traditions in personal, highly efficacious manner. Other recordings which demonstrate his skills to excellent effect include **Live At The Cookery, The Stride Piano Of Dick Wellstood, Jazz At The New School, From Dixie To Swing** and **Uptown & Lowdown** – last two demonstrating his capabilities as band pianist.

Recordings:
**Bob Wilber, From Dixie To
Swing** *(Music Minus One/—)*
**The Stride Piano Of Dick
Wellstood** *(Riverside/London)*
Sidney Bechet 1949 *(Barclay)*
**Eddie Condon, Jazz At The New
School** *(Chiaroscuro/—)*
**(Cliff Jackson)/Dick Wellstood,
Uptown & Lowdown**
(Prestige–Swingville/—)
From Ragtime On
(Chiaroscuro/—)
**Dick Wellstood & His Famous
Orchestra Featuring Kenny
Davern** *(Chiaroscuro/—)*
Dick Wellstood Alone
(Jazzology/—)
Walkin' With Wellstood
(—/77 Records)
**Dick Wellstood/Billy
Butterfield, Rapport**
(—/77 Records)
**Dick Wellstood/Peter Ind,
Some Hefty Cats** *(Hefty Jazz)*

Mike Westbrook

One of Britain's most vital energy centers, alternately praised and damned, composer-band leader Mike Westbrook started out with a sextet which included baritone saxophonist John Surman, altoist Mike Osborne, trombonist Malcolm Griffiths, bassist Harry Miller and drummer Alan Jackson. Bringing the group up to eleven, Westbrook recorded an extended work **(Celebration)** in 1967. This was followed by a big band work **(Marching Song)** which incorporates brass band sections, and the brilliantly eclectic piece for twelve instruments **(Release)**, ranging from free ensembles to the saxophone chorus from **Flying Home**. His preoccupation with presentation began to show in stage back-projections, light shows and sections of rock 'n' roll, all culminating in the unrecorded **Earthrise**.

Above: Randy Weston in Tangier with Ed Blackwell and Vishnu Wood. From Brooklyn to Africa in search of roots.

Another composition from that period, **Metropolis,** was written with Arts Council assistance, and makes brilliant use of shifting key centers. Forming another unit, including rock musicians like tenorman George Khan and guitarist Chris Spedding, Westbrook demonstrated that fun was a cardinal tenet in making music **(Solid Gold Cadillac).** One of his finest works was commissioned by Swedish Radio **(Citadel/Room 315),** and makes brilliant use of soloists like the great baritonist John Surman on **Outgoing,** tenorman Alan Wakeman on the driving **Pastorale** as well as blending borrowings from Ellington and Gil Evans. Westbrook currently leads a brass band.

Recordings:
Celebration (—/Deram)
Marching Song (—/Deram)
Release (—/Deram)
Metropolis (—/RCA Neon)
Citadel/Room 315 (—/RCA)
Love, Dreams & Variations (—/Transatlantic)
Mike Westbrook Brass Band Plays For The Record (—/Transatlantic)
Goose Sauce (—/Original Records)

Randy Weston

Randy Weston ran a restaurant in Brooklyn frequented by the giants of Bebop, and was encouraged by customers like Bird and Max Roach to take up the piano. Like his friends Herbie Nichols and Valdo Williams, Weston idolized The-

lonious Monk, and that influence – along with Duke Ellington and Fats Waller – can be found in his style. After R&B experience with Bull Moose Jackson and Eddie Cleanhead Vinson, he launched out on a jazz career, winning the Down Beat New Star category in 1955. Most of his early work for Riverside has vanished with the collapse of that label, but a recent Blue Note re-issue **(Little Niles)** reveals the strength and charm of his keyboard and compositions. **Pam's Waltz** and **Little Niles** are classics of impressionistic writing. In 1961, Weston, always deeply conscious of his African heritage, took a band on tour to Africa, the first of several visits leading to his settling in Morocco in 1968. An album made in 1964, **African Cookbook,** shows the all-pervading African influence. **Congolese Children** is adapted from a traditional Bashai folk song, though the outstanding piece is **Portrait Of Vivian,** a

Randy Weston's Music – Little Niles (Blue Note).

vehicle for the overwhelming tenor of Booker Ervin. Subsequent albums have featured works dedicated to Africa and Ellington **(Blues** and **Carnival),** and the solo piano album **Blues To Africa** shows the spectrum of his talents from stride to Bebop.

A highly articulate man and something of a trailblazer in terms of the Afro-American search for cultural heritage, Randy Weston has been performing in Europe since 1974. His music is as distinctive as his 6 foot 7 inch frame.

Recordings:
Little Niles (Blue Note/Blue Note)
African Cookbook (Atlantic/Atlantic)
Blues (Trip/—)
Carnival (Freedom/Freedom)
Blues To Africa (Freedom/Freedom)

George Wettling
♦ *Eddie Condon*

Arthur Whetsol

Arthur Parker 'Artie' Whetsol (born Punta Gorda, Florida, 1905), in comparison with many of the stalwart, long-serving Elingtonians, spent fairly short period within the ranks. Was member of

the trumpet section of Ellington Orchestra between 1928–36. During that time Whetsol, personal friend of the leader from their earliest days as professional musicians, never was a major soloist. Yet whenever called upon to make individual statements his sensitive, beautifully structured contributions always compared favorably with such as Cootie Williams (♦), Rex Stewart (♦), or Bubber Miley (♦). Usually, Ellington used Whetsol, muted, as eloquent presenter of themes including the uniquely voiced introduction to first-ever version of **Mood Indigo (Rockin' In Rhythm 1929-1931)** with Whetsol's muted trumpet voiced inimitably with Barney Bigard's (♦) clarinet, and Joe Nanton's (♦) trombone (also muted). Whetsol was also given opportunity to use plunger mute (à la Miley), as on **Take It Easy (The Beginning, 1926-1928),** or to take an unusually aggressive open solo, like that on **Jungle Jamboree (Jungle Jamboree).** Other fine Whetsol solos include **Saturday Night Function (The Works Of Duke, Vol 2)** and **Stevedore Stomp (The Works Of Duke, Vol 3).** More typical, though, are Whetsol's poignant contributions to **Awful Sad (Hot In Harlem 1928-1929); The Dicty Glide (The Works Of Duke, Vol 3); Reminiscin' In Tempo (The Ellington Era, 1927-1940, Vol 2)** and, best of all, **Rocky Mountain Blues (Rockin' In Rhythm 1929-1931).**

Whetsol, who was raised in Washington, DC, and also worked with Claude Hopkins Orchestra, first worked with Duke Ellington for brief period in 1923, leaving to study medicine at Washington's Howard University. He returned to the ranks in 1928, remaining until forced to retire through illness in 1937. Whetsol, also a fine lead trumpet, died in New York City from brain illness in 1940.

Recordings:
Duke Ellington, The Works Of Duke, Vols 1-7
(RCA Victor – France)
Duke Ellington, The Beginnings (1926-1928)
(Decca/MCA – Germany)
Duke Ellington, Hot In Harlem (1928-1929)
(Decca/MCA – Germany)
Duke Ellington, Rockin' In Rhythm (1929-1931)
(Decca/MCA – Germany)
Duke Ellington, The Ellington Era, 1927-1940, Vols 1, 2
(Columbia/CBS)
Duke Ellington, Jungle Jamboree *(—/Parlophone)*
Duke Ellington In Harlem *(Jazz Panorama/ – Sweden)*
Duke Ellington, Masterpieces (1928-1930)
(RCA Victor – France)
Various (Including Duke Ellington), The Big Bands – 1933 *(Prestige)/*
Ridin' In Rhythm
(World Records)

Paul Whiteman

Paul Whiteman (born Denver, Colorado, 1890) remains, a decade after his death (in Doylestown, Pennsylvania) as controversial a figure as he was during his halcyon days as bandleader during 1920s-to-mid-1930s. With regard to the standard of musicianship within Whiteman-led bands, or indeed the quality of much of the music featured over the years, there can be few, if any, complaints. That is, until it is remembered that Whiteman was billed as the King of Jazz. It is within the jazz genre that the controversy begins – and no doubt will continue for as long as his music is available on record and discussed. For Whiteman's 'symphonic jazz' appears to have little but superficial resemblance to more obvious jazz music that was to be heard during the period when he was leading a succession of sizeable orchestras (1919 until early-1940s). Whiteman's band's deficiencies – especially its often elephantine rhythm – are thrown in stark relief when recordings from 1920s are compared with those of big bands led by such as Fletcher Henderson (♦), Duke Ellington (♦) and Don Redman (♦) during same decade. And Whiteman's predilection for using strictly non-jazz, non-swinging and semi-symphonic string sections helped not one iota in this respect. That the band occasionally swung in a generally accepted sense is true when listening to rare airshot material available on record in more recent years (**Jack Teagarden – Frankie Trumbauer**), but this was not the norm.

Whiteman himself was an accomplished musician. Studied violin

Paul Whiteman & His Orchestra (RCA Victor). The Great Pretender to the apocryphal title King of Jazz.

and viola as youngster, becoming proficient enough to take his place in the ranks of Denver Symphony Orchestra (1912). Moved to San Francisco in 1915. Played in both World's Fair Orchestra and San Francisco Symphony Orchestra. After brief period in US Navy (during World War I), became leader of houseband at Fairmont Hotel, San Francisco. Moved to Atlantic City and New York (1920). Took his orchestra to Europe on two occasions (1923, 1926). In February 1924 he played his most prestigious concert; he premièred George Gershwin's **Rhapsody In Blue,** with the composer at piano. Whiteman and his orchestra were starred in much-talked-about 1930 movie *King of Jazz* (from whence came his own appellation). Financially, Whiteman Orchestra was by far best-paid (it has been reported that Whiteman, in 1920s, could ask for – and get – $5,000 for one broadcast appearance). Despite the pseudo-jazz his orchestra produced, Whiteman's love for jazz was genuine. It is said he was personally responsible for ensuring that great jazz soloists such as Bix Beiderbecke (♦), Jack Teagarden (♦) and Frankie Trumbauer (♦) were members of the Whiteman aggregation at one time or another during its lifetime. And it was the individual contributions of these and others – like Mildred Bailey (♦), Bunny Berigan (♦), Joe Venuti (♦), Tommy Dorsey (♦), Jimmy Dorsey (♦), Charlie Teagarden (♦), Eddie Lang (♦), Andy Secrest, and the jazz-based Bing Crosby (♦) – that justified any jazz tag

accorded to Paul Whiteman & His Orchestra. Beiderbecke, in particular, was responsible for a string of beautifully conceived, totally memorable solos with the band. Arranger-composer Don Redman wrote **Whiteman Stomp** (also recorded by Fletcher Henderson) specially for Whiteman Orchestra. Paul Whiteman succeeded, on several occasions, in reforming during 1940s and 1950s but time had long since passed the Whiteman concept by, and these were one-off, or at least short-lived, ventures.

During 1950s, employed as director of American Broadcasting Company. Put together own bands on two further occasions at beginning of 1960s, but was in retirement during last few years of his life.

Recordings:
Paul Whiteman *(RCA Victor/—)*
The Bix Beiderbecke Legend
(RCA Victor – France)
Featuring Jack Teagarden *(—/MCA)*
Jack Teagarden – Frankie Trumbauer *(Totem – Canada)*
Jack Teagarden, Vol 2 (1928-1957): 'Prince Of The Bone' *(RCA Victor – France)*

Bob Wilber

During past decade Robert Sage Wilber (born New York City, 1928) finally has emerged from being merely a highly-accomplished musician, with little or no voice of

his own, into a saxist-clarinettist whose talents have attained marked degree of individuality. Certainly, his work, with the World's Greatest Jazzband (The WGJB of Yank Lawson & Bob Haggart, **The WGJB Of Yank Lawson & Bob Haggart – Live At The Roosevelt Grill** and **In Concert),** and more recently, as co-leader of Soprano Summit (**Chalumeau Blue** and **Soprano Summit In Concert)** has demonstrated an astonishing maturity, both as clarinettist and, in particular, as exponent of small, curved soprano-sax. And his neat arrangements for WGJB, Soprano Summit, along with those, on record, for singer Maxine Sullivan (♦) (**The Music Of Hoagy Carmichael, Close As Pages In A Book** and Bud Freeman's **Song Of The Tenor)** have shown improvement commensurate with his playing. Wilber, who moved from NYC to Scarsdale, NY, at seven, first played clarinet in 1941. Nucleus of his high school band became Wilber's Wild Cats, band specializing in interpretations of New Orleans jazz classics. Two-year period of study, both at Juilliard and Eastman Schools of Music; also received tuition, on clarinet and soprano-sax from his idol Sidney Bechet (♦). Also played with Bechet's band of 1947-8, taking part in concert performances with great Creole reedman, as well as recording sessions (**Sidney Bechet With Bob Wilber's Wildcats, Creole Reeds** and **The Rarest Sidney Bechet, Vol 1).** Later, together with musicians such as Dick Wellstood (♦), Vic Dickenson

Lee Wiley Sings Rodgers & Hart And Harold Arlen (Monmouth-Evergreen). Wiley's singing '. . . exuded warmth'.

(♦), recorded own tribute to Bechet **(Spreadin' Joy - The Music Of Bechet).** After regular work, leading own group, at Boston's Savoy Club (1948–50 – during which time worked with Mezz Mezzrow at Nice Jazz Festival), Wilber was member of band which worked (in 1951) at Storyville Club, Boston, and which included Big Sid Catlett (♦), and brothers Wilbur and Sidney De Paris (♦). Studied with Lennie Tristano (♦), after becoming interested in more contemporary jazz sounds. Following service in US Army (1952–4), during which taught theory and led Fort Dix jazz band, studied clarinet with Leon Russianoff at Manhattan School of Music. Two years as member of The Six, co-operative combo **(The Six),** one other member of which was trumpeter Johnny Glasel (ex-colleague in Scarsdale Jazz Band, 1945, 1946). Worked with Eddie Condon (♦) at latter's club, and toured UK with Condon in '57. Played sax, clarinet, vibes, with Bobby Hackett (♦) Band ('57). With Max Kaminsky (♦) ('58), then, played tenor-sax with Benny Goodman (♦) Orchestra (1958–9). Free-lanced through 1960s, recorded, again, with Condon, and was involved with Music Minus One albums. Member of reactivated Bob Crosby (♦) Bob Cats (1966–8) before joining World's Greatest Jazzband of Yank Lawson & Bob Haggart (1969), with whom he was to remain for around six years. Together with fellow clarinettist/saxist Kenny Davern (♦), put together Soprano Summit three years ago. Since when it has received much critical and fan acclaim, with two co-leaders providing marvellous interplay and up-front textures by constant changing of their respective instruments (including alto-sax, which Wilber has added to his personal armoury in recent times).

Recordings:
The Rarest Sidney Bechet, Vol 1 *(After Hours – Italy)*
Spreadin' Joy - The Music Of Bechet *(Classic Jazz/—)*

Sidney Bechet/(Albert Nicholas), Creole Reeds *(Riverside/Riverside)*
Bob Wilber & His Wildcats *(Riverside/Riverside)*
Jim Chapin *(Classic Editions/—)*
Sidney Bechet With Bob Wilber's Wildcats *(Columbia/CBS – France)*
Bobby Hackett/(Duke Ellington), Jazz Concert *(Good Year/Good Year)*
Bob Wilber/Maxine Sullivan, The Music Of Hoagy Carmichael *(Monmouth-Evergreen/Parlophone)*
Bob Wilber/Maxine Sullivan, Close As Pages In A Book *(Monmouth-Evergreen/Parlophone)*
Buck Clayton Jam Session, Vol 2 *(—/Vogue)*
Soprano Summit Live At Concord '77 *(Concord Jazz/—)*
The WGJB Of Yank Lawson & Bob Haggart, Live At The Roosevelt Grill *(Atlantic/Atlantic)*
Soprano Summit *(World Jazz/—)*
Soprano Summit In Concert *(Concord Jazz/—)*
Soprano Summit, Chalumeau Blue *(Chiaroscuro/Pye)*
Bud Freeman, Song Of The Tenor *(—/Philips)*

Lee Wiley

Lee Wiley (born Port Gibson, Oklahoma, 1915) possessed one of the most delightful jazz-based voices to become a familiar sound during 1930s – decade when Billie Holiday (♦), Mildred Bailey (♦), Maxine Sullivan (♦) and Ella Fitzgerald (♦) came of age, musically speaking. Of the many singers over the years with pronounced vibrato, Wiley used hers to most musical advantage. Her singing exuded warmth, she had an involvement with words which must have induced genuine tears of joy to any self-respecting lyricist's eyes and never was guilty of any act of musical bad taste. In pre-LP days,

Lee Wiley was making 78rpm albums of standard songwriters like George & Ira Gershwin, Cole Porter **(Lee Wiley Sings George Gershwin & Cole Porter);** Richard Rodgers & Lorenz Hart and Harold Arlen **(Lee Wiley Sings Rodgers & Hart & Harold Arlen),** on which invariably she was accompanied by a first-class array of leading jazz musicians. The Gershwin-Porter album, for instance, is enhanced by the presence of such as Bunny Berigan (♦), Max Kaminsky (♦), Joe Bushkin, Bud Freeman (♦), Pee Wee Russell (♦) and Fats Waller (♦), latter providing sole accompaniment to **Someone To Watch Over Me** on organ, beautifully too.

Was married to pianist Jess Stacy (♦) between 1943–8. Wiley, of part Cherokee extraction, received schooling in Tulsa, Oklahoma then, at 15, left home to sing in Paramount Show, New York. Became band singer with Leo Reisman in 1931; also sang and did dramatic acting on radio. Broadcast with Paul Whiteman (♦) and later with songwriter Willard Robison. Became associated with Eddie Condon (♦) at end of 1930s, singing often with various bands fronted by guitarist-leader **(Eddie Condon Town Hall Concerts With Lee Wiley).** Became moderately successful songwriter, writing lyrics to Victor Young's music. Best-known of these are **Eerie Moan, Got The South In My Soul** and **Anytime, Anyday, Anywhere,** latter revived through hit single by R&B specialists Joe Morris & Laurie Tate, in 1963. Sang with Stacy's short-lived big band (1945–6). Made regular nightclub circuit during late-1940s, into the 1950s. Then became semi-active for next decade, making only special appearances, on television, radio and, even more rarely, in person.

Made something of a comeback during early-1970s, with in-person appearances and a record or two. Her first recording since 1957 was released in '71 **(Back Home Again)** and received justifiable rave reviews. Once again, Lee Wiley performed in company of first-class jazz instrumentalists (eg Dick Hyman, Rusty Dedrick, George Duvivier) and once again she responded in that beautifully understated way she treated every song – good or bad. Her timing and phrasing were unimpaired either by passage of time or her prolonged inactivity. It hardly seemed 27 years had passed since Eddie Condon announced her appearance at one of his regular Town Hall concerts and Lee Wiley had stepped forward to the microphone to sing an enchanting version of **Someone To Watch Over Me (Eddie Condon & His All Stars, Vol 7),** surrounded by the kind of jazz background that was a perfect complement to a singer whose standard of performance, in any context, never was anything but impeccable. The voice of Lee Wiley was silenced for ever in 1975, when she died (in Sloan Kettering Memorial Hospital, NYC) from cancer.

Recordings:
Lee Wiley Sings Rodgers & Hart And Harold Arlen *(Monmouth-Evergreen/—)*
Lee Wiley Sings George Gershwin & Cole Porter *(Monmouth-Evergreen/—)*

Sweet & Lowdown *(Halcyon)*
Eddie Condon Town Hall Concerts With Lee Wiley *(Chiaroscuro/—)*
Lee Wiley, Back Home Again *(Monmouth-Evergreen/—)*
Lee Wiley 'On The Air' *(Totem – Canada)*

Clarence Williams

New Orleans pianist-composer Clarence Williams, 1893–1965, has tended to be eclipsed by the musical company he kept. He accompanied Bessie Smith on her recording debut, **Downhearted Blues** and **Gulf Coast Blues (The World's Greatest Blues Singer)** and worked with her on and off throughout her career, writing or co-writing many of her songs including **Baby Won't You Please Come Home.** Based in New York, he managed Okeh's race label, arranging recording sessions and recruiting talent, adapting the New Orleans style to the new environment and market. His ensemble-writing for various combinations was always professional and often

Country Goes To Town (1929-1941) (RCA Victor).

highly resourceful, while his piano playing remained retiring and functional. Williams turns up on numerous sessions featuring Sidney Bechet, Louis Armstrong, Coleman Hawkins, Buster Bailey, King Oliver, Eddie Lang and Tommy Ladnier, lending his distinctive touch to the arrangements.

Recordings:
Bessie Smith, The World's Greatest Blues Singer *(Columbia/CBS)*
Jazz Sounds Of The Twenties, Vols 3 & 4 *(—/Parlophone)*
Clarence Williams! Jazz Kings 1927-9 *(—/VJM)*

Cootie & His Rug Cutters 1937-40 (Tax - Sweden).

Louis Armstrong, Sidney Bechet With The Clarence Williams Blue Five
(—/CBS – France)
Adam & Eve Had The Blues
(—/CBS – France)
Jugs & Washboards
(—/Ace of Hearts)
West End Blues
(—/CBS – France)
Clarence Williams & His Washboard Band, Vols 1 & 2
(—/Classic Jazz Masters)

Cootie Williams

Despite an absence of 23 years, Charlie Melvin 'Cootie' Williams was able to return to the ranks of the Duke Ellington (♦) Orchestra in 1962 and resume his role as one of its most potent and important soloists – almost as though he had never been away at all. Williams (born Mobile, Alabama, 1910), first joined Ellington in 1929, after first gaining playing experience with Fletcher Henderson (♦), Chick Webb (♦) and James P. Johnson (♦) (on record at least), as well as with the exquisitely-named Eagle Eye Shields. Remained an Ellingtonian until 1940 when he accepted lucrative offer to join Benny Goodman (♦) with whom he was employed as featured soloist, in small-combo and big-band settings, for just under a year. Williams' departure from Ellington shocked the jazz scene at the time, and event was documented, musically, by bandleader-composer Raymond Scott, who composed the self-explanatory **When Cootie Left The Duke**.

During his stay with Goodman, Williams, together with the youthful Charlie Christian (♦), gave immeasurable inspiration to various of the clarinettist's bands – particularly the Sextets and Septets of 1940–1 period. Amongst recorded titles to which trumpeter contributed typical pungent statements were **Wholly Cats, Blues In B, A Smo-o-o-oth One, Airmail Special** and the extraordinary **Waiting For Benny** (all **Charlie Christian With The Benny Goodman Sextet & Orchestra**); and **I Can't Give You Anything But Love, On The Alamo, Royal Garden Blues** and **Solo Flight** (with big band) (all **Solo Flight - The Genius Of Charlie Christian/Solo Flight**). In between his Goodman sojourn and the reunion with Ellington, Williams fronted own big band. This latter outfit, often R&B-orientated, was only partially successful, in terms of commercial acceptance, but there were some interesting moments. For instance, Williams' big band and sextet of 1944 contained, trumpeter-leader apart, several interesting musicians, including altoist-vocalist Eddie 'Cleanhead' Vinson (♦), tenorist Eddie 'Lockjaw' Davis (♦), singer Pearl Bailey (♦) and, most interesting of all, a 20-year-old pianist named Earl 'Bud' Powell (♦). Both big band and small combo of 1944 were recorded and results show (**Cootie Williams Sextet & Orchestra**) it was a more than capable band, collectively as well as individually. Williams' trumpet playing brings the best out of his former section colleague Rex Stewart (♦) during the all-star (**The Big Challenge**) which found

Above: A tremendously exciting player, Cootie Williams' use of plunger mute with trumpet was devastating.

both trumpeters as joint leaders for the occasion. From earlier days, Williams' fierce blowing stood out on many record dates featuring top jazzmen, including several hosted during late-1930s by Lionel Hampton (♦) (**The Complete Lionel Hampton/Lionel Hampton's Best Records, Vols 1, 5**) and those celebrating annual jazz popularity polls (in which Williams often has featured strongly) including **Benny Carter 1945 + Metronome All-Stars** and **The Metronome All Stars/The Esquire All Stars**.

Of numerous solos by Williams in his pre-Goodman period with Ellington, many feature his superb use of plunger mute. Williams replaced Bubber Miley (♦) in this role, and in very short time had made himself as irreplaceable as his predecessor. Amongst his most impressive solos, using plunger and also demonstrating his powerful, Armstrong (♦)-influenced open style, the following are particularly memorable: **Saratoga Swing** (**The Works Of Duke, Vol 3**); **Double Check Stomp** (**The Works Of Duke, Vol 4**); **Ring Dem Bells** (also with Williams vocal), (**The Works Of Duke, Vol 5**); **Blue**

Feeling (**The Works Of Duke, Vol 8**); **Concerto For Cootie, Never No Lament, Harlem Airshaft** (**The Works Of Duke, Vol 10**); **Sepia Panorama, In A Mellotone** (**The Works Of Duke, Vol 11**); **Echoes Of Harlem, Harmony In Harlem, Ridin' On A Blue Note, Grievin'** (**The Ellington Era, 1927-1940, Vol 1**); **Sweet Chariot, A Gypsy Without A Song** and **Tootin' Through The Roof** (magnificent duet with Stewart) (**The Ellington Era, 1927-1940, Vol 2**).

His post-1962 work sometimes lacked the flexibility of a quarter-century before but if anything it was even more powerful. Both on record and in person he contributed his quota of torrid solos, including **Let's Get Together** (**Recollections Of The Big Band Era**): **Tutti For Cootie** and a re-working of **Concerto For Cootie** (**The Great Paris Concert**); **Intimacy Of The Blues** (**. . . And His Mother Called Him Bill**); **Night Flock** and another **Tutti For Cootie** (**Greatest Jazz Concert In The World**); **Satin Doll** (**Duke Ellington's 70th Brithday Concert**); **Portrait Of Louis Armstrong, Portrait Of Mahalia Jackson** (**New Orleans Suite**); and **I Got It Bad, C-Jam Blues, In A Mellotone** (**Togo Brava Suite/ The English Concert**). During his first tenure with Ellington,

Williams recorded with his Rug Cutters and Gotham Stompers, using mostly colleagues from Ducal sources. These recordings produced some exquisite, timeless jazz, with the trumpeter performing at peak of his game (**Cootie & The Boys From Harlem** and **Cootie & His Rug Cutters, 1937-1940**). With his own big bands Williams has not always been captured on record at his very best. However, there is much fine trumpet to be found during majority of **Big Band Bounce** and **Big Sound Trumpets**. Interesting, too, that Williams' big band of 1942 recorded what surely must be the very first version of Thelonious Monk's (♦) **Epistrophy** (**The New York Scene In The '40s: From Be-Bop To Cool**).

In recent years, Williams has been dogged by persistent ill-health and has been hospitalized at least on one occasion. Not surprisingly, his playing has tended to be intermittent and there have been times when his work has been inconsistent and considerably less controlled and effective than in the past. Significantly, perhaps, Cootie Williams' trenchant trumpet playing was heard on the first album to be made (**Continuum**) following Duke Ellington's death, when son Mercer Ellington (♦) had taken over the remnants of a band in the process of disintegration . . .

Recordings:
Duke Ellington, The Works Of Duke, Vols 3-5, 8, 10, 11 *(RCA Victor – France)*
Duke Ellington, The Ellington Era, 1927-1940, Vols 1, 2 *(Columbia/CBS)*
Duke Ellington, The Complete Duke Ellington, Vols 2-7 *(CBS – France)*
Duke Ellington, Cotton Club Days - 1938, Vols 1, 2 *(Jazz Archives/—)*
Duke Ellington, Recollections Of The Big Band Era *(Atlantic/—)*
Duke Ellington, The Great Paris Concert *(Atlantic/—)*
Duke Ellington, . . . And His Mother Called Him Bill *(RCA Victor/RCA Victor)*
Duke Ellington's 70th Birthday Concert *(Solid State/United Artists)*
Duke Ellington, New Orleans Suite *(Atlantic/Atlantic)*
Various (Including Duke Ellington), The Greatest Jazz Concert In The World *(Pablo/Pablo)*
Duke Ellington, Togo Brava Suite *(United Artists)/* **The English Concert** *(United Artists)*
Charlie Christian With The Benny Goodman Sextet & Orchestra *(Columbia/CBS)*
Charlie Christian/Benny Goodman, Solo Flight – The Genius Of Charlie Christian *(Columbia)/* **Solo Flight** *(CBS)*
Benny Goodman Plays Solid Instrumental Hits *(Columbia/CBS)*
The Complete Lionel Hampton *(Bluebird)/* **Lionel Hampton's Best Records, Vols 1, 5** *(RCA Victor – France)*
Johnny Hodges, Hodge Podge *(Epic/CBS – Realm)*
Various, The Metronome All Stars/Esquire All Stars *(RCA Victor – France)*
Various, Benny Carter 1945+ The Metronome All-Stars *(Queen Disc – Italy)*
Various (Including Cootie Williams), The New York Scene In The '40s: From Be-Bop To Cool *(CBS – France)*
Cootie Williams Sextet & Orchestra *(Phoenix)*
Cootie Williams/(Hot Lips Page), Big Sound Trumpets *(RCA Victor – France)*
Cootie Williams/Rex Stewart, The Big Challenge *(Jazztone/Concert Hall)*
Various (Including Cootie Williams), Big Band Bounce *(Capitol/Capitol – Holland)*
Cootie Williams, Cootie & The Boys From Harlem *(Tax – Sweden)*
Cootie Williams, Cootie & His Rug Cutters *(Tax – Sweden)*

Mary Lou Williams

Although, in truth, there might well be few claimants to such a title as First Lady of Jazz, there is little doubt that Mary Lou Williams (born Mary Elfrieda Winn, Atlanta, Georgia, 1910) most deserves such a hypothetical accolade. For one thing, she is a pianist to rank with the highest company. Hers is not a gentle, effete style one might

Above: Mary Lou Williams – First Lady of Jazz. Composer, arranger, pianist, hers is indeed a unique talent.

expect from a lady. True, her touch is as elegant as she is harmonically sophisticated, but Mary Lou Williams is noted for her driving, two-fisted piano playing – as powerful in execution as most male practitioners. She is also a composer and arranger of the first order, having written straight-forward jazz pieces as well as more extended works, including at least two religious masses. Her arranging skills have been manifested in the repertoire of many famous bands, including Duke Ellington (♦), Benny Goodman (♦), Louis Armstrong (♦), Tommy Dorsey (♦), Earl Hines (♦), Glen Gray, and Andy Kirk (♦). It is little short of amazing to remember that she first played for and recorded with a band led by Kirk as long ago as 1929, or indeed that Mary Lou Williams led her own band for the first time two years before that date. Moreover, perhaps the most heart-warming aspect of Williams' art – an art undiminished by time or the many changes that have taken place in jazz since she first began to play professionally, in mid-1920s – is that musically as well as personally she refuses to grow old. For instance, her piano playing runs the whole history of jazz, from stride to boogie woogie to bop to

post-bop impressionism. And what is even more important, there is ample evidence of her abilities within each of these (and other) jazz idioms. Her praiseworthy musical catholicity is, not surprisingly, carried over into her writing.

Together with mother and sister, Mary Lou Williams moved from from Atlanta to Pittsburgh when she was four. Studied piano at four and was playing live engagements not too many years later. Toured with TOBA circuit as pianist-accompanist, working under name of Mary Lou Burleigh (surname was stepfather's).

Toured with several other bands, including one led by John Williams (who became her first husband – they were divorced during 1930s). It was this band with which Mary Lou Williams made her band-leading debut when Williams left (1928). Contributed arrangements in 1929 to a band led by Andy Kirk, occasionally sitting in on piano at recording dates and gigs. Joined full-time, as pianist and chief arranger, in 1931; she was to remain with Kirk's band (soon to be known as his 12 Clouds of Joy) from 1931–42, an unbroken period apart from time off for hospital treatment in 1938. Amongst her

first charts for Kirk, **Messa Stomp, Corky Stomp** and **Blue Clarinet Stomp** (all **Clouds Of Joy**), register, especially in retrospect, far more convincingly than the performances of band which plays them.

By 1936, both as pianist and writer, she had improved more than marginally. There is a freshness and originality about items like **Walkin' & Swingin', Lotta Sax Appeal, Bearcat Shuffle** and **Steppin' Pretty** (all **Andy Kirk & His 12 Clouds of Joy March – 1936**), that makes them sound good even today. Also during '36, Williams recorded (together with Booker Collins and Ben Thigpen, her rhythm section colleagues with Kirk) a series of piano tracks, of which **Overhand, Swingin' For Joy** and the inappropriately titled **Corny Rhythm** (all **Jazz Pioneers 1933-36/Andy Kirk & His 12 Clouds Of Joy - March 1936**) are intriguing examples of her instrumental talents.

Married trumpeter Harold 'Shorty' Baker (♦), and for a time the two co-led own small combo, before Baker joined Duke Ellington (♦) Orchestra and in 1945 Mary Lou contributed an electrifying **Trumpet No End (The Golden Duke)** to Ellington book. (In 1937 had enhanced repertoire of Benny Goodman band by producing **Camel Hop, Roll 'Em** (both **Benny Good-**

man, **Vol 7**) writing superior arrangements for both). Also in '46, led an all-female quintet (**The Greatest Of The Small Bands, Vol 2**) which produced fine music, thus giving lie to any possible accusations of gimmickry. Became deeply involved in Bebop evolution during 1945, having become close friends with Dizzy Gillespie (♦), Thelonious Monk (♦) Bud Powell (♦). Her **Zodiac Suite** premièred at New York's Town Hall, played by New York Philharmonic; 12 years later, Gillespie persuaded her to sit in on piano during performance (featuring his big band) of the work, played at Newport Jazz Festival (**Dizzy Gillespie At Newport**). Between 1944–8, became more or less resident at both Cafe Society clubs, New York.

During early 1950s, active in New York clubs before leaving US to spend time (1952–4) in Britain and France. Recorded in Paris with Don Byas (♦) (**Don Carlos Meets Mary Lou**) and in London took part in two separate piano-quartet dates (**Mary Lou Williams Plays In London** and **I Love A Piano**). Back in US she decided to leave music business altogether, becoming deeply immersed in religious instruction and charity work for needy musicians. Her musical comeback took place in August, 1957 and since then she has undertaken regular visits, mostly leading own combos, at clubs, concerts and festivals. Thankfully too she has continued to make appearances on record, either as guests of musicians like Gillespie, Bobby Hackett (♦) (**Giants/The Great Modern Jazz Trumpet**) and Buddy Tate (♦) (**Buddy & His Buddies**) or by herself. In latter category, a 1971 solo piano date (**From The Heart**) provides a rare treat. A perfect showcase for her timeless artistry, with First Lady Of Jazz improvising brilliantly on widely varied selection of her own compositions: old (**Scratchin' In The Gravel, Little Joe From Chicago, Morning Glory**) and new (**Blues For John, Offertory, A Fungus Amungus**). In a totally different vein, her comprehensive involvement – writing, arranging, playing – with two splendid Masses (**Black Christ Of The Andes** and **Music For Peace**) brought forth impressive results. Three further examples of the multi-faceted career of one of jazz's most durable – and important – personalities.

Recordings:
Andy Kirk, Clouds Of Joy
(Ace of Hearts/Ace of Hearts)
Various (Including Mary Lou Williams), Jazz Pioneers, 1933-36 *(Prestige)/*
Andy Kirk & His 12 Clouds Of Joy - March 1936 *(Parlophone)*
Andy Kirk, Twelve Clouds Of Joy *(Ace of Hearts/ Ace of Hearts)*
Benny Goodman, Vol 7: 'The Kingdom Of Swing' (1935-1939) *(RCA Victor – France)*
Duke Ellington, The Golden Duke *(Prestige/Prestige)*
Various (Including Mary Lou Williams), The Greatest Of The Small Bands, Vol 2 *(RCA Victor – France)*
Dizzy Gillespie At Newport *(Verve/Columbia – Clef)*
Don Byas/Mary Lou Williams, Don Carlos Meets Mary Lou *(Storyville/Vogue – EP)*
Various (Including Mary Lou

Williams), **I Love A Piano** *(—/Esquire)*
Mary Lou Williams, Black Christ Of The Andes *(MPS)*
Various (Including Mary Lou Williams, Cafe Society *(Onyx/—)*
Dizzy Gillespie/Bobby Hackett, Giants *(Perception)/* **The Great Modern Jazz Trumpet** *(Festival)*
Buddy Tate, Buddy & His Buddies *(Chiaroscuro/—)*
Mary Lou Williams, From The Heart *(Chiaroscuro/Storyville)*

Dick Wilson
♦ Andy Kirk

Teddy Wilson

Theodore 'Teddy' Wilson (born Austin, Texas, 1912) will go down in jazz history as one of the music's finest keyboard soloists, a pianist whose unflashy sophisticated approach is immediately recognizable and whose delicate but firm touch only rarely strays into the realms of the cocktail piano brigade. Basically, Wilson's style is a personal refinement of the more virtuosic and extrovert interpretations of Art Tatum (♦) and Earl Hines (♦) with more than a passing reference to the more basic deliberations of Fats Waller (♦) and James P. Johnson (♦). Always, Wilson's piano-playing is neat, economic and, some would say, over-precise. He is equally talented as an accompanist or band pianist, and has worked and recorded with most of the great innovators in jazz from beginning of 1930s up to and including the bop era. Moreover, Wilson's reputation for putting together all-star record dates, resulting in music of classic proportions, has long since passed into jazz lore.

Only as leader of his own bands has Wilson achieved but minimal results. For example, his experiences in fronting own big band lasted only a year (1939–40). As good a band as it was – and its personnel, leader apart, included, at various times Ben Webster (♦), Doc Cheatham (♦), J. C. Heard and Harold 'Shorty' Baker (♦), with arrangements by Wilson, Edgar Sampson (♦), Buster Harding and Webster – its music was too refined and lacked real dynamics and basic excitement (**Teddy Wilson & His Big Band 1939/40**). Another facet of Teddy Wilson's

musical career of much importance has been his ability to provide well nigh perfect accompaniments for, and thus further the respective careers of, an impressive number of jazz or jazz-based vocalists, several of the highest quality. Included in any such list of singers must be the following: Billie Holiday (♦), Mildred Bailey (♦), Ella Fitzgerald (♦), Sarah Vaughan (♦), Lena Horne and, of lesser import, Midge Williams and Putney Dandridge. The accompaniments Wilson provided for Holiday – especially those he assembled for record dates between 1935–8 – never were less than superb, reaching heights of sublimity with presence of Lester Young (♦). Wilson him-

Above: Teddy Wilson – one of the great jazz pianists. An ace entrepreneur for some great lady jazz singers.

The Teddy Wilson (CBS Sony, Japan) - 'impressive' combos.

self contributed numerous introductions and solos whose content was beyond reproach. Certainly, leaving aside Young's unsurpassed contributions, no-one did more than Teddy Wilson to make the majority of Billie Holiday recordings (at a most important time during her career) the all-time masterpieces they are (**Billie Holiday, The Golden Years, Vols 1, 2, The Lester Young Story, Vol 1** and **The Billie Holiday Story, Vol 1**).

Mildred Bailey often seemed at her most relaxed and happy when Teddy Wilson was pianist on her record dates of mid- and late-1930s (**Her Greatest Performances 1929-1946**) and one of the most rewarding of the earlier Ella Fitzgerald dates was that which Wilson supervised – arranged in 1936 (**Ella, Billie, Lena, Sarah: 4 Grandes Dames Du Jazz**). And Horne, never really a jazz singer, sounded as if she might have become one at a 1941 recording date with Teddy Wilson & His Orchestra (**Ella, Billie, Lena, Sarah: 4 Grandes Dames Du Jazz**). In following decade, a youthful Sarah Vaughan (**Tenderly**) was afforded the kind of sympathetic, respectful support which already was a byword in jazz circles. The galaxy of musicians which Wilson used both at the vocal as well as purely instrumental dates (often sessions were devoted to both) was, to say the least, impressive. Just a few choice names of the many involved: Roy Eldridge (♦), Buster Bailey (♦), Johnny Hodges (♦), Harry James (♦), Pee Wee Russell (♦), Gene Krupa (♦), Harry Carney (♦) (**The Teddy Wilson** and **Teddy Wilson & His All-Stars**).

Wilson's other claim to jazz fame was as pianist with Benny Goodman's (♦) Trio and Quartet, of which he was vitally important member, from 1936–9. (He was to rejoin Goodman in '45, for record dates and to appear in Broadway production of *Seven Lively Arts.*) As immaculate and beautifully conceived as are Wilson's Trio/Quartet studio-made solos (**The Complete Benny Goodman, Vols 1-3/ Benny Goodman, Vols 1-3, Trio & Quartet 1935-1938**) airshot versions of identical (and other) repertoire find him in even greater form. This is true of Wilson's dazzling pianistics during live performances of such as **Dizzy Spells, Moonglow, Body & Soul, Time On My Hands** and **China Boy** (**Benny Goodman Trio & Quartet, Vol II**); **Runnin' Wild, Have You Met Miss Jones?** and **I'm A Ding Dong Daddy** (**Vol I**); and **Smiles, Limehouse Blues** and **Tea For Two** (**Kings Of Swing, Vol 1**). And his individual contributions to celebrated **1938 Carnegie Hall Jazz Concert** are uniformly outstanding. It seemed absolutely right that, 24 years after the Carnegie Hall triumph, Goodman should take Wilson to Russia, as part of a star-studded entourage which made an historic working visit there (**Benny Goodman In Moscow, Vols 1, 2**).

After demise of his own big band, Wilson led a succession of superior small combos, including a 1944 sextet which included Hot Lips Page (♦) and Benny Morton (♦) (**The Radio Years/Teddy Wilson & His Orchestra 1944**) and another, equally satisfying six-piecer following year which included in its line-up Charlie Shavers (♦) and Red Norvo (♦)

(**Stompin' At The Savoy**). Started work for CBS radio in 1946, a position which lasted for some years; he was studio musician at WNEW four years, from 1949. Had recorded with Charlie Parker (♦) and Dizzy Gillespie (♦) in 1945 (**Red Norvo's Fabulous Jam Session**) but had made no attempt to adjust his style to meet the demands of the 'new music'. Wisely, he had decided to continue along a tried-and-trusted musical pathway which was unlikely to be fraught with the kind of problems which beset many of his generation who tried, with disastrous results, to embrace the intricacies of bop.

Played series of well-received concerts in Scandinavia (1952), and visited Britain (1953). Took part in 1955 biopic, *The Benny Goodman Story*, and, whilst in Hollywood, was re-united for recorded tribute to Goodman with Lionel Hampton (♦) and Gene Krupa (**Krupa-Wilson-Hampton/Kings Of Swing, Vol 1**) during which he produced some of his finest playing of past 25 years. During this quarter-century period, continued touring – home and broad – mostly in trio setting. From time to time, has also played invitation dates with Goodman. Has continued to be recorded at frequent intervals, including two exceptional sessions – one quartet, one septet – headlined by Lester Young (**Pres & Teddy & Oscar/Prez & Teddy**) which took place in January 1956. Few of own latterday recordings have matched sparkle, drive of earlier efforts, like **The Teddy Wilson Piano Solos** comprising 11 beautifully poised performances recorded between 1935–7. But when occasion has moved him, has recaptured – temporarily at least – much of the effervescence of yore as proven with **Runnin' Wild!**, taped live at 1973 Montreux Jazz Festival, with trio of British musicians; plus two excellent solo albums, **Striding After Fats** and **With Billie In Mind**. Listening to these 1970s recordings, it seems scarcely credible that Teddy Wil-

son's first professional engagement took place in 1929, or even that he worked with orchestra of Louis Armstrong (♦) and Benny Carter (♦) (**Benny Carter - 1933/ Ridin' In Rhythm**) in 1933, and with Willie Bryant Orchestra, between 1934–5 (**Willie Bryant & His Orchestra**).

Recordings:
Willie Bryant & His Orchestra
(*RCA Victor – France*)
Benny Carter - 1933 (*Prestige*)/
Various (Including Benny Carter), Ridin' In Rhythm
(*World Records*)
The Teddy Wilson Piano Solos
(*CBS – France*)
**The Complete Benny Goodman, Vols 1-3/
Benny Goodman, Vols 1-3**
(*RCA Victor – France*)
Benny Goodman Trio & Quartet, Vols I, II
(*CBS – France*)
Various (Including Benny Goodman/Lionel Hampton/ Gene Krupa/Teddy Wilson), Kings Of Swing, Vol 1
(*Verve/Verve*)
Benny Goodman, 1938 Carnegie Hall Jazz Concert
(*Columbia/CBS*)
Billie Holiday, The Golden Years, Vols 1, 2
(*Columbia/CBS*)
The Billie Holiday Story, Vol 1
(*Columbia/CBS*)
The Lester Young Story, Vols 1-3
(*Columbia/CBS*)
Mildred Bailey: Her Greatest Performances 1929-1946, Vols 1-3 (*Columbia/CBS*)
Various (Including Ella Fitzgerald/Billie Holiday/ Lena Horne), Ella, Billie, Lena, Sarah: 4 Grandes Dames Du Jazz (*CBS – France*)
Teddy Wilson & His Big Band 1939/40 (*Tax – Sweden*)
The Teddy Wilson
(*CBS/Sony – Japan*)
Teddy Wilson & His All Stars
(*Columbia/CBS*)
The Radio Years/Teddy Wilson & His Orchestra 1944
(*—/London*)

Teddy Wilson, Stompin' At The Savoy (*—/Ember*)
Sarah Vaughan, Tenderly
(*—/Bulldog*)
Red Norvo's Fabulous Jam Session (*Charlie Parker*)
Krupa-Wilson-Hampton
(*—/Verve*)
Lester Young/Teddy Wilson, Pres & Teddy & Oscar
(*Verve*)/
Pres & Teddy (*Verve*)
Benny Goodman In Moscow, Vols 1, 2
(*RCA Victor/RCA Victor*)
Teddy Wilson, Runnin' Wild!
(*Black Lion/Black Lion*)
Teddy Wilson, Striding After Fats (*Black Lion/Black Lion*)
Teddy Wilson, With Billie In Mind (*Chiaroscuro*)/
Body & Soul (*Vogue*)

Jimmy Witherspoon

James 'Jimmy' Witherspoon (born Gurdon, Arkansas, 1923) is one of the most compelling blues singers extant – a situation which has prevailed for around 30 years. 'Spoon', who received no formal music training and started in music at seven, as member of local Baptist choir, is a charismatic in-person performer, invariably responding to the presence of blues-playing instrumentalists of the calibre of Ben Webster (♦), Buddy Tate (♦), Hampton Hawes (♦), and Teddy Edwards, each of whom has worked with singer at some time during his career. Witherspoon's musical education came from Church music as well as from bluesmen – instrumentalists and singers – who visited his home town in particular and Arkansas in general.

At 18, was drafted into US Merchant Marine, serving majority of his time (1941–3) in Pacific Area. On leave in Calcutta, met pianist Teddy Weatherford, who had lived in Far East since 1926. Sang with Weatherford's band, at leader's invitation. Following release from Marines, decided to make career out of blues-singing. Career received first impetus when he joined Jay McShann (♦) Orchestra, in place of Walter Brown. For next four years, Witherspoon gained valuable experience as McShann's principal blues vocalist (even though, in '45, two other singers – Crown Prince Waterford, Numa Lee Davis – also featured with band). Record debut, with band, in 1947, for Down Beat–Swing Time label. Apart from first-class interpretations of blues classics like **How Long, How Long Blues** and **Ain't Nobody's Business,** his expressive voice was well served by two of his own compositions: **Skidrow Blues** and **Money's Getting Cheaper** (all **Ain't Nobody's Business!**). Same year, Witherspoon–McShann combination put together equally fine versions of **Frog-I-More, In The Evening,** and **Backwater Blues** (**Ain't Nobody's Business!**). In 1948, came two further beauties from same source, both again Spoon originals, **Spoon Calls Hootie** and **Destruction Blues.**

After deciding to leave McShann to pursue solo career, progress was slow-but-steady. A hit record in 1952 – a re-recording of **Ain't Nobody's Business** – helped to make his one of the big names in

The Teddy Wilson Piano Solos (CBS, France). Delightful album 'comprising 11 beautifully poised performances . . .'

memorable moments during the Prestige period, not the least being **Baby, Baby, Baby, Blue Spoon** and **Some Of My Best Friends Are The Blues**. And a brief association with Wilbur De Paris Band produced a more than respectable album, **Callin' The Blues**. Singer's on-off involvement with more blues-rock ventures have proved less successful, although his admirable flexibility (of blues singers Spoon's actual singing voice is best) has resulted in singing of real interest, to be found on perusal of such recordings as **Love Is A Five-Letter Word** and **Handbags & Gladrags**.

With the 1980s fast approaching, Jimmy Witherspoon seems eminently capable of producing superior, genuinely exciting singing that will encompass blues, jazz, R&B, soul and rock. But whatever happens during next decade, he remains, as of now, a major talent in a fast diminishing field.

Recordings:
Jimmy Witherspoon, Ain't Nobody's Business
(—|Black Lion)
Jimmy Witherspoon, A Spoonful Of Blues
(RCA Victor – France)
Jimmy Witherspoon/(Count Basie), Blue Moods In The Shade Of Kansas City
(RCA Victor – France)
Jimmy Witherspoon, The Spoon Concerts *(Fantasy)/*

1959 Monterey Jazz Festival
(Ember)
Witherspoon At The Renaissance *(HiFi|Ember)*
Buck Clayton & Jimmy Witherspoon Live In Paris
(Vogue/Vogue)
Evenin' Blues
(Prestige/Stateside)
Baby, Baby, Baby *(Prestige/—)*
Blues Around The Clock
(Prestige/Stateside)
Some Of My Best Friends Are The Blues *(Prestige/—)*
Blue Spoon *(Prestige/—)*
Singin' The Blues
(World Pacific)/
There's Good Rockin' Tonight
(Fontana)
Jimmy Witherspoon & Ben Webster *(Atlantic/Atlantic)*
Jimmy Witherspoon/Wilbur De Paris, Callin' The Blues
(Atlantic/London)
Spoonful *(Blue Note/—)*
Handbags & Gladrags
(Probe/Probe)
Love Is A Five Letter Word
(Capitol/Capitol)

Phil Woods

Born 1931 in Massachusetts, Phil Woods inherited his first alto from a dead uncle. He spent four years at Juilliard Music College, and gained experience with Charlie Barnet, Neal Hefti and Jimmy Raney, before cutting his debut

Above: Jimmy Witherspoon's magnificent singing and his personal charisma make him a bluesman to remember.

R&B circles; other successes came later (eg **Big Fine Girl, The Wind Is Blowing** and **No Rollin' Blues**). But his overall acceptance by a more jazz-type market came only at end of 1950s, when Witherspoon produced at least two of his greatest recordings. The first **(Singin' The Blues/There's Good Rockin' Tonight)** was a studio-made affair, for World Pacific, with Spoon's vibrant singing of a superior selection of blues material complemented admirably by sterling instrumental support from Harry Edison (♦), Teddy Edwards, Gerald Wilson, Hawes, and Henry McDode; in most ways, better than a two session date from the previous year (1957) **(Blue Moods In The Shade Of Kansas City)**. Better too than another album dating from '57 **(A Spoonful Of Blues)** with support on this occasion from Jesse Stone's band. As good as the World Pacific LP undoubtedly turned out to be, a live recording from late-1950s **(Witherspoon At The Renaissance)** was even better. Taped at former Sunset Strip club, it found Spoon, in magnificent voice, delivering the goods at optimum level of performance, more than ably supported by a rhythm section (Jimmie Rowles, Mel Lewis, Leroy Vinnegar) that is unflagging in its buoyant, constantly stimulating support, and with exceptional

solos and obbligatos from Ben Webster and Gerry Mulligan (♦), latter producing blues playing of a quality which must have astonished even his keenest admirers.

Webster, key instrumental figure during the Renaissance gig, was to be catalyst during recording of two LPs made for Reprise in 1961, 1962, especially so with **Jimmy Witherspoon & Ben Webster**. During 1960s and indeed in more recent times, Witherspoon has continued to record, for a variety of labels – including many album dates for Prestige during 1960s – but this work has not always retained consistency of Renaissance–World Pacific sets, or indeed another live date (1961) **(Buck Clayton & Jimmy Witherspoon Live In Paris)** with its accompaniments cast in comfortably swinging 'mainstream' idiom. Still, there were

Witherspoon At The Renaissance (Vogue) – 'magnificent'.

Above: altoist Phil Woods, one of the best of the Hard Boppers in the '50s, and still a force to be reckoned with.

album – long deleted – with trumpeter Jon Eardley in 1955. Basically a Charlie Parker disciple, Woods is a direct, charging player who conveys few of the emotional depths of a contemporary like Jackie McLean, but can always be relied upon to dominate the session with his fiercely strident tone and sense of structure. The re-release of Hard Bop sessions from the '50s shows Woods as one of the most inventive swingers around, from the excellent George Wallington Quintet **(The New York Scene** and **Jazz For The Carriage Trade)**; the Donald Byrd–Phil Woods–Al Haig session, **House Of Byrd**; to the chases with fellow altoist Gene Quill, **Phil Woods**. He was completely at home with mainstream musicians like Benny Carter and Coleman Hawkins **(Further Definitions)** and undaunted by the challenging Thelonious Monk scores **(In Person)** in an orchestral setting, where his jumping attack dominates **Friday The 13th.**

Woods leads a large group through his own extended composition, **Rights Of Swing,** which features beautiful trumpet from Benny Bailey, some darkly sombre voicings for baritone and French horn, and Woods' own linking alto.

In 1968 Phil Woods left America for Paris, where he formed a new quartet, The Rhythm Machine, which included composer-pianist Gordon Beck, bassist Ron Matthewson and drummer Daniel Humair. A recording from 1972 **(Live From Montreux)** shows all the old ebullience and the incorporation of some of the New Wave's expressive tonal devices. **The Executive Suite** is a tour de force of alto playing – unaccompanied sections, great command from screaming top to plangent bottom of the horn. Later work with Michel Legrand **(The Concert Legrand),** tends to be submerged in the string sections.

Recordings:
George Wallington Quintet:
 The New York Scene
  (Prestige/—)
 Jazz For The Carriage Trade
  (Prestige/—)
Donald Byrd, House Of Byrd
 (Prestige/Prestige)
Phil Woods *(Prestige/Prestige)*
Thelonious Monk, In Person
 (Milestone/Milestone)
Benny Carter, Further
 Definitions *(Impulse/Impulse)*
Rights Of Swing *(CBS–Barnaby/
 CBS-Barnaby)*
Live From Montreux
 (Verve/Verve)
The Concert Legrand
 (RCA/RCA)
Musique Du Bois *(Muse/—)*

Frank Wright

Tenorman Frank Wright, currently the Reverend, is an expatriate New Thinger living in Paris. His first albums for ESP **(Frank Wright Trio** and **Your Prayer)** show the conventional Rollins–Coltrane influence, plus a wild bag of freak effects. Over the years, he seems to have developed very little in the line of structure or melodic interest, but the furious overblowing, honking and squealing does

have an initial impact. Both albums with his regular group, Bobby Few on piano, the great Alan Silva on bass, and Muhammad Ali on drums, offer multi-directional support to his locomotive-heavy charge, but – depending on your tolerance for total freedom in extremis – pall before the end **(Center Of The World** and **Last Polka In Nancy).** His work with front-line partner Noah Howard, an altoist of disciplined and lyrical gifts, raises the climate without steamrollering the

variety of interaction **(One For John** and **Space Dimension).**

Recordings:
Frank Wright Trio *(ESP/—)*
Your Prayer *(ESP/—)*
Center Of The World
 (Sun Records – France)
Last Polka In Nancy
 (Sun Records – France)
One For John *(BYG/BYG)*
Noah Howard, Space Dimension
 (America – France)

Jimmy Yancey

James Edward 'Jimmy' Yancey (born Chicago, Illinois, 1894) was a pianist with limited technical skills and limited musical vocabulary. Yet he was a master of understatement, and a great blues player within an area bounded by boogie woogie and basic blues. His playing, often poignant and invariably full of expression, was so personal as to give the listener a sense of intruding into Yancey's private world – a world that seemed to contain an aura of sadness.

Yancey came from musical family – father was musician and singer, brother a pianist – and before World War I, starting when he was six, had been a dancer-singer. He visited Europe as dancer prior to 1914. Back to Chicago (1915) and taught himself to play piano. Worked at rent parties and clubs in Chicago until 1925 when he retired from music full-time to become groundsman at headquarters of Chicago White Sox baseball club. Re-discovered after late-1930s success of **Yancey Special**, written by fellow pianist Meade Lux Lewis (♦). Versions of number by Lewis and Bob Crosby (♦) band attained much popularity. Yancey's comeback was achieved first by records. In 1939 recorded for Solo Arts, series of piano solos, of which **Yancey's Getaway, Lucille's Lament, 2 O'Clock Blues** and **Janye's Joys** are superior illustrations of Yancey's sensitivity, combining two-handed strength with delicacy of touch **(Lost Recording Date / Piano Solos)**. Recorded again, later same year, with even more consistently rewarding results **(Boogie Woogie Man)**, with outstanding piano-playing on **Yancey Stomp, Five O'Clock Blues** and **State Street Special,**

plus a bonus in most moving vocal performances by Yancey on **Death Letter Blues** and **Crying In My Sleep**. Recorded equally moving performances for Session in 1943 **(The Immortal: 1898-1951),** including **35th & Dearborn, I Love To Hear My Baby Call My Name** (another Jimmy Yancey vocal), plus three examples of Mama Yancey's equally moving singing, but topped by Jimmy's pain-filled **How Long, How Long Blues.**

Accompanied Mama Yancey (his wife) at various gigs during 1940s, including joint appearance at 1948 Carnegie Hall concert. Suffered from ill-health during final year of his life (he died in Chicago in 1951) but during same year was fit enough to record again – as it turned out, for last time. Accompanied throughout, with great taste and understanding, by fellow Chicagoan, Israel Crosby (♦), Yancey's final record date was suitably memorable, if not redolent of his very best playing. Certainly, though, his accompaniments for Mama Yancey were furnished with loving care and infinite good taste, and latter's high-pitched vocals on **Make Me A Pallet On The Floor,** and four other titles, were projected with tenderness and dignity that obviates any slight diminution in technical qualities **(Lowdown Dirty Blues).**

Recordings:
Jimmy Yancey, Lost Recording Date *(Riverside)*/
Piano Solos *(Joker – Italy)*
Various (Including Jimmy Yancey); Boogie Woogie Man *(RCA Victor – France)*
Various (Including Jimmy Yancey), Boogie Woogie Man Originaux *(RCA Victor – France)*
Jimmy Yancey, 'The Immortal' (1898-1951) *(Oldie Blues – Holland)*
Jimmy Yancey/(Cripple Clarence Lofton), The Yancey/ Lofton Sessions, Vols 1, 2 *(Storyville)*
Jimmy Yancey, Lowdown Dirty Blues *(Atlantic)*

Piano Solos (Joker, Italy) – the artistry of Jimmy Yancey.

Lester Young

When Lester Willis Young (born Woodville, Missouri, 1909) first came into prominence in mid-1930s, his talent seemed to be fully developed. That was in 1936, when he recorded for first time as member of a small band calling itself Smith-Jones, Inc (actually, a contingent from Count Basie (♦) Orchestra of which Young was soon to be recognized as its most important soloist). Those early Young solos, on **Shoe Shine Boy, Evenin', Boogie Woogie** and **Lady Be Good,** still rank with the very finest produced by anyone in the entire history of jazz – a situation hardly likely to change at any time in the future. They had (and have) a quality of flowing logicality that is as near to perfection as anything produced by other comparable giants (eg Parker (♦), Hawkins (♦), Tatum (♦), Armstrong (♦), Coltrane (♦), etc). Their rhythmic impact, in particular, remains as vital and as deliciously subtle as when the recordings first were released, and the solos have provided a constant inspiration to subsequent generations of saxophonists through the years. Strange, perhaps, but Young's period of strongest influence on others came over ten years after those 1936 recordings. Though it might be over-stressing the case to say that Young's seemingly detached way of purveying (real) emotion was entirely responsible for advent of so-called 'cool' school of jazz at beginning of 1950s, certainly his playing was prime mover in helping shape styles and approach taken by numerous (mostly white) tenor players, notably Stan Getz (♦), Brew Moore, Al Cohn (♦), Allen Eager (♦), and Zoot Sims (♦). But great though these and other Lester-minded saxophonists have been (and that list would also include Lee Konitz (♦), an alto-saxophonist), none has succeeded in surpassing his mentor's uniqueness in implying as much as he actually said, or indeed his rhythmic subtlety and drive.

Young – whose brother, Lee Young, was an active drummer during 1930s-1950s – came from a musical family. His father gave Lester, Lee and sister Irma a basic music education. Lester Young tried drums (at ten),

giving them up after three years because, he said, he grew tired of packing and unpacking the kit before and after each gig. Admired Frankie Trumbauer's (♦) playing, and it is said he tried to assimilate the former Beiderbecke (♦) associate's flowing lines on C-melody sax on first, alto, then tenor. Young had schooled in Minneapolis (the Young family had moved from New Orleans, having previously left Woodville), and before taking up saxophone had drummed with family band in carnival minstrel shows – the kind of jobs his father, W. H. Young, had been undertaking for years. At 18, Lester Young wanted out, then joined Art Bronson's Bostonians; on baritone-sax, at the beginning, then switching to tenor. After returning to Young family band for a while, rejoined Bronson, in 1930. Subsequently, worked with various bands in and around Minneapolis, Minnesota, playing alto, baritone, but mostly tenor. Became member of Original Blue Devils in 1932, leaving following year to link up with Bennie Moten (♦). Other engagements followed, including short spell with band of a then fading King Oliver (♦). After first-time work with a Count Basie-led band, offered chance to replace Coleman Hawkins (♦) with prestigious Fletcher Henderson (♦) Orchestra. Joined Henderson at beginning of '34 – only to leave three-and-a-half months later. Reason for this sudden departure was that some of Henderson's sidemen found Young's more airy, almost bland tone no substitute for rich, majestic

Prez & Teddy (Verve, Polydor). Lester, Teddy & Friends (circa 1956), make superb, timeless jazz, as of old.

tone of Hawkins. Young then became member of Andy Kirk (♦) Orchestra, thence to Boyd Atkins and others. Finally, in 1936, joined Basie again, in Kansas City, with which band he was to establish an enviable reputation as an absolutely valid and vital alternative approach to the tenor-saxophone styles of, say, Hawkins, Ben Webster (♦) and Bud Freeman (♦).

During his four-and-a-half-year stay with Basie, Young became not only its most celebrated soloist but one of the great instrumental voices in jazz. Apart from the initial quartet of sides, Young produced a series of remarkable solos with the band that not only helped to re-write the art of saxophone playing but also did much to point in the directions jazz was to take during next decade. His solos with full Basie orchestra are too numerous to mention in full, but those which must be considered of inestimable importance are the following: **Honeysuckle Rose, Roseland Shuffle, Every Tub (The Best Of Count Basie, 1937-1938); Panassie Stomp, Jive At Five, Swinging The Blues, You Can Depend On Me** (a Basie Sextet track), **Jumpin' At The Woodside (You Can Depend On Basie);** and **Taxi War Dance, Clap Hands, Here Comes Charlie, Ham 'N' Eggs, Pound Cake, Hollywood Jump, Blow Top, Tickle-Toe, Moten Swing, Let Me See, I Never Knew, Broadway** (all **Lester Young With Count Basie & His Orchestra).** Basically, there was nothing to separate Young and Hawkins at the time, in terms of all-round ability, musicianship, and total individuality, except perhaps that at this period Young was a superior blues-player. A fact that is apparent during blues performances by Jimmy Rushing (♦) with Basie **(Blues I Love To Sing)** with Young providing choice obbligatos and solos in support.

It was during the late-1930s that the unforgettable Lester Young – Billie Holiday (♦) partnership was forged. Holiday had much in common with Young, not the least of which was impeccable, subtle time. Holiday's matchless singing was perfectly complemented by the tenorist's totally sympathetic, equally poignant contributions. And Young's solos themselves often sounded like an extension of the vocal they succeeded. Their on-record achievements added new dimensions to a phrase like 'musical togetherness'. On a purely instrumental front, just how omnipotent Lester Young could sound was demonstrated – comprehensively, exquisitely – during a Carnegie Hall concert at which he performed during a specially organized jam session. After a typical introduction to **Honey-**

suckle Rose (1938 Carnegie Hall Jazz Concert) by Count Basie, another of the guest performers. Young takes off on a three-chorus solo that demolishes successfully everything else that follows.

During 1939, was as persuasively brilliant as at any time during his career at recording dates featuring Count Basie & His Kansas City Seven (**Lester Young With Count Basie & His Orchestra**), gloriously so on his own **Lester Leaps In**. Apart from tenor-sax, Young occasionally soloed on a metal clarinet at this time with which he produced a haunting, wistful, almost eerie sound. Used this instrument on earlier Basie sides like **Blue & Sentimental, Texas Shuffle (Jumpin' At The Woodside)**, also on a 1938 edition of **Kansas City Six (Lester Young & The Kansas City Five)**; and equally beguiling on **I Want A Little Girl, Pagin' The Devil** and **Countless Blues**.

Left Basie in 1940; worked with own bands, first in New York (at Kelly's Stables), then, with brother Lee on drums, in California (at Billy Berg's). Took part in a most rewarding recording session in Los Angeles with pianist Nat Cole (♦) **(Nat Cole Meets The Master Saxes)** including a tender **I Can't Get Started**. Young and Cole were to record together three years later **(The Genius Of Lester Young)** but the overall quality of the music was a notch below earlier meeting. Young was back in New York summer of '42, worked with fellow tenorist Al Sears' (♦) big band following year, also with Dizzy Gillespie (♦) on 52nd Street; then, for best part of a year, was back with Basie.

In October, '44, Young was inducted into US Army. Apparently, he was to suffer degradation, mental and physical hardship during his approximately one-year period as serviceman; certainly, the experience was a traumatic one which thereafter affected him personally; it also was to change him musically. A particularly sensitive man anyway, Young's general demeanor had changed dramatically following a court-martial, period of detention, and subsequent discharge. He became even more sensitive; often withdrawn and prone to eccentricities in dress, speech and behavior (including something of a drink problem). His first recordings following his return to civilian life **(The Aladdin Sessions)** give an indication of the kind of change he had undergone personally. His playing had become laconic, indolent – even morose in places. There was a wry, sometimes caustic humor, and an overall feeling of resignation that later

Lester Young With Count Basie & His Orchestra (Epic, France). Classic tenor statements by the immortal 'Pres'.

'Prez' or 'Pres') was a significant link between pre-war jazz and bebop of the 1940s. He was an important influence on bop musicians – particularly Charlie Parker (♦) – as well as younger musicians who were as much influenced by Young (sometimes more so) as Parker. His forward-looking playing ran on parallel lines with that of guitarist Charlie Christian (♦) which makes listening to the few recordings featuring both men together instructive as well as absorbing **(Charlie Christian/Lester Young: Together, 1940** and **John Hammond's Spirituals To Swing).**

Recordings:
Lester Young With Count Basie & His Orchestra
(Epic/Epic – France)
Count Basie, The Best Of Count Basie 1937-1938
(MCA Coral – Germany)
Count Basie, You Can Depend On Basie *(—/Coral)*
Various, 1938 Carnegie Hall Jazz Concert *(Columbia/CBS)*
Count Basie, Jumpin' At The Woodside *(Brunswick/Ace of Clubs)*
Lester Young & The Kansas City Five (sic) *(Mainstream/Stateside)*
Various, Nat Cole Meets The Master Saxes *(Phoenix/Spotlite)*
Various (Including Lester Young), Jammin' With Lester
(Jazz Archives)
Lester Young, Lester Leaps Again! *(EmArcy/Fontana)*
Charlie Christian/Lester Young: Together, 1940 *(Jazz Archives/—)*
Lester Young, Pres/The Complete Savoy Recordings *(Savoy/—)*
Various, Jazz At The Philharmonic 1944-46 *(—/Verve)*
Various, Jazz At The Philharmonic 1946, Vol 2 *(—/Verve)*
Lester Young/(Coleman Hawkins), Classic Tenors
(Contact/Stateside)
Lester Young/(Coleman Hawkins/Ben Webster), The Big Three
(Bob Thiele Music/RCA Victor)
The Lester Young Story, Vols 1-3 *(Columbia/CBS)*
Lester Young, The Genius of . . . *(Verve)*
Coleman Hawkins/Lester Young *(Zim/Spotlite)*
Lester Young, The Aladdin Sessions *(Blue Note/—)*
Lester Young, Prez In Europe *(Onyx/Onyx)*
Lester Young, Pres & Teddy & Oscar *(Verve/—)*
Lester Young, Prez & Teddy *(—/Verve)*
Jimmy Rushing/Count Basie, Blues I Love To Sing *(Ace of Hearts)*

Lester Young (Vogue) – 'great instrumental voice'.

The Lester Young Story, Vol 1 (CBS) – tenor genius.

was to approach despair. Much of the lightness in his playing prior to Army Service would rarely return, likewise with the quicksilver dexterity of **Lester Leaps In** or **Jumpin' At The Woodside** of a few years before. There was a difference in approach between **D.B. Blues** (an obvious reference to his incarceration in Army detention block), **After You've Gone** and **Jumpin' At Mesners** and pre-Army recordings such as **Blue Lester, Jump Lester Jump, Basie English (Pres/The Complete Savoy Recordings); I Never Knew, Lester Leaps Again, Just You, Just Me (Lester Young Leaps Again!);** or his uniformly superb playing during a celebrated jazz movie, **Jammin' The Blues (Jamming With Lester).** All of which is not to suggest, as has been the habit over the years in some critical circles, that Young was finished as a major soloist after 1945. If anything, his playing had become even more emotionally enriched, as was personified in his ballad playing during his membership of Jazz At The Philharmonic in 1946 on **I Can't Get Started (Jazz At The Philharmonic 1946, Vol 2)**. That he had lost none of the running excitement at faster tempos can be judged from his fine solo on **After You've Gone** from same concert **(Jazz At The Philharmonic 1944-46)**. True, subsequent recordings by Young did tend to be inconsistent, but there was sufficient top-class tenor playing during his 'declining' years to negate any accusations that he was but a pale shadow of his former great self.

Of later years, his finest recordings took place in 1956, on two consecutive dates. On both, he was re-united with Teddy Wilson (♦) with whom he had worked during those memorable Billie Holiday sessions. The second of the '56 dates was in quartet setting with Wilson pacing Young's tenor in masterfully sympathetic fashion. For the first, Wilson, Young and the same rhythm section (Jo Jones, Gene Ramey) were joined by Vic Dickenson (♦), who had performed so admirably on Young's first post-Army recordings, Roy Eldridge (♦) and Basie's long-serving guitarist Freddie Green. On the slower numbers (eg **This Year's Kisses, I Didn't Know What Time It Was**) Young's phrasing was masterful, the emotional content of his playing very moving. No problems either with the up-tempo numbers, with his volatile playing on **Gigantic Blues** comparable with practically any of his earlier classic solos.

Poor health dogged Young during the last years of his life and he was hospitalized on several occasions. Upon completion of a not altogether successful engagement at Blue Note Club, Paris, he returned to New York; one day later he was dead. Lester Young (known affectionately as

Eugene 'Snooky' Young
♦ *Count Basie*

Joe Zawinul
♦ *Weather Report*

Zawinul (Atlantic): the wizard of the keyboards.

Right: Lester Young.

INDEX

This index does not set out to be comprehensive, but concentrates on those personalities whose names recur throughout. It also provides an alphabetical guide to any acts and artists of stature not given their own entry in the book, and supplements the cross-reference system (denoted by ◗ or ◖) used throughout. The main A–Z entries are not all included so please check with the main listing first. References to main entries are indicated here by **bold** type.

221

PRINTED IN BELGIUM BY

proost
INTERNATIONAL BOOK PRODUCTION

PRINTED IN BELGIUM

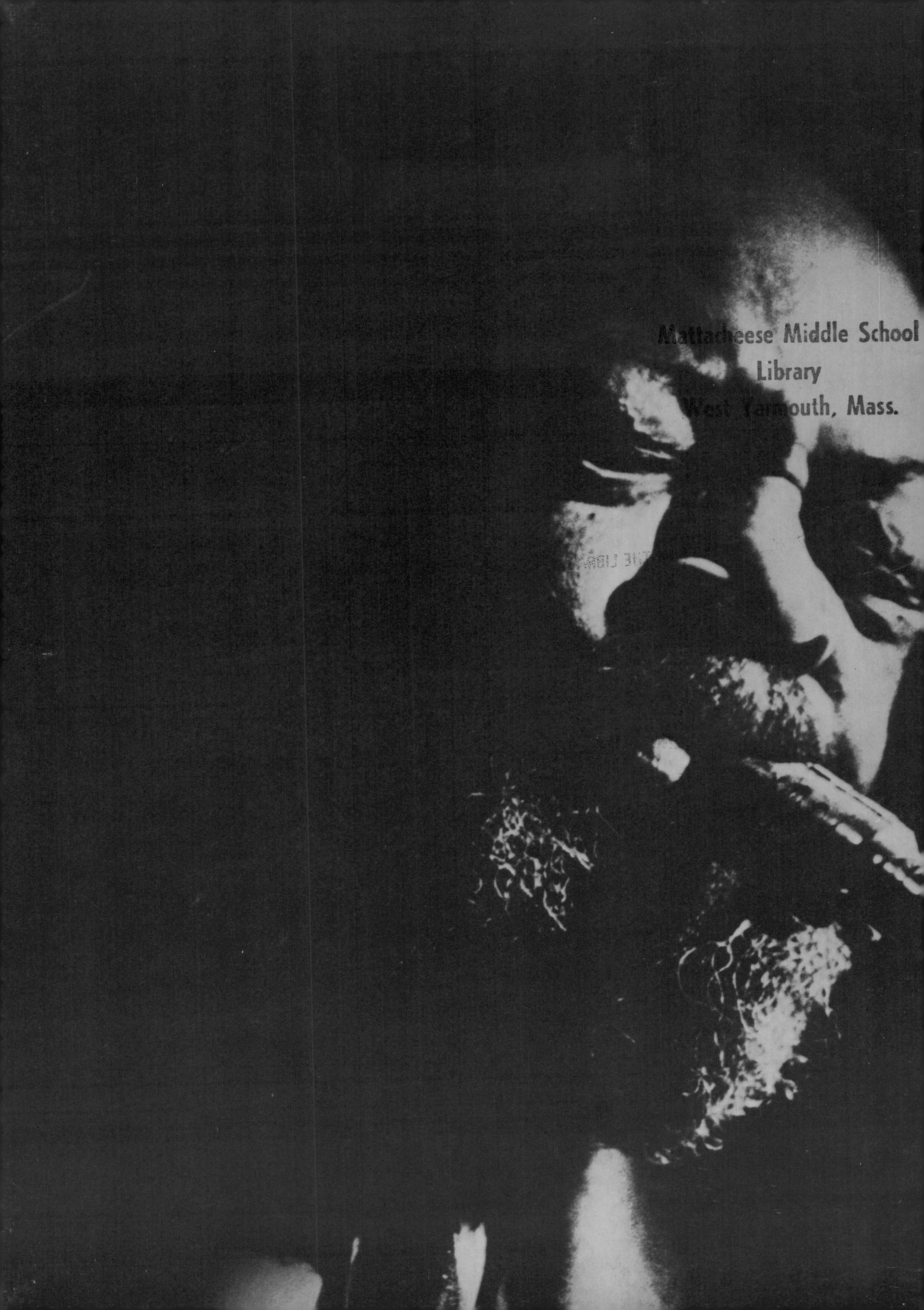